Crime and Social Institutions

International Library of Criminology, Criminal Justice and Penology - Second Series
Series Editors: Gerald Mars and David Nelken

Titles in the Series:

Gender and Prisons
Dana M. Britton

Quantitative Methods in Criminology
Shawn Bushway and David Weisburd

Detecting Deception
David Canter and Donna Youngs

Offender Profiling
David Canter and Michael Davis

Insurgent Terrorism
Gerald Cromer

Criminal Courts
Jo Dixon, Aaron Kupchick and Joachim Savelsberg

Crime and Security
Benjamin Goold and Lucia Zedner

Crime and Regulation
Fiona Haines

Recent Developments in Criminological Theory
Stuart Henry

Gun Crime
Richard Hobbs and Robert Hornsby

The Criminology of War
Ruth Jamieson

The Impact of HIV/AIDS on Criminology and Criminal Justice
Mark M. Lanier

Burglary
Robert Mawby

Domestic Violence
Mangai Natarajan

Women Police
Mangai Natarajan

Crime and Immigration
Graeme Newman and Joshua Freilich

Surveillance, Crime and Social Control
Clive Norris and Dean Wilson

Crime and Social Institutions
Richard Rosenfeld

The Death Penalty, Volumes I and II
Austin Sarat

Gangs
Jacqueline Schneider and Nick Tilley

Corporate Crime
Sally Simpson and Carole Gibbs

Crime and Deviance in Cyberspace
David Wall

Green Criminology
Nigel South and Piers Beirne

Crime and Social Institutions

Edited by

Richard Rosenfeld

University of Missouri-St Louis, USA

ASHGATE

Published by
Ashgate Publishing Limited
Gower House
Croft Road
Aldershot
Hampshire GU11 3HR
England

Ashgate Publishing Company
Suite 420
101 Cherry Street
Burlington, VT 05401-4405
USA

Ashgate website: http://www.ashgate.com

British Library Cataloguing in Publication Data
Crime and social institutions. – (International library of criminology, criminal justice and penology. Second series)
1. Crime – Sociological aspects 2. Social institutions – United States 3. Criminology – United States
I. Rosenfeld, Richard
364.2'5'0973

Library of Congress Cataloging-in-Publication Data
Crime and social institutions / edited by Richard Rosenfeld.
p. cm. – (International library of criminology, criminal justice, and penology. Second Series)
Includes bibliographical references.
1. Crime– Sociological aspects. 2. Social Institutions. 3. Crime– United States. 4. Criminology – United States. I. Rosenfeld, Richard. II. International library of criminology, criminal justice & penology. Second series.

HV6150.C743 2006
364.973– dc22

2005057082

ISBN 0 7546 2501 X

Printed in Great Britain by TJ International Ltd, Padstow, Cornwall

Contents

PART III US-BASED TESTS OF INSTITUTIONAL-ANOMIE THEORY

PART IV CRIME AND INSTITUTIONAL DYNAMICS AT THE LOCAL LEVEL

PART V IMPLICATIONS FOR PUNISHMENT

Acknowledgements

The editor and publishers wish to thank the following for permission to use copyright material.

American Society of Criminology for the essays: Jukka Savolainen (2000), 'Inequality, Welfare State, and Homicide: Further Support for the Institutional Anomie Theory', *Criminology*, **38**, pp. 1021–42. Copyright © 2000 American Society of Criminology; Travis C. Pratt and Timothy W. Godsey (2003), 'Social Support, Inequality, and Homicide: A Cross-National Test of an Integrated Theoretical Model', *Criminology*, **41**, pp. 611–43. Copyright © 2003 American Society of Criminology; Mitchell B. Chamlin and John K. Cochran (1995), 'Assessing Messner and Rosenfeld's Institutional Anomie Theory: A Partial Test', *Criminology*, **33**, pp. 411–29. Copyright © 1995 American Society of Criminology; Michael O. Maume and Matthew R. Lee (2003), 'Social Institutions and Violence: A Sub-National Test of Institutional Anomie Theory', *Criminology*, **41**, pp. 1137–72. Copyright © 2003 American Society of Criminology; Mitchell B. Chamlin and John K. Cochran (1997), 'Social Altruism and Crime', *Criminology*, **35**, pp. 203–28. Copyright © 1997 American Society of Criminology; Thomas D. Stucky (2003), 'Local Politics and Violent Crime in U.S. Cities', *Criminology*, **41**, pp. 1101–35. Copyright © 2003 American Society of Criminology; María B. Vélez (2001), 'The Role of Public Social Control in Urban Neighborhoods: A Multi-Level Analysis of Victimization Risk', *Criminology*, **39**, pp. 837–64. Copyright © 2001 American Society of Criminology; Karen F. Parker (2004), 'Industrial Shift, Polarized Labor Markets and Urban Violence: Modeling the Dynamics Between the Economic Transformation and Disaggregated Homicide', *Criminology*, **42**, pp. 619–45. Copyright © 2004 American Society of Criminology; Dina R. Rose and Todd R. Clear (1998), 'Incarceration, Social Capital, and Crime: Implications for Social Disorganization Theory', *Criminology*, **36**, pp. 441–79. Copyright © 1998 American Society of Criminology.

American Sociological Association for the essay: John R. Sutton (2004), 'The Political Economy of Imprisonment in Affluent Western Democracies, 1960–1990', *American Sociological Review*, **69**, pp. 170–89.

Copyright Clearance Center for the essays: Steven F. Messner and Richard Rosenfeld (2004), '"Institutionalizing" Criminological Theory', *Advances in Criminological Theory*, **13**, pp. 83–105; John B. Cullen, K. Praveen Parboteeah and Martin Hoegl (2004), 'Cross-National Differences in Managers' Willingness to Justify Ethically Suspect Behaviors: A Test of Institutional Anomie Theory', *Academy of Management Journal*, **47**, pp. 411–21. Copyright © 2004 Academy of Management Journal.

Oxford University Press for the essay: Jón Gunnar Bernburg (2002), 'Anomie, Social Change and Crime: A Theoretical Examination of Institutional-Anomie Theory', *British Journal of Criminology*, **42**, pp. 729–42. Copyright © 2002 Centre for Crime and Justice Studies.

Taylor & Francis for the essay: Francis T. Cullen (1994), 'Social Support as an Organizing Concept for Criminology: Presidential Address to the Academy of Criminal Justice Sciences', *Justice Quarterly*, **11**, pp. 527–59. Copyright © 1994 Academy of Criminal Justice Sciences.

University of North Carolina for the essay: Steven F. Messner and Richard Rosenfeld (1997), 'Political Restraint of the Market and Levels of Criminal Homicide: A Cross-National Application of Institutional-Anomie Theory', *Social Forces*, **75**, pp. 1393–416. Copyright © 1997 University of North Carolina Press.

Every effort has been made to trace all the copyright holders, but if any have been inadvertently overlooked the publishers will be pleased to make the necessary arrangement at the first opportunity.

Preface to the Second Series

The first series of the International Library of Criminology, Criminal Justice and Penology has established itself as a major research resource by bringing together the most significant journal essays in contemporary criminology, criminal justice and penology. The series made available to researchers, teachers and students an extensive range of essays which are indispensable for obtaining an overview of the latest theories and findings in this fast changing subject. Indeed the rapid growth of interesting scholarly work in the field has created a demand for a second series which like the first consists of volumes dealing with criminological schools and theories as well as with approaches to particular areas of crime criminal justice and penology. Each volume is edited by a recognised authority who has selected twenty or so of the best journal articles in the field of their special competence and provided an informative introduction giving a summary of the field and the relevance of the articles chosen. The original pagination is retained for ease of reference.

The difficulties of keeping on top of the steadily growing literature in criminology are complicated by the many disciplines from which its theories and findings are drawn (sociology, law, sociology of law, psychology, psychiatry, philosophy and economics are the most obvious). The development of new specialisms with their own journals (policing, victimology, mediation) as well as the debates between rival schools of thought (feminist criminology, left realism, critical criminology, abolitionism etc.) make necessary overviews that offer syntheses of the state of the art.

GERALD MARS
Visiting Professor, Brunel University, Middlesex, UK

DAVID NELKEN
Distinguished Professor of Sociology, University of Macerata, Italy;
Distinguished Research Professor of Law, University of Cardiff, Wales;
Honourary Visiting Professor of Law, LSE, London, UK

Introduction

> … there is a kind of reductionism in our traditional way of thinking about society. We think in the first place that the problem is probably with the individual; if not, then with the organization. This pattern of thinking hides from us the power of institutions and their great possibilities for good and evil (Bellah *et al.*,1992, p. 11).

American criminologists have always had a special fascination with the individual criminal or delinquent. In this, American criminology reflects the strong individualistic strain in American culture generally. Alongside the cult of the individual in the United States is an equally persistent aversion to social institutions. Sociologist Robert Bellah and his colleagues observe that 'the very idea of institutions is often repugnant to Americans' (Bellah *et al.*, 1992, p. 38). A corresponding avoidance of, if not disdain for, institutions also is reflected in contemporary American criminology. Social institutions are largely missing from contemporary theory and research on crime in the United States.

The purpose of this volume is to highlight recent theoretical developments and research contributions in American criminology[1] that run counter to the individualistic bias of the field. Much of the literature reproduced here assesses the theoretical claims and empirical implications of the only current criminological perspective devoted explicitly to examining the institutional sources of crime: the so-called *institutional-anomie* theory (Messner and Rosenfeld, 2001a; Rosenfeld and Messner, 2006). Other essays address somewhat parallel theoretical developments or report research on the institutional sources of variation in crime and punishment across neighbourhoods, cities and nations. The volume contains what I consider to be some of the best recent macro-level work in American criminology, and yet it also reveals how much further we Americans have to go in 'putting institutions to work' in the study of crime and punishment. In this Introduction to *Crime and Social Institutions*, I offer a working conception of social institutions and summarize the institutional-anomie theory of crime. I then briefly describe the following chapters, each of which points the way – even if none has completed the journey – towards a fully 'institutional' understanding of crime.

What are Social Institutions?

The term 'institution' has varied meanings and applications, even among social scientists. As Messner and Rosenfeld point out in Chapter 1 of this volume, institutions are often confused with the concept of 'organization', as when the local college is referred to as an 'institution of higher education' or a prison is called a 'correctional institution'. As Messner and Rosenfeld suggest, the confusion of institutions with organizations is widespread in American criminology and can obscure the social origins of crime.

---

[1] The term 'American criminology' is a shorthand reference to the theories, explanations, data and methods typically used by criminologists who have been trained and work in the United States.

Institutions are not organizations, although concrete organizations are part of institutions. The concept of social institutions is much more abstract. It refers to the broad value patterns and accompanying beliefs, goals and norms that coalesce around a society's basic needs. Institutions also encompass the social structures – the interrelated statuses and roles – through which values, beliefs, and norms are enacted. All societies must adapt to their environment, attain collective goals, maintain social solidarity and socialize members in the society's core value commitments. Adapting to the environment is the primary function of the economy, goal attainment is the function of the political system or 'polity', and solidarity and value transmission are accomplished through the family system, education, law and religion (see Messner and Rosenfeld, 2001b, pp. 64–68). The economy, polity, family, education, law and religion are the major social institutions found, in one form or another, in every complex human society.

Many readers will recognize this highly abstract conception of social institutions, with its emphasis on social 'needs' and institutional 'functions', as rooted in the structural functionalist theory of Talcott Parsons (1951). I plead guilty. Parsons' sociology has been accused of serving conservative political ends, exaggerating the degree of value consensus in society, minimizing social conflict, and being so abstract and vague as to be useless in the study of concrete societies (see Mills' (1959) classic critique of Parsons' 'grand theory'). There is some truth to these charges, but they should not prevent criminologists – Americans in particular – from recovering those aspects of Parsons' sociology that are essential in the study of crime as a macro-social phenomenon. Crime is a characteristic of societies. As such, it cannot be studied adequately in isolation from a conception of the structure and functioning of whole societies. Parsons offers such a conception that, even with its flaws, is better than no conception at all. Unfortunately, one searches in vain for a working model of society in contemporary American criminology. A coherent vision of society is utterly absent from the dominant theories and research on individual criminal behaviour and only partially visible in more macro-level work. American criminologists, whether we like it or not, badly need Parsons.

They also need Marx, Durkheim and Weber. The classical sociologists had visions, competing visions to be sure, but full-blown visions of the social whole. For them, all social practices of any consequence had to be studied in the context of the society in which they are situated. The capacity to link a given social act to the broad outlines of the larger society is what C. Wright Mills (1959) called the 'sociological imagination'. Ironically, even though American criminology sprang from the discipline of sociology, it lacks the sociological imagination.

What does the sociological imagination bring to the study of crime? First and foremost, it brings the capacity to locate the origins of crime and punishment in the structure, functioning and interrelationships among social institutions. Institutions are the building blocks of whole societies, the basis on which one society may be distinguished from another, the source of both social stability – the maintenance of a given society as a going concern – and social change. Institutions are distinct from one another, in the sense that their primary functions differ, but at the same time they are interdependent; they cannot function in isolation from one another. The polity secures the social order required for a functioning economy. The family and education system transmit the values, knowledge and skills required to perform occupational roles. The economy provides the material resources required to feed, house and clothe families. If one institution fails, the effects ramify through the others and threaten the whole society.

Institutional-Anomie Theory

If institutions are necessarily interdependent, they are never in perfect balance. Every society is characterized by a more or less distinctive 'institutional balance of power' in which one institution assumes dominance over the others (Messner and Rosenfeld, 2001a). In the United States the economy dominates the institutional structure in the sense that its needs receive priority over those of other institutions and its particular mode of action or 'logic' penetrates other institutional realms (Messner and Rosenfeld 2001b). In the former Soviet Union and socialist Eastern Europe, the polity dominated the institutional balance of power. In contemporary Western Europe, Canada, Australia and Japan, cultural differences notwithstanding, the free-market economy and democratic polity are in somewhat greater balance. In many Middle Eastern countries and throughout the rest of the world, the so-called primordial institutions of kin, religion, ethnicity and village are dominant. The basic argument of the institutional-anomie theory of crime is that each of the differing institutional configurations gives rise to a characteristic type of crime.

Free-market economies, by definition, operate relatively unrestrained by other institutions. Societies in which such freedom from institutional regulation is extreme tend to have high levels of 'anomic' crime such as robbery and homicide, or they must maintain huge prison systems to keep crime rates at manageable levels. Free-market economies cultivate an innovative ethic and 'bottom-line' mentality in members of society, thereby encouraging a technical, rather than moral, orientation to norms that facilitates criminal behaviour on the part of upper- and lower-status persons alike. They also, when unchecked, tend to undermine the capacities of other institutions to exercise social control and provide social support (Messner and Rosenfeld, 2001b). Messner and Rosenfeld (2001b) maintain that the United States is exemplary of such societies, but post-Soviet Russia's 'deadly capitalism' also fits this pattern (Gordon, 1996, p. A3; Bohlen, 1992; Holmes, 1997). Societies in which the polity is dominant tend to have much lower rates of street crime but high levels of official and unofficial corruption. Finally, where religion (or ethnicity or clan) dominates the institutional structure, including the legal system, crime as such may not be particularly prevalent, but crimes of social control in the form of the repression of minorities and women and human rights violations are often observed under such conditions (Messner and Rosenfeld, 2001a).

If each form of institutional imbalance or dominance gives rise to a more or less distinctive type of crime, that does not mean that other types of crime are absent or even that the characteristic type always or necessarily surpasses the levels found under differing institutional arrangements. A good example is the dramatic fall in violent crime rates in the United States during the 1990s. Indeed, the gap between the United States, once the developed world's leader in violent crime, and other nations has begun to close (Messner and Rosenfeld, forthcoming). A number of factors probably contributed to this decline in crime, but one of the most important is the unprecedented expansion of the prison and jail systems, which now hold well over 2 million people (Blumstein and Wallman, 2000; Harrison and Beck, 2005; Levitt, 2004). In fact, no society on record has ever incarcerated as large a fraction of its population as does the United States today. However, the Americans pay a high price for suppressing crime through mass incarceration, and the price reflects a set of institutional arrangements that not only result in a high volume of criminal activity but also close off alternative ways of addressing the crime problem (Messner and Rosenfeld, forthcoming). We might say, then, that a given set of institutional arrangements creates a 'social propensity' (or what Elliot Currie (Chapter 4) terms the 'criminality rate') for a particular type of crime, and that societies with a given propensity will find it more difficult than others to suppress that type of crime.

Theoretical Considerations

The essays in Part I of *Crime and Social Institutions* set forth some of the basic theoretical issues in the study of crime at the institutional level of analysis. In Chapter 1 Steven Messner and Richard Rosenfeld advocate 'institutionalizing' criminological theory in the sense of thinking about the levels and types of crime that arise when social institutions are operating normally. They contrast this way of thinking about crime with theoretical approaches that view crime as a consequence of institutional breakdown or dysfunction, as, for example, when juvenile delinquency is attributed to poor parenting or schooling. Their institutional-anomie theory is intended to explain crime with reference to the 'rules of the game' associated with normal institutional functioning. Following on from this, Jón Bernburg (Chapter 2) presents a detailed description of institutional-anomie theory and suggests that, in their effort to extend Merton's classical anomie perspective beyond the social stratification system to encompass other social institutions, Messner and Rosenfeld divert attention from the 'objective conditions' of material deprivation and inequality under which decisions to engage in crime are made. In Chapter 3 Barbara Sims argues that Marxist criminology is the theoretical 'missing link' – missing, that is, from institutional-anomie theory – capable of explaining why American society is excessively materialistic, unequal and crime-ridden.

In the next chapter, Elliott Currie proposes provocatively that official crime rates are deceptive because they exclude the imprisoned population, which underwent massive expansion in the United States when crime rates were plummeting in the 1990s. Excluding prisoners from the crime statistics, Currie suggests, makes as little sense as excluding hospital patients from health statistics, especially since prisons rarely 'cure' crime but simply shift it from social locations where it is counted to those where it is hidden. Although official crime rates may have fallen, he concludes that the 'criminality rate' – the propensity to commit crime – may have remained constant during the 1990s. Part I concludes with Francis Cullen's discussion of the relationship between crime and 'social support' (Chapter 5). Cullen proposes that communities and societies that are more supportive of their members will experience less crime. He suggests that the theme of social support is implicit in other theoretical perspectives, including Messner's and Rosenfeld's institutional-anomie theory, and that social support may condition the effect of social control on crime: controls applied in a supportive context, similar to Braithwaite's (1989) idea of 'reintegrative shaming', should be more likely to reduce crime than when applied without social support.

Cross-national Tests of Institutional-Anomie Theory

Part II presents several cross-national empirical investigations of the institutional-anomie perspective. In Chapter 6 Messner and Rosenfeld hypothesize that nations whose political systems are less dominated by the institutional claims and requisites of the free-market economy should have lower crime rates than those in which market imperatives more fully circumscribe political action. Drawing on the political economist Gosta Esping-Andersen's (1990) work on 'decommodified' social policies, they measure the degree to which the polity has 'tamed the market' with generous, broad and inclusive social welfare benefits and services. Consistent with theoretical expectations, they find that nations with stronger social welfare policies have lower homicide rates than those with weaker polices, when other conditions related to homicide rates are controlled for. Next, Jukka Savolainen (Chapter 7) extends the logic of Messner's and Rosenfeld's analysis, hypothesizing that economic and social inequality should not be as closely associated with homicide rates in nations with strong social welfare policies as in those with more restrictive policies. He finds evidence for this hypothesis in an analysis of two cross-national samples. Drawing on the institutional-anomie perspective, Cullen's social support theory, and Agnew's general strain theory (Agnew, 1992, 1999), Travis Pratt and Timothy Godsey obtain similar results in their study reported in Chapter 8.

In Chapter 9 John B. Cullen and his colleagues apply the institutional-anomie perspective in a cross-national investigation of managers' willingness to justify unethical behaviour. Their results offer mixed support for the theory. Managers in 'welfare socialist' societies are perhaps more likely than those elsewhere to justify unethical behaviour, the authors reason, because they are more apt to regard themselves as 'net losers' under socialist policies. Managers committed to the values of universalism and pecuniary materialism are more likely to justify unethical behaviour but, contrary to theoretical expectations, those committed to achievement and individualism are less willing than others to justify such behaviour.

US-based Tests of Institutional-Anomie Theory

Part III of the volume presents several US-based tests of institutional-anomie theory with differing units of analysis. In Chapter 10 Mitchell Chamlin and John Cochran derive from the theory the proposition that the impact of adverse economic conditions on crime should be conditioned by the strength of non-economic institutions. Where such institutions retain their vitality, they reason, the effect of poverty on crime should be smaller than in circumstances where non-economic institutions are weaker. They find support for this proposition in an analysis of American states. Following the same logic, Alex Piquero and Nicole Piquero (Chapter 11) find support for the theory when certain indicators of the strength of non-economic institutions are employed but not when alternative measurements are used. They conclude that institutional-anomie theory may be sensitive to how its major concepts are operationalized.

Michael Maume and Matthew Lee propose in Chapter 12 that the strength of non-economic institutions mediates, rather than moderates, the influence of adverse economic conditions produced by the free-market economy on crime rates, and their analysis of US counties produces evidence in support of this argument (see also Hannon and DeFronzo, 1998).

The US-based studies presented thus far evaluate empirical implications of institutional-anomie theory with cross-sectional data on states or counties. In the next chapter, Candice Batton and Gary Jensen investigate the impact on crime of changes over time in indicators of the dominance of the free-market economy in the United States. Their results indicate that such effects may be limited to specific historical periods. Part III concludes with another study by Mitchell Chamlin and John Cochran (Chapter 14) that examines the effect of a measure of 'social altruism' on city crime rates. Consistent with expectations from institutional-anomie theory, they find an inverse relationship between social altruism and both property and violent crime rates.

Crime and Institutional Dynamics at the Local Level

Part IV presents studies that investigate the impact of local 'institutions' on crime. As noted earlier, institutions are commonly confused with organizations by American criminologists. Although several of the studies in this section refer to 'institutions' of one kind or another, they in fact incorporate measures of organizations such as local businesses, recreation facilities and the like. Nonetheless, these studies represent an important advance over prior community-level research on crime in that they investigate how the presence of organizations in a community mediates or moderates the effects of economic disadvantage on community crime rates. The logic of the approach is similar to that of the studies discussed earlier that focus on the role of non-economic institutions in reducing crime. All of these studies emphasize the functions of organizations, or the broader institutions in which they are embedded, in imposing social controls or providing social supports that affect crime rates.

Thomas Stucky (Chapter 15) derives hypotheses from both institutional-anomie theory and systemic social disorganization theory (Bursik and Grasmick, 1993) indicating that local political structures that are more responsive to citizens should not only reduce crime rates directly, but also reduce the effect of deprivation on crime. He finds evidence in support of both hypotheses in an analysis of American cities. In Chapter 16 Ruth Peterson and her colleagues find, in a study of Columbus, Ohio neighbourhoods, that the presence of recreation facilities reduces neighbourhood crime rates, when other community characteristics are controlled for, and that the crime reductions are greatest in the most disadvantaged areas. They also report, however, that strong direct effects of deprivation on crime remain when the presence of recreation facilities is statistically controlled.

María Vélez (Chapter 17) investigates the impact of 'public social control' on criminal victimization in a study of 60 neighbourhoods in three American cities. Public social control refers to the ties between residents in local neighbourhoods and extra-community entities such as city government and police. The stronger such ties are, according to systemic disorganization theory (Bursik and Grasmick, 1993), the better local residents are able to control crime. Vélez finds that neighbourhood residents' perceptions of the responsiveness of city officials and police are negatively related to the frequency of victimization. Consistent with other research, she also finds that the crime-reducing effects of public social control are greatest in the most disadvantaged neighbourhoods.

Part IV concludes with Karen Parker's examination of the effect on homicide rates of institutional transformations in the US economy – specifically, the decline of employment in manufacturing and the corresponding rise in the service sector. Her study of American cities indicates that the decline in manufacturing is associated with a rise in homicides among black males, and that the growth of the service sector is associated with an increase in homicides among black females. This study highlights both the importance of investigating the relationship between crime and institutional change and of modelling the racially disparate consequences of economic change on crime rates.

Implications for Punishment

The two essays in Part V focus on punishment rather than crime. Just as crime rates should be responsive to the nature of, and balance among, social institutions, so should punishment policies and processes. If anything, formal punishment policies should be *more* responsive than crime rates to the institutional context, because punishment of law violations is an explicit and important function of the state. Yet, as John Sutton points out in Chapter 19, American criminologists have characteristically avoided studying the institutional sources of the leading punitive instrument for serious crimes: imprisonment.[2] In a cross-national study of imprisonment rates, Sutton finds that the association between various economic outcomes and imprisonment is largely a function of institutional context. The association is attenuated in nations with strong labour unions and left-wing political parties compared with nations in which unions and social democratic parties are weaker.

The final essay is Dina Rose's and Todd Clear's provocative discussion of how formal punishment policies – incarceration in particular – may in fact lead to more, rather than less, crime because they reduce community social capital. They argue that high rates of incarceration weaken families and communities through the coerced removal of young men and that these effects are concentrated in the very communities that already suffer from elevated rates of economic deprivation, family disruption and reduced social control. The institutional message in Rose's and Clear's assessment of incarceration is that formal social control mechanisms may interfere with the informal controls of family and community. Rose's and Clear's argument has not yet received extensive empirical evaluation, but, by calling attention to the unintended institutional consequences of incarceration, their contribution – especially when viewed in the context of the other studies reproduced in this volume – promises to enrich theory and research on crime and punishment for years to come.

References

Agnew, Robert (1992), 'Foundation for a General Strain Theory of Crime and Delinquency', *Criminology*, **30**, pp. 47–87

Agnew, Robert (1999), 'A General Strain Theory of Community Differences in Crime Rates', *Journal of Research in Crime and Delinquency*, 36, pp. 123–55.

Bellah, Robert N., Madsen, Richard, Sullivan, William M., Swidler, Ann and Tipton, Steven M.. (1992), *The Good Society*, New York: Knopf.

Blumstein, Alfred and Wallman, Joel (eds) (2000), *The Crime Drop in America*, New York: Cambridge University Press.

Bohlen, Celestine (1992), 'The Russians' New Code: If It Pays, Anything Goes', *New York Times*, 30 August, pp. 1, 6.

Braithwaite, John (1989), *Crime, Shame, and Reintegration*, Cambridge: Cambridge University Press.

Bursik, Robert J. Jr and Grasmick, Harold G. (1993), *Neighborhoods and Crime: The Dimensions of Effective Community Control*, New York: Lexington Books.

Esping-Andersen, Gosta (1990), *The Three Worlds of Welfare Capitalism*. Princeton, NJ: Princeton University Press.

---

[2] David Garland's (2001) work on punishment is an exception, but in as much as Garland was trained in Europe, it is an exception that proves the rule.

Garland, David (2001), *The Culture of Control: Crime and Social Order in Contemporary Society*, Chicago: University of Chicago Press.

Gordon, Michael R. (1996), 'Slaying Tells of Russia's Deadly Capitalism', *New York Times*, 5 November, p. A3.

Hannon, Lance and DeFronzo, James (1998), 'The Truly Disadvantaged, Public Assistance, and Crime', *Social Problems*, **45**, pp.383–92.

Harrison, Paige M. and Beck, Allen J. (2005), *Prison and Jail Inmates at Midyear 2004*, Washington, DC: US Department of Justice.

Holmes, Stephen (1997), 'What Russia Teaches Us Now', *American Prospect*, July–August, pp. 30–39.

Levitt, Steven D. (2004), 'Understanding Why Crime Fell in the 1990s: Four Factors that Explain the Decline and Six that Do Not', *Journal of Economic Perspectives*, **18**, pp. 163–90.

Messner, Steven F. and Rosenfeld, Richard (2001a), 'An Institutional-Anomie Theory of Crime' in R. Paternoster and R. Bachman (eds), *Explaining Criminals and Crime*, Los Angeles: Roxbury, pp. 151–60.

Messner, Steven F. and Rosenfeld, Richard (2001b), *Crime and the American Dream* (3rd edn), Belmont, CA: Wadsworth.

Messner, Steven F. and Rosenfeld, Richard (forthcoming), *Crime and the American Dream* (4th edn), Belmont, CA: Wadsworth.

Mills, C. Wright (1959), *The Sociological Imagination*, New York: Oxford University Press.

Parsons, Talcott (1951), *The Social System*, New York: Free Press.

Rosenfeld, Richard and Messner, Steven F. (2006), 'The Origins, Nature, and Prospects of Institutional-Anomie Theory',in Stuart Henry and Mark Lanier (eds), *The Essential Criminology Reader*, Boulder, CO: Westview, pp. 164-173.

Part I
Theoretical Considerations

[1]

"Institutionalizing" Criminological Theory[1]

Steven F. Messner and Richard Rosenfeld

Introduction

The influence of sociology as a discipline on criminology as a field of study is hard to exaggerate. As Ronald Akers observed in his presidential address at the annual meetings of the Southern Sociological Society, criminology was essentially incorporated into sociology by the middle of the twentieth century.[2] Subsequent developments, such as the emergence of criminal justice programs and the spread of criminological journals, have rendered sociology a less dominant force in the study of crime. Nevertheless, it seems fair to assert that "sociological perspectives still constitute...the intellectual center of gravity in criminology" (Akers, 1992: 4).

However, despite the profitable exchanges between criminology and sociology, the full potential of the sociological perspective for an understanding of crime has not been realized. That is because inadequate attention has been directed to one of the core concepts of sociology: *social institutions*. Of course, institutions have not been neglected in criminology. Conflict and labeling perspectives in particular have offered keen insights on how the institution of law plays a critical role in the criminalization process by defining the subset of behaviors and persons officially recognized as "crimes" and "criminals" (Quinney, 1974, 1977; Turk, 1969; Vold, 1958). Nevertheless, institutional analysis has been seriously underdeveloped in *etiological* analyses of crime because the concept of institutions has been invoked in criminological theory in a confusing or an overly restrictive manner.

To develop these arguments, we briefly review the more important macro-level approaches to explaining the causes of crime in sociological criminology. We attempt to show that the concept of institutions has not been applied rigorously in any of these approaches. We then explicate a formal concept of institutions and show how this concept is often confounded with related concepts. Finally, we illustrate promising issues for a distinctively institutional analysis of crime and discuss some of the more important challenges that must be met if criminological theory is to be more fully "institutionalized."

The Underdevelopment of Institutional Inquiry in Criminological Theory

Criminological theories are often distinguished on the basis of levels of explanation and corresponding units of analysis. Some theories attempt to explain why a given person rather than another commits a crime and adopt the individual as the unit of analysis. Other theories attempt to explain variation in rates of crime across socially meaningful collectivities or aggregates. These theories are formulated at a macro-level of analysis. Institutions are intrinsically properties of organized collectivities and not individuals, and thus institutional processes generally play a greater role in macro-level theorizing than in individual-level theorizing. We thus focus on the three most influential macro-level perspectives on the causes of crime: social disorganization, anomie, and cultural deviance theories.[3]

Social Disorganization Theory

The etiological perspective in criminology in which institutional processes are invoked most prominently is social disorganization theory. As Kornhauser (1978) explains, institutions play a critical mediating role in classical social disorganization theory. It is precisely the "disruption" or "decay" (pp. 64, 79) of conventional institutions that links structural conditions such as residential mobility, population heterogeneity, and poverty with weak social control and high rates of crime and delinquency. This basic argument has proven to be quite fruitful as far as it goes. Empirical variation in crime rates across urban neighborhoods can be explained to some degree with reference to the structural variables identified by classical social disorganization theory (Sampson and Groves, 1989; Sampson, Morenoff, and Gannon-Rowley, 2002; but see also Veysey and Messner, 1999).

However, the fundamental limitation associated with the type of analysis characteristic of classical social disorganization theory is that the actual *nature* and *structure* of conventional institutions themselves are neither described fully, nor incorporated into the analysis of crime. The structures of social institutions are pretty much taken as given. To the extent that institutions are considered in any detail, the focus lies with their *functioning* rather than their defining characteristics and the implications of those characteristics for crime.

Recent studies informed by elaborated versions of social disorganization theory similarly incorporate institutions in a highly restricted manner. In an extensive review of the "neighborhood effects" literature that has appeared since the mid-1990s, Sampson et al. (2002: 459) point out that most studies that attend explicitly to institutions are limited to assessments of the "mere presence of neighborhood institutions." To some extent, this is a consequence of limited data availability, but it also reflects the lack of clear conceptualizing about institutions and a common confounding of institutional structure with institutional functioning. The absence of an institution is taken as prima facie evidence that any functions associated with that institution are not being fulfilled. This relative neglect of the actual structure of institutions, in contrast with their effective functioning, is not surprising given the focus in the social disorganization tradition on explaining variation in crime at the community level. Although institutions might vary markedly in their strength across neighborhoods within a particular city, variation in basic *institutional structure* across these units is likely to be limited because institutions commonly reflect features of the larger society.

Moreover, disorganization perspectives provide little guidance with respect to the level or type of crime that should be expected when institutions are operating normally. Disorganization theories, virtually by definition, are "breakdown" theories of crime. Crime results when institutions do not function the way they are supposed to function. This conception leaves no way of determining the expected level of crime when institutions are functioning pretty much as they should.

One response to this criticism is simply to assume that the expected level of crime when a community or society is well organized and institutions are functioning effectively is zero. This approach is problematic, however, for two reasons. One, it easily leads to tautological reasoning. If a researcher begins with the premise that there would be no crime under conditions of strong social organization, then the very existence of crime would seem to signal some *dis*-organization. Indeed, the classical social disorganization theorists have been faulted for precisely this logical flaw—treating crime as both a consequence and an indicator of social disorganization (Pfohl, 1994: 210; see also Bursik, 1988).

Two, the very notion that the level of crime for a well-organized community could conceivably be zero is implausible upon careful examination. The classic formulation of the argument that a certain, non-zero level of crime can be regarded as "normal" for different types of social organization is of course Durkheim's (1966a [1895]: 64-75). Durkheim argues persuasively that crime is the outcome of conditions that are essential for social life and that crime is functional for society in a number of respects. Durkheim's insistence that some amount of crime necessarily is found in all societies is faithfully recorded in criminology textbooks, but is largely absent from contemporary criminological theories. In the case of social disorganization theories, this omission results in a basic analytical problem: How can one know how much "excess" crime is produced by institutional "decay" or "disruption" when no baseline level of crime has been established, that is, the level associated with normal institutional functioning?

An instructive illustration of how a "normal" crime rate might be viewed by criminologists is provided by the concept of *frictional unemployment* in economics. Economists differ with respect to the optimum level of unemployment in a modern, complex economy, but hardly any maintain that the optimum level is zero. Some unemployment is inevitable because people change jobs and are searching for new jobs, and because people often take a break before beginning a job with a new employer.[4] This so-called frictional unemployment is an expected outcome of the normal workings of a healthy economy. The economist, therefore, can determine whether too much unemployment exists by comparing the actual level of unemployment with the frictional level. Indeed, the level of unemployment might be deemed too low, if it suggests insufficient mobility in the labor market. The criminologist working from the perspective of social disorganization theory, in contrast, is unable to determine in any analogous fashion whether crime rates are too high and cannot begin to comprehend crime rates that are too low.

Anomie Theory

Anomie theory as formulated by Merton (1938, 1968) is typically cited as an exemplar of the sociological approach to the explanation of crime and deviance (Rosenfeld, 1989), and thus it might be expected that institutions would play a particularly prominent role in this theory. At the most general level, Merton argues that pressures for "aberrant behavior" are generated when there is "dissociation between culturally prescribed aspirations and socially structured avenues for realizing these aspirations" (1968: 188). To illustrate his argument, Merton selects the United States as essentially a case study of a social system characterized by such "dissociation," and he directs attention to the fundamental nature of one particular institution in American society: the distribution of economic opportunities and rewards, or the economic *stratification system.*

In his well-known formulation, Merton identifies a profound internal contradiction between the motivational mechanism of the stratification system in the United States—universal cultural prescriptions for material success—and its allocative mechanism—earnings generated in labor markets, where irrelevant status characteristics influence opportunities.[5] People are socialized to aspire to goals that are inaccessible given their structural location. This contradiction generates pressures for deviant behavior, including crime. Similar arguments appear in Marxist discussions of the dialectics of a capitalist economy (Bonger, 1916).

Merton's theory thus treats institutional structure in a way that it is lacking in social disorganization theory. A relatively high level of crime is the normal, expected outcome of the very nature of a given institutional arrangement, albeit a somewhat "disjunctured" arrangement (Merton 1968: 216). Merton's institutional analysis is limited, however, in two very important respects. First, as we have argued elsewhere (Messner and Rosenfeld, 2001a; see also Cohen, 1985: 233), Merton's theory largely ignores the relevance for crime of institutions other than the stratification system (e.g., the family, polity, education, religion). He does refer briefly to the role of the family when attempting to account for the individual adaptation of "ritualism" in contrast with "innovation," the latter being the adaptation that typically involves criminal behavior. He speculates that parents in the lower middle class "exert continuous pressure upon children to abide by the moral mandates of the society" (1968: 205), thereby increasing the likelihood that those from lower middle-class families will become ritualists rather than criminals. However, Merton never describes what it is about families in the respective social classes that accounts for the differences in socialization practices. He simply notes that "much sociological research" is needed on this topic (1968: 207).

Moreover, his sketchy remarks on the role of the family in the selection of modes of adaptation conform rather closely to the "breakdown" logic of social disorganization theory. He explains that innovation, in contrast with ritualism, "...presupposes that individuals have been imperfectly socialized so that they abandon the institutional means while retaining the success-aspiration" (1968: 203). Merton thus fails to attend explicitly to the ways in which the basic structure of the family, rather than its effective functioning as a socializing agent, might be related to crime. By way of contrast, consider the explanation of the gender differential in delinquency contained in power-control theory (Hagan, Gillis, and Simpson, 1985; Hagan, Simpson, and Gillis, 1987). Different family structures—patriarchal and egalitarian—lead to more or less control of daughters in comparison with sons, corresponding gender differences in preferences for risk, and a greater or lesser gender differential in delinquency. This explanation for delinquency directs attention precisely to the implications of *effective* socialization across different family structures.

A second major limitation of Merton's analytic framework is that it focuses narrowly on the stratification of *economic outputs* (monetary rewards) and neglects other important aspects of the economy. As his Marxist critics have pointed out (Sims, 1997), Mertonian anomie theory undervalues the organization of *production*—the essence of the capitalist economy as an institution—and directs sole emphasis to the system of distribution. One does not have to accept all of the implications of the Marxist critique to agree that Mertonian theory requires not only a conception of the structure and interrelated functions of the broad range of social institutions, but a richer conception of the economy as an institution as well.

Cultural Deviance Theory

Cultural deviance theories postulate that criminal behavior is acquired through the more-or-less normal processes of socialization in deviant or criminal subcultures. The focus on normal learning in these perspectives, at first glance, appears to be compatible with explanations of crime emphasizing the structure of institutions and not merely their faulty functioning. But cultural deviance accounts differ from "institutional" explanations of the causes of crime in two important ways.

First, cultural deviance theories of crime invariably direct attention away from -the dominant institutional order in a society toward deviant or criminal *subcultures* which, by definition, are comprised of values and norms at odds with the conventional or "legitimate" moral order. Rarely do such perspectives consider the criminogenic properties of the dominant order itself.[6] Instead, cultural deviance theories often entail a "mixed model" that combines social disorganization organization themes with subcultural dynamics: the subcultural sources of criminal behavior emerge in response to institutional deficiencies of one kind or another.[7] A good example is Elijah Anderson's (1999) influential account of violent "codes of the street" (see also Kubrin and Weitzer, 2003; Sampson and Wilson, 1995). These codes emerge in deprived inner-city neighborhoods where "the rules of civil law have been severely weakened" and neighborhood residents have become alienated from conventional institutions (Anderson, 2002: 1547).

A second subtle but telling distinction between cultural deviance and institutional explanations is that institutional explanations of crime do not require culturally sanctioned deviance. The distinction turns on whether the content of the cultural rules directly promotes or supports criminal activity. In cultural deviance theories they do, whereas they need not in institutional explanations. This distinction can be clarified by considering Durkheim's (1966b [1897]) classic explanation for higher suicide rates among Protestants than Catholics in Europe. Durkheim maintains that Protestantism as a "religious system" does not directly promote suicide. On the contrary, Protestantism and Catholicism "prohibit suicide with equal emphasis" (p.

157). Rather, the emphasis placed on free inquiry and individual salvation in Protestantism diminishes group solidarity, freeing individuals to engage in the ultimate form of social withdrawal. Durkheim locates the causes of suicide in the nature of cultural rules, to be sure, but not in rules that require, condone, or are unconcerned with suicide.

A criminological illustration of the difference between cultural deviance and institutional explanations comes from our own work on the cultural sources of the high rates of serious, predatory crime in the United States (Messner and Rosenfeld, 2001a). We argue that the strong emphasis placed on individual, competitive achievement in the American Dream contributes to higher rates of violent crime in the United States than in other developed societies, but not because the dominant cultural rules require people to commit homicide and robbery. Our institutional explanation of crime may be wrong on the facts, but conceptually it is quite distinct from explanations, such as Anderson's (1999), that attribute high levels of violent behavior to violent conduct codes.

The Concept of an Institution

A major reason for the limited incorporation of institutional analysis in macro-sociological theories of crime such as social disorganization and anomie theory is conceptual imprecision and ambiguity. Proponents of these approaches have failed to explicate the intended meaning of "institution" and have failed to apply the concept rigorously. This has led to conceptual confusion, which has, in turn, inhibited productive theorizing about the relationship between social institutions and crime. In an effort to overcome these limitations, it is instructive to review a classic treatment of the concept of institutions in sociology and more recent applications in other social science disciplines.

Institutions as "Rules"

In the sociological literature, Parsons (1990 [1934]) provides the most elaborate and rigorous discussion of the concept of an institution (see also Bellah et al., 1991: 287-306). Parsons argues for a strict analytic distinction between institutions and behavior. Institutions in the formal sense refer to the regulatory norms that guide behavior, or more precisely, that govern the choice of the ends of social action (1990 [1934]: 324). Institutions are formalized to varying degrees, and compliance with institutional norms is empirically variable. Nevertheless, institutions establish an encompassing framework of rules within which individual action occurs.

A very similar approach appears in the "new institutionalism" that has emerged in economics, political science, and economic sociology over recent decades. As Douglass North (1990: 3) puts it, "institutions are the rules of the game in a society or, more formally, are the humanly devised constraints that shape human interaction." Criminologists (and, we might add, many other social scientists) clearly have not understood institutions in this way, that is, as a system of rules that govern behavior. Rather, they have confounded the rules upon which there is widespread (albeit imperfect) agreement with the degree of behavioral conformity with the rules. As a result, criminologists have focused almost exclusively on institutional functioning and have been largely blinded to the consequences of *institutional structure* for crime.

Analytic Distinction between "Institutions" and "Organizations"

In many ways, this blind spot in criminology is understandable because the concept of a social institution is highly abstract and is easily confused with less abstract concepts that are easier to grasp. To avoid this kind of confusion, Parsons (1990 [1934]: 320) cautioned long ago that it is critically important to distinguish between an institution as "an analytic category" and any "class of concrete phenomena." Concrete social behaviors are caused by many factors. Accordingly, to be able to isolate the distinctive contribution of institutions in explaining these phenomena, the institutional element must be distinguished from the phenomena themselves.

Failure to retain a clear distinction between institutions and concrete behavioral phenomena often directs attention away from institutions to the more familiar concept of *organizations*. Organizations are comprised of networks of actors performing a variety of tasks oriented towards a common purpose. It is, of course, instructive to analyze the structure and functioning of organizations. However, as Bellah et al. (1991) have argued, studying organizations is no substitute for studying institutions. Indeed, to do so "runs the risk of confusing the organizations with the institutional patterns that define their purposes and meanings" (p. 302).

In the economics literature, Douglass North has similarly explicated the distinction between organizations and institutions through the use of the game analogy:

> Conceptually, what must be clearly differentiated are the rules from the players. The purpose of the rules is to define the way the game is played. But the objective of the team within that set of rules is to win the game—by a combination of skills, strategy, and coordination; by fair means and sometimes by foul means. Modeling the strategies and the skills of the team as it develops is a separate process from modeling the creation, evolution, and consequences of the rules. (pp. 4-5)

To develop this analogy further, consider the game of football as an institutionalized activity. The institution of football, in the sense of the rules of the game, is different from the organizations that play the game, the teams. Following North, it is useful to examine how the strategies and choices of a given set of players and coaches, such as those on the New York Giants or the Toronto Argonauts, affect outcomes within their leagues, the National Football League (NFL) and the Canadian Football League (CFL), respectively. This entails an organizational analysis and is in keeping with the analytical scope of disorganization theories of crime. In the example given here, the disorganization theorist would search for impediments to team success in the relationships among players and between players and team management. A "disorganized" team is likely to have difficulty winning many games. However, it is also useful to ask, and this is a different kind of analytical question, how the *institutional framework*, the defining rules associated with Canadian and American football, structures the incentives for behaviors and defines opportunities, thereby producing distinctive kinds of strategies and outcomes (more points, more injuries, more penalties, etc.).

The analytic distinction between institutions and organizations is typically blurred in criminological explanations. The reference to "weak institutions" usually refers to poorly functioning organizations, either formal or informal. For example, social disorganization theorists who attribute weak social control to the failure of the educational "institution" are typically invoking organizational failure: the *schools* in the neighborhood as organizations are not effectively supervising students or bonding them to school rules. The argument does not entail an analysis of the *institution* of education, as a set of rules governing the transmission and acquisition of knowledge. Similarly, criminological theories that postulate a role for the "family" in the genesis of crime typically refer to concrete social phenomena—weak or disrupted families as informal organizations or social groups—rather than to the institution of the family per se. The institution of the family refers to the basic rules that govern sexual activity, entry to and exit from marital roles, child-rearing, nurturance across generations, and so on.

Dimensions of Institutions

Once institutions have been clearly conceptualized as rules, or the system of norms that govern behavior, different dimensions of institutions can be identified that can inform criminological inquiry. Three particularly important dimensions of institutions are: (1) institutional *structure*, (2) institutional *regulation*, and (3) institutional *performance*. Institutional structure encompasses the actual content of the rules and their internal consistency, or what Parsons (1990 [1930]: 332) refers to as "structural integration." The greater the degree of "harmony" of the rules constituting an institution, the greater is its structural integration. Institutional regulation refers to the degree of conformity with the rules themselves, that is, the extent to which institutional roles are enacted faithfully. Institutional regulation depends on the moral force of the rules and the extrinsic sanctions and incentives that can be applied to influence behavior. The third dimension, institutional performance, refers to the extent to which the enactment of institutional roles fosters the realization of the goals associated with a particular institutional domain.

The distinctions among these three dimensions of institutions—structure, regulation, and performance—are perhaps not obvious but are critically important for understanding how institutions affect the level and types of crime in a society. To illustrate from the field of economics, a society might have economic institutions that specify a structurally coherent set of rules for how people should go about meeting their material needs. Moreover, these rules governing economic behavior might have considerable moral force: people enact the economic roles faithfully. The economy, however, might perform very poorly in terms of actually producing goods and services. Indeed, this is a key analytic issue for institutional economists: what kinds of rules are more or less conducive to economic productivity and growth?

This is precisely the kind of question that has been largely absent from criminological inquiry, where the analytic focus neglects institutional structure in favor of institutional regulation and performance. It is also the kind of question that bears upon the "normal" level of crime associated with a given institutional configuration referred to earlier.

For example, assuming that parents enact their institutional roles as expected (they follow the rules for bringing up children), how much and what kinds of deviant behavior should we expect their children to engage in? Note the difference between this analytic question, which asks about the deviant behavior associated with effective socialization, and that typically posed by social disorganization and control perspectives, which ask about the deviance produced by ineffective socialization. In the latter case, the rules of the game are taken for granted; in the former, they are at the center of the analysis. The bulk of contemporary research on the relationship between family functioning and delinquency is informed by learning or attachment theories that attribute child misbehavior to criminal or antisocial parents, inadequate parental supervision, or "disrupted" families (Farrington, 2002). The nature of the family as an institution rarely enters the analysis. By sharp contrast, power-control theory, as noted above, and feminist theories more generally view conventional gender role socialization as responsible for higher rates of delinquency and crime, violent crime in particular, among boys and men compared with girls and women. Boys and young men are socialized in the family and in other settings to display independence, courage, physical strength, and aggressiveness—attributes compatible with much criminal behavior, if not criminogenic per se. Girls and young women, on the other hand, are "socialized to be patient, understanding, sensitive, passive, dependent, and nurturing" (Beirne and Messerschmidt, 2000: 204). From these perspectives, we would expect "normal" (i.e., properly socialized) boys to be more criminally active than normal girls given the nature of the conventional "rules of the game" of gender role socialization.

General Issues for Institutional Inquiry on Crime

We suggest that the adoption of a more formal conceptualization of institutions and their various dimensions will open up new and exciting avenues for criminological theorizing and research. To develop this point, we pose questions about institutions and crime and pursue further the "game analogy." This facilitates a comparison between approaches that attend explicitly to institutional structure with the more limited approaches commonly adopted in criminological inquiry.

Institutional Structure, Institutional Integration, and the Volume of Crime

One rather obvious question for institutional analysis in criminology is this: what are the consequences of the structure of a given institution for overall levels of criminal activity?

Continuing with our sports analogy, we might ask: Why does the number of fouls in a professional basketball game typically exceed the number of penalties in a professional football game? An important reason for this empirical phenomenon is the different nature of the rules of the two types of games. In basketball, there is a very fine line between permitted behavior and prohibited behavior, making frequent violations virtually inevitable. In addition, rules about stopping the clock near the end of the game create an incentive structure wherein infractions can be deployed strategically. Note also that the moral authority associated with the rules ("regulatory integration") varies across these two sports. In basketball, moral prohibitions against most fouls are relatively weak, and coaches quite openly countenance fouling under certain circumstance. Similar behavior is much rarer in football. If coaches or players engage in these acts intentionally, they do so surreptitiously.[8]

Now consider how social disorganization or conventional anomie theories might approach the problem of more fouls in basketball than penalties in football. The disorganization theorist would be drawn to the relative weaknesses in the structure of basketball teams that loosen the controls over players, "freeing" them to foul. The anomie theorist would search for unequal opportunities or an excessive emphasis on winning in basketball. Neither approach necessarily would be wrong, of course, but the analytical limitations of any approach that neglected the differences in the rules of the games of basketball and football in explaining patterns and levels of infractions should be apparent. Such an approach would miss the fundamental point that the "normal" basketball game will produce more fouls than the "normal" football game.

A second important criminological question pertains to the interrelation of institutions, or institutional integration. What are the consequences for crime of differences in the articulation of institutions?

Elsewhere (Messner and Rosenfeld, 2001a, 2001b), we have advanced an institutional-anomie theory that attempts to address this kind of question. It "puts institutions to work" by explaining different levels and forms of crime with reference to three analytically distinct types of institutional configurations that reflect differences in the articulation of institutions, or differences in the "institutional balance of power." In the first type, a free-market economy dominates the institutional structure, and the society is characterized by a strong emphasis on personal liberty (in the economic realm), the competitive allocation of rewards, and an emphasis on the ends versus the means of individual action. The rules of the economy are awarded highest priority in the system of institutions. High levels of individualistic, predatory crime are the expected outcome of this institutional configuration. In the second institutional type, the state dominates other institutions, as reflected in the high priority given to the rules for the exercise of power. High levels of corruption and related forms of manipulation of personal relationships for unfair advantage are the likely result of this type arrangement. The third institutional type is characterized by the dominance of civil institutions, notably religion or the kinship system. Rules associated with in-group loyalty and the protection of honor dominate social interaction under such circumstances. These institutional arrangements are hypothesized to produce high levels of crime-equivalents in the form of human rights violations and repression of personal freedoms.

The hypotheses enumerated above are just that—hypotheses. They have yet to be substantiated through comprehensive empirical analysis (for partial assessments, see Messner and Rosenfeld, 1997; Savolainen, 2000). Nevertheless, they illustrate a distinctive kind of explanation of the nature and level of crime, one that directs attention to the relevant "rules of the game" associated with institutional structures and their interrelationships.

Institutional Structure as the Context for Individual Criminal Behavior

Our emphasis in the analysis of institutions thus far has been at the macro-level. However, attention to institutional structure is essential not only for an analysis of macro-level patterns and levels of crime but also for understanding individual-level criminal behavior. As Albert Cohen (1985: 223) reminds us, a basic premise in contemporary criminology—indeed a "platitude"—is that "all crime is a function of some properties of the actor and some properties of the situation in which the actor acts." Features of the situation activate and channel propensities of individuals. Thus, given that institutions constitute a salient feature of the situation or social environment in all societies, explaining individual behavior requires an understanding of the institutional context.

Returning to the sports analogy, the individual determinants of the commission of infractions are likely to be very different in basketball than in football. Consider "self-control" as a cause of deviant behavior (Gottfredson and Hirschi, 1990). In basketball, low self-control is likely to be a poorer predictor of fouls than in football because the rules of the game entail a more favorable mix of rewards relative to sanctions for infractions. Indeed, late in the game, it may very well be the more self-controlled basketball players who foul more frequently for strategic purposes. In football, where penalties generally lead to greater costs and fewer benefits for the team, individual impulsiveness or low self-control should be a better predictor of violations.

A criminological illustration of the importance of institutional structure for understanding individual criminal behavior entails the differential effect of school failure on delinquency in relation to the articulation of the educational system with the economy. The consequences of school failure for criminal behavior and life chances are dependent on the nature of the relationship between the system of formal education and the occupational structure. Where the two institutions are tightly coupled in the sense that occupational achievement is highly dependent on academic success, we would expect school failure to be strongly related to delinquency and crime. In contrast, where education and the occupational structure are loosely coupled, occupational success, and the associated material rewards, are less dependent on school achievement, and a weak relationship between school failure and criminal behavior would be expected. A concrete illustration of the two institutional configurations is the contrast between Germany, where a strong apprenticeship system reduces reliance on academic achievement for occupational success, and the United States, where academic achievement strongly influences occupational placement and outcomes.[9]

Conclusions

Despite the continuing influence of sociology on criminology, criminological theory and research on the causes of crime remain "under-institutionalized." What passes for institutional analysis typically entails a restricted focus on institutional functioning or performance, with little attention to institutional structure, that is, the nature of the rules themselves and how adherence to the rules is related to the normal or expected patterns and level of crime in a society. In fact, criminological investigations with a professed emphasis on social "institutions" very often ignore institutions per se and focus instead on organizations. The result is a kind of thinking about crime that is at once misleading and impoverished. Institutions should not be confused with their concrete organizational manifestations, and a richer understanding of the nature of institutions and their interconnections will enable criminologists to address key analytical issues that traditionally have been bypassed. Among the most important of such issues, we have proposed, is the amount and type of crime that results when institutions function the way they are supposed to.

We do not wish to minimize the difficulties inherent in conducting studies of crime with a more explicit and rigorous institutional orientation. It is far easier to call for more and better institutional analysis in criminology than to indicate precisely what such analysis should look like and how it ought to be implemented. By way of closing, we outline what we consider to be some of the essential features of fruitful institutional inquiry and identify some of the more important challenges that must be met to conduct such inquiry.

Essential Features of Institutional Inquiry

Institutional assessments of crime must, in our view, incorporate at least three key analytical elements. They must be *comparative*, in order to expand and maximize variation in institutional structure; *multilevel*, by focusing on the interplay of individual behavior and institutional context; and *integrative*, by attending to the full array of institutional domains, thereby drawing from a wide range of scholarly disciplines and specializations.

Comparative research is fundamental to a genuinely institutional analysis of crime or any other aspect of social behavior. From an institutional perspective, we have maintained, crime varies according to the nature of the "rules of the game." Therefore, criminological inquiry requires sufficiently broad variation in the rules governing behavior for reliably assessing how differences in the structure, regulatory force, and performance of distinct systems of rules are associated with observed patterns and levels of crime. A comparative approach to the study of crime will, in turn, ordinarily require research at the cross-cultural level of analysis or historical research that encompasses time periods long enough to insure genuine institutional change. This means that neighborhood-level research, whatever its other merits, is not particularly well suited for institutional analysis in the full sense, because as subunits of individual cities, neighborhoods ordinarily do not exhibit variation in the structure of institutional rules. It follows, however, that neighborhoods would be appropriate units of institutional analysis when it can be shown that they do, in fact, exhibit different institutions. Such would be the case, for example, if immigrant populations settle in different neighborhoods of the city and sustain the distinctive institutional arrangements of their countries of origin.

As we noted earlier, institutional analysis does not necessarily ignore variation in individual behavior. Rather, it forces the analyst's attention to the institutional origins and context of individual action. Studies of individual criminal behavior from an institutional perspective, therefore, will nearly always require multilevel methods. Such methods, in principle, allow for the partitioning of individual behavior into a component associated with differences in social context and a component associated with variation across individuals within a given context. Returning to the example of immigrant settlement patterns offered above, once it has been determined that neighborhoods can be distinguished on the basis of institutional differences, the measurement of those differences becomes a primary analytical task of institutional research on individual criminal behavior. The underlying premise is that such behavior can be fully understood only in institutional context. At the same time, a cross-level orientation serves as a reminder that institutions are ultimately created and changed by individual action.

A final methodological principle of institutional analysis is an explicit focus on the interrelationships among social institutions. Institutions do not operate in isolation from one another. The structure of a single institution can be understood only with reference to its interdependence with those of others in a social system (cf. Parsons, 1951). Institutional analysis is in this sense necessarily integrative and must draw on the perspectives, methods, and empirical materials of different disciplines, such as economics and political science, and different specializations within disciplines, such as the sociology of the family, religion, and educational sociology. This is a tall intellectual order, but certainly one that criminology cannot easily avoid, given its avowed self-definition as an "interdisciplinary" field of study.

But how should criminology go about implementing its interdisciplinary promise, as well as the comparative and multilevel approaches that are central to institutional inquiry? If these were straightforward or simple directives, we suspect institutional analysis would be more prominent in contemporary criminology, and our criticisms would center on technical questions concerning particular institutional applications rather than the avoidance of institutional analysis as such. In fact, several impediments stand in the way of "institutionalizing" criminology.

Challenges for Institutional Inquiry

Perhaps the most important challenge is the abstractness of the concept of social institutions. The concept of "institutions" is highly abstract, often serving more as a heuristic devise than an analytical construct suitable for comparative, cross-level, interdisciplinary research. If the abstract nature of "institutions" offers possibilities for comprehensive, general explanations, it also raises the danger of "grand theory" as discussed by C. Wright Mills (1959) in his classic critique of Parsons' sociology. Mills was rightly critical of a kind of theorizing that sacrifices precise and detailed examination of concrete social structures for grandiloquent pronouncements about the nature of "social action." A basic problem in institutional analysis is measurement of the concept of social institutions. As Bellah and his colleagues (1991: 302) observe, the social sciences have "well-developed methods for studying individuals" and "rudimentary methods for studying organizations." Techniques for measuring features of institutions are more primitive still.

Institutional analysis remains underdeveloped in American criminology not simply because an "institution" is a highly abstract concept that defies easy measurement but also because the strong individualistic bias of American culture and social science renders collective phenomena inherently suspect. Indeed, the ideology of individualism is largely responsible for why many American tend to view social institutions as ethereal entities that have little bearing on their everyday lives. What the historian Stanley Elkins said of the peculiarly rugged brand of individualism that characterized early nineteenth-century America continues to apply nearly two centuries later. The early American (male) could believe that he did not "draw from society his traditions, his culture, and all his aspirations.... Miraculously, all society then sprang to his aid in celebration of that conceit" (Elkins, 1956/1969: 33; see, also, Messner and Rosenfeld, 2001a: 68-69).

The strong ideological commitment to individualism in American culture inhibits thinking about collective phenomena such as institutions and inclines criminologists in the United States to approach crime from the standpoint of individual actors, often understood in "universal" terms rather than in terms of distinctive social and cultural contexts (Nelken, 1994: 10). The individualistic bias in American criminology is reflected in the predominance of survey research as the method of choice for studying criminal behavior. Sample surveys do have a role in the study of social institutions, but not in isolation from other methods, favored by historians and anthropologists, that are designed to capture the features of whole societies. Institutional analysis will require that criminologists learn the methods and standards of historiography and engage in "longitudinal" research that spans more than a few decades. It will also mean becoming familiar with the methods and materials of comparative ethnography.

An example of the application of ethnographic data to the concerns of criminologists is a study of ours on the social sources of homicide in different types of societies (Rosenfeld and Messner, 1991). We use data from the Human Relations Area Files (HRAF) to examine the relationship between indicators of inequality and the frequency of homicide for a maximum sample of thirty-two small, non-industrial, "simple" societies—the kinds of societies typically studied by anthropologists. The results reveal that indicators of social inequality are not positively related to levels of socially disapproved homicides in these types of societies, contrary to the widely observed pattern for advanced nation-states (LaFree, 1999). Thus, consistent with a general theme of this chapter, the consequences of forms of social stratification for violence appear to be contingent on the larger institutional context.

Borrowing the methods and material from other disciplines is likely to be particularly fruitful because rigorous institutional analysis of crime is alive and well outside of criminology. This is reflected, for example, in the lively debates over the quality of thirteenth-century European homicide records at a recent meeting of the Social Science History Association (http://www.ssha.org), and in the similarly animated discussions about alternative measurements of the prevalence of "wife beating" at a recent meeting of the Society for Cross-Cultural Research (http://www.fit.edu/CampusLife/clubs-org/sccr). Once having acquired some knowledge of the institutional structures of different societies, more criminologists might then turn profitably to the World Values surveys (http://wvs.isr.umich.edu) for evidence of similarities and differences in the "rules of the game" across nations in the contemporary period.

None of these suggestions for invigorating institutional analysis will amount to much, however, without a renewed appreciation for the relevance of large-scale social systems for an understanding of crime. This will require a tempering of the individualistic bias in American criminology and a broadening of macro- and multi-level theory and research to include analyses that extend beyond the census-defined "neighborhood." Not only will such an enlarged analytical scope produce valuable intellectual payoffs, it would seem to be an especially pressing practical task at a time when the social sources of crime and violence are not easily contained within porous political borders.

Notes

1. Presented at the 54th Annual Meeting of the American Society of Criminology, Chicago, Illinois, 13-16 November 2002. We are grateful to David H. Bayley and Joan McCord for comments on an earlier draft of this chapter.
2. Akers (1992) offers a particularly insightful review of the interconnections between sociology and criminology. The discussion in this paragraph is based upon Akers' review.
3. Macro-level theories of crime are inevitably predicated on premises about individual-level behavior, and it is thus useful to think of the dominant sociological

theories of the causes of crime as "hybrid" theories that combine logically consistent processes across levels of analysis. Elsewhere (Messner and Rosenfeld, 2001a), we have argued that macro-level criminological theories can be paired with individual-level theories as follows: social disorganization/control, anomie/strain, cultural deviance/social learning. For purposes of the present analysis, we assume that the macro-level component of the hybrid perspective describes institutional dynamics, while the individual-level analogue explains the processes through which institutional dynamics are translated into criminal behavior.

4. See the entry for "frictional unemployment" online at: http://www.economist.com/research/.
5. Merton illustrates his theory with reference to a strong cultural emphasis on monetary success goals and structural obstacles to the realization of these goals in the United States, but the theory is intended to have more general relevance. In his essay on "Continuities in the Theory of Social Structure and Anomie," he explains that "it is the conflict between cultural goals and institutional means—whatever the character of the goals—which produces a strain toward anomie" (1968: 220).
6. Variants of cultural deviance theories that emphasize political processes, such as Sellin's (1938) culture conflict theory, depict the dominant institutional order as "criminogenic" in the sense of establishing the legal standards that ultimately define crime. As noted above, we focus on institutional processes that might explain the origins of the behaviors that are susceptible to criminal definitions rather than on the criminalization process.
7. Kornhauser (1978:62-69) argues that the classic social disorganization theory of Shaw and McKay invokes a "mixed model" wherein an autonomous delinquent subculture is both a cause and a consequence of social disorganization.
8. Just as Protestantism does not countenance suicide, the rules of basketball do not directly promote fouling opponents; as in football, they penalize fouls. In this way, an institutional explanation of rule-breaking in the two sports differs from a cultural-deviance explanation. It also might be observed, from an institutional perspective, that basketball is a more "Protestant" sport than football in the sense of allowing for more individuality in performance.
9. Martin Killias contrasted these institutional features of Germany and the United States and discussed their implications for crime in a Presidential Plenary at the annual meetings of the American Society of Criminology (Killias, 2001).

References

Akers, Ronald L. 1992. "Linking Sociology and Its Specialties: The Case of Criminology." *Social Forces* 71: 1-16.

Anderson, Elijah. 1999. *Code of the Street: Decency, Violence, and the Moral Life of the Inner City*. New York: W. W. Norton & Company.

_____. 2002. "The Ideologically Driven Critique." *American Journal of Sociology* 107: 1533-50.

Beirne, Piers, and Messerschmidt, James. 2000. *Criminology*, 3rd ed. Boulder, CO: Westview.

Bellah, Robert N., Marsden, Richard, Sullivan, William M., Swidler, Ann, and Tipton, Steven M. 1991. *The Good Society*. New York: Knopf.

Bonger, Willem A. 1916. *Criminality and Economic Conditions*. Boston: Little, Brown.

Bursik, Robert J., Jr. 1988. "Social Disorganization and Theories of Crime and Delinquency: Problems and Prospects." *Criminology* 26: 519-551.

Cohen, Albert K. 1985. "The Assumption that Crime Is a Product of Environments: Sociological Approaches." Pp. 223-243 in *Theoretical Methods in Criminology*, edited by Robert F. Meier. Beverly Hills, CA: Sage.

Durkheim, Emile. 1966a [1895]. *The Rules of Sociological Method.* New York: Free Press.

_______. 1966b [1897]. Suicide: A Study in Sociology. New York: Free Press.

Elkins, Stanley M. 1956/1969. *Slavery: A Problem in American Institutional and Intellectual Life*, 2nd ed. Chicago: University of Chicago Press.

Farrington, David P. 2002. "Families and Crime." Pp. 129-148 in *Crime: Public Policies for Crime Control*, edited by James Q. Wilson and Joan Petersilia. Oakland, CA: ICS Press.

Gottfredson, Michael, and Hirschi, Travis. 1990. *A General Theory of Crime*. Stanford, CA: Stanford University Press.

Hagan, John, Gillis, A. R., and Simpson, John. 1985. "The Class Structure of Gender and Delinquency: Toward A Power-Control Theory of Common Delinquent Behavior." *American Journal of Sociology* 90: 1151-1178.

Hagan, John, John Simpson, and A. R. Gillis. 1987. "Class in the Household: A Power-Control Theory of Gender and Delinquency." *American Journal of Sociology* 92:788-816.

Killias, Martin. 2001. Presidential Plenary. Fifty-third Annual Meeting of the American Society of Criminology, 7-10 November, Atlanta, GA.

Kornhauser, Ruth R. 1978. *Social Sources of Delinquency: An Appraisal of Analytic Models.* Chicago: University of Chicago Press.

Kubrin, Charis E., and Weitzer, Ronald. 2003. "Structural Covariates of Homicide Rates: Does Type of Homicide Matter?" *Homicide Studies* 40: 139-170.

LaFree, Gary. 1999. "A Summary and Review of Cross-National Comparative Studies of Homicide." Pp. 125-145 in *Homicide: A Sourcebook of Social Research*, edited by M. Dwayne Smith and Margaret A. Zahn. Thousand Oaks, CA: Sage.

Merton, Robert K. 1938. "Social Structure and Anomie." *American Sociological Review* 3: 672-682.

_____. 1968. *Social Theory and Social Structure*. New York: Free Press.

Messner, Steven F., and Rosenfeld, Richard. 1997. "Political Restraint of the Market and Levels of Criminal Homicide: A Cross-National Application of Institutional-Anomie Theory." *Social Forces* 75: 1393-1416.

_____. 2001a. *Crime and the American Dream*, 3rd ed. Belmont, CA: Wadsworth.

_____. 2001b. "An Institutional Anomie Theory of Crime." Pp. 151-160 in *Explaining Criminals and Crime*, edited by R. Paternoster and Ronet Bachman. Los Angeles: Roxbury.

Mills, C. Wright. 1959. *The Sociological Imagination*. Oxford: Oxford University Press.

Nelken, David. 1994. "Reflexive Criminology?" Pp. 7-42 in *The Futures of Criminology*, edited by David Nelken. Thousand Oaks, CA: Sage.

North, Douglass C. 1990. *Institutions, Institutional Change and Economic Performance*. Cambridge: Cambridge University Press.

Parsons, Talcott. 1951. *The Social System*. New York: Free Press.

_____. 1990 [1934]. "Prolegomena to a Theory of Social Institutions." *American Sociological Review* 55: 319-333.

Pfohl, Stephen. 1994. *Images of Deviance and Social Control*, 2nd ed. New York: McGraw-Hill.

Quinney, Richard. 1974. *Critique of Legal Order*. Boston: Little, Brown.

_____. 1977. *Class, State, and Crime*. New York: David McKay.

Rosenfeld, Richard. 1989. "Robert Merton's Contributions to the Sociology of Deviance." *Sociology Inquiry* 59, 4: 453-466.

Rosenfeld, Richard, and Messner, Steven F. 1991. "The Social Sources Homicide in Different Types of Societies." *Sociological Forum* 6: 51-70.

Sampson, Robert J., and Groves, W. Byron. 1989. "Community Structure and Crime: Testing Social-Disorganization Theory." *American Journal of Sociology* 94: 774-802.
Sampson, Robert J., and Wilson, William Julius. 1995. "Toward a Theory of Race, Crime, and Urban Inequality." Pp. 37-54 in *Crime and Inequality*, edited by John Hagan and Ruth D. Peterson. Stanford, CA: Stanford University Press.
Sampson, Robert J., and Morenoff, Jeffrey D., Gannon-Rowley, Thomas. 2002. "Assessing 'Neighborhood Effects': Social Processes and New Directions in Research." *Annual Review of Sociology* 28: 443-78.
Savolainen, Jukka. 2000. "Inequality, Welfare State, and Homicide: Further Support for the Institutional Anomie Theory." *Criminology* 38: 1021-1039.
Sellin, Thorsten. 1938. *Culture Conflict and Crime*. New York: Social Science Research Council.
Sims, Barbara A. 1997. "Crime, Punishment, and the American Dream: Toward a Marxist Integration." *Journal of Research in Crime and Delinquency* 34: 5-24.
Turk, Austin T. 1969. *Criminality and Legal Order*. Chicago, IL: Rand McNally.
Veysey, Bonita M., and Messner, Steven F. 1999. "Further Testing of Social Disorganization Theory: An Elaboration of Sampson and Groves' 'Community Structure and Crime.'" *Journal of Research in Crime and Delinquency* 36: 156-74.
Vold, George B. 1958. *Theoretical Criminology*. New York: Oxford University Press.

[2]

ANOMIE, SOCIAL CHANGE AND CRIME

A Theoretical Examination of Institutional-Anomie Theory

JÓN GUNNAR BERNBURG*

The last decade has seen a revived interest in using anomie theory in crime and deviance research. The present paper contributes to this development by offering an examination of a particular extension of anomie theory, namely, Messner and Rosenfeld's Institutional-Anomie theory. Explicating Institutional-Anomie theory relative to the sociologies of Durkheim, Merton and Polanyi, I find that this theory goes beyond Merton by using a strain of thought that is critical of liberal society. By bringing in the notion of the disembedded market economy, a central notion in the institutionalism of Polanyi and Durkheim, this theory links crime, anomie, and contemporary social change. I also discuss some of the limitations of linking crime with societal level processes in a Durkheimian rather than Mertonian manner.

The classical sociological notion of anomie has long been a conceptual tool to understand the relationship between social structure, culture and deviant behaviour. Central to different versions of anomie theory is the premise that humans are normative beings. People act and think on the basis of commonly shared definitions and traditions. To a greater and lesser extent the common meanings that emerge in social life have sentimental value for people; they constitute morality and ethics. Shared cultural values define and sanction people's goals and the means they use in reaching the goals. Anomie results when the power of social values to regulate the ends and the means of human conduct is weakened.

But anomie perspectives are not a unified body of theory. While Durkheim is usually seen as the founder of the sociological tradition of anomie theory, his notion of anomie changed fundamentally in the hands of American sociology (Orrù 1987; Besnard 1990). Durkheim's (1951) understanding of anomie derives from his concern about the disruptive tendencies of fundamental features of modern, industrial society. Durkheim argues that specific features of industrial society, particularly in the sphere of economic activity, produce a chronic state of normative deregulation. As a result, valued goals become ill conceived and the society fails to provide people with normative limits on their desires. In contrast, American anomie theorists have not emphasized anomie as the widespread lack of socially valued goals. Thus Merton's (1967/1994) influential essay, *Social Structure and Anomie,* does not cast in doubt the fundamental cultural ends of the society, that is, the normative ends of action. In Merton's theory social values are clearly defined in the mainstream egalitarian ideology and in the universal emphasis on monetary success. On the cultural level, Merton emphasizes the lack of equilibrium between socially described means and ends of action. Anomie is caused by the imbalance

* Bergthorugata 5, 101 Reykjavik, Iceland; JB7992@CSC.ALBANY.EDU. The writer thanks Steve Messner for helpful comments on earlier drafts of this paper.

that results when cultural goals are overemphasized at the expense of institutionalized means. As Agnew (1997) puts it, 'for Merton, normlessness refers to regulating goal achievement, whereas for Durkheim it refers to those norms regulating goals' (p. 37).

Marco Orrù (1987: 118–19) explains this fundamental change in anomie theory in reference to the prevalent intellectual orientation on each continent. Thus the social historical conditions in America differed greatly from those in Europe. In contrast to European intellectuals, who were expected to be critical of social arrangements, American intellectuals were expected not to criticize the socially described ends of American society. In America, there has been a much more forceful ideology of social ends as given and therefore beyond dispute. Orrù further observes that

> Durkheim's concept of anomie and the one found in contemporary American sociology differ exactly in this crucial way: for Durkheim anomie refers to the ill-conceived cultural goals of industrial societies, whereas for American sociologists anomie refers to the inadequacy of means for the fulfillment of society's culturally sanctioned goals. These goals, by and large, have been implicitly adhered to in American sociology. This shift of focus implies an abandonment of the European sociological tradition of 'Grand Theory' which sketches the blueprint of a utopian society in favor of a piecemeal social engineering which looks for technical improvements in an otherwise sound social structure. (p. 119)

Orrù's analysis on the nature of the American anomie tradition is of some significance in light of the recent interest in anomie theory in the study of crime and deviance. After a long recess the past decade has seen a revived interest in using anomie perspectives to explain crime and deviant behaviour. Several prominent theorists and researchers have again put the issue of normative regulation and deregulation to the fore of the study of deviance. Anomie perspectives have recently informed research in so disparate fields as delinquency (Agnew 1992), white-collar and corporate crime (Passas 1990), cross-national comparative studies of homicide (Chamblin and Cochran 1995; Messner and Rosenfeld 1997b), organizational deviance (Vaughan 1983, 1997) and suicide (Thorlindsson and Bjarnason 1998). Recent books with titles such as *The Legacy of Anomie Theory* (Adler and Laufer 1995) and *The Future of Anomie Theory* (Agnew and Passas 1997) also signify a revival of this theoretical tradition.

The recent revitalization of anomie theory brings the problem of the normlessness of ends and means of social action to the fore of theoretical considerations. A question that arises is whether in fact there are strains of thought within some of these recent efforts to refine and extend anomie theory that go beyond Orrù's description of the American anomie tradition. In other words, have any of the recent developments in American anomie theory moved beyond the 'consolation of liberal society'; have they shifted from focusing on Mertonian normlessness of means and to Durkheimian normlessness of ends? At stake here is how different conceptions of anomie draw our attention to different features of social organization.

While this question integrates the present paper, it is nevertheless beyond its scope to provide a conclusive answer to it. That would require a thorough investigation of all of the major revisions of anomie theory. Not withstanding this ideal aim, the present paper examines one particular extension of anomie theory as a likely candidate for an affirmation of the thesis stated above, namely, Institutional-Anomie theory (Messner and Rosenfeld 1994, 1997a). A few points guide this decision. First, while some of the most significant recent revisions of anomie theory aim to explain between-individual variation in deviance (Agnew 1992, 1997: Menard 1995, 1997), Institutional-Anomie theory is a macro level theory that aims to account for societal level processes. Furthermore, as I argue below, this theory specifies how the emergence of anomie is related to specific institutional arrangements of contemporary society (Messner and Rosenfeld 1994: 44–57). By so doing the theory creates a conceptual framework that renders contemporary changes in industrial societies—declining political restraints on market economy, globalization, decline of the welfare state, neoliberal social policy, and so on—relevant to the study of crime and deviance. Finally, Institutional-Anomie theory has recently inspired empirical research that lends support to its central claims (Chamblin and Cochran 1995; Messner and Rosenfeld 1997; Savolainen 2000), making it relevant for theoretical scrutiny.

To shed light on the thesis stated above, I ask the following questions. How does Institutional-Anomie theory differ from prior anomie theories of crime and deviance? Does this theoretical effort signal a concern for the 'soundness' of modern social structure, in contrast to Orrú's description of the intellectual orientation of American sociologists? More generally, is this line of theorizing a response to profound social changes or conditions that bring us back to Durkheim's notion of 'pathologic' trends in modern society? What are some of the problems and prospects associated with this intellectual orientation?

The paper proceeds as follows. First, I discuss how Institutional-Anomie theory departs from Merton's *Social Structure and Anomie*. The point of this discussion is to see how it differs from traditional American anomie theories. I point out that Institutional-Anomie theory goes beyond this tradition by offering a theory of the societal sources of the anomic ethic. I then discuss how Institutional-Anomie theory relates to some profound critiques of modern social organization—in particular to Durkheim's discussion of anomic suicide, but also to Polanyi's notion of the disembedded market economy. I find that there is a shared understanding among these authors that anomic cultural characteristics emerge because the market economy is left unchecked by non-economic institutions. In the fourth section, I discuss how the shift to the institutional level reflects social change. I suggest that bringing back in the notion of the disembedded economy, highlighted by Durkheim and Polanyi, reflect societal changes currently taking place. Finally, however, I take a more critical look at some of the implications of Institutional-Anomie theory vis-à-vis Merton by identifying some limitations of linking crime with societal level processes in a Durkheimian rather than Mertonian manner.

Institutional-Anomie Theory

Messner and Rosenfeld's (1994, 1997a) Institutional-Anomie theory of crime attempts to comprehensively account for the interplay between the 'fundamental' features of social organization, namely, culture and social structure. On the one hand, these authors stay faithful to Merton in that they see specific cultural values giving rise to anomic pressures. These are the value-orientations of the 'American Dream', namely, 'a broad cultural ethos that entails a commitment to the goal of material success, to be pursued by everyone in society, under conditions of open, individual competition' (1994: 6). In line with Merton, this cultural ethos 'encourages an exaggerated emphasis on monetary achievement while devaluing alternative criterion of success, it promotes a preoccupation with the realization of goals while de-emphasizing the importance of the ways in which these goals are pursued' (p. 10). Thus the American Dream creates pressure to achieve, but minimizes the pressure to play by the rules. Under these circumstances people become more likely to use the 'most technically efficient means necessary' in reaching their goals. The result is a higher rate of predatory crime.[1]

However, Messner and Rosenfeld depart from Merton in that they see the structural sources of this anomic cultural ethos in the nature of the capitalist market economy, more specifically, in the relationship between the economy and non-economic institutions. They argue that when the market economy is an unusually powerful social institution relative to vital non-economic institutions, as seems to be the case in the United States, it disrupts the normal functioning of the other institutions. Specifically, the value-orientations of the market economy, that is, the pursuit of self-interest, attraction to monetary rewards, and competition, become exaggerated relative to the value-orientations of institutions such as the family, the education, and the polity. This manifests in (1) the devaluation of non-economic institutional functions and roles (2) the accommodation of institutions by economic requirements, and (3) the penetration of economic norms into other institutional domains. That the dominance of the economy in the institutional balance of power weakens the ability of the other social institutions to exercise social control has important implications for the rate of deviant behaviour. These institutions serve to 'mobilize and deploy resources for the achievement of collective goals' and 'socialize members to accept the society's fundamental normative patterns' (p. 65). The invasion of the market economy into the other institutions obstructs the functioning of these vital institutions. When this happens, the society fails to regulate the conduct of its members effectively by means of societal norms and roles.

Institutional-Anomie theory stipulates a reciprocal causal relationship between the culture and the institutional structure. Most importantly, it holds that the dominance of the market economy supports and even breeds a cultural ethos characterized by the American Dream. Note, however, that in Messner and Rosenfeld's recent statements the anomic cultural ethos is not, it seems, specifically American. Rather, it is the result of the dominance of the capitalist market economy in other capitalist countries as well (Messner and Rosenfeld 1997a: 213; this theme is also emphasized by Hagan *et al.* 1998).

To be sure, Messner and Rosenfeld explicitly stay faithful to Merton's influential means-ends schema. Institutional-Anomie theory does not hold that anomie result from deregulated ends, but from the deregulated means of social action. The basic social values in question—the ends of the market ethos—are not problematic *per se*, but they become so only because of the normlessness of means.

> There is nothing inherently criminogenic about the market values of competition and materialism . . . Market values of competition and materialism lead to crime, we suggest, only when they occur in combination with what can be termed an 'anomic ethic.' Following Merton, the anomic ethic refers to the excessive emphasis on the goals of social action regardless of the moral status of the means used to achieve social goals. (Messner and Rosenfeld 1997a: 214)

[1] There is some debate in the literature about the scope of applicability of Institutional-Anomie theory. Messner and Rosenfeld mention that it applies to serious predatory crime, both violent and property crime. Chamblin and Cochran (1995), in contrast, have argued that Institutional-Anomie theory applies most directly to property crime.

Nevertheless, Institutional-Anomie theory does give us a theory of the emergence of the 'anomic ethic'—contra Merton—and thus goes beyond the means-ends schema in an important way. Thus, whereas Merton sees the anomic ethic as a cultural deficit in American society (which rhymes nicely with Orrù's description of American anomie theory as occupied with 'technical improvements in an otherwise sound social structure'), Institutional-Anomie theory specifies institutional arrangements give rise to the emergence of the anomic ethic. Moreover, the anomic ethic emerges from institutional conditions that are a defining feature of modern society. 'Economic dominance stimulates the emergence of anomie at the cultural level' (p. 213). The valued ends of social action are thus not 'given' in Institutional-Anomie theory, rather the theory attempts to explain their relative emphasis in the culture. Economic dominance creates an 'exaggerated' emphasis on particular ends, but, being disembedded from other social institutions, it fails to provide normative limits on these ends.

In conclusion, Institutional-Anomie theory follows Merton's notion of the anomic ethic (the American Dream), but focuses on very different structural sources for anomie. On the structural level, an important part of Merton's notion of anomie is the uneven distribution of opportunities throughout the social structure. The social structure is problematic insofar as it fails to live up to its promise of equal opportunity. Institutional-Anomie theory goes up a level of analysis by focusing on the institutional sources of the anomic ethic itself. The theory attempts to explain the institutional arrangements that sustain and reinforce this ethic. As I discuss in the following section, the theory does so by using a strain of thought that is highly critical of liberal society.

Anomie and the Notion of the Disembedded Economy

Institutional-Anomie theory incorporates a strain of social thought that sees the market economy, if left unregulated by other social institutions, as inherently obtrusive to human organization. For our purposes, this strain of thought is most clearly expressed in the work of Karl Polanyi (1944/1957, 1947/1968, 1957/1968) and Emile Durkheim (1897/1951), both of which are concerned with the social consequences of the unchecked market.[2]

In *The Great Transformation*, Polanyi (1957) argues that modern society is fundamentally different from pre-existing societies in that the economic system is not embedded or regulated by other social institutions. In pre-modern societies, through the principles of reciprocity or redistribution, the economic system was a function of social organization: 'Custom and law, magic and religion co-operated in inducing the individual to comply with rules of behaviour which, eventually, ensured his functioning in the economic system' (p. 55). Since, however, the market pattern is related to a specific motive of its own, namely, 'the motive to truck and barter', this pattern can create an institution of its own. Hence, when the market economy is unregulated by non-economic institutions, the principles of the market become the dominating principle of society, subjugating social relations to market principles (in particular, treating people as commodities). This happens because 'once the economic system is organized in separate institutions, based

[2] In subsequent work, Messner and Rosenfeld (1997c) have made explicit linkage between Institutional-Anomie theory and Polanyi's writing on self-regulating markets.

on specific motives and conferring a special status, society must be shaped in such a manner as to allow that system to function according to its own laws' (p. 57). In short, Polanyi argues that as the market economy becomes decoupled from other social institutions, it tends to dominate them. If left unchecked the market economy penetrates and disrupts the functioning of other institutions. Much as Institutional-Anomie theory stipulates, when the market becomes self-regulating social relationships are embedded in the economic system 'instead of the economic system being embedded in social relationships' (Polanyi 1968: 70).

Polanyi recognizes that the disembedded economy has profound influence on society's culture. At times, even, Polanyi's argument implies that the very cultural characteristics discussed by Merton and later Messner and Rosenfeld emerge from the disembeddedness of the market economy. Drawing on anthropological evidence, Polanyi is convinced that modern economic motives, realized in profit-seeking individuals, are the creation of the decoupling of the market economy from other social institutions. On the one hand, then, a disembedded market economy colonizes all other aspects of social life and thus places great emphasis on economic motives in the culture:

> Since no human aggregation can survive without a functioning productive apparatus, its embodiment in a distinct and separate sphere had the effect of making the 'rest' of society dependent upon that sphere . . . As a result, the market mechanism became determinative for the life of the body social . . . '*Economic motives' reigned supreme in a world of their own, and the individual was made to act on them under pain of being trodden under foot by the juggernaut market.* Such a forced conversion to a utilitarian outlook fatefully warped Western man's understanding of himself. (Polanyi 1968; italics added)

On the other hand, the disembedded market economy leaves economic motives unchecked by other social institutions:

> The market pattern . . . being related to a peculiar motive of its own, the motive of truck or barter, is capable of creating a specific institution, namely, the market. Ultimately, that is why the control of the economic system by the market is of overwhelming consequence to the whole organization of society: it means no less than the running of the society as an adjunct to the market. *Instead of economy being embedded in social relations, social relations are embedded in the economic system.* (Polanyi 1957: 57; italics added)

Although Polanyi is not interested in the degree to which the disembeddedness of the economy affects the rate of deviant behaviour,[3] he nevertheless suggests that both the goals of monetary success and the absence of institutionalized means to reach these goals emerge when the economy becomes disembedded from other social institutions. Such motives, moreover, are not a natural condition as envisioned by Adam Smith. A disembedded economy organizes social relationships in its fashion and therefore the 'value-orientations' of the market gain dominance, to use Messner and Rosenfeld's

[3] Nevertheless, Polanyi vaguely hints at the potential consequences for crime and deviant behaviour. Thus, in *The Great Transformation* (1957: 73) he writes: 'To allow the market mechanism to be sole director of the fate of human beings and their natural environment, indeed, even of the amount and use of purchasing power, would result in the demolition of society . . . Robbed of the protective covering of cultural institutions, human beings would perish from the effects of social exposure; they would die as the victims of acute social dislocation through vice, perversion, crime, and starvation.'

terminology. A disembedded economy is by definition weakly governed by social norms and therefore there are weak norms governing the means of reaching the goals thus emphasized.

The same trend of thought is found in Durkheim's classic statements on anomic suicide. In the context of our discussion, Durkheim's work is even more revealing than Polanyi's is because in fact he was very much interested in explaining anomie and patterns of deviant behaviour. In *Suicide*, Durkheim argues that the modern economy is in a state of chronic deregulation. No longer regulated by religion or government, the economy is in fact detached from other social 'organs' [institutions]. Durkheim claims that the modern economy has the 'power to subordinate other social organs to itself and to make them converge toward one dominant aim' (1951: 255). Moreover,

> industry, instead of being still regarded as a means to an end transcending itself, has become the supreme end of individuals and societies alike. Thereupon the appetites thus excited have become freed of any limiting authority . . . Ultimately, this liberation of desires has been made worse by the very development of industry and the almost infinite extension of the market. (p. 255)

The resemblance of Durkheim's discussion to Polanyi and to Institutional-Anomie theory is striking. All these authors rely on the notion of the disembedded market economy in one form or another. Moreover, Durkheim explicitly (if not very systematically) recognizes that the disembedded economy—which for him is a defining feature of modernity—is a major source of social deregulation, or anomie.

Durkheim does not define anomie as just one thing. On the one hand, he argues that anomie is the normlessness of goals. In the absence of a social authority 'our capacity for feeling is in itself an insatiable and bottomless abyss' (1951: 247). To the extent that society exerts authority over individuals, it creates boundaries for their desires, and only then can they be content. Thence, when regulation fails 'we see society gripped by a dejection and pessimism reflected in the curve of suicides' (1925/1961: 68). On the other hand, particularly where Durkheim is concerned with the disembedded economy in *Suicide*, anomie arises when the socially prescribed goals are practically unattainable, by definition. 'To pursue a goal which is by definition unattainable is to condemn oneself to a state of perpetual unhappiness' (1951: 248). In this case, the ends are not really undefined, but nevertheless by definition limitless. The disembedded economy is an important source of this kind of anomie:

> Such is the source of excitement predominating in this part of society, and which has thence extended to other parts. There, the state of crisis and anom[ie] is constant and, so to speak, normal. From top to bottom of the ladder, greed is aroused without knowing where to find ultimate foothold. Nothing can calm it, since its goal is for beyond all it can attain . . . A thirst arises for novelties, unfamiliar pleasures, nameless sensations, all of which lose their savor once known. (p. 256)

There is a striking resemblance between Institutional-Anomie theory and Durkheim's theory in the very nature of the anomic ethic that has its roots in the disembedded economy. Durkheim indeed recognizes that the disembedded economy produces infinite goals, but also that these goals are morally sanctioned. For Durkheim, the anomic ethic indeed contains normatively sanctioned ends (as opposed to normless ends), but these ends are by definition limitless:

. . . these dispositions are so inbred that society has grown to accept them and is accustomed to think them *normal.* It is everlastingly repeated that it is in man's nature to be eternally dissatisfied, constantly to advance, without relief or rest, toward an indefinite goal. *The longing for infinity is daily represented as a mark of moral distinction, whereas it can only appear with unregulated consciences which elevate to a rule the lack of rule from which they suffer.* The doctrine of the most ruthless and swift progress has become an article of faith . . . praising the advantages of instability. (p. 257; italics added)

In essence, then, Durkheim identifies the same cultural characteristics as Merton and later Messner and Rosenfeld identify in the 'American Dream'. In this context, Horton observes that 'a pathological urge for constant advancement and the promotion of a passion for the indefinite as a mark of moral distinction were discussed by Durkheim [and Merton alike,] . . . but Durkheim questioned the very values which Merton holds constant' (Horton 1964, cited in Passas 1995: 96). Just as Messner and Rosenfeld recognize, then, for Durkheim the anomic ethic exaggerates monetary success, but nevertheless compels people to adhere to this end. In this sense, the ends are not normless, but normatively sanctioned. In Messner's and Rosenfeld's account, this cultural ethos is characterized by four 'value-orientations' (1994, pp. 62–5): (1) An overriding pressure on the individuals to achieve at any cost; (2) intense individualism, where one's fellow member becomes one's competitor; (3) universalism; the standards of success apply equally to all members of society; and (4) monetary 'fetishism', where money is the metric of success, a social fact that gives rise to a 'never-ending' achievement—in principle, it is always possible to have more. As Durkheim (1951) would have it, the anomic ethic describes goals that are limitless and which are no longer bounded by clear distribution of statuses (they are universal).

In short, Institutional-Anomie theory makes use of Merton's elaboration of anomie, but brings us back to the type of social criticism that Durkheim and Polanyi emphasize. Whereas Merton emphasizes imbalance between components of a given social fabric (capitalist market society), Durkheim and Polanyi focus on the nature of the social fabric itself—in comparison with a different kind of social organization. Messner and Rosenfeld's institutional framework clearly brings us back to the latter's level of thinking. And, if implicitly, by so doing their notion of anomie becomes very similar to that of Durkheim and Polanyi.

Anomie Theory in Society

Recently, Nicos Passas has pointed out that the differences between the anomie theories of Durkheim and Merton reflect the different social environments of these authors (1995: 93–4). Thus Durkheim observes the rootlessness of rapid industrial growth in French society at the turn of the century and sees these forces as the major source of anomie. He argues that rapid industrial growth, combined with a less speedy growth of moral forces to regulate it, produces relentless status-seeking and limitless aspirations—anomie. Merton, in contrast, observes these forces after they are institutionalized. Therefore, he sees them as normal—given, if you will—and focuses on how the culture can be viewed as a more stable source of anomie.

Passas's observation adds an important historical dimension to my discussion. As Polanyi (1957) so vigorously argues, the nineteenth century witnessed the development of the self-regulated market. Social relations became 'embedded in the economic system' (p. 57), and political economists praised the motive of individual profit seeking as humanity's natural condition. In point of fact, this is the social reality that Durkheim faces. And, as I have argued above, it is precisely this social condition that Durkheim sees as a major social source of anomie. Merton, in contrast, theorizes anomie in the aftermath of the Great Depression. This is a period when the market's self-destructive tendency was held in check by the nation state (Polanyi 1957). Therefore Merton focuses on factors that were more internal to the social system, namely, imbalance between the given ends and means of social action, on the one hand, and the opportunity structure, on the other.

Above I argued that Institutional-Anomie theory brings us back to the concerns of Durkheim and Polanyi about the disembedded economy. I suggest that this move indeed reflect important societal changes currently taking place. The conditions faced by sociologists today are increasingly similar to those that Polanyi describes in nineteenth century England, and those that Durkheim faced in the late nineteenth and the early twentieth century—namely, the trend toward the dominance of the market logic in social institutions. These current social changes manifest in the increasingly unregulated flow of capital, which results in the decreasing power of nation states over capital and labour (Teeple 1995) and decline of public welfare spending (Olsen 1996). 'Faced with the power of globalized production and international finance, including dept structures, leaders are constrained to concentrate on enhancing national conditions for competing forms of capitalism' (Mittelman 1996: 7). In turn, the decreasing power of the state combined with the increasing power of neoliberal rhetoric (Block 1990; Wolfe 1989) results in 're-commodification' of labour, where people are increasingly left unguarded against market forces (Messner and Rosenfeld 1997b). On the organizational level, furthermore, this change has been described in many organizational fields as an institutional shift to a market logic (Thornton and Ocasio 1999). This is manifested, for example, in the overriding emphasis on the goal of profit making and delegitimization of alternative goals and decreased commitment to professional values other than those of professionals educated in business and management (Useem 1996; Oakes *et al.* 1998; Thornton and Ocasio 1999). Institutional-Anomie theory calls our attention to these societal processes, claiming that there are consequences for the rate of crime and deviant behaviour—like Durkheim did in the beginning of the twentieth century.

Thus far my focus has been on how Institutional-Anomie theory goes 'beyond' Merton. I have discussed how this theory identifies linkages that are absent in Merton's formulation, namely, how it identifies the institutional source of anomic culture, and how it thus offers a link between crime and social change. This important contribution can inform empirical research of crime rates as reflection of changes in the institutional environments across societies and time periods. In particular, this approach is relevant for studying the impact of the current societal drifting toward the market logic. In the following section, however, I develop a more critical view of Institutional-Anomie theory vis-à-vis Merton's anomie theory. An important implication of Institutional-Anomie theory—as it aims to link crime with societal level processes in a Durkheimian, rather than Mertonian, manner—is that it shifts the focus away from Merton's emphasis on social stratification (Gesualdi 1996–7).

Gains and Losses: Another Look at Institutional-Anomie Theory vis-à-vis Merton

Merton focuses on the discrepancy between the ethic of universal goals and unequal opportunity structure. In this view, social structure is a stable pattern of human relations; it refers to the distribution of social-economic statuses. In contrast, Messner and Rosenfeld focus on social structure as the balance of power between the major institutions of society. Following a Parsonian approach, these authors do not conceptualize social structure as a stable pattern of relations between people, but rather functional relations between stable patterns of norms. That the two theories focus on social structure in such a different manner is of major importance. How social structure is understood has important implications for the explanatory scope of each theory. Thus Institutional-Anomie theory specifies the institutional arrangements that contribute to the emergence of anomic culture. Merton's theory specifies the objective conditions that indeed translate anomic norms and goals—culture—into patterns of deviant and conforming behaviour.

In Institutional-Anomie theory, anomic pressures arise when a nexus of reinforcing cultural patterns develops, producing an overemphasis on the market ethic and undermining the regulatory power of social norms (because of the weakening the regulatory function of the family, the education system, and the political system). As a result, individuals feel an overriding pressure to achieve and at the same time are confronted with weak normative restrains on legitimate means to achieve. This theorizing elaborates and expands Merton's explanation of anomie on the cultural level. Merton does not specify the structural features that bring about cultural anomie (Taylor *et al.* 1973: 103). Institutional-Anomie's structural-functional approach offers an explanation of both the societal sources of the overriding goals of achievement and the weakening of norms guiding the means.[4]

However, while Institutional-Anomie theory clarifies the processes that Merton identifies on the cultural level, it makes no use of his key innovative discussion of the discrepancy between culture and social structure. Messner and Rosenfeld ignore Merton's insight on the role of the unequal distribution of people's objective conditions in translating the anomic ethic into crime and deviant behaviour. Thus Institutional-Anomie theory claims that on the individual level the anomic ethic (culture) is a sufficient condition for anomic pressure. The cultural impact of the anomic ethic is not specified by a position in the distribution of social statuses. As we have seen above, this notion of anomie is very much in accordance with Durkheim's notion of anomic suicide. The crux of this approach, from Durkheim on, is that the anomic ethic compels individuals to aspire beyond their capabilities, regardless of what the latter may be. By definition, the social goal of monetary success is never accomplished.

But thus limiting the theory to the cultural level—the proximate cause of crime encompassed by the theory is the cultural emphasis on limitless goals in combination with weak norms—renders vague the relationship between the anomic ethic and crime. In the absence of the notion of opportunity distribution it becomes unclear why

[4] Moreover, the theory makes important contribution in clarifying how institutional arrangement affect social structural control on the individual level (Hirschi 1969; Sampson and Groves 1989; Sampson and Laub 1993).

predatory crime is ever perceived as a more efficient means to achievement than legitimate forms of behaviour. If the moral of the anomic ethic is 'by any means necessary', which means actually are necessary, advantageous, or even possible, depends on the distribution of people's objective conditions and opportunities. The genius of Merton's approach is indeed the recognition that *objective conditions in which goals and norms operate are crucial in specifying their effect on action.* Thus,

> the distinctive prediction to be derived from Merton's theory is that structural and cultural variables affect rates of deviance in an 'interactive' manner. The theory stipulates that certain structural conditions, *in combination with* certain cultural conditions, generate anomie and high rates of deviant behaviour. (Messner 1988: 47; italics in original)

Let me use a simple example. A wealthy stockbroker is unlikely to commit an armed robbery as a means of reaching unsatisfied aspirations beyond his or her legitimate means, but to a member of the disadvantaged classes (Wilson 1987) this may sometimes seem as a viable option. Of course, as some anomie theorists have emphasized (Passas 1997), the stockbroker may consider using his position in other, though no less destructive, ways. The latter does not render social stratification irrelevant, but precisely the opposite. Social stratification specifies how anomic culture is translated into action, and what type of action. This example should also remind us of Cloward's (1959/1994) argument that both legitimate and illegitimate opportunity structures are crucial in specifying the effect of culture on action. This line of reasoning thus also offers opportunities to use the core ideas of Institutional-Anomie theory and Merton's anomie theory to inform research on white-collar crime and organizational deviance.

In this context, we should note that Merton's anomie theory has produced supportive empirical findings (Blau and Blau 1982; Krahn *et al.* 1986; Messner 1988), that is, when understood as a macro level theory of crime rates (Messner 1988).

Recognizing the limitations of Institutional-Anomie theory vis-à-vis Merton—and the limitations of Merton vis-à-vis Institutional-Anomie theory—we reach the following conclusion. Institutional-Anomie theory explains how the anomic culture emerges and how it is sustained and amplified. The strategy of this approach is linking the emergence of this cultural pattern with institutional arrangements, and therefore offering an important link to social change. In this sense the theory highlights the strength of Durkheimian sociology. However, as a theory of criminal action, Institutional-Anomie theory risks slipping into an 'oversocialized view' (Granovetter 1985) of how norms and goals affect behaviour. In contrast, Merton's theory is guided by a notion of people making choices in the context of their socially structured realities (Nee and Brinton 1998). Merton specifies the objective conditions that translate norms and goals—culture—into crime. Merton's approach is thus more suitable in specifying how anomic culture—given in Merton but explained in Institutional-Anomie theory—creates pressure to innovate because of incompatibility of culture with people's objective conditions.

In this sense, therefore, these theoretical arguments—Merton's and Messner and Rosenfeld's—may be seen as supplementing each other. In fact, recent empirical work suggests that together these theories provide a richer macro level explanation of crime and deviance than each does on its own. Although studies have not been guided by an explicit integration of the theories provided by Merton on the one hand and Messner and Rosenfeld on the other, the evidence suggests that such integration may be a fruitful endeavour. Two recent studies indicate that social stratification specifies the effect of market dominance in the institutional balance of power on crime rates (Chamblin and Cochran 1995; Savolainen 2000). A strong anomic ethic—which, in turn, has structural underpinnings in the weakening of non-economic institutions relative to the market economy—only creates real life situations conducive to predatory street crime when a substantial part of the population experiences such crime as a means to the end of monetary achievement.

Conclusion

Social analysts have focused on different social structural conditions in their attempt to link crime and social structure through the medium of anomie theory. I have discussed how different formulations turn our attention to different features of social structure and social change. Institutional-Anomie theory clearly transcends Orrù's description of the American anomie tradition, offering an attempt to bring back the institutional tradition in explaining deviant behaviour. The theory brings us back to the enterprise of European sociologists of the nineteenth century, Durkheim in particular, for which a sociology of deviance was also a study of contemporary societal changes. Most importantly the theory opens up the possibility of studying crime and deviance in direct relation to important social concerns of our time, such as the penetration of the market logic and market arrangements into other social spheres (Block 1990; Wolfe 1989) and the decline of the welfare state (Messner and Rosenfeld 1997). The revitalization of the institutional level of analysis is also a fresh contribution to contemporary research on crime and deviance, which often offers tenuous linkages between crime and social organization (Walton 1998; Young 1998). As Messner (1988) has pointed out, informing research with a theory of social organization has been the 'the road not taken' in crime and deviance research. The anomie tradition continues to be a medium to understand the impact of contemporary social change on crime. I have argued that contemporary patterning of social organization highlights the strength of Durkheimian sociology and the anomie theory tradition more generally. The future of this work, however, is likely to depend on appreciation for the limitations associated with this intellectual heritage.

References

AGNEW, R. (1992), 'Foundation for a General Strain Theory of Crime and Delinquency', *Criminology*, 30: 47–87.

—— (1997), 'The Nature and Determinants of Strain: Another Look at Durkheim and Merton', in N. Passas and R. Agnew, eds., *The Future of Anomie Theory*, 27–51. Boston, MA: Northeastern University Press.

AGNEW, R. and PASSAS, N. (1997), 'Introduction', in N. Passas and R. Agnew, eds., *The Future of Anomie Theory*, 1–26. Boston, MA: Northeastern University Press.

BESNARD, P. (1990), 'Merton in Search of Anomie', in J. Clark, C. Modgil and S. Modgil, eds., *Robert K. Merton: Consensus and Controversy*. London: The Falmer Press.

BLAU, J. R. and BLAU, P. M. (1982), 'The Cost of Inequality: Metropolitan Structure and Violent Crime', *American Sociological Review*, 47: 114–29.

BLOCK, F. (1990), *Postindustrial Possibilities: A Critique of Economic Discourse.* Berkeley, CA: University of California Press.

CHAMBLIN, M. B. and COCHRAN, J. K. (1995), 'Assessing Messner and Rosenfeld's Institutional-Anomie Theory: A Partial Test', *Criminology*, 33: 411–29.

CLOWARD, R. A. (1959/1994), 'Illegitimate Means, Anomie, and Deviant Behavior', in S. H. Traub and C. B. Little, eds., *Theories of Deviance*, 4th edn., 148–69. Itasca, IL: F. E. Peacock Publishers, Inc.

COHEN, A. K. (1997), 'An Elaboration of Anomie Theory', in N. Passas and R. Agnew, eds., *The Future of Anomie Theory*, 54–61. Boston, MA: Northeastern University Press.

DURKHEIM, E. (1897/1951), *Suicide: A Study in Sociology.* New York: The Free Press.

—— (1895/1982), *The Rules of Sociological Method.* New York: The Free Press.

—— (1893/1984), *The Division of Labor in Society.* New York: The Free Press.

—— (1925/1961), *Moral Education.* New York: The Free Press of Glencoe.

ESPING-ANDERSEN, G. (1990), *The Three Worlds of Welfare Capitalism.* Princeton, NJ: Princeton University Press.

GESUALDI, L. (1996–97), 'Crime and the American Dream: A Book Review', *Crime, Law, and Social Change*, 26/1: 96–7.

GRANOVETTER, M. (1985), 'Economic Action and Social Structure: The Problem of Embeddedness', *American Journal of Sociology*, 91:481–510.

HAGAN, J., HEFFLER, G., CLASSEN, G., BOEHNKE, C. and MERKEN, H. (1998), 'Subterranean Sources of Delinquency: Beyond the American Dream', *Criminology*, 36: 309–42.

HIRSCHI, T. (1969), *Causes of Delinquency.* Berkeley, CA: University of California Press.

KRAHN, H., HARTNAGEL, T. F. and GARTRELL, J. W. (1986), 'Income Inequality and Homicide Rates: Cross-National Data and Criminological Theories', *Criminology*, 24: 269–95.

MENARD, S. (1995), 'A Developmental Test of Merton's Anomie Theory', *Journal of Research in Crime and Delinquency*, 32: 136–74.

—— (1997), 'A Developmental Test of Cloward's Differential-Opportunity Theory', in N. Passas and R. Agnew, eds., *The Future of Anomie Theory*, 142–86. Boston, MA: Northeastern University Press.

MERTON, R. K. (1967/1994), 'Social Structure and Anomie', in S. H. Traub and C. B. Little, eds., *Theories of Deviance*, 4th edn., 114–48. Itasca, IL: F. E. Peacock.

MESSNER, S. F. (1988), 'Merton's Social Structure and Anomie: The Road Not Taken', *Deviant Behavior*, 9: 33–53.

MESSNER, S. F. and ROSENFELD, R. (1994), *Crime and The American Dream*, 2nd edn. Belmont, CA: Wadsworth Publishing Company.

—— (1997a), 'Markets, Morality, and an Institutional-Anomie Theory of Crime', in N. Passas and R. Agnew, eds., *The Future of Anomie Theory*, 207–27. Boston, MA: Northeastern University Press.

—— (1997b), 'Political Restraints of the Market and Levels of Criminal Homicide: A Cross-National Application of Institutional-Anomie Theory', *Social Forces*, 75: 1393–416.

—— (1997c), 'Market Dominance, Crime, and Globalization', presented at the workshop on 'Social Dynamics and Regulatory Order in Modern Societies', International Institute for the Sociology of Law, Spain, 23–24 October.

MITTELMAN, J. H. (1996), 'The Dynamics of Globalization', in J. H. Mittelman, ed., *Globalization: Critical Reflections*, 1–19. Boulder, CO: Lynne Rienner Publishers.

NEE, V. and BRINTON, M. C. (1998), 'Introduction', in M. C. Brinton and V. Nee, eds., *The New Institutionalism in Sociology*, xv–xix. New York: Russel Sage Foundation.

Oakes, L. S., Townley, B. and Cooper, D. J. (1998), 'Business Planning as Pedagogy: Language and Control in a Changing Institutional Field', *Administrative Science Quarterly*, 43: 257–92.

Olsen, G. M. (1996), 'Re-modelling Sweden: The Rise and Demise of the Swedish Compromise in a Global Economy', *Social Problems*, 43: 1–20.

Orrù, M. (1987), *Anomie: History and Meanings*. Boston, MA: Allen and Unwin.

Passas, N. (1990), 'Anomie and Corporate Deviance', *Contemporary Crises*, 14: 157–78.

—— (1995), 'Continuities in the Anomie Tradition', in F. Adler and W. S. Laufer, eds., *The Legacy of Anomie Theory*. New Brunswick and London: Transaction Publishers.

—— (1997), 'Anomie, Reference Groups, and Relative Deprivation', in N. Passas and R. Agnew, eds., *The Future of Anomie Theory*, 62–94. Boston, MA: Northeastern University Press.

Polanyi, K. (1944/1957), *The Great Transformation: The Political and Economic Origins of Our Time*. Boston, MA: Beacon.

—— (1947/1968), 'Our Obsolete Market Mentality', in G. Dalton, ed., *Primitive, Archaic, and Modern Economies: Essays of Karl Polanyi*, 59–77. Garden City, NY: Anchor Books.

—— (1957/1968), 'The Economy as an Instituted Process', in G. Dalton, ed., *Primitive, Archaic, and Modern Economies: Essays of Karl Polanyi*, 139–74. Garden City, NY: Anchor Books.

Sampson, R. J. and Groves, W. B. (1989), 'Community Structure and Crime: Testing Social-Disorganization Theory', *American Journal of Sociology*, 94: 774–802.

Sampson, R. J. and Laub, J. H. (1993), *Crime in the Making: Pathways and Turning Points Through Life*. Cambridge, MA: Harvard University Press.

Savolainen, J. (2000), 'Inequality, Welfare State, and Homicide: Further Support for the Institutional-Anomie Theory', *Criminology*, 38: 1021–42.

Taylor, I., Walton, P. and Young, J. (1973), *The New Criminology: For a Social Theory of Deviance*. London and Boston: Routledge and Keegan Paul.

Teeple, G. (1995), *Globalization and the Decline of Social Reform*. Atlantic Highlands, NJ: Humanities Press.

Thorlindsson, T and Bjarnason, T. (1998), 'Modeling Durkheim on the Micro Level: A Study of Youth Suicidality', *American Sociological Review*, 63: 94–110.

Thornton, P. H. and Ocasio, W. (1999), 'Institutional Logics and the Historical Contingency of Power in Organizations: Executive Succession in the Higher Education Publishing Industry, 1958–1990', *American Journal of Sociology*, 105: 801–43.

Useem, M. (1996), *Investor Capitalism: How Money Managers are Changing the Face of Corporate America*. New York: Basic Books.

Vaughan, D. (1983), *Controlling Unlawful Organizational Behavior*. Chicago, IL: University of Chicago Press.

—— (1997), 'Anomie Theory and Organizations: Culture and the Normalization of Deviance at NASA', in N. Passas and R. Agnew, eds., *The Future of Anomie Theory*, 95–123. Boston, MA: Northeastern University Press.

Walton, P. (1998), 'Big Science: Distopia and Utopia—Establishment and New Criminology Revisited', in P. Walton and J. Young, eds., *The New Criminology Revisited*, 1–13. New York: St Martin's Press.

Wilson, W. J. (1987), *The Truly Disadvantaged*. Chicago, IL: University of Chicago Press.

Wolfe, A. (1989), *Whose Keeper?: Social Science and Moral Obligation*. Berkeley, LA: University of California Press.

Young, J. (1998), 'Breaking Windows: Situating the New Criminology', in P. Walton and J. Young, eds., *The New Criminology Revisited*, 14–46. New York: St Martin's Press.

[3]

CRIME, PUNISHMENT, AND THE AMERICAN DREAM: TOWARD A MARXIST INTEGRATION

BARBARA A. SIMS

In their book Crime and the American Dream, *Messner and Rosenfeld suggest that the American economy sets up a society conducive to conflict and crime. The authors argue throughout their work that social, educational, and political institutions take a backseat to the economy. When building the theoretical foundation for their argument, however, Messner and Rosenfeld fail to adequately address the contribution of Marxist criminology to their "sociological paradigm." In the present article, the author attempts to supply that missing link by suggesting that Marxist criminology can explain how social and economic inequalities are a naturally occurring event in the American system of capitalism. Having done so, she then examines how the theoretical foundation constructed in the first part of the article could be applied to address the manner in which punishment is meted out in American society.*

According to a 1994 Gallup poll, 52% of Americans believe that crime is the most important problem facing the United States today. In spite of research that has shown a great disparity between individuals' fear of crime and the chance of them actually becoming victims, the media, legislators, and U.S. presidents have continued to paint a picture of "soaring crime rates" (Walker 1994:4). In his State of the Union Address in January 1994, President Bill Clinton placed a great emphasis on crime and announced that he was introducing a new crime bill. During the months that followed, as the U.S. Congress began considering the bill, extensive media coverage kept the issue of crime alive in the minds of Americans.

This "fear of crime" is not a new social phenomenon. Some 20 years ago, 51% of Americans already felt that crime was getting worse instead of better (Walker 1994). To what extent the public's concern for crime can be attributed to politicians and the media cannot be clearly discerned. It is difficult to

The author expresses her appreciation to Laura Myers and three anonymous reviewers for editing contributions to this article.

disentangle the true incidence level of crime from official reports of crime, no doubt. It is equally difficult to get a clear picture of crime from self-report data. Yet the public rarely looks firsthand at either published *Uniform Crime Reports* or results of the National Crime and Victimization Survey. The public instead gets most of its information about crime from the media and at election time from politicians, both of which are in the business of selling something to the public. The media wants to be seen, read, or listened to—thus a greater chance of convincing the public to buy the products of advertisers that keep them in operation. The politicians clearly are selling themselves.

With so much at stake for both the media and politicians, it is no wonder that the public ends up being saturated with an anecdotal picture of crime in America; the media paint it and the politicians use it as a convenient political tool. This unlikely marriage of the media to politicians could play a major role in the continuing concern Americans express about crime.

Although the picture of crime that Americans are left with may be distorted and used to feed a politically fruitful "get tough" approach to crime, the fact is that crime is a major problem in the United States. Whether or not crime is increasing in such drastic measures, as has been portrayed by the press and politicians, is a question that is not answered in this article. Instead, an argument is made that the resulting "lock 'em up" policy—fueled by the media, politicians, and the public's increased punitiveness toward offenders—has diverted attention away from a close examination of a social structure and culture that produces criminal activity in the first place. This punitive approach to crime has had a tremendous impact on the criminal justice system (police, courts, and corrections)—an impact that has been felt throughout other social institutions across U.S. communities.

To lay the theoretical foundation for this argument, I apply Messner and Rosenfeld's (1994) "sociological paradigm" in *Crime and the American Dream* to Irwin and Austin's (1994) "imprisonment binge" in *It's About Time: America's Imprisonment Binge.* I first suggest, however, that Messner and Rosenfeld did not go far enough in framing their paradigm and propose a substantial contribution to their work by Marxist criminology. I attempt to include Marxist theory with the theories used by Messner and Rosenfeld to develop a more comprehensive theoretical foundation on which to examine crime in American society. I then apply the new paradigm to a new approach to crime developed in the first part of the article with the crime control policies as discussed by Irwin and Austin. I conclude by offering suggestions for future theory development and its application in the American crime arena.

THE MISSING LINK IN MESSNER AND ROSENFELD'S "SOCIOLOGICAL PARADIGM"

In *Crime and the American Dream*, Messner and Rosenfeld (1994:8) argue that there is a "dark side" to the American Dream. The thesis of their book is that the American Dream itself

> encourages an exaggerated emphasis on monetary achievements while devaluing alternative criteria of success; it promotes a preoccupation with the realization of goals while deemphasizing the importance of the ways in which these goals are pursued; and it helps create and sustain social structures with limited capacities to restrain the cultural pressures to disregard legal restraints. (pp. 8-10)

Out of their thesis, the authors form the hypothesis that high crime rates in America are intrinsic to the basic cultural commitments and institutional arrangements of American society. Both the cultural and structural underpinnings of U.S. communities are, for Messner and Rosenfeld, "organized for crime" (p. 6).

The intellectual roots of *Crime and the American Dream* are found in Durkheim and his examination of the critical role that social forces play in explaining human behavior. For Durkheim (1933), any explanation of human behavior must take into account the various social forces surrounding the individual. His key concept, anomie (a sense of normlessness brought about by the breakdown in social institutions), is a natural result, a state of *confusion*, when societies are transformed from the mechanical (traditional/rural) to the organic (modern/urban).

Messner and Rosenfeld rely on the later works by Merton (1938, 1964, 1968), however, and his expansion of Durkheim's anomie, to provide the underlying premise for their own work. They accept Merton's notion that motivations for crime do not result simply from the flaws, failures, and/or free choices of individuals and that a complete examination of crime ultimately must consider the sociocultural environments in which people are located. They suggest, however, that Merton's argument, by itself, is not enough because it does not provide a "fully comprehensive, sociological explanation of crime in America" (Messner and Rosenfeld 1994:15).

To achieve this comprehensive, sociological explanation (their sociological paradigm), Messner and Rosenfeld look to the "levels of explanation" in social research, namely, micro and macro. Primarily, micro explanations of crime focus on individual behavior, whereas macro explanations shift attention from individuals to social collectivities (Messner, Krohn, and Liska 1989). Messner and Rosenfeld (1994) integrate six theories across these levels of explanations to form the theoretical argument for *Crime and the American Dream.* Their assumptions are detailed in the following.

1. *Social learning* (micro) theories are associated with *cultural deviance* (macro) theories that explain crime as the product of cultural (or subcultural) values and norms.
2. *Social control* (micro) theory is most closely connected with *social disorganization* (macro) theory as it refers to the inability of groups or communities to realize collective goals, including the goal of crime control.
3. *Anomie* (macro) is a result of *strain* (micro) experienced as a result of a differential distribution of opportunities to achieve highly valued goals.

Thus, for Messner and Rosenfeld (1994), as communities become socially disorganized, they lose their ability to maintain sufficient control (both formal and informal) over their members such as to deter them from adopting delinquent lifestyles. As a result, subcultures can arise that create a new set of values and norms that can be learned in the same manner that values and norms in the mainstream culture are learned. In a situation of this sort, with institutions in decay, the problem is further exacerbated by an unequal opportunity structure in which not only the institutions but also the individuals who compose them are likely to suffer strain, the result of which is Durkheim's state of *confusion* (anomie).

According to these assumptions, Messner and Rosenfeld (1994) suggest that the answer to America's crime problem is to be found in a strengthening of its institutions (family, school, and polity) through social reorganization. Part of this reorganization process will entail the reassessing of the cultural values found in American society with its "exaggerated emphasis on monetary success" (p. 76). For too long, say the authors, the economy has maintained such a grip on American life in general as to shortchange families, schools, local communities, and even the one institution that is supposed to give a voice to Americans themselves—the political arena.

In their discussion on social structure and culture, Messner and Rosenfeld (1994) refer briefly to Marx. They draw from Marx's "insight that the distribution of the means of consumption is ultimately dependent on the conditions of production themselves" (p. 108). However, they fail to make the necessary link between Marx and their own arguments. A brief discussion of Marxist criminology should make this point.

Crime in a Capitalist Economic Structure

As Greenberg (1993) points out, the question of what specifically Marxism has to offer criminologists is hotly debated. He admits that "although Marx and Engels wrote about crime, law, and criminal justice from time to time, they gave them no systematic treatment" (p. 11). This debate has led to a consensus of sorts in the idea that an understanding of the way in which social conflict is generated, is sustained, and produces criminal activity is found in Marx's general *economic* theory.

For Marx, each economic system is divided into those who own the means of production and those who are dependent on them for their economic existence (the "haves" and the "have-nots"): free citizens versus slaves, nobles versus serfs, bourgeoisie versus proletariat. History becomes a series of economic systems in which classes are structured according to the social relations of production. The relationship between them is one of antagonism, with those "owning the most" able to secure a great amount of power and domination over those who are less fortunate (Lynch and Groves 1989).

Through the use of a *base structure* metaphor, Marx (1904) argues that "the mode of production in material life determines the general character of the social, political, and spiritual processes of life" (p. 11). Like a building with different levels rising up and out of its base foundation, societies are formed with the economic mode of production providing the base foundation for its social institutions. Just as each floor in a building may alter its individual structure within certain limits as established by its foundation, societal institutions take on a life of their own (Greenberg 1993). Yet, social institutions are restricted by the economic base in the degree to which they can shift and change. Marx and Engels (1969) explain this metaphor further.

> Political, juridical, philosophical, religious, artistic, etc. development is based on economic development. But all these react upon one another and also upon the economic basis. It is not that the economic situation is *cause, solely active*, while everything else is only passive effect. There is, rather, interaction on the basis of economic necessity, which *ultimately* always asserts itself. (p. 502; emphasis added)

Among these societal institutions (political, juridical, philosophical, religious, artistic, family, community, education, and economic), contradictions and conflicts are sure to exist. In a capitalist economy, fueled by competitiveness and the importance of material success, conflict increases. This conflict is internal to society, then, and will over time have a destabilizing effect on its social institutions and the individual members that compose them.

In this "history of class struggles," Marxist criminologists argue that the haves have "exploited and oppressed the have-nots through economic, political, and legal mechanisms" (Lynch and Groves 1989:5). In a capitalist economy, the means of subsistence accrue to labor in the form of wages with the surplus product distributed among capitalists, financiers, and landlords in the form of profit, interest, and rent (Roberts and Stephenson 1970). With the differences in distribution, class differences emerge and conflict is inevitable. Those in power have more than just the larger slice of the *economic* and *political* pies; they also are able to accrue power in the *legal* system, wherein the very laws under which they must live are developed. These laws often are tilted in favor of the ruling class and more punitive toward the lower classes.

The first question for Marxist criminologists, then, is as follows: How have laws and criminal justice, as forms of social control, been used to contain class struggle and maintain class divisions at different times in different societies? Lynch and Groves (1989) point out, for example, that there is no reason to believe that crime in the Roman Empire (slaves and free citizens) would be the same as crime in a mercantile system. It follows, then, that crime in a socialist economic structure would be different from crime in a capitalist economic structure.

Under capitalism, as Lynch and Grove (1989) point out, "private ownership and respect for private property are very important concepts, and today the state takes an active interest in protecting rights through criminal justice prosecution" (p. 6). Before capitalism (early mercantilism), for example, theft was treated as a civil matter, with a dispute over property settled in a civil rather than a criminal court. After capitalism, theft became a crime against the state. Because theft usually was a crime committed by the poor, the state's "intrusion into this matter pitted the poor against the propertied class and their ally—the state itself" (Lynch and Groves 1989:6).

Marx's Contribution to Messner and Rosenfeld

As mentioned earlier, Messner and Rosenfeld (1994) do not fail to give some credit to Marx. Yet, their brief mention of the contribution Marxist criminology makes to their own work is more *implicit* than *explicit* and, therefore, easy for the reader to miss. To synthesize, this contribution stems from an argument that the economic mode of production in America (i.e., capitalism) sets up a society for conflict and crime. It forms the foundation of a society from which other social institutions arise—the institutions that, for Messner and Rosenfeld, become so important.

Marxist criminologists align with strain, social disorganization, and cultural theories at this juncture and with the assumptions in *Crime and the American Dream*. When Messner and Rosenfeld (1994) talk about value patterns such as achievement, individualism, universalism, and the fetishism of money, Marxists point out that these values are derivatives of a capitalist mode of production. Its members are socialized to overemphasize materialism, which quite often leads to greed. Yet, for Marxists, it is not the consciousness of men that determines their existence; rather, it is their social existence that determines their consciousness (Marx 1978). The cause of crime, then, is determined by social forces outside the control of individuals. Those who engage in criminal activity may be "freely acting," but, for Marxists and for Messner and Rosenfeld, they are acting within a determined social, political, and economical setting.

Figure 1 argues conceptually that Marxist criminology can provide an explanation of how social relationships in a capitalist economic system (the *social formation* for Marx) can produce structural and economic inequalities. The economic and structural inequalities that arise in the social environment can produce a state of confusion (anomie). Within this anomic cultural environment, individuals are likely to suffer strain, and institutions (schools, communities, families, and the criminal justice system) lose their ability to control their members. As a result, a new culture may form whose members reject the norms and values of the mainstream culture. Within this subculture and, in particular, a *delinquent* subculture, a new set of norms and values are adopted that could provide fertile ground for the learning of criminal behavior.

The basic premise for this article is that Messner and Rosenfeld (1994), in building the theoretical foundation for their argument in *Crime and the American Dream*, fail to adequately address the system under which social and economic inequalities arise, namely, a capitalist economy. This effort to call attention to the missing link (Marxist criminology) in their sociological paradigm is not completely at odds with the not-too-distant literature.

In an attempt to "build a few bridges between traditional and radical criminology," Groves and Sampson (1987:181) closely examine similarities between traditional and radical theories of crime. They point out, for example, that Merton's assertion that societal structures can pressure certain individuals in society to engage in nonconformist conduct makes for an "immediate affinity between strain and radical theories" (p. 188). Recast in Marxist terms, behavior must be viewed in the structural context in which it occurs; the two cannot be separated. As pointed out by Groves and Sampson, when "crimi-

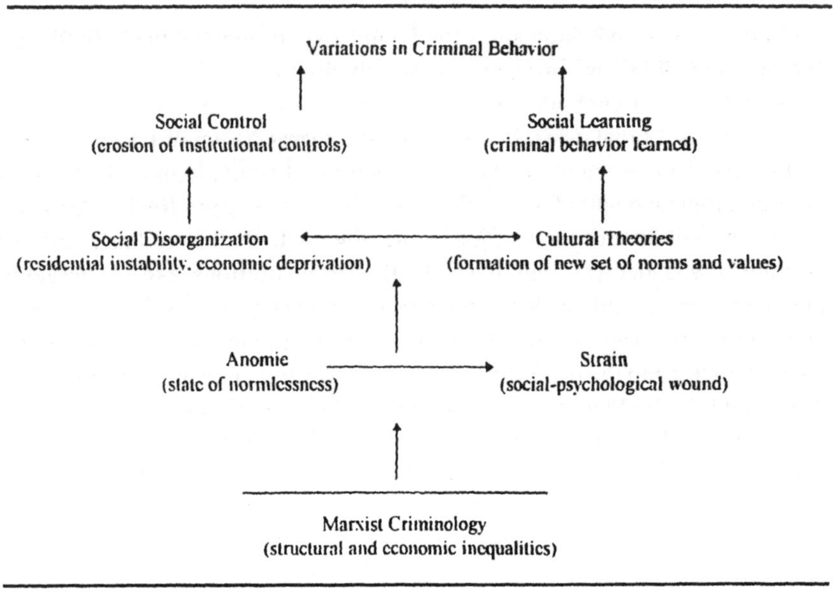

Figure 1: An Integrated Theory of Crime

nologists suggest that social structure has causal effects that are independent of culture, their arguments carry materialist overtones that are consistent with generally accepted Marxist methodology" (p. 189).

Examining further the similarities between traditional and radical criminological theories, Lynch and Groves (1989) argue that Merton failed to address exactly where the goals—which he argues are not capable of being achieved by all in society—originate. Nor did Merton explain how various social classes are formed. Goals, according to Marxists, are materialistic in nature and, as such, can be traced to the "economic requirements of capitalism" (Lynch and Groves 1989:74). Opportunity structures are, in Marxist terms, distributed along class lines created by stratifications that are dictated by society's economic structure. Classes are not created equally and, as pointed out by Lynch and Groves, do not "pop out of thin air" (p. 75). Thus they amend strain theory by supplying an explanation of how they are formed and further suggest the following.

> Consistent with radical expectations, strain theorists suggest that crimes are not sporadic occurrences committed by isolated and abnormal individuals, but are regular and institutionalized features of a social system characterized by intense stratification and pervasive class conflict. (p. 75, citing Taylor, Walton, and Young 1975; Bernard 1987)

Both Groves and Sampson (1987) and Lynch and Groves (1989) also bridge social disorganization and control theories with Marxist criminology. This bridge, for Lynch and Groves, is based on Durkheim's argument that when there is a breakdown in institutional integration, an imbalance occurs and social disorganization is the result. Marxists criminologists view *imbalance* as a logical result of a capitalist economic mode of production. Messner and Rosenfeld do an excellent job of picking up the ball from this point and arguing how, under a system in which all other institutions take a backseat to the economic system, such an imbalance can occur. Social disorganization and control theories are solid arguments for a breakdown in community characteristics and the resulting loss of control over its members, an argument discussed fully by Messner and Rosenfeld (1994). Yet, as suggested by Lynch and Groves (1989) and as would receive little argument from Groves and Sampson (1987), communities cannot be viewed out of the social context that produces them. Poverty and inequality, two characteristics most often associated with a socially disorganized community, can, as argued earlier, be traced to a disproportionate distribution of goods and services in a capitalist economic system. This simple but much overlooked fact does nothing to detract from Durkheim's original theory and certainly is not at odds with it.

In the context of a community in which poverty and inequality are a way of life, a new set of values may form that seem to be in direct opposition to those of the larger society (criminogenic in nature). Sutherland (1947) suggested that persons engage in criminal behavior because it is demanded by their culture; they commit crimes because they have learned that it is the correct thing to do. Marxist's criminologists ask the question: Where do these criminogenic values come from? Like cultural goals, class strata, and socially disorganized institutions, they originate somewhere. Miller (1979) attempts to answer the question by arguing that "lower class structure is a distinctive tradition many centuries old with an integrity all its own" (p. 167).

As pointed out by Groves and Sampson (1987:185), however, Miller and other cultural theorists would have us believe that lower class culture is "something that floats through history and just happens to be adhered to by those at the bottom of the class hierarchy." Argued from a Marxist perspective, persons are in fact motivated by their values, beliefs, and ideas, which in turn are determined by structurally defined conditions of life. Cultural theorists ignore what produces the idea of an act, or of a particular value system, and draw a line straight from the idea of committing a crime to the criminal act itself. Once again, the structural factors that could explain the existence of variations in values are ignored (Groves and Sampson 1987).

In Messner and Rosenfeld's (1994) sociological paradigm, they include social learning theory as the micro analog of cultural theories; that is, criminal behavior is learned just like any other behavior is learned. They also include social control theory as the micro analog of social disorganization theory; that is, when a person's bond to society is weak or broken, he or she is more likely to engage in deviant behavior. When discussing these two theories, they are not slack in addressing the issue of social structure. At the individual level, both social learning and social control variables are able to explain much of the variance in deviant behavior. This is to be expected given that those variables are the most proximate to the act itself. What researchers fail to recognize, however, is the fact that the more distal variables (i.e., the structural or macro-level variables) are contributing much to any model of crime. What is it about the way in which society is structured that allows—or disallows—social bonding to take place? What is it about the way in which society is structured that produces variation in value systems where social learning takes place? Only a theoretical foundation that includes a close examination of how differentials in the social structure are produced can begin to explore the answer to these questions.

The Interaction of Culture With Economic and Structural Components

In *Crime and the American Dream*, Messner and Rosenfeld (1994) state that the "American Dream is a broad cultural ethos that entails a commitment to the goal of material success to be pursued by everyone in society under conditions of open, individual competition" (p. 6). This cultural ethos sets up all members of American society to want the same things, to view success in terms of material items, with other success criteria (educational achievement, artistic talent, etc.) taking a backseat to monetary success. Messner and Rosenfeld call this phenomenon the "fetishism of money" and argue that the American Dream, then, can never actually be realized by anyone given that members of society always are working to accumulate more material goods.

Marxist criminologists ask the question: Just what is it about American society that produces this fetishism of money? Messner and Rosenfeld (1994) argue that in American society, individuals are encouraged to succeed "by any means necessary" (p. 9). They talk about *universalism* (clearly a concept with Mertonian overtones) in which members of American society are socialized to "embrace the tenets of the dominant cultural ethos" (p. 9), an ethos that says that, regardless of your position in society, you can, and in fact should, achieve the American Dream.

The question arises, then: Just how is it that success, in American culture, became so entangled with material goods? From a Marxist perspective, that question is not difficult to answer. During the Industrial Revolution, as

American society moved from an agrarian to a market economy, individual workers were transformed from producers of goods for their own consumption to producers of goods that would produce profits for the factory owners. During this process, the early proletariats were twice "duped" by the capitalists. First, they were transformed into a "disposal industrial army" (Marx 1967:632) to be used by the industrialists in the *production* of various commodities. Second, and here is the rub, the workers then again were transformed, through a massive advertising campaign that took root during the 1920s, into the *consumers* of the very products they were producing. Workers were paid wages that barely kept their families housed, fed, and clothed and then were taught that no longer was it enough to have what they needed in life to survive; rather, somehow they could be more "civilized," and not "social failures," once a certain amount of the produced commodities were accumulated (Ewen 1976:42-44).

For industry to succeed, it had to create in workers a desire to consume. What better way to mobilize the desires of individuals than through massive advertising. In 1926, U.S. President Calvin Coolidge remarked that advertising, if applied correctly, could be the "method by which the desire is created for better things" (quoted in Ewen 1976:37). The new advertising age was up and running, and with it came a host of ads that were meant to keep the workers dissatisfied with their way of life; dissatisfied customers, after all, "are much more profitable than satisfied ones" (p. 39).

According to Ewen (1976), the ads constantly bombarded the workers with messages that the new commodities of industry would somehow lift them out of the working class and into the more accepted mainstream of American society. This created a culture in which the *economy* began to ride roughshod over all other institutions. In its wake, industry left behind the

> indigenous networks of social structure that carried premises and values which generated mistrust or open opposition to the corporate monopolization of culture, . . . traditional family structures, immigrant values, and the traditional realms of aesthetic expression. (p. 58)

A new culture was created with industry, and thus the economy, becoming the "captain of consciousness" for the new army of workers (Ewen 1976). A sense of "excessiveness" replaced "thrift" as the *old ways* were usurped by this new culture of mass consumption, a social phenomenon that many would argue is very much alive and well in American society today. In *Crime and the American Dream*, Messner and Rosenfeld (1994) argue that this drive to accumulate material goods contributes greatly to the dark side of the American Dream. From a Mertonian standpoint, the authors suggest that all are equally encouraged to consume but that there is a "relatively weak emphasis on the importance of using the legitimate means to do so" (p. 69).

Given an overemphasis on monetary success coupled with an unequal means to achieve it, it is more likely than not that individuals could, under these circumstances, become frustrated over the inability to accumulate material goods. The concept of "relative deprivation" has a rich history in much of the literature and describes just such a situation. Gurr (1970) defines relative deprivation as "actors' perception of discrepancy between their value *expectations* and their value *capabilities*" (p. 24). Value is a term used to describe the goods, and the conditions of life in general, to which individuals believe they are entitled. Gurr uses relative deprivation to argue that the potential for collective violence could vary strongly with the "intensity and scope" (p. 24) of relative deprivation among members of a group.

Cloward and Ohlin (1960), in talking about deprivation, argue that a sense of being unjustly deprived of access to opportunities to which they are entitled is common among delinquent subcultures. The psychological wound of relative deprivation, Cloward and Ohlin argue, could play a "significant role in the withdrawal of attributions of legitimacy from official norms" (p. 117). This withdrawal could, in turn, result in individuals engaging in illegitimate activities (i.e., crime) as a means of accumulating those goods and conditions of life that their culture has led them to believe are, in fact, their heritage.

If, as has been argued, there is as much a cultural component that produces crime in one capitalist country—namely, in America—as there is a structural component, then one question comes quickly to mind: How is it that in other capitalist nations, the crime rates have not soared to the same heights as the crime rate seemingly has soared in America? Is it because the institutions themselves vary greatly from one country to the other, or could it be that not so heavy an emphasis is placed on mass consumerism and the accumulation of material goods in other countries relative to that found in the United States?

Initial reactions to this question might produce, and not unrightfully so, answers coming from perspectives based on the easy accessibility of guns in American society or the fact that minorities are disproportionately represented in arrest reports in the United States. Messner and Rosenfeld (1994) address both of these issues in great detail. They argue that although rates of gun ownership are much higher in America than they are in other industrial nations, if gun-related homicides were left out of the U.S. homicide rate, then the United States still would have a non-gun homicide rate higher than the total homicide rates of other industrial nations.

Messner and Rosenfeld (1994) argue further that although lethal violence among young African American men is extremely high, this, in and of itself, does not explain the differences in homicide rates between the United States and other industrial societies. Excluding African Americans from the equation, Messner and Rosenfeld state that the "homicide rate for *Whites* is more than four times the average rate of homicide" among other industrial nations (p. 29). Thus the answer to the question of what explains the high rate of violent crime in the United States cannot be reduced to guns and ethnicity.

When opponents of a Marxist perspective attempt to show how the argument that "capitalism produces crime" fails, they usually point to the Japanese society. As pointed out by Braithwaite (1989), Japan might be expected to have a crime rate given its history of rapid industrialization following World War II and the fact that it very quickly became highly urbanized in densely packed cities. In making an argument for "reintegrative shaming," Braithwaite points out that shaming is fundamental to Japanese society: "When an individual is shamed in Japan, the shame is often born by the collectivity to which the individual belongs as well—the family the company, the school—particularly by the titular head of the collectivity" (p. 63).

In Japan, then, the other social institutions play as much a role in society as does the economy in the level of control they are able to exert over individuals. The Japanese culture, although one existing in a capitalist backdrop, supports a highly developed sense of community—a situation far removed from the heavy emphasis on individualism found in the United States. Even though Japan, like the United States, has grown into one of the most highly developed societies in the world, what sets it apart from the United States is its ability to hold on to its historical traditions surrounding behavioral expectations (Adler 1983).

In spite of low levels of crime in Japanese society, however, the fact remains that the country is not crime free. According to Fenwick (1985), Japan does have concerns in areas such as juvenile delinquency, drug abuse, and organized crime. Although much lower than other industrial nations, the Japanese crime rate has been on the increase since the late 1970s (Fenwick 1985). Looking specifically at increases in juvenile crime, Chang (1988) offers the following reason for this increase. In Tokyo, the Japanese city with the highest mobility rate, the value system of youth has begun a transformation of sorts. No longer is personal interdependence the key to social status and satisfaction; *money* quickly has become the ticket to personal success. Youths commute long distances to schools and neighborhoods where their families are not known. Instead of living in houses owned by their forefathers for generations, they live in crowded multiple-family housing units—a situation not conducive to pride and healthy self-images. Under these circumstances, the notion of honor, so important in the Japanese culture, begins to break down, and the responsibility to the community and the family is weakened.

As pointed out by Chang (1988), this may all sound familiar as it describes, in essence, the evolution of Japanese youths away from a "vertical, Confucian-based society" and toward a more individualistic Western model (p. 148). As countries adopt a more "Americanized" type of capitalism, in which success is measured in dollars and the community, family, and school begin to play "second fiddle" to this economic success, institutions suffer, cultural methods of social control break down, and the end result is a society "organized for crime."

PUNITIVE CRIME CONTROL: AMERICA'S IMPRISONMENT BINGE

In a society with its institutions in disarray and thus unable to maintain control over its members, and in a society where the cultural expectations are geared toward the accumulation of material goods with unequal means to achieve those goods, crime often is an unintended consequence. As crime increases, so too does the method of social control over members of society. It follows, then, that America's "war on crime" would result in higher numbers of incarceration for members of its lower classes given that this war has been waged on "street crime" as opposed to white-collar crime. Marxist criminologists view laws in a capitalist society as tilted in favor of the ruling class and more punitive toward the lower classes.

Greenberg (1993) argues this point well in a discussion on crime and punishment. Through a historical development of crime control measures, Greenberg is able to show how, when necessary to protect the new economic order, the state takes action. For example, throughout the 16th through 18th centuries, when those individuals who had been driven from their lands by the rural landlords turned to begging and thievery for their existence, the state created a host of laws against vagrancy, begging, idleness, and petty forms of theft (Greenberg 1993). These laws benefited capitalists because they forced individuals into a wage-labor relationship with them.

This taking of the lands from the people was, for Marx, codified into law that eventually became the instrument for the great dispossession that continued to occur into the 19th century. The state thus "conquered the field for capitalistic agriculture and created for the town industries the necessary supply of an outlawed proletariat" (cited in Greenberg, 1993:47).

Hahn (1982) writes about an 1875 South Carolina law that restricted individuals' use of land. In an effort to reclaim the lost labor of the now freed

African American slaves, southern states moved to create laws that would punish anyone caught hunting or fishing. The coercive arm of the state resulted in restriction of mobility and access to the means of survival. This again forced individuals into a working relationship with the large landowners. As Hahn points out, this "plantation mentality" did not stop in the South; rather, it carried over into the industry of the North.

The dispossessed of the South, African Americans as well as White owners of small parcels of land, migrated to the North in record numbers during the late 19th and early 20th centuries. This social phenomenon provided even more workers for the industrialists of the expanding cities and, in turn, a small band of individuals who took to begging in the streets as an alternative to working in the factories. The state then intervened with laws against vagrancy, and these laws left the workers with no other possible sources of income other than wage labor (Humphries and Greenberg 1980).

The more recent American history shows how many urban areas have been hit by a new economic transition—the withdrawal of industry from the inner cities to cheaper labor markets. This transition has been seen as a contributing factor to the development and continuation of urban youth gangs. Jackson (1991) argues, for example, that the failure to retrain inner-city youths for a more service-related industry with substantial changes in technology worsens economic opportunities for unskilled urban youths.

Inner-city youths have been, and often unrightfully so, connected with the use and sale of illegal drugs. The war on drugs, with its more punitive sentencing policies for drug offenders, has focused heavily on crack cocaine. Because this drug is mainly sold and used in inner-city communities, Hispanics and African Americans are the ones who have felt the strong arm of the law. As of 1989, the African American prison population, for example, had increased to 46%—from 21% of all prison admissions in 1926, when the race of the prison population began to be recorded (Irwin and Austin 1994).

In *It's About Time: America's Imprisonment Binge*, Irwin and Austin (1994) argue that punitive approaches to crime have left America's correctional institutions overburdened and unable to meet the demands of a coerced public. This coercion stems from a public misperception about crime brought about primarily by the attention paid to such by politicians and the media. Marxist criminologists would relate this misperception to the concept of "false consciousness." The attention politicians have paid to crime has acted as a smokescreen—a diversion tactic of sorts. With the public's attention focused on crime, and with a public willing to pay whatever cost it must to get the crime rate down, issues such as the threat of nuclear war, unemployment, high living costs, and the economy are placed on the back burner. Irwin and Austin (1994) point out that any attempts made to solve these problems, along with a host of other social problems, would be met by the powerful forces of political, legal, and economic interest groups—an argument with which Marxist criminologists would readily agree.

The result of this diversion tactic is exponential growth in America's correctional institutions—be it incarceration, probation, community corrections, or parole. Primarily, as Irwin and Austin (1994) point out and as backed up by Marxist criminology, the population that composes the greatest increase is drawn from the lower classes. The crimes of the "powerless" (street crimes) are controlled by punitive governmental measures, although they cost society far less than do the crimes of the "powerful" ("suite crimes").

As Messner and Rosenfeld (1994) point out, white-collar crime costs society approximately $200 billion a year—roughly 20 times the annual monetary loss or damage due to street crimes in the United States. Irwin and Austin (1994) cite a 1990 report by the U.S. Department of Justice's National Crime Victim Survey that puts the cost of crimes to victims at about $19.2 billion. Still, it is not chief executive officers or the owners (including stockholders) of major corporations who form the bulk of the U.S. inmate population.

Nor do those comprising the upper 1% of American society seem overly concerned with street crime. The powerful are segregated from the "invisible lower class masses" and, as such, are far removed from the likelihood of becoming victims of street crime. As individuals move downward in the class stratification system under capitalism, however, that likelihood increases (not in the drastic proportion that the politicians and media would lead the public to believe, but it does increase nonetheless). The powerful, unconcerned with street crime, use it as a tool of deception and as a way of maintaining control of the lower strata of society: The lower classes are controlled through incarceration, and the middle classes are controlled by diverting their attention away from the crimes of the powerful and to the crimes of the powerless.

Messner and Rosenfeld (1994), as well as Irwin and Austin (1994), move down the crime continuum and look closely at the inequalities in America's social structure that lead individuals to the threshold of the criminal justice system. The former spend a great amount of energy arguing that America's social system is tilted in favor of the economy—an argument with which Marxist criminologists would not disagree. The latter argue that America must begin to rethink its punitive approach to crime because it cannot afford the price tag of exponential incarceration—an argument that would get no disagreement from Marxist criminologists. To "catch criminals and lock them up; if they hit you, hit them back" may seem a *commonsense* approach to crime (Menninger 1969:5). As expressed by Menninger (1969), it is also a commonsense approach that if it gets dark, you go to bed. Yet, the *uncom-*

monsense of science has made it no longer necessary to go to bed when it gets dark and has taught us that simply to lock up individuals who commit crimes does little to curtail them (p. 5).

Both Messner and Rosenfeld (1994) and Irwin and Austin (1994) offer solutions to the problem of crime in America. Many of these solutions have been suggested by Marxist criminologists over the past two decades. A discussion of these solutions, along with recommendations for future directions in theory construction and application, concludes this article.

THEORY AND ITS APPLICATION IN THE REDUCTION OF CRIME IN AMERICAN SOCIETY

Before moving to a discussion of solutions for America's crime problem, there is one clarification with regard to Marxist criminology that should be made. Some factions of Marxist criminology believe that no solution outside of an overthrow of the current economic mode of production in America (i.e., capitalism) can expect to turn around the crime tide—be it street crime or suite crime. Neo-Marxists, however, take a more realistic approach through the realization that, as Marx himself proclaimed, history will usher in a new economic order in its own good time. In the meantime, while we

> wait and agitate for large-scale transformation [as outlined by both Messner and Rosenfeld 1994 and Irwin and Austin 1994], there is a great deal to be accomplished in terms of middle-range policy alternatives which do not compromise any overall design for fundamental social change. (Lynch and Groves 1989:128-129)

What follows is a list of these policy alternatives offered up by Marxist criminologists. Many of them mirror the solutions suggested by Messner and Rosenfeld (1994) and Irwin and Austin (1994).

1. Crime should be defined according to the amount of harm inflicted on society. The definition of crime and the practice of crime control should no longer be organized along class lines (Michalowski 1985).
2. Reduce the capacity of capital to displace labor. Develop tax initiatives to establish a surcharge on any industry attempting to close plants or permanently reduce the workforce in a given community, introduce legislation requiring the retraining and placement of displaced workers, and increase minimum wages to a sufficient amount so as to decrease the numbers of working poor (Michalowski 1983).

3. Reduce inequality in the existing social structure, because it is a strong predictor of U.S. homicide rates (Messner 1989).
4. Abolish mandatory sentences that discriminate against lower class America and greatly overburden its correctional institutions (Platt 1982).
5. Curb white-collar crime by improving enforcement through the allocation of more resources to regulatory agencies, implementing structural reforms, and enacting political reforms designed to minimize conflict of interest (Coleman 1989).
6. Take a closer look at the enactment of laws that require punitive governmental intervention such as those that create new classes of criminals, for example, laws that criminalize the homeless (Barak and Bohm 1989)

This condensed version of Marxist criminologists' solutions to America's crime problem shortchanges a host of theorists who have attempted to attack the problem at its roots rather than on its branches. It does, however, make the point that these solutions are not out of alignment with those of the more mainstream theorists. The better direction for theorists, then, would be a reconciliation of both camps. These two camps, often referred to as conflict versus consensus, quite often appear to be reading from the same sheet of music. The underlying point of contention is found in one faction of conflict theory, namely, critical theory (sometimes referred to as Marxist or radical theory).

Critical theorists are not content to remain behind the walls of universities; rather, they feel the responsibility to take their findings to the public arena by openly, and continually, critiquing the existing social order. In their passion for seeking social change, however, critical theorists quite often make the same mistake as their more conservative counterparts. They wrap themselves in a rhetoric that is overbearing and quite often misunderstood by fellow theorists as well as the public and decision makers. The result often is deadlock; nothing is accomplished, and society continues down a spiraling path of institutional decay and loss of control over its members.

The future of theoretical development should take a two-prong approach. One is to be found in a coming together of consensus and conflict theorists. As shown here, both camps are closer to agreement than much of the literature would dictate. The other approach is to move the research findings out of the secluded halls of academe and into the halls of the body politic. With the increase in social science techniques, criminologists, sociologists, psychologists, and biologists all have produced a sufficient amount of evidence supporting possible solutions to the problem of crime in America. Until the message reaches the public, however, these findings will forever be concealed in the dustbins of academe.

REFERENCES

Adler, Freda. 1983. *Nations Not Obsessed With Crime*. Littleton, CO: Fred B. Rothman.

Barak, Gregg and Robert M. Bohm. 1989. "The Crimes of the Homeless or the Crime of Homelessness? On the Dialectics of Criminalization, Decriminalization, and Victimization." *Contemporary Crisis* 13:275-88.

Bernard, T. 1987. "Testing Structural Strain Theories." *Journal of Research in Crime and Delinquency* 24:262-80.

Braithwaite, John. 1989. *Crime, Shame, and Reintegration*. New York: Press Syndicate of the University of Cambridge.

Chang, Dae H. 1988. "Crime and Delinquency Control Strategy in Japan: A Comparative Note." *International Journal of Comparative and Applied Criminal Justice* 12 (Winter): 139-49.

Cloward, Richard A. and Lloyd E. Ohlin. 1960. *Delinquency and Opportunity: A Theory of Delinquent Gangs*. New York: Free Press.

Coleman, W. J. 1989. *The Criminal Elite: The Sociology of White Collar Crime*. New York: St. Martin's.

Durkheim, Emile. 1933. *The Division of Labor in Society*. New York: Free Press.

Ewen, Stuart. 1976. *Captains of Consciousness: Advertising and the Social Roots of the Consumer Culture*. New York: McGraw-Hill.

Fenwick, Charles R. 1985. "Culture, Philosophy and Crime: The Japanese Experience." *International Journal of Comparative and Applied Criminal Justice* 9 (Spring): 67-81.

Greenberg, David F. 1993. *Crime and Capitalism: Readings in Marxist Criminology*. Philadelphia: Temple University Press.

Groves, W. Byron and Robert J. Sampson. 1987. "Traditional Contributions to Radical Criminology." *Journal of Research in Crime and Delinquency* 24:181-214.

Gurr, Ted Robert. 1970. *Why Men Rebel*. Princeton, NJ: Princeton University Press.

Hahn, Steven. 1982. "Hunting, Fishing and Foraging: Common Rights and Class Relations in the Postbellum South." *Radical History Review* 26:37-64.

Humphries, Drew and David F. Greenberg. 1980. "Social Control and Social Formations." In *Toward a General Theory of Social Control*, edited by Donald Black. New York: Academic Press.

Irwin, John and James Austin. 1994. *It's About Time: America's Imprisonment Binge*. Belmont, CA: Wadsworth.

Jackson, Pamela Irving. 1991. "Crime, Youth Gangs, and Urban Transition: The Social Dislocations of Postindustrial Economic Development." *Justice Quarterly* 8 (September): 379-97.

Lynch, Michael J. and W. Byron Groves. 1989. *A Primer in Radical Criminology* (2nd ed.). Albany, NY: Harrow & Heston.

Marx, Karl. 1967. *Capital* (Vol. 1). New York: International.

———. 1978. *The Marx Engels Reader* (2nd ed.), edited by Robert C. Tucker. New York: Norton.

———. 1904. *Contribution to a Critique of Political Economy*, translated by N. I. Stone. Chicago: Charles H. Kerr.

Marx, Karl and Frederick Engels. 1969. *Selected Works* (Vol. 3). Moscow: Progress.

Menninger, Karl. 1969. *The Crime of Punishment*. New York: Viking.

Merton, Robert K. 1938. "Social Structure and Anomie." *American Sociological Review* 3:672-82.

———. 1964. "Anomie, Anomia, and Social Interaction." Pp. 213-42 in *Anomie and Deviant Behavior*, edited by Marshall Clinard. New York: Free Press.

———. *Social Theory and Social Structure*. New York: Free Press.

Messner, Steven F. 1989. "Economic Discrimination and Societal Homicide Rates: Further Evidence on the Cost of Inequality." *American Sociological Review* 54:597-611.

Messner, Steven F., Marvin D. Krohn, and Allen E. Liska. 1989. *Theoretical Integration in the Study of Deviance and Crime: Problems and Prospects*. Albany: State University of New York Press.

Messner, Steven F. and Marvin Rosenfeld. 1994. *Crime and the American Dream*. Belmont, CA: Wadsworth.

Michalowski, Raymond J. 1983. "Crime Control in the 1980s: A Progressive Agenda." *Crime and Social Justice* 19 (Summer): 13-23.

———. 1985. *Order, Law, and Crime: An Introduction to Criminology*. New York: Random House.

Miller, Walter. 1979. "Lower Class Culture as a Generating Milieu of Gang Delinquency." Pp. 155-68 in *Classics of Criminology*, edited by Joseph E. Jacoby. Prospect Heights, IL: Waveland.

Platt, Anthony. 1982. "Crime and Punishment in the United States: Immediate and Long-Term Reforms From a Marxist Perspective." *Crime and Social Justice* 18:38-45.

Roberts, Paul Craig and Matthew A. Stephenson. 1970. *Marx's Theory of Exchange, Alienation and Crisis*. Stanford, CA: Hoover Institutional Press.

Sutherland, Edwin H. 1947. *Principles of Criminology*. Philadelphia: Lippincott.

Taylor, Ian, P. Walton, and Jock Young. 1975. *Critical Criminology*. London: Routledge and Kegan Paul.

Walker, Samuel. 1994. *Sense and Nonsense About Crime and Drugs*. Belmont, CA: Wadsworth.

[4]

Reflections on Crime and Criminology at the Millenium*

Elliott Currie

Citation: Currie, Elliott. 1999. "Reflections on Crime and Criminology at the Millenium." *Western Criminology Review* 2(1). [Online]. Available: http://wcr.sonoma.edu/v2n1/currie.html.

Keywords: criminology, criminal justice, social change, public policy, crime trends, social problems, incapacitation and crime

Reflections on Crime and Criminology at the Millenium*

A funny thing kept happening every time I sat down to put this talk together. I kept finding that my thoughts were coming out a lot more negative than I expected; and I felt sort of guilty about that: I thought that, in the spirit of celebrating the millenium, I should be more upbeat.

After all, aren't things pretty good as we close out this century? The economy's booming, stock market's good, crime is down--right? But when I sat down to really think through how I felt about where we stand with respect to crime and the justice system today, the truth is that no matter how valiantly I tried, I just didn't feel all that upbeat. So I decided to stop fighting it and share with you some of the reasons why.

The truth is that I find myself very troubled about the state of crime and justice in America. And I'm troubled both as a citizen and as a criminologist. As a citizen, I'm troubled by the drift of our crime policy and by the shoulder-shrugging inattention to the massive injustices we have tolerated, or precipitated, in the name of fighting crime. As a criminologist--as a professional--I'm troubled by the drift of our public discourse about these issues--a discourse that seems to me to be increasingly removed from most of what you and I in this room actually *know* about crime.

And I'm also convinced that we are making mistakes today in our approach to crime and punishment that will probably come back to haunt us in the future. I say "probably," because nobody, in this peculiar and volatile age, should profess to be able to predict what's going to happen next week, much less a few years down the road. But what I'm sure of is that we're doing our best to mess things up, big time. We might, for reasons I'll get into, be able to escape some of the consequences of that. But then again, we might not.

Those mistakes are masked by the recent declines in serious crime in the United States. And let me be clear about this--I think that for the most part those declines are real ones. We know that there are places like New York and Philadelphia where they've fudged some of the statistics, but the overall decline is mainly genuine. And it matters, in the real world: it means that a lot of lives will be saved, and a lot of real-life tragedies will be avoided.

But there is a great danger of exaggerating our "successes" --and, above all, of *misinterpreting* them--of drawing the wrong lessons from them. And that's what I think I see happening today.

THE NEW TRIUMPHALISM

In the last few years we've seen the emergence of a new kind of *triumphalism* about crime, and the capacity of the criminal justice system to control it. You don't see this so much among criminologists, or among practitioners who actually work in the trenches of the justice system every day. But you see it, in spades, among pundits and politicians and in the media.

The new triumphalism about crime is connected to the broader triumphalism--even smugness--about the "American Model" generally. There is a sense that we've got it "fixed" here in the United States--that we possess the secret of how to organize your economy and society successfully, and that everyone else in the world ought to learn to do things the way we do. When it comes to the economy, our secret is usually said to be things like a "flexible" labor market, a minimal welfare state, a willingness to deregulate economic life whenever and wherever we can. In the triumphalist view about crime, the secret of our supposed success is variously said to be our "tough" policing strategies--"zero tolerance," "quality of life"--and/or that our enormous investment in incarceration is finally paying off in a big way. And as a result we are now sometimes compared favorably to other countries that, unlike us, still have crime.

The lesson we're supposed to ingest from all of this "success" on the crime front is that it's *ok* now: after years and years of doing it wrong, we're finally doing it *right*. And the even deeper implication is that we've now proven that we *can* indeed control crime through the criminal justice system alone. The flip side of that being that we've also proven that you don't, after all, need to address such problems as poverty or social exclusion or other supposed "root causes" of violent crime. Mayor Giuliani has proven all those carping sociologists wrong. It may indeed have been true until recently that the criminal justice system wasn't doing much to reduce crime, but that's because we didn't let it. Now we've shaken off our self-imposed shackles, and it's "working."

As the former New York Police Commissioner, William Bratton, was quoted the other day in the New York *Times*, "we've learned we can manage our way out of the crime problem."

Now of course these aren't new ideas, in themselves; some people have been making similar arguments for decades. But what's new is that now a lot of people--outside this profession, at least--*believe* them. In fact some version of this view now dominates the official political discourse on crime in the United States. And this is a thoroughly bipartisan consensus. In the turmoil around the Clinton impeachment, when the Republicans and Democrats have been consistently polarized and at each others' throats, it may be easy to forget that when it comes to crime, the two parties have for the most part followed virtually identical policies, and produced virtually identical rhetoric, for years.

Virtually all candidates for major political office, whether Democrat or Republican, are pretty much the same things--enforcing the death penalty, tough sentencing, drug mandatories, denial of welfare benefits to minor drug offenders--and on and on.

There is no significant national-level political debate on the most critical issues of criminal justice policy today--the swelling of the correctional complex, the massive overrepresentation of black Americans in the justice system, the chronic revelations of terrible abuses in our prisons, jails, and juvenile facilities, the increasing resort to the death penalty in the face of the opposite trend in every other Western democracy, or the increasing use of the penal system as a substitute for more constructive approaches to the structural social ills of American society: and very little real debate about these things at the state level either. The one partial exception to this is gun control, where there is a good deal of interesting and long overdue stirring. But aside from that, these are not issues that exactly convulse the Congress or state legislatures--or the White House--these days.

And again I find this absence of debate enormously troubling, on several levels at once. As a social scientist, I have to say I'm appalled, frankly, by the intellectual shallowness and shoddiness of many of the arguments that underlie the triumphalist consensus; as a citizen of what I'd like to think of as a democratic nation, I'm chilled by its values, or lack thereof; as a member of the community--and a parent--I'm frightened by the heedlessness it displays about the future.

Put simply, I think we're in a lot worse shape than the new triumphalism is willing to recognize. And we will not get much better until and unless we reject that triumphalism and, finally, get to work to deal with the deeper ills that our present situation both reflects and exacerbates. The good news is that we could do that. We're at a point in our history when we actually have the wherewithal--both the knowledge and the material resources--to launch an honest and effective attack on the violent crime that still shames us, in a way that's both enduring and humane. And we have the knowledge and the resources to shape our justice systems into institutions that we could--of all things--be proud of, rather than the globally recognized scandal that they are today.

But make no mistake--we'll never get there if we keep trying to fool ourselves that we're there already.

So I want to touch on three things today: first, I want to talk about where I think we really stand with respect to serious violent crime in the United States as we close this century; second, to talk about what we really know about why things have recently improved to the extent that they have; and third, to say just a little about what all of that tells us about what we need to do now if we want both a safer society and a more humane--and more honorable--justice system.

DECLINING VIOLENCE COMPARED TO WHAT?

Let me start with a couple of thoughts on our current situation. I wish I could believe the hype about our crime rates, which are now universally described as "plummeting" or "plunging" (there's something interestingly Freudian about that sort of language, which somebody ought to explore, or delve into...). But while there is an important reality beneath the hype, it's hype nonetheless, and it obscures some very important home truths.

Home Truth Number One is that despite the declines in violent crime since the early nineties, we remain a far more violent place than the rest of the advanced industrial world. That particular home truth gets obscured for a variety of reasons; partly because in our public discourse about social problems we very rarely look anywhere else in the world for a basic reality check on our own condition (that's especially rare in the mass media); and partly because of some rather misleading empirical claims that have been made about the level of crime in other industrial societies.

There are now people who will tell you in all seriousness that crime is worse in Switzerland than in the United States. (Anybody who believes that hasn't been there; well, they may have been to Geneva, or they may have been to New Orleans, but they surely haven't been to both). Even when it comes to property crime and less serious violence, there's a lot to be skeptical about in some of this research. But when it comes to really serious violence--homicide, gun assaults, forcible rape, armed robbery--nobody who's serious denies that we still stand out, that we are in fact an anomaly--an outlier--among the advanced industrial countries.

And that reality forces us to put the recent declines in violence in the United States in proper perspective. It doesn't make us any less glad that those declines have happened, but it does serve as a check against going overboard in interpreting them. A few years ago our homicide death rate among young men aged 15-24 was 36 per 100,000. By 1996 it had dropped to about 30 per 100,000. With any luck, it's probably more like 25 now. That's good. It means that a lot of young men are alive who would be dead at the earlier rate. But it's still higher than it was in 1987. And more importantly, it's still out of the ballpark by comparison with every other industrial democracy.

A drop from 36 to 25 per 100,000 would mean that the relative risk of homicide death for our young men versus those in England has fallen from 33 to 1 to only... 23 to 1. In 1996, 5,665 young American men aged 15-24 died of homicide. If the United States had had the English youth homicide death rate there would have been roughly 210 of them. And over 5,400 young men--disproportionately young men of color--would be alive today. A little black *girl* aged 1-4 in the United States, at last count, was seven times as likely to die by homicide as a teenaged to young adult *male* in England. There is a limit to how much we can celebrate these realities.

Home Truth Number Two is that even measured against our own norms the recent declines are not exactly what they are sometimes described as being. In the media discussion of the recent trends, you often see them presented as if they represented a sudden fall from a plateau--which appears quite spectacular, and also rather mysterious--when the reality is that they mainly represent a falling-off from an extraordinary peak, which is both less wonderful and less mysterious.

Seen this way, what's very clear is that we had an epidemic of serious violence which started in the late 1980s and peaked in the early 1990s; we're at the tail end of that now, which is a lot better than being in the middle of it, but which also puts us back at close to the very high endemic levels of violence we've been suffering for thirty-odd years.

The age-adjusted homicide death rate was just fractionally lower in 1997 than it was in 1985, despite the redoubling of the prison population during that time, and almost exactly the same as it was in 1969, despite the enormous increases in the prison population--and despite the very significant medical improvements in our ability to keep people from dying if they are badly hurt in an assault.

Home Truth Number Three is more subtle, and explaining it can get a little more technical. It's that in a very real sense we have *hidden* our crime problem, not beaten it. The fact that we don't pay much attention to this basic reality is due both to the nature of the public response to crime and, also, to some of the conventions of measurement in criminology. Since the public is most interested in getting criminals off the street and safely away from view, the public discourse about crime rarely counts the people behind bars as part of our crime problem. Instead they are usually counted as part of the solution, if they are counted at all. But as a result, the issue of what it means for our assessment of ourselves as a society--as a civilization--that we have such a big proportion of our population behind bars, rarely comes up.

But there is also a more complicated empirical and conceptual peculiarity in the way we measure crime that tends to obscure the extent of the problem--and to exaggerate our success against it.

This is a tricky issue, and I find myself struggling frequently over how best to express it. It's the kind of thing, I find, that you either get or you don't; people who *do* get it, get it right away and think it's obvious, while those who don't get it, *never* get it. But the basic issue is simple. When we try to assess the severity of our crime problem, we usually fail to include that part of the problem that's represented by the people currently behind bars. We do this so naturally that it's completely unreflective, but on reflection this is actually very odd.

One of the most distinctive things about the United States with respect to crime and punishment, after all, is that we not only have an unusually high level of serious violent crime--but we maintain that high level of violent crime despite the fact that we also boast the highest level of incarceration of any country in the world but one (and when it comes to ordinary street crimes, we probably even beat Russia).

Now our common sense, I think, would tell us that this means that our real crime problem is even worse than our measured crime "rate" itself would indicate. Because that measured rate leaves out all of the "criminality" that's represented by those masses of people behind bars. I'm not talking here about the crimes they actually commit while behind bars--though that's of course very important itself in understanding our real crime rate; for example, most of us would shudder to think what would happen to our official rate of rape if we counted what goes on in jails and prisons.

But the more important conceptual problem is that we measure our crime rate without factoring in the reality that we've simply *shifted* some of the total "pool" of criminals in our society from one place to another. We haven't stopped producing them. We've just moved them. Put in a shorthand way, the problem is that we traditionally measure the "crime rate" rather than what we might call the "criminality rate." What we call the "crime rate" measures the activity of criminals still on the street: and of course, that kind of measure is useful in many ways. But as an measure of the overall *criminality* problem--as an indicator of the tendency of our society to produce criminals--it's obviously defective.

It's like measuring the extent of some physical illness in our society while systematically excluding from the count all those people who are so sick we've had to put them in the hospital. Nobody would do that, in the field of public health. We do it all the time in the field of criminology.

This point is often lost in that triumphalist consensus I've been talking about. I was struck by this not too long ago when I heard some remarks by an official in the Clinton administration, who was waxing enthusistic about the great state of the country around the time the President was running for his second term. He was ticking off all the good social indicators that showed how successful his adminstration had been and, presumably, why we should vote for them again. So he very triumphantly declared that "more people are at work, more people are off the welfare rolls, and more people are in prison."

So on one level there is a sort of philosophical "disconnect" here. You'll recall how people used this term "disconnect" as a noun when talking about the gap between the House Republicans and a lot of other people on the issue of Bill Clinton's impeachment. Well, I have to say there is a "disconnect" between me and those who think that having a lot of people in prison is a *positive* social indicator.

But this isn't just a philosophical issue, because it significantly affects how we think about the problem of crime in our society and how we assess the meaning of the recent trends. And it's an issue that can be framed in empirical terms and studied. You could come up a number of ways of actually measuring the "criminality rate" in quantitative terms, and in fact we have some bits and pieces of research that suggest how we might do that.

The basic strategy is pretty straightforward; we need a measure of the amount of criminality represented by the offenders currently on the street combined with the amount of criminality represented by offenders currently incarcerated. The key is to get a good estimate of the individual crime rates, what some criminologists call "lambda," of offenders behind bars and add to it the lambda of those on the outside. (There is in fact a recent attempt to calculate some similar figures, by Jose Canela-Cacho, Alfred Blumstein and Jacqueline Cohen, which you may have seen published in *Criminology* not long ago.)

I won't go into detail, but suppose, just for the sake of argument, that we assume that the average number of reported robberies committed by incarcerated robbers is, say, 5 a year. Well, there were about 135,000 inmates in state and federal prisons with robbery as their most serious charge in 1995. That means that other things being equal, those robbers, had they been on the street, would have been responsible for an additional 5 x 135,000, or 675,000, reported robberies--on top of the 580,000 we actually had in 1995. So factoring in the level of criminality in the incarcerated population to arrive at what we might call the "latent" robbery rate more than doubles the conventional rate.

And looking at crime this way obviously forces us to think differently about the trends in recent years. By my extremely rough calculation, our "criminality index" for reported robbery in 1995 was about 1,250,000--that's adding the 675 to the 580 thousand. Now let's go back to 1985, and do the same calculation. In that year imprisoned robbers accounted for an estimated 94,000 X 5 robberies, or 470,000, because there were fewer robbers in prison; add to that the 498,000 reported, and you get 968,000. So our index increased by 287,000, or about 30 percent, between 1985 and 1995. Measured the conventional way, the number of robberies increased too in those years, but by only 16 percent. So the rate of increase in the robbery problem, by this measure, was twice the conventionally reported one.

Now again there are lots of technical uncertainties to this kind of measurement; but I'll leave all that to people who are better at this sort of thing than I am. But I think the general point is beyond serious doubt. If we measure our crime problem by our tendency to produce *criminality*, then we may be in a real sense losing the "war" on crime even as we have successfully hidden some of the losses behind prison walls--and therefore appear superficially to be winning it.

That obviously gives us a very different sense of what's going on in our society. And again, I think looking at matters this way is only common sense. We feel that there's got to be something especially wrong here if we have *both* very high rates of violent crime *and* very high incarceration rates, at the same time--something that isn't captured in the conventional crime rate alone. Suppose two countries have the same official rate of violent crimes, but one country has, proportionally, four times as many violent offenders behind bars. Do they really have the same violent crime problem? I don't think so.

"Well," some people might say, "this isn't fair. You're just manipulating the statistics to make things look bad." But--again--the reality is that this is the way we actually go about measuring most other social ills--with the exception of criminality. In a reasonable culture we would not say we had won the war against disease just because we've moved a lot of sick people from their homes to hospital wards. And in a reasonable culture we would not say we've won the war against crime just because we've moved a lot of criminals from the community into prison cells.

There is another way in which we have shoved the crime problem out of sight, rather than really improving it; one which I'll only touch on now, but which I think will become more and more difficult to ignore in the 21st century. There's a sense in which we've hidden some of the tendency of our current social order to produce crime by displacing some of the problem into other countries. As a result, it doesn't appear in our crime statistics, although it has a lot to do with us.

As everyone knows, we are no longer an isolated national economy--no longer a socio-economic system that's contained within our national borders (indeed we never were, but we are less and less so today). We're part of a global system that is tied together in increasingly fateful and intricate ways--as the recent near-meltdown of the global financial system reminded us. In fact, as many economists have pointed out, our current economic good fortune is partly dependent on the *misfortune* of other countries, especially in the developing world--because it means lower prices for the imports we buy from them, from oil to blue jeans to jumbo shrimp.

But those low prices reflect the near-collapse of the standard of living in some other countries, especially for low-income people. That in turn aggravates a variety of social processes that tend to boost their rate of crime. It creates a lot of family poverty and family disruption, massive joblessness, resulting migration, and the growth of illicit occupations, especially the drug trade. And those social processes have sent violent crime through the roof in a number of countries whose economies are intimately connected to ours, notably Mexico.

We don't count any of this when we think about our crime rate, of course, until some of it comes back across our borders--which it invariably does, in a variety of ways. But surely it's time to start acknowledging these connections, if we want to understand the real impact of our present social and economic model on crime, much less to grapple with it.

So one problem I have with the new "triumphalism" about crime is that I think that to some extent it represents a state of denial--in which we exaggerate our recent successes against serious crime and strategically ignore the implications of our comparative standing vis-a-vis other countries. But there's also what may be an even more crucial problem. Granting that there have been significant reductions in violence, the new triumphalism puts a highly misleading "spin" on the *why* of those declines--a spin which is not only misleading but dangerous, because it could lead us to adopt (or to continue) all the wrong anticrime policies while ignoring the things we really ought to be doing.

MISINTERPRETING DECLINES IN VIOLENCE

There are two facets of that misleading "spin": first, it exaggerates the role of some kinds of criminal justice strategies in accounting for the declines; second, it underestimates the role of other, social factors which are probably more important. Put those together, and you have the core of a new ideology about crime control that could lead us to policy mistakes that, once made, are very difficult to correct.

Let's take the exaggeration of the criminal justice effects first. As everyone here knows, two things in particular, in some combination, have often been given the bulk of the credit for our recent declines in violent crime. One is tough sentencing laws which have dramatically boosted incarceration rates; the other is tough policing, especially the so-called "zero tolerance" approach most famously, or notoriously, adopted in New York City. You can read about the supposed great effects of both of these in the media practically any day of the week, and not only in the United States, but all over the world.

But the reality, of course, is that ascribing too much effect to either our booming incarceration rates or our famous zero tolerance policing flies in the face of the evidence--or maybe more precisely, flies in the face of the lack of evidence.

Take the impact of incarceration first. I'm sure I don't have to spend too much time talking about the limits of incarceration to this audience. But let me just make a few points. I'm not suggesting that there have been *no* effects of our mushrooming prison population on rates of violence. I think there are effects, and I've gone on record as saying so. I don't think you can lock up everybody and their brother--and increasingly their sister--and not have *some* impact on rates of violent crime. Indeed that's what the serious research on incapacitation effects has told us for many years, and I have no real quarrel with that research. (In fact what I just said about the "latent" crime rate or "criminality" rate implies that there's such a thing as incapacitation). But that's very different from believing that mass incarceration is the major reason for the declines in serious violence in America; or that we could drive our rates of violence even lower if we just did more of the same.

The idea that booming prison populations are the key reason for the declines in serious criminal violence runs up against a number of stubborn realities. One is that the magnitude of the declines varies enormously across different states--and doesn't vary in any consistent fashion with those states' use of incarceration relative to their crime rates. Some of the slowest declines in violence (and in index crime generally) have been in Southern states with very high and very rapidly rising incarceration rates; some of the fastest declines have been in the Northeast, which traditionally incarcerates relatively sparingly. Some of the most spectacular successes against youth violence have taken place in Boston, in a state with a traditionally low incarceration rate relative to its crime rate.

And the more complicated research we have so far backs up that common-sense "eyeball' observation. If you boost your state prison population a lot, you will probably get moderate effects on some "high rate" crimes, notably burglary and perhaps one violent crime, robbery--but astonishingly small effects on most other serious crimes of violence, including homicide, serious assault and forcible rape. Yet it's homicide that has fallen the fastest among violent offenses in the last few years. Can our sixfold increase in the prison population explain some of the decline in homicide? Probably. Can it explain most of it? No.

There are similar problems, only worse, with the assertion that it's aggressive "zero tolerance" policing that's responsible for the declines in serious violence. I find myself gritting my teeth about this one several times a week. There are plenty of legitimate controversies about the effects of police on violent crime. But this is different. This, to my mind, is one of the most egregious examples I know of the triumph of public relations hype over evidence.

And in this case it has a lot of nasty consequences--including the justification of police behavior that nobody should be justifying. I've just read, for example, an opinion column saying that, sure, it's too bad that a young African immigrant was shot nineteen times by the NYPD's street crimes unit even though he didn't do anything wrong--but we've got to accept that kind of thing occasionally if we want to have the declines in crime that the NYPD has achieved. After all, if the police take a less aggressive role, then crime will go back up--and when it does, the worst victims will be other black people!

To put it in the most technical methodological language I can, I'd say this argument is B.S. It's B.S. because nobody has in fact ever shown that nasty policing is responsible for declining rates of violent crime in our cities--even less, that you *have* to have nasty police to have declines in crime. We know that many cities have seen sharp drops in violence *without* resorting to the heavy-handed and heedless methods that all too many people today are too quick to credit. That includes a number of cities here in California--some of which have indeed done innovative things with their police, but in very different, more positive and community-oriented ways; I recently spent about a week hanging around with a San Diego cop whose opinion of the New York version of "zero tolerance" policing is even lower than mine, and expressed much less politely. There are also cities in which the police have done practically *nothing* that's new, and still the levels of violent crime have dropped strikingly.

This isn't to say that nothing the NYPD does is relevant to their crime declines; I'm pretty convinced that some things they do, notably the strong emphasis on crime analysis and targeting resources on hot spots, have been part of the story, and those things make a great deal of sense. But what is too often forgotten, especially in the media's treatment of these issues, is that we utterly lack evidence that rousting squeegee men or harassing homeless people--or emptying your weapons into innocent young immigrants--has anything whatever to do with reducing serious violent crime. I've asked for such evidence over and over again, and so far I've come away empty-handed. Can the police help to prevent crime? Yes, and probably more than we once thought. Is zero tolerance policing mainly responsible for the drop in the national homicide rate since 1992? No.

The flip side of the exaggeration of the effect of tough sentencing and macho policing is the underestimation of the impact of deeper social forces in producing the recent declines in violence. And again, there's an ideological purpose being served by this underestimation. It helps to bolster the claim that "root causes" don't matter and that those of us who believe that we'd have less violence if we began treating people better, rather than just treating them rougher, are obsolete. Because the implications of these declines for social policy are very different if you believe, as I do, that the most important factor in producing them is probably the extraordinary economic boom we've enjoyed for the last seven years.

It's very important to bear in mind the magnitude of this burst of prosperity. As the New York *Times* put it in an editorial the other day, these are "astounding" economic times. This is by now more than seven years of sustained economic growth, which has produced unprecedented levels of employment--which of course have made us the wonder of most of the rest of the post-industrial world. It's true that the wonderfulness of our job picture relative to that of, say, Europe is routinely exaggerated, not least because we get to remove our nearly two million incarcerated people from our unemployment count. But the job gains since the late 1980s *have* been extraordinary.

And these economic gains have not been confined to the affluent. It's true that they've been concentrated among the rich. But they have also significantly changed the economic condition and the economic prospects--at least the short-term prospects--of low-income Americans, in many parts of the country. Unemployment rates have fallen sharply, even among people who have traditionally had the worst employment problems: the unemployment rate among black teenagers has fallen by close to twenty per cent since 1992, for example--rather nicely paralleling the drops in reported robbery and homicide.

Beyond that, the boom has begun to pull people into the labor force who until recently were too far out of it to even be counted as unemployed. It has also begun, more recently, to push up wages and hence family incomes for people underemployed in low-wage jobs, and, among blacks, to shift some people out of contingent work into more or less steady jobs. All of this has begun to make at least a noticeable dent in our rates of family poverty.

And from a variety of criminological perspectives, we know that this matters. It matters because it gives people, especially young people on the edges of the economy, a better stake in legitimate occupations as opposed to illegitimate ones. If you're a smart kid who now has a realistic opportunity to go to work at Banana Republic where before your only economic opportunity was on the corner with a beeper, pretty soon Banana Republic can start to look pretty good by comparison, given the dangers and uncertainties--and moral quandaries--of the street life. It matters also because it pulls many people--especially young men--out of settings that have a high risk for them to become either offenders or victims of violence, like bars and street corners, and into the workplace. It matters because it diminishes the risks of intimate violence behind closed doors.

And as a result it provides a much better explanation for the pattern of our recent crime declines. Again, I'm not suggesting it explains all of them, or that criminal justice strategies are unimportant. But the economic boom as explanation has the supreme virtue of actually fitting the reality. It fits, for example, with the otherwise perplexing fact that homicide has fallen faster than some property crimes. If putting lots of people in prison were the main explanation, then we'd expect big drops in property crimes and small ones in homicide, since, again, that's what all of our incapacitation research would predict. Instead the biggest drops are in homicide, a crime notoriously resistant to incapacitation effects. On the other hand, in a booming economy with rising employment, we could predict contradictory effects on some property crime--because there's more to steal--but falling homicide rates, for all of the reasons I just mentioned.

Another crucial part of the explanation for the recent declines in violence is related to the economic boom--it's the waning of the crack epidemic. I think the research--by Al Blumstein, Richard Rosenfeld, Janet Lauritsen, and others--is pretty clear on this. It makes sense that as the crack epidemic swamped the cities, especially the big ones, after the mid 1980s, and brought the huge escalation in the gun trade with it, violence would go through the roof--and it did. It's in the cities where the crack epidemic started *later* that rates of serious violence have proven most stubborn. The waning of the crack epidemic, of course, is itself a very complicated phenomenon: it's certainly not unrelated to criminal justice tactics, but it's also related to the growth of realistic opportunities for legitimate work for people ready to abandon the crack trade.

Now, both of those factors--the booming economy and the waning of the crack epidemic--are very positive developments, and very welcome. But virtually by definition they also contain a warning. And the warning is pretty obvious: if indeed we have been rescued from our recent crime epidemic mainly by two basically fortuitous trends--then, by the same token, that means that we're in trouble if those beneficent trends should change.

IS THE FUTURE INEVITABLE?

It's true that this current economic boom is unusual and has lasted a long time, and there are people who say that the whole traditional business cycle may have become a thing of the past. Well, maybe. But don't bet the farm on it. And if, as most of us expect, the inevitable downturn comes--whether it's triggered in Sao Paulo or Jakarta or Guadalajara or wherever around the increasingly volatile globe--does anyone here really doubt that violent crime will get worse--probably sooner rather than later? I suspect that if and when that happens, we will relearn rather quickly that root causes do indeed matter. What exactly would we expect if we throw all those young men back on the street, out of their new-found legitimate jobs, and keep them there for a long time--especially since we have simultaneously steadily chipped away at what remains of our social safety net?

I was in Brazil recently, and I spent some time in the *favelas* of Rio de Janeiro. It was among the most sobering experiences of my life. Not just because of the extraordinary level of deprivation there and the almost total absence of a public commitment to even the most minimal social protection for the poor. Not just because of the terribly glaring gap between large numbers of affluent people and even larger numbers of desperately poor people. But also because I kept having this chilling sense of *recognition*. Rio's problems, of poverty and violence and drugs, are extreme. But to an American, they are not, unfortunately, altogether unfamilar.

And I couldn't help but think that there's a very real sense in which that could be where we are going--or where we *could* go if indeed we suffer a major reversal of our recent economic fortunes. A society that tolerates vast inequalities, that enforces extreme social exclusion, that then uses its criminal justice system--notably an "unleashed" police--to keep the whole thing contained, and then justifies all of that in the name of some notion of economic necessity: well, that's Brazil all right; but to an uncomfortable degree, it's also *us*, and my fear is that it could be even more "us" in the future. Unless, of course, we take serious steps now to avoid it.

The good news is that we could do that, if we so choose. How? I've talked too long already, so I won't go into great detail--and in any case I've tried to do that elsewhere. But for now, let me just say that two big jobs seem to me to especially critical for us as criminologists in the coming century. The first is to push, and push relentlessly, to insure that this nation makes those preventive social investments that can reduce violent crime in enduring and humane ways, rather than simply suppressing it, hiding it, or denying it. The second--related, of course--is to push equally hard and equally relentlessly to end the systemic abuses in our institutions of criminal justice and, beyond that, to foster a new kind of revolution in those institutions--so that their job number one is understood to be the dedicated effort to rebuild the lives and enhance the productive capacities of the people who have to go through them.

Neither of these tasks is exactly a hot-button issue in most of the public arena today. And so in both of these tasks we have a very special, and indispensable, role. I'm increasingly afraid that if somebody doesn't push, and push very hard, then nobody's going to do these things--at least not to the extent that they need doing. And I think it may be us who've got to do the pushing.

For my money, within those general parameters there are some especially crucial things that need our most immediate and sustained attention. I want to see us invest seriously in family support programs of the kind that can prevent child abuse and neglect and thus stop a lot of our worst violent crime before it starts. I want to see serious investment in intensive work with kids already in trouble, along the lines of Multisystemic Therapy, and I want to see that kind of help available to the kids who need it in every community in the United States. I want to see a real commitment to helping those people we do put behind bars to become literate, skilled in some meaningful line of work, and with their substance abuse under control. (To make that possible, I want to see the people who don't belong in prison taken out, and those serving absurd sentences for minor crimes get shorter ones, if they get any sentence at all.) I want to see a fundamental legislative and judicial re-examination of three strikes and other mandatory sentencing schemes.

On the broader, societal level, what I most want to see is a serious and sustained challenge to our scandalous levels of child poverty, far the worst in the advanced industrial world--which I am thoroughly convinced are the soil out of which our appalling levels of violence grow. And I want to see a real, not rhetorical, commitment to a package of family-friendly social policies--including better child care, flexible and shorter work time, and living wages for honest work--so that we can (a) cut the roots of family violence and (b) help to insure that the next century's kids grow up with better support and better nurturance than a lot of them have in this century. (I've just read a study, by the way, that estimates that if women were paid the same as men doing comparable work in the paid labor force, the poverty rate among single mothers would be cut almost exactly in half.)

Most of these suggestions aren't new. Many people have made them before, including me (I note with interest that James Q. Wilson has recently been coming out in support of some early family intervention programs; if something is supported by me *and* James Q. Wilson, I think it's probably going to be supported by quite a lot of people). But what may be different about saying them now is that we really do have the resources to make them happen.

There was a time, not too long ago, when a lot of states could plead poverty in explaining why they didn't invest in preventive work with families and kids, for example. There were massive budget deficits, and so we "couldn't afford" it. You'd go to legislators, and they would shake their heads sadly and say, gee, we agree with you, it would be great if we could do these things, but our hands are tied. Come back when (or if) things get better. Well, it's hard to get off the hook that way in 1999. I've just read that the states now have a combined budget surplus of over $30 billlion, and that doesn't, I think, count the largesse they're going to get from from the recent tobacco settlements.

But my guess is that this situation is temporary, and that means we have a window of opportunity now to make some of those critical social investments we should have been making forty years ago. And we should use that opportunity very soon, because we could also lose it very soon. Right now, many states have so much money because of the economic boom that they literally don't know what to do with it. I think we should tell them.

We, criminologists, should tell them. Because the last point I want to emphasize is that I hope that in the next century criminologists will have a stronger, and louder, voice in shaping our social policy than they have usually had in this one. It's no secret that an awful lot of the crime policies that have been launched in our recent history have been almost diametrically opposed to what most of *us* think we know about crime. How exactly that happened is not so easy to answer. But what's crystal clear is that it *shouldn't* happen. If there's one task that we as professional criminologists should set for ourselves in the new millenium, it's to fight to insure that stupid and brutal policies that we know don't work are--at the very least--challenged at every turn and in every forum that's available to us.

I especially hope than in the next century we will take the lead in fighting to end the blatant abuses of human rights that scar our prisons, our juvenile facilities, our police departments. I know many of us individually have done a lot of that already. But I want to see us doing so not as scattered individuals, but as a unified profession. If we act together as a profession we can provide a kind of clout and credibility that the movement against those abuses badly needs. It's one thing if a handful of underfunded nonprofits take on some egregious violation of human rights in a state's prison system all by themselves (though more power to them). It's another if the entire Western Society of Criminology, or the entire American Society of Criminology, does--loudly and visibly. An abusive criminal justice system is the way a neglectful society keeps its casualties in line. We need to do our best to put a stop to that.

If we *don't* take on a more forceful role in advocating for intelligent and decent policy, then it's not only bad for the country: it's bad for *us* too. Because if we don't challenge the way things are now, we can get caught in the web of what I sometimes call the "criminology of the absurd." By that I mean that we're put into the hugely frustrating position of seeing, from our vantage point as professionals, the same depressing and tragic scene unfolding before us, year after year after year. We see the same kinds of people, coming from the same kinds of quite predictable environments, churning through our justice systems, and through the related agencies of control and emergency assistance, where they get very little serious help of the kind that could realistically change anything in their lives: and then we accordingly bemoan, over and over again, our inability to make much of a difference in this depressing pattern.

There comes a point when, as a practitioner or a scholar watching this process year in, year out, you can become deeply alienated, sometimes in ways that are very subtle but very profound. You can begin to feel like Sisyphus pushing that rock; or like one of what Lee Rainwater, following the sociologist Everett Hughes, famously called the "dirty workers" of society--the people charged with keeping the lid on--which is not something that most of us really want to do for the rest of our lives. So for our own mental health, as well as our integrity as a profession, we have to struggle against getting put in the position of simply being the containers, and/or the chroniclers, of massive and deepening social exclusion.

To some extent, this will mean redefining what the criminologist's *job* is. We will need, I think, to shift some emphasis away from the accumulation of research findings to better dissemination of what we already know, and to more skillful promotion of sensible policies based on that knowledge--policies both in and out of the criminal justice system, including policies to directly attack social exclusion and inequality. That doesn't mean, by the way, just increasing our "access" to elected officials; first and foremost, it means raising public awareness--enhancing the public's criminological IQ. We need to think through more intensive and creative ways of doing that, because the only way that we will get our political systems to move is if they are facing an already informed and mobilized public.

For too long, we've been accustomed to being in a one-down position, always lamenting the fact that politicians pay no attention to us and ignore what we know. I think that could change. But it will change only if, and when, we develop the organizational capacity to raise public consciousness on these issues to a level that neither politicians, nor anyone else, can ignore.

[5]

SOCIAL SUPPORT AS AN ORGANIZING CONCEPT FOR CRIMINOLOGY: PRESIDENTIAL ADDRESS TO THE ACADEMY OF CRIMINAL JUSTICE SCIENCES*

FRANCIS T. CULLEN
University of Cincinnati

Although "social support" is present as a theme in many criminological writings, it has not been identified explicitly as a concept capable of organizing theory and research in criminology. Drawing on existing criminological and related writings, this address derives a series of propositions that form the foundation, in a preliminary way, for the "social support paradigm" of the study of crime and control. The overriding contention is that whether social support is delivered through government social programs, communities, social networks, families, interpersonal relations, or agents of the criminal justice system, it reduces criminal involvement. Further, I contend that insofar as the social support paradigm proves to be "Good Criminology"—establishing that nonsupportive policies and conditions are criminogenic—it can provide grounds for creating a more supportive, "Good Society."

Chicago strikes me as a particularly appropriate gathering place for criminologists, since so many of our intellectual roots extend to the scholars who explored the lives of offenders earlier in this century and mapped the distribution of their crimes. As Kurtz (1984:72) observes in his analysis of the contributions of the Chicago school, "[E]xcept for strain models of deviance, delinquency theory originated at the University of Chicago" (also see Kornhauser 1978).

---

* Address delivered on March 9, 1994, at the annual meetings of the Academy of Criminal Justice Sciences, held in Chicago. Direct correspondence to Division of Criminal Justice, Mail Location 389, University of Cincinnati, Cincinnati, OH 45221-0389. A preliminary statement of these ideas was presented at the 1992 meetings of the American Sociological Association, held in Pittsburgh. With apologies to those whose help I may have failed to record, I would like to acknowledge the assistance of Robert Agnew, Ronald Akers, Joanne Belknap, Michael Benson, John Braithwaite, Michael Braswell, Velmer Burton, John Broderick, Leo Carroll, Mitchell Chamlin, Albert Cohen, Paula Dubeck, David Farrington, Richard Felson, Karen Feinberg, Bonnie Fisher, James Frank, Lynne Goodstein, Stuart Henry, Robert Langworthy, Bruce Link, Brendan Maguire, Tina Mawhorr, M. Joan McDermott, Robert Regoli, Richard Rosenfeld, Joachim Savelsberg, James Short, Sally Simpson, Quint Thurman, Patricia Van Voorhis, John Wozniak, and John Wright.

In preparing this address, it thus seemed appropriate to revisit the writings of these early Chicago school theorists—such as Frederick Thrasher and Clifford Shaw and Henry McKay—as well as those of prominent social reformers, such as Jane Addams, who influenced the development of this school (Bulmer 1984:23-24). I was reminded of their enduring influence on our understandings of the origins of crime. Most notably, their research on social disorganization laid the foundation for ecological studies and for control theories, and their investigations of the cultural transmission of criminal values and skills gave rise to work on gangs, subcultural theory, and illegitimate opportunity structures.

This theoretical legacy has been cataloged by numerous criminological texts—including my own (Cullen 1984; Lilly, Cullen, and Ball 1989; Sykes and Cullen 1992)—and we now pass on stock summaries of the Chicago school to our students, as I do each year. My purpose is not to argue that past accounts of the Chicago school are incorrect or need revision. But I suggest that we are missing something important when we reduce these theorists' perspectives to the sterile interplay of the concepts of disorganization, control, and cultural values. The underlying humanity of their criminology and (I believe) their insights on the importance of social support are overlooked.

Perhaps because I was reading with a different lens, the landscape appeared to have changed on my latest excursion through the Chicago school's writings. I saw depictions of how the powerful social forces that tore apart communities and families left youths to fend for themselves in an inhospitable environment. In Thrasher's ([1927] 1963:32) view, for example, "gangs represent the spontaneous efforts of boys to create a society for themselves where none adequate to their needs exists"; invariably, he noted, a delinquent's family "fails to hold the boy's interest, neglects him, or actually forces him into the street" ([1927] 1963:340). Shaw's life histories of Stanley, the "jack-roller," and of Sidney's "natural delinquent career" similarly document the inordinate neglect that many youths experienced ([1930] 1966, [1931] 1976).

In short, the writings of The Chicago School suggest that a lack of social support—not simply exposure to criminal cultures or a lack of control—is implicated in crime. Not surprisingly, the Chicago school's policy prescriptions embodied the view that support, not punishment, was integral to reducing crime. In retrospect we may see their policies as misguided, naive, and shaped by class interests (Platt 1969; Rothman 1980). But we should not take this revisionism too far; to do so would be to miss the humanity, decency, and caring that informed these reform efforts (see Garland 1990). Settlement houses in the slums, the saving of youths in the juvenile court, the Chicago Area Project's attempt to help residents reconstruct their neighborhoods—all contrast sharply with contemporary discourse on crime, which has ranged in the past two presidencies from "Willie Horton" to "three strikes and you're out." Further, on a more personal dimension, members of the Chicago school moved beyond scientific analysis to helping others (Addams 1910). As Snodgrass (1982:146) points out in *The Jack-Roller at Seventy*, Stanley, the offender interviewed by Clifford Shaw, "attributes his turning from a life in crime and his personal ontology in no small measure to Shaw's kindness and support."

I do not mean to single out the Chicago school as the only source of insights on social support; quite the opposite. My intention is to argue that notions of social support appear in diverse criminological writings. In some works, the concept is used explicitly (Agnew 1992; Astin, Lawrence, and Foy 1993; Brownfield and Sorenson 1991). In others, such as feminist and peacemaking/humanist writings that focus on caring, connectedness, and responsiveness, allusions to social support can be detected easily (Braswell 1989, 1990; McDermott 1994; Pepinksy and Quinney 1991). In still others, social support can be recognized by considering the reverse of the central theoretical concept of a perspective, such as the opposite of the labeling theory concept of stigmatization (Braithwaite 1989) or of Regoli and Hewitt's (1994) concept of "differential social oppression." Finally, in many other works, I suspect that valuable insights on social support can be uncovered with some mining.

What is lacking, however, is an attempt to integrate these diverse insights on social support into a coherent criminological paradigm. In the sociology of mental illness, for example, considerable progress has been made in this direction (Lin, Dean, and Ensel 1986; Vaux 1988). But in criminology the insights linking social support to crime remain disparate, and are not systematized so far as to direct theoretical and empirical investigation. Indeed, I can offer one (nonetheless significant) indicator of the latency of this concept: virtually no introductory or theoretical textbook lists "social support" in its index (see, for example, Akers 1994; Barlow 1993; Beirne and Messerschmidt 1991; Empey 1982; Lilly et al. 1989; Pfohl 1985; Sheley 1991; Sutherland, Cressey, and Luckenbill 1992; Vito and Holmes 1994; Vold and Bernard 1986).

My goal, then, is to argue that social support, if approached systematically, can be an important organizing concept for criminology. In the pages ahead, I will discuss propositions that might form the parameters, in a preliminary way, for a criminological paradigm, which draws on existing knowledge to illuminate new research vistas.

WHAT IS SOCIAL SUPPORT?

As a prelude to this discussion, let me comment on the concept of social support. Since detailed analyses of the concept are readily available (House 1981; Lin et al. 1986; Vaux 1988), I will sketch out only the major dimensions.

Lin (1986:18) defines social support as "the perceived or actual instrumental and/or expressive provisions supplied by the community, social networks, and confiding partners." Dissection of this definition reveals three major dimensions of support. The first is the distinction between the objective delivery and the perception of support. Taking perceptions into account is important because it leads to the insight that people do not receive support in a mechanical way but interpret, appraise, and anticipate it in the context of social situations (see Matsueda 1992).

Second, although different typologies exist, social support is usually divided into two broad rubrics: instrumental and expressive. According to Lin (1986:20), "the instrumental dimension involves the use of the relationship as a means to a goal, such as seeking a job, getting a loan, or finding someone to babysit." Vaux (1988:21) suggests that "instrumental functions may be served through the provision of goods or money (material aid or financial assistance) and through providing information, making suggestions, and clarifying issues (advice and guidance)."

The expressive dimension, again according to Lin (1986:20), "involves the use of the relationship as an end as well as a means. It is the activity of sharing sentiments, ventilating frustrations, reaching an understanding on issues and problems, and affirming one's own as well as the other's worth and dignity." Vaux (1988:21) notes that the "affective functions" of support "include meeting the needs for love and affection, esteem and identity, and belonging and companionship. These needs are met respectively through emotional support, feedback and social reinforcement, and socializing."

Third, Lin's definition indicates that support occurs on different social levels. Micro-level support can be delivered by a confiding individual, such as a spouse or a best friend. But social support also can be viewed as a property of social networks and of communities and larger ecological units in which individuals are enmeshed.[1]

A fourth dimension, not discussed by Lin, must be added: whether the support is delivered by a formal agency or through informal relations (Vaux 1988). Informal social support would occur through social relationships with others who lack any official status relative to the individual. Formal social support might be provided by schools, governmental assistance programs, and—perhaps most interesting to us—the criminal justice system.[2]

THE ECOLOGY OF SOCIAL SUPPORT

In the past decade, scholars have shown a renewed interest in studying the social ecology of crime, as did Shaw and McKay (1942) (Bursik and Grasmick 1993a; Byrne and Sampson 1986; Reiss and Tonry 1986). This research has shown that crime rates vary across nations and, within a single nation, across communities. It is noteworthy, if unsurprising, that the United States has higher rates of serious crime, especially violent offenses, than other Western industrialized nations (Adler 1983; Archer and Gartner 1984; Currie 1985; Messner and Rosenfeld 1994; also see Lynch 1995). This finding prompts my first proposition:

1. America has higher rates of serious crime than other industrialized nations because it is a less supportive society.

I am not claiming that Americans, as individuals, are ungenerous in giving their money to charity or their time to voluntary organizations; quite the opposite appears to be the case (Wuthnow 1991). Even so, I assert that American society is not *organized*, structurally or culturally, to be socially supportive. This conclusion receives confirmation from several sources, which make interrelated or complementary points.

First, Braithwaite (1989:100) observes that societies differ in their "communitarian" quality—that is, in the extent to which "individuals are densely enmeshed in interdependencies which have the special qualities of *mutual help and trust*" (emphasis added). With a mobile, heterogeneous, urban population, the United States is low in communitarianism. Accordingly the structural basis for creating and sustaining supportive social relations is weak.

1 Social support is not identical to social networks, social integration, or social ties. The distinctive quality of social support is not the mere existence of social relationships but the extent to which such relations deliver instrumental and expressive assistance.

2 Again, this discussion presents only the bare bones of the concept of social support. Thus other dimensions of social support could be introduced: consistency, quality, depth, source, and the difference between chronic and situational.

Second, numerous commentators—often referred to as communitarians—have documented the corrosive effects of America's culture of excessive individualism (Bellah et al. 1985, 1991; Coles 1993; Etzioni 1993; Reich 1988; Wuthnow 1991). In the influential *Habits of the Heart*, Bellah et al. (1985) decry in particular "utilitarian individualism"—the dominance of individual self-interest in the pursuit of desired, usually material ends (also see Messner and Rosenfeld 1994). "We have committed," say Bellah et al. (1985:285), "what to the republican founders of our nation was the cardinal sin: we have put our own good, as individuals, as groups, as a nation, above the common good." Building a "good society," in which concern for community and mutuality of support dominate, awaits a fundamental "transformation of American culture" (Bellah et al. 1985:275-96, 1991).

Wuthnow (1991) notes that even compassion is "bounded" by the culture of individualism. Compassionate behavior is managed by being segmented into limited roles (e.g., a few hours of volunteer work). If pursued so extensively that it interferes with a person's self-interest, such behavior is regarded as an unhealthy obsession (1991:191-220). As a result, while "some of the work—the work that can be divided up into limited commitments—is accomplished, much of it remains to be done" (1991:220). Wuthnow expresses this point nicely:

> Although millions of hours are donated to volunteer activities each year, this effort falls far short of what is needed. I mentioned earlier that two-thirds of American people have visited someone in the hospital in the past year and a quarter have taken care of someone seriously ill in their homes. But thousands of people have no one to care for them. Substantial numbers in our society fear they could not count on anyone for help if they or a member of their family became seriously ill. Nearly four in ten (37 percent) feel that they could not count on their immediate neighbors . . . One person in three doubts it would be possible to count on relatives outside the immediate family . . . Half the population think volunteers in their community could not be counted on for help; two people in three think this about social welfare agencies.
>
> As a society we pay lip service to altruistic values, but these values must be seen in the context of other pursuits, the majority of which focus on ourselves rather than others (1991:11).

In short, Wuthnow suggests that the demand for support in America exceeds the supply. This observation leads to a corollary to the first proposition: *The more a society is deficient in the support needed, the higher its crime rate will be.*[3]

Third, Currie (1985, 1989, 1993) makes perhaps the most compelling case that support is low in America and is linked inextricably to the country's high violent crime rate. As Currie points out, America's past and recent economic development has disrupted the traditional "private cushions" provided by networks of social support. Unlike other Western nations, however, America's welfare state has been stingy, if not mean-spirited, in the support it offers to the casualties of the social dislocation and wide inequalities bred by this development (also see Block et al. 1987). The cost of undermining the delivery of support, argues Currie, is an inordinately high rate of violent crime:

> It isn't accidental, then, that among developed countries, the United States is afflicted simultaneously with the worst rates of violent crime, the widest spread in income inequality, and the most severe public policies toward the disadvantaged. The industrial societies that have escaped our extremes of criminal violence tend either to have highly developed public sectors with fairly generous systems of income support, relatively well-developed employment policies, and other cushions against the "forces of the market," or (like Japan) to accomplish much the same ends through private institutions backed by an ethos of social obligation and mutual responsibility (1985:171-72).

Currie also challenges attempts to relate America's high crime rate to a weakness in control. Because other Western nations are more socially integrated, the argument goes, they are better able to exercise informal controls over their citizens (Adler 1983; Bayley 1976). Although this view may have merit, it overlooks the role of support in reducing crime. Japan offers an instructive example. Currie (1985:46) notes that previous analyses have neglected "the ways in which Japanese society is more *supportive* than ours, not simply more 'controlling'" (author's emphasis). In particular, he points both to Japan's "private mechanisms of social obligation" and to Japan's efforts to limit inequality and to provide lifetime job security to most workers (also see Beirne and Messerschmidt 1991:608-609).[4]

---

3 The limits of compassion are evident in the recent discussions of Americans' "compassion fatigue" regarding the homeless. Further, Link et al. (1992) question the assumption of compassion fatigue, largely on the grounds that Americans never showed unmixed compassion toward the homeless in the first place.

4 In a related issue, Currie (1985) disputes the conservatives' claim that permissiveness accounts for America's high crime rate. Currie observes that many Western nations are more permissive than the United States, both culturally and in their criminal justice systems, and he reasserts that the distinctive quality of American social policy is the grudging nature of its support for the impoverished. Also see Beirne and Messerschmidt (1991).

As I will discuss again later, the broader point here is that criminologists often confound the effects of informal control with those of social support. These concepts are not necessarily rivals in explaining criminal behavior; in reality, support and control may be mutually reinforcing in reducing crime. Still, the distinction between the two is important both for achieving theoretical precision and because their policy implications can differ dramatically.

In a similar vein, a social support perspective leads us to reconsider the connection to crimes of inequality, which research indicates is a salient predictor of cross-cultural variations in violent offenses (Braithwaite 1979; Braithwaite and Braithwaite 1980; Currie 1985; Messner 1980). This relationship often is interpreted from a strain theory perspective: inequality breeds feelings of relative deprivation and, in turn, criminal involvement (Bailey 1984; Blau and Blau 1982: Rosenfeld 1986). As stated by Currie (1985), however, economic inequality can generate crime not only by exposing people to relative deprivation but also by eviscerating and inhibiting the development of social support networks.[5]

The social ecology of support and crime varies not only across but also within nations (Currie 1985). Thus I offer a second proposition:

2. The less social support there is in a community, the higher the crime rate will be.

This thesis is buttressed by several pieces of evidence. Admittedly, quantitative research on communities and crime has not systematically explored the relationship of social support to crime (Bursik and Grasmick 1993a; Byrne and Sampson 1986; Reiss and Tonry 1986; but see Zuravin 1989). Nonetheless, variables employed in various studies may be viewed as operationalizing the concept of support.

First, there is evidence that governmental assistance to the poor tends to lessen violent crime across ecological units (DeFronzo 1983; Messner 1986; see Rosenfeld 1986). Thus, contrary to conservatives' claims that welfare corrodes individual initiative and fosters irresponsibility, including lawlessness (Murray 1984; but see Block et al. 1987; Ellwood 1988), it appears that state support buffers against criminogenic forces (also see Currie 1985, 1989, 1993).

---

[5] The relationship of relative deprivation to crime is problematic. Within the United States, support for a relationship between relative deprivation and crime is inconsistent for both individual-level studies (Burton et al. 1994; Burton and Dunaway 1994) and macro-level studies (see, for example, Bailey 1984). Further, it is not clear that inequality causes crime by deprivation, through other processes such as routine activities (Cao and Maume 1993; Carroll and Jackson 1983; Maume 1989), or (as I suggest) by undermining social support networks.

Second, research reveals that crime rates are higher in communities characterized by family disruption, weak friendship networks, and low participation in local voluntary organizations (Sampson 1986a, 1986b; Sampson and Groves 1989). Sampson interprets these findings as an indication that such communities are unable to exert informal social control over their residents (also see Bursik and Grasmick 1993b). Although this perspective may have merit, it is unclear why these variables are measures of control and not of support. It is telling that the mental illness literature uses neighborhood interaction and participation in voluntary organizations to assess "community and network support" (Lin, Dumin, and Woelfel 1986). Further, high rates of family disruption may operationalize not only adults' ability to exert surveillance over youths but also the availability to youths of both adult support networks and the opportunity to develop intimate relations. In short, existing ecological studies can be interpreted as containing measures of social support and, in turn, as showing that support reduces rates of criminal involvement.

Zuravin's (1989) study on the "ecology of child abuse and neglect" across Baltimore neighborhoods provides a useful example of this line of inquiry. "High-risk neighborhoods," she theorizes, "are characterized by demographic, social, and physical characteristics that negatively impact on family and individual stress levels by decreasing the availability as well as the adequacy of support systems" (1989:102). In contrast, families in low-risk neighborhoods are "embedded in informal helping networks," a situation which, in turn, reduces stress and "protects against child maltreatment" (1989:102). Incorporating ecological measures of "inadequate support" into her analysis, Zuravin presents preliminary data suggesting that child maltreatment is related inversely to the ecology of support.

Quantitative and ethnographic research on the "underclass" or the "truly disadvantaged" also is relevant to the social ecology of crime and support. This research documents the powerful social forces—deindustrialization, joblessness, persisting racial segregation, migration to the suburbs—that have created socially and economically isolated inner-city enclaves (Devine and Wright 1993; Jencks and Peterson 1991; Lemann 1991; Massey and Denton 1993; Sullivan 1989; Wilson 1987). This trend, which has been described as a continuing process of social and cultural "disinvestment" in these neighborhoods, has enormous social consequences (Hagan 1993a; Short 1990, 1991).

The literature essentially documents the erosion of community social institutions and of their ability to provide social support.

Wilson (1987:144) notes, for example, that the departure of many middle-class families from inner-city neighborhoods reduced the "social buffer" or human capital needed to "absorb the shock or cushion the effect of uneven economic growth and periodic recessions." Similarly, in his review of Anderson's (1990) *Street Wise*, an ethnography of the Philadelphia neighborhood of "Northton," Hagan (1993a:329) shows how "structural and cultural disinvestment" has frayed the supportive relations between adults and youths that previously protected youths against crime. In the past, writes Hagan of Northton,

> The mentor and protégé relationship between old heads and young boys was . . . a defining feature of the social organization of Northton. The old heads were respected older women and men of the community who, as *guides* and role models, *encouraged* youth to invest in conventional culture. However, as structural investment in Northton and other such neighborhoods declined, the moral authority of the old heads and their emphasis on "honesty, independence, hard work, and family values" diminished. . . The result is a form of cultural disinvestment, *as old heads and young boys go their separate ways, each losing the opportunity of investment from the other* (1993a:329, emphasis added; also see Duneier 1992:59-62).[6]

Sullivan's (1989) *"Getting Paid"* illuminates how differences in support structures across neighborhoods either divert youths from a criminal life course or set them on such a course (also see Hagan 1993b:471-73). Sullivan studied Latino, African-American, and white youths in three Brooklyn neighborhoods. In contrast to the more impoverished minority youths, whose access to support was structurally limited, white juveniles from the working-class area of "Hamilton Park" were able to mobilize social networks to provide the resources they needed to escape being deeply embedded in a criminal role. Thus they avoided legal sanctions through "personal connections. . . . When in trouble, many of them went immediately to relatives on the police force or in the courts for advice and aid" (1989:197). Even more telling, they were able to join the legitimate workforce because their family ties provided entry into "extensive labor market networks" (1989:218; also see Kasinitz 1993). Accordingly, observes Sullivan,

---

6 A risk of emphasizing the deteriorating conditions of inner cities is that the existence and importance of social support networks in these areas are often overlooked. See, in particular, *Slim's Table* (Duneier 1992). This sometimes touching ethnography not only reveals supports among African-American men but also challenges stereotypes about ghetto males by making working-class blacks and their respectability visible.

> The Hamilton Park youths found a relatively plentiful supply of temporary, part-time, almost always off-the-books work through relatives, friends and local employers during their middle teens, most of it in the local vicinity. As these youths reached their late teens, they employed these same networks to gain access to a substantial if diminishing supply of desirable blue-collar jobs characterized by high pay, strong unions, and job protection. The minority youths suffered during both periods from their lack of comparable job networks (1989:103).

In short, my thesis is that both across nations and across communities, crime rates vary inversely with the level of social support. The social ecologists of crime have largely overlooked this possibility, but (as I hope I have revealed) their work contains evidence favoring the social support thesis and offers important clues for future investigation. In the next section I explore ways in which the presence or absence of support is implicated in individuals' involvement in crime.

SUPPORT AND CRIME

Since the inception of American criminology, interest in the criminogenic effects of family life has ebbed and flowed (Wilkinson 1974). Over the past decade, attention has increased once again, in part because of the American family's beleaguered status (Sykes and Cullen 1992) and in part because of the emergence of salient criminological findings showing that the pathway to serious adult criminality begins in childhood (Loeber and Le Blanc 1990; Nagin and Farrington 1992; Nagin and Paternoster 1991; Sampson and Laub 1993).

This renewed interest has prompted not only numerous empirical studies on family correlates of crime (Loeber and Stouthamer-Loeber 1986; Wells and Rankin 1991) but also widely read theoretical frameworks. Although these theories differ fundamentally, they emphasize the criminogenic role that the family plays by the way it exercises or instills *control* (Colvin and Pauly 1983; Gottfredson and Hirschi 1990; Hagan 1989; Regoli and Hewitt 1994; Wilson and Herrnstein 1985). These perspectives are earning a measure of empirical confirmation (see, for example, Akers 1994; Burton et al. 1994; Grasmick et al. 1993; Hagan 1989; Hagan, Gillis, and Simpson 1990; Messner and Krohn 1990); thus I will not argue against their value. At the same time, as a result of criminologists' emphasis on control, virtually no theoretical attention has been paid to how family-related social support, or its absence, is involved in crime causation. Accordingly I offer my third proposition:

3. The more support a family provides, the less likely it is that a person will engage in crime.

We have considerable evidence that parental expressive support diminishes children's risk of criminal involvement. Glueck and Glueck (1950:113-15, 125), for example, found that in comparison with nondelinquents, delinquents had less "warm" relations with their parents, were less likely to engage in family activities, and came from families that were less "cohesive, that is, evincing strong emotional ties among the members, joint interests, pride in their home, and a 'we' feeling in general." Similarly, Alexander (1973) reported that "supportive" as opposed to "defensive" communication was present more often in nondelinquents' than delinquents' families. More recently, Walsh and Petee's (1987) study revealed that "love deprivation" was an important predictor of violence in a sample of juvenile probationers.

The firmest empirical evidence, however, can be drawn from Loeber and Stouthamer-Loeber's (1986) comprehensive meta-analysis of family correlates of delinquency: factors indicating a lack of parental support clearly increase delinquent involvement. (Also see Feldman's [1993:196] discussion of "positive parenting.") Loeber and Stouthamer-Loeber conclude that delinquency is related inversely to "child-parent involvement, such as the amount of intimate communication, confiding, sharing of activities, and seeking help" (1986:42). Similarly, their analysis indicates that measures of parental rejection of children, such as "rejection, not warm, lack of love, lack of affection, less affectionate," were "consistently related to delinquency and aggression" (1986:54; also see Sampson and Laub 1993:119). These "support" elements, moreover, were among the most powerful family factors related to delinquency; their effects exceeded those of parental criminality, marital discord, parental absence, parental health, and family size (1993:120-23).[7]

Also relevant are criminological studies of the social bond theory concept of "attachment to parents." Research reveals that attachment is generally, though not uniformly, related inversely to delinquency (Burton 1991; Mawhorr 1992). As Mawhorr points out, interpreting this relationship is difficult because attachment has been conceptualized and operationalized in diverse ways. Notably, measures of attachment often confound "indirect control," bonds that make youths not wish to disappoint parents by getting into trouble (Rankin and Wells 1990), with youths' perceptions of parental support, such as expressing love, being nurturant, and providing

[7] Evidence suggesting the harmful effects of nonsupportive parents also is present in research linking physical abuse to delinquency and adult violence. See, for example, Regoli and Hewitt (1994), Straus (1990), and Widom (1989).

a confiding relationship. Although the results are not fully consistent (Mawhorr 1992) and the concept of support has not been measured systematically, at least some evidence exists to suggest that perceived parental support mitigates delinquency (Van Voorhis et al. 1988; also see Barnes 1984).

In contrast to expressive support, criminological research contains few empirical studies on the impact of instrumental family support on crime (see, for example, Loeber and Stouthamer-Loeber 1986). It is premature to conclude that instrumental support is as salient as expressive support, and possibly these forms of support vary in their effects across the life cycle. In any case, the literature contains some clues as to the importance of instrumental family support. Thus, if we revisit Glueck and Glueck (1950:129-30), we discover that delinquents were more likely than nondelinquents to have parents who "had not given any thought to the boys' futures." Further, as noted above, family-based networks are an important source of entry into the job market; this, in turn, can undermine continued involvement in crime (Sullivan 1989; also see Curtis 1989:155).

Finally, any discussion of families and crime must be careful to avoid what Currie (1985:185) calls the "fallacy of autonomy—the belief that what goes on inside the family can usefully be separated from the forces that affect it from the outside: the larger social context in which families are embedded for better or for worse." Indeed, large social forces have transformed many American families in ways that often have reduced their capacity to support children (see, for example, Hewlett 1991; Wilson 1987). For example, adolescents today are much less likely than in the past to eat evening meals with parents or to spend time at home (Felson 1994:104; Messner and Rosenfeld 1994:103); the potential time that parents have to spend with children is declining (Hewlett 1991:90-92); and "less than 5 percent of all families have another adult (e.g., grandparent) living in the home, compared to 50 percent two generations ago. This reduces the backup support that might otherwise be available to working parents" (Panel on High-Risk Youth 1993:56).

Most disconcerting, however, is the concentration of forces that have ripped apart families of the underclass, or the "truly disadvantaged" (Devine and Wright 1993; Wilson 1987), and have made inner-city youths vulnerable to crime, drugs, and an array of unhealthy behaviors (Currie 1985, 1993; Panel on High-Risk Youth 1993). The Panel on High-Risk Youth states,

> Perhaps the most serious risk facing adolescents in high-risk settings is isolation from the nurturance, safety, and guidance that comes from sustained relationships with adults. Parents are the best source of support, but for

> many adolescents, parents are not positively involved in their lives. In some cases, parents are absent or abusive. In many more cases, parents strive to be good parents, but lack the capacity or opportunity to be so (1993:213).

Accordingly I offer this as a corollary to my third proposition: *The more support is given to families, the less crime will occur.* As Rivara and Farrington (forthcoming) observe, "increased social support to families can take the form of information (e.g., parenting programs), emotional support (e.g., home visitors), provision of material needs (e.g., food stamps, housing) or instrumental help (e.g., day care)." They also note that the "most successful interventions appear to be those which offer more than one type of social support service, thereby affecting a number of risk factors for the development of delinquency and violence" (forthcoming; also see Farrington 1994). Echoing this theme, Currie (1989:18-19, 1993:310-17) argues persuasively that the government should institute a "genuinely supportive national family policy," including, for example, child care, family leaves, and special programs for families at risk for mistreating children.

Currie's (1985, 1989, 1993) analyses and the above discussion on changing levels of support within the American family lead to a second corollary: *Changes in levels of support for and by families have contributed since the 1960s to increases in crime and to the concentration of serious violence in high-risk inner-city neighborhoods.* This statement contradicts the thinking of Murray (1984), who blames the "generous revolution" of the Great Society programs for eroding individual responsibility and for fostering criminal and other deviant behaviors (see Lemann 1991; Lupo 1994).

Beyond the family, Krohn (1986) contends that social networks may provide a "web of conformity" (also see Sampson and Laub 1993). Krohn emphasizes how dimensions of networks operate to control behavior; scholars in the sociology of mental illness study how these characteristics of networks are an important source of social support (Lin et al. 1986; Vaux 1988). In short, the web of conformity involves not only constraints but also supports (Sullivan 1989; also see Zuravin 1989). This point leads to my fourth proposition:

4. The more social support in a person's social network, the less crime will occur.

Social support theorists have examined most extensively how supports mitigate the effects of strain or "stress." The relationships are complex, but social supports can prevent stresses from arising or can lessen negative consequences if stresses should emerge (House 1981; Vaux 1988). These findings are important in light of the recent revitalization of strain theory, particularly empirical research linking strain to criminal behavior (Agnew 1985a, 1989; Agnew and White 1992; Burton and Cullen 1992; Farnworth and Leiber 1989; McCarthy and Hagan 1992; Vaux and Ruggiero 1983).

Most important is Agnew's (1992) attempt to lay the foundation for a "general strain theory." Agnew argues that in focusing almost exclusively on the Mertonian or status frustration version of strain theory, criminologists have conceptualized criminogenic strain too narrowly. In addition to the blockage of desired (success) goals emphasized by the Mertonian tradition, Agnew demarcates two other general categories of strain: removal of positively valued stimuli, and the presentation of noxious stimuli (also see Agnew 1985a, 1989; Agnew and White 1992; McCarthy and Hagan 1992; Vaux and Ruggiero 1983).

The remaining issue, largely ignored by strain theorists (Cullen 1984), is how people respond to this range of stressful conditions. Building on the social support literature (e.g., Vaux 1988), Agnew (1992) suggests that the ability to cope with criminogenic strains is contingent on access to supports. "Adolescents with conventional social support," he observes, "should be better able to respond to objective strains in a nondelinquent manner" (1992:72). This contention suggests my fifth proposition:

5. *Social support lessens the effects of exposure to criminogenic strains.*

In their important reassessment of Glueck and Glueck's longitudinal data, Sampson and Laub (1993) study not only sources of the stability of crime across the life course but also the "turning points" at which offenders depart from the criminal "pathway." Their analysis shows that during adulthood, job stability and attachments to spouse contribute to desistance from crime. They interpret these findings as indicating that "adult social bonds" provide offenders with social capital which subjects them to "informal social controls" (1993:140-43). "Adult social ties," they observe, "create interdependent systems of obligation and restraint that impose significant costs for translating criminal propensities into action" (1993:141).

I will not take issue with the control theory set forth by Sampson and Laub, but I observe that their *Crime in the Making* also contains insights on the salience of adult *social supports*. Thus Sampson and Laub (1993:141) take note of the "social capital invested by employers and spouses," not simply that invested by offenders. With regard to marriage, for example, life histories on offenders in Glueck and Glueck's sample reveal that this investment took the form of wives' providing "material and emotional *support*" (Sampson and Laub 1993:205, 220, emphasis added; also see Vaux 1988:173).[8] Two points follow from this observation.

First, marital and employment "social supports" may reduce crime by increasing social capital and thus expanding the basis for informal social controls. Second, these social supports may exert independent (main) effects on crime not by facilitating control but by reducing other sources of crime (e.g., lessening emotional difficulties, relieving strains, transforming deviant identities). More broadly, I offer my sixth proposition:

6. *Across the life cycle, social support increases the likelihood that offenders will turn away from a criminal pathway.*

I do not mean to confine this proposition to the role of adult social supports in crime desistance. In particular, accounts of at-risk youths suggest that supports can trigger their turning away from crime (see also Dubow and Reid 1994). Such supports may involve a youth's special informal relationship with an adult (e.g., teacher, coach), participation in a mentorship program (Kuznik 1994; Panel on High-Risk Youth 1993:213-14), or placement in a community program (Curtis 1989:154-60).

Commentary on impoverished juveniles at risk for crime also frequently emphasizes the sense of isolation felt by these youths. The Panel on High-Risk Youth (1993:217), for example, notes that "young people from high-risk settings" often "confront the emotional pain and feelings of hopelessness that can interfere with positive development." Echoing this theme, Curtis (1989:158) observes that inner-city minority youths think "the cards are stacked hopelessly against them. These youths believe that fate will not permit them to 'make it' in any legitimate form."

This isolation might be viewed as a detachment from social bonds that lessens control and increases criminal involvement, but another process also may be operating: These youths may perceive

---

[8] Criminological research paints a complicated picture of the relationship of marriage to criminal involvement (see, for example, Farrington, Ohlin, and Wilson 1986:56; Rand 1987; Wright and Wright 1992). A weakness in this research is the shortage of studies measuring marital quality and, in particular, the personal characteristics and behavior of spouses in the relationship. In the social support literature, marriage is often used as a proxy measure for support (as opposed to control). Even in this research, however, the quality of marital support has not been explored extensively. As Vaux (1988:200) points out, "marriage often provides individuals with a readily accessible source of each important mode of support in the context of a long-standing relationship based on love, mutual obligation, and intimate knowledge." At the same time, continues Vaux (1988:200), "many marriages survive for a lifetime but perform these support functions poorly. Many others prove so unrewarding or aversive that they are terminated."

that they will always lack the instrumental and expressive supports needed to change the circumstances in which they are enmeshed.[9] This possibility leads to my seventh proposition:

7. *Anticipation of a lack of social support increases criminal involvement.*

Thus far I have concentrated on how *receiving* support diminishes criminality, but it also seems important to consider how *giving* support affects involvement in crime. The logic of writings from the peacemaking/humanist and feminist perspectives suggests that providing support should reduce criminal propensities (McDermott 1994). Pepinsky (1988), in fact, regards crime as the opposite of "responsiveness" to others. Further, in *The Call of Service,* Coles (1993) tells how the experience of supporting others can transform selves, inculcate idealism, foster moral purpose, and create long-standing interconnections—all of which would seem anti-criminogenic.

I know of no systematic empirical investigation of the link between giving support and crime, but some insights can be gleaned from the research. Sampson and Laub (1993:219-20), for example, note that the offenders in their study were likely to desist from crime when they were devoted to their spouses and children, and were "financially responsible not only to their spouses, but also to parents and siblings if the need arose." That is, as offenders assumed a role as providers of expressive and instrumental support, their involvement in crime ceased.

Ward's (1988) research on "urban adolescents' conceptions of violence" also is relevant. Youths were asked to describe a violent event they had witnessed and whether those involved were "right or wrong in what they did." Of the youths who interpreted the episode with a "care" as opposed to a "justice" logic,[10] "none found violence justifiable in any way . . . care calls for an injunction *against* hurt" (1988:193; author's emphasis). There is a clear distinction, of course, between caring behavior and caring attitudes, but these results at least indicate that a caring or supportive orientation toward others facilitates connectedness and makes victimization incongruous (see McCord 1992).

---

9 These perceptions would be classified as "appraisals of support" (Vaux 1988). Here, however, the focus is on appraising not only current support but future support as well. On the potential importance of anticipations of support and rejection, see Link et al. (1989).

10 This distinction in moral orientations has been made by Gilligan (1982; Gilligan and Attanucci 1988), who argues that moral issues tend to be viewed by males in terms of "justice" (an emphasis on rules, reciprocity, and fair treatment) and by females in terms of "care" (an emphasis on interconnections and on responsiveness to others' needs) (also see McDermott 1994).

Lynne Goodstein (personal communication, January 2, 1994) offers another pertinent insight: "Women's traditional responsibility for the delivery of social support and nurturance to others (children, elders, partners) and the dramatically lower crime rates for women is an interesting association." Although this association is open to differing interpretations,[11] it suggests that the experience of providing support creates sentiments (e.g., compassion), identities, role expectations, and problem-solving skills that are generally incompatible with the "seductions of crime" (Katz 1988; also see Gilligan, Ward, and Taylor 1988).

In any event, these various considerations lead to my eighth proposition:

8. *Giving social support lessens involvement in crime.*

Finally, Albert Cohen (personal communication, January 29, 1994) has alerted me to the need to consider the broader concept of "differential social support."[12] To this point, I have largely explored the role of supports in making conformity possible. Cohen, however, observes

> that social support is equally important to non-conformity, to crime. Indeed, the burden of much of the literature on causation is that associations, the situation of company, provide much of the support that makes it possible to break the law, more effectively to thwart the justice process and reduce the "hurtfulness" and other consequences of punishment.

Indeed, insights on support for crime are evident in the literature on peers and co-offending (Reiss 1988), on the acquisition and performance of criminal roles (Cloward 1959; Steffensmeier 1983), and on the organizational conditions that make corporate crime possible (Hills 1987; Sutherland 1949). Differential social support also might operate in situational contexts. As shown by Richard Felson (1982; Felson and Tedeschi 1993), "third parties" to interpersonal conflict can support the escalation of violence or can mediate tensions and diminish subsequent aggression. These observations lead to my ninth proposition:

9. *Crime is less likely when social support for conformity exceeds social support for crime.*

In a related vein, Ronald Akers (personal communication, January 1994) has cautioned that social supports are likely to be most effective when they are linked to "conformity-inducing outcomes."

[11] For example, Hagan's (1989) power-control theory might suggest that females confined to supportive, domestic roles are subjected to greater control and thus are involved in less crime.

[12] Ronald Akers (personal communication, January 1994) has made a similar observation.

The *source* of the support may be particularly important. For instance, support from conformist sources may not only address criminal risk factors (e.g., strain) but also provide an opportunity for prosocial modeling (Andrews and Bonta 1994:202-205). Conversely, support from criminal friends (e.g., comfort in the face of a stressful life event) may be counteracted if these associations also expose youths to criminogenic influences.

On this point, the research on the effects of marriage provides relevant data. Although the findings are not fully consistent (Sampson and Laub 1993), we find some evidence that marriage—conceptualized here as a social support—reduces crime only if spouses are not themselves deviant or criminal (Farrington, Ohlin, and Wilson 1986:56; West 1982:100-104). Thus I offer this corollary to Proposition 9: *Social support from conformist sources is most likely to reduce criminal involvement.*

SUPPORT AND CONTROL

As stated earlier, recent advances in criminological theory have been dominated by attempts to link control with crime. I have tried to show that these perspectives overlook social support and potentially confound the effects of control and with the effects of support. Now I wish to make a different, but related, argument, which is set forth in my tenth proposition:

10. Social support often is a precondition for effective social control.

The criminological literature contains numerous illustrations of this proposition. Braithwaite's (1989) influential theory of "reintegrative shaming," however, is perhaps the most noteworthy example (also see Braithwaite and Mugford 1994; Makkai and Braithwaite 1994). In brief, Braithwaite contends that legal violations often evoke formal and informal attempts at "shaming," which he defines as "all processes of expressing disapproval which have the intention or effect of invoking remorse in the person being shamed and/or condemnation by others who become aware of the shaming" (1989:9). Braithwaite observes, however, that shaming takes two general forms. Disintegrative shaming is criminogenic; as labeling theory would predict, it stigmatizes, excludes, and ensures the exposure of offenders to criminogenic conditions. Reintegrative shaming, in contrast, achieves conformity. After the act is condemned, attempts are made "to reintegrate the offender back into the community of law-abiding or respectable citizens through words or gestures of forgiveness or ceremonies to decertify the offender as deviant" (1989:100-101). Even if repeated efforts are required, the goal is to avoid exclusion and thus to embed the offender in conventional, accepting relationships (Braithwaite and Mugford 1994).

In the language of the social support paradigm, Braithwaite is asserting that control can be effective only in the context of support (see Sherman 1992). Further, the very likelihood that reintegrative shaming will be used depends on the extent to which the larger society is supportive or, as Braithwaite puts its, "communitarian." Not surprisingly, shaming in the United States tends to be disintegrative (also see Benson 1990).

A related insight can be gained from the correctional literature. It appears that family support of offenders during and after incarceration improves chances of successful completion of parole supervision (Farrington et al. 1986:147; Wright and Wright 1992:54). In short, control with support is more effective than control by itself.

The family socialization literature also offers useful information. Wilson and Herrnstein (1985:237-40) argue that "restrictive" parenting is important in detecting and discouraging rule transgressions and thus in teaching that behavior has consequences. But restrictiveness is most effective when coupled with parental warmth. "A warm parent," they state, "is approving and supportive of the child, frequently employs praise as a reinforcement for good behavior, and explains the reasons for rules" (1985:237). In this case, warmth (support) empowers restrictiveness (control): when children care about their parents, obedience is rewarding and disobedience is unrewarding (1985:239). As Maccoby puts it,

> A common theme in these various findings seems to be that parental warmth binds children to their parents in a positive way—it makes children responsive and more willing to accept guidance. If the parent-child relationship is close and affectionate, parents can exercise what control is needed without having to apply heavy disciplinary pressure. It is as if parents' responsiveness, affection, and obvious commitment to their children's welfare gave them the right to make demands and exercise control (cited in Braithwaite 1989:166-67).

These observations suggest a broader conclusion about the correction of crime:

11. A supportive correctional system lessens crime.

Braithwaite's (1989) theoretical work on reintegrative shaming suggests this proposition (also see Braithwaite and Mugford 1994). Experiences in the United States, however, offer additional, substantive confirmatory evidence. Over the past two decades, American policy makers have engaged in what Clear (1994) calls an experiment in "penal harm," largely on the assumption that inflicting pain on offenders rather than supporting them will lessen the crime problem (also see Currie 1989). Policy makers have attempted to increase the scale of imprisonment (Zimring and Hawkins 1991) and to replace community *corrections* with intermediate *punishments* (Byrne, Lurigio, and Petersilia 1992). This experiment in reducing crime through nonsupport must be termed a failure: America's crime rates have stubbornly resisted the intended effects of penal harm (Clear 1994; Cullen and Wright forthcoming; Currie 1985; Irwin and Austin 1994; Petersilia 1992; Steffensmeier and Harer 1993; Visher 1987; Zimring and Hawkins 1991; but see Wright 1994).

Evaluations of correctional interventions also are instructive. It is rather clear that punishment-oriented programs have virtually no effect on recidivism—indeed, they may actually increase it (Andrews and Bonta 1994; Byrne and Pattavina 1992; Cullen, Wright, and Applegate 1993; Petersilia and Turner 1993). In contrast, meta-analyses show clearly that rehabilitation programs reduce recidivism across programs by 10 to 12 percent (Palmer 1992:158), and by about 50 percent when interventions are based on principles of effective treatment (Andrews and Bonta 1994; also see Lipsey 1992).

These findings are important for two reasons. First, although rehabilitation is often criticized for justifying coercive practices (Cullen and Gilbert 1982), it represents a correctional philosophy that embodies sentiments of "doing good." It implies a genuine concern for protecting the social order, but with the understanding that this goal is best achieved by addressing offenders' criminogenic needs and assisting their reintegration into conventional roles. In short, rehabilitation is a supportive, not a punitive, correctional approach (Cullen and Gilbert 1982; Cullen and Wright forthcoming).

Second, as Andrews and Bonta (1994) point out, support is an integral part of effective correctional treatment programs. In behavioral programs, for example, they note that counselors should "give at least four positive supportive statements for every punishing one" (1994:205). They also observe the importance of "high quality relationships" characterized by "mutual liking, respect and caring . . . openness, warmth and understanding" (1994:203-204). These supportive relationships, contend Andrews and Bonta (1994:204-205), provide a basis for effective modeling and for increasing the chances that expressions of disapproval will matter to offenders.[13]

---

13 For a compelling statement of the value of a supportive correctional system, see Miller (1991).

Although the evidence for this point is less highly developed, I speculate in my twelfth proposition that support also is integral to law enforcement:

12. Social support leads to more effective policing.

This proposition reflects the belief that law enforcement works more effectively—to reduce crime, to serve community needs—when police and citizens are involved in a mutually supportive relationship. In this case, the goal is to encourage the "co-production" of order by police and citizens acting in concert.

The "community-policing" movement is the most obvious example of mutually supportive policing (see Bayley 1976). Traditional policing emphasizes largely impersonal, reactive, centralized law enforcement. In contrast, community policing views officers as located in the community, where they can interact with and listen to local residents; as building personal, trusting relationships with citizens; and as attempting proactively to work with citizens to solve community problems related to crime (Skolnick and Bayley 1988; Sparrow 1988; Wycoff 1988).

It is premature to conclude that supportive policing ventures will reap the anticipated benefits, especially if they are implemented with unrealistic expectations and without program integrity (Mastrofski 1988). Still, initial results show some promise: community-policing ventures appear to reduce citizens' crime-related fears and perceptions of disorder (Spelman and Eck 1987; Wycoff 1988). Further, although solid evaluations are lacking, it seems reasonable to anticipate that community-oriented policing which actually delivers meaningful support to the community will diminish crime rates (National Institute of Justice 1992; Skolnick and Bayley 1988; Spelman and Eck 1987; but see Bowers and Hirsch 1987). As Thurman concludes:

> Co-producing solutions to crime and related social problems seems the best means at hand for bringing human resources together with the police for mutual benefit, while at the same time engendering respect for the ability of residents within communities to make an important contribution to community-based problem-solving (1993:22).

In connection with this point, Guarino-Ghezzi (1994) argues that the police could become more effective in reducing juvenile lawlessness by participating in a "model of reintegrative surveillance" (see Braithwaite 1989). Drawing on the results from "model programs for juveniles"—"pockets of innovation that involve aggressive outreach efforts by police" (1994:146)—Guarino-Ghezzi illuminates the benefits that accrue when officers are involved more fully in the lives of community members, especially youthful offenders. By building interpersonal bonds and increasing their understanding of urban youths, officers can 1) exercise more consistent surveillance over, and impose graduated sanctions on, problem youths and 2) foster the reintegration of offenders through caring responses and the provision of services—that is, by delivering social supports. "In short," observes Guarino-Ghezzi (1994:149), "the police role needs to be reexamined as an important *resource* for juvenile offender reintegration and crime prevention, particularly in high-crime neighborhoods where *other vital supports are lacking* and disorder is prevalent" (emphasis added; also see Myers and Chiang 1993).

SUPPORT AND VICTIMIZATION

My general thesis is that social support, both ecologically and in individuals' lives, reduces the number of persons motivated to break the law. A reduction in persons with criminal propensities should limit the crime rate and, by implication, should decrease victimization in society. This point leads into my thirteenth proposition:

13. Social support lessens criminal victimization.

As Cohen and Felson (1979:589) point out, however, the presence of "motivated offenders" is only one of the elements necessary for victimization; there also must be a "suitable target" and "the absence of capable guardians against a violation" (also see Garofalo 1987). Although it is speculative, I offer the following corollary to my proposition: *Social support reduces victimization by decreasing suitable targets and by increasing guardianship.*

I contend that the provision of social support potentially builds connectedness among community members; in particular, it fosters bonds of reciprocity and intimacy. Under these conditions, "targets" become less attractive for two reasons. First, if a motivated offender previously received support from a potential target, a victimization would violate reciprocity norms and would exact a psychic cost. Second, intimacy creates the possibility that a target could identify an offender; again, the target's attractiveness would be decreased by increasing the costs of a victimization (see Felson 1986).

In the same vein, the more widespread the provision of social support and thus of interpersonal knowledge in an area, the greater the overall level of guardianship. Because of investments in relationships, high levels of social support provide the social capital for guardianship. Further, interpersonal knowledge stemming from support creates a larger pool of potential "informants" (Felson

1986), who are available to report those who otherwise might contemplate victimizing others. "A tight community—where people know people, property, and their linkages," observes Felson (1986:123), "offers little opportunity for common exploitive crime."

Finally, I offer another corollary: *A more supportive society reduces exposure to victimization.* Here I draw on Maume's (1989) research revealing that "one of the hidden costs of inequality is that some people are constrained to live risk-prone lifestyles," which make their victimization more likely (also see Cao and Maume 1993; Carroll, personal communication, December 29, 1993; Carroll and Jackson 1983). A supportive society, which presumably would diminish racial and economic inequalities (Currie 1985), thus would provide disadvantaged citizens with resources to follow less risky lifestyles and to commensurately reduce their exposure to victimization.[14]

There also is evidence that social support mitigates the effects of crime victimization. As Agnew (1985b:234) notes, "[D]ata indicate that fear of crime is lower when social support is high." Although relationships are often complex, other studies suggest that social support improves victims' psychological adjustment (Astin et al. 1993; Testa et al. 1992). Support to victims can be expressive, as in providing comfort and helping to neutralize self-blame, or instrumental, as in supplying information on how to avoid future victimizations or providing the resources to escape the threat of continuing abuse (e.g., shelters for battered women) (Agnew 1985b; Saunders and Azar 1989:494-508; also see Nurius, Furrey, and Berliner 1992). These considerations lead to my final proposition:

14. Social support lessens the pains of criminal victimization.

NEXT STEPS

I have outlined only the broad parameters suggesting how social support might serve as an organizing concept for criminology. If a social support paradigm is to bear fruit, I suspect that my initial ideas will warrant empirical scrutiny, revision, and perhaps reversal. Here I want to identify three steps that might be taken by criminologists interested in advancing the paradigm of social support and crime.

First, scholars must conceptualize and study which forms of social support are implicated most deeply in diminishing criminal involvement. Social support is a multifaceted concept (see Vaux 1988), which undoubtedly has a complex relationship to crime.

---

[14] Although this idea is not developed here systematically, I would propose that opportunities for victimization would be related inversely to ecological and individual-level measures of support (especially of social networks).

Although my thesis is that social support generally reduces lawbreaking, we must learn to recognize when the provision of various types of support, and by whom, has no effect or has the unanticipated consequence of increasing criminal involvement (e.g., when support is of poor quality or comes from a source enmeshed in crime).

Second, I have stopped far short of developing a formal theory of social support and crime—in part because my thinking has not progressed to that point and in part because I suspect that social support operates as a general protective factor across a variety of criminogenic risk factors. Even so, the theoretical task is still the identification of the precise mechanisms by which social support does, or does not, decrease criminal behavior.

I hope I have provided reasonable clues about the nature of these mechanisms. Thus, among other proposals, I have suggested that the provision of social supports reduces criminogenic strains, fosters effective parenting and a nurturing family life, supplies the human and social capital needed to desist from crime, creates opportunities for prosocial modeling, strengthens efforts at informal and formal control, and reduces opportunities for victimization. Research must discern which of these hunches have merit, and to what degree.

Third, to advance the social support paradigm, criminologists must incorporate measures of support into their research designs. With secondary data sets, the challenge is to reexamine questions on surveys and other variables (e.g., census data) while considering how these data operationalize various dimensions of social support. In collecting new data, the challenge is to devise measures of support—with considerable help from the existing sociological literature on social support (Cleary 1988; Lin et al. 1986; Vaux 1988)—and to incorporate them into empirical studies of crime causation and into tests of rival criminological theories.

GOOD CRIMINOLOGY AND THE GOOD SOCIETY

Over the past decade, an increasing number of voices have joined in a national conversation about the requirements for what Robert Bellah and his colleagues call the "Good Society" (Bellah et al. 1991; also see Bellah et al. 1985; Coles 1993; Etzioni 1993; Reich 1988; Wuthnow 1991). Fundamental to this ongoing conversation is a critique of the excessive individualism in the United States, which too often degenerates into a politics justifying either the crass pursuit of rights or materialistic self-aggrandizement. In this context, there is a lack of attention to the public good, service to others, and an appreciation for our need for connectedness. Accordingly there is a call to revitalize our common bonds and to build a society supportive of all its citizens.

I realize the risk in linking one's criminology to a larger social agenda: regardless of how crime is affected, attempts to build a Good Society certainly should stand or fall on their own merits (Felson 1994:12-13). Still, it is equally misguided to assume that criminological ideas have no consequences (Bohm 1993; Lilly et al. 1989). A criminology that emphasizes the need for social supports thus may have the potential to make a difference.

Indeed, if the social supports paradigm proves to be "Good Criminology," it will provide empirical grounds for suggesting that an important key to solving the crime problem is the construction of a supportive social order—the Good Society. Accordingly this paradigm may present an opportunity to challenge the current hegemony of punitive policy in criminal justice. It may prompt us to consider that the cost of a nonsupportive society, exacerbated by mean-spirited or neglectful public policies, is a disgraceful level of crime and violence (Currie 1985). And, hopefully, it may provide the basis for criminal justice and public policies which help to create a society that is more supportive and hence safer for its citizens.

REFERENCES

Addams, J. (1910) *Twenty Years at Hull-House.* New York: Signet.

Adler, F. (1983) *Nations Not Obsessed with Crime.* Littleton, CO: Rothman.

Agnew, R. (1985a) "A Revised Strain Theory of Delinquency." *Social Forces* 64:151-67.

——— (1985b) "Neutralizing the Impact of Crime." *Criminal Justice and Behavior* 12:221-39.

——— (1989) "A Longitudinal Test of Revised Strain Theory." *Journal of Quantitative Criminology* 5:373-87.

——— (1992) "Foundation for a General Strain Theory of Crime and Delinquency." *Criminology* 30:47-86.

Agnew, R. and H. R. White (1992) "An Empirical Test of General Strain Theory." *Criminology* 30:475-99.

Akers, R. L. (1994) *Criminological Theories: Introduction and Evaluation.* Los Angeles: Roxbury.

Alexander, J. F. (1973) "Defensive and Supportive Communications in Normal and Deviant Families." *Journal of Consulting and Clinical Psychology* 40:223-31.

Anderson, E. (1990) *Street Wise: Race, Class, and Change in an Urban Community.* Chicago: University of Chicago Press.

Andrews, D. A. and J. Bonta (1994) *The Psychology of Criminal Conduct.* Cincinnati: Anderson.

Archer, D. and R. Gartner (1984) *Violence and Crime in Cross-National Perspective.* New Haven: Yale University Press.

Astin, M. C., K. J. Lawrence, and D. W. Foy (1993) "Posttraumatic Stress Disorder among Battered Women: Risk and Resiliency Factors." *Violence and Victims* 8:17-28.

Bailey, W. C. (1984) "Poverty, Inequality, and City Homicide Rates." *Criminology* 22:531-50.

Barlow, H. D. (1993) *Introduction to Criminology*. 6th ed. New York: HarperCollins.
Barnes, G. M. (1984) "Adolescent Alcohol Abuse and Other Problem Behaviors: Their Relationships and Common Parental Influences." *Journal of Youth and Adolescence* 13:329-47.
Bayley, D. H. (1976) *Forces of Order: Police Behavior in Japan and the United States*. Berkeley: University of California Press.
Beirne, P. and J. Messerschmidt (1991) *Criminology*. San Diego: Harcourt Brace Jovanovich.
Bellah, R. N., R. Madsen, W. M. Sullivan, A. Swidler, and S. M. Tipton (1985) *Habits of the Heart: Individualism and Commitment in American Life*. Berkeley: University of California Press.
——— (1991) *The Good Society*. New York: Knopf.
Benson, M. L. (1990) "Emotions and Adjudication: Status Degradation among White-Collar Criminals." *Justice Quarterly* 7:515-28.
Blau, J. R. and P. M. Blau (1982) "The Cost of Inequality: Metropolitan Structure and Violent Crime." *American Sociological Review* 47:114-29.
Block, F., R. A. Cloward, B. Ehrenreich, and F. F. Piven (1987) *The Mean Season: The Attack on the Welfare State*. New York: Pantheon.
Bohm, R. M. (1993) "On the State of Criminal Justice: 1993 Presidential Address to the Academy of Criminal Justice Sciences." *Justice Quarterly* 10:529-40.
Bowers, W. J. and J. H. Hirsch (1987) "The Impact of Foot Patrol Staffing on Crime and Disorder in Boston: An Unmet Promise." *American Journal of Police* 6:17-44.
Braithwaite, J. (1979) *Inequality, Crime and Public Policy*. London: Routledge and Kegan Paul.
——— (1989) *Crime, Shame and Reintegration*. Cambridge, UK: Cambridge University Press.
Braithwaite, J. and V. Braithwaite (1980) "The Effect of Income Inequality and Social Democracy on Homicide." *British Journal of Criminology* 20:45-53.
Braithwaite, J. and S. Mugford (1994) "Conditions of Successful Reintegration Ceremonies: Dealing with Juvenile Offenders." *British Journal of Criminology* 34:139-71.
Braswell, M. C. (1989) "Correctional Treatment and the Human Spirit: A Focus on Relationship." *Federal Probation* 53 (June):49-60.
——— (1990) "Peacemaking: A Missing Link in Criminology." *The Criminologist* 15 (May-June):1, 3-5.
Brownfield, D. and A. M. Sorenson (1991) "Religion and Drug Use among Adolescents: A Social Support Conceptualization and Interpretation." *Deviant Behavior* 12:259-76.
Bulmer, M. (1984) *The Chicago School of Sociology: Institutionalization, Diversity, and the Rise of Sociological Research*. Chicago: University of Chicago Press.
Bursik, R. J., Jr. and H. G. Grasmick (1993a) *Neighborhoods and Crime: The Dimensions of Effective Community Control*. New York: Lexington Books.
——— (1993b) "Economic Deprivation and Neighborhood Crime Rates, 1960-1980." *Law and Society Review* 27:263-83.
Burton, V. S., Jr. (1991) "Explaining Adult Criminality: Testing Strain, Differential Association, and Control Theories." Doctoral dissertation, University of Cincinnati.
Burton, V. S., Jr. and F. T. Cullen (1992) "The Empirical Status of Strain Theory." *Journal of Crime and Justice* 15 (2):1-30.
Burton, V. S., Jr., F. T. Cullen, T. D. Evans, and R. G. Dunaway (1994) "Reconsidering Strain Theory: Operationalization, Rival Theories, and Adult Criminality." *Journal of Quantitative Criminology* 10:213-39.
Burton, V. S., Jr. and R. G. Dunaway (1994) "Strain, Relative Deprivation, and Middle-Class Delinquency." In G. Barak (ed.), *Varieties of Criminology: Readings from a Dynamic Discipline*, pp. 79-96. Westport, CT: Praeger.
Byrne, J. M., A. J. Lurigio, and J. Petersilia, eds. (1992) *Smart Sentencing: The Emergence of Intermediate Sanctions*. Newbury Park, CA: Sage.
Byrne, J. M. and A. Pattavina (1992) "The Effectiveness Issue: Assessing What Works in the Adult Community Corrections System." In J. M. Byrne, A. J. Lurigio, and J. Petersilia (eds.), *Smart Sentencing: The Emergence of Intermediate Sanctions*, pp. 281-303. Newbury Park, CA: Sage.
Byrne, J. M. and R. J. Sampson, eds. (1986) *The Social Ecology of Crime*. New York: Springer-Verlag.

Cao, L. and D. J. Maume Jr. (1993) "Urbanization, Inequality, Lifestyles and Robbery: A Comprehensive Model." *Sociological Focus* 26:11-26.

Carroll, L. and P. I. Jackson (1983) "Inequality, Opportunity, and Crime Rates in Central Cities." *Criminology* 21:178-94.

Clear, T. R. (1994) *Harm in American Penology: Offenders, Victims, and Their Communities.* Albany: SUNY Press.

Cleary, P. D. (1988) "Social Support: Conceptualization and Measurement." In H. B. Weis and F. H. Jacobs (eds.), *Evaluating Family Programs*, pp. 195-216. New York: Aldine.

Cloward, R. A. (1959) "Illegitimate Means, Anomie, and Deviant Behavior." *American Sociological Review* 24:164-76.

Cohen, L. E. and M. Felson (1979) "Social Change and Crime Rate Trends: A Routine Activity Approach." *American Sociological Review* 44:588-608.

Coles, R. (1993) *The Call of Service: A Witness to Idealism.* New York: Houghton Mifflin.

Colvin, M. and J. Pauly (1983) "A Critique of Criminology: Toward an Integrated Structural-Marxist Theory of Delinquency Production." *American Journal of Sociology* 89:513-51.

Cullen, F. T. (1984) *Rethinking Crime and Deviance Theory: The Emergence of a Structuring Tradition.* Totowa, NJ: Rowman and Allenheld.

Cullen, F. T. and K. E. Gilbert (1982) *Reaffirming Rehabilitation.* Cincinnati: Anderson.

Cullen, F. T. and J. P. Wright (forthcoming) "The Future of Corrections." In B. Maguire and P. Radosh (eds.), *The Past, Present, and Future of American Criminal Justice.* New York: General Hall.

Cullen, F. T., J. P. Wright, and B. K. Applegate (1993) "Control in the Community: The Limits of Reform?" Paper presented at the annual meeting of the International Association of Residential and Community Alternatives, Philadelphia.

Currie, E. (1985) *Confronting Crime: An American Challenge.* New York: Pantheon.

——— (1989) "Confronting Crime: Looking toward the Twenty-First Century." *Justice Quarterly* 6:5-25.

——— (1993) *Reckoning: Drugs, the Cities, and the American Future.* New York: Hill and Wang.

Curtis, L. A. (1989) "Race and Violent Crime: Toward a New Policy." In N. A. Weiner and M. E. Wolfgang (eds.), *Violent Crime, Violent Criminals*, pp. 139-70. Newbury Park, CA: Sage.

DeFronzo, J. (1983) "Economic Assistance to Impoverished Americans: Relationship to Incidence of Crime." *Criminology* 21:119-36.

Devine, J. A. and J. D. Wright (1993) *The Greatest of Evils: Urban Poverty and the American Underclass.* New York: Aldine.

Dubow, E. F. and G. J. Reid (1994) "Risk and Resource Variables in Children's Aggressive Behavior: A Two-Year Longitudinal Study." In L. R. Huesmann (ed.), *Aggressive Behavior: Current Perspectives*, pp. 187-211. New York: Plenum.

Duneier, M. (1992) *Slim's Table: Race, Respectability, and Masculinity.* Chicago: University of Chicago Press.

Ellwood, D. T. (1988). *Poor Support: Poverty in the American Family.* New York: Basic Books.

Empey, L. T. (1982) *American Delinquency: Its Meaning and Construction.* 2nd ed. Homewood, IL: Dorsey.

Etzioni, A. (1993) *The Spirit of Community: Rights, Responsibilities, and the Communitarian Agenda.* New York: Crown.

Farnworth, M. and M. J. Leiber (1989) "Strain Theory Revisited: Economic Goals, Educational Means, and Delinquency." *American Sociological Review* 54:263-74.

Farrington, D. P. (1994) "Delinquency Prevention in the First Few Years of Life." Plenary address presented at the Fourth European Conference on Law and Psychology, Barcelona.

Farrington, D. P., L. E. Ohlin, and J. Q. Wilson (1986) *Understanding and Controlling Crime: Toward a New Research Strategy.* New York: Springer-Verlag.

Feldman, P. (1993) *The Psychology of Crime: A Social Science Textbook.* Cambridge, UK: Cambridge University Press.

Felson, M. (1986) "Linking Criminal Choices, Routine Activities, Informal Control, and Criminal Outcomes." In D. B. Cornish and R. V. Clarke (eds.), *The Reasoning Criminal: Rational Choice Perspectives on Offending*, pp. 119-28. New York: Springer-Verlag.

——— (1994) *Crime and Everyday Life: Insight and Implications for Society*. Thousand Oaks, CA: Pine Forge Press.

Felson, R. B. (1982) "Impression Management and the Escalation of Aggression and Violence." *Social Psychology Quarterly* 45:245-54.

Felson, R. B. and J. T. Tedeschi (1993) "A Social Interactionist Approach to Violence: Cross-Cultural Applications." *Violence and Victims* 8:295-310.

Garland, D. (1990) *Punishment and Modern Society: A Study in Social Theory*. Chicago: University of Chicago Press.

Garofalo, J. (1987) "Reassessing the Lifestyle Model of Criminal Victimization." In M. R. Gottfredson and T. Hirschi (eds.), *Positive Criminology*, pp. 23-42. Newbury Park, CA: Sage.

Gilligan, C. (1982) *In a Different Voice: Psychological Theory and Women's Development*. Cambridge, MA: Harvard University Press.

Gilligan, C. and J. Attanucci (1988) "Two Moral Orientations." In C. Gilligan, J. V. Ward, and J. M. Taylor (eds.), with B. Bardige, *Mapping the Moral Domain: A Contribution of Women's Thinking to Psychological Theory and Education*, pp. 73-86. Cambridge, MA: Harvard University Press.

Gilligan, C., J. V. Ward, and J. M. Taylor (eds.) with B. Bardige (1988), *Mapping the Moral Domain: A Contribution of Women's Thinking to Psychological Theory and Education*. Cambridge, MA: Harvard University Press.

Glueck, S. and E. Glueck (1950) *Unraveling Juvenile Delinquency*. Cambridge, MA: Harvard University Press.

Gottfredson, M. R. and T. Hirschi (1990) *A General Theory of Crime*. Stanford: Stanford University Press.

Grasmick, H. G., C. R. Tittle, R. J. Bursik Jr., and B. J. Arneklev (1993) "Testing the Core Empirical Implications of Gottfredson and Hirschi's General Theory of Crime." *Journal of Research in Crime and Delinquency* 30:5-29.

Guarino-Ghezzi, S. (1994) "Reintegrative Police Surveillance of Juvenile Offenders: Forging an Urban Model." *Crime and Delinquency* 40:131-53.

Hagan, J. (1989) *Structural Criminology*. New Brunswick: Rutgers University Press.

——— (1993a) "Structural and Cultural Disinvestment and the New Ethnographies of Poverty and Crime." *Contemporary Sociology* 22:327-32.

——— (1993b) "The Social Embeddedness of Crime and Unemployment." *Criminology* 31:465-91.

Hagan, J., A. R. Gillis, and J. Simpson (1990) "Clarifying and Extending Power-Control Theory." *American Journal of Sociology* 95:1024-37.

Hewlett, S. A. (1991) *When the Bough Breaks: The Cost of Neglecting Our Children*. New York: HarperCollins.

Hills, S. L., ed. (1987) *Corporate Violence: Injury and Death for Profit*. Totowa, NJ: Rowman and Littlefield.

House, J. L. (1981) *Work Stress and Social Support*. Reading, MA: Addison-Wesley.

Irwin, J. and J. Austin (1994) *It's About Time: America's Prison Binge*. Belmont, CA: Wadsworth.

Jencks, C. and P. E. Peterson, eds. (1991) *The Urban Underclass*. Washington, DC: Brookings Institution.

Kasinitz, P. (1993) "The Real Jobs Problem." *Wall Street Journal*, November 26, p. A-6.

Katz, J. (1988) *Seductions of Crime: Moral and Sensual Attractions of Doing Evil*. New York: Basic Books.

Kornhauser, R. R. (1978) *Social Sources of Delinquency: An Appraisal of Analytic Models*. Chicago: University of Chicago Press.

Krohn, M. D. (1986) "The Web of Conformity: A Network Approach to the Explanation of Delinquent Behavior." *Social Problems* 33:581-93.

Kurtz, L. R. (1984) *Evaluating Chicago Sociology: A Guide to the Literature with an Annotated Bibliography*. Chicago: University of Chicago Press.

Kuznik, F. (1994) "An Uncommon Bond." *USA Weekend*, January 14-16, pp. 4-5.

Lemann, N. (1991) *The Promised Land: The Great Black Migration and How It Changed America*. New York: Knopf.

Lilly, J. R., F. T. Cullen, and R. A. Ball (1989) *Criminological Theory: Context and Consequences*. Newbury Park, CA: Sage.

Lin, N. (1986) "Conceptualizing Social Support." In N. Lin, A. Dean, and W. Edsel (eds.), *Social Support, Life Events, and Depression*, pp. 17-30. Orlando: Academic Press.

Lin, N., A. Dean, and W. Ensel, eds. (1986) *Social Support, Life Events, and Depression*. Orlando: Academic Press.

Lin, N., M. Y. Dumin, and M. Woelfel (1986) "Measuring Community and Network Support." In N. Lin, A. Dean, and W. Ensel (eds.), *Social Support, Life Events, and Depression*, pp. 153-70. Orlando: Academic Press.

Link, B. G., F. T. Cullen, E. Struening, P. E. Shrout, and B. G. Dohrenwend (1989) "A Modified Labeling Theory Approach to Mental Disorders: An Empirical Assessment." *American Sociological Review* 54:400-23.

Link, B. G., S. Schwartz, R. E. Moore, J. Phelan, E. L. Struening, C. A. Stueve, and M. E. Colton (1992) "Public Knowledge, Attitudes, and Beliefs toward Homeless People: Evidence for Compassion Fatigue?" Paper presented at the annual meeting of the American Public Health Association, Washington, DC.

Lipsey, M. W. (1992) "Juvenile Delinquency Treatment: A Meta-Analytic Inquiry into the Variability of Effects." In T. D. Cook, H. Cooper, D. S. Cordray, H. Hartmann, L. V. Hedges, R. J. Light, T. A. Louis, and F. Mosteller (eds.), *Meta-Analysis for Explanation: A Casebook*, pp. 83-127. New York: Russell Sage.

Loeber, R. and M. Le Blanc (1990) "Toward a Developmental Criminology." In M. Tonry and N. Morris (eds.), *Crime and Justice: A Review of Research*, vol. 12, pp. 375-473. Chicago: University of Chicago Press.

Loeber, R. and M. Stouthamer-Loeber (1986) "Family Factors as Correlates and Predictors of Juvenile Conduct Problems and Delinquency." In M. Tonry and N. Morris (eds.), *Crime and Justice: An Annual Review of Research*, vol. 7, pp. 29-149. Chicago: University of Chicago Press.

Lupo, A. (1994) "Still Yearning for the Great Society." *Boston Globe*, January 30, p. 66.

Lynch, J. (1995) "Crime in International Perspective." In J.Q. Wilson and J. Petersilia (eds.), *Crime*, pp. 11-38. San Francisco: ICS Press.

Makkai, T. and J. Braithwaite (1994) "Reintegrative Shaming and Compliance with Regulatory Standards." *Criminology* 32:361-85.

Massey, D. S. and N. A. Denton (1993) *American Apartheid: Segregation and the Making of the Underclass*. Cambridge, MA: Harvard University Press.

Mastrofski, S. D. (1988) "Community Policing as Reform: A Cautionary Tale." In J. D. Greene and S. D. Mastrofski (eds.), *Community Policing: Rhetoric or Reality*, pp. 47-68. New York: Praeger.

Matsueda, R. L. (1992) "Reflected Appraisals, Parental Labeling, and Delinquency: Specifying a Symbolic Interactionist Theory." *American Journal of Sociology* 6:1577-1611.

Maume, D. J., Jr. (1989) "Inequality and Metropolitan Rape Rates: A Routine Activity Approach." *Justice Quarterly* 6:513-27.

Mawhorr, T. L. (1992) "Unraveling the Attachment-Delinquency Link." Doctoral dissertation, Bowling Green State University.

McCarthy, B. and J. Hagan (1992) "Mean Streets: The Theoretical Significance of Situational Delinquency among Homeless Youths." *American Journal of Sociology* 98:597-627.

McCord, J. (1992) "Understanding Motivations: Considering Altruism and Aggression." In J. McCord (ed.), *Facts, Frameworks, and Forecasts: Advances in Criminological Theory*, vol. 3. New Brunswick, NJ: Transaction.

McDermott, M. J. (1994) "Criminology as Peacemaking, Feminist Ethics and the Victimization of Women." *Women and Criminal Justice* 5 (2):21-44.

Messner, S. F. (1980) "Income Inequality and Murder Rates: Some Cross-National Findings." *Comparative Social Research* 3:185-98.

——— (1986) "Geographical Mobility, Governmental Assistance to the Poor, and Rates of Urban Crime." *Journal of Crime and Justice* 9:1-18.

Messner, S. F. and M. D. Krohn (1990) "Class, Compliance Structures, and Delinquency: Assessing Integrated Structural-Marxist Theory." *American Journal of Sociology* 96:300-28.

Messner, S. F. and R. Rosenfeld (1994) *Crime and the American Dream*. Belmont, CA: Wadsworth.

Miller, J. G. (1991) *Last One Over the Wall: The Massachusetts Experiment in Closing Reform Schools.* Columbus: Ohio State University Press.

Murray, C. (1984) *Losing Ground: American Social Policy, 1950-1980.* New York: Basic Books.

Myers, L. B. and C. P. Chiang (1993) "Law Enforcement Officer and Peace Officer: Reconciliation Using the Feminine Approach." *Journal of Crime and Justice* 16 (2):31-41.

Nagin, D. S. and D. P. Farrington (1992) "The Stability of Criminal Potential from Childhood to Adulthood." *Criminology* 30:235-60.

Nagin, D. S. and R. Paternoster (1991) "On the Relationship of Past to Future Participation in Delinquency." *Criminology* 29:163-89.

National Institute of Justice (1992) *Community Policing in Seattle: A Model Partnership between Citizens and Police.* Washington, DC: National Institute of Justice.

Nurius, P. S., M. Furrey, and L. Berliner (1992) "Coping Capacity among Women with Abusive Partners." *Violence and Victims* 7:229-43.

Palmer, T. (1992) *The Re-Emergence of Correctional Intervention.* Newbury Park, CA: Sage.

Panel of High-Risk Youth (1993) *Losing Generations: Adolescents in High-Risk Settings.* Washington, DC: National Academy Press.

Pepinsky, H. E. (1988) "Violence as Unresponsiveness: Toward a New Conception of Crime." *Justice Quarterly* 4:539-63.

Pepinsky, H. E. and R. Quinney, eds. (1991) *Criminology as Peacemaking.* Bloomington: Indiana University Press.

Petersilia, J. (1992) "California's Prison Policy: Causes, Costs, and Consequences." *The Prison Journal* 72:8-36.

Petersilia, J. and S. Turner (1993) "Intensive Probation and Parole." In M. Tonry (ed.), *Crime and Justice: A Review of Research,* vol. 17, pp. 281-335. Chicago: University of Chicago Press.

Pfohl, S. J. (1985) *Images of Deviance and Social Control: A Sociological History.* New York: McGraw-Hill.

Platt, A. M. (1969) *The Child Savers: The Invention of Delinquency.* Chicago: University of Chicago Press.

Rand, A. (1987) "Transitional Life Events and Desistance from Delinquency and Crime." In M. E. Wolfgang, T. P. Thornberry, and R. M. Figlio (eds.), *From Boy to Man, from Delinquency to Crime,* pp. 134-62. Chicago: University of Chicago Press.

Rankin, J. H. and E. L. Wells (1990) "The Effect of Parental Attachments and Direct Controls on Delinquency." *Journal of Research in Crime and Delinquency* 27:140-65.

Regoli, R. M. and J. D. Hewitt (1994) *Delinquency in Society.* 2nd ed. New York: McGraw-Hill.

Reich, R. B., ed. (1988) *The Power of Public Ideas.* Cambridge, MA: Harvard University Press.

Reiss, A. J., Jr. (1988) "Co-Offending and Criminal Careers." In M. Tonry and N. Morris (eds.), *Crime and Justice: An Annual Review of Research,* vol. 10, pp. 117-70. Chicago: University of Chicago Press.

Reiss, A. J., Jr. and M. Tonry, eds. (1986) *Communities and Crime.* Chicago: University of Chicago Press.

Rivara, F. P. and D. P. Farrington (forthcoming) "Prevention of Violence: Role of the Pediatrician." *Archives of Pediatrics and Adolescent Medicine.*

Rosenfeld, R. (1986) "Urban Crime Rates: Effects of Inequality, Welfare Dependency, Region, and Race." In J. M. Byrne and R. J. Sampson (eds.), *The Social Ecology of Crime,* pp. 116-30. New York: Springer-Verlag.

Rothman, D. J. (1980) *Conscience and Convenience: The Asylum and Its Alternatives in Progressive America.* Boston: Little, Brown.

Sampson, R. J. (1986a) "Neighborhood Family Structure and the Risk of Personal Victimization." In J. M. Byrne and R. J. Sampson (eds.), *The Social Ecology of Crime,* pp. 25-46. New York: Springer-Verlag.

——— (1986b) "Crime in Cities: The Effects of Formal and Informal Social Control." In A. J. Reiss Jr. and M. Tonry (eds.), *Communities and Crime,* pp. 271-311. Chicago: University of Chicago Press.

Sampson, R. J. and W. B. Groves (1989) "Community Structure and Crime: Testing Social-Disorganization Theory." *American Journal of Sociology* 94:774-802.

Sampson, R. J. and J. H. Laub (1993) *Crime in the Making: Pathways and Turning Points through Life*. Cambridge, MA: Harvard University Press.

Saunders, D. G. and S. T. Azar (1989) "Treatment Programs for Family Violence." In L. Ohlin and M. Tonry (eds.), *Family Violence*, pp. 481-546. Chicago: University of Chicago Press.

Shaw, C. R. ([1930] 1966) *The Jack-Roller: A Delinquent Boy's Own Story*. Chicago: University of Chicago Press.

Shaw, C. R., with M. E. Moore ([1931] 1976) *The Natural History of a Delinquent Career*. Chicago: University of Chicago Press.

Shaw, C. R. and H. D. McKay (1942) *Juvenile Delinquency and Urban Areas*. Chicago: University of Chicago Press.

Sheley, J. F., ed. (1991) *Criminology: A Contemporary Handbook*. Belmont, CA: Wadsworth.

Sherman, L. W., with J. D. Schmidt and D. P. Rogan (1992) *Policing Domestic Violence: Experiments and Dilemmas*. New York: Free Press.

Short, J. F., Jr. (1990) "Cities, Gangs, and Delinquency." *Sociological Forum* 5:657-68.

——— (1991) "Poverty, Ethnicity, and Crime: Change and Continuity in U.S. Cities." *Journal of Research in Crime and Delinquency* 28:501-18.

Skolnick, J. H. and D. H. Bayley (1988) "Theme and Variation in Community Policing." In M. Tonry and N. Morris (eds.), *Crime and Justice: A Review of Research*, vol. 10, pp. 1-37. Chicago: University of Chicago Press.

Snodgrass, J. (1982) *The Jack-Roller at Seventy: A Fifty-Year Follow-Up*. Lexington, MA: Lexington Books.

Sparrow, M. K. (1988) *Implementing Community Policing*. Washington, DC: National Institute of Justice.

Spelman, W. and J. E. Eck (1987) *Problem-Oriented Policing*. Washington, DC: National Institute of Justice.

Steffensmeier, D. J. (1983) "Organization Properties and Sex-Segregation in the Underworld: Building a Sociological Theory of Sex Differences in Crime." *Social Forces* 61:1010-32.

Steffensmeier, D. J. and M. D. Harer (1993) "Bulging Prisons, An Aging U.S. Population, and the Nation's Crime Rate." *Federal Probation* 57 (June):3-10.

Straus, M. A. (1990) "Discipline and Deviance: Physical Punishment of Children and Violence and Other Crimes in Adulthood." *Social Problems* 38:133-54.

Sullivan, M. L. (1989) *"Getting Paid": Youth Crime and Work in the Inner City*. Ithaca: Cornell University Press.

Sutherland, E. H. (1949) *White Collar Crime*. New York: Holt, Rinehart and Winston.

Sutherland, E. H., D. R. Cressey, and D. F. Luckenbill (1992) *Principles of Criminology*. 11th ed. Dix Hills, NY: General Hall.

Sykes, G. M. and F. T. Cullen (1992) *Criminology*. 2nd ed. Fort Worth: Harcourt Brace Jovanovich.

Testa, M., B. A. Miller, W. R. Downs, and D. Panek (1992) "The Moderating Impact of Social Support Following Childhood Sexual Abuse." *Violence and Victims* 7:173-86.

Thrasher, F. M. ([1927] 1963) *The Gang: A Study of 1,313 Gangs in Chicago*. Abridged ed. Chicago: University of Chicago Press.

Thurman, Q. C. (1993) "The Police as a Community-Based Resource." Paper presented to the Oberman Faculty Seminar, University of Iowa.

Van Voorhis, P., F. T. Cullen, R. A. Mathers, and C. C. Garner (1988) "The Impact of Family Structure and Quality on Delinquency: A Comparative Assessment of Structure and Functional Factors." *Criminology* 26:235-61.

Vaux, A. (1988) *Social Support: Theory, Research, and Intervention*. New York: Praeger.

Vaux, A. and M. Ruggiero (1983) "Stressful Life Change and Delinquent Behavior." *American Journal of Community Psychology* 11:169-83.

Visher, C. A. (1987) "Incapacitation and Crime Control: Does a 'Lock 'Em Up' Strategy Reduce Crime?" *Justice Quarterly* 4:513-43.

Vito, G. F. and R. M. Holmes (1994) *Criminology: Theory, Research, and Policy*. Belmont, CA: Wadsworth.

Vold, G. B. and T. J. Bernard (1986) *Theoretical Criminology*. 3rd ed. New York: Oxford University Press.

Walsh, A. and T. A. Petee (1987) "Love Deprivation and Violent Juvenile Delinquency." *Journal of Crime and Justice* 10 (2):45-61.
Ward, J. V. (1988) "Urban Adolescents' Conceptions of Violence." In C. Gilligan, J. V. Ward, and J. M. Taylor (eds.) with B. Bardige, *Mapping the Moral Domain*, pp. 175-200. Cambridge, MA: Harvard University Press.
Wells, L. E. and J. H. Rankin (1991) "Families and Delinquency: A Meta-Analysis of the Impact of Broken Homes." *Social Problems* 38:71-93.
West, D. J. (1982) *Delinquency: Its Roots, Careers and Prospects.* Cambridge, MA: Harvard University Press.
Widom, C. S. (1989) "The Cycle of Violence." *Science* 244 (April 14):160-66.
Wilkinson, K. (1974) "The Broken Family and Juvenile Delinquency: Scientific Explanation or Ideology?" *Social Problems* 21:726-39.
Wilson, J. Q. and R. J. Herrnstein (1985) *Crime and Human Nature.* New York: Simon and Schuster.
Wilson, W. J. (1987) *The Truly Disadvantaged: The Inner City, the Underclass, and Public Policy.* Chicago: University of Chicago Press.
Wright, K. N. and K. E. Wright (1992) "Does Getting Married Reduce the Likelihood of Criminality? A Review of the Literature." *Federal Probation* 56 (September):50-56.
Wright, R. A. (1994) *In Defense of Prisons.* Westport, CT: Greenwood.
Wuthnow, R. (1991) *Acts of Compassion: Caring for Others and Helping Ourselves.* Princeton: Princeton University Press.
Wycoff, M. A. (1988) "The Benefits of Community Policing: Evidence and Conjecture." In J. R. Greene and S. D. Mastrofski (eds.), *Community Policing: Rhetoric or Reality*, pp. 103-20. New York: Praeger.
Zimring, F. and G. Hawkins (1991) *The Scale of Imprisonment.* Chicago: University of Chicago Press.
Zuravin, S. J. (1989) "The Ecology of Child Abuse and Neglect: Review of the Literature and Presentation of Data." *Violence and Victims* 4:101-20.

Part II
Cross-National Tests of Institutional-Anomie Theory

[6]

Political Restraint of the Market and Levels of Criminal Homicide: A Cross-National Application of Institutional-Anomie Theory *

STEVEN F. MESSNER, *University at Albany, SUNY*
RICHARD ROSENFELD, *University of Missouri — St. Louis*

Abstract

This article examines the effects on national homicide rates of political efforts to insulate personal well-being from market forces. Drawing upon recent work by Esping-Andersen and the institutional-anomie theory of crime, we hypothesize that levels of homicide will vary inversely with the "decommodification of labor." We develop a measure of decommodification based on levels and patterns of welfare expenditures and include this measure in a multivariate, cross-national analysis of homicide rates. The results support our hypothesis and lend credibility to the institutional-anomie perspective. The degree of decommodification is negatively related to homicide rates, net of controls for other characteristics of nations.

Interest in explaining differences among nations in rates of crime and violence is as old as the sociology of crime itself. The quantitative measurement of these differences by the nineteenth-century moral statisticians Quetelet and Guerry marks the beginning of scientific criminological inquiry (Beirne 1993). Marx also refers to national crime data in the course of developing his critique of the inherent flaws of capitalism. "There must be something rotten in the very core of a social system," Marx (1859) writes, "which increases its wealth without diminishing its misery, and increases in crimes even more rapidly than in numbers" (*New York Daily Tribune*).

In recent decades, there has been a resurgence of interest in cross-national criminological inquiry as reflected in a growing body of literature on the structural determinants of homicide rates.[1] Although there are some

Presented at the 46th annual meeting of the American Society of Criminology, 9-12 November, 1994, Miami, FL. We are grateful to the anonymous referees for helpful comments on an earlier draft of this manuscript. *Direct correspondence to Steven F. Messner, Department of Sociology, SUNY-Albany, Albany, NY 12222.*

1394 / *Social Forces* 75:4, June 1997

discrepancies in this literature, the research is supportive of Marx's general suspicion that fundamental features of the economic system affect societal levels of crime. A finding that has emerged with remarkable consistency is that high rates of homicide tend to accompany high levels of inequality in the distribution of income (Krahn, Hartnagel & Gartrell 1986; Neuman & Berger 1988). The cross-national research also indicates that there are additional features of a society's political economy, beyond that of income dispersion, that are systematically related to homicide rates. For example, evidence suggests that levels of homicide are associated with measures of the degree of economic discrimination against social groups (Messner 1989) and measures of the generosity of social welfare policies (Fiala & LaFree 1988; Gartner 1990, 1991).

The present article explores further the relationship between basic features of the economic and political systems of societies and levels of criminal homicide. Our specific focus is on the role of the market as a mechanism for distributing the material resources for personal well-being. Markets play a vital role in all capitalist societies, but, in some of these, physical survival and social position are not as dependent on market considerations as in others. Esping-Andersen (1990) has recently used the concept of the "decommodification of labor" to refer to policies that promote reliance on, or insulation from, pure market forces, and he has developed techniques for measuring this concept for a small sample of advanced capitalist nations. In this research, we build upon Esping-Andersen's work and propose a proxy measure of the decommodification of labor that can be used in multivariate analyses for a reasonably large sample of nations. We link the decommodification of labor specifically with crime by drawing upon a recently proposed macrosocial perspective in criminology: institutional-anomie theory. Our basic hypothesis is that homicide rates and decommodification vary inversely: the higher the level of political protection from the vicissitudes of the market, the lower the national homicide rate.

Decommodification and Crime in Market Society

Esping-Andersen's work on decommodification is part of a long standing intellectual and political tradition that emphasizes the importance of the welfare state in stabilizing market societies (e.g., Bellah et al. 1992; Marshall 1950; Polanyi 1944; Tawney 1920). Decommodification refers in the most general sense to the empowerment of the citizenry against the forces of the market. Decommodified social policies permit actions and choices by citizens — to get married, have children, seek higher education, engage in political activity — that are, in principle, unconstrained by market considerations. Decommodification frees people from the market.

There is some irony in this conception of the interrelation between the market and the state. In the classical writings of Enlightenment thinkers such as Adam Smith and David Hume, markets are depicted as social arrangements that liberate individuals from the restraints imposed by traditional institutions: the "free market" is an arena for the unfettered pursuit of self-interest (see Hirschman 1992). That the market itself impedes the exercise of free choice is a key intellectual claim of Marxist and social-democratic critics of modern capitalism. That citizens possess social rights and entitlements that transcend market considerations is the principal institutional claim made on the modern capitalist economy by the welfare state (Marshall 1950).

The basic issue of accommodating the market to the functioning of other social institutions is also relevant to the concerns of modernization theorists. In Parsons's (1966) influential formulation, modernization entails the increasing differentiation and interdependence of institutional subsystems. The decommodification policies of the welfare state can be viewed from this perspective as an equilibrating mechanism in highly differentiated societies.[2] In general, the concept of decommodification has been highly useful in attempts to understand the institutional functioning of modern market societies.

In Esping-Andersen's usage, decommodification refers to the granting of services and resources to citizens as a matter of right, thereby reducing their reliance on the market for sustenance and support (1990). It entails "emancipation" of citizens from the market in the most fundamental sense: "citizens can freely, and without potential loss of job, income, or general welfare, opt out of work when they themselves consider it necessary" (23). Decommodification involves considerably more than a society's level of expenditure on social welfare policies and programs. It reflects the quality as well as the quantity of social rights and entitlements. Three essential dimensions of entitlements are encompassed by decommodification: ease of access to them, their income-replacement value, and the range of social statuses and conditions they cover (Esping-Andersen 1990).

It is useful to think of a continuum of decommodified social policies along which societies may be arrayed. Near one end would be societies with highly decommodified policies, defined by nearly universal and nonconditional entitlements, with benefit levels close to average market incomes[3], covering most or all of the relevant causes and conditions for assistance (e.g., sickness, old age, unemployment, parenthood). Societies located near the other end would display correspondingly weaker decommodification, reflected in strict eligibility criteria for assistance, benefit levels well below prevailing market incomes, and a narrow range of statuses and conditions meriting assistance. At the extremes, fully decommodified policies would pay everyone a "social wage" guaranteeing a socially acceptable level of earnings regardless of market participation, and fully "commodified" policies would require strict and complete dependence on the market for the resources necessary for survival. Although no existing society can be found at either of the ideal-typical extremes of the continuum, market societies are enormously variable with respect to the level and types of social assistance available to their populations and the associated degree of decommodification.

Esping-Andersen does not relate the notion of decommodification directly to the phenomenon of crime. However, Messner and Rosenfeld's institutional-anomie perspective provides a plausible theoretical basis for predicting a relationship between the levels of serious crime in market society and the extent to which labor has been decommodified.

Institutional-anomie theory builds upon the classical anomie tradition, attributing high levels of crime to interrelated cultural and structural dynamics (Messner & Rosenfeld 1997; Rosenfeld & Messner 1994; cf. Chamlin & Cochran 1995). With respect to culture, a basic premise of the theory is that market mechanisms and arrangements are conducive to anomic pressures. Markets presuppose a materialistic goal-orientation among actors, and they promote a calculating, utilitarian orientation towards social relationships (Hirschman 1992:139). When these orientations develop to an extreme degree, anomie in the Mertonian sense is likely to ensue (Merton 1968). Goals — especially, but not exclusively, materialistic ones — receive strong cultural support, whereas the normative means regulating conduct begin to lose "their savor and their force" (Merton 1964:226). In such an anomic environment, actors are preoccupied with "outcomes" (Merton 1968:211), and the efficiency rather than the legitimacy of the means governs behavior. The resulting attenuation of normative controls is likely to lead to high levels of deviant behavior, including crime.[4]

Institutional-anomie theory also assigns a critical role to structural dynamics and, more specifically, to the balance among major social institutions (e.g., the economy, the family, the polity). In all societies of any complexity, the integration of social institutions is inherently problematic. This is because the claims of the social roles associated with the respective institutions are potentially contradictory and competing. For example, the demands and value-orientations associated with economic roles are at times incompatible with those of familial roles. The resolution of these conflicting claims in the course of ongoing social interaction yields a distinctive pattern of institutional relationships for the society at large — a distinctive "institutional balance of power" (Messner & Rosenfeld 1997:68-79).

According to institutional-anomie theory, the form of institutional structure that is particularly conducive to high levels of crime is one in which the economy dominates the institutional balance of power.[5] Economic dominance occurs when: (1) economic goals are assigned high priority in comparison with noneconomic goals; (2) the claims of economic roles are typically honored at the expense of those of noneconomic roles when conflicts occur; (3) social standing tends to be more highly dependent on the performance of economic roles than of noneconomic roles; and (4) the calculating, utilitarian logic of the marketplace penetrates other institutional realms.[6]

Economic dominance leads, in turn, to high rates of crime via two complementary processes. First, this type of institutional imbalance provides fertile soil for the growth of the anomic cultural pressures associated with market arrangements. This is because the noneconomic institutions that bear primary responsibility for cultivating respect for social norms, such as families and schools, are less capable of fulfilling their distinctive socialization functions. Second, economic dominance weakens the external social controls associated with institutional attachments. When the economy dominates the institutional balance of power, noneconomic roles become relatively unattractive. The result is relatively tenuous institutional engagement, weak social control, and high rates of crime.

This concept of economic dominance in the institutional balance of power, we propose, can be joined with Esping-Andersen's notion of decommodification to derive a hypothesis about societal levels of crime. As noted above, decommodification signals that the balance of institutional power in market society has shifted from the economy toward the polity; it implies that purely economic values and criteria are accommodated to collective, political considerations. The market is not permitted to operate according to its inherent logic alone but rather is subjected to political restraints. In other words, the decommodification of labor can serve as an indicator of one important dimension of the institutional balance of power — the balance between the economy and the polity. A greater degree of decommodification indicates a lower level of economic dominance in this particular institutional interrelationship. Given the general logic of institutional-anomie theory, then, the decommodification of labor should vary inversely with societal levels of crime, including the most serious of crimes — homicide.

We are aware of no previous efforts to join institutional-anomie theory with the concept of decommodification in the analysis of cross-national variation in homicide rates. Nevertheless, there is evidence consistent with our basic hypothesis. Fiala & LaFree (1988) find that measures of welfare expenditures are inversely related to child homicide rates in a cross-sectional analysis of 39 developed countries. Research by Gartner (1990) indicates that these beneficial effects of welfare policies apply to homicide victimization more generally. In a pooled, cross-sectional time-series analysis of 18 capitalist societies observed at five-year intervals between 1950-80, Gartner discovers significant negative effects of indicators of welfare spending on homicide rates for all age-sex-specific groups. Finally, Pampel and Gartner (1995) have examined the effects of a scale of "collectivism" on homicide rates in a cross-national analysis of the same 18 advanced capitalist societies studied by Gartner. The collectivism scale combines Esping-Andersen's decommodification index with indicators of corporatism, consensus government, Leftist political rule, and "governability" (the absence of violent political conflict). The collectivism scale has negative main effects on homicide rates, and it reduces the positive effect of the relative size of the youthful population on annual changes in homicide rates.

1398 / *Social Forces* 75:4, June 1997

These studies lend plausibility to our general hypothesis, but they are limited in important respects. As noted, the research by Fiala & LaFree (1988) is restricted to child homicide (see also Gartner 1991), while the results of the research by Gartner (1990) and Pampel & Gartner (1995) pertain only to the experiences of the 18 most advanced capitalist nations (albeit with observations for multiple time periods). The present study goes beyond these earlier efforts by developing a theoretically grounded measure of decommodification that can be employed in a multivariate analysis of overall homicide rates for a reasonably large sample of contemporary nations.

Before describing our measure of decommodification, it is important to confront a key conceptual issue. Esping-Anderson (1990) explicitly focuses his analyses on "advanced" nations and, more specifically, on the "advanced capitalist democracies" (1-2). He does so because these are the nations with the economic and political capacity to achieve a high degree of decommodification. The advanced capitalist democracies have sufficiently large economic surpluses to enable appreciable segments of the population to withdraw from the market, and they have political structures that are conducive to the emergence of class coalitions supportive of decommodification.

A legitimate question to raise, therefore, is whether the very concept of decommodification can be applied to a heterogeneous sample of nations at very different levels of development. We base our analysis on the assumption that decommodification is a meaningful property with which to describe industrial and industrializing nations in general because the provision of basic social security is a concern in virtually all such societies. This assumption is consistent with the underlying rationale for the comparative data sets on social transfers published by the International Labour Office (ILO), which serve as the source for our proxy measure of decommodification. The ILO observes that social security has become an important feature of the economy for member states in "nearly every country" (ILO 1992:3). To assess the applicability of decommodification to industrial nations generally, we have examined whether the effects of our decommodification measure on homicide rates differ significantly for the 18 nation subsample studied by Esping-Andersen and the remaining subsample of nations. As reported below, comparable effects are observed across these subsamples, which is consistent with our assumption that the concept of decommodification can be usefully applied to lesser-developed nations as well as to the advanced capitalist democracies.

Data and Methods

MEASURING DECOMMODIFICATION

Esping-Andersen's measure of decommodification encompasses three primary dimensions of the underlying concept: the ease of access to welfare benefits, their income-replacement value, and the expansiveness of coverage across different statuses and circumstances. A complex scoring system is used to operationalize each of these dimensions of decommodification for the three most important social welfare programs: pensions, sickness benefits, and unemployment compensation (1990). This scoring system reflects the "prohibitiveness" of conditions for eligibility, the disincentives for and duration of entitlements, and the degree to which benefits replace normal levels of earnings (1990). The indices for these three types of social welfare programs are then aggregated into a combined index reflecting the overall decommodification characteristic of a given nation's social welfare system.

Esping-Andersen is able to operationalize decommodification in this unique way by using highly detailed information on social policies from an original data source — the Svensk Socialpolitik i International Bleysning (the SSIB data files). The data were collected at the Swedish Institute for Social Research over an eight-year period, beginning in 1981, through contacts with numerous officials in government departments and statistical offices in different nations (1990). Although Esping-Andersen's approach to measuring decommodification is highly appealing from a theoretical standpoint, his measure has been constructed for only 18 capitalist nations. The explanatory scope using this measure will therefore apply to only the most highly developed market societies, and the small size of the resulting sample will seriously limit the possibilities for including decommodification in multivariate statistical analyses. Moreover, the procedures employed by Esping-Andersen to construct his index require data on social policies that are not available in published sources.

To overcome these limitations, we have developed a proxy measure of decommodification for an appreciably larger sample of nations (maximum $N = 45$). The proxy measure is based on data compiled by the International Labor Office (ILO) on the financial operations of national social security systems. These data include information on absolute and relative levels of expenditures for social security programs, on funding sources for these programs, and on the distribution of the expenditures across different program types (e.g., unemployment benefits, family allowances, work-related injuries). Our approach is based on the assumption that general expenditure patterns reflect the underlying logic of social welfare systems. Consequently, indicators of these general patterns are likely to be correlated with the more refined and theoretically informed measure of decommodification developed by Esping-Andersen.

We have examined the relationships between Esping-Andersen's decommodification index and a variety of indicators of social security expenditures in the 1980s for the 18 advanced capitalist nations included in the SSIB data files. The indicators encompass four important features of the social security systems: (1) the priority given to social welfare spending, as reflected in expenditures as a percent of total gross domestic product (ILO 1992, Table 3); (2) the generosity of social welfare spending, as reflected in

1400 / *Social Forces* 75:4, June 1997

average annual expenditures per head of population in U.S. dollars (Table 5); (3) the financing of social security systems, as reflected in the percentage of total receipts according to origin (Table 8); and (4) the range of entitlements, as reflected in the percentage distribution of benefit expenditures across different program types (Table 10).[7]

Esping-Andersen's decommodification index is strongly associated with three of the indicators of expenditure patterns. Expenditure levels as a percent of GDP and average annual expenditures per capita exhibit large positive correlations with the decommodification index (.75 and .81, respectively). An indicator of the distribution of expenditures across program types — the percent of total benefit expenditures allocated to employment injuries — also yields a sizeable correlation with the decommodification index: r =.-.67. The negative sign of this coefficient is theoretically meaningful because it implies that a large share of welfare benefits is not available to all citizens as a basic entitlement but, rather, is contingent on participation in the labor market. Only employed workers can receive benefits for employment injuries. Welfare systems that impose this type of restriction on access are therefore less decommodifying than those covering a wider range of circumstances independent of market participation (e.g., programs such as family allowances and maternity benefits).

Analogous results are obtained in a principal components factor analysis of the decommodification index and the full range of expenditure indicators. The decommodification index, average annual benefits per household, expenditures as a percent of GDP, and the percent of benefit expenditures allocated to employment injuries all load highly on the same factor. These four measures thus exhibit a high level of shared variance, suggesting that they converge on a common, underlying dimension.[8]

Given these results, we have computed a proxy decommodification index by summing the z-scores for the three indicators of expenditure patterns that are highly intercorrelated with Esping-Andersen's index and that cluster along the same dimension.[9] The resulting composite index is highly correlated with Esping-Andersen's original decommodification measure: r = .84. Our proxy measure thus exhibits strong predictive validity for the 18 nations with data from the Swedish data source, the SSIB.

It is possible to compute the decommodification proxy measure for a fairly large sample of nations (a maximum of 55) using ILO (1992) data for the mid-1980s. The presence of missing data on other variables (explained below) limits the sample size for the analysis to 45 cases. The proxy measure of decommodification yields a respectable level of reliability for this sample: alpha coefficient = .702.

DEPENDENT VARIABLE

The dependent variable for the analysis is the homicide rate per 100,000 population as reported in the World Health Organization's (WHO) *World*

Health Statistics Annual (various years). WHO defines homicide as death by injury purposely inflicted by others. One limitation of the WHO data on homicide is that underdeveloped nations, especially those in Africa and Asia, are not well represented in this data source (Krahn, Hartnagel & Gartrell 1986). Therefore caution should be exercised in generalizing our findings to the larger population of nations. In addition, the WHO data on homicide may be biased because they necessarily exclude deaths with undetermined cause, some of which may be homicides. Nevertheless, Kalish (1988) argues that the WHO data serve as the best source of information on homicide for international comparisons because they are "based on an actual count of deceased persons" and therefore are not susceptible to biases resulting from intercountry differences in the treatment of "attempted homicides."[10]

To minimize the effect of random yearly fluctuations in homicide levels, we follow the conventional practice of computing multi-year averages (Kick & LaFree 1985; Krahn, Hartnagel & Gartrell 1986). The averages refer to the 1980-90 period, or in cases with missing data, to the subset of years within that period for which data are available. We employ an extended time period for measuring homicide (a maximum of 11 years) because decommodification is conceptualized as a basic structural feature of societies that is not likely to vary in a meaningful way over the short run.

Examination of the univariate distribution for homicide rates reveals considerable skewness. The value for the highest nation (Colombia, 41.2) is approximately 6.5 times the mean value for the sample at large (6.27). We accordingly convert homicide rates to natural logarithms to reduce skewness and induce homogeneity in error variance.[11] Although the log transformation successfully reduces the overall degree of skewness in the homicide distribution, a possible outlier remains at the lower tail of the distribution. The logged value for Syria (-3.00; untransformed value = .05) is considerably smaller than the value for the nation (Egypt) with the next smallest value (-.38; untransformed value = .69). The possibility that this case is an atypical one that distorts the regression estimates is addressed in the statistical analysis.

CONTROL VARIABLES

Data have also been collected on additional characteristics of nations to serve as controls. Previous comparative research on homicide typically includes some combination of indicators of the general economic well-being of national populations and of demographic structure (see LaFree & Kick 1986, and Neuman & Berger 1988, for comprehensive reviews). Consistent with this research, we have collected information on the following socioeconomic and demographic characteristics of nations:[12] gross national product per capita in U.S. dollars; infant mortality rate (under age 1); life expectancy at birth; percent of the population over 64 years of age; average annual population growth 1980-85; percent of the population urban; males per 100 females.

GNP per capita and the sex ratio are logged transformed to reduce the effect of cases with extreme values. With the exception of the measure of population growth, the time of measurement for these socioeconomic and demographic characteristics is 1985, the midpoint of the 1980-90 period, or the closest year with available data. The sources for the sex ratio and percent over 64 years of age are the Population Reference Bureau's (1987) *Population Data Sheet* and United Nations' (various years) *Demographic Yearbook*. The other measures are taken from the World Bank's (1987) *World Development Report*.

In the comparative homicide literature, age structure is typically measured by an indicator of the relative size of the young population. This approach is based on the assumption that the young population is at a relatively high risk of offending (see Krahn, Hartnagel & Gartrell 1986). We employ a measure of the relative size of the elderly population because this variable has been identified as a key determinant of welfare expenditures (Wilensky 1975; see also Pampel, Williamson & Stryker 1990), and because the elderly are likely to have low homicide offending rates (thereby creating the possibility of spuriousness in the bivariate relationship between homicide rates and social welfare measures). Not surprisingly, measures of the youthful population and the elderly population are strongly correlated. The correlation between percent less than 15 years of age and the percent over 64 for the sample of 45 nations is -.90. Thus, the results of our regression analyses are highly similar if the former measure of age structure is substituted for the latter.

Several of the control variables are strongly intercorrelated. To simplify the regressor space and lessen the problem of multicollinearity (Land, McCall & Cohen 1990), a principal components analysis has been performed on these socioeconomic and demographic variables. The results reveal that all the measures except the sex ratio cluster along a single dimension (the eigenvalue for the principal component is 4.2, and the variance explained is 71%). The positive pole of this dimension reflects socioeconomic development, as indicated by high life expectancy, high GNP/capita, low infant mortality, relatively large elderly populations, slow population growth, and high levels of urban development. These measures have been combined into a "development index" using the loadings from the principal components analysis as weights.

Two additional variables are also relevant to the analysis on both empirical and theoretical grounds. As noted earlier, previous cross-national research indicates that economic inequality is one of the more important structural correlates of homicide rates. It seems likely that decommodification and economic inequality are inversely related to one another. Decommodification should reduce the dispersion in incomes as well as lessen reliance on the market for economic well-being. However, to the degree that decommodified social welfare practices reflect the broader balance of power between the polity and the economy, as suggested by institutional-anomie theory, decommodification is expected to have an effect on the level of crime independent of its relationship with inequality.

FIGURE 1: Scatterplot of Homicide Rates and Decommodification Scores for Esping Andersen's 18 Nation Sample

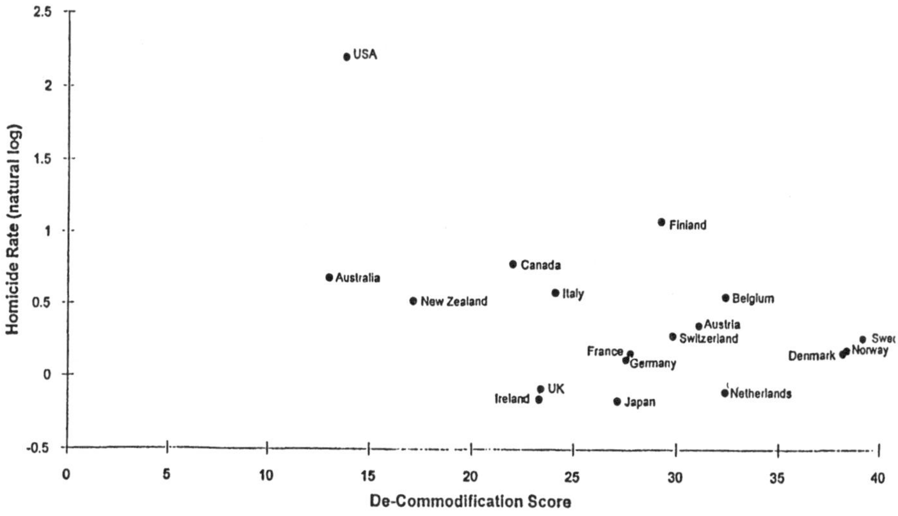

We include two measures of economic inequality. One is the commonly used Gini coefficient of household income distribution. The primary data source for this measure is Hoover (1989), supplemented in a few cases with data from Krahn, Hartnagel & Gartrell (1986). Unfortunately, the available data for the Gini coefficient of income inequality refer to the period "circa 1969" (Hoover 1989), which is earlier than our time period of interest (1980-90). Although income distribution is a reasonably stable feature of societies (Muller 1988), the measurement error associated with this time lag could attenuate the effects of income inequality in our analyses.

The second measure reflects an ascriptive form of economic inequality: economic discrimination against social groups. The specific measure is an ordinal rating scale based on expert judgments about the extent to which groups experience objective economic disadvantages that are attributable to deliberate discrimination. A nation's score represents the most extreme level of economic discrimination experienced by any minority group in that nation. The economic discrimination index is based on information contained in the "Minorities at Risk" data file compiled by Gurr (Gurr & Scarritt 1989).

Data for all variables except the Gini coefficient and economic discrimination are available for the maximum sample of 45 nations (see Appendix A). In the analysis of this sample, mean substitution is applied to cases with missing data on the two measures of economic inequality. We also conduct parallel analyses on the subsample of nations with complete data across all variables to assess the sensitivity of the results to mean substitution.

1404 / *Social Forces* 75:4, June 1997

TABLE 1: OLS Regressions of the Average Homicide Rate, 1980-90, on the Proxy Decommodification Index and Controls

	Equation			
	1	2	3	4
Independent variable				
Development index	-.104* [-.342]	-.017 [-.057]	-.097* [-.355]	-.097* [-.363]
Gini coefficient of income inequality	3.802 [.246]	3.274 [.212]	1.474 [.108]	1.432 [.108]
Economic discrimination index	.213* [.226]	.172 [.182]	.151* [.180]	.146 [.176]
Sex ratio (ln)	-5.709* [-.248]	-5.754* [-.250]	-5.509* [-.268]	-5.551 [-.157]
Decommodification index	—	-.209* [-.386]	- .161* [-.334]	-.161* [-.337]
R^2	.357	.402	.547	.548
Adjusted R^2	.293	.326	.487	.480
N	45	45	44	39

[a] Standardized regression coefficients are reported in brackets. Homicide rates are log (ln) transformed.

* Unstandardized regression coefficient is at least 1.5 times its standard error.

Results

Before turning to the multivariate analysis of homicide rates for the full sample of nations, it is instructive to examine the bivariate relationship between levels of homicide and Esping-Andersen's original decommodification index for the 18 advanced capitalist nations with available data. As expected, the Pearson correlation coefficient is inverse and statistically significant at the .05 level despite the small sample: r = -.48.[13] Nations with greater decommodification scores thus tend to have lower homicide rates.

Figure 1 presents the scatterplot for these two variables. A striking feature of the scatterplot is the distinctiveness of the U.S. Even with homicide rates expressed in natural logarithms, the rate for the U.S. is unusually high. The U.S. also has a very low decommodification score (the second from the bottom), suggesting that this case plays a major role in producing the observed inverse association.[14] It is thus important to determine whether decommodification exhibits the predicted association with homicide rates in a larger sample of nations not as sensitive to the influence of any single case.

The bivariate relationship between the decommodification proxy measure and homicide rates for the sample of 45 nations is highly similar to that observed with the original measure in the smaller 18-nation sample: $r = -.52$ (see Appendix B). Of course, the nations in this larger sample are quite heterogeneous, raising the possibility that at least some of the simple association between decommodification and homicide is confounded with the effects of other structural characteristics of nations.

To assess this possibility, we turn to the multivariate analyses. Table 1 reports the estimates from four multiple regressions. The first column of the table provides a baseline model that includes only the control variables. Consistent with past research (Krahn, Hartnagel & Gartrell 1986; Messner 1989), the two indicators of economic inequality — the Gini coefficient of income dispersion and the index of economic discrimination against social groups — yield moderate positive effects on homicide rates, although the coefficient for the Gini coefficient does not quite reach statistical significance. Both the development index and the sex ratio are negatively related to homicide rates. The negative coefficient for development is consistent with the "modernization thesis" on crime, which predicts a decline in rates of violent crime with greater urbanization and industrialization (Gurr 1989; Shelley 1981). This finding is similarly compatible with arguments that development is associated with reduced opportunities for the kinds of interpersonal contacts that lead to homicide (LaFree & Kick 1986). In addition, the negative effect of development probably reflects demographic factors captured by the composite index (an elderly population and low population- growth rates).

The negative association observed for the sex ratio is counter-intuitive. It indicates that low homicide rates tend to be found in nations with large numbers of males relative to females. This association is contrary to individual-level research on criminal violence, which shows higher levels of victimization and offending for males, but it is compatible with arguments by Messner & Sampson (1991). They suggest that low sex ratios may promote family arrangements that are conducive to crime and that counterbalance the crime-reducing compositional effect at the macro-level of relatively small male populations.

In equation 2, the decommodification proxy index is added to the baseline model. The results are consistent with theoretical predictions. Decommodification exhibits a significant, negative relationship with homicide rates net of the control variables. The standardized coefficient ($B = -.386$) is moderately strong and is the largest for any of the predictors in this model.[15] Comparing across equations 1 and 2, including the decommodification measure in the model reduces slightly the effect of the Gini coefficient and the economic discrimination index, while the coefficient for the sex ratio remains virtually unchanged. The most dramatic change is observed for the development index, the effects of which become trivial in equation 2.

Equation 3 estimates the same model as equation 2 for the subsample of 44 nations without Syria, an outlier on homicide. Excluding this case raises

1406 / *Social Forces* 75:4, June 1997

TABLE 2: Effects of the Proxy Decommodification Index on the Average Homicide Rate, 1980-90, across Alternative Specifications

	Sample[a]		
Model	A	B	C
1. Excluding the development index	-.227* [-.419]	-.258* [-.535]	-.232* [-.487]
2. Excluding the Gini coefficient	-.225* [-.414]	-.166* [-.345]	-.159* [-.333]
3. Excluding the economic discrimination index	-.240* [-.443]	-.187* [-.387]	-.187* [-.392]
4. Excluding the sex ratio (ln)	-.208* [-.383]	-.160* [-.331]	-.175* [-.367]
N	45	44	39

[a] Standardized regression coefficients are reported in brackets. Homicide rates are log (ln) transformed.
[b] Sample A is the maximum sample yielded with mean substitution for income inequality and economic discrimination; sample B excludes Syria; sample C is the sample yielded with listwise deletion of cases with missing values.
* Unstandardized regression coefficient is at least 1.5 times its standard error.

the explanatory power of the model appreciably (compare the adjusted R^2s) and increases the observed effect of the development index in comparison with the previous model. The effect for the decommodification index is lessened slightly in equation 3 in comparison with equation 2, but it remains significant and moderately strong.

In the final equation (equation 4), the analysis is repeated without mean substitution, which is required in the analysis of the larger samples for cases with missing values on the Gini coefficient and the economic discrimination index. The results for the theoretically strategic measure prove to be very similar to those in the previous equations. Nations with high scores on the decommodification index tend to have low homicide rates, net of the effects of the other variables in the models.[16]

To assess further the sensitivity of the effects of the decommodification proxy to alternative specifications, we re-estimate the regressions deleting each of the control variables, one at a time. These analyses are performed on the full sample of nations, the subsample without Syria, and the subsample without mean substitution. Table 2 reports the regression coefficients for the decommodification proxy across these alternative specifications for the respective samples. The results reveal a highly robust pattern. Consistent with our theoretical argument, the coefficients for decommodification are negative, significant, and moderately strong in all specifications.

Our findings for other predictors of homicide are less stable, as shown in Table 1, although the overall patterns of relationships are theoretically meaningful. The instability in the estimates for the development index may reflect problems of multicollinearity. Despite our efforts to simplify the covariance structure of predictors through principal components indexing, a troublesome degree of multicollinearity remains for this variable.[17] We also suspect that the rather unimpressive effects of income inequality are attributable, at least in part, to measurement error (noted earlier) resulting from the time lag between the measurement of inequality and homicide rates.

Finally, we consider the possibility that the observed effect of decommodification applies only to the nations originally studied by Esping-Andersen and not to other nations in the sample. We do so by creating a dummy variable coded 1 for nations in Esping-Andersen's sample and 0 for the other nations, and by constructing a product term for this dummy variable and the decommodification proxy. The product term is then added to the regression models for each of the three samples reported in Table 1, along with the constituent terms. In all cases, the coefficients for the product term fail to attain statistical significance. This finding suggests that the net effect of decommodification on homicide rates for the nations originally studied by Esping-Andersen is comparable to the effect observed for the other nations in the analysis.

SUMMARY AND CONCLUSIONS

In this article, we have addressed the consequences of political restraints on the market for societal levels of lethal violence. Drawing upon recent work on the nature of welfare state regimes, the institutional-anomie theory of crime, and previous cross-national analyses of homicide, we have derived a specific hypothesis that overall levels of homicide will be lower in capitalist societies that have decommodified labor by reducing dependence on the market for personal well-being. This hypothesis has been tested in cross-national regression analyses using a theoretically grounded measure of decommodification, along with relevant controls.

The results support our basic hypothesis. Controlling for a wide range of other structural characteristics of nations, the decommodification measure exhibits a significant negative effect on homicide rates. This effect is moderately strong and is robust across alternative specifications and varying subsamples. Our analyses thus replicate the findings of previous cross-national studies of homicide that have incorporated measures of social welfare spending, and they indicate that these earlier findings are generalizable to larger samples of nations and to more inclusive measures of homicide.

Our research also lends credibility to the theoretical perspective informing the analysis — the institutional-anomie theory of crime — and helps to empirically distinguish this perspective from more conventional stratification-based accounts of variation across societies in the level of homicide. Although these perspectives are in many respects complementary, there are two important distinctions between them.

First, institutional-anomie theory broadens the *structural* focus of traditional economic stress or deprivation perspectives by directing attention to aspects of the economic organization of market societies beyond the stratification system, and to the interplay of the economy and other social institutions. In this article, we have restricted our attention to restraints imposed on market economies by the political system. Additional research is needed on the role of other institutions, such as the kinship, religious, and educational systems, in fostering or curbing crime in market societies. Such an expanded institutional focus might help to account for nations such as Japan and Ireland, which have exceptionally low levels of homicide among the developed countries, and yet only moderate scores on the decommodification index (see Figure 1). In the case of Japan, we would attribute the low rate of homicide to the prominent role of the family and its restraining influence on the anomic forces emanating from the market (cf. Adler 1983). It would seem promising to pursue in further research the corresponding role of organized religion in a nation such as Ireland.

A second difference between institutional-anomie theory and more traditional economic perspectives on societal levels of crime involves the significance assigned by institutional-anomie theory to *cultural* orientations, which ostensibly operate in tandem with features of economic stratification. It is not possible to document any such cultural effects with the existing data because valid and reliable measures of culture are not available for cross-national analysis, but it is interesting to note that our development index captures to some extent levels of economically induced deprivation via the indicators of overall economic resources (GDP/capita) and life chances (infant mortality and life expectancy). The effects of decommodification on homicide rates net of the development index are thus at least suggestive of the kinds of cultural dynamics postulated by institutional-anomie theory.[18] Nevertheless, further research is clearly needed to clarify the precise nature of the social mechanisms linking the welfare state, institutional balance, and levels of crime and violence in market societies.

We close with a final comment on the practical implications of our analysis. It is hardly an exaggeration to claim that the current era is one of profound social change in the history of capitalism. With the fall of the Soviet empire and with the economic reforms taking place in the People's Republic of China, a much larger segment of the world's population is exposed to market arrangements. Moreover, in the U.S. and other advanced capitalist societies, there have been growing concerns about the scope, cost, and even the very logic of the welfare state (e.g., Stevenson 1995; Whitney 1995). If the findings reported here are sustained in subsequent research, then proposals to substantially reduce social welfare spending and deregulate market economies should be considered with due regard for unintended social consequences, including possibly higher rates of criminal violence.

Notes

1. See, for example, Archer & Gartner (1984); Avison & Loring (1986); Braithwaite & Braithwaite (1980); Conklin & Simpson (1985); Fiala & LaFree (1988); Gartner (1990); Groves, McCleary & Newman (1985); Kick & LaFree (1985); Krahn, Hartnagel & Gartrell (1986); Krohn (1976); LaFree & Kick (1986); Messner (1980, 1982, 1989); and Wellford (1974).

2. From a more critical perspective, the function of the welfare state is to stabilize the capitalist economic order and legitimate class rule (Habermas 1989; O'Connor 1973). See Esping-Andersen (1990:12-14) for a discussion of the similarities between structural functionalist and Marxist approaches to the modernization process.

3. Esping-Andersen (1990) defines the market replacement value of social entitlements as the difference between benefit levels and "normal earnings or the standard of living considered adequate and acceptable in the society" (47).

4. Merton directs attention to the contemporary U.S. in his discussion of the nature and sources of anomie, as do Messner and Rosenfeld (1997) in their discussion. However, as Gouldner (1970) suggests, Merton's arguments (and by extension Messner and Rosenfeld's) can be applied more generally to societies dominated by a market economy, i.e., to "bourgeois utilitarian societies." In Gouldner's words: "The 'almost exclusive concern with outcomes' to which Merton refers is a distinctive characteristic of utilitarian culture; it is not an aberration of utilitarian society but its normal cultural emphasis" (1970:68; see also Rosenfeld & Messner 1997).

5. Messner and Rosenfeld's discussion of economic dominance in the institutional balance of power raises themes similar to those contained in Currie's analysis of a "market society" as distinct from a "market economy." According to Currie (1991:255), a market society refers to "one in which the pursuit of private gain becomes the organizing principle of all areas of social life — not simply a mechanism that we may use to accomplish certain circumscribed economic ends."

6. John Gagnon comments on the general tendency in market societies for the logic of the economy to permeate discourse over an ever widening range of social phenomena, both inside and outside academic social science: "Within the social sciences there has been a 100-year struggle to extend the reach of economic metaphors and analyses to include all aspects of mental and social life. Outside the social sciences, in practical society, a parallel attempt to subject all forms of conduct to the discipline of commodification and pricing has become part of the normal order" (Gagnon 1994:1078).

7. The categories for the origin of social security receipts are: contributions from insured persons, contributions from employers, special taxes, state participation, other public participation, income from capital, and "other" receipts. The categories for the distribution of benefits are: sickness-maternity, employment injuries, pensions, unemployment, and family allowances.

8. The factor loadings for the decommodification index, average annual benefits per household, expenditures as a percent of GDP, and the percent of benefit expenditures allocated to employment injuries are .90, .86, .82, and -.82 respectively. Although these loadings are reasonably high, some unshared variance obviously remains. This probably reflects the limitations of expenditure data as indicators of the "theoretical substance of

the welfare state," as well as random measurement error. See Esping-Andersen (1990:18-21).

9. In the construction of the index, we reverse the polarity of the item on the distribution of benefits by using the percentage of benefits distributed to categories other than employment injuries (i.e., 100 — "the percent distributed to employment injuries"). This ensures that all items are scored in a consistent direction.

10. See Bennett and Lynch (1990), Huang (1993), Kalish (1988), and Messner (1992) for discussions of the quality and comparability of international crime statistics.

11. We plotted the residuals from an OLS regression of the untransformed homicide rate against predicted *Y* values. The scatterplot conforms to a classic heteroskedastic "fan" pattern, with greater variance in residuals for higher predicted *Y* values (Hamilton 1992:117). The plot for residuals with the transformed homicide rates reveals a more homoskedastic distribution. The transformation of homicide rates implies that the modeled relationship between homicide and other variables is curvilinear with respect to the original metrics. For a discussion of the interpretation of regression coefficients under different transformations, see Hamilton (1992:145-82).

12. Three additional controls were considered in preliminary analyses but were excluded because they consistently failed to yield appreciable net associations with homicide rates: population size, population density, and Gurr's institutionalized democracy index (ICPSR 1990).

13. Although tests of statistical significance are not technically applicable given the nonrandom nature of the sample, we nevertheless follow the common practice of reporting significance as a rule-of-thumb to identify nontrivial relationships. The criterion for significance in the regression analysis is a *t* ratio of 1.5, which corresponds approximately to the .05 level (one-tailed test).

14. With the U.S. removed from the sample, the correlation between the homicide rate and decommodification score drops to $r = -.25$. Although still in the expected direction and moderately strong, this correlation is not statistically significant for the remaining 17 nation sample. The outlier status of the U.S. in the homicide distribution depicted in Figure 1 is consistent with the hypothesis derived from institutional-anomie theory that a society characterized by economic dominance will have unusually high levels of serious crime. See Messner and Rosenfeld (1997). More generally, the proposition that the U.S. is distinctive on a number of social and cultural dimensions when compared with other advanced industrial nations is part of the thesis of "American exceptionalism." See Lipset (1996) for a recent statement.

15. In this larger sample of nations, removing the U.S. has a minor impact on the observed relationship between the decommodification proxy and homicide rates. The association is still moderately inverse and statistically significant. The unstandardized regression coefficient without the U.S. is -.200; the *B* coefficient is -.361.

16. We computed values of Cook's D for each of the three subsamples in Table 1 to search for influential cases in the estimation of regression parameters. No case reaches the generally accepted critical value of "1" on this diagnostic statistic. As a further check for a disproportionate impact of a single case or a small number of cases on the parameter estimates, we performed a robust regression on the full sample using the Huber iteratively reweighted least squares technique (Hamilton 1992:183-216). The robust WLS results for the decommodification index are virtually identical to those obtained through OLS: the unstandardized coefficients are -.217 and -.209, respectively.

Institutional-Anomie Theory / 1411

17. Appendix C reports variance inflation factors (VIF) for the independent variables in the analyses of the respective samples. The values for the development index in all instances exceed the conventional threshold for high multicollinearity of 4.0. This problem is particularly severe in the analysis of the 39 nation sample without mean substitution. The VIFs for the decommodification proxy, however, are always below the conventional criterion.

18. Similarly, in her analysis of the relationships between family structure, welfare expenditures, and child homicide, Gartner (1991) proposes a broader interpretation of indicators of welfare practices, suggesting that "perhaps spending on social programs should be thought of as an indicator of a cultural orientation or social ideology inhibiting personal violence" (238).

References

Adler, Freda. 1983. *Nations Not Obsessed with Crime*. Rothman.

Archer, Dane, and Rosemary Gartner. 1984. *Violence and Crime in Cross-National Perspective*. Yale University Press.

Avison, William R. and Pamela L. Loring. 1986. "Population Diversity and Cross-National Homicide: The Effects of Inequality and Heterogeneity." *Criminology* 24:733-49.

Beirne, Piers. 1993. *Inventing Criminology*. SUNY Press.

Bellah, Robert N., Richard Madsen, William M. Sullivan, Ann Swidler, and Steven M. Tipton. 1992. *The Good Society*. Knopf.

Bennett, Richard R. and James P. Lynch. 1990. "Does Difference Make a Difference? Comparing Cross-National Crime Indicators." *Criminology* 28:153-81.

Braithwaite, John and V. Braithwaite. 1980. "The Effect of Income Inequality and Social Democracy on Homicide." *British Journal of Criminology* 20:45-53.

Chamlin, Mitchell B. and John K. Cochran. 1995. "Assessing Messner and Rosenfeld's Institutional Anomie Theory: A Partial Test." *Criminology* 33:411-29.

Conklin, George H. and Miles E. Simpson. 1985. "A Demographic Approach to the Cross-National Study of Homicide." *Comparative Social Research* 8:171-85.

Currie, Elliot. 1991. "Crime in the Market Society." *Dissent* (Spring):254-59.

Esping-Andersen, Gosta. 1990. *The Three Worlds of Welfare Capitalism*. Princeton University Press.

Fiala, Robert and Gary LaFree. 1988. "Cross-National Determinants of Child Homicide." *American Sociological Review* 53:432-45.

Gagnon, John H. 1994. "Review Essay: The Dismal Science and Sex." *American Journal of Sociology* 99:1078-82.

Gartner, Rosemary. 1990. "The Victims of Homicide: A Temporal and Cross-National Comparison." *American Sociological Review* 55:92-106.

____. 1991. "Family Structure, Welfare Spending, and Child Homicide in Developed Democracies." *Journal of Marriage and the Family* 53:231-40.

Gouldner, Alvin W. 1970. *The Coming Crisis of Western Sociology*. Basic Books.

Groves, W. Byron, Richard McCleary, and Graeme R. Newman. 1985. "Religion, Modernization, and World Crime." *Comparative Social Research* 8:59-78.

Gurr, Ted Robert. 1989. "Historical Trends in Violent Crime: Europe and the United States." Pp. 21-54 in *Violence in America*. Vol. 1, edited by T.R. Gurr. Sage.

Gurr, Ted Robert, and James R. Scarritt. 1989. "Minorities at Risk: A Global Study." *Human Rights Quarterly* 11:375-405.

Habermas, Jurgen. 1989. "The Crisis of the Welfare State and the Exhaustion of Utopian Energies." Pp. 284-99 in *Jurgen Habermas On Society and Politics: A Reader*, edited by Steven Seidman. Beacon Press.

Hamilton, Lawrence C. 1992. *Regression with Graphics: A Second Course in Statistics*. Duxbury Press.

Hirschman, Albert O. 1992. *Rival Views of Market Society and Other Recent Essays*. Harvard University Press.

Hoover, Gary A. 1989. "International Inequality: A Cross-National Data Set." *Social Forces* 67:1008-26.

Huang, W.S. Wilson. 1993. "Are International Murder Data Valid and Reliable? Some Evidence to Support the Use of Interpol Data." *International Journal of Comparative and Applied Criminal Justice* 17:77-89.

ICPSR. 1990. "Polity II: Political Structure and Regime Change, 1800-1986: Summary." *Inter-University Consortium for Political and Social Research*, Machine-Readable Datafile (Study #9263; Principal Investigator: Ted Robert Gurr).

ILO (International Labour Office). 1992. *The Cost of Social Security*. International Labour Office.

Kalish, Carol B. 1988. *International Crime Rates*. U.S. Department of Justice.

Kick, Edward L., and Gary D. LaFree. 1985. "Development and the Social Context of Murder." *Comparative Social Research* 8:37-58.

Krahn, Harvey, Timothy F. Hartnagel, and John W. Gartrell. 1986. "Income Inequality and Homicide Rates: Cross-National Data and Criminological Theories." *Criminology* 24:269-95.

Krohn, Marvin D. 1976. "Inequality, Unemployment, and Crime: A Cross-National Analysis." *Sociological Quarterly* 17:303-313.

LaFree, Gary D., and Edward L. Kick. 1986. "Cross-National Effects of Developmental, Distributional, and Demographic Variables on Crime: A Review and Analysis." *International Annals of Criminology* 24:213-35.

Land, Kenneth C., Patricia L. McCall, and Lawrence E. Cohen. 1990. "Structural Covariates of Homicide Rates: Are There Any Invariances Across Time and Social Space?" *American Journal of Sociology* 95:922-63.

Lipset, Seymour Martin. 1996. *American Exceptionalism: A Double-Edged Sword*. Norton.

Marshall, T.H. 1950. *Citizenship and Social Class*. Cambridge University Press.

Marx, Karl. 1859. "Europe: Population, Crime, and Pauperism." *New York Daily Tribune* (16 Sept.).

Merton, Robert K. 1964. "Anomie, Anomia, and Social Interation." Pp. 213-42 in Anomie and Deviant Behavior, edited by Marshall Clinard. Free Press.

_____. 1968. *Social Theory and Social Structure*. Free Press.

Messner, Steven F. 1980. "Income Inequality and Murder Rates: Some Cross-National Findings." *Comparative Social Research* 3:185-98.

_____. 1982. "Societal Development, Social Equality, and Homicide: A Cross-National Test of a Durkheimian Model." *Social Forces* 61:225-40.

_____. 1989. "Economic Discrimination and Societal Homicide Rates: Further Evidence on the Cost of Inequality." *American Sociological Review* 54:597-611.

_____. 1992. "Exploring the Consequences of Erratic Data Reporting for Cross-National Research on Homicide." *Journal of Quantitative Criminology* 8:155-73.

Messner, Steven F., and Robert J. Sampson. 1991. "The Sex Ratio, Family Disruption, and Rates of Violent Crime: The Paradox of Demographic Structure." *Social Forces* 69:693-713.

Messner, Steven F., and Richard Rosenfeld. 1997. *Crime and the American Dream*. 2d ed. Wadsworth.

Muller, Edward N. 1988. "Democracy, Economic Development, and Income Inequality." *American Sociological Review* 53:50-68.

Neuman, W. Lawrence, and Ronald J. Berger. 1988. "Competing Perspectives on Cross-National Crime: An Evaluation of Theory and Evidence." *Sociological Quarterly* 29:281-313.

O'Connor, James. 1973. *The Fiscal Crisis of the State*. St. Martin's Press.

Pampel, Fred, and Rosemary Gartner. 1995. "Age Structure, Socio-political Institutions, and National Homicide Rates." *European Sociological Review* 11:243-60.

Pampel, Fred, John B. Williamson, and Robin Stryker. 1990. "Class Context and Pension Response to Demographic Structure in Advanced Industrial Democracies." *Social Problems* 37:535-50.

Parsons, Talcott. 1966. *Societies: Evolutionary and Comparative Perspectives*. Prentice-Hall.

Polanyi, Karl. 1944. *The Great Transformation*. Rinehart.

Population Reference Bureau. Various years. *World Population Data Sheet*. Population Reference Bureau.

Rosenfeld, Richard, and Steven F. Messner. 1994. "Crime and the American Dream: An Institutional Analysis." *Advances in Criminological Theory* 6:81-103.

____. 1997. "Markets, Morality, and an Institutional-Anomie Theory of Crime." In *The Future of Anomie Theory*, edited by Nikkos Passas and Robert Agnew. Northeastern University Press.

Shelley, Louise I. 1981. *Crime and Modernization*. Southern Illinois University Press.

Stevenson, Richard W. 1995. "A Deficit Reins in Sweden's Welfare State." *New York Times* (2 Feb.), A1, A5.

Tawney, R.H. 1920. *The Acquisitive Society*. Harcourt Brace.

United Nations. Various years. *Demographic Yearbook*. United Nations Publishing Service.

Wellford, Charles F. 1974. "Crime and the Dimensions of Nations." *International Journal of Criminology and Penology* 2:1-10.

Whitney, Craig R. 1995. "In Europe, Touches of Leanness and Meanness." *New York Times* (1 January), p. E5.

Wilensky, Harold L. 1975. *The Welfare State and Equality: Structural and Ideological Roots of Public Expenditures*. University of California Press.

World Bank. 1987. *World Development Report*. Oxford University Press.

World Health Organization. 1980-90. *World Health Statistics Annual*. World Health Organization.

1414 / *Social Forces* 75:4, June 1997

APPENDIX A: Sample of Nations

Argentina	Mauritius
Australia	Mexico
Austria	Netherlands
Belgium	New Zealand
Brazil	Norway
Canada	Panama
Chile	Peru
Colombia	Portugal
Costa Rica	Singapore
Denmark	Spain
Dominican Republic	Sri Lanka
Ecuador	Sweden
Egypt	Switzerland
El Salvador	Syria
Finland	Thailand
France	Trinidad
Germany, Federal Republic	United Kingdom
Greece	United States
Guatemala	Uruguay
Ireland	Venezuela
Israel	
Italy	
Jamaica	
Japan	
Kuwait	

APPENDIX B: Correlations and Univariate Statistics

I. Correlation Matrix

	Y	X1	X2	X3	X4	X5
(Y) Average homicide rate (ln)	1.00	-.52	-.44	.51	.34	-.02
(X1) Decommodification index		1.00	.82	-.63	-.28	-.38
(X2) Development index			1.00	-.68	-.19	-.46
(X3) Gini coefficient				1.00	.34	.17
(X4) Economic discrimination index					1.00	.13
(X5) Sex ratio (ln)						1.00

(N = 45)

II. Univariate Statistics

	Mean	Standard Deviation
Average homicide rate (ln)	.97	1.29
Decommodification index	.00	2.38
Development index	.00	4.24
Gini coefficient	.40	.08
Economic discrimination index	1.63	1.37
Sex ratio (ln)	4.59	.06

(N = 45)

1416 / *Social Forces* 75:4, June 1997

APPENDIX C: Variance Inflation Factors for Fully Specified Models across Different Samples of Nations

	Sample		
Predictors	Maximum	Excluding Syria	No Mean Substitution
Development index	4.2	4.3	7.6
Gini coefficient	2.2	2.3	2.9
Economic discrimination index	1.2	1.2	1.3
Sex ratio (ln)	1.4	1.3	2.6
Decommodification index	3.3	3.3	3.4
N	45	44	39

[7]

INEQUALITY, WELFARE STATE, AND HOMICIDE: FURTHER SUPPORT FOR THE INSTITUTIONAL ANOMIE THEORY*

JUKKA SAVOLAINEN
New York City Criminal Justice Agency

Building directly on key insights from two prior tests of the institutional anomie theory, we predict that the positive effect of economic inequality on the level of lethal violence is limited to nations characterized by relatively weak collective institutions of social protection. This hypothesis is tested with two complementary cross-national data sets. Both settings reveal a negative interaction effect between economic inequality and the strength of the welfare state. Nations that protect their citizens from the vicissitudes of market forces appear to be immune to the homicidal effects of economic inequality. This finding provides critical support for the institutional anomie theory.

The anomie theoretical tradition of sociological criminology appears to be particularly vibrant in two distinct research programs operating at different levels of explanation. The general strain theory pursues the tradition at the individual level of analysis, whereas the institutional anomie theory is in the process of reforming the macrolevel elements of Merton's legacy. Formulated by Robert Agnew in 1992, the general strain theory has generated several empirical applications, many of which support the core assumptions of this perspective (e.g., Agnew and Raskin, 1992; Brezina, 1996; Broidy and Agnew, 1997; Hoffmann and Miller, 1998; Paternoster and Mazerolle, 1994). By contrast, only two prior studies have been conducted specifically to test the institutional anomie theory: Chamlin and Cochran (1995) and Messner and Rosenfeld (1997b). Building directly on the unique features of both contributions, the purpose of our research is to perform a more compelling appraisal of the institutional anomie theory (IAT).

THEORY

As argued by Messner (1988), Merton's statement of anomie theory actually inheres two analytically independent causal arguments: one that concerns the *distribution* of crime within the social unit ("strain theory")

* I am grateful to Steve Messner and Rick Rosenfeld for sharing their data with me. This paper has benefited from thoughtful comments by Steve Messner, James Inverarity, the Editor of *Criminology*, and two anonymous reviewers.

and one addressing variation in the *level* of crime across social units ("anomie theory"). As Messner points out, much of the subsequent work pursuing Merton's legacy has focused on the strain theoretical argument (according to Messner, the macrolevel component of Merton's theory is compatible with a number of individual-level aggregation mechanisms, including social bonding and differential association theory). A defining agenda of the IAT is to develop the neglected anomie theoretical element of Merton's contribution.

The conceptual model of the IAT is articulated in Messner and Rosenfeld's book, *Crime and the American Dream* (1997a). With Merton's statement as its point of departure, the IAT retains the core assumption that the level of crime in a social unit depends on the balance between elements of culture and social structure. Although offering a more systematic treatment of the cultural component of Merton's theory, Messner and Rosenfeld have not significantly altered the original meaning of "the American Dream." It still refers to a value orientation characterized by the universal achievement goal of personal monetary success (Messner and Rosenfeld, 1997a:61–65). The main revision suggested by the IAT concerns the conceptualization of social structure.

In Merton's theory, the anomic pressures inherent in the American Dream channel into criminal behavior depending on the stratification of legitimate economic opportunities. The more unequal the opportunities, the higher the strain and, in consequence, the level of criminal offending. Instead of focusing on this aspect of the social structure, Messner and Rosenfeld expand the concept to include a more comprehensive set of institutional contexts, such as the family, education, and the political sphere. According to the IAT, the relative strength between institutions is the most salient aspect of the social structure. Indeed, with its emphasis on the relationships among functionally different elements of the society, Messner and Rosenfeld's concept of anomie bears close resemblance to Durkheim's discussion of anomic division of labor (Besnard, 1987:31–36).

An institutional balance of power in which the economy dominates other institutions is assumed to be the most conducive to high rates of serious crime because such an arrangement is the least capable of restraining criminal motivations stimulated by the logic of egalitarian market capitalism. At the level of culture, institutional imbalance of this description generates value orientations that emphasize efficiency norms at the expense of moral considerations; the "mood" of the society becomes more predatory. At the level of social structure, weak noneconomic institutions are less capable of providing stakes in conformity in the form of meaningful social roles.

INEQUALITY, WELFARE STATE, AND HOMICIDE1023

PRIOR RESEARCH

As Chamlin and Cochran (1995) point out, Messner and Rosenfeld's model is rather complex and virtually impossible to test directly because of the lack of appropriate measures for each of its concepts. However, drawing on the fundamental aspects of this perspective, they have derived a hypothesis that captures the empirical core of the IAT accurately. According to Chamlin and Cochran, Messner and Rosenfeld's model implies that in the presence of strong noneconomic institutions, economic stress will be less salient as a predictor of serious crime. More specifically, they hypothesize that the impact of poverty on property crime is moderated by the strength of religious, political, and family institutions. Results from their state-level analysis are consistent with this hypothesis: high church membership, low divorce rate, and high voting percentage significantly reduced the effect of poverty rate on property crime.

Messner and Rosenfeld (1997b) have produced their empirical application of the IAT. It relies on Esping-Andersen's (1990) decommodification index as the indicator of economic dominance in the institutional balance of power. In the most basic sense of the term, decommodification refers to the degree to which the state protects the personal well-being of its citizens from market dynamics (the quality and quantity of social rights and entitlements). From the perspective of the IAT, decommodification "signals that the balance of institutional power in market society has shifted from the economy toward the polity; it implies that purely economic values and criteria are accommodated to collective, political considerations" (Messner and Rosenfeld, 1997b:1397). According to Messner and Rosenfeld, decommodification taps only one dimension of the institutional balance of power, the relationship between the economy and the polity. In our judgment, however, public policies associated with high levels of decommodification, such as universal health care and parental leave arrangements, are likely to improve the relative strength of other institutions as well, particularly the family.

Redistribution of income and wealth is obviously a direct outcome of the decommodification process. A strong negative association between the level of decommodification and economic inequality is therefore expected. However, as a novel prediction derived from the IAT, Messner and Rosenfeld argue that decommodification should influence crime independently of economic stratification. They propose that economic dominance in the institutional balance of power "provides fertile soil for anomic cultural pressures" while weakening "the external social control associated with institutional attachments" (Messner and Rosenfeld, 1997b:1396–1398). Their findings based on cross-national data support this hypothesis: The index of decommodification has a relatively strong negative effect on national homicide rates controlling for economic discrimination, income inequality, and the level of socioeconomic development.

We find both of these studies strong contributions to a promising theoretical research program. They differ from each other in three significant respects. First, according to Chamlin and Cochran (1995), the IAT implies an interaction effect between economic stratification and the strength of noneconomic institutions. By contrast, Messner and Rosenfeld (1997b) attend to the main effect of institutional balance of power net of economic conditions. Second, the study by Chamlin and Cochran is based on American data with states as the units of analysis, whereas Messner and Rosenfeld apply the theory in a cross-national setting. Finally, the dependent variable in Chamlin and Cochran is property crime, whereas Messner and Rosenfeld explain variation in homicide rates.

RESEARCH DESIGN

In their statement of the theory, Messner and Rosenfeld (1997a:39–44) are explicit about its intended scope: Institutional anomie theory is meant to explain macrolevel variation in serious criminal offending. In light of this statement, the dependent variable and the unit of analysis are theoretically sound in both studies. Both homicide and index property crimes are clear instances of crimes located at the serious end of the offending continuum, and states and nation-states are both examples of macrolevel entities.

To be sure, because Messner and Rosenfeld rely exclusively on cross-national data to illustrate macrolevel variation in serious offending, one could argue, from a purely dogmatic standpoint, that nation-states constitute more appropriate units of analysis than do the states of the Union. As defined in the preface to *Crime and the American Dream* (Messner and Rosenfeld, 1997a:*x*), the primary purpose of the book is to "present a plausible explanation of the exceptionally high levels of serious crime in the United States," a goal that clearly calls for international comparisons. Indeed, because international variation in the dominant cultural orientation is one of the key assumptions of the IAT, using states as the units of analysis could be criticized for missing the point.

With its emphasis on the dominance of economic imperatives in the social system, the IAT appears to provide a plausible account of the variation in the levels of property crime, but how can the relevance of this model be extended to lethal interpersonal violence? Within the framework of the classic Mertonian anomie theory, the link to violent crime is typically achieved by some version of the frustration-aggression hypothesis. For example, at the macrolevel of analysis, Blau and Blau (1982:119) have argued that groups that "cannot find realistic expression in striving to achieve desired goals" may find an outlet in "diffuse aggression." Although still consistent with these types of assumptions, it should be emphasized that the IAT attends more broadly to the role of social institutions as agents of social control (Messner and Rosenfeld, 1997a:77 and 78):

> Impotent families and schools are severely handicapped in their efforts to promote allegiance to social rules, including legal prohibitions. . . . The anomie associated with this cultural ethos thus tends to neutralize and overpower normative restraints more generally, and the selection of the means for realizing goals of any type, not simply monetary goals, tend to be guided mainly by considerations of technical expediency. . . .
>
> Institutions such as the family, schools, and the polity bear responsibility not only for socialization, and hence the normative control associated with culture, but also for the more external type of social control associated with social structure. . . . [T]o the degree that noneconomic institutions are relatively devalued, the attractiveness of the roles that they offer for the members of society is diminished. There is, accordingly, widespread detachment from these institutions and weak institutional control.

Among other things, according to Messner and Rosenfeld (1997a:78), this "generalized anomie" explains the unusually high levels of gun-related violence in the United States.

The most significant discrepancy between the two studies has to do with the causal form of the assumed effect: Should it be characterized as additive or interactive? Does the institutional balance of power affect crime rates directly, or does this variable moderate the impact of economic stratification? We are unable to resolve this question simply by drawing on the original source of the IAT. Messner and Rosenfeld (1997a:77) provide an analytical model, which is meant to describe the relationships among the key concepts of this theory. Featuring as many as nine causal paths, including two reciprocal relationships, we find this model too general and ambiguous for the problem at hand. Indeed, in our judgment, conceptual clarification remains one of the more urgent tasks in the development of this research program.

However, in our reading, a number of concrete statements in Messner and Rosenfeld's (1997a) discussion seem to imply an interaction effect. For example, as cited by Chamlin and Cochran (1995:415), Messner and Rosenfeld argue that "war on poverty or on inequality of opportunity is not likely to be an effective strategy for crime control in the absence of other cultural and structural changes." Even in their research, Messner and Rosenfeld come very close to inferring effects that are interactional in nature when discussing the findings from their additive models:

"[I]nstitutional-anomie theory broadens the structural focus of traditional economic stress or deprivation perspectives by directing attention to aspects of the economic organization of market societies beyond the stratification system, and to the *interplay of the economy and other social institutions*" (Messner and Rosenfeld, 1997b:1408; emphasis added).

Although both specifications seem compatible with the current statement of the theory, in our judgment, the hypothesis involving an interaction effect constitutes a more compelling rendering of the spirit of the IAT than does the additive formulation. Moreover, in the absence of theoretical clarity, we deem it prudent to choose a test that is more stringent and theoretically distinct. A mere negative relationship between the strength of noneconomic institutions and the national homicide rate is consistent with different interpretations. For example, given the obvious link between the strength of the welfare state and economic marginalization, decommodification could be conceived as an indicator of *post-transfer* inequality in contrast to the income-based Gini index. According to this interpretation, the research by Messner and Rosenfeld merely restates one of the best-documented findings in cross-national criminology with a more complete set of measures. The interactional version of the hypothesis appears to hinge on a more unique kind of evidence and, therefore, constitutes a more critical test of the theory.

HYPOTHESIS

To summarize the discussion so far, a critical test of the institutional anomie theory should estimate the moderating effect of the institutional context on the relationship between economic inequality and serious crime, preferably at the cross-national level of analysis. Both of the prior studies feature an appropriate dependent variable. From the perspective of the ideal test, the main strength of Chamlin and Cochran's (1995) contribution is the interactional nature of the hypothesis, whereas the use of cross-national data constitutes the unique strength of Messner and Rosenfeld's research. The basic purpose of our research is to combine these two desirable properties in a single study. Specifically, we will test the hypothesis that the positive effect of economic inequality on the level of lethal violence is strongest in nations where the economy dominates the institutional balance of power. This hypothesis implies a negative interaction effect between economic stratification and the relative strength of noneconomic institutions.

Our study shares important characteristics with research occurring outside of the specific domain of the institutional anomie theory. First, recent work by LaFree (1998) joins Messner and Rosenfeld's perspective in emphasizing the role of institutions as primary sources of macrolevel variation in serious crime. According to his analysis, postwar trends in the U.S. street crime rate reflect changes in the legitimacy of family, economy, and the political institutions. On the other hand, a cross-national study by Pampel and Gartner (1995) found strong support for the hypothesis that the effect of the population age structure on the nations' homicide rate depends significantly on the sociopolitical context. Specifically, nations featuring strong institutions for collective social protection were found to be relatively immune to the criminogenic effects of changing age structure, whereas the percentage of young people proved to be positively related to the homicide rates of nations with low levels of collectivism. Our study expects to find a similar conditional effect for economic stratification as Pampel and Gartner found for age structure.

DATA AND METHODS

In criminological research, choosing nations as units of analysis entails serious limitations for measures and sample characteristics. In order to reduce these problems, the hypothesis will be tested with two complementary data sets. The sample from the Messner and Rosenfeld (1997b) study constitutes the primary source of data in our research. To improve the reliability and validity of these findings, a parallel set of analyses is conducted with another data set, featuring a different sample of nations and a partially different set of measures.

MESSNER AND ROSENFELD'S DATA

Adhering to a conventional practice in cross-national homicide research, Messner and Rosenfeld measure national homicide rates by calculating multiyear averages to eliminate the impact of short-term fluctuations in the dependent variable. These data are obtained from the World Health Organization (WHO) cause of death statistics covering the 10-year period between 1980 and 1990. As the only source audited by a uniform procedure, the WHO data are generally considered the most valid source of international homicide statistics (LaFree, 1997). It should be noted, though, that by treating homicide as a one-dimensional outcome, these statistics provide a relatively crude picture of the phenomenon. For example, the WHO data do not distinguish between murder and manslaughter. The most serious limitation with this source, however, is the number and the composition of nations reporting homicide data. Only 47 nations were included in the 1995 edition of the WHO report (LaFree, 1997:123). The maximum sample size in Messner and Rosenfeld's data is 45. Twenty of these nations are advanced industrialized countries, whereas only six of them represent either Asia or Africa. To reduce the skewness in the distribution of these data, the dependent variable has been transformed into a natural logarithmic scale.

The data for Esping-Andersen's (1990) original measure of decommodification are available only for 18 advanced welfare states. His index is generated by a sophisticated scoring system reflecting a large number of national characteristics, including the level of political corporatism, universalism of public benefits, and the nature of health care regimes. To tap the essential elements of decommodification for a broader sample of nations, Messner and Rosenfeld (1997b:1399) have developed a proxy measure based on the data on the financial operations of national social security systems collected by the International Labor Organization (ILO). Reflecting both the level and the (universal) distribution of social security spending, this measure is highly correlated (r = .84) with the original decommodification index in the 18-nation sample.

The other independent variables in this data set include income inequality, economic discrimination, development index, and sex ratio. Income inequality is measured with Gini coefficients from the period "circa 1969," which is more than a decade earlier than the period of interest. To complement the Gini-based measure, Messner and Rosenfeld use economic discrimination as another indicator of economic inequality. Economic discrimination refers to inequality based on an ascribed group characteristic (race, ethnicity, religion, language, etc.). As such, this variable measures the "consolidated" nature of economic inequality. Previous research by Messner (1989) found that economic discrimination is a stronger predictor of the national homicide rate than is the Gini index. The data on economic discrimination were obtained from the Minorities at Risk data file (Gurr and Scarritt, 1989). The specific indicator is an ordinal index based on "expert judgements about the extent to which groups experience objective economic disadvantages that are attributable to deliberate discrimination" (Messner and Rosenfeld, 1997b:1403). The data on either income inequality or economic discrimination are not available for 6 of the 45 nations.

To preserve degrees of freedom and to reduce the problem of multicollinearity, Messner and Rosenfeld combine several necessary control variables under a single index of socioeconomic development. A high value on this index reflects high life expectancy, high GNP per capita, low infant mortality, large elderly population, slow population growth, and high levels of urban development. Of all the control variables of interest, only the sex ratio of the population failed to cluster along this dimension of socioeconomic development. In consequence, Messner and Rosenfeld model it as a separate factor. As a way to reduce positive skewness in the distribution, a natural log conversion is applied to the sex ratio scores.

INEQUALITY, WELFARE STATE, AND HOMICIDE1029

SUPPLEMENTARY SAMPLE

After testing the hypothesis with the data collected by Messner and Rosenfeld, the analyses are replicated with our own data set. This supplementary file differs from Messner and Rosenfeld's in the following respects. First, it includes a different set of nations as units of analysis. The most significant change is the inclusion of seven emerging market economies of Eastern Europe. Because Messner and Rosenfeld's sample does not contain any cases from this geopolitical context, this represents a non-trivial improvement in the diversity of the national experience. (The lists of nations included in the two samples are provided in Appendix 1). On the other hand, because much of the data of interest have not been available from these countries until recently, all of the variables, including the dependent variable, are based on a single-year statistic (i.e., 1990), as opposed to a multiyear average.

Second, using national homicide rates disaggregated by sex, these data feature two dependent variables: the male and the female homicide victimization rate. As stated previously, one of the limitations with the WHO data is the crude definition of homicide. One way to improve the situation is to use disaggregated rates. Gartner (1990:94) suggests that, compared with men, women are more likely to be victimized in situations arising from domestic or romantic disputes, whereas men are more likely to be killed by strangers and for instrumental gain. In general, because the profile of lethal violence may vary significantly across nations, it is advisable to use disaggregated data for any comparative purposes (Zimring and Hawkins, 1997:34–50). To be sure, the use of sex-specific rates is but a minor step in that direction.

Third, the supplementary data file contains only one indicator of economic inequality, the Gini index of income distribution. On the other hand, based on observations from the period of interest (i.e., 1990), it should be a more valid measure than is the one available in Messner and Rosenfeld's file. Fourth, the institutional balance of power is measured by the amount of government spending on social security and other welfare programs as a percentage of total public expenditures. Although it is a conceptually crude rendering of the institutional context, empirically, this variable overlaps reasonably well with Messner and Rosenfeld's proxy decommodification index. Using data from the same time period (mid-1980s), we created a sample of 36 nations and computed a Pearson's correlation of .71 between the two variables. The data on income inequality and welfare spending are obtained from the 1998 World Development Indicators CD-ROM (World Bank, 1998).

The supplementary data set features two control variables included as elements in Messner and Rosenfeld's development index: GDP per capita and population age structure. All else equal, nations with a large elderly population are likely to spend a larger proportion of the budget on pension benefits and health care programs than do nations with a young age structure. On the other hand, because we expect to obtain a negative association between age and criminal offending, it is necessary to control for the differences in the age structure of nations. This variable is measured as the number of people at ages 15 to 24 as a percentage of the total population around 1990 (United Nations, various years). Because the GDP per capita is a general indicator of the nations' socioeconomic status, it may influence the relationships among economic inequality, welfare spending, and homicide rate (World Bank, 1998). Finally, consistent with Messner and Rosenfeld, we have also included sex ratio as a control variable. However, we differ from them in measuring sex ratio by its natural units, as it is even less skewed in our data than is the log-transformed equivalent in Messner and Rosenfeld's data. The descriptive statistics for the variables from both data files are provided in Appendix 2.

The sample of nation-states included in these two data sets is far from representative of the nations of the world. The ones that are missing from these analyses tend to be among the economically least developed or politically least democratic nations. However, it can be argued that the findings from this research can be generalized fairly well to the population of nations characterized by a market-driven economy and a democratic political regime.

METHOD OF ESTIMATION

The multivariate models have been estimated in accordance with the assumptions of the ordinary least-squares (OLS) regression. Given the small size of our samples, we feel justified to adopt a more liberal standard of statistical significance than usual. Following the standard used in Messner and Rosenfeld's research, a regression coefficient that is more than 1.5 times larger than its standard error will be accepted as statistically significant. Along more conventional lines, we shall also report if the *p*-value of an estimate is .10 or smaller in a two-tailed test.

In order to reduce multicollinearity among the elements of the interaction terms, all of the variables involved in the estimated interaction effects have been centered, a practice recommended by Jaccard et al. (1990:30–31). Centering is a form of additive transformation in which the mean value of a variable is subtracted from each of its scores. In the Messner-Rosenfeld data, this procedure is applied to the following variables: income inequality, economic discrimination, and decommodification. In the supplementary data, the scores for income inequality and social security spending have been centered. Appendix 3 displays the bivariate associations among the variables from these two data sets.

With one exception, the independent variables in Messner and Rosenfeld's data file appear to be free from potential collinearity problems: The correlation between the indices of development and decommodification is .83. By comparison, the highest bivariate correlation coefficient among the independent variables in the supplementary data set is –.71 (between income inequality and welfare spending). To address the issue of multicollinearity more formally, we computed variance inflation factors for each of the estimated models. According to the rule of thumb suggested by Fisher and Mason (1981:105–106), predictors that score above 4.0 on the VIF are associated with serious collinearity problems (this rule is also consistent with the discussion in Fox, 1991:10–13). In light of this standard, only the development index, a control variable featured in the Messner and Rosenfeld's data file, is biased by multicollinearity. The analyses conducted with the supplementary data set are entirely free from serious collinearity.

FINDINGS

Models 1 through 3 in Table 1 describe results from the analysis of the maximum sample from the Messner-Rosenfeld data set. The *N* of 45 is accomplished by way of means substitution for the missing values of income inequality or economic discrimination. Model 1 estimates the main effects of each independent variable. This model corresponds to equation 2 of Table 1 in Messner and Rosenfeld's original study (Messner and Rosenfeld, 1997b:1404). As expected, the coefficients as well as the fit of these two models are identical. Two variables, sex ratio and the decommodification index, are statistically significant (at the .10 level). Model 1 explains 32.6% of the cross-national variation in homicide rate. Our specification of the institutional anomie theory predicts that the level of decommodification moderates the effect of economic inequality on the national homicide rate. To test this hypothesis, we have estimated interaction effects between the Gini index of income inequality and decommodification (model 2) and between economic discrimination and decommodification (model 3). Our prediction implies a negative coefficient for both interaction terms.

As reported in Table 1, a negative interaction effect emerges in both models, although it is statistically significant only in model 3. The magnitude of this coefficient indicates that for one standard deviation unit increase in decommodification, the estimated effect of economic discrimination declines by .224 units. In order to examine the nature of this interaction effect in more concrete terms, we calculated point estimates for the conditional effect of economic discrimination on the national homicide rates of Finland and Mexico, two nations representing opposite ends (but

Table 1. Main and Interactive Effects of Income Inequality, Economic Discrimination, and Decommodification on Average Homicide Victimization Rate (1980–1990), Controlling for Nations' Socioeconomic Development and Sex Ratio. OLS Regression Coefficients

Independent Variable	Model 1		Model 2		Model 3		Model 4		Model 5		Model 6	
	b	*β*	*b*	*β*	*b*	*β*	*b*	*β*	*b*	*β*	*b*	*β*
Development Index	–.017	–.057	–.016	–.052	–.021	–.070	–.095	–.350	–.103	–.365	–.093	–.329
	(.077)		(.078)		(.075)		(.088)		(.089)		(.086)	
Sex Ratio (ln)	–5.755	–.250**	–5.937	–.257**	–5.545	–.240**	–5.290	–.150	–6.159	–.174	–4.912	–.139
	(3.330)		(3.356)		(3.239)		(6.482)		(6.609)		(6.303)	
Income Inequality	3.274	.212	3.278	.212	3.714	.240	1.496	.112	1.389	.104	2.025	.152
	(2.836)		(2.850)		(2.767)		(2.615)		(2.633)		(2.560)	
Economic Discrimination	.172	.182	.170	.180	.141	.149	.147	.177	.148	.179	.127	.153
	(.128)		(.128)		(.125)		(.109)		(.109)		(.106)	
Decommodification Index	–.210	–.386**	–.215	–.396**	–.179	–.330	–.163	–.342*	–.166	–.349*	–.143	–.300
	(.122)		(.123)		(.120)		(.102)		(.102)		(.100)	
Income Inequality × Decommodification			–.744	–.097					–.626	–.095		
			(.954)						(.788)			
Economic Discrimination × Decommodification					–.092	–.224**					–.072	–.200**
					(.051)						(.042)	
Adjusted R^2	.326		.319		.363		.480		.374		.509	
N	45		45		45		39		39		39	

*$b > 1.5$ (S.E.); **$p < .10$ (two-tailed test).
Note: Numbers in parentheses are standard errors.

not the extreme values) of the decommodification scale.[1] With decommodification at –2.16, the predicted effect of economic discrimination for Mexico equals .340. By comparison, scoring 2.66 on the decommodification index, the corresponding estimate for Finland equals –.104. In other words, economic inequality based on ascribed group characteristics proves to be a relatively strong positive determinant of the homicide rate in nations characterized by low levels of decommodification, while having a small negative effect among nations featuring strong collective institutions of social protection.

Residing over three standard deviations below the predicted value, Syria emerges as a potential outlier in these analyses. However, removing this case did not affect the pattern of findings reported in models 1 through 3. These models were next reestimated with a reduced sample excluding the six cases with missing values. As reported in models 4 through 6 of Table 1, both interaction terms remain negative, and the one involving economic discrimination is still the only statistically significant one. The only major difference between the results from the two samples concerns the fit of the multivariate models: The adjusted R^2 is systematically about 15% higher in models estimated with casewise deletion of missing values. Throughout these analyses, the inclusion of the interaction terms has little impact on the main effects of the independent variables, which suggests that multicollinearity is not a problem.

So far, our research has failed to demonstrate a statistically significant negative interaction effect between income inequality and the institutional balance of power. The weaker success associated with this measure of economic stratification may have to do with the fact that it is based on data that are 10–20 years older than are the data used to measure decommodification and homicide. Time-appropriate measurement of income inequality is one of the distinguishing characteristics of our supplementary data file. Results from the analyses of these data are presented in Table 2.

Models 1 and 2 feature the male homicide victimization rate as the dependent variable. In the baseline model (model 1), sex ratio, income inequality, and welfare spending emerge as the variables with statistically significant regression coefficients. The effect of sex ratio is negative, which implies that, all else equal, nations with a higher number of men than women tend to have lower rates of homicide. It is likely that at least a part of this relationship is causally reverse; i.e., a low male homicide rate may have a positive impact on the sex ratio of a population. As predicted,

1. The point estimates have been calculated in accordance with the following formula provided by Jaccard et al. (1990:26): β_1 at $X_2 = \beta_1 + \beta_3 X_2$, where β_1 is the regression coefficient for X_1 (economic discrimination), β_3 refers to the coefficient for the product term, and X_2 is the value of the moderating variable (decommodification).

Table 2. Main and Interactive Effects of Income Inequality and Welfare Spending on Sex-Specific Homicide Victimization Rates, Controlling for GNP, Age Structure, and Sex Ratio. OLS Regression Coefficients ($N = 32$)

Independent Variable	Model 1 (Men)		Model 2 (Men)		Model 3 (Women)		Model 4 (Women)	
	b	β	b	β	b	β	b	β
GNP per Capita	–.018	–.135	–.037	.277**	–.008	–.095	–.022	–.261
	(.019)		(.018)		(.017)		(.017)	
% at Ages 15 to 24	–.003	–.060	.000	.005	–.002	–.058	.000	.018
	(.005)		(.004)		(.004)		(.004)	
Sex Ratio	–15.481	–.405**	–13.610	–.356**	–14.815	–.607**	–13.423	–.550**
	(5.321)		(4.719)		(4.773)		(4.455)	
Income Inequality	.064	.568**	.073	.651**	.024	.340*	.031	.436**
	(.018)		(.016)		(.016)		(.016)	
Welfare Spending	–.048	–.442**	–.028	–.259*	–.033	–.474**	–.018	–.261
	(.019)		(.018)		(.017)		(.017)	
Income Inequality × Welfare Spending			–.003	–.298**			–.003	–.347**
			(.001)				(.001)	
Adjusted R^2	.685		.756		.379		.468	

*b > (12 × S.E.); **$p < .10$ (two-tailed test).
Note: Numbers in parentheses are standard errors.

income inequality has a positive and welfare spending a negative main effect on male homicide rate.

Featuring an interaction term between income inequality and welfare spending, model 2 constitutes a more critical test of the institutional anomie theory. Consistent with the hypothesis, a negative interaction effect is obtained that is statistically highly significant. Adding this product term in the equation improves the fit of the model from 69% to 76%. Models explaining cross-national variation in female homicide victimization rates generate the same basic findings. The interaction effect between income inequality and welfare spending is strong, negative, and statistically significant, and the increase in the R^2 is nine percentage points. (Note, however, that this set of independent variables explains variation in male victimization about 30 percentage points better.)

As previously, we calculated point estimates for the conditional effects of income inequality for Finland and Mexico. During the period of interest, the Finnish government spent 47.4% of the total budget on various welfare programs, which is 20.1 percentage points above the average score in this sample. As a result, the predicted effect of income inequality on the Finnish male homicide victimization rate is –5.34 and –6.54 on the female homicide rate. The corresponding estimates for Mexico, scoring –12.9 on the centered measure of welfare spending, equal 4.50 and 4.91, respectively.

The strong positive effects of income inequality on the homicide rate of Mexico makes immediate sense from the perspective of the institutional anomie theory. However, indicating that income inequality may actually reduce the level of homicide, the point estimates for Finland may seem counterintuitive. Why should economic equality reduce lethal violence in the presence of strong collective institutions of social protection?

First of all, this effect is largely theoretical, given that, not surprisingly, nations featuring the most generous welfare programs tend also to have the lowest levels of income inequality. In this sample, only one nation (Chile) with higher than average welfare spending ranks above the average level of income inequality. However, theoretically speaking, it is conceivable that nations that safeguard their citizens from the vicissitudes of market capitalism may actually benefit from income inequality. As a matter of fact, this finding is consistent with one of the most influential modern statements of social justice, *A Theory of Justice* by John Rawls (1972). As a key aspect of his theory, Rawls proposes the *maximin* principle, which states that a just society is one that maximizes the well-being of the worst off. Under this principle, income inequality, however large, may be acceptable, insofar as it stimulates hard work, innovation, and economic productivity in general, and, by way of tax revenues, improves the situation of the poorest segment of the society (Kangas, 1998). The strong negative point estimate associated with Finland could be seen as an empirical illustration of the maximin principle.

CONCLUSIONS

Drawing on the unique strengths of two prior tests of the institutional anomie perspective, we developed a hypothesis predicting a negative interaction effect between economic inequality and the strength of the welfare state. Specifically, we hypothesized that economic inequality is a strong determinant of the national homicide rates in societies characterized by weak institutions of social protection, but should not be a salient predictor among the more collectivist nations. This hypothesis was tested with two complementary data sets featuring slightly different samples of nations and sets of measures.

Results from both samples provide support for the institutional anomie theory. Each of the estimated interaction terms between an indicator of economic inequality and the strength of the welfare state turned out negative. In the first sample, the interaction between economic discrimination and decommodification was statistically significant, whereas the interaction between the Gini index of income inequality and decommodification was not. However, there emerged a strong and statistically significant negative interaction effect between income inequality and the level of welfare spending in the supplementary data set, which features more appropriate national measures of the Gini index.

To examine the nature of these interaction effects, we calculated conditional effects of economic inequality at different levels of decommodification/welfare spending. The values of these point estimates confirmed the hypothesized effects. Indeed, the negative point estimates at high values of welfare spending suggest that economic inequality may actually lower the homicide rates under such conditions. This finding, although largely theoretical, is consistent with Rawls's theory of social justice.

In light of a large body of prior research, economic inequality is one of the most robust determinants of cross-national variation in homicide (LaFree, 1997:132). Attending to the sociopolitical context of this relationship, the results from our research suggest an important qualification for this basic finding. The fact that the effect of economic inequality on lethal violence appears to be limited to nations characterized by low levels of decommodification and welfare spending is inconsistent with a pure relative deprivation argument. It seems that the average distance between the rich and the poor is not as significant a factor as the presence of an economically marginalized population. Because of their generous welfare programs, the nations that appear to be immune to the detrimental effects of economic inequality have a very small or nonexistent underclass population. In light of our research, the size of the population living significantly below the normative standard of economic well-being may be the critical characteristic explaining the inequality effect in cross-national criminology. In our view, this conclusion is consistent with the spirit of Merton's anomie theory and the letter of Messner and Rosenfeld's institutional anomie theory.

REFERENCES

Agnew, Robert
1992 Foundation for a general strain theory of crime and delinquency. Criminology 30:47–87.

Agnew, Robert and Helene Raskin White
1992 An empirical test of general strain theory. Criminology 30:475–499.

Besnard, Philippe
1987 L'anomie: Ses Usages et Ses Fonctions dans la Discipline Sociologique depuis Durkheim. Paris: Presses Universitaires de France.

Blau, Judith R. and Peter M. Blau
1982 The cost of inequality: Metropolitan structure and violent crime. American Sociological Review 47:114–129.

Brezina, Timothy
1996 Adapting to strain: An examination of delinquent coping responses. Criminology 34:39–60.

Broidy, Lisa and Robert Agnew
1997 Gender and crime: A general strain theory perspective. Journal of Research in Crime and Delinquency 34:275–306.

Chamlin, Mitchell B. and John K. Cochran
1995 Assessing Messner and Rosenfeld's institutional anomie theory: A partial test. Criminology 33:411–429.

Esping-Andersen, Gösta
1990 Three Worlds of Welfare Capitalism. New York: Princeton University Press.

Fisher, Joseph E. and Robert L. Mason
1981 The analysis of multicollinear data in criminology. In James A. Fox (ed.), Methods in Quantitative Criminology. New York: Academic Press.

Fox, John
1991 Regression Diagnostics: An Introduction. Vol. 79. Quantitative Applications in the Social Sciences. Newbury Park, Calif.: Sage.

Gartner, Rosemary
1990 The victims of homicide: A temporal and cross-national comparison. American Sociological Review 55:92–106.

Gurr, Ted Robert and James R. Scarritt
1989 Minorities at risk: A global study. Human Rights Quarterly 11:375–405.

Hoffmann, John P. and Alan S. Miller
1998 A latent variable analysis of general strain theory. Journal of Quantitative Criminology 14:83–110.

Jaccard, James, Robert Turrisi, and Choi K. Wan
1990 Interaction Effects in Multiple Regression. Vol. 72. Quantitative Applications in the Social Sciences. Thousand Oaks, Calif.: Sage.

Kangas, Olli
1998 Distributive Justice and Social Policy Models: Rawls in International Comparisons. University of Turku, Department of Social Policy Working Paper. Series B:13. Turku, Finland.

LaFree, Gary
1997 Comparative cross-national studies of homicide. In M. Dwayne Smith and Margaret A. Zahn (eds.), Homicide Studies: A Source Book of Social Research. Beverly Hills, Calif.: Sage.
1998 Losing Legitimacy: Street Crime and the Decline of Social Institutions in America. Boulder, Colo.: Westview Press.

Messner, Steven F.
1988 Merton's 'Social structure and anomie': The road not taken. Deviant Behavior 9:33–53.
1989 Economic discrimination and societal homicide rates: Further evidence on the cost of inequality. American Sociological Review 54:597–611.

Messner, Steven F. and Richard Rosenfeld
1997a Crime and the American Dream. 2d ed. Belmont, Calif.: Wadsworth.
1997b Political restraint of the market and levels of criminal homicide: A cross-national application of institutional-anomie theory. Social Forces 75:1393–1416.

Pampel, Fred and Rosemary Gartner
1995 Age-structure, socio-political institutions, and national homicide rates. European Sociological Review 11:243–260.

Paternoster, Raymond and Paul Mazerolle
1994 General strain theory and delinquency: A replication and extension. Journal of Research in Crime and Delinquency 31:235–263.

Rawls, John
1972 A Theory of Justice. Oxford, U.K.: Oxford University Press.

United Nations
Demographic Yearbook. New York: United Nations.

World Bank
1998 World Development Indicators 1998. CD-ROM.

Zimring, Franklin E. and Gordon Hawkins
1997 Crime is Not the Problem: Lethal Violence in America. New York: Oxford University Press.

INEQUALITY, WELFARE STATE, AND HOMICIDE1039

Jukka Savolainen is a Senior Research Analyst at the New York City Criminal Justice Agency. In addition to cross-national homicide and anomie theory, his current research includes a study of criminal recidivism among participants in alternative-to-incarceration programs. Contact information: 52 Duane Street, 8th Floor, New York, N.Y. 10007; jsavolainen@nycja.org.

Appendix 1. Samples of Nations

A. Messner and Rosenfeld's Data Set (full sample, N = 45)

Argentina	France	Panama
Australia	Germany, Federal Republic	Peru
Austria	Greece	Portugal
Belgium	Guatemala	Singapore
Brazil	Ireland	Spain
Canada	Israel	Sri Lanka
Chile	Italy	Sweden
Colombia	Jamaica	Switzerland
Costa Rica	Japan	Syria
Denmark	Kuwait	Thailand
Dominican Republic	Mauritius	Trinidad
Ecuador	Mexico	United Kingdom
Egypt	Netherlands	United States
El Salvador	New Zealand	Uruguay
Finland	Norway	Venezuela

B. The Supplementary Data Set (N = 32)

Australia	Ireland
Austria	Israel
Brazil	Latvia[a]
Bulgaria[a]	Lithuania[a]
Canada	Mexico
Chile	Netherlands
Colombia	Nicaragua[a]
Costa Rica	Norway
Czech Republic[a]	Panama
Denmark	Paraguay[a]
Ecuador	Poland[a]
El Salvador	Romania[a]
Finland	Spain
France	Sweden
Germany	United Kingdom
Hungary[a]	United States

[a]These nations are not included in Messner and Rosenfeld's sample.

Appendix 2. Descriptive Statistics

Messner and Rosenfeld Data	Mean	S.D.	*N*
Homicide Rate (ln)	.97	1.29	45
Development Index	.00	4.24	45
Sex Ratio (ln)	4.59	5.59	45
Income Inequality[a]	.00	.09	40
Economic Discrimination[a]	.00	1.40	43
Decommodification[a]	.00	2.37	45
Income Inequality × Decommodification	–.14	.18	40
Economic Discrimination × Decommodification	–.93	3.21	43
The Supplementary Data	Mean	S.D.	*N*
Male Homicide Rate (ln)	1.56	1.23	43
Female Homicide Rate (ln)	.35	.77	43
GNP per Capita	11.15	10.12	44
Percent at Ages 15 to 24	20.59	24.86	41
Sex Ratio	.97	.04	44
Income Inequality[a]	.00	10.99	47
Welfare Spending[a]	.00	15.91	48
Income Inequality × Welfare Spending	–108.19	109.21	39

[a]These variables have been centered to reduce multicollinearity in the estimation of interaction effects.

Appendix 3. Bivariate Correlations.

A. Messner and Rosenfeld's Sample (Missing Values Deleted Listwise).

	Y	X1	X2	X3	X4	X5	X6	X7
(Y) Average Homicide Rate (ln)	1.00	–.66	.35	.60	.38	–.68	–.07	–.31
(X1) Development Index		1.00	–.68	–.73	–.28	.83	.02	.13
(X2) Sex Ratio (ln)			1.00	.29	.28	–.52	–.13	–.10
(X3) Income Inequality[a]				1.00	.35	–.64	.01	–.04
(X4) Economic Discrimination[a]					1.00	–.32	–.02	–.13
(X5) Decommodification Index[a]						1.00	–.02	.18
(X6) X3 * X5							1.00	.64
(X7) X4 * X5								1.00

[a]These variables have been centered to reduce multicollinearity in the estimation of interaction effects.

B. The Supplementary Sample (Missing Values Deleted Listwise).

	Y1	Y2	X1	X2	X3	X4	X5	X6
(Y1) Male Homicide Rate (ln)	1.00	.86	–.67	–.04	.18	.70	–.72	–.13
(Y2) Female Homicide Rate (ln)		1.00	–.49	–.08	–.15	.35	–.46	–.26
(X1) GNP per Capita			1.00	.01	–.17	–.54	.66	–.25
(X2) Percent at Ages 15 to 24				1.00	.19	.06	–.15	.17
(X3) Sex Ratio					1.00	.61	–.51	.14
(X4) Income Inequality[a]						1.00	–.71	.22
(X5) Welfare Spending[a]							1.00	–.01
(X6) X4 * X5								1.00

[a]These variables have been centered to reduce multicollinearity in the estimation of interaction effects.

[8]

SOCIAL SUPPORT, INEQUALITY, AND HOMICIDE: A CROSS-NATIONAL TEST OF AN INTEGRATED THEORETICAL MODEL*

TRAVIS C. PRATT
Washington State University

TIMOTHY W. GODSEY
University of Cincinnati

Social support, institutional anomie, and macrolevel general strain perspectives have emerged as potentially important explanations of aggregate levels of crime. Drawing on insights from each of these perspectives in a cross-national context, the analyses show that 1) our measure of social support is inversely related to homicide rates, 2) economic inequality also maintains a direct relationship with homicide rates, and 3) social support significantly interacts with economic inequality to influence homicide rates. The implications of the analysis for ongoing discourse concerning the integration of these criminological theories and the implications for the development of effective crime control policies are discussed.

KEYWORDS: Social support, inequality, macro-level crime rates.

Beginning in the late 1970s and early 1980s, macrolevel (or "ecological") criminological theory and research "reemerged" and has since earned sustained attention from the academic community. Indeed, following the dominance of individual-level explanations of crime and deviance during the 1960s and 1970s, Bursik and Grasmick (1993:ix) argue that "the pendulum has begun to swing in the other direction, and there has been a relatively recent acceleration in the number of studies that have been conducted with an explicit focus on [macrolevel] dynamics." At least in part, this resurgence of interest in macrolevel approaches has been encouraged by four primary contributions: Cohen and Felson's (1979) development of routine activities theory; the seminal work of Blau and Blau (1982) on inequality and violent crime; the rediscovery in the 1980s of Shaw and McKay's social disorganization theory by scholars such as Bursik (1986,

---

* A previous version of this manuscript was presented at the 2001 Annual Meeting of the American Society of Criminology. Please direct all correspondence to Travis C. Pratt, Department of Political Science/Criminal Justice, Washington State University, 801 Johnson Tower, Pullman, WA 99164-4880 (e-mail: tpratt@mail.wsu.edu).

1988), Sampson and Groves (1989), and Wilson (1987); and, finally, brought on by rational choice theorists such as Gary Becker (1968) and by a concern over what impact the growing level of imprisonment has on crime rates, the late 1970s and early 1980s experienced a renewed interest in deterrence-rational choice theory at the macro level (see, e.g., Blumstein, Cohen, and Nagin, 1978; Wilson, 1983).

As a result of these important works, new theoretical vistas have been explored, including social support (or "altruism") theory (Chamlin and Cochran, 1997; Cullen, 1994), institutional-anomie theory (Messner and Rosenfeld, 2001), and even a macrolevel variant of general strain theory (Agnew, 1999). Each of these perspectives is distinct in their own right, and yet there is considerable conceptual overlap between them. To be sure, to a certain extent, these theories—either explicitly or implicitly—draw upon each other when specifying their core theoretical propositions. Although still relatively new on the criminological scene, empirical tests of the social support and institutional anomie perspectives have begun to emerge in the published literature (see, e.g., Chamlin and Cochran, 1997; Chamlin et al., 1999; Messner and Rosenfeld, 1997; Piquero and Piquero, 1998; Savolainen, 2000). Agnew's macrolevel general strain theory, however, has yet to be formally tested on a sample of social aggregates;[1] thus, the present analysis represents the first effort toward building a body of empirical tests of this paradigm.

Drawing on each of these three theoretical perspectives, this article has two major objectives. First, we wish to demonstrate how each of these three criminological theories—social support, institutional anomie, and macrolevel general strain—specify similar relationships among measures of social support, economic inequality, and crime. It is not the purpose of the work presented here to play arbiter over which theories may rightfully claim "ownership" over these empirical relationships. Rather, our discussion seeks to highlight the similarities across these theories in terms of how they view—albeit for different reasons—the dynamics of social support, inequality, and crime. Accordingly, the second objective of this article is to empirically test the core propositions shared by these theories concerning the relative effects of social support and economic inequality on homicide rates, and the interaction effect between social support and economic inequality on homicide rates. In particular, our analysis addresses the following three issues: 1) whether social support and economic inequality

1. The multilevel analysis of youths' aggressive behavior in school conducted by Brezina et al. (2001)—which was guided by Agnew's (1999) discussion of community strain—was not an explicitly macrolevel study (the dependent variable was measured at the individual level) and is therefore not considered here to be a macrosocial test of the theory.

maintain significant *independent* effects on homicide rates, 2) whether controlling for the effects of either social support or economic inequality *moderate* the effects for either variable, and 3) whether there is a significant *interaction* effect between social support and economic inequality on homicide rates in the cross-national setting.

THEORETICAL FRAMEWORK

Consistent with the first objective of this article, this section outlines the major tenets of the social support, institutional anomie, and macrolevel general strain perspectives. In describing the core propositions specified by each theory, two interrelated issues will be addressed: how each theory 1) specifies a direct effect for both social support and economic inequality on crime, and 2) how each specifies an interaction between measures of social support and economic inequality on crime.

SOCIAL SUPPORT THEORY

Social support/altruism theory is rooted primarily in the works of Braithwaite's (1989) theory of reintegrative shaming, Coleman's (1990) discussion of social capital, Cullen's (1994) development of social support as an organizing concept for criminology, Messner and Rosenfeld's (2001) institutional anomie theory, and Chamlin and Cochran's (1997) discussion and empirical test of "social altruism" theory. Each of these theoretical statements is somewhat conceptually distinct when viewed in isolation, and yet they all draw on the common proposition that social aggregates—from communities to nations—vary in their degree of cohesiveness, support, shared values, and willingness to come to the aid of those in need (Cullen and Wright, 1997; Etzioni, 1993). Such variations, in turn, are assumed to be related to crime (Barrera and Li, 1996; Sampson et al., 1997; Wilson, 1987).

Defined as "the perceived or actual instrumental and/or expressive provisions supplied by the community, social networks, and confiding partners" (Lin, 1986:18; see also Apter and Propper, 1986; Cullen et al., 1999), the exact mechanisms by which higher levels of social support should reduce criminal involvement are numerous. Indeed, a higher level of social support may increase family efficacy and promote better parenting practices (Currie, 1985; Loeber and Stouthamer-Loeber, 1986; Wright et al, 2001), it may aid in the prosocial adaptation to criminogenic strains (Agnew, 1992, 1999), it may facilitate earlier criminal desistance patterns over the life course (Sampson and Laub, 1993), and it may even be a necessary precondition for effective social control (Braithwaite, 1989). Regardless of the precise processes that may be the result of higher levels of social support, Cullen (1994:537) is clear in his statement that "across nations and across communities, crime rates vary inversely with the level of social support."

As such, much of the scholarly discussion surrounding social support theory focuses on the potential "main effects" of social support—often in the form of measures of economic assistance—on crime (e.g., compare Chamlin and Cochran, 1997; Chamlin et al., 1999; DeFronzo, 1983, 1996, 1997; Devine et al., 1988; Hannon and DeFronzo, 1998a; Zuravin, 1989). Less attention has been paid, however, to the possible interaction effects that levels of social support may have with other structural characteristics of social aggregates. In particular, social support theorists are well aware of the link between economic inequality and crime. Cullen (1994:534) notes that "economic inequality can generate crime not only by exposing people to relative deprivation but also by eviscerating and inhibiting the development of social support networks" (see also Colvin, 2000; Currie, 1985). In essence, therefore, the core tenets of social support theory—when taken to the next logical step—indirectly specify an interaction effect between levels of economic deprivation and social support on crime. Indeed, the theoretical statements of Cullen (1994) and of Chamlin and Cochran (1997) both center on the notion that the effect of economic deprivation (i.e., economic inequality) on crime should be most pronounced within macrosocial units characterized by low levels of social support.[2]

Although not necessarily couched in the language of social support theory, the recent work of Hannon and DeFronzo (1998b) reveals a certain measure of empirical support for this interaction hypothesis. Their analysis of large U.S. counties indicated that the effect of resource/economic deprivation on crime rates was significantly reduced in areas with higher levels of welfare assistance (even when disaggregated to violent and property crime rates).

INSTITUTIONAL ANOMIE THEORY

Messner and Rosenfeld published *Crime and the American Dream* in 1994. In this important work, Merton's (1938) anomie/strain theory was extended and partially reformulated. Although Messner and Rosenfeld agreed with Merton's view of an American culture obsessed with economic success, they found his analysis of social structure incomplete. Merton held that the American system of *stratification* was responsible for

2. Cullen's (1994) work also seems to indicate a potentially indirect relationship among inequality, social support, and crime, where inequality may lead to low levels of social support and, in turn, higher levels of crime—a proposition that researchers may address in the future. Nevertheless, he is clear in his assertion that the criminogenic effects of economic deprivation (inequality) should be most intense when coupled with low levels of social support. It is this latter statement that guides the present analysis.

restricting individuals' access to legitimate opportunities for upward socioeconomic mobility, which, in turn, resulted in high levels of criminogenic anomie in society. What was missing from the anomie tradition, argued Messner and Rosenfeld (2001), was an understanding of how the American Dream creates and reproduces an institutional structure in which one social institution—the economy—assumes dominance over all others. This apparent imbalance in the institutional structure limits the ability of other social institutions, such as the family, education, or the political system, to insulate members of society from the criminogenic pressures of the American Dream. What Messner and Rosenfeld have created, therefore, is a version of anomie/strain theory that sees crime rates as a function of the American Dream's cultural emphasis on economic success in combination with an institutional structure dominated by the economy.

Accordingly, Messner and Rosenfeld (2001) explicitly cite inequality as an indicator of the presence of structural barriers to the universal access of social collectives to the legitimate means to achieve economic success. Furthermore, their theoretical statement indicates that an emphasis on promoting social support may alter the institutional imbalance of power (i.e., the dominance of the economy over other social institutions), where the strengthening of noneconomic institutions should translate into stronger "institutional controls" (Messner and Rosenfeld, 2001:77). Thus, consistent with the major propositions set forth by social support theory, institutional anomie theory also predicts that social support and inequality should exert direct independent effects on crime rates across macrosocial units.

Using "indirect" measures of the central concepts, there have been four explicit tests of institutional anomie theory conducted thus far (Chamlin and Cochran, 1995; Messner and Rosenfeld, 1997; Piquero and Piquero, 1998; Savolainen, 2000)—all of which at least partially support the main propositions of the theory (cf. Jensen, 1996).[3] Although these tests are certainly not identical methodologically, a common thread running across each is the analytical approach involving estimating main effects and interaction terms between the proxy for the strength of noneconomic institutions and some measure of economic deprivation. Indeed, Messner and Rosenfeld (2001) are clear in their assertion that the effects of economic deprivation should be most pronounced when coupled with weak noneconomic institutions (see also Chamlin and Cochran, 1996).

---

3. This is not to say that other macrolevel studies have not been conducted that may bear, to a degree, some importance to anomie theory. Indeed, many studies have included measures of economic deprivation—in some form—to predict crime rates (e.g., for comprehensive reviews of the poverty and inequality literature, see Hsieh and Pugh, 1993; Vieraitis, 2000; and see Chiricos, 1987 for a review of the unemployment-crime literature).

Accordingly, each of these empirical tests revealed—albeit somewhat inconsistently—an inverse interaction effect between various measures of economic deprivation (including measures of poverty, economic inequality) and the strength of noneconomic institutions (including various measures of family dynamics, educational support, and indicators of religious and political participation). Thus, to the extent that indicators of "social support" can be reasonably substituted as indicators of the "strength of noneconomic institutions," social support and institutional anomie theories may be reasonably integrated with regard to their similar stances on the dynamics of social support, inequality, and crime.

MACROLEVEL GENERAL STRAIN THEORY

Another branch that has recently grown out of the resuscitated anomie tradition is Agnew's macrolevel version of general strain theory. Originally conceptualized as an individual-level explanation of crime and delinquency (see, e.g., Agnew, 1985, 1992), general strain theory views crime primarily as the result of frustration-induced anger. Although the microlevel version of the theory has been fairly well tested in recent years (e.g., see the discussion by Mazerolle and Maahs, 2000), Agnew (1999) has also set forth a macrolevel variant of general strain theory as an explanation of aggregate crime rates that has yet to be formally tested on a sample of social aggregates.

Consistent with the individual-level version of general strain theory, Agnew (1999) argues that strain (or stress) is a major source of the motivation to commit crime. In particular, variations in crime across macrosocial units can be explained in terms of "differences in strain and in those factors that condition the effect of strain on crime" (Agnew, 1999:126). This perspective draws heavily on the relative deprivation tradition (Bernard, 1990; Blau and Blau, 1982; Hagan and McCarthy, 1997a) in that "high levels of income or socioeconomic inequality lead some individuals to experience stress or frustration" (Angew, 1999:123). Such feelings of relative deprivation, argues Angew (1999:127), can lead to high levels of "negative affect" among social collectives and to increased frequencies of interactions between "angry/frustrated individuals," which, in turn, lead to higher rates of crime. As such, social aggregates characterized by high levels of crime "are more likely to select and retain strained individuals, produce strain, and foster criminal responses to strain" (Agnew, 1999:126).

Agnew (1999) is also extremely clear in terms of what the relationships should look like between crime rates and variables assumed to both induce (inequality) and condition (social support) strain. Economic inequality is specified by Agnew (1999:127) as a structural source of strain in that inequality tends to "increase one's absolute level of goal blockage [and may] also increase one's feelings of relative deprivation." Furthermore, Agnew (1999:134) contends that "when inequality is high, people compare themselves to advantaged others, decide that they want and deserve what these others have, and decide that they cannot get what these others have through legitimate channels." Thus, a direct effect of economic inequality on aggregate crime rates should be found according to macrolevel general strain theory.

In addition to the main effects of economic inequality on crime rates, Agnew (1999) holds that indicators of social support should also maintain a direct effect on crime. To be sure, social support is implicated in general strain theory as having "an important effect on the ability of individuals to cope with strain" (Agnew, 1999:144; see also Hagan and McCarthy, 1997b). As such, macrolevel general strain theory—similar to the social support and institutional anomie perspectives—also specifies a direct and inverse effect of social support on crime. Consistent with the theoretical framework thus far, macrolevel general strain theory also specifies an interaction effect between measures of inequality and social support on crime. Indeed, as social support is viewed as a "conditioning variable" between aggregate structural characteristics (e.g., inequality) and crime, Agnew (1999) therefore contends that the effect of inequality on crime rates should be most pronounced when coupled with low levels of social support (see also Cullen and Wright, 1997; Hagan and McCarthy, 1997a).

RESEARCH STRATEGY

Given this integrated theoretical framework, our analysis addresses three main issues that emerge out of the social support, institutional anomie, and macrolevel general strain paradigms. First, we examine whether social support and economic inequality maintain significant *independent* effects on homicide rates. Second, we assess whether controlling for the effects of either social support or economic inequality *moderate* the effects for either variable. In other words, we are interested in whether controlling for either variable dampens—or "washes out"—the effects of the other. Finally, our analysis uncovers whether there is a significant *interaction* effect between social support and economic inequality on homicide rates in the cross-national setting.

METHODS

UNIT OF ANALYSIS

Criminologists have long debated the relative merits of various levels of aggregation for criminological research. Part of the problem often lies in the ambiguities contained in macrolevel criminological theories as to what the appropriate unit of analysis should be (Short, 1998). In the present case, we test the integrated theoretical model discussed above in the cross-national setting. Although it is certainly true that considerable within-nation variation exists with regard to social support, economic inequality, and homicide rates, our choice of nations as the unit of analysis was based on propositions contained in the theories under investigation. In particular, institutional anomie theory is explicit about how American social organization causes the United States to have high crime rates "compared with those of other developed nations" (Messner and Rosenfeld, 2001:42). Indeed, Messner and Rosenfeld (2001:80) themselves note how their perspective is "proposed for explaining the distinctive position of the United States when considered in [an] international perspective."

Furthermore, although perhaps slightly less explicit about optimal level of aggregation for theory testing, Cullen (1994:531) notes that the tenets of social support theory are applicable to "communities and *larger ecological units* in which individuals are enmeshed" (emphasis added). Following suit, Agnew (1999:124) states that his macrolevel general strain theory can "explain differences in crime rates across units like cities, SMSAs, and *beyond*" (emphasis added). Thus, although we acknowledge the existence of substantial within-nation heterogeneity with regard to the key variables of interest in the present case, testing this integrated perspective in the cross-national context is most appropriate for institutional anomie theory and is, at minimum, compatible with the social support and macrolevel general strain perspectives.

SAMPLE

Given the limited existence of reliable national-level proxies of social-structural characteristics, researchers are typically handcuffed by the availability of data when generating cross-national samples (Barclay, 2000; Killias and Rau, 2000; Neapolitan, 1997, 2001). Although sample sizes vary among the cross-national studies that have appeared in the criminological literature, reliable data that could be used in a multivariate statistical context is generally available for fairly well-developed industrialized nations only (LaFree, 1999; see also Gartner and Parker, 1990; Marenin, 1997; Messner and Rosenfeld, 1997; Savolainen, 2000). Accordingly, the data for the variables used in the analysis were drawn from the World Health Organization (2000) and the United Nations Statistics Division (2000). Thus, our sample of nations was based on our ability to gather reliable values for the dependent and independent variables of interest from these well-established cross-national data sources. Given the nature of our research question and the availability of data to measure our key concepts (i.e., the ability to obtain data for our independent and dependent variables for each nation in the sample),[4] the present sample is composed of 46 nations.[5]

DEPENDENT VARIABLE

The dependent variable of violent crime is operationalized using each nation's *homicide rate* (homicides per 100,000 citizens) drawn from the World Health Organization's (WHO) 2000 report. Homicides are used as a proxy for violent crime in this setting for three reasons. First, researchers have long noted the relative reliability of cross-national homicide rates over data on other types of offenses (LaFree, 1999; Neapolitan, 1997, 1999; see also Bennett and Lynch, 1990; Boswell and Dixon, 1993; Fiala and LaFree, 1988; Gartner, 1990; Lynch, 1995; Merriman, 1991; Neapolitan, 1998). Second, although recent data from the International Crime Survey (Lee, 2000) on offenses other than homicide (e.g., assault, burglary, theft) are now available for a select group of nations, there is little overlap between the nations included in this dataset with those from the WHO and United Nations Statistics Division sources. In the end, victimization data from the International Crime Survey were available for only 17 of the nations in the present sample, which would make any multivariate modeling techniques inappropriate.

Finally, it would seem that the institutional anomie and social support perspectives—with their similar emphases on the consequences of economic deprivation and cultural arrangements stressing the desirability of achieving economic success—would be most suited to the explanation of property offenses.[6] Messner and Rosenfeld (2001:86), however, explicitly

4. Given the limitations on the availability of data covering the time frame for the study, the listwise deletion of cases due to missing data would have dropped our sample size to 39. Using LISREL 8.50 for Windows and the EM algorithm, we imputed values for the missing cases. The EM algorithm generates values based on the covariance structure of the full set of variables included in the analysis. Thus, as opposed to an alternative method such as mean replacement, the variance estimates produced through imputation methods are not biased downward (which would otherwise increase the probability of obtaining statistically significant results).

5. The nations comprising the sample include Argentina, Australia, Austria, Belgium, Brazil, Canada, Chile, Colombia, Costa Rica, Denmark, Dominican Republic, Ecuador, Egypt, El Salvador, Finland, France, Germany, Greece, Guatemala, Ireland, Israel, Italy, Jamaica, Japan, Kuwait, Mauritius, Mexico, The Netherlands, New Zealand, Norway, Panama, Peru, Portugal, Russian Federation, Singapore, Spain, Sri Lanka, Sweden, Switzerland, Syria, Thailand, Trinidad (and Tobago), United Kingdom, United States, Uruguay, and Venezuela.

6. Relative to the institutional anomie and social support perspectives, Agnew's (1999) focus on the role of negative affect—or anger—in the explanation of aggregate crime rates appears on the surface to be most directly applicable to the explanation of homicide rates.

discuss how factors such as economic deprivation may inhibit "long-term integration in the economic, social, and *moral* life of a community" (emphasis in the original) in their explanation of the youth violence (primarily homicide) "epidemic" in the United States during the 1990s. In particular, in social contexts characterized by an absence of legitimate economic opportunities, illegitimate opportunities—particularly those associated with drug markets—become the preferred vehicle for securing the American Dream. As a result, Messner and Rosenfeld (2001:84) note how economic deprivation, inner city drug markets, and levels of homicide and other forms of firearm violence are not only intertwined, but "causally symmetrical: they account for both the increase and decrease in violence." Thus, institutional anomie theory does provide a plausible explanation for why social aggregates vary in terms of their homicide rates.

Similarly, Cullen's (1994) discussion of social support theory emphasizes the "generality" of how social support—at any level of aggregation—reduces crime and victimization. Indeed, Cullen (1994) notes that social support may be treated as an "organizing concept for criminology" (p. 529), and that it "*generally* reduces lawbreaking" (emphasis added, p. 551). Accordingly, although Cullen's perspective is not necessarily a theory of homicide, it has been articulated as a general theory of crime that, like institutional anomie theory, should account for differences in homicide rates across nations.

INDEPENDENT VARIABLES

Social Support Measure

In the absence of direct measures for key theoretical concepts, macrolevel researchers are generally faced with the task of developing proxy measures of the constructs under investigation. Although certain researchers have been able to "aggregate up" individual-level responses within particular social and geographic settings (see, e.g., Rosenfeld et al., 2001; Sampson and Groves, 1989), it is the norm in cross-national research to employ proxy measures of key concepts because of the inability to obtain direct measures due to the limited availability of reliable data—an approach that is also taken here (see also Chamlin and Cochran, 1995, 1997; Chamlin et al., 1999; Hoskin, 2001; Messner and Rosenfeld, 1997; Savolainen, 2000).

The research literature does not currently specify a uniform measure of social support at any level of aggregation. Although researchers have used creative measures such as charitable contributions (Chamlin and Cochran, 1997) and tax ratios (Chamlin et al., 1999) at lower levels of aggregation within the United States, it is questionable whether such indicators would be applicable in the cross-national setting even if they were available (which they are not). Even so, our reading of the social support perspective indicates that the concept could be measured in terms of the importance—or "value"—that social collectives will afford social institutions that, when emphasized, may combat the criminogenic effects of certain social-structural arrangements. Accordingly, our indicator of social support is the percent of the nation's gross domestic product (GDP) spent on health care. As the World Bank database provides disaggregated estimates of health care spending—including private, public, and total spending—we use the estimates of public spending on health care because it more closely approximates the concept of social support articulated above (as opposed to either private or total health care expenditures, which could simply be driven by individual spending).

Although we certainly admit that such an indicator comes with a degree of estimation error, we believe that our measure serves as a reasonably valid proxy of social support for three reasons. First, researchers have noted that the spending priorities of nations are generally reflective of the social priorities of their citizens (Aaron, 1992; Kingdon, 1999; Skocpol, 1992; Steinmo, 1993). Thus, we are operating on the working assumption that supportive societies are more likely to devote higher levels of economic resources toward supportive, noneconomic social institutions than those that are characterized by low levels of social support. Second, and relatedly, we view health care as a supportive, noneconomic social institution (see also Galbraith, 1996; Wilson, 1999). Indeed, scholars have noted the importance of health-related issues for promoting and enhancing intellectual and social development—especially among children—yet such efforts are often undermined by the lack of access or cultural preference for linking such programs to crime reduction (Currie, 1998; Yoshikawa, 1994). Finally, previous research has included a health care component in measures of "decommodification" (Esping-Anderson, 1990), a concept that has recently appeared in the criminological literature (Messner and Rosenfeld, 1997; Savolainen, 2000). In short, as stated above, nations that are "decommodified" are more likely to emphasize the importance of social support (Messner and Rosenfeld, 1997), and should therefore be less likely to create and maintain a criminogenic social structure.

Economic Inequality Measure

Consistent with the theoretical framework outlined above, our analysis includes a measure of economic inequality (Blau, 1977; Blau and Blau, 1982). Researchers have noted that the Gini index of economic inequality—the most common measure of inequality employed in aggregate studies of crime—tends to be unreliable in the cross-national setting (e.g., see the discussions by Hsieh and Pugh, 1993; Vieraitis, 2000). To improve the reliability (and predictive validity) of this measure, therefore, our indicator of economic inequality is measured as the ratio of the median incomes of the richest to the poorest 20% of citizens (for similar reasons, income differential-based inequality measures have been used by others; see, e.g., Blau and Blau, 1982; Blau and Golden, 1986; Braithwaite, 1979; Messner and South, 1986; Parker and McCall, 1999; Smith and Bennett, 1985; Vieraitis, 2000).

Structural Covariates

A number of structural covariates were included in the analysis as statistical controls in order to isolate the effects of the social support index and levels of economic inequality on homicide rates. The control variables included in the analysis are those typically employed by researchers when conducting cross-national analyses of crime (for reviews, see LaFree and Kick, 1986; Neuman and Berger, 1988). In particular, to maximize the available degrees of freedom and to minimize the potential problems associated with multicollinearity (Land et al., 1990), the structural covariates included in our models are intended to generally mirror those found in the most recent cross-national tests of the major criminological theories (Messner and Rosenfeld, 1997; Savolainen, 2000).

The first structural characteristics controlled in the analysis is each nation's *sex ratio* (measured as the number of men per 100 women), which has been shown to be related to national-level crime rates in prior criminological research (see Avakame, 1999; Guttentag and Secord, 1983; O'Brien, 1991). Consistent with prior research in this area, our analyses also control for the *percentage of the population living in urban areas* (Fischer, 1975). Finally, we also control for the effect of general socioeconomic development with the *human development index* (for similar approaches, see Messner and Rosenfeld, 1997; Bennett, 1991). Controlling for development is important for determining whether or not the theoretical propositions discussed above are limited to fully developed nations only (see also Savolainen, 2000). The four factors comprising the human development index (HDI), which is compiled by the WHO, include average life expectancy at birth; adult literacy rates; combined primary, secondary, and tertiary education enrollment, and the GDP per capita measured in U.S. dollars. Aside from serving as a control for socioeconomic development, by taking into account the average life expectancy at birth—which is based on age cohort trajectories over time—the HDI also adjusts for the age composition of each nation. This is critically important for the current study because Savolainen (2000:1030) notes that "nations with a large elderly population are likely to spend a larger proportion of the budget on . . . health care programs." Controlling for the HDI, therefore, removes the potentially spurious shared variation between our social support measure and homicide rates that may be due to differences in the age structures across the nations in our sample.

RESULTS

Table 1 contains the descriptive statistics for the variables included in the analysis. As indicated, the natural log of each nation's homicide rate was taken to correct for skewness in the variable's univariate distribution. Furthermore, prior to presenting the results of the multivariate model testing the relationship between social support and homicide, it is first necessary to explore whether the problems associated with multicollinearity between the independent variables may be present. Following the section addressing the collinearity diagnostics we conducted, the results of the multivariate analysis are presented. Finally, this section concludes with a series of additional statistical diagnostic analyses intended to determine the adequacy of the multivariate statistical models when subjected to changes in model specification and sample composition.

Table 1. Descriptive Statistics and Zero-Order Correlations for Variables Included in the Analysis (N = 46).

Variable	1	2	3	4	5	6	7
1. Homicide Rate (ln)	—						
2. Sex Ratio	.094	—					
3. Percent Urban	.027	–.114	—				
4. HDI	–.205	–.089	.302*	—			
5. Social Support	–.407**	–.330*	.326*	.424**	—		
6. Economic Inequality	.477**	.168	–.117	–.293*	–.380**	—	
7. Support-Inequality Interaction	–.553**	–.122	–.259†	.121	.281†	–.325*	—
Mean	1.383	98.13	70.00	.831	0.00	0.00	.630
SD	1.169	3.28	19.28	.009	1.00	1.00	.488

* = $p < .05$; ** = $p < .01$; † = $p < .10$

TESTING FOR MULTICOLLINEARITY

Table 1 also contains the zero-order correlation coefficients between each of the variables to be included in the multivariate analysis. Extremely high intercorrelations between independent variables in a multivariate context may result in unstable and biased parameter estimates (Blalock, 1972; Hanushek and Jackson, 1977). Although it is certainly not the final step for identifying whether multicollinearity will be present in a statistical model, examining the bivariate correlations between the predictor variables may be a useful first step in this process (Fox, 1994).

A zero-order correlation of at least .70 between two independent variables is generally treated as the threshold for when multicollinearity becomes a mathematical certainty (where each variable explains more than of the variation in the other; see Hanushek and Jackson, 1977). As indicated in Table 1, none of the bivariate correlations exceed .70. Nevertheless, in a multivariate model, when the effects of each of the covariates are controlled statistically, multicollinearity may still emerge between predictor variables that were highly correlated—although not above .70—at the bivariate level (Farrar and Glauber, 1967; Maddala, 1992). Accordingly, the correlations between economic inequality and social support (r = –.380), and between the human development index and social support (r = .424) are both high enough that the risk of multicollinearity may still be present in a multivariate model.

As an explicit test for multicollinearity, therefore, we computed the variance inflation factors (VIFs) for each of the weighted least-squares (WLS) regression models presented in Tables 2 and 3. None of the VIFs exceed the threshold of 4—the standard "cutoff" point indicating when multicollinearity is present (Fox, 1991).[7] Given the potential limitations of VIF values (see Maddala, 1992)—in particular, the restricted relevance of the VIF to individual coefficients of direct interest with no applicability to "sets" of regressors (Fox and Monette, 1992:478)—we also examined the condition index scores from each predictor. Each of these scores fell well below the threshold of 30 specified by Belsley et al. (1980). Thus, despite the relatively large bivariate correlations between certain predictors included in the multivariate models, we are confident that the parameter estimates were not biased due to multicollinearity.

THE MULTIVARIATE MODELS

Table 2 contains the results of the WLS regression models testing the relationship among social support, economic inequality, and homicide at the national level. The square root of each nation's population size is used as the weight variable in the WLS models to adjust for the problems associated with heteroscedasticity that often accompany aggregate-level research when ordinary least-squares (OLS) regression is used (Lyon and Tsai, 1996).[8]

7. Some researchers hold that a VIF value of over 10 indicates the presence of multicollinearity (Neter et al., 1990). To err on the side of statistical conservatism, we have chosen the lower threshold of 4 as our indicator of multicollinearity.

8. Residual analysis did reveal unequal variances across fixed values of the dependent variable using studentized score tests proposed by Breusch and Pagan (1979) and by Cook and Weisberg (1983)—an approach generally considered to be considerably robust because it does not require the assumption of normally distributed error terms in the OLS solution (Lyon and Tsai, 1996).

Table 2. WLS regression models of social support, economic inequality, and structural covariates predicting homicide rates (ln). Standardized effects (β) shown (N = 46).

Independent Variable	Model 1	Model 2	Model 3	Model 4
Sex Ratio	–.321*	–.213†	–.311*	–.220†
Percent Urban	.274†	–.018	.112	–.047
HDI	.075	.061	.157	.206
Social Support	–.690**	—	–.399*	–.281†
Economic Inequality	—	.688**	.541**	.383**
Social Support-Economic Inequality Interaction	—	—	—	–.359*
Model F	5.141**	8.812**	9.336**	10.21**
Model R-square	.334	.462	.539	.611

NOTE: all WLS regression models estimated using the square root of each nation's population as the weight. * = $p < .05$; ** = $p < .01$; † = $p < .10$

Model 1 is fairly robust (r-square = .334; $p < .01$). In this equation, we are interested in whether social support is significantly related to homicide rates after controlling for the specified structural characteristics of each nation. As can be seen in Table 2, a statistically significant inverse relationship between social support and homicide rates was revealed by the multivariate model. Furthermore, the strongest relationship contained in the model was between social support and homicide (standardized β = –.690). Thus, net of statistical controls, the analysis reveals a strong inverse effect of social support on homicides at the national level.

Model 2 assesses whether economic inequality significantly predicts homicide rates after controlling for the structural covariates. Like the previous equation, the full model is robust (r-square = .462, $p < .01$). Furthermore, model 2 indicates that economic inequality also exerts a strong independent effect on homicides (β = .688), where higher levels of economic inequality are associated with higher homicide rates.

In model 3, we are interested in what happens to the effects of both social support and economic inequality on homicide rates when controlling for the effects of both key theoretical variables. In essence, model 3 addresses whether social support or economic inequality moderate the effects of the other variable (i.e., does controlling for the effects of each dampen the predictive capacity of either variable?). In answering this question, both social support and economic inequality still maintain statistically significant relationships with homicide rates after controlling for the effects of each, and the full statistical model explains a substantially larger proportion of the variation in the dependent variable (r-square = .539, $p <$ .01). Nevertheless, the magnitudes of the effects for both variables are reduced (social support $\beta = -.399$, economic inequality $\beta = .541$) in this model. Even so, the direct effects of both social support and economic inequality on homicide rates in model 3 suggest that both variables still exert a strong and fairly stable influence on homicide rates.

Aside from these "main effects," the theoretical integration presented above suggests that social support, institutional anomie, and macrolevel general strain theories all posit a significant interaction effect between social support and economic inequality on crime. Accordingly, model 4 adds a social support-economic inequality interaction term to the WLS regression equation. Taking the approach suggested by Jaccard et al. (1990), the variables contributing to the interaction term were centered—a practice generally assumed to reduce multicollinearity among predictor variables. Nevertheless, a VIF above 4.00 emerged in the WLS model using the centered interaction term (VIF = 4.265), which suggests the presence of multicollinearity with the constituent components of the interaction term—a finding not uncommon in aggregate research using relatively small sample sizes. To avoid the estimation problems associated with multicollinearity for these analyses, the interaction term was recoded into a dummy variable where a value of 0 reflects high levels of economic inequality and low levels of social support relative to all others in the sample.

As with each of the three previous equations, the full model is certainly robust (r-square = .611, $p < .01$). Also, consistent with the theoretical integration, the interaction between social support and economic inequality is both strong and significant ($\beta = -.359$, $p < .05$). The negative sign of the coefficient for the interaction term indicates that the effect of economic inequality on homicide rates is significantly reduced in the presence of high levels of social support. Finally, including the interaction term did not "wash out" the main effects for either social support ($\beta = -.281$, $p < .10$) or economic inequality ($\beta = .383$, $p < .05$). Thus, taken together, the four WLS regression models presented in Table 2 indicate that social support and economic inequality are strongly and independently related to homicide rates and that the interaction between the two variables also plays a role in explaining variation in national-level homicide rates.[9]

MODEL SPECIFICATION DIAGNOSTICS

In addition to the collinearity diagnostics discussed above, two sets of additional statistical diagnostic analyses were conducted to examine the

9. It is important to note that the sex ratio also maintained a consistent inverse effect on homicides across each of the models presented in Table 2. This means that a higher proportion of males relative to females in the population is associated with lower levels of homicide—a finding that is consistent with Messner and Sampson's (1991) discussion of the supply of marriage partners in a given social context.

adequacy of the multivariate models presented in Table 2. The results of these analyses are presented in Table 3. First, in model 1, we reestimated the full main and interaction effects model from Table 2 after deleting the United States from the analysis. This was done to test for whether the United States—which is often viewed as "exceptional" with regard to limited access to public social support along with high rates of violent crime (see, e.g., Kingdon, 1999; Zimring and Hawkins, 1997)—is really "driving" the results. None of the parameter estimates differed significantly from the previous model using equality of coefficients tests (for detailed discussions of the method for comparing the equality of parameter estimates, see Clogg et al., 1995).[10] This may not be terribly surprising. Indeed, Rose (1991) and Wilson (1998) have argued that a number of European and Pacific Rim nations, including Switzerland, Finland, Canada, Japan, and Australia, are similar to the United States in terms of their general economic structure and the overall scope of the state. Thus, despite the American desire to view itself as such, it may not be essentially unique.[11]

The second set of analyses concerned the issue of potential spuriousness. We addressed this issue by estimating three additional WLS regression models under different specifications. First, model 2 in Table 3 includes an explicit measure for the *age structure* of each nation (proportion of the population aged 15 to 59). As stated above, researchers have noted the potential problem that nations with a larger proportion of older residents are more likely to spend more on health care (Savolainen, 2000). Although our measure of overall development—the HDI—contains an item related to each population's age structure, it is possible that when included in such an index, its potential effects on homicides are obscured. Upon including the measure of age structure in model 2 the direct effect of social support is no longer statistically significant. The inclusion of the age structure, however, does not fully moderate either the direct effect of economic inequality or the social support-inequality interaction effect on homicides. Thus, the overall pattern of significance-nonsignificance for the relationships among social support, economic inequality, and the interaction between the two on homicides—although fairly consistent—is not completely invariant across this alternative model specification.

10. This method differs from that discussed by Brame et al. (1998) in that the Clogg et al. (1995) test is designed for coefficient comparisons using the same sample. The test discussed by Brame et al. (1998) is intended for independent samples.

11. Similar analyses were conducted after deleting the Russian Federation, Trinidad and Tobago, and The Netherlands (all of which contained either extreme values on key variables of interest) with results that did not significantly differ from those presented in model 1 from Table 3.

Table 3. Standardized WLS regression coefficients for social support and economic inequality (main and interaction effects) on homicide rates across sample specifications. Standardized effects (β) shown.

Independent Variable	Model 1	Model 2	Model 3	Model 4
Sex Ratio	–.246*	–.302*	—	–.220†
Percent Urban	.001	.031	—	–.054
HDI	.033	—	—	.213
Percent Measles Immunized	—	—	—	–.021
Age Structure	—	.394*	—	—
Incarceration Rate	—	—	.292**	—
Disorganization Index	—	—	–.089	—
Social Support	–.308*	–.042	–.255†	–.287†
Economic Inequality	.298*	.202†	.344*	.381**
Social Support-Economic Inequality Interaction	–.433**	–.337*	–.348*	–.357*
Model F	14.036**	11.488**	11.599**	8.546**
Model R-square	.689	.639	.641	.612

NOTE: Model 1: United States excluded from the analysis. * = $p < .05$; ** = $p < .01$; † = $p < .10$

In taking this inquiry a step further, model 3 in Table 3 includes a composite measure of factors typically used in macrolevel criminological studies limited to the United States referred to as a *disorganization index*. The disorganization index is a factor consisting of five items: age structure, the sex ratio, the infant mortality rate, the percent of the population (aged 15–19 never married), and a five-year rural-urban population change (as a proxy for residential mobility). Each of these items was highly correlated and loaded onto a single factor (64.25% explained variance)—each with a factor loading above .70. This factor is assumed to tap into the social problems that tend to be associated with urbanization, high levels of family disruption, and increased residential mobility (see, e.g., Bursik and Grasmick, 1993; Sampson, 1986; Shaw and McKay, 1972).[12] This model also includes a measure of each nation's *incarceration rate*—a measure that, in addition to being a proxy for the general punitiveness of a society (Young and Brown, 1993), has also been interpreted to be an indicator of the degree to which social collectives experience intense social and political conflict (Donziger, 1996; Rose and Clear, 1998; Tonry, 1995). The

12. As the sex ratio, age structure, and urbanism variables were included in the disorganization index, they were excluded from model 2 to avoid multicollinearity.

results of this analysis are generally consistent with those revealed in Table 2. Specifically, although the incarceration rate emerges as a significant predictor of homicides (the disorganization index was not), the general trends for statistical significance and strength for the measures of social support, economic inequality, and the interaction between the two remained consistent.

Finally, we reestimated the final WLS regression model from Table 2 using an "identification restriction" (Fisher, 1966; see also Nagin, 1998a) to remove the potentially spurious portion of shared variation between our measure of social support and homicide rates (see also Nagin, 1998b). In particular, as our proxy of social support includes a health care component, an inverse association between social support and homicides may reflect, in part, a "hospital effect," where citizens living in nations with a higher quality of health care are less likely to die as a result of a potentially fatal interpersonal encounter (similar arguments and methodological approaches have been taken by Loftin and Hill, 1974; Nagin, 1978, 1998a). Thus, to control for the risk of a hospital effect, we use the *proportion of one-year-olds that have been immunized for measles* as our identification restriction, the results of which are presented in model 4 in Table 3. Upon doing so, equality of coefficients tests again revealed that none of the parameter estimates differed significantly as a result of including the identification restriction.[13]

DISCUSSION

Criminological theorists have made major strides in recent years, including the emergence of new theoretical traditions, the development of sophisticated multilevel explanations of crime, and the refinement and reformulation of well-established (even if not well-tested) criminological theories. One of the most visible trends in the development of macrolevel criminological theory is movement toward theoretical integration. Social support (Chamlin and Cochran, 1997; Cullen, 1994), institutional anomie

13. In additional analyses, we created a composite index for social support that included an item for the percent of the GDP spent on education in addition to health care. These additional models generally mirrored the results of the original analyses with two minor exceptions. First, the direct effects of social support were slightly weaker (yet still statistically significant) in all of the models presented in Table 2 (and the first two models in Table 3). This is likely because of the introduction of a certain degree of measurement error with this index (the two items are strongly, yet not extremely highly, correlated at .54). Second, the effects of the composite index were slightly stronger in the final model presented in Table 3. As the identification restriction employed in model 4 in Table 3 was specifically directed to the health care component of the social support measure, it is not surprising that its corrective effects were dampened a bit with the composite measure.

(Messner and Rosenfeld, 2001), and macrolevel general strain theory (Agnew, 1999) all exist as integrated alternatives to the more narrowly defined perspectives such as routine activity, subcultural, deterrence/rational choice, and relative/absolute deprivation theories. According to a recent discussion by Tittle (2000:86), the advantage of the integrated approach is that it has "led to overlaps among various theories, along with wider recognition of the advantages of bringing diverse ideas together and of borrowing from various extant accounts to create theories with more scope and more precise explanatory application." Tittle (2000:87) goes on to note, however, that "there is an emerging awareness that research practice is now lagging behind theory." Thus, it is critical that we not only seek to clarify such theoretical integration efforts on conceptual grounds, but that we subject them to empirical analysis as well (see also Hay, 2001; Liska, 1987).

With this goal in mind, the central purpose of this article was not to settle the debate concerning which criminological theory may rightfully claim "ownership" over the relationships among social support, inequality, and crime. To be sure, one of the major objectives of this article was to demonstrate how social support, institutional anomie, and macrolevel general strain theories can be successfully integrated with regard to these key concepts. What the present analysis does show is that significant relationships among social support, inequality, and crime rates do in fact exist. In particular, measures of both social support and economic inequality maintain strong and stable main and interaction effects with homicide rates. Even more important, the interaction effects revealed in the analyses indicate that the criminogenic effects of economic inequality are enhanced when found in conjunction with low levels of social support (see also Hannon and DeFronzo, 1998b). Furthermore, these relationships remained stable when assessed under different sampling conditions and under different methodological specifications.

Taken together, we are therefore confident that our results were not idiosyncratic to a particular sample or method of estimation; rather, they reflect ongoing social phenomena in the cross-national context. Nevertheless, it still remains to be seen whether similar results would be found regarding the dynamics of economic inequality, social support, and crime in cross-national tests when using crime measures other than homicides. To a certain extent, this process has already begun. Lee's (2000) analysis of the 1992 wave of the International Victimization Survey for 15 nations revealed a fairly consistent inverse effect for "community cohesion"—a concept akin to Sampson et al.'s (1997) "collective efficacy"—on the victimization risk for robbery and assault. In the absence of comparative data on homicide victimization, however, it is still unclear (both theoretically and empirically) whether the general pattern of statistical significance/nonsignificance of the relationships found in the present study would hold when predicting crime types other than homicides (see also the review by LaFree, 1999).

Accordingly, scholars should continue to clarify the core propositions of the theories tested here—possibly with the intent of further integration (Bernard and Snipes, 1996; Liska et al., 1989). Colvin's (2000) integrated perspective on crime and coercion, coupled with the emerging research on the relationship between social capital and crime (Rosenfeld et al., 2001), are both illustrative of the trend toward merging concepts from alternative criminological perspectives under a common umbrella. It is still, however, incumbent upon researchers to subject the core propositions specified by these theories to empirical analysis—only in doing so can the relative empirical validity of these theories be established.

In addition to these implications for the continued development of criminological theory, the policy implications of the research presented here are fairly straightforward. First, our analysis echoes the statement by Chamlin et al. (1999:441) in their test of social support (referred to as altruism) theory that "unlike the crime reduction strategies one might deduce from motivational and opportunity theories of crime, social [support] theory does not call for a radical transformation of the social structure." This is not to say that crime rates could not be substantially reduced within and across macrosocial units by altering certain social-structural arrangements. Indeed, ample empirical evidence exists that points to the criminogenic effects of both absolute (poverty) and relative (inequality) economic deprivation at multiple levels of aggregation (see, e.g., Bailey, 1999; Blau and Blau, 1982; Carroll and Jackson, 1983; Crutchfield, 1989; Fowles and Merva, 1996; Harer and Steffensmeier, 1992; Kovandzic et al., 1998; Land et al., 1990; Piquero and Piquero, 1998; Pratt and Lowenkamp, 2002; Warner and Roundtree, 1997). Even so, the present research affirms the notion that increases in levels of social support are capable of producing a concomitant reduction in crime rates even in the absence of a social and economic revolution, and that higher levels of social support can help to reduce the harmful effects of economic inequality on crime.

We also hasten to note that an emphasis on social support does not necessarily render social control mechanisms—when either formal or informal in nature—as unimportant in explaining variations in crime rates. To be sure, there is ample empirical evidence demonstrating the ability of certain types of policing practices (Nagin, 1998b; cf. Eck and Maguire, 2000), situational crime prevention strategies (e.g., see Brantingham and Brantingham, 1991; Felson and Clarke, 1997; Mazerolle et al., 1998), and other institutions of informal social control (e.g., the dynamics of family disruption and "collective efficacy") to affect levels of crime within macrosocial units (Bursik, 1986; Friedman, 1998; LaFree, 1998; Sampson, 1986; Sampson and Groves, 1989; Sampson et al., 1997; Veysey and Messner, 1999). Nevertheless, the problem—at least according to social support theorists—is that macrolevel theories premised on notions of control often err in their assumption that the only effective approach to crime prevention "requires doing something *to* a person rather than *for* a person" (Cullen et al., 1999:189; emphasis in the original).

In the case of the United States, the "control" perspective has been translated (or perhaps perverted) into a series of repressive crime control policies aimed at increasing the potential risks associated with crime (Beckett, 1997; Gordon, 1990). Rooted in the "common sense" notion that would-be offenders are sufficiently contemplative in the moments before typical criminal events, the architects of such policies assume that the fear of incarceration, harsh community-level sanctions, or intense physical exercise (e.g., boot camps) will keep crime rates in check (Bennett et al., 1996; Reynolds, 1997; cf. Clear, 1994; Cullen and Gilbert, 1982; Cullen et al., 1996). As a conceptual alternative to this theoretical framework (and concomitant policy prescriptions), a core proposition shared by the social support, institutional anomie, and macrolevel general strain paradigms is that a more useful method for increasing our understanding of why crime rates vary across macrosocial units is to assess how crime may be, in part, a function of the degree of social support that is afforded to social collectives.

On a related note, this study also indicates that state-based crime control efforts do not necessarily have to come in a punitive form. Nevertheless, a nagging barrier holding back the momentum of a more progressive crime control policy agenda—especially in the United States—is the considerable amount of scholarly attention that academics have devoted toward attempting to demonstrate the ineptitude and potentially coercive nature of the "softer" side of public policies aimed at reducing crime (e.g., correctional rehabilitation programs; see Logan and Gaes, 1993; Martinson, 1974; Whitehead and Lab, 1989; cf. Cullen and Gendreau, 2001; Pratt, 2002). Additional empirical research addressing the emerging social support, institutional anomie, and macrolevel general strain paradigms may, however, help to show that collective efforts to provide social support to citizens represents a promising and progressive method for reducing crime.

SOCIAL SUPPORT, INEQUALITY, AND HOMICIDE 633

REFERENCES

Aaron, Henry J.
1992 Health care financing. In Henry J. Aaron and Charles L. Schultze (eds.), Setting Domestic Priorities: What Can Government Do? Washington, D.C.: The Brookings Institution.

Agnew, Robert
1985 Neutralizing the impact of crime. Criminal Justice and Behavior 12:221–239.
1992 Foundation for a general strain theory of crime and delinquency. Criminology 30:47–86.
1999 A general strain theory of community differences in crime rates. Journal of Research in Crime and Delinquency 36:123–155.

Apter, Steven J. and Cathy A. Propper
1986 Ecological perspectives on youth violence. In Steven J. Apter and Arnold P. Goldstein (eds.), Youth Violence: Programs and Prospects. New York: Pergamon.

Avakame, Edem F.
1999 Sex ratios, female labor force participation, and lethal violence against women. Violence Against Women 5:1321–1341.

Bailey, William C.
1999 The socioeconomic status of women and patterns of forcible rape for major U.S. cities. Sociological Focus 32:43–63.

Barclay, Gordon C.
2000 The comparability of data on convictions and sanctions: Are international comparisons possible? European Journal on Criminal Policy and Research 8:13–26.

Barrera, Manuel and Susan A. Li
1996 The relation of family support to adolescents' psychological distress and behavior problems. In Gregory R. Pierce, Barbara R. Sarason, and Irwin G. Sarason (eds.), Handbook of Social Support and the Family. New York: Plenum.

Becker, Gary S.
1968 Crime and punishment: An economic approach. The Journal of Political Economy 76:169–217.

Beckett, Katherine
1997 Making Crime Pay. New York: Oxford University Press.

Belsley, David A., Edwin Kuh, and Roy E. Welsch
1980 Regression Diagnostics. New York: Wiley.

Bennett, Richard R.
1991 Development and crime: A cross-national, time-series analysis of competing models. The Sociological Quarterly 32:343–363.

Bennett, Richard R. and James Lynch
1990 Does a difference make a difference? Comparing cross-national crime indicators. Criminology 28:153–181.

Bennett, William J., John J. DiIulio, and John P. Walters
1996 Body Count. New York: Simon and Schuster.

Bernard, Thomas J.

1990 Angry aggression among the "truly disadvantaged." Criminology 28:73–96.

Bernard, Thomas J. and Jeffrey B. Snipes

1996 Theoretical integration in criminology. In Michael Tonry (ed.), Crime and Justice: A Review of Research. Chicago: University of Chicago Press.

Blalock, Hubert M.

1972 Social Statistics. 2d ed. New York: McGraw-Hill.

Blau, Peter M.

1977 Inequality and Heterogeneity. New York: The Free Press.

Blau, Peter M. and Judith R. Blau

1982 The cost of inequality: Metropolitan structure and violent crime. American Sociological Review 47:114–129.

Blau, Peter M. and Reid M. Golden

1986 Metropolitan structure and criminal violence. Sociological Quarterly 27:15–26.

Blumstein, Alfred, Jacqueline Cohen, and Daniel Nagin

1978 Deterrence and Incapacitation: Estimating the Effects of Criminal Sanctions on Crime Rates. Panel on Research on Deterrent and Incapacitative Effects, National Research Council. Washington, D.C.: National Academy of Sciences.

Boswell, Terry and William J. Dixon

1993 Marx's theory of rebellion: A cross-national analysis of class exploitation, economic development, and violent revolt. American Sociological Review 58:681–702.

Braithwaite, John

1979 Inequality, Crime and Public Policy. London: Routledge and Kegan Paul.

1989 Crime, Shame, and Reintegration. Cambridge, U.K.: Cambridge University Press.

Brame, Robert, Raymond Paternoster, Paul Mazerolle, and Alex Piquero

1998 Testing for the equality of maximum-likelihood regression coefficients between two independent equations. Journal of Quantitative Criminology 14:245–261.

Brantingham, Paul J. and Patricia L. Brantingham

1991 Environmental Criminology. Revised edition. Prospect Heights, Ill.: Waveland.

Breusch, T.S. and A.R. Pagan

1979 A simple test for heteroscedasticity and random coefficient variation. Economietrica 47:1287–1294.

Brezina, Timothy, Alex R. Piquero, and Paul Mazerolle

2001 Student anger and aggressive behavior in school: An initial test of Agnew's macro-level general strain theory. Journal of Research in Crime and Delinquency 38:362–386.

Bursik, Robert J.
1986 Ecological stability and the dynamics of delinquency. In Albert J. Riess and Michael Tonry (eds.), Communities and Crime. Chicago: University of Chicago Press.
1988 Social disorganization and theories of crime and delinquency: Problems and prospects. Criminology 26:519–551.

Bursik, Robert J. and Harold G. Grasmick
1993 Neighborhoods and Crime: The Dimensions of Effective Community Control. New York: Macmillan.

Carroll, Leo and Pamela Irving Jackson
1983 Inequality, opportunity, and crime rates in central cities. Criminology 21:178–94.

Chamlin, Mitchell B. and John K. Cochran
1995 Assessing Messner and Rosenfeld's institutional anomie theory: A partial test. Criminology 33:411–429.
1996 Reply to Jensen. Criminology 34:133–134.
1997 Social altruism and crime. Criminology 35:203–228.

Chamlin, Mitchell B., Kenneth J. Novak, Christopher T. Lowenkamp, and John K. Cochran
1999 Social altruism, tax policy, and crime: A cautionary tale. Criminal Justice Policy Review 10:429–446.

Chiricos, Theodore G.
1987 Rates of crime and unemployment: An analysis of aggregate research evidence. Social Problems 34:187–212.

Clear, Todd R.
1994 Harm in American Penology: Offenders, Victims, and Their Communities. Albany: State University of New York Press.

Clogg, Clifford C., Eva Petkova, and Adamantios Haritou
1995 Statistical methods for comparing regression coefficients between models. American Journal of Sociology 100:1261–1293.

Cohen, Lawrence E. and Marcus Felson
1979 Social change and crime rate trends: A routine activities approach. American Sociological Review 44:588–608.

Coleman, James S.
1990 Foundations of Social Theory. Cambridge, Mass.: Harvard University Press.

Colvin, Mark
2000 Crime and Coercion: An Integrated Theory of Chronic Criminality. New York: St. Martin's.

Cook, R. Dennis and Sanford Weisberg
1983 Diagnostics for heteroscedasticity in regression. Biometrika 70:1–10.

Crutchfield, Robert D.
1989 Labor stratification and violent crime. Social Forces 68:489–512.

Cullen, Francis T.
1994 Social support as an organizing concept for criminology: Presidential address to the academy of criminal justice sciences. Justice Quarterly 11:527–559.

Cullen, Francis T. and Paul Gendreau
2001 From nothing works to what works: Changing professional ideology in the 21st century. The Prison Journal 81:313–338.

Cullen, Francis T. and Karen E. Gilbert
1982 Reaffirming Rehabilitation. Cincinnati, Ohio: Anderson.

Cullen, Francis T. and John Paul Wright
1997 Liberating the anomie-strain paradigm: Implications from social-support theory. In Nikos Passas and Robert Agnew (eds.), The Future of Anomie Theory. Boston: Northeastern University Press.

Cullen, Francis T., John Paul Wright, and Brandon K. Applegate
1996 Control in the community: The limits of reform? In Alan T. Harland (ed.), Choosing Correctional Options that Work. Thousand Oaks, Calif.: Sage.

Cullen, Francis T., John Paul Wright, and Mitchell B. Chamlin
1999 Social support and social reform: A progressive crime control agenda. Crime and Delinquency 45:188–207.

Currie, Elliott
1985 Confronting Crime: An American Challenge. New York: Pantheon.
1998 Crime and Punishment in America. New York: Owl Books.

DeFronzo, James
1983 Economic assistance to impoverished Americans: Relationship to incidence of crime. Criminology 21:119–136.
1996 Welfare and burglary. Crime and Delinquency 42:223–230.
1997 Welfare and homicide. Journal of Research in Crime and Delinquency 34:395–406.

Devine, Joel A., Joseph F. Sheley, and M. Dwayne Smith
1988 Macroeconomic and social-control policy influences on crime rate changes, 1948–1985. American Sociological Review 53:407–420.

Donziger, Steven R.
1996. The Real War on Crime. New York: Harper Collins.

Eck, John and Edward Maguire
2000 Have changes in policing reduced violent crime? An assessment of the evidence. In Alfred Blumstein and Joel Wallm-n (eds.), The Crime Drop in America. Cambridge, U.K.: Cambridge University Press.

Esping-Anderson, Gosta
1990 Three Worlds of Welfare Capitalism. New York: Princeton University Press.

Etzioni, Amatai
1993 The Spirit of Community: Rights, Responsibilities, and the Communitarian Agenda. New York: Crown.

Farrar, Donald E. and Robert R. Glauber
1967 Multicollinearity in regression analysis: The problem revisited. Review of Economics and Statistics 49:92–107.

Felson, Marcus and Ronald V. Clarke
1997 Business and Crime Prevention. Monsey, N.Y.: Criminal Justice Press.

Fiala, Robert and Gary LaFree
1988 Cross-national determinants of child homicides. American Sociological Review 53:432–445.

Fischer, Claude S.
1975 Toward a subcultural theory of urbanism. American Journal of Sociology 80:1319–1341.

Fisher, Franklin M.
1966 The Identification Problem in Econometrics. New York: McGraw Hill.

Fowles, Richard and Mary Merva
1996 Wage inequality and criminal activity: An extreme bounds analysis for the United States, 1975-1990. Criminology 34:163–182.

Fox, John
1991 Regression Diagnostics. Newbury Park, Calif.: Sage.
1994 Linear Statistical Models and Related Methods. New York: Wiley.

Fox, John and Georges Monette
1992 Generalized collinearity diagnostics. Journal of the American Statistical Association 87:178–183.

Friedman, Warren
1998 Volunteerism and the decline of violent crime. Journal of Criminal Law and Criminology 88:1453–1474.

Galbraith, John Kenneth
1996 The Good Society: The Humane Agenda. New York: Houghton Mifflin.

Gartner, Rosemary
1990 The victims of homicide: A temporal and cross-national comparison. American Sociological Review 55:92–106.

Gartner, Rosemary and Robert Nash Parker
1990 Cross-national evidence on homicide and the age structure of the population. Social Forces 69:351–371.

Gordon, Diana R.
1990 The Justice Juggernaut. New Brunswick, N.J.: Rutgers University Press.

Guttentag, Marcia and Paul Secord
1983 Too Many Women? The Sex Ratio Question. Beverly Hills, Calif.: Sage.

Hagan, John and Bill McCarthy
1997a Mean Streets. Cambridge, U.K.: Cambridge University Press.
1997b Anomie, social capital and street crime. In Nikos Passas and Robert Agnew (eds.), The Future of Anomie Theory. Boston: Northeastern University Press.

Hannon, Lance and James DeFronzo
1998a Welfare and property crime. Justice Quarterly 15:273–288.
1998b The truly disadvantaged, public assistance, and crime. Social Problems 45:383–392.

Hanushek, Eric A. and John E. Jackson
1977 Statistical Methods for Social Scientists. San Diego, Calif.: Academic Press.

Harer, Miles D. and Darrell Steffensmeier
1992 The differing effects of economic inequality on Black and White rates of violence. Social Forces 70:1035–1054.

Hay, Carter
2001 An exploratory test of Braithwaite's reintegrative shaming theory. Journal of Research in Crime and Delinquency 38:132–153.

Hoskin, Anthony W.
2001 Armed Americans: The impact of firearm availability on national homicide rates. Justice Quarterly 18:569–592.

Hsieh, Ching-Chi and M.D. Pugh
1993 Poverty, income inequality, and violent crime: A meta-analysis. Criminal Justice Review 18:182–202.

Jensen, Gary F.
1996 Comment on Chamlin and Cochran. Criminology 34:129–131.

Jaccard, James, Robert Turrisi, and Choi K. Wan
1990 Interaction Effects in Multiple Regression. Thousand Oaks, Calif.: Sage.

Killias, Martin and Wolfgang Rau
2000 The European sourcebook of crime and criminal justice statistics: A new tool in assessing crime and policy issues in comparative and empirical perspective. European Journal on Criminal Policy and Research 8:3–12.

Kingdon, John W.
1999 America the Unusual. New York: St. Martins.

Kovandzic, Tomislav V., Lynne M. Vieraitis, and Mark R. Yeisley
1998 The structural covariates of urban homicide: Reassessing the impact of income inequality and poverty in the post-Reagan era. Criminology 36:569–599.

LaFree, Gary
1998 Social institutions and the crime "bust" of the 1990s. Journal of Criminal Law and Criminology 88:1325–1368.
1999 A summary and review of cross-national comparative studies of homicide. In M. Dwayne Smith and Margaret A. Zahn (eds.), Homicide: A Sourcebook of Social Research. Thousand Oaks, Calif.: Sage.

LaFree, Gary D. and Edward L. Kick
1986 Cross-national effects of developmental, distributional, and demographic variables on crime: A review and analysis. International Annals of Criminology 24:213–235.

Land, Kenneth C., Patricia L. McCall, and Lawrence E. Cohen
1990 Structural covariates of homicide rates: Are there any invariances across time and space? American Journal of Sociology 95:922–963.

Lee, Matthew R.
2000 Community cohesion and violent predatory victimization: A theoretical extension and cross-national test of opportunity theory. Social Forces 79:683–688.

Lin, Nan
1986 Conceptualizing social support. In Nan Lin, Alfred Dean, and Walter Edsel (eds.), Social Support, Life Events, and Depression. Orlando: Academic Press.

Liska, Allen E.
1987 A critical examination of macro perspectives on crime control. Annual Review of Sociology 13:67–88.

Liska, Allen E., Marvin D. Krohn, and Steven F. Messner
1989 Strategies and requisites for theoretical integration in the study of crime and deviance. In Steven F. Messner, Marvin D. Krohn, and Allen E. Liska (eds.), Theoretical Integration in the Study of Crime and Deviance: Problems and Prospects. Albany: State University of New York Press.

Loeber, Rolf and Magda Stouthamer-Loeber
1986 Family factors as correlates and predictors of juvenile conduct problems and delinquency. In Michael Tonry and Norval Morris (eds.), Crime and Justice: An Annual Review of Research. Vol. 7. Chicago: University of Chicago Press.

Loftin, Colin and Robert H. Hill
1974 Regional subculture and homicide: An examination of the Gastil-Hackney thesis. American Sociological Review 39:714–724.

Logan, Charles H. and Gerald G. Gaes
1993 Meta-analysis and the rehabilitation of punishment. Justice Quarterly 10:245–263.

Lynch, James
1995 Crime in international perspective. In James Q. Wilson and Joan Petersilia (eds.), Crime. San Francisco, Calif.: Institute for Contemporary Studies.

Lyon, John D. and Chih-Ling Tsai.
1996 A comparison of tests for heteroscedasticity. The Statistician 45:337–349.

Maddala, G.S.
1992 Introduction to Econometrics. New York: Macmillan.

Marenin, Otwin
1997 Victimization surveys and the accuracy and reliability of official crime data in developing countries. Journal of Criminal Justice 25:463–475.

Martinson, Robert
1974 What works?—Questions and answers about prison reform. The Public Interest (Spring):22–54.

Mazerolle, Lorraine G., Colleen Kadleck, and Jan Roehl
1998 Controlling drug and disorder problems: The role of place managers. Criminology 36:371–404.

Mazerolle, Paul and Jeff Maahs
2000 General strain and delinquency: An alternative examination of conditioning influences. Justice Quarterly 17:753–778.

Merriman, David
1991 An economic analysis of the post World War II decline in the Japanese crime rate. Journal of Quantitative Criminology 7:19–39.

Merton, Robert K.
1938 Social structure and anomie. American Sociological Review 3:672–682.

Messner, Steven F. and Richard Rosenfeld
1997 Political restraint of the market and levels of criminal homicide: A cross-national application of institutional anomie. Social Forces 75:1393–1416.
2001 Crime and the American Dream. 3d ed. Belmont, Calif.: Wadsworth.

Messner, Steven F. and Robert J. Sampson
1991 The sex ratio, family disruption, and rates of violent crime: The paradox of demographic structure. Social Forces 69:693–713.

Messner, Steven F. and Scott J. South
1986 Economic deprivation, opportunity structure, and robbery cictimization: Intra- and inter-racial patterns. Social Forces 64:975–991.

Nagin, Daniel
1978 Crime rates, sanction levels, and constraints on the prison population. Law and Society Review 12:341–366.
1998a Criminal deterrence research at the outset of the twenty-first century. In Michael Tonry (ed.), Crime and Justice: A Review of Research. Vol. 23. Chicago: University of Chicago Press.
1998b Deterrence and incapacitation. In Michael Tonry (ed.), The Handbook of Crime and Punishment. New York: Oxford University Press.

Neapolitan, Jerome L.
1997 Cross-National Crime: A Research Review and Sourcebook. Westport, Conn.: Greenwood Press.
1998 Cross-national variation in homicides: Is race a factor? Criminology 36:139–156.
1999 A comparative analysis of nations with low and high levels of violent crime. Journal of Criminal Justice 27:259–274.
2001 An examination of cross-national variation in punitiveness. International Journal of Offender Therapy and Comparative Criminology 45:691–710.

Neter, John, William Wasserman, and Michael H. Kutner
1990 Applied Linear Statistical Models. Homeland, Ill.: Irwin.

Neuman, W. Lawrence and Ronald J. Berger
1988 Competing perspectives on cross-national crime: An evaluation of theory and evidence. Sociological Quarterly 29:281–313.

O'Brien, Robert M.
1991 Sex ratios and rape rates: A power control theory. Criminology 29:99–115.

Parker, Karen F. and Patricia L. McCall
1999 Structural conditions and racial homicide patterns: A look at the multiple disadvantages in urban areas. Criminology 37:447–478.

Piquero, Alex and Nicole Leeper Piquero
1998 On testing institutional anomie theory with varying specifications. Studies on Crime and Crime Prevention 7:61–84.

Pratt, Travis C.
2002 Meta-analysis and its discontents: Treatment destruction techniques revisited. Journal of Offender Rehabilitation 35:23–40.

Pratt, Travis C. and Christopher T. Lowenkamp
2002 Conflict theory, economic conditions, and homicide: A time series analysis. Homicide Studies 6:61–83.

Reynolds, Morgan O.
1997 Crime and Punishment in America: 1997 Update. Dallas, Tex.: National Center for Policy Analysis.

Rose, Dina R. and Todd R. Clear
1998 Incarceration, social capital, and crime: Implications for social disorganization theory. Criminology 36:441–479.

Rose, Richard
1991 Is American public policy exceptional? In Byron E. Shafer (ed.), Is America Different? A New Look at American Exceptionalism. New York: Oxford University Press.

Rosenfeld, Richard, Steven F. Messner, and Eric P. Baumer
2001 Social capital and homicide. Social Forces 80:283–309.

Sampson, Robert J.
1986 Neighborhood family structure and the risk of personal victimization. In Robert J. Sampson and James M. Byrne (eds.), The Social Ecology of Crime. New York: Springer-Verlag.

Sampson, Robert J. and W. Byron Groves
1989 Community structure and crime: Testing social disorganization theory. American Journal of Sociology 94:774–802.

Sampson, Robert J. and John H. Laub
1993 Crime in the Making: Pathways and Turning Points Through Life. Cambridge, Mass.: Harvard University Press.

Sampson, Robert J., Stephen W. Raudenbush, and Felton Earls
1997 Neighborhoods and violent crime: A multilevel study of collective efficacy. Science 277:918–924.

Savolainen, Jukka
2000 Inequality, welfare state, and homicide: Further support for the institutional anomie theory. Criminology 38:1021–1042.

Shaw, Clifford R. and Henry D. McKay
1972 Juvenile Delinquency and Urban Areas. Chicago: University of Chicago Press.

Short, James F.
1998 The level of explanation problem revisited: The American Society of Criminology 1997 Presidential Address. Criminology 36:3–36.

Skocpol, Theda
1992 Protecting Soldiers and Mothers: The Political Origins of Social Policy in the United States. Cambridge, Mass.: Harvard University Press.

Smith, M. Dwayne and Nathan Bennett
1985 Poverty, inequality, and theories of forcible rape. Crime and Delinquency 31:295–305.

Steinmo, Sven
1993 Taxation and Democracy: Swedish, British, and American Approaches to Financing the Modern State. New Haven, Conn.: Yale University Press.

Tittle, Charles R.
2000 Theoretical developments in criminology. In Criminal Justice 2000. Washington, D.C.: National Institute of Justice.

Tonry, Michael
1995 Malign Neglect: Race, Crime and Punishment. New York: Oxford University Press.

United Nations Statistics Division
2000 Infonation. Available online: www.un.org/pubs/cyberschoolbus/information/e_infonation.htm.

Veysey, Bonita M. and Steven F. Messner
1999 Further testing social disorganization theory: An elaboration of Sampson and Groves's "Community Structure and Crime." Journal of Research in Crime and Delinquency 36:156–174.

Vieraitis, Lynne M.
2000 Income inequality, poverty, and violent crime: A review of the empirical evidence. Social Pathology: A Journal of Reviews 6:24–45.

Warner, Barbara D. and Pamela Wilcox Roundtree
1997 Local ties in a community and crime model: Questioning the systemic nature of informal social control. Social Problems 44:520–536.

Whitehead, John T. and Steven P. Lab
1989 A meta-analysis of juvenile correctional treatment. Journal of Research in Crime and Delinquency 26:276–295.

Wilson, Graham K.
1998 Only in America: The Politics of the United States in Comparative Perspective. Chatham, N.J.: Chatham House.

Wilson, James Q.
1983 Thinking About Crime. New York: Basic.

Wilson, William Julius
1987 The Truly Disadvantaged: The Inner City, The Underclass, and Public Policy. Chicago: University of Chicago Press.
1999 The Bridge Over the Racial Divide: Rising Inequality and Coalition Politics. Berkeley: University of California Press.

World Health Organization
2000 World Health Report 2000.

Wright, John Paul, Francis T. Cullen, and Jeremy T. Miller
2001 Family social capital and delinquent involvement. Journal of Criminal Justice 29:1–9.

Yoshikawa, Hirokazu
1994 Prevention as cumulative protection: Effects of early family support and education on chronic delinquency and its risks. Psychological Bulletin 115:28–54.

Young, Warren and Mark Brown
1993 Cross-national comparisons of imprisonment. In Michael Tonry (ed.), Crime and Justice: A Review of Research. Vol. 17. Chicago: University of Chicago Press.

Zimring, Franklin E. and Gordon Hawkins
1997 Crime Is Not the Problem: Lethal Violence in America. Oxford, N.Y.: Oxford University Press.

Zuravin, Susan J.
1989 The ecology of child abuse and neglect: A review of the literature and presentation of data. Violence and Victims 4:101–120.

Travis C. Pratt is an Assistant Professor in the Department of Political Science/Criminal Justice at Washington State University. His research focuses on macrolevel and structural theories of crime and delinquency and correctional policy. His recent work has appeared in *Criminology*, the *Journal of Criminal Justice*, the *Journal of Research in Crime and Delinquency*, and *Justice Quarterly*.

Timothy W. Godsey is a doctoral student in the Division of Criminal Justice at the University of Cincinnati. His research interests include criminological theory and cross-national comparisons of prison use. His recent research has appeared in the *Journal of Criminal Justice*.

[9]

CROSS-NATIONAL DIFFERENCES IN MANAGERS' WILLINGNESS TO JUSTIFY ETHICALLY SUSPECT BEHAVIORS: A TEST OF INSTITUTIONAL ANOMIE THEORY

JOHN B. CULLEN
Washington State University

K. PRAVEEN PARBOTEEAH
University of Wisconsin—Whitewater

MARTIN HOEGL
Bocconi University

With globalization, understanding unethical conduct from a cross-national perspective is becoming more important. We used institutional anomie theory to develop hypotheses relating four national culture variables (achievement, individualism, universalism, and pecuniary materialism) and social institutions (economy, polity, family, and education) to managers' willingness to justify behaviors generally considered ethically suspect. Data from 3,450 managers from 28 countries support our hypotheses for universalism, pecuniary materialism, economy, family, and education. Implications for future research and practice are discussed.

The increasing concern for managerial ethics in the context of globalization calls for a better cross-national understanding of ethical issues related to management (Beyer & Nino, 1999). To date, previous research on cross-national ethical issues has focused mostly on national culture (e.g., Husted, Dozier, McMahon, & Kattan, 1996). However, many researchers have argued that cross-national differences are understood best by considering *both* national culture and social institutions (Hofstede, 2001; Parboteeah & Cullen, 2003; Schooler, 1996). In addition, although theorists (e.g., Schwartz, 1994) have identified an array of cultural dimensions for possible consideration, cross-national ethics research has used Hofstede's (2001) cultural dimensions almost exclusively, often without theoretical justification for specific dimensions (Vitell, Nwachukwu, & Barnes, 1993).

To address these shortcomings, we introduce institutional anomie theory, as developed by Messner and Rosenfeld (2001; Rosenfeld & Messner, 1997) as an innovative approach to guide our understanding of how both social institutions (such as political systems) and national culture affect ethical issues related to managers. *Institutional anomie theory* is a sociological theory that explains rates of crime and deviance in social units on the basis of specific social institutions and cultural values. In this work, the first application of institutional anomie theory to managers, we tested hypotheses based on the theory predicting the criterion of managerial ethical reasoning. Our cross-national test of institutional anomie theory used data from 28 nations and 3,450 managers.

We wish to thank Associate Editor Marshall Schminke and the *AMJ* anonymous reviewers for their constructive comments on this paper. We also acknowledge the Inter-University Consortium for Political and Social Research (ICPSR) for making available a significant portion of the data used in this study.

ETHICAL REASONING AND INSTITUTIONAL ANOMIE THEORY

Below, we explain the general tenets of institutional anomie theory, specify the issues regarding managerial ethical reasoning, and offer specific hypotheses regarding the effects of national culture and social institutions on managerial ethical reasoning.

Institutional Anomie Theory

Foundations: The sociological theory of anomie. The sociological theory of anomie (Durkheim, 1893/1964, 1897/1966) provides the theoretical roots of institutional anomie theory. Durkheim observed that institutional and cultural changes associated with modernization encourage a decline of traditional social controls that are based on family and social relationships. The result is anomie—the weakening of norms—and, in turn, increased rates of deviance.

In a later formulation of anomie theory, Robert

Merton (1968), like Durkheim earlier, saw a pressure for deviance both in the institutional structure of society and in cultural values. Merton, however, focused on the cultural values that emphasize achieving ends (primarily materialistic and economic ends) over the legitimacy (that is, the ethicality) of the means employed to achieve these ends. Merton went on to argue that choice of a deviant means to achieve an end is particularly likely when a social stratification system prevents people from goal achievement in areas encouraged by cultural values.

Institutional anomie theory: Basic assumptions. In formulating institutional anomie theory, Messner and Rosenfeld (2001; Rosenfeld & Messner, 1997) argued that Merton did not give sufficient emphasis to the institutional drivers of anomie. Thus, institutional anomie theory specifies both the social institutions and the cultural values that affect rates of deviant behavior. Institutional anomie theory does not address the role of social stratification systems.

In general, institutional anomie theory identifies cultural and institutional factors that propagate more egoistic rather than principled or benevolent ethical reasoning in a society. These cultural and institutional systems enable cognitive separation from traditional social rules and norms, based, for example, on education and the family. This separation in turn increases the willingness of more people to "have no moral qualms" (Rosenfeld & Messner, 1997: 214) about choosing any means necessary to achieve their goals.

Evidence shows that institutional anomie theory is predictive of deviant outcomes such as homicide rates and property crimes both within and between nations (e.g., Messner & Rosenfeld, 1997; Savolainen, 2000). However, institutional anomie theory's concern for the roots of moral decision making in society (Rosenfeld & Messner, 1997) suggests broader applications to all forms of outcomes with ethical consequences, including managerial ethical reasoning.

Managerial ethical reasoning: Issues considered. In this study, we considered cross-national differences as one step in the ethical reasoning processes of managers: the extent to which managers report that they are willing to justify behaviors that are generally considered ethically suspect solutions to ethical dilemmas.

Prior research shows that managers from different national cultures identify similar business practices as ethically suspect (Husted et al., 1996). This research and our findings below suggest there may be cultural universalism or convergence on the belief that certain acts violate "hypernorms." Donaldson and Dunfee (1994, 1999) posited that hypernorms represent prescriptions that are accepted by all cultures and organizations, although the degrees to which hypernorms are enforced and to which the violation of such norms is justifiable vary. These authors noted, for example, that bribery is universally ethically suspect, yet ethical reactions to bribery differ around the globe. Donaldson and Dunfee's arguments are consistent with the perspective of our research. Institutional anomie theory, in turn, provides a theoretical model in which institutional and cultural contexts account for such differences in managers' perceptions of ethically suspect acts as justifiable.

Institutional anomie theory and its precursors provide strong theoretical and empirical explanations of national differences in rates of crime (homicide, violent crimes in general, delinquency) and other outcomes termed "deviant" in the sociological literature (for example, alcohol abuse and suicide) (Lilly, Cullen, & Ball, 2002) and "illegitimate" in the ethical perspectives of Donaldson and Dunfee (1994). Thus, most prior research has focused on outcomes generally accepted as deviant behaviors rather than on the steps in the ethical reasoning process that lead to such behaviors—although it is reasonable to hypothesize that the effects of national cultures and social institutions on ethical outcomes result from ethical reasoning processes. In this study, we considered the deliberative reasoning (Thorne & Saunders, 2002) processes of managers regarding the degree to which they believed that ethically suspect acts were justifiable. We labeled that degree of belief "managers' willingness to justify ethically suspect behaviors."

National Cultural Values and Managers' Willingness to Justify Ethically Suspect Behaviors

Institutional anomie theory, as noted above, identifies four cultural values as predictors of deviance: achievement, individualism, universalism, and pecuniary materialism (Messner & Rosenfeld, 2001: 61). Broadly, the theory's argument is that these cultural values create anomic conditions that encourage egoistic goal achievement at the expense of a concern for the ethical consequences of the means chosen to achieve goals.

National cultures can be characterized as ranging from "achievement-oriented" to "ascription-oriented" (Trompenaars & Hampden-Turner, 1998). Achievement refers to assessment of personal worth on the basis of the outcome of efforts. Ascription, in contrast, refers to assessment of worth on the basis of location in social networks and inherited statuses. The more achievement values dominate a culture, the greater the value given to outcomes typifying personal goals and the less the concern given to the means of achieving these outcomes. According to Messner and Rosenfeld, achievement values are "conducive to the mentality that 'it's not how you play the game: it's whether you win or lose' " (2001: 63). Achievement values are thus more likely than ascription values to encourage an obsession with the pursuit of material and other competitive goals (Passas, 2000).

As a cultural value, individualism encourages disengagement from the collective and, as a consequence, weakens bonds of social control. Individualism subordinates relationships to personal goals and likely leads to more egoistic ethical decision making. The prime orientation is to self rather than to common ends (Trompenaars & Hampden-Turner, 1998) as the values of autonomy, self-sufficiency, and competitiveness become more eminent (Hofstede, 2001). According to institutional anomie theory, competition in individualistic cultures pressures people to ignore traditional normative restrictions in the pursuit of personal success (Messner & Rosenfeld, 2001).

The cultural value of universalism promotes equality of opportunity in that it creates expectations that all will be judged on similar criteria rather than on particularistic relationships (Trompenaars & Hampden-Turner, 1998). However, the expectation of equality of opportunity in a universalistic society also encourages more individuals to strive to achieve their goals. In contrast, in a particularistic society, preferential treatment may discourage ambition. Thus, the increased ambition and drive inherent in a universalistic society are more likely to promote an egoistic concern for advancement. The proposition of institutional anomie theory is that universalism also leads to a concern for outcomes at the expense of the ethicality of achieving these ends.

The final value considered by institutional anomie theory is pecuniary materialism, or a focus on monetary rewards. Messner and Rosenfeld (2001) argued that, to the degree cultural values promote money as a valued end independent of other material rewards, the desire for this end becomes insatiable. Additionally, pecuniary materialism encourages assessing self-worth on the basis of a personal economic metric that is not linked to group welfare.

Thus, according to the logic of institutional anomie theory, the cultural values of achievement orientation, individualism, universalism, and pecuniary materialism encourage a breakdown of traditional social ties, the attendant weakening of traditional social norms, and a general legitimization of putting goal achievement ahead of concern for the welfare of others. That is, these cultural values encourage self-serving, unethical decision making and, ultimately, a greater willingness to justify ethically suspect behaviors. Consequently, we hypothesize:

Hypothesis 1. The stronger the achievement values in a nation, the greater the willingness of its managers to justify ethically suspect behaviors.

Hypothesis 2. The stronger the individualism values in a nation, the greater the willingness of its managers to justify ethically suspect behaviors.

Hypothesis 3. The stronger the universalism values in a nation, the greater the willingness of its managers to justify ethically suspect behaviors.

Hypothesis 4. The stronger the pecuniary materialism values in a nation, the greater the willingness of its managers to justify ethically suspect behaviors.

Social Institutions and Managers' Willingness to Justify Ethically Suspect Behaviors

In addition to the four cultural values, institutional anomie theory identifies four social institutions that are "central to what may be called an institutional understanding of crime" (Messner & Rosenfeld, 2001: 66). These include a nation's economy, polity, prevailing family structure, and educational system.

The economy. A nation's economy is the social institution (Turner, 1997) that organizes the production and distribution of goods and services (Messner & Rosenfeld, 2001). A major tenet of institutional anomie theory (Messner & Rosenfeld, 2001; Rosenfeld & Messner, 1997) is that the dominance of the economy breaks down traditional normative controls. Theoretical and empirical evidence suggests that level of industrialization is a major indicator of what economic system is dominant in a nation. (Esping-Anderson, 1990).

According to institutional anomie theory (Messner & Rosenfeld, 1997; Rosenfeld & Messner, 1997), when individuals' economic roles dominate their other roles in society, such as family membership, the calculating and utilitarian logic of the marketplace leads to a loss of social control and more egoistic seeking of ends through deviant means. Industrialization more often presents managers with situations that encourage the pursuit of egoistic goals when competitive pressures provide justification for deviance or unethical behaviors (Passas, 2000). As such, in industrial societies one would expect managers to be more likely to justify ethically suspect behaviors in their ethical reasoning. Furthermore, industrialization also encourages emphasis on security, affluence, and economic well-being (Inglehart, 1997), all egoistic goals. Consequently, we hypothesize:

Hypothesis 5. The more industrialized a nation, the greater the willingness of its managers to justify ethically suspect behaviors.

Polity and the economy. A political system, or polity, "mobilizes and distributes power to attain collective goals" (Messner & Rosenfeld, 2001: 65). Cross-national tests of institutional anomie theory have suggested that a national polity's promotion of different economic systems affects national levels of crime (Messner & Rosenfeld, 1997; Pampel & Gartner, 1995).

A government policy of less active intervention in a nation's economy implies a more capitalist polity in which the institutional logic is that the market provides the necessary rewards to stimulate individual efforts. The result, as Ralston, Holt, Terpstra, and Kai-Cheng noted, is that the capitalist system is a "self-serving economic system where everyone looks out for his/her own interests" (1997: 180). In turn, according to institutional anomie theory, this self-interest reduces social control and leads a society's members to increasingly accept more unethical or criminal means of achieving their goals.

In contrast, more socialist political systems have more active government intervention in economic coordination and the appropriation and redistribution of economic wealth (Turner, 1997). According to institutional anomie theory, welfare socialism provides security nets that protect people from the "vicissitudes of the market" (Messner & Rosenfeld, 1997: 1394), thereby preventing people's dependency on competitive market forces (Savolainen, 2000). Providing services and resources to citizens as entitlements rather than as outcomes of egocentrism-creating competitive market forces in turn reduces the need of the members of a society to use more deviant or ethically suspect means to achieve desired ends. We hypothesize that similar processes affect managerial ethical reasoning:

Hypothesis 6. The more welfare socialist a nation's political system, the less willing its managers to justify ethically suspect behaviors.

Family. According to institutional anomie theory (Messner & Rosenfeld, 2001) and supporting empirical evidence (Chamlin & Cochran, 1995), stronger traditional social institutions, such as stable families, oppose the egocentrism-creating pressures produced by economic dominance. Stable families provide emotional support and normative control by socialization. They also provide a noneconomic basis of self-worth that offsets the cultural values and institutional systems that define self-worth as dependent on economic market performance (Messner & Rosenfeld, 2001). That is, stronger family units counteract the forces that encourage managers to adopt ethically suspect means to achieve their goals. Similarly, from the opposite perspective, extensive evidence indicates that marital and family disruption creates social disorganization that reduces informal social controls and increases criminal activity and other forms of deviance (Stack & Eshleman, 1998). Consequently, we hypothesize:

Hypothesis 7. The lower the family strength in a nation, the greater the willingness of its managers to justify ethically suspect behaviors.

Education. Education is a key social institution that shares with the family many of the important socialization functions of transmitting basic societal norms and beliefs from generation to generation (Messner & Rosenfeld, 2001; Turner, 1997). Institutional anomie theory suggests that educational systems transmit values that reduce anomie pressures and thus should decrease willingness to justify unethical behaviors (Chamlin & Cochran, 1995; Messner & Rosenfeld, 2001). Such values discourage egoism and include, for example, respect for others, politeness, and a rejection of violence (Van Deth, 1995). Similarly, Rest (1986) found that education was the most powerful predictor of higher levels of moral development. He reasoned that education helps people "take responsibility for themselves and their environs" (Rest, 1986: 57). Thus, formal education provides a challenging and stimulating environment that encourages people to take more interest in the welfare of their communities and in their larger societal context (Rest & Narvaez, 1991).

Evidence also shows that educational systems encourage postmaterialist values that prioritize quality of life and self-expression over economic and material achievements (Inglehart, 1997). Proponents of institutional anomie theory have argued that exposure to education generally contradicts the materialist and egocentric values that promote achievement by any means.

Nations vary in the general educational attainment of their populations, both in terms of highest degrees attained and years spent in the educational system. Managers are typically among the more educated members of a population. Thus, it follows that managers in nations with more comprehensive educational systems are likely more socialized to espouse postmaterialist values and, from an institutional anomie theory perspective, less willing to justify ethically suspect behaviors. Consequently, we hypothesize:

Hypothesis 8. The greater a nation's educational attainment level, the less the willingness of managers to justify ethically suspect behaviors.

METHODS

Sample

The sample included individual-level data from 3,450 managers and nation-level data from 28 nations. The nations were Austria, Belgium, Britain, Bulgaria, Canada, China, Denmark, France, Germany, Hungary, Iceland, India, Italy, Ireland, Japan, Mexico, The Netherlands, Nigeria, Norway, Portugal, Romania, The Russian Federation, South Korea, Spain, Sweden, Switzerland, Turkey, and the United States.

Managers. The sample of managers was a subset of the national probability samples collected approximately every five years by the World Values Study Group (2000) and made available by the Inter-University Consortium for Political and Social Research. A collaborative effort of research groups from 43 nations, the World Values Survey (WVS) represents nearly 70 percent of the world's population.

WVS data were gathered with face-to-face interviews conducted by professional survey organizations, typically the Gallup organization in Western countries, and national academies of science or university-based institutes in other countries. The World Values Study Group (2000) provides more detail on the data-gathering procedures.

Nations. We selected our nation sample on the basis of the availability of reliable individual-level data for our dependent variable. To check for construct equivalence across countries and to ensure comparable within-nation data (Singh, 1995), we computed the reliability of our dependent measure, managers' willingness to justify ethically suspect behaviors, separately for each nation. We eliminated from the study countries with alpha coefficients below .7 for our dependent measure. This measurement standard reduced the nations in the sample to 28 of the original 43.

Variables and Data Sources

Dependent variable: Manager's willingness to justify ethically suspect behaviors. The WVS provided information on the ethical decision making process of mangers by asking them the extent to which they thought that certain ethically suspect behaviors were justifiable. Seven items presented ethically suspect behaviors, such as "claiming government benefits which you are not entitled to," "cheating on taxes if you have the chance," and "Accepting bribes in the course of your duty." Responses were made on a 1–10 scale.

Consistent with previous evidence suggesting that managers from different countries perceive similar behaviors as ethically suspect (Husted et al., 1996), our data also showed a cross-national consistency of perceptions regarding ethically suspect behaviors. Factor analysis produced single-factor solutions for all nations separately and for the combined data.

National culture. Among the various models of national culture (Hofstede, 2001; Schwartz, 1994), the model proposed recently by Trompenaars and Hampden-Turner (1998) has the best theoretical match with institutional anomie theory. This model identifies three of the four relevant cultural dimensions (achievement, universalism, and individualism).

We measured the *achievement* versus ascription orientation of a nation with three indicators. Two items, from Trompenaars and Hampden-Turner (1998: 107–109), used the percentages of people who disagreed with the following statements: "The respect a person gets is highly dependent on their family background" and "The most important thing in life is to think and act in the ways that best suit the way you really are, even if you do not get things done." A third item, from the World Values Study Group (2000), was the percentage of people surveyed by the WVS who agreed with the statement, "One does not have the duty to respect and love parents who have not earned it by their behavior and attitudes."

The measure of *individualism* consisted of three items that used the percentage of respondents in a nation making the individualism choice on three issues. The issues and items were (1) quality of life: "It is obvious that if individuals have as much freedom as possible and the maximum opportunity to develop themselves, the quality of their life will improve as a result"; (2) typical job: "Everyone is allowed to work individually and individual credit can be received"; and (3) negligence of a team member: "The person causing the defect by negligence is the one responsible." For our nation sample, the correlation of this measure with Hofstede's individualism measure was .70.

The *universalism* measure posed two dilemmas, and a respondent selected either a particularistic or a universalistic option. One dealt with testifying truthfully regarding the driving speed of a friend involved in an accident (the universalistic choice). The other asked whether a journalist should write a positive review for a friend's restaurant (the particularistic choice) (Trompenaars & Hampden-Turner, 1998: 35–37). Each item used the percentage of respondents from a nation responding in the universalistic direction.

Materialism is not a cultural value included in any of the popular cultural models of Hofstede (2001), Schwartz (1994), or Trompenaars and Hampden-Turner (1998). However, writing in the political science tradition, Inglehart (1997) developed a measure of national value change from materialism to postmaterialism. To measure *pecuniary materialism,* we used the materialist items from Inglehart's measure. Indicators came from questions asking respondents to prioritize the following goals for their nation: "stable economy" and "progress toward a society where ideas count more than money" (reverse-coded). To improve reliability, we also added an indicator from the WVS, the proportion of people in a nation choosing "good pay" as "important in a job."

Social institutions. Our measures of nation-level social institutions borrowed directly from those commonly used in the extensive comparative research in political science (Duch & Taylor, 1993), economics (Temple & Voth, 1998), and sociology (Rau & Wazienski, 1999).

In keeping with theoretical explanations and descriptions of industrialization, we crafted a measure that reflected the physical and human resource inputs and outputs that characterize an industrial economy (Turner, 1997). Indicators selected included degree of urbanization, measured by the percentage of urban population (Duch & Taylor, 1993); energy use, measured in coal-equivalent units (Parboteeah & Cullen, 2003); and demographic distribution of the workforce into nonagricultural sectors, measured as the percentage of workers in the nonagricultural sector (Temple & Voth, 1998). Data were collected from annual world development indicators reported by the World Bank (2002).

Our measure of *welfare socialism* included three items: tax collected as a percentage of gross domestic product, government expenditure as a percentage of gross domestic product, and government revenues as a percentage of gross domestic product. Following theoretical arguments of Turner (1997), we reasoned that countries whose political systems are more welfare socialist have more governmental intervention, which will be reflected in government expenditures and revenues. The 1992 *United Nations Statistical Yearbook* and the World Bank's annual world development indicators (http://publications.worldbank.org/ecommerce/products) provided the data for this measure.

As have previous researchers conducting nation-level comparative research (e.g., Stack & Eshleman, 1998), we used the ratio of marriages to divorces to assess institutionalized *family strength.* Since the work of Durkheim (1897), marriage and divorce rates have been used as macrolevel indicators of social integration that predict an array of societal outcomes, from general well-being to suicide. Divorce-to-marriage ratios were computed as the number of marriages divided by the number of divorces per 1,000 population. Data were obtained from *Euromonitor* (2002).

We measured *educational attainment* with the United Nations Development Program's (1991) educational attainment score, which is generally accepted as indicating access to education in a country (Parboteeah & Cullen, 2003). This score is computed as two-thirds of the adult literacy rate plus one-third of the mean years of schooling. To adjust for differences in the metrics of component indicators, we standardized all composite measures for national culture and institutional variables.

Individual-level control variables. Although institutional anomie theory does not address individual differences, criminology and ethics research has shown relationships between most forms of crime and most forms of ethical behavior with age, gender, marital status, and individual religiosity (e.g., Evans, Cullen, Dunaway, & Burton, 1995; Serwinek, 1992). To control for such individual-level effects, we used a number of individual-level variables available from the WVS: age (measured in years), gender (0 = "male," 1 = "female", and marital status (0 = "single," 1 = "married, divorced, or widowed"). Attendance at religious services more than once a week measured individual religiosity.

Analysis techniques: Hierarchical linear modeling. Given that our dependent variable and control variables were measured at the individual level (level 1) and the independent variables (culture and social institutions) were measured at the nation level (level 2), we chose hierarchical linear modeling (HLM; Bryk & Raudenbush, 2002) as the appropriate technique to assess these cross-level relationships.

To assess some of the collinearity diagnostics available with regression analysis, we also estimated a multiple regression model. In spite of the strong correlation between educational attainment and industrialization, the variance inflation factors were less than 10 for all parameter estimates, suggesting that multicollinearity was not a problem (Studenmund, 1992). In addition, for both our HLM and regression models, the estimates for educational attainment and industrialization remained significant and in the same direction when included in separate models without the other as a control.

RESULTS

Table 1 shows a matrix of correlations and sample statistics of the level 1 and level 2 variables used in this study. Table 2 shows the results of an intercept-as-outcomes HLM model. It includes standardized coefficients of country and individual-level variables predicting managers' willingness to justify ethically suspect behaviors. Since hypotheses were tested with level 2 variables, it is important to note that level 2 statistical tests in HLM are not based on total sample size, as would be the case in an OLS approach with country-level variables assigned to each individual. Rather, HLM parameter estimates and standard errors are based on a combination of group-level sample size weighted by the reliabilities of the individual-level dependent variable in each group. Although parameter estimates are usually similar, the HLM approach counters the tendency of OLS to underestimate standard errors of level 2 variables because of the larger size of the individual-level sample (Hofmann, Griffin, & Gavin, 2000).

HLM partitions explained variance between levels rather than estimating total variance explained.

TABLE 2
Results of Hierarchical Linear Modeling for Managers' Willingness to Justify Ethically Suspect Behaviors

Variables	Estimates: Coefficient	s.e.
Individual-level		
Religiosity	−0.13***	0.03
Marital status	−0.06*	0.02
Gender	0.02**	0.06
Age	−0.19***	0.02
Nation-level		
National culture		
Achievement	−0.17***	0.02
Individualism	−0.16***	0.02
Universalism	0.23***	0.03
Pecuniary materialism	0.11***	0.03
Social institutions		
Economy: Degree of industrialization	0.44***	0.03
Polity: Degree of socialism	0.12***	0.03
Family: Degree of breakdown	0.12***	0.03
Educational attainment	−0.50***	0.04

* $p < .05$
** $p < .01$
*** $p < .001$

TABLE 1
Descriptive Statistics and Cross-Level Correlations[a, b]

Variable	Mean	s.d.	1	2	3	4	5	6	7	8	9	10	11	12
1 Age	45.16	15.14												
2. Gender	0.32	0.51	−.03											
3. Marital status	0.88	0.33	.34	−.00										
4. Religiosity	5.78	3.26	.16	.04	.03									
5. Willingness to justify ethically suspect behaviors	2.30	1.41	−.24	−.04	−.13	−.12	(.77)							
6. Achievement	0.13	2.57	.13	−.04	.07	−.06	−.06	(.75)						
7. Individualism	−0.24	2.69	.09	.02	.05	.03	.03	.28	(70)					
8. Universalism	0.14	2.19	.17	−.07	.02	.13	.06	.49	.53	(.85)				
9. Pecuniary materialism	−1.64	2.26	−.12	−.03	.01	−.06	.02	.02	−.23	−.39	(.79)			
10. Economy	0.05	0.95	.18	.08	.07	−.06	.08	.47	.51	.52	−.50	(.91)		
11. Polity	−0.23	0.87	.11	.06	.06	−.23	.14	.23	.40	.22	.14	.34	(.87)	
12. Family breakdown	0.32	0.17	.18	.07	.09	−.11	−.08	.39	.51	.57	−.24	.57	.49	
13. Education attainment	0.07	0.99	.22	.08	.10	−.15	−.02	.48	.46	.57	−.51	.79	.29	.67

[a] $n = 3{,}450$, level 1; $n = 28$, level 2. To compute correlations, we assigned country-level variables to each individual in that country. However, to weigh each country equally, we counterweighted by sample size. With counterweighting, the nation-level correlations are equivalent to correlations based on the nation-level sample size.

[b] Correlations greater than .04 are significant at $p < .05$, and correlations greater than .05 are significant at $p < .01$. Alpha reliabilities are in parentheses on the diagonal.

Level 2 variables explained 35 percent of the variance between countries, estimated by the formula suggested by Bryk and Raudenbush (2002: 106). For approximate estimates of total variance explained, we computed the correlation between predicted dependent variable scores (from HLM coefficients) and the actual dependent variable scores. The value of the correlation was .40, almost identical to the regression multiple correlation of .41. Given this calculation and the results of an analysis of covariance (ANCOVA) and regression analyses, our estimate of the total explained variance between individuals was 16–24 percent.

Hypotheses 1, 2, 3, and 4 propose positive relationships between managers' willingness to justify ethically suspect behaviors and the cultural values of achievement, individualism, universalism, and pecuniary materialism, respectively. Table 2 reports results that support Hypothesis 3 (universalism) and Hypothesis 4 (pecuniary materialism) but do not support Hypothesis 1 (achievement) and Hypothesis 2 (individualism).

Hypotheses 5 and 7, which posit positive relationships between managerial justifications of ethically suspect behaviors and industrialization and family breakdown, respectively, were both supported. Hypotheses also suggest negative relationships between managers' willingness to justify ethically suspect behaviors and welfare socialism (Hypothesis 6) and national levels of educational attainment (Hypothesis 8). Results supported the hypothesis for education but rejected the hypothesis for the degree of welfare socialism.

DISCUSSION AND CONCLUSIONS

The major objective of this study was to test the propositions of institutional anomie theory as applied to managers' willingness to justify ethically suspect behaviors. Following institutional anomie theory, we proposed that four cultural dimensions and four social institutions are related to managers' willingness to justify ethically suspect behaviors. Our results provided support for five of our eight hypotheses, confirming that institutional anomie theory applies, with some modification, to managers. In addition, since HLM statistical estimation techniques are not solely dependent on individual-level sample size, the analysis showed that the significant nation-level effects explained substantively important variance between nations.

Cultural Values

Results for universalism and pecuniary materialism confirmed the hypotheses and suggested support for institutional anomie theory's basic argument (Messner & Rosenfeld, 2001) that these cultural values lead to more egoistic ethical reasoning and a greater likelihood of managers believing that ethically suspect behaviors are justifiable.

Results for the cultural values of individualism and achievement were, however, surprising. Contrary to institutional anomie theory, these cultural values negatively predicted the willingness to justify ethically suspect behaviors. A possible explanation of these findings is found within the anomie theoretical tradition but rests on Merton's (1968) view of anomie rather than on the view proposed in institutional anomie theory. Like the proponents of institutional anomie theory, Merton argued that the cultural values of individualism and achievement orientation promote increased deviance (and hence unethical reasoning) because of the pressure of increased aspirations. Unlike institutional anomie theory's proponents, however, he noted that these values encourage illegitimate means to seeking ends primarily when a stratification system blocks aspirations.

This is a pertinent argument for this study, as managers seem less likely to face blocked aspirations stemming from society-level social stratification than might other groups, such as inner city youth. Thus, for the managerial class of a society, the cultural values of individualism and an achievement orientation may produce no pressure to use illegitimate or unethical means to achieve desired ends. In fact, the data suggest that managers, who are likely to be in a society's upper echelons, have the luxury of engaging in little questionable ethical reasoning and ethically suspect behavior.

Social Institutions

Results for industrialization, family strength, and educational attainment were consistent with institutional anomie theory predictions. As argued, it seems that social norms are weakened in more industrialized nations where economic roles dominate the societal structure (Passas, 2000). Industrialization's promotion of a win-at-all-costs mentality likely leads to more egoistic ethical reasoning and, consequently, managers in more industrialized nations seemingly have a greater willingness to justify ethically suspect behaviors.

In societies in which the institution of the family is weaker, its role in social integration and providing emotional support is also weakened. Thus, managers in such societies seemingly develop more egoistic attitudes and, in turn, seem more willing to justify ethically suspect behaviors. Finally, as argued in institutional anomie theory, societies with more developed educational systems likely socialize managers to have a more benevolent orientation toward others. Educational levels are also associated with postmaterialist values, whereby the quality of life takes precedence over more materialistic values (Inglehart, 1997). Thus, managers in societies with widely accessible and comprehensive educational systems are less willing to justify ethically suspect behaviors.

Our results for the effects of polity (degree of welfare socialism) were contrary to institutional anomie theory. Following the logic of the theory, we expected that the redistributive benefits provided by more socialist polities and the resulting reduced dependence on competitive market forces would reduce the incentives for egoistic ethical reasoning and thus the willingness of managers to justify ethically suspect behaviors. However, contrary to previous tests of institutional anomic theory in general populations, we found a strong, positive relationship between the degree of socialism and managers' willingness to justify ethically suspect behaviors.

Again, the position of managers in a social structure and an appeal to the Mertonian view of anomie theory (Merton, 1968) may explain why this finding is counter to institutional anomie theory. The general Mertonian argument is that destratification policies remove barriers to achieving culturally and institutionally induced goals, alleviating people's need to seek illegitimate means to achieve these ends. Savolainen (2000) provided evidence for this argument, showing that social welfare policies had a greater effect on reducing homicide in more stratified societies.

However, the redistributive benefits of more socialist polities that may result in less traditional crime also require by definition the transfer of wealth from the more affluent to the less affluent. Thus, since the members of managerial classes are more likely to hold greater wealth, they may be net losers in more socialist societies. Higher tax rates and policies such as those that restrict stock options limit managerial benefits. Consequently, although evidence suggests the institutional incentives of more socialist nations reduce the need for the majorities of their populations to seek illegitimate ways to achieve goals (Savolainen, 2000), the same logic suggests the opposite may be true for managers.

Conclusions

Institutional anomie theory has its roots in what is generally considered the strongest theoretical tradition in sociology, anomie. Following the same tradition, this study demonstrates the potential of the most recent variant of anomie theory, institutional anomie theory, as a theoretical framework for explaining cross-national differences in managers' ethical reasoning. Additionally, from a practical perspective, the findings suggest a more complex basis for identifying when to adjust processes for ethical management in different nations. In particular, the study highlights the importance of managers' considering the effects on ethics not just of culture but also of social institutions when conducting business operations in different national contexts.

However, we also conclude that institutional anomie theory must be modified in its application to managers. One modification, consistent with earlier views of anomie theory, is to take into account the position of managers in the social structure of a society. That is, the cultural and institutional incentives that may promote or deter deviance in the general population may have different effects on managers because they have different incentives, given their higher position in the stratification system. Future research based on institutional anomie theory might contrast the effects of national culture and social institutions on workers and managers.

Besides introducing institutional anomie theory to the study of managerial ethics, our study suggests that considering the effects of both national culture and social institutions provides a more comprehensive understanding of nation-level effects not only on ethical issues but also on other management-related phenomena. Additionally, our findings for national cultural dimensions that are not part of the more commonly used Hofstede (2001) model suggest potential benefits for future research using other conceptual schemes.

Although we were able to develop theoretically grounded and reliable measures for our test of institutional anomie theory, our use of secondary data limited the study's selection of variables and nations. As more cross-national data such as the GLOBE study (House, Javidan, Hanges, Dorfman, 2002) become available, we suggest that future research apply the theoretical reasoning of institutional anomie theory to the consideration of more individual control variables and other behaviors with ethical consequences, such as whistle blowing. Cross-level study of the *relationships* between individual variables as criteria (a "slopes-as-outcome" model) may also provide a more subtle understanding of institutional and cultural effects on managerial ethical reasoning.

REFERENCES

Beyer, J. M., & Nino, D. 1999. Ethics and cultures in international business. ***Journal of Management Inquiry,*** 8: 287–297.

Bryk, A. S., & Raudenbush, S. W. 2002. ***Hierarchical linear models.*** Newbury Park, CA: Sage.

Chamlin, M. B., & Cochran, J. K. 1995. Assessing Messner and Rosenfeld's institutional anomie theory: A partial test. ***Criminology,*** 33: 411–426.

Donaldson, T., & Dunfee, T. W. 1994. Toward a unified conception of business ethics: Integrative social contracts theory. ***Academy of Management Review,*** 19: 252–284.

Donaldson, T., & Dunfee, T. W. 1999. ***Ties that bind: A social contracts approach to business ethics.*** Boston: Harvard Business School Press.

Duch, R., & Taylor, M. 1993. Postmaterialism and the economic condition. ***American Journal of Political Science,*** 37: 747–779.

Durkheim, É. 1893/1964. ***The division of labor in society.*** New York: Free Press.

Durkheim, É. 1897/1966. ***Suicide: A study in sociology.*** New York: Free Press.

Euromonitor. 2002. http://www.euromonitor.com.

Esping-Anderson, G. 1990. ***The three worlds of welfare capitalism.*** Princeton, NJ: Princeton University Press.

Evans, D. T., Cullen, F. T., Dunaway, R. G., & Burton, V. S. 1995. Religion and crime reexamined: The impact of religion, secular controls, and social ecology on adult criminality. ***Criminology,*** 33: 195–215.

Hofstede, G. 2001. ***Culture's consequences.*** Thousand Oaks, CA: Sage.

Hofmann, D. A., Griffin, M. A., & Gavin, M. B. 2000. The application of hierarchical linear modeling to organizational research. In K. J. Klein & S. W. J. Kozlowski (Eds.), ***Multilevel theory, research, and methods in organizations:*** 467–511. San Francisco: Jossey-Bass.

House, R., Javidan, M., Hanges, P., & Dorfman, P. 2002. Understanding cultures and implicit leadership theories across the globe: An introduction to project GLOBE. ***Journal of World Business,*** 37: 3–10.

Husted, B., Dozier, J. B., McMahon, J. T., & Kattan, M. W. 1996. The impact of cross-national carriers of business ethics on attitudes about questionable practices and form of moral reasoning. ***Journal of International Business Studies,*** 27: 391–411.

Inglehart, R. 1997. ***Modernization and postmodernization: Cultural, economic, and political change in 43 societies.*** Princeton, NJ: Princeton University Press.

Lilly, J. R., Cullen, F. T., & Ball, R. A. 2002. ***Criminological theory: Context and consequences.*** Thousand Oaks, Sage.

Merton, R. K. 1968. ***Social theory and social structure.*** New York: Free Press.

Messner, S., & Rosenfeld, R. 1997. Political restraint of the market and levels of criminal homicide: A cross-national application of institutional-anomie theory. ***Social Forces,*** 75: 1393–1416.

Messner, S. F., & Rosenfeld, R. 2001. ***Crime and the American dream.*** Belmont, CA: Wadsworth.

Pampel, F., & Gartner, R. 1995 Age structure, socio-political institutions, and national homicide rates. ***European Sociological Review,*** 11: 243–60.

Parboteeah, K. P., & Cullen, J. B. 2003. Social institutions and work centrality: Explorations beyond national culture. ***Organization Science,*** 14: 137–148.

Passas, N. 2000. Global anomie, dysnomie, and economic crime: Hidden consequences of neoliberalism and globalization in Russia and around the world. ***Social Justice,*** 27(2): 16–44.

Ralston, D. A., Holt, D. H., Terpstra, R. H., & Kai-Cheng, Y. 1997. The impact of national culture and economic ideology on managerial world values: A study of the United States, Russia, Japan, and China. ***Journal of International Business Studies,*** 28 (1): 177–207.

Rau, W., & Wazienski, R. 1999. Industrialization, female labor force participation, and the modern division of labor by sex. ***Industrial Relations,*** 38: 504–521.

Rest, J. 1986. ***Moral development: Advances in research theory.*** New York: Praeger.

Rest, J., & Narvaez, D. 1991. The college experience and moral development. In W. Kurtines & J. Gewirtz (Eds.), ***Handbook of moral behavior and development:*** 229–245. New Jersey: Hillsdale.

Rosenfeld, R., & Messner, S. F. 1997. Markets, morality, and an institutional anomie theory of crime. In N. Passas & R. Agnew (Eds.), ***The future of anomie theory:*** 207–224. Boston: Northeastern University Press.

Savolainen, J. 2000. Inequality, welfare state, and homicide: Further support for the institutional anomie theory. ***Criminology,*** 38: 1021–1042.

Schooler, C. 1996. Cultural and social-structural explanations of cross-national psychological differences. In J. Hagan & K. S. Cook (Eds.), ***Annual review of sociology,*** vol. 22: 323–349. Palo Alto, CA: Annual Reviews.

Schwartz, S. H. 1994. Cultural dimensions of values: Towards an understanding of national differences. In U. Kim, H. C. Triandis, C. Kagitcibasi, S. C. Choi, & G. Yoon (Eds.), ***Individualism and collectivism:***

Theoretical and methodological issues: 85–199. Thousand Oaks, CA: Sage.

Serwinek, P. J. 1992. Demographic and related differences in ethical views among small business. ***Journal of Business Ethics,*** 11: 555–566.

Singh, J. 1995. Measurement issues in cross-national research. ***Journal of International Business Studies,*** 26: 597–620.

Stack, S., & Eshleman, J. R. 1998. Marital status and happiness: A 17-nation study. ***Journal of Marriage and Family,*** 60: 527–536.

Studenmund, A. H. 1992. ***Using econometrics: A practical guide.*** New York: Harper Collins.

Temple, J., & Voth, H. 1998. Human capital, equipment investment, and industrialization. ***European Economic Review,*** 42: 1343–1362.

Thorne, L., & Saunders, S. B. 2002. The socio-cultural embeddedness of individuals' ethical reasoning in organizations (cross-cultural ethics). ***Journal of Business Ethics,*** 35: 1–14.

Trompenaars, F., & Hampden-Turner, C. 1998. ***Riding the waves of culture: Understanding cultural diversity in global business.*** New York: McGraw Hill.

Turner, J. H. 1997. ***The institutional order.*** New York: Addison-Wesley.

United Nations Development Program. 1991. ***Human development report.*** New York: United Nations Development Program.

Van Deth, J. W. 1995. A macro setting for micro politics. In J. W. Van Deth & E. Scarbrough (Eds.), ***The impact of values:*** 48–75. New York: Oxford University Press.

Vitell, S. J., Nwachukwu, S. L., & Barnes, J. H. 1993. The effects of culture on ethical decision-making: An application of Hofstede's typology. ***Journal of Business Ethics,*** 12: 753–760.

World Values Study Group. 2000. ***World values surveys and European values surveys: 1981–1984 and 1990–1993, and 1995–1997*** (computer file). Ann Arbor, MI: Inter-University Consortium for Political and Social Research.

John B. Cullen *(cullenj@cbe.wsu.edu)* is a professor of management at Washington State University. He received his Ph.D. from Columbia University. His major research interests include the effects of social institutions and national culture on ethical outcomes and work values, the management of trust and commitment in international strategic alliances, ethical climates in multinational organizations, and the dynamics of organizational structure.

K. Praveen Parboteeah *(parbotek@uww.edu)* is an assistant professor of management at the University of Wisconsin—Whitewater. He received his Ph.D. in international management and organizational behavior from Washington State University. His research interests include development of alternative cross-level models of national culture to explain cross-national differences in individual behaviors. He is also interested in ethics, ethical climates, and team dynamics in innovative projects.

Martin Hoegl *(martin.hoegl@uni-bocconi.it)* is an assistant professor at the Institute of Organization and Information Systems at Bocconi University, Milan. He received his Ph.D. from the University of Karlsruhe, Germany. Before joining Bocconi University, he served on the faculty of the Department of Management and Decision Sciences at Washington State University. His research interests include collaboration, leadership, and knowledge processes in team-based innovation projects, the management of interorganizational research and development, and the role of cross-national differences in explaining organizational, group, and individual behavior.

Part III
US-Based Tests of Institutional-Anomie Theory

[10]

ASSESSING MESSNER AND ROSENFELD'S INSTITUTIONAL ANOMIE THEORY: A PARTIAL TEST*

MITCHELL B. CHAMLIN
University of Cincinnati

JOHN K. COCHRAN
University of South Florida

In Crime and the American Dream, *Messner and Rosenfeld contend that culturally and structurally produced pressures to secure monetary rewards, coupled with weak controls from noneconomic social institutions, promote high levels of instrumental crime. Empirically, they suggest that the effects of economic conditions on profit-related crime depend on the strength of noneconomic institutions. This investigation evaluates this proposition with cross-sectional data for U.S. states. In brief, the nonlinear models show considerable, indirect support for Messner and Rosenfeld's institutional anomie theory, revealing that the effects of poverty on property crime depend on levels of structural indicators of the capacity of noneconomic institutions to ameliorate the criminogenic impact of economic deprivation. The implications of these findings are discussed.*

Functional theories of social control assume that most members of society share a common value system, including the belief that the violation of law is wrong (Durkheim, 1858a; Dahrendorf, 1959; Merton, 1938, 1957). If this presumption holds any validity, then one must confront a seemingly insoluble question. Specifically, why do rates of illegal activity vary so dramatically across time and space (see, e.g., Bonger, 1916; Blau and Blau, 1982; Land et al., 1990)? After all, if behavioral choices are rooted in universally held norms and values, then there is little reason to expect to find much variation in the level of crime across macrosocial units.

One of the more intriguing answers to this apparent paradox focuses on the inherent contradictions that permeate the cultural and social structures of the American social system. That is to say, the decision to follow certain cultural prescriptions may compel some to ignore other cultural proscriptions. In essence, this is the creative insight that guides Merton's statement of anomie theory.

In brief, Merton (1938, 1957) recognizes that the social structure cannot

---

* We would like to thank Frank Cullen, John Wooldredge, Steve Messner, and the anonymous reviewers for their comments on an earlier draft of this paper.

effectively deliver what the dominant value system promises: universal access to legitimate means to secure material success goals. According to Merton, American culture places a preeminent emphasis on monetary rewards (i.e., the "American Dream"). Although socially accepted methods for acquiring property are also instilled in the populace, a preoccupation with the "ends" often relegates the norms associated with the "means" to a position of lesser importance. When the social structure fails to provide sufficient means to achieve success goals in the prescribed fashion, an increase in the rate of crime is the anticipated result. In the context of blocked opportunities, the contradictions between the values concerning means and ends produce a state of anomie, which in turn, frees some segments of society to engage in criminal behavior to procure monetary goals.

In a recently published book, *Crime and the American Dream*, Messner and Rosenfeld (1994) extend Merton's ideas concerning the relationships among culture, social structure, anomie, and rates of crime. This work is certain to generate important theoretical debates and research. Moreover, it reflects the resurgence of interest within criminology in the relationship between anomie and levels of illegal behavior (Agnew, 1985, 1992; Bernard, 1984; Messner, 1988; Rosenfeld, 1989). After a review of the theoretical arguments developed in this work, we assess the efficacy of this approach with a cross-sectional sample of U.S. states.

INSTITUTIONAL ANOMIE THEORY: THE MESSNER–ROSENFELD THESIS

Messner and Rosenfeld (1994), like Merton, contend that American culture places a disproportionate emphasis on material success goals. Also consistent with Merton, they maintain that the contradictions implicit in the dominant value system produce strong pressures to employ the most efficient means available to achieve monetary rewards (pp. 84–85). However, as we discuss below, their conceptualization of the impact of the social structure on the level of anomie and, in turn, levels of instrumental crime departs dramatically from that of Merton's.

In brief, Messner and Rosenfeld question Merton's decision to restrict his analysis of the relationship between social structure and anomie to only one facet of this dimension of the social system, the legitimate opportunity structure (p. 15). More to the point, they argue that an expansion of economic opportunities, rather than lessening the level of anomie in society, may actually intensify culturally induced pressures to use extralegal means to acquire monetary rewards. Insofar as economic vitality reinforces the societal preoccupation with the goal of material success, it is likely to heighten the level of anomie within a collectivity (pp.62, 99–101).

Hence, they conclude that the elimination of structural impediments to the legitimate opportunities cannot, in and of themselves, do much to reduce crime rates (p. 108).

Rather than focusing solely on the limitations of the economic structure as the primary source of structural pressure to innovate, Messner and Rosenfeld's analysis centers on the criminogenic influence of a variety of social institutions in American society. Drawing heavily on Marxist theory, they argue that the cultural penchant for pecuniary rewards is so all-encompassing that the major social institutions (i.e., the polity, religion, education, and the family) lose their ability to regulate passions and behavior. Instead of promoting other social goals, these institutions primarily support the quest for material success (i.e., the "American Dream"). For example, Messner and Rosenfeld contend that "education is regarded largely as a means to occupational attainment, which in turn is valued primarily insofar as it promises economic rewards" (p. 78). In short, to the extent that social institutions are subservient to the economic structure, they fail to provide alternative definitions of self-worth and achievement that could serve as countervailing forces against the anomic pressures of the American Dream.

To summarize, Messner and Rosenfeld's institutional anomie theory holds that culturally produced pressures to secure monetary rewards, coupled with weak controls from noneconomic social institutions, promote high rates of instrumental criminal activity (pp. 103–108). At first glance, the derivation of empirical hypotheses from this theoretical statement would seem to be a simple matter. However, as we discuss in the next section, this perspective does not readily lend itself to direct empirical evaluation.

OPERATIONALIZING INSTITUTIONAL ANOMIE THEORY: A RESEARCH STRATEGY

Messner and Rosenfeld (1994) are quite clear about the types of behavior that their perspective is designed to predict and explain. Specifically, institutional anomie theory pertains to rates of "criminal behavior with an instrumental character, behavior that offers monetary rewards" within the United States (pp. 68, 85). Thus, both common-law and white-collar offenses, as long as they are profit motivated, fall within the scope of Messner and Rosenfeld's theoretical approach.

What is less discernible, however, is the strategy one should employ to measure the effects of culture, social structure, and institutional controls on rates of instrumental crime. Consider Messner and Rosenfeld's (1994:84) summary statement concerning the linkages among culture, institutional structure, and rates of crime:

> Both of the core features of the social organization of the United States—culture and institutional structure—are implicated in the genesis of high levels of crime. At the cultural level, the dominant ethos of the American Dream stimulates wants and desires that are difficult to satisfy within the confines of legally permissible behavior while at the same time promoting a weak normative environment (anomie). The American Dream thus simultaneously generates certain types of criminal motivations while undermining normative restraints against crime. At the institutional level, the dominance of the economy in the institutional balance of power fosters weak social control. And, as just explained, both culture and institutional structure are themselves interdependent.

In brief, Messner and Rosenfeld describe a rather complex model of relationships among highly abstract concepts. Schematically, the model is presented in the following manner: Culture (the American Dream) promotes intense cultural pressures for monetary success and anomie, which in turn, are expected to influence each other. Social structure (the dominance of the economic structure) weakens institutional controls. Culture and social structure are hypothesized to influence each other. Lastly, anomie and weak institutional controls mediate the effects of culture and social structure on rates of instrumental crime, respectively (see Messner and Rosenfeld, 1994:85 for a path diagram of these linkages).

RESEARCH STRATEGY

Regardless of its complexities, we believe that institutional anomie theory has the potential to make a major contribution to the understanding of variations in the rate of crime across, and within, macro social units. Interestingly, as Messner (1988) points out, macro-level anomie theory in general, and Merton's anomie theory in particular, was a "road not taken" by criminologists. Instead, the social structure and anomie paradigm was largely reduced, with arguable benefit, to a social-psychological level "strain theory" (see, e.g., Agnew, 1985, 1992; Bernard, 1984; Burton and Cullen, 1992). Meanwhile, with the possible exception of Cloward's (1959) work on "illegitimate means," the macrosocial aspect of Merton's paradigm was left relatively underdeveloped (Messner, 1988). In this context, institutional anomie theory represents a salient attempt to revitalize Merton's anomie theory.

An attraction of the individual-level strain theory is that it was readily amenable to empirical tests (Hirschi, 1969; see also Burton and Cullen, 1992). Merton's anomie theory, however, has been more difficult to assess empirically, and this may well have retarded its development. At least as currently stated, Messner and Rosenfeld's (1994) institutional anomie theory risks suffering the same fate. Although they developed the theoretical portion of their work with sophistication, they provide little guidance on how their theory might be tested or how their key theoretical constructs might be operationalized. For example, using macro-level data, how does one measure the dominance of the economy in the institutional balance of power, the effectiveness of noneconomic institutional controls, or anomie?

More problematic, the obstacles to locating data that would facilitate a comprehensive test of their full model are daunting. As Sampson and Groves (1989) have lamented, the cost associated with the collection of aggregate-level information concerning mechanisms of informal social control is prohibitive. At least within the United States, macrosocial measures of the central theoretical constructs of institutional anomie theory are unavailable (see also Bursik, 1988; Heitgard and Bursik, 1987; Reiss, 1986).

These difficulties do not mean, however, that Messner and Rosenfeld's theory cannot be subjected to empirical scrutiny. Although a comprehensive test is beyond reach at this point, it is possible to derive empirical propositions from their work. If they are supported, then the larger theory would gain credence (Braithwaite, 1955).

Accordingly, our research strategy is to assess a proposition that can be derived from, and thus reflects on, the core assumptions of institutional anomie theory. As noted above, Messner and Rosenfeld (1994:101, 108) argue that the expansion of economic opportunities is expected to reduce rates of instrumental crime only when coupled with a revitalization of noneconomic institutions:

> We have maintained that greater equality of opportunity is not likely to eliminate, and in fact may aggravate, pressures to turn to illegitimate means to realize the goal of economic success . . . . Our point is simply that a war on poverty or on inequality of opportunity is not likely to be an effective strategy for *crime control* in the absence of other cultural and structural changes.

Taken together, these statements suggest evaluating the following hypothesis: The effect of economic conditions on instrumental crime rates will depend on the vitality of noneconomic institutions. That is to say, we would expect an improvement in economic conditions to result in a reduction of instrumental crime only when there is a simultaneous strengthening of noneconomic institutions. The proceeding analyses attempt to test this proposition by assessing the multiplicative effects of economic conditions and structural indicators of noneconomic institutions on instrumental crime.

RELATED RESEARCH

While there are numerous published works, often rooted in the social disorganization and functionalist perspectives, that have examined the additive, partial effects of economic conditions and/or community cohesion on economic crime rates (see, e.g., Bursik and Webb, 1982; Crutchfield et al., 1982; Jacobs, 1981; Sampson and Groves, 1989), few studies have considered the joint impact of these predictors on crime within a macrosocial context.

Interestingly, Stack (1984), in an analysis that somewhat parallels our own, examined the extent to which the effect of economic inequality on property crime rates depends on the cultural climate of nation-states. Specifically, Stack (1984) has argued that high levels of relative economic deprivation, when coupled with a radical value system that views economic inequality as illegitimate, increase the level of property crime. Contrary to expectations, the results from multiplicative models provide no support for the contention that the effects of relative economic deprivation, as estimated by the Gini index, are conditioned by measures of the cultural system.

Similarly, Tittle and Welch's (1983) contextual analyses of the relationship between religiosity and deviant behavior suggest that this association is not tempered by the level of economic deprivation. While their findings indicate that the effects of religious participation on self-reported deviance are conditioned by some social contexts (e.g., the level of normative dissensus), the results also reveal that level of status inequality (the standard deviation of the socioeconomic status scores of individuals within 24 contexts) has no appreciable effect on the religiosity-deviance relationship.

Taken together, Stack's (1984) and, to a lesser extent, Tittle and Welch's (1983) results may raise some concerns about our research strategy. However, as Stack (1984) notes in an explanation for his null findings, the egalitarian-radical dichotomy may be too broad to capture the conditioning effects of the cultural climate on the inequality-crime relationship. Consistent with Messner and Rosenfeld's (1994) approach, Stack (1984:250–251) suggests that future studies explore the conditional effects of political involvement on the economic deprivation-property crime association. As we discuss below, the level of participation in the political process is one of the noneconomic institutions we explicitly take into account in our model specifications.

DATA AND VARIABLES

Institutional anomie theory seeks to explain and predict rates of instrumental crime. Hence, aggregate-level data are appropriate. The sample for this investigation consists of the entire universe of 50 U.S. states for 1980. Although there is some concern that states are too heterogeneous to allow for an assessment of macrosocial theory (Bailey, 1984), we believe that they are adequate for the task at hand. Institutional anomie theory, unlike other macrostructural approaches such as general deterrence (Chamlin et al., 1992; Greenberg et al., 1981), focuses on social dynamics that are likely to operate across various levels of social aggregation (cf. Durkheim, 1858b; Messner and Rosenfeld, 1994). Moreover, as a practical matter, one of our indicators of noneconomic institutions, voting behavior, is only available for states, and another, religious membership, is best measured at this level of aggregation and for this time period (Stark, 1987).

DEPENDENT VARIABLE

As elucidated above, institutional anomie theory pertains to profit-motivated crime. Hence, we examine the effects of the predictor variables on the property crime rate. The property crime rate is measured as the total number of reported robbery, burglary, larceny, and auto theft offenses per 1,000 population (1980).

ECONOMIC DEPRIVATION

Typically, measures of relative (e.g., the Gini index) and/or absolute (e.g., the percentage of families below the poverty level) deprivation are used to estimate the economic structure of macrosocial units. Over the years there have been frequent debates about which indicator of economic deprivation is the most appropriate for the purpose of evaluating anomie theory (cf. Bailey, 1984; Messner, 1982). Given that institutional anomie focuses on the influence of structured opportunities to acquire material wealth rather than the level of inequality within a collectivity, our analyses employ the latter measure of economic deprivation. Absolute economic deprivation is measured as the percentage of families below the poverty level (1979).

NONECONOMIC INSTITUTIONS

As we argued above, direct measures of the extent to which noneconomic institutions provide alternative definitions of self-worth that could serve as countervailing forces against the anomie produced by the unbridled pursuit of the American Dream are not available. Consequently, we employ structural indicators that attempt to measure the capacity of social institutions to provide a bulwark against culturally induced pressures to secure monetary gain by illegal means. The presumption here is that certain structural arrangements are more likely than others to promulgate nonmaterialistic values. Each of these measures is discussed in turn.

According to institutional anomie theory, families can function to mitigate anomic pressures to secure material wealth by illegal means by providing emotional support for their members, as well as by inculcating noneconomic definitions of self-worth (Messner and Rosenfeld, 1994:73–75). Family disruption (e.g., divorce), insofar as it impedes these functions, is likely to increase the rate of instrumental crime (Messner and Rosenfeld, 1994:81). Hence, we contend that social aggregates that contain a higher rate of disrupted families relative to the rate of intact families are potentially less effective at providing values that serve as an alternative to the American Dream. There is a substantial body of scholarship that suggests that this may be so. Specifically, theory and research indicate that marital and family disruption decrease the level of informal social control (a dimension of weak institutional controls) and thereby increase the rate of economic crime (Blau and Blau, 1982; Blau and Golden, 1986; Felson and Cohen, 1980; Sampson, 1986, 1987; Sampson and Groves, 1989; see also Braithwaite, 1989; Sampson and Laub, 1993). We operationalize family structure as the ratio of the yearly divorce rate per 1,000 population (1980) to the yearly marriage rate per 1,000 population (1980).

Like families, religious institutions are important transmitters of values and norms that can counteract the anomic pressures produced by the economy (Messner and Rosenfeld, 1992:74). According to Stark et al. (1980, 1982) macrosocial units that have greater proportions of their population actively involved in religious organizations are more likely than others to develop a moral climate that promotes conformity. Consistent with this view, they report that upon controlling for the racial composition of standard metropolitan statistical areas, the rate of church membership is negatively related to property crime (Stark et al., 1980). Thus, we believe participation in formal religious organizations is a reasonable structural proxy for the capacity of religious institutions to reduce the level of anomie and, in turn, the rate of instrumental crime (see also, Tittle and Welch, 1983).

Participation in religious institutions is measured as the "adjusted" rate of church membership per 1,000 population (1980). Stark (1987) argues that the best available source of information concerning church membership, the Glenmary data (Quinn et al., 1982) substantially underestimates black and Jewish participation in formal religious organizations. Hence, we use Stark's (1987) modified church membership rate in lieu of the crude rate published by Quinn and his associates.

Lastly, Messner and Rosenfeld (1994:106–108) suggest that increased involvement in political institutions can produce a sense of public altruism and thereby reduce the level of anomie within macrosocial units. We indirectly measure the level of commitment to the political process as the percentage of voting age individuals who actually voted in the 1980 congressional contests. We focus on congressional elections, as opposed to the presidential contest, because the former are more likely than the latter to reflect an interest in local and statewide matters.

We recognize, as do Messner and Rosenfeld (1994:79–80), that voting behavior may be motivated by particularistic, pecuniary concerns and, consequently, may actually result in an *increase* in the level of anomie within a community. However, it is possible, if not likely, that participation in the political process may inadvertently promote some extrafinancial stakes in the community. Thus, we assume that states that have a greater proportion of voting age citizens actually exercising their franchise will be more insulated from the anomic effects of the economy than those that do not. Regardless, in the absence of more content-laden measures of political activity, we use voting behavior as the best available measure of commitment to the polity. Clearly, we have less confidence in this indicator than in the other two structural measures of noneconomic institutions.

CONTROL VARIABLES

Following previous research (e.g., Devine et al., 1988; Felson and Cohen, 1980; Sampson, 1987), indicators of the racial and age composition of the state are included as control variables. Racial heterogeneity is measured as the percentage of the population that is black (1980), and the age structure is measured as the percentage of the population aged 18 to 24 (1980).

INTERACTION EFFECTS

As argued above, we hypothesize that the effects of economic conditions on rates of instrumental crime will depend on the values of the noneconomic, institutional variables. First, we hypothesize that the effect of the poverty rate on economic crime will depend on family structure. Specifically, improvements in economic conditions (low poverty rates) are expected to reduce economic crime rates when the ratio of divorces to marriages is low. Second, we predict that the effect of the poverty rate on economic crime will depend on levels of the membership in religious organizations. That is to say, improvements in economic conditions (low poverty rates) are expected to reduce economic crime rates when the religious membership rate is high. Lastly, we predict that the effect of the poverty rate on economic crime will depend on levels of participation in elections. Improvements in economic conditions (low poverty rates) are expected to reduce economic crime rates when voter participation is high. To evaluate these interaction effects, we constructed three product terms (poverty rate

× church membership rate, poverty rate × divorce-marriage ratio, and poverty rate × percentage voting) and examine their increment to the explained variance (Allison, 1977).

DATA SOURCES

Information concerning the official count of property crimes was obtained from the Uniform Crime Reports (Federal Bureau of Investigation, 1981). With the exception of the adjusted church membership rates, which were gathered from a published source (Stark, 1987), data for each of the predictor variables were obtained from *State and Metropolitan Area Data Book* (Bureau of the Census, 1982b, 1986).

ESTIMATION PROCEDURES

As sometimes occurs with ordinary least squares (OLS) regression analyses of ecological data, an examination of the model residuals reveals that the variance of the error terms is not constant. Hence, we use weighted least squares regression procedures to increase the efficiency of our parameter estimates. Each case is weighted by the square root of the 1980 population size of the state (Greene, 1993).

The analyses proceed as follows. First, to establish a baseline for comparison, we estimate the additive effects of the structural variables on the property crime rate. Second, to evaluate indirectly institutional anomie theory, we reestimate the equations, introducing each of the product terms into the model. The inclusion of several multiplicative terms in a single equation substantially increases problems with multicollinearity and parameter redundancy (i.e., the variation associated with the poverty rate would be distributed among four separate variables). Therefore, we evaluate the unique contribution of each product term to the additive model separately.

RESULTS

Column one of Table 1 presents the weighted least squares estimates of the additive effects of the predictor variables on the property crime rate. In general, the additive model is quite efficacious, accounting for 96% of the variation in property crime rates across states. Consistent with past research (e.g., Land et al., 1990), the percentage of population aged 18 to 24 positively affects ($b = 3.82$, $p < .05$) the endogenous variable. Two of the three indicators of the structure of noneconomic institutions, the ratio of divorces to marriages and church membership, affect property crime in a manner consistent with Messner and Rosenfeld's (1994) approach. Specifically, the ratio of divorces to marriages ($b = 1.19$, $p < .05$) is positively, while church membership ($b = -.05$, $p < .05$) is negatively, related to the property crime rate. More important, the parameter estimate for the poverty rate is small and insignificant, indicating that economic conditions have no independent effect on instrumental crime.

Table 1. Weighted Least Squares Regression Estimates for Property Crime Rates: Additive and Multiplicative Models

	Equation 1	Equation 2	Equation 3	Equation 4
Percent Black	0.17[a]	0.29	0.27	0.18
	0.58[b]	1.91	0.93	0.65
Percent 18–24	3.82	.55	4.37	0.47
	2.75*	0.36	3.19*	0.25
Poverty	0.86	8.26	−0.48	6.17
	0.88	3.88*	−0.41	2.75*
Church Membership	−0.05	0.05	−0.06	−0.72
	−3.16*	1.61	−3.55*	−3.98*
Family Structure	1.19	0.74	−4.79	1.20
	2.82*	1.91	−1.60	3.03*
Percent Voting	0.38	0.11	0.51	1.53
	1.51	0.46	2.04	3.04*
Poverty ×	—	−0.01	—	—
Church Membership	—	−3.79*	—	—
Poverty ×	—	—	0.66	—
Family Structure	—	—	2.03*	—
Poverty ×	—	—	—	−0.12
Percent Voting	—	—	—	−2.59*
Adjusted R^2	.96	.98	.98	.98

[a] Metric coefficient.
[b] t value.
* $p < .05$.

Regardless of the efficacy of the additive model in explaining variations across states in the rate of property crime, it has little bearing on the evaluation of institutional anomie theory. Rather, it primarily serves as a baseline for the determination of the contribution of the joint influence of economic conditions and measures of noneconomic institutions on instrumental crime. The remainder of our presentation of the findings focuses on this issue.

Columns two through four of Table 1 contain the results from the nonlinear models of the property crime rate. As suggested by institutional anomie theory, each of the product terms significantly affects the property crime rate. In each equation, the increment to the explained variance is 2%.

While increases in the explained variance can be used to assess the statistical significance of interaction effects, they do not reveal the direction of those effects. However, as Stolzenberg (1978) demonstrates, one can derive the conditional effects of a variable of interest by taking the first-order partial derivative of Y with respect to each of the additive and multiplicative components of the product terms within a model. For example, the conditional effect of the poverty rate on property crime rates, controlling for levels of the church membership, is $b_1 + b_3X_2$; where b_1 is the unstandardized coefficient for the poverty rate, b_3 is the unstandardized coefficient for the product term, and X_2 is the church membership rate (see also, Tate, 1984).

To explicate the nonlinear influence of economic conditions on the property crime rate, we calculated the point estimates of the conditional effects of the poverty rate at the maximum and minimum values of the church membership rate, the divorce-marriage ratio, and the percentage of voters, respectively. The results of these analyses are presented in Table 2.

Table 2. Point Estimates of the Conditional Effects of Poverty on the Property Crime Rate

	Property Crime
Poverty Rate	
Church Membership (Maximum)	0.51
Church Membership (Minimum)	5.15
Poverty Rate	
Divorce-Marriage Ratio (Maximum)	9.42
Divorce-Marriage Ratio (Minimum)	–0.41
Poverty Rate	
Percent Voting (Maximum)	–1.75
Percent Voting (Minimum)	4.67

To reiterate, institutional anomie theory suggests that strong noneconomic institutions counteract the anomic pressures produced by the economic structure. As predicted, the findings reveal that higher levels of church membership, lower levels of the divorce-marriage ratio, and higher levels of voting participation reduce the criminogenic effects of poverty on economic crime. Specifically, the point estimate for the conditional effect of poverty at the maximum value of church membership remains positive, but it is approximately one-tenth the magnitude of the point estimate at the minimum value of this variable. Moreover, the point estimates for poverty, at the minimum value of the divorce-marriage ratio and the maximum value of the percentage of voters, are negative.

In short, these findings are consistent with Messner and Rosenfeld's (1994:63, 67–88) core theoretical insight concerning the interrelationships among social structure, culture, and crime. Indeed, the nonlinear analyses support their contention that it is inappropriate to focus solely on the relationship among the economic structure, anomie, and instrumental crime. Rather, it appears that it is the interplay between economic and other social institutions that determines the level of anomie within a collectivity and, in turn, the level of crime.

ALTERNATIVE SPECIFICATIONS

In the absence of observable indicators of anomie and institutional controls, the cogency of our findings rests heavily on how effectively we operationalize the structural antecedents of these theoretical constructs. Consequently, to assuage concerns that the results reported above reflect idiosyncratic measurement decisions, we performed a number of supplementary analyses.

Although we believe that within the context of anomie theory economic deprivation is best measured as the level of poverty within a political unit (Bailey, 1984), we recognize that other indicators are often used to estimate this concept. Therefore, to facilitate comparisons with other research and to assess partially the robustness of our initial findings, we reestimated the equations presented in Table 1 replacing the percentage of families below the poverty level with the level of economic inequality (estimated by the Gini index of economic concentration, 1980) and unemployment (1980), respectively.

With the exception of the conditional effects associated with family structure, the alternative measures of economic deprivation yield findings comparable to those reported above. Contrary to the initial findings, the economic inequality × divorce-marriage ratio product term is insignificant. Although the inclusion of the unemployment × divorce-marriage ratio produces a significant increment to the explained variance, the sign of the coefficient for this product term is opposite to that predicted by institutional anomie theory. That is to say, higher levels of family disruption appear to reduce, rather than increase, the criminogenic influence of unemployment. However, the results for the remaining nonlinear models are consistent with those reported in Table 1. Specifically, the economic inequality × church membership rate, economic inequality × voting participation, unemployment × church membership rate, and the unemployment × voting participation product terms are each statistically significant. Moreover, the signs of these coefficients, as predicted, are negative. Thus, higher levels of church membership and voting participation appear to reduce the criminogenic influence of economic inequality and unemployment.

Since, as in this case, voter turnout tends to be higher for presidential contests than for local ones (mean difference = 5.19, t = 5.34), we also examined the joint effects of economic deprivation and voting participation in the 1980 presidential election on property crime. For each of the three measures of economic deprivation, the analyses reveal that the product terms add significantly to the explained variance. More important, the sign of each of the coefficients is negative, indicating that greater levels of voter participation in presidential elections, as with congressional elections, militates against the disruptive effects of economic deprivation.

Lastly, we decided to explore further Stack's (1984) arguments concerning the joint effects of economic deprivation and cultural conditions on property crime. To review, Stack (1984) contends that economic inequality is expected to increase the level of property crime within the context of a radical cultural climate that views such inequalities as illegitimate. Following Stack (1984), we measured the presence of a radical value system in terms of union membership (i.e., the percentage of nonagricultural workers belonging to unions, 1980). Consistent with Stack's (1984) cross-national research, we found no evidence to support the claim that the effect of economic deprivation (measured as the Gini index, poverty level, or unemployment) depends on levels of union membership.**

In sum, with the exception of the conditional effects associated with family disruption, the overall pattern of the supplementary analyses suggests that the conditional effects of economic deprivation on property crime do not depend on how one measures this construct. Rather, these findings lend further credence to the contention that noneconomic institutions can reduce the level of anomie and crime across U.S. states.

** With the exception of the Gini index, each of the predictors used in the supplementary analyses was ascertained from the *State and Metropolitan Area Data Book* (Bureau of the Census, 1982b, 1986). The Gini index was calculated from household income data obtained from the *Census of Population* (Bureau of the Census, 1982). A more detailed exposition of the supplementary analyses is available upon request from the first named author.

DISCUSSION

In his discussion of the relationship between anomie and suicide, Durkheim (1858b) notes that even during periods of relative stability society can fail to regulate effectively the behavior of its members. He convincingly argues that the desire for "more" is so insatiable that regardless of how much property one acquires it is rarely enough (Durkheim, 1858b:346–347). Thus, in the absence of external, socially created constraints, anomic pressures to commit suicide become pronounced.

Further, Durkheim laments that the striving for material rewards has become so dominant in modern industrial society that noneconomic social institutions have lost their capacity to moderate the passions of the citizenry. As Durkheim (1858b:255) observes, "religion has lost most of its power. And government instead of regulating economic life, has become its tool and servant."

In Messner and Rosenfeld's institutional anomie theory, we find an application and extension of Durkheim's conceptualization of the social sources and consequences of anomie to instrumental criminal behavior. Like Durkheim, Messner and Rosenfeld assume that, regardless of how much wealth one is able to accumulate, the impetus to secure more wealth continues unabated. Also consistent with Durkheim, they contend that social institutions have become subservient to the economic structure and consequently have lost much of their ability to counteract the anomic pressures that emerge from the desire for "more" (Messner and Rosenfeld, 1994:62, 72–88). Hence, they conclude that culturally produced pressures to secure monetary rewards, coupled with weak controls from noneconomic social institutions, promote high rates of instrumental crime (Messner and Rosenfeld, 1994:103–108). It is this contention that is the focus of our investigation.

In the absence of direct measures of anomie and institutional controls, we indirectly evaluate institutional anomie theory by examining the joint effects of their structural antecedents on instrumental crime. Drawing on the logic of Messner and Rosenfeld's theoretical discussion, we hypothesized that the effect of the poverty rate (a measure of blocked opportunities) on the property crime rate depends on levels of church membership, the ratio of divorces to marriages, and voting behavior (structural proxies for the capacity of religious, family, and political institutions to reduce anomie).

Although the nonlinear and supplementary analyses lend credibility to Messner and Rosenfeld's (1994) extension of anomie theory, the failure to replicate fully the results reported in Table 1 when we replaced the percentage of families below the poverty level with the alternative measures of economic deprivation points to the need for further research. Clearly, an optimal strategy would entail devising cost-efficient means of collecting direct measures of the manner in which social institutions strengthen inhibitions against engaging in profit-motivated crime. However, insofar as direct, macrosocial indicators of the value orientations of social institutions are unobtainable, we recommend continuing to attempt, as we have done here, to make use of available data to evaluate empirical propositions that reflect on the core assumptions of institutional anomie theory. More specifically, it may prove useful to use alternative research designs (e.g., longitudinal data, city-level data) and reexamine the conditional effects of economic deprivation on instrumental crime. Clearly, the only remaining option is simply to reject institutional anomie, along with other approaches which contain unmeasurable, abstract constructs (e.g., routine activity theory, Mertonian anomie theory), as inherently nonfalsifiable. We believe that the former strategy is more productive.

REFERENCES

Agnew, Robert
1985 A revised theory of strain. Social Forces 68:435–451.
1992 Foundation for a general strain theory of crime and delinquency. Criminology 30:47–87.

Allison, Paul D.
1977 Testing for interaction in multiple regression. American Journal of Sociology 83:144–153.

Bailey, William C.
1984 Poverty, inequality, and city homicide rates. Criminology 22:531–550.

Bernard, Thomas J.
1984 Control criticisms of strain theories: An assessment of theoretical and empirical adequacy. Journal of Research in Crime and Delinquency 21:353–372.

Blau, Judith R. and Peter M. Blau
1982 The cost of inequality: Metropolitan structure and violent crime. American Sociological Review 47:114–129.

Blau, Peter M. and Reid M. Golden
1986 Metropolitan structure and criminal violence. The Sociological Quarterly 27:15–26.

Bonger, Willem
1916 Criminality and Economic Conditions. Boston: Little, Brown.

Braithwaite, John
1989 Crime, Shame and Reintegration. New York: Cambridge University Press.

Braithwaite, Richard B.
1955 Scientific Explanation. London: Cambridge University Press.

Bureau of the Census
1982a Census of the Population. Washington, D.C.: U.S. Government Printing Office.
1982b State and Metropolitan Area Data Book, 1982. Washington, D.C.: U.S. Government Printing Office.
1986 State and Metropolitan Area Data Book, 1986. Washington, D.C.: U.S. Government Printing Office.

Bursik, Robert J., Jr.
1988 Social disorganization and theories of crime and delinquency: Problems and prospects. Criminology 26:519–551.

Bursik, Robert J., Jr. and Jim Webb
1982 Community change and patterns of delinquency. American Journal of Sociology 88:24–42.

Burton, Velmer S., Jr. and Francis T. Cullen
1992 The empirical status of strain theory. Journal of Crime and Justice 15:1–30.

Chamlin, Mitchell B., Harold G. Grasmick, Robert J. Bursik, Jr., and John K. Cochran
1992 Time aggregation and time lag in macro-level deterrence research. Criminology 30:377–395.

Cloward, Richard
1959 Illegitimate means, anomie, and deviant behavior. American Sociological Review 24:164–176.

Crutchfield, Robert D., Michael R. Geerken, and Walter R. Gove
1982 Crime rate and social integration: The impact of metropolitan mobility. Criminology 20:467–478.

Dahrendorf, Ralf
1959 Class and Class Conflict in Industrial Society. Stanford, Calif.: Stanford University Press.

Devine, Joel A., Joseph F. Sheley, and M. Dwayne Smith
1988 Macroeconomic and social-control policy influences on crime rate changes, 1948–1985. American Sociological Review 53:407–420.

Durkheim, Emile
1858a The Division of Labor in Society. 1933. New York: Free Press.
1858b Suicide. 1951. New York: Free Press.

Federal Bureau of Investigation
1981 Crime in the United States. Uniform Crime Reports. Washington, D.C.: U.S. Government Printing Office.

Felson, Marcus and Lawrence E. Cohen
1980 Human ecology and crime: A routine activity approach. Human Ecology 8:389–406.

Greenberg, David F., Ronald C. Kessler, and Charles H. Logan
1981 Aggregation bias in deterrence research: An empirical analysis. Journal of Research in Crime and Delinquency 18:128–137.

Greene, William H.
1993 Econometric Analysis. 2nd ed. New York: Macmillan.

Heitgard, Janet L. and Robert J. Bursik, Jr.
1987 Extracommunity dynamics and the ecology of delinquency. American Journal of Sociology 92:775–787.

Hirschi, Travis
1969 Causes of Delinquency. Berkeley: University of California Press.

Jacobs, David
1981 Inequality and economic crime. Sociology and Social Research 66:12–28.

Land, Kenneth C., Patricia L. McCall, and Lawrence E. Cohen
1990 Structural covariates of homicide rates: Are there any invariances across time and space? American Journal of Sociology 95:922–963.

Merton, Robert K.
1938 Social structure and anomie. American Sociological Review 3:672–682.
1957 Social Theory and Social Structure. 1968. New York: Free Press.

Messner, Steven F.
1982 Poverty, inequality, and the urban homicide rate: Some unexpected findings. Criminology 20:103–114.
1988 Merton's "Social Structure and Anomie": The road not taken. Deviant Behavior 9:33–53.

Messner, Steven F. and Richard Rosenfeld
1994 Crime and the American Dream. Belmont, Calif.: Wadsworth.

Quinn, Bernard, Herman Anderson, Martin Bradley, Paul Goetting, and Peggy Shriver
1982 Churches and Church Membership in the United States 1980. Atlanta, Ga.: Glenmary Research Center.

Reiss, Albert J., Jr.
1986 Why are communities important in understanding crime? In Albert J. Reiss, Jr. (ed.), Communities and Crime. Chicago: University of Chicago Press.

Rosenfeld, Richard
1989 Robert Merton's contributions to the sociology of deviance. Sociological Inquiry 59:453–466.

Sampson, Robert J.
1986 Crime in Cities: The effects of formal and informal social control. In Albert J. Reiss, Jr., and Michael Tonry (eds.), Crime and Justice. Chicago: University of Chicago Press.
1987 Urban black violence: The effect of male joblessness and family disruption. American Journal of Sociology 93:348–382.

Sampson, Robert J. and W. Byron Groves
1989 Community structure and crime: Testing social-disorganization theory. American Journal of Sociology 94:774–802.

Sampson, Robert J. and John H. Laub
1993 Crime in the Making: Pathways and Turning Points through the Life Course. Cambridge, Mass.: Harvard University Press.

Stack, Steven
1984 Income inequality and property crime. Criminology 22:229–257.

Stark, Rodney
1987 Correcting church membership rates: 1971 and 1980. Review of Religious Research 29:69–77.

Stark, Rodney, Daniel P. Doyle, and Lori Kent
1980 Rediscovering moral communities: Church membership and crime. In Travis Hirschi and Michael Gottfredson (eds.), Understanding Crime: Current Theory and Research. Beverly Hills, Calif.: Sage.

Stark, Rodney, Daniel P. Doyle, and Lori Kent
1982 Religion and delinquency: The ecology of a "lost" relationship. Journal of Research in Crime and Delinquency 19:4–24.

Stolzenberg, Ross M.
1978 Bringing the boss back in: Employer size, employee schooling, and socioeconomic achievement. American Sociological Review 43:813–828.

Tate, Richard L.
1984 Limitations of centering for interactive models. Sociological Methods & Research 13:251–271.

Tittle, Charles R. and Michael R. Welch
1983 Religiosity and deviance: Toward a contingency theory of constraining effects. Social Forces 61:653–682.

Mitchell B. Chamlin is Associate Professor of Criminal Justice at the University of Cincinnati. His research interests and recent publications focus on changes, over time, in mechanisms of formal social control within municipalities.

John K. Cochran is Associate Professor of Criminology at the University of South Florida. His current research interests lie in examining the impact of sentencing reforms on offender populations and the deterrent/brutalization effects of executions.

[11]

On Testing Institutional Anomie Theory with Varying Specifications

By Alex Piquero and Nicole Leeper Piquero

Abstract

In their recent book *Crime and the American Dream,* Messner and Rosenfeld suggest that anomic tendencies inherent in the American Dream, defined as the commitment to the goal of material success to be pursued by everyone under conditions of open, individual competition, both produce and are reproduced by an institutional balance of power dominated by the economy over other institutions such as the family, the polity, and education. Termed Institutional Anomie Theory (IAT), the result of this interplay between the cultural commitments of the American Dream and the companion institutional arrangements is a) widespread anomie, b) weak social controls, and most importantly, c) high levels of crime. In this paper, we provide a preliminary assessment of IAT with cross-sectional data from the United States. In so doing, we employ a series of alternative operationalizations of key IAT variables in an effort to determine how sensitive our test of IAT is to a variable measurement strategy. The results indicate that the conclusions one draws from IAT may be subject to the operationalization of variables. The theoretical implications and future research directions are discussed. *(Studies on Crime and Crime Prevention, Vol. 7 No. 1 1998. National Council for Crime Prevention).*

Keywords: institutional anomic theory, cross-sectional research, theory testing, American Dream, crime.

INTRODUCTION

Merton's statement of anomie theory advanced the notion that two elements of United States society interacted to produce anomic conditions: culture and social structure. To Merton, culture specified the approved norms that all individuals were expected to follow in pursuing cultural goals whereas the social structure specified the means or legitimate opportunities through which cultural goals would be obtained. According to Merton, U.S. society is goal-oriented, particularly with regards to its emphasis on wealth and material goods. At the same time, not all persons in the U.S. have the means with which to obtain these goals. To many of these people, the "ends" are to be obtained through any means possible. As a result, for Merton, the distribution of crime in U.S. society is explained by the distribution of legitimate opportunities in the social structure. When legitimate means to monetary success are unavailable or unobtainable, people will tend to choose illegitimate means (Bernard, 1987:266). Under an anomic condition, people are encouraged to use whatever means to attain all types of goals and outcomes (Merton, 1968:189,211).

In an effort to explain the high levels of serious crime in the United States relative to other highly developed nations, Messner and Rosenfeld (1994) have put together a revision and expansion of Merton's classic, macro-level anomic theory with their book *Crime and the American Dream.* These authors claim that high levels of crime in the U.S. are produced by cultural and structural factors found in the organization of American society. Following Merton's position that American culture is characterized by a strong emphasis on (monetary) success and a weak emphasis on the importance of legitimate means for the pursuit of success, Messner and Rosenfeld claim that this "American Dream" contributes to crime by encouraging people to employ illegal means to achieve the goals that are culturally approved (Merton, 1997:519). To Messner and Rosenfeld (1994:69), the American Dream refers to a commitment to the goal of material success, to be pursued by everyone in society, under conditions of open, individual competition. Similarly, Hochschild (1995:xi) defines the *American Dream* as the promise that all Americans have a reasonable chance to achieve success as they define it – material or otherwise – through their own efforts, and to attain virtue and fulfillment through success.

Guided by the large difference in rates of serious crimes in the United States relative to other western nations, Messner and Rosenfeld extend Merton's ideas concerning the inter-relationships among culture, social structure, anomie, and the rate of crime in advancing a thesis of the production of crime that stems largely from an institutional imbalance of power marked by the strong emphasis of the economy. The purpose of this paper is to provide a preliminary assessment of some of the central tenants of Messner and Rosenfeld's institutional anomie theory (hereafter referred to as IAT). After a brief review of IAT, as well as the research undertaken to assess its merits, we examine the validity of Messner and Rosenfeld's arguments in the explanation of property and violent crime rates in the United States. In addition, we perform a number of supplementary analyses which contain different operationalizations of key IAT variables. In this way, we are in a position to determine if the conclusions we draw are sensitive to different variable measurement strategies.

INSTITUTIONAL ANOMIE THEORY

The fact that the United States has higher levels of crime, particularly higher levels of lethal violence, has been well documented (Lynch, 1995). What is in question, however, are the reasons for this trend. While some explanations have been advanced to account for this, IAT attributes the cause of crime to the interplay of two macro-level characteristics, culture and social structure. While culture refers to values and goals, social structure consists of patterned relationships among persons and groups defined and organized through social institutions (Messner and Rosenfeld, 1994:49). The thesis driving *Crime and the American Dream* is quite straightforward: the American Dream exerts pressures toward crime by encouraging an anomic cultural environment, an environment in which people are encouraged to adopt an "anything goes" mentality in the pursuit of personal goals (Messner and Rosenfeld, 1994:68; see also Derber's, 1992, description of "wilding").

To be sure, the *American Dream* may mean different things to different people such that various examples of the *American Dream* permeate U.S. society. Hochschild (1995) discusses the presence of the American Dream in recent speeches by Presidents Reagan and Clinton, as well re-producing a number of advertisements suggesting that "dreams come true in America", "dream big", "go for it", and "like it or not, success often means stepping over others". Furthermore, a recent U.S. Department of Housing and Urban Development document (HUD, 1996) entitled "Moving up to the *American Dream:* From Public Housing to Private Homeownership" contains a forward written by former HUD secretary Henry Cisneros stating that "..as we prepare to enter the 21st century in a time of profound change, homeownsership is still the *American Dream.* It is one of the most powerful and enduring values in all our lives." As can be seen, while the *American Dream* may not merely be material success in terms of dollars, it nevertheless seems to give a promise of sorts that all Americans have the chance to achieve success, as they define it, through their own efforts (Hochschild, 1995:xi).

To Messner and Rosenfeld, the *American Dream* is the embodiment of four distinctive cultural values: achievement, individualism, universalism, and materialism. Achievement refers to success. As Messner and Rosenfeld (1994:69-70) suggest, people are encouraged to make something of themselves and failure to do so is equated with a failure of the individual to contribute to society. Individualism concerns the basic belief in individual autonomy and rights. This value suggests a situation where everyone has to make it on their own. For example, in many places of employment, particularly in the business world, individuals tend to look out for themselves for fear that someone else will step on them to reach the top. The third cultural value for Messner and Rosenfeld concerns universalism. This value suggests that *everyone* is encouraged to aspire to success. According to Messner and Rosenfeld (1994:71), "virtually no one is exempt from the cultural mandate for individual achievement." The final but most important value concerns materialism, or what Messner and Rosenfeld refer to as the "fetishism" of money. They contend that success is signified by the accumulation of monetary rewards. Taken together, these four characteristics comprise the core elements of the *American Dream.*

The cultural ethos (i.e., the American Dream), however, is not the only reason for high levels of crime in the United States. For Messner and Rosenfeld (1994:63), social institutions have to place limits on the cultural imperative to succeed. Institutions, as defined by Messner and Rosenfeld (1994:72), refer to "relatively stable sets of norms and values, statuses and roles, and groups and organizations that regulate human conduct to meet the basic needs of society." By expanding Merton's work on the broader institutional structure of society – and not solely the role of inequality – Messner and Rosenfeld focus on the criminogenic influences of a variety of social institutions: the family, education, the political system, and the economy.[1]

The family has the primary responsibility for the regulation of sexual activ-

1. In his most recent book, *When Work Disappears,* William Julius Wilson (1996) also discusses the arrangement of the same four institutions implicated by Messner and Rosenfeld but with a focus on unemployment and social problems in urban cities. Nevertheless, this list is not exhaustive of all of the institutions in society. Other institutions like religion may play an important role as well.

ity and for the replacement of members of society (Messner & Rosenfeld, 1994: 73). In addition, the family has the responsibility of nurturing and socializing its children into the values and beliefs of society (Gottfredson & Hirschi, 1990; Hirschi, 1995). Perhaps the most important function of the family is to counterbalance the competitive conditions of public life (Rosenfeld & Messner, 1995:167).

The education institution is very similar to the family in its socialization function. Schools are to transmit basic cultural standards to new generations (Messner & Rosenfeld, 1994:73), and in an ideal world, give its members the tools necessary to make a contribution to society within their adult occupational roles.

The polity mobilizes and distributes power to attain collective goals, and has a major responsibility for crime control and the maintenance of public safety (Messner & Rosenfeld, 1994:73). In addition, the polity has the responsibility to take general care of its residents. The theme uniting these noneconomic institutions is to confer moral legitimacy on the means of social action (Rosenfeld & Messner, 1997).

The fourth and final institution is the economy, an institution which consists of activities organized around the production and distribution of goods and services needed to satisfy the basic material requirements of human existence (Messner & Rosenfeld, 1994:73; Rosenfeld & Messner, 1995:167). To them, the economy is what characterizes the essence of the American Dream and the most important feature of the economy is its capitalist nature. For Messner and Rosenfeld, the capitalist nature of the economy cultivates a competitive spirit.[2] While they have no main quarrel with capitalism per se, they assert that the United States, and their brand of capitalism in particular, places an exaggerated emphasis on monetary success and an unrestrained receptivity to innovation such that the goal of monetary success, relative to other non-economic goals, becomes the primary measuring rod for achievements (Rosenfeld & Messner, 1995:170). This is similar to Bonger's (1916) notion that capitalism legitimizes selfishness and develops egoism at the expense of altruism. Therefore, the goal of monetary success is put above all other goals, such as being educated and serving the community, and becomes that which everyone is compared against. The economy, dominates the other social institutions such that the institutional balance of power is tilted toward the economy and weakens social control (Messner & Rosenfeld, 1994:76; Rosnefeld & Messner, 1997).[3]

---

2. The relationship between capitalist markets and the moral order can be both good and bad. According to Rosenfeld and Messner (1997), markets may civilize behavior so that individuals in society become mutually dependent. Still, markets may demoralize economic activities and social relations by unleashing individuals from institutional control. Nevertheless, markets distribute material sources for personal well-being while presupposing a materialistic goal-orientation among individuals (Messner & Rosenfeld, 1997b; Hirschman, 1992).
3. For historical reasons, the economy in the United States has enjoyed a dominance of power that is manifested in three different ways: 1) the devaluation of non-economic institutional functions and roles, 2) the accommodation to economic requirements by other institutions, and 3) the penetration of economic norms into other institutional domains. Those interested in an expanded discussion of this issue should consult Messner and Rosenfeld (1994:78-84).

Economic dominance, then, leads to high rates of crime via two processes (Messner & Rosenfeld, 1997a). First, the dominance of the economy relative to the other institutions leads to an increase in anomic and cultural pressure such that noneconomic institutions become less capable of their socialization function. Second, this same economic dominance weakens external social control; therefore, noneconomic institutions become less attractive. The unfortunate result of these processes include, but may not be limited to, high rates of serious crime.

By drawing attention to the disproportionate emphasis placed on material success in American society, Messner and Rosenfeld (1994:85-86) suggest that the pressure to succeed is so strong that other major social institutions lose their ability to regulate behavior and/or perform their socialization function, even though this is one of their primary goals. As a result, these social institutions mimic the economy and support the quest for material success since the institutional structure diminishes the capacity of these noneconomic institutions to curb criminogenic pressures.[4] Thus, the universal application of the goal of monetary success creates a dilemma for a large number of individuals in a social structure characterized by appreciable economic inequality.

Messner and Rosenfeld suggest that the capitalist economy of the United States orients members toward an unrestrained pursuit of economic achievement such that the cultural emphasis on pursuing and achieving the American Dream is done so without regard to the normative means to obtain success. Strong cultural pressures to reach the American Dream, coupled with weak controls from noneconomic social institutions, promote high rates of crime (Messner & Rosenfeld, 1994; Chamlin & Cochran, 1995:413).[5] Perhaps the most salient policy implication emerging from the theory that could lead to a significant reduction in crime concerns the policies that promote a rebalancing of social institutions (Messner & Rosenfeld, 1997a:103). In other words, the current emphasis placed on the economy as the dominant institution, especially in the U.S., would have to take a backseat to noneconomic institutions and the exaggerated emphasis placed on the accumulation of material goods needs to be lessened.

In sum, IAT does not reject traditional anomie theory; it merely tries to extend it. Therefore, IAT is not proposed as a radically new theory of criminal behavior. It is intended to be a synthetic theory that recasts contemporary explanations of crime in a broad macrosociological framework (Messner & Rosenfeld, 1997a:44).

4. For example, education may be viewed as a way of advancement in the labor market as opposed to a means for learning and knowledge. Likewise, in the family, it is the homeowner rather than the homemaker that is admired and envied (Messner & Rosenfeld, 1994: 78,83).
5. Since IAT begins with a premise that bonds to institutions regulate human conduct, in some sense, IAT could be seen as an integration of macrolevel control and anomie theory. What IAT offers that macrolevel control theory does not, however, is its attempt to specify the macro-social conditions which more or less regulate human behavior (Rosenfeld & Messner, 1997).

RESEARCH ON IAT

In a recent paper, Sims (1997) suggests that Messner and Rosenfeld underrated the Marxist component of their argument. Sims claims that Marxist criminology can be a useful addition to an 'integrated theory of crime' in the sense that structural and economic inequalities help to explain how success, in American culture, has become entangled with material goods. In essence, she claims that goals in American society became materialistic because of the economic requirements of capitalism.

In a related manner, Messner and Rosenfeld (1997a:102-104) suggest that it is not merely the rewards that contribute to crime, but rather the "mechanism by which rewards are distributed". Drawing heavily upon the work of Karl Marx, Messner and Rosenfeld (1997a:102) claim that the conditions of production in American society dictate that the distribution of rewards be tied to economic functions such that the wealth that is produced within the economy is also distributed almost exclusively with economic criteria by labor and capital markets.

Within the empirical realm, Chamlin and Cochran (1995) were the first to assess IAT by using cross-sectional data for U.S. states. Although they did not have direct measures of specific IAT variables, Chamlin and Cochran indirectly evaluated IAT by examining the joint effects of structural antecedents on the property crime rate. The results suggested that the property crime rate depended upon levels of church membership, the ratio of divorces to marriages and voting behavior. In addition, Chamlin and Cochran (1995:422) calculated point estimates of the conditional effects of the poverty rate at the maximum and minimum values of the church membership rate, the divorce-marriage ratio, and the percentage of voters. As predicted by IAT, the findings revealed that higher levels of church membership, lower levels of the divorce-marriage ratio, and higher levels of voting participation reduced the criminogenic effects of poverty on economic crime (Chamlin & Cochran, 1995:423).[6]

Next, Chamlin and Cochran performed some sensitivity analyses by replacing the poverty level measure with other economic indicators such as the level of economic inequality as measured by the Gini index and unemployment. When doing so, they found comparable results with regard to church membership and voting participation. However, the divorce-marriage ratio effect was in the opposite direction: "higher levels in family disruption appear to reduce, rather than increase, the criminogenic influence of unemployment" (Chamlin & Cochran, 1995:423).[7]

Messner and Rosenfeld (1997b) report on a limited application of IAT to cross-national homicides with regard to the political restraint of the market. Political restraint refers to government

6. For example, at its maximum level, the divorce-marriage ratio had an effect of 9.42 on property crime, while the effect of the divorce-marriage ratio at its minimum level was -.41. Similarly, at its minimum value, church membership had an effect of 5.15 on property crime while at its maximum value, church membership had an effect on property crime of .51.
7. For a slightly different interpretation of the Chamlin and Cochran study, readers should consult Jensen (1996).

efforts to 'tame the market' by providing guarantees of minimal levels of material well-being (Messner & Rosenfeld, 1997a:102). Drawing upon the recent work of Esping-Andersen (1990), Messner and Rosenfeld (1997b) hypothesize that levels of homicide vary inversely to the "de-commodification of labor", a concept referring to policies which promote reliance on, or insulation from, pure market forces. In other words, de-commodification simply means that citizens empower themselves against the forces of the market such that the polity grants services and resources to citizens as a matter of right thereby reducing their reliance on the market for support (see Esping-Andersen, 1990:21-22).[8]

Therefore, the more resources the polity puts towards de-commodification and away from the economy, the less crime there should be. This index reflects the ease of access to welfare entitlements, income replacement value, and the range of social statuses covered by public assistance policies (Messner & Rosenfeld, 1997a:103). High scores on this index reflect comprehensive and unrestrictive welfare policies while low scores indicate low benefit levels and strict eligibility requirements. Using a de-commodification index based in part from Esping-Andersen's measure, Messner and Rosenfeld (1997b) examine the relative merits of this measure in the prediction of the homicide rate across forty-five nations. The results emanating from their work presents considerable support for one of the central tenants of IAT.

First, and consistent with their hypothesis, countries with higher de-commodification also had a lower homicide rate, and this was especially true of the United States which had one of the lowest de-commodification rates as well as the highest homicide rate. Second, after controls for a number of theoretically relevant variables were introduced into the model, the de-commodification index continued to exert a significant and negative effect on the homicide rate. That is, countries with a higher level of de-commodification had a lower homicide rate.

A review of the recent research on IAT suggests that the theory has some promise for the explanation of serious crime rates. IAT takes into consideration both cultural and structural variables by pointing to the importance of the interplay between the economy and other social, non-economic institutions. This paper seeks to contribute to the small but growing body of literature on IAT in a number of ways. First, we examine the scope conditions of the theory and assess whether or not IAT can explain property *and* violent crime rates. Second, we have access to particular variables within IAT which refer to certain non-economic institutions that have not been assessed in previous tests of the theory. Third, our data are from 1990, ten years after Chamlin and Cochran's data which was the first empirical examination of IAT with state level data from the United States. If the results from the present research are similar to those obtained by Chamlin and Cochran, this would argue for the enduring characteristics of IAT. Finally, and perhaps most important, we operationalize variables deduced from IAT in a number of different ways to

8. Examples of services and resources associated with de-commodification include welfare support, provision of basic social security, pensions, sickness benefits, and unemployment compensation.

determine if our conclusions are sensitive to the form of variable measurement we employ.

DATA AND VARIABLES

Since IAT is a theory of the aggregate and not the individual, specific pieces of information are required. For example, measures of the four institutions discussed in IAT, as well as rates of crime are needed. For this paper, we collected information for all 50 states in the U.S., as well as the District of Columbia. Some observers may initially question our state-level, cross-sectional test of IAT because the theory implicitly asserts that culture and (and to a lesser degree) structure within the United States is largely invariant. However, to the extent that Messner and Rosenfeld are correct, culture should be regarded largely as a constant for the purposes of testing IAT with cross-sectional U.S. data. At the same time, state-level variation is likely to be found in the structural variables that are part of IAT. Thus, the effects of culture may be differentially channeled through structural antecedents (Menard, 1995:137). As Chamlin and Cochran (1995:417) noted in their cross-sectional test of IAT with state-level data, IAT focuses on the social dynamics that are likely to operate across various levels of social aggregation. Messner and Rosenfeld (1997a:40) agree:

> ...analysis at the macrolevel focuses on questions about groups and populations. The relevant questions here include the following: Why do levels of crime vary across social systems (for example, nations, cities, neighborhoods)?

Insofar as the structural level variables operate in a manner consistent with Messner and Rosenfeld across different types of social systems, a test of IAT with state-level data should be sensitive enough to detect differences in the impact of such variables on crime rates.

While our data contain fairly reasonable indicators of IAT variables, they are not direct measures of these variables. As Chamlin and Cochran (1995:-415) note, "At least within the United States, macrosocial measures of the central theoretical constructs of institutional anomie theory are unavailable." This concern, however, should not dissuade researchers from attempting to assess the viability of a theory, particularly through its early development. Even though Messner and Rosenfeld provide little instruction as to the measurement of the institutions in IAT, we utilize various indicators that appear to be theoretically and empirically relevant.

DEPENDENT VARIABLE

Messner and Rosenfeld (1994:46, 84-85) limit the scope of the dependent variable to violations of the criminal law involving significant bodily injury, the threat of bodily injury, or in the case of nonviolent offenses, significant economic harm to victims – both individual and collective – that offer monetary rewards. By limiting the scope of its dependent variable, the theory seems to be concentrating its efforts to explain both property (economic harm) and violent (bodily injury) types of crime. For some people, the crimes they commit may serve instrumental, or monetary needs. However, for others who are not concerned with instrumental needs, or who do not define success in terms of monetary goals, they may turn to violence as an escape from anomic conditions (see also Agnew, 1992). The two empirical tests of IAT have examined both of these paths; Chamlin and Cochran (1995) focused on instrumental crime, while Messner and Rosenfeld (1997b) examined homicide rates. We use two operationalizations of crime as dependent variables in this paper. The first is the property crime rate per 100,000. The property crime rate includes the following offenses: burglary, larceny-theft and motor-vehicle theft. The second dependent variable is the violent crime rate per 100,000, which includes murder, forcible rape, robbery and aggravated assault. Both rates are from 1990, and are taken from the *Sourcebook of Criminal Justice Statistics* (Flanagan & Maguire, 1992).

INDEPENDENT VARIABLES

Recall that IAT posits the interplay between economic and noneconomic institutions of power. Aside from the economy, noneconomic institutions include the polity, education, and the family. As stated earlier, the extant literature on IAT is virtually silent on how and why particular variables serve as adequate representations of these four institutions. As a form of sensitivity analysis, we operationalize the institutions discussed in IAT in a variety of ways to determine if our conclusions are a function of the variable measurement strategy.

In terms of the polity, Messner and Rosenfeld (1994:106) argue that increased involvement in political institutions can reduce the level of anomie (and crime) within society by producing a sense of public altruism (see also Chamlin & Cochran, 1995:418; 1997). Research has shown that nations with broader and more generous social welfare policies have lower rates of crime (particularly homicide) (Fiala & LaFree, 1988; Gartner, 1990; Rosenfeld & Messner, 1997), and cutbacks or low funding from the polity could be viewed as tipping the institutional balance of power toward the economy and away from the polity (Rosenfeld & Messner, 1997). For the polity, we employ two different conceptualizations. First, we use the percentage of the population who receive public aid. Taken from the U.S. Bureau of the Census (1996), this item includes total recipients of Aid to Families with Dependent Children and of Federal Supplemental Security Income. This item reflects the vitality of the polity insofar as it is able to help its citizens in need (e.g., Messner & Rosenfeld, 1997b). Yet, some scholars may observe that this measure is amenable to a number of different interpretations. To account for this, we employ another measure of the polity that is based on involvement by the public in their governance. As Messner and Rosenfeld (1994:106-108) suggest, increased involvement in political institutions can produce a sense of public altruism which reduces the level of anomie within macrosocial units. We use the percentage of the population who cast a vote in the 1988 presidential election (U.S. Bureau of Census, 1992).

The next social institution concerns education, a component of IAT which no existing research has attempted to measure. IAT predicts that the institution of education prepares youths for adult and occupational roles. To the extent that the education succeeds in doing so, it should suppress crime in part by exposing its constituents to a different set of values and orientations, one based on the pursuit of knowledge and not necessarily on securing a high-paying job. According to IAT, education should serve to reduce property and violent crime rates by creating an increase in the percentage of people who through their education, can become productive, non-criminal members of society. We employ three different measures for education. The first is the proportion of the population enrolled full-time in college. This variable is taken from the U.S. Bureau of Census (1996). This variable is also susceptible to some measurement error as well. For example, college may be viewed as a means to achieve the *American Dream* than as a place that provides alternatives definitions of success.

Therefore, we also measure education through the percentage of high school dropouts. Taken from the U.S. Bureau of Census (1990), this variable indexes the vitality of the educational system. When the noneconomic institution of education is out of balance, people will be more likely to drop out of school. However, individuals who drop out of school may do so in an effort to join the armed forces, or enter the employment sector. Therefore, our third and final measure is referred to as comparative salary. This measure reflects a teacher's salary relative to the average annual pay of citizens. The logic of using teacher's salaries as a measure of the importance of education is that, in a market society, the status of institutional roles is reflected in their market value. States that pay teachers more relative to other occupations, it follows, place greater emphasis on the importance of non-economic institutions.[9] This measure was calculated by taking the ratio of the average salaries of public elementary and secondary teachers to the average annual pay of citizens (U.S. Bureau of Census, 1996).

The last non-economic institution discussed by Messner and Rosenfeld is the family. According to IAT, the family functions to insulate its members from the anomic pressures evident in society. As Chamlin and Cochran (1995: 418) note, family disruption may impede the important functions of the family and is likely to increase the rate of crime (Messner & Rosenfeld, 1994: 81). Moreover, a large amount of research has found that family cohesion is a very important socialization mechanism and the breakdown of such cohesion, usually in the form of divorce, separation, or the presence of single parent families, results in a decrease of social control and effective socialization (Blau & Blau, 1982; Glueck & Glueck, 1950; Sampson & Laub, 1993). To measure the family, we use the percentage of single parent families (Bureau of Census, 1993). Since a good deal of research has shown that single-parent families do not effectively socialize or supervise their children (Messner & Rosenfeld, 1997a:78; National Research Council, 1993: 155-156), this measure appears to be a reasonable proxy for family disruption given its risk factor for crime (Sampson & Lauritsen, 1994: 56).

The final institution discussed by Messner and Rosenfeld concerns the economy. The economy sets the stage for the anomic condition prevalent in society where this institution dominates all others. While there has been some discussion as to which measure of economic deprivation is most appropriate for the purpose of assessing macrolevel anomie theory (Messner, 1982), we utilize one measure of the economy that comes from U.S. Bureau of the Census (1996): the percentage of persons below the poverty level. The prediction that higher percentages of people below the poverty level should increase the property and violent crime rates follows most directly from conventional Mertonian theory. Also, since urban areas have the highest rates of crime (National Research Council, 1993:75), we also include the percentage of the

9. We would like to thank Rick Rosenfeld for bringing this to our attention.

population residing in urban areas (Bureau of the Census, 1996) as a control variable in our model estimations.

Although the measures we rely on are designed to provide a preliminary assessment of IAT, some readers may observe that these variables are common to other macrosociological theories of crime. For example, many macrolevel theories claim "economic deprivation" as a causal factor in one sense or another. In addition, the family structure hypothesis is also consistent with Sampson and Laub (1993), classic social disorganization theory (Shaw & McKay, 1969), and routine activities (Cohen & Felson, 1979). As previously mentioned, IAT is not a radically new theory of crime. Its contribution lies in its synthesis of explanations of crime within a broad macrosociological framework. The key difference between IAT and these other macrolevel theories of crime lies in IAT's attribution of the effect of these variables on crime. For example, increases in education, decreases in family disruption and so on can be expected to reduce anomie and crime if they are able to offer alternative definitions of success to that of material wealth. The theory is quite emphatic about the interrelationships between the economic and non-economic institutions. The effects of economic conditions on rates of crime will depend on the values of the non-economic, institutional variables (Chamlin & Cochran, 1995:419). As such, not only are additive effects important, but perhaps the more important effects are those that index the interplay between economic and non-economic institutions (Chamlin & Cochran, 1995: 423; Messner & Rosenfeld, 1994: 63, 67-88, 101,108) We present expanded reasons for the importance of interactions in the pages that follow.

Sometimes with cross-sectional data, heteroscedasticity occurs when the variance of the disturbances ε_i is not constant, but changing. To detect heteroskedasticity, it is useful to plot each predicted y-value against its corresponding residual. Visual inspection of the plots would reveal heteroskedasticity if the plots are fan shaped or if the cases lie outside the boundary lines (±2.5). In the present analysis, the plots did not exceed these lines. In addition, formal tests of heteroskedasticity (Breusch & Pagan, 1979) were also calculated and they yielded the same conclusion--heteroskedasticity was not present in the data.[10] All of the models were estimated in LIMDEP 7 (Greene, 1995) with the GLS (generalized least squares) estimator. Descriptive statistics for the variables may be found in Table 1.[11]

RESULTS

Property crime

In the first set of estimations, polity is measured by the percentage of the population who are public aid recipients, education is measured as the percentage of the population enrolled in college, family is measured by the percentage of single parent families, economy is measured as the percentage of people living below the poverty level, and the control variable is the percentage of people residing in an urban area. The estimates for the effects of the independent variables on the property crime rate may be found in the first

10. All of the diagnostic results are obtainable by writing to the senior author.
11. Correlations are available upon request.

TABLE 1. *Descriptive statistics (N=51)*

Variable	Mean	Std. Dev.
Economy		
- Percentage of population living below the poverty level	13.28	4.27
Family		
- Percentage of single parent families	23.41	5.31
Polity		
- Percentage of public aid recipients	5.76	2.00
- Percentage of population voting in 1988 presidential election	51.94	6.35
Education		
- Percentage of population enrolled full-time in college	59.82	9.81
- Percentage of high-school dropouts	10.40	2.41
- Comparative salary	1.41	.10
Percentage of population residing in urban areas	67.37	22.09
Property crime rate per 100,000	4734.82	1193.35
Violent crime rate per 100,000	571.78	389.34

column of Table 2. As can be seen, all five variables have their expected effects, both in terms of sign and significance. With regard to the four institutions postulated by IAT, both education (estimate=-21.10) and polity (estimate=-254.46) exert negative effects on the property crime rate. Therefore, the more individuals who are enrolled full-time in college and the higher the percentage of public aid recipients, the lower the property crime rate. The percentage of individuals living below the poverty level (estimate=98.44), as well as the higher the percentage of single parent families (estimate=110.74), exert positive effects on the property crime rate. Therefore, both high poverty levels and family disruption serve to increase property crime rates. In addition, and as expected, the higher the percentage of individuals living in urban areas (estimate=26.23), the higher the property crime rate.

While the additive findings appear supportive of IAT, Chamlin and Cochran (1995: 421) assert that it is the interplay or interactive effects hypothesized in IAT that are of the most interest. Specifically, we examine three interactions in the explanation of property crime rates. In creating the interactions, we followed the approach outlined by Jaccard and his colleagues (1990: 31) in mean-centering the raw scores of the component factors in or-

TABLE 2. *GLS estimates for property crime rate*

Variable	Estimate	Std Error	Estimate	Std Error	Estimate	Std Error	Estimate	Std Error
Urban	26.23	974.95*	25.25	6.04*	26.67	6.40*	24.93	6.22*
Polity	-254.46	77.04*	-237.77	75.04*	-251.70	77.57*	-236.01	77.38*
Education	-21.10	12.33*	-23.93	12.02*	-22.63	13.41*	-19.38	12.23
Economy	98.44	37.43*	117.12	37.55*	100.91	38.38*	100.94	36.94*
Family	110.74	27.67*	109.70	26.76*	99.72	47.29*	121.60	28.66*
Constant	1795.0	974.95*	1787.0	942.99*	2050.7	1319.9	1449.9	1000.8
Economy-Education			-4.98	2.66*				
Economy-Family					1.53	5.32		
Economy-Polity							-11.80	9.58
R-Square	.64		.67		.64		.65	

* p<.05

der to rid the measures of non-essential ill-conditioning (i.e., the multicollinearity between the component variables produced by the noncenteredness) which would inevitably cause multicollinearity between the component variables and their product terms. Columns 2 to 4 of Table 2 contain these results.

The first interaction term was for the effect of *education-economy*. It is hypothesized that the effect of the poverty rate on property crime will depend on the percentage of individuals enrolled in college. As such, lower percentages of people living below the poverty level should reduce property crime rates when the percentage of individuals enrolled in college is high. As can be seen, the effect of this variable is consistent with expectations from IAT. That is, the interaction term exerted a negative (estimate=-4.98) and significant effect on the property crime rate. In other words, the higher the percentage of individuals enrolled full-time in college, the less the effect of the poverty level on the property crime rate. The increase in explained variance is a little over 2% and is significant. All of the other variables exerted the same effects as they did in the additive model.

Our second interaction term, *family-economy*, may be found in the third column of Table 2. IAT would predict that a lower percentage of people living below the poverty level should reduce property crime rates when there is a low percentage of single parent families. This interaction term (estimate=1.53) fails to significantly affect property crime rates. The final interaction term, *polity-economy*, may be found in the fourth column of Table 2. Improvements in the conditions of the economy (lower percentage of people living below the poverty level) should reduce the property crime rate when there is a higher number of public aid recipients because the polity is taking care of its citizens. While the sign of this interaction (estimate=-11.80) is in the right direction, it fails to reach statistical significance.

The additive results for the property

crime estimation appear supportive of the effects of economic and non-economic institutions. However, only one of the three interaction terms exerted a significant effect on the property crime rate. This is not to say that all non-economic institutions are incapable of minimizing the domination of the economy since education appeared to be able to do so. Similar to Chamlin and Cochran (1995), we also calculate point estimates of the effect of the economy at the minimum and maximum levels of the non-economic institution of education which significantly affected the property crime rate. To calculate point estimates, Neter and his colleagues (1989:231) give the following formula:

$$ß_1 + ß_3X_2$$

where $ß_1$ is the unstandardized coefficient for the percentage of individuals living below the poverty level, $ß_3$ is the product term between the percentage of individuals living below the poverty level and the non-economic institution of education, and X_2 is the minimum or maximum level of education. Higher levels of the interaction are met with lower levels of the property crime rate. When full-time college enrollments are at their lowest level, the conditional effect of the economy on the property crime rate is -31.92; at the maximum level of full-time college enrollments, the conditional effect of the economy on the property crime rate is -280.67.

Violent crime

As was the case for property crimes, we estimate the effect of the same variable operationalizations on the violent crime rate. The results may be found in Table 3. For the most part, the results, are similar to those for the property crime rate. Higher percentages of people residing in urban areas (estimate=6.78), higher percentages of people living below the poverty level (estimate=21.06), and a higher percentage of single parent families (estimate=50.91) increased violence crime rates. It is interesting to note that the effect of single parent families on the violent crime rate is markedly stronger for the violent crime rate than it was for the property crime rate. On the other hand, and consistent with the results for property crime, higher percentages of public aid recipients (estimate=-27.57) and higher full-time college enrollments (estimate=-2.42) served to decrease violent crime rates. However, the effect for education was not statistically significant.

As we did for the property crime rate, we computed the same three sets of interactions, the results of which may be found in the final three columns of Table 3. For the interaction of *education-economy*, the result is the same as it was for the property crime rate. That is, the interaction (estimate=-1.52) exerted a negative effect on the violent crime rate. Therefore, education, indexed as a higher percentage of individuals enrolled full-time in college, appears to lessen the impact of the economy on the violent crime rate. The addition of the interaction term adds a significant amount of explanatory power to the model by 2%. The additive effects were substantively the same as they were prior to the inclusion of the interaction term except that the effect of polity on the violent crime rate becomes marginally significant ($p<.06$).

Similar to the second interaction effect for the property crime rate, the effect for *economy-family*, (estimate=-.38) did not exert a significant effect on the violent crime rate. In the final column of Table 3, the interaction for *polity-economy* (estimate=-5.09) produces a significant and negative effect on the vio-

TABLE 3. *GLS Estimates for violent crime rate*

Variable	Estimate	Std Error	Estimate	Std Error	Estimate	Std Error	Estimate	Std Error
Urban	6.78	1.24*	6.48	1.15*	6.67	1.28*	6.22	1.17*
Polity	-27.57	15.40*	-22.48	14.29	-28.26	15.49*	-19.60	14.60
Education	-2.42	2.46	-3.28	2.29	-2.04	2.68	-1.68	2.31
Economy	21.06	7.48*	26.76	7.15*	20.44	7.67*	22.14	6.97*
Family	50.91	5.53*	50.59	5.10*	53.66	9.45*	55.60	5.41*
Constant	-1053.0	194.85*	-1055.4	179.62*	-1116.9	263.67	-1202.0	188.81*
Economy-Education			-1.52	.51*				
Economy-Family					-.38	1.06		
Economy-Polity							-5.09	1.81*
R-Square	.87		.89		.87		.88	

* p<.05

lent crime rate. Consistent with Messner and Rosenfeld (1997b; see also, Rosenfeld & Messner, 1997), the polity appears to reduce the criminogenic effect of the economy on the violent crime rate. While we do not produce the conditional effects for the violent crime rate, they tell the same substantive story as they did for the property crime rate.[12]

THE IMPACT OF ALTERNATIVE VARIABLE OPERATIONALIZATIONS

In order to determine if our conclusions are sensitive to the variable measurement strategy, we turn to another set of results which substitutes alternative measures of the polity and education. We estimate the influence of these alternative conceptualizations on both the property and violent crime rate for additive and interactive models.

Property crime rate

In the first column of Table 4, we present the estimates for the additive model with two new measures. In this model, polity is conceptualized as the percentage of the population who voted in the 1988 presidential election, while education is measured as the percentage of high school dropouts. In this model, only two variables are statistically significant. The higher the percentage of the population residing in urban areas

12. We also estimated the influence of urban, poverty level, single parent families, public aid recipients, and the two other measures of education (high school dropouts first, then comparative salary) on both the property and violent crime rate in two different equations. All of the variables exerted their expected effects (both in terms of sign and significance), however, neither of the two education variables were significant. These results are available upon request.

TABLE 4. *GLS estimates for property crime rate with alternative variable operationalizations*

Variable	Column 1		Column 2		Column 3		Column 4		Column 5	
	Estimate	Std Error	Estimate	Std Error	Estimate	Std Error	Estimate	Std Error	Estimate	Std Error
Urban	18.94	7.12*	21.11	6.97*	25.25	6.84*	27.27	6.35*	26.84	6.10
Polity	-4.79	26.59	-25.67	22.08	30.59	11.50*	30.25	11.61*	36.52	11.52*
Education	106.83	74.49	-1504.3	1356.3	-2294.3	1421.1*	-1948.2	1350.1	-2046.4	1250.1*
Economy	-17.99	37.95	-22.59	40.45	18.64	41.69	28.10	39.83	41.95	38.15
Family	82.62	29.51*	88.04	29.54*	116.16	47.82*	88.15	30.31*	113.70	31.05*
Constant	903.16	2084.1	5005.4	2691.9*	1594.5	2260.6	1498.20	2306.0	633.22	2179.2
Economy-Family					-4.89	5.75				
Economy-Polity							2.72	6.22		
Economy-Education									653.12	326.57*
R-Square	.56		.55		.60		.59		.62	

* p<.05

(estimate=18.94), the higher the property crime rate. Similarly, the higher the percentage of single-parent families (estimate=82.62), the higher the property crime rate. The two new conceptualizations of education and polity, as well as the economy failed to significantly influence property crime rates. In the second column of Table 4, we alternate the education measures, this time inserting comparative salary. Once again, the only two variables that significantly influenced the property crime rate were urban (estimate=21.11) and single parent families (estimate= 88.04). None of the other variables exerted a significant effect on the property crime rate.

Using the alternative measures, we next turn to the interaction effects for property crime rates. In the third column of Table 4, we present the results of the interaction term for *economy-family* while controlling for the alternative measures of education and polity. While four variables exerted a significant effect on the property crime rate, the interaction term (estimate=-4.89) failed to significantly influence property crime rates. Moreover, the additive effect of our alternative measure of the polity, percentage of people voting in the 1988 presidential election, had a significant and positive effect (estimate=30.59) on the property crime rate. In the fourth column of Table 4, we computed the second interaction term, *economy-polity,* where polity is the percentage of people who voted in the 1988 presidential election. While the results are essentially the same as the preceding analysis, the interaction term in this model did not significantly influence property crime rates (estimate= 2.72). In the final column of Table 4, we report the results for the final interaction term (economy-education) on property crime rates. In this model, education is conceptualized as the ratio of teacher salaries to average annual pay for citizens. The results are essentially the same. While three variables exerted significant effects on the property crime rate, the interaction term exerted a significant and positive effect on property crime rates (estimate= 653.12). The sign of this coefficient is counterintuitive. It suggests that higher ratios of teacher salaries to average annual pay for citizens in the population increase the criminogenic effect of the economy on property crime rates. We also estimated interactions between economy and education with education measured as the percentage of high school dropouts. None of the interaction effects were significant, and all of the other results were substantively the same. These results are available upon request.

Violent crime rate

The alternative specifications for violent crime rates may be found in Table 5. In the first column, we report the additive effects for the alternative specification of education (high school dropouts) and polity (percentage of people who voted in the 1988 presidential election). Two variables exert significant effects on violent crime rates: urban (estimate=5.97) and single parent families (estimate=48.03). While the signs of the alternative measures are in the correct direction, both education and polity failed to significantly affect violent crime rates (estimates= 3.67 and -6.94 respectively). Substituting the comparative salary variable for education, the second column of Table 5 reveals the same substantive story. Once again, neither polity (estimate=-6.07) or education (-253.44) exerted a significant effect on the violent crime rate.

Using the alternative specifications for education (comparative salary) and polity (percentage of population vot-

TABLE 5. *GLS estimates for violent crime rate with alternative variable operationalizations*

Variable	Column 1		Column 2		Column 3		Column 4		Column 5	
	Estimate	Std Error	Estimate	Std Error	Estimate	Std Error	Estimate	Std Error	Estimate	Std Error
Urban	5.97	1.31*	5.85	1.26*	6.18	1.30*	6.88	1.22*	6.66	1.16*
Polity	-6.94	4.88	-6.07	3.98	2.36	2.19	2.51	2.22	3.64	2.19*
Education	-3.67	13.67	-253.44	244.57	-424.55	270.82	-237.0	258.85	-340.73	237.55
Economy	8.21	6.96*	4.73	7.29	7.85	7.94	12.10	7.63	13.60	7.25*
Family	48.03	5.41*	47.96	5.33*	57.32	9.11*	47.00	5.81*	54.87	5.90*
Constant	-666.02	382.43*	-335.31	485.39	-814.0	430.80*	-969.63	442.10*	-1040.9	414.11*
Economy-Family					-1.34	1.09				
Economy-Polity							-.68	1.19		
Economy-Education									140.63	62.06*
R-Square	.86		.86		.86		.86		.84	

* p<.05

ing in the 1988 presidential election), the third column reports on the interaction *economy-family*. As can be seen, the interaction term (estimate=-1.34) failed to significantly influence the violent crime rate. In the next column, we computed the *economy-polity* interaction. This term (estimate=-.68) also failed to significantly influence violent crime rates. In the final column, we report on the interaction between *economy-education*. As was the case in the property crime analysis, this variable exerted a significant and positive (estimate= 140.63) on the violent crime rate. Similar to property crime rates, we also estimated the interactions between economy and education where education was the percentage of high school dropouts. All of the interaction terms failed to exert a significant effect on the violent crime rate. These results are available upon request.

DISCUSSION AND CONCLUSION

Using cross-sectional data from the United States, and different indicators of key IAT variables, we set out to examine the relationship between IAT and the property and violent crime rate. Our results concerning IAT are somewhat mixed. In an early analysis using a particular operationalization strategy, the hypothesized relationships of the effect of economic and non-economic institutions on both the property and violent crime rate were evident. In an additive fashion, both education, measured as the percentage of the population enrolled full-time in college, and the polity, measured as the percentage of the population who receive public aid, reduced the property and violent crime rate. On the other hand, the economy, measured as the percentage of the population living below the poverty level, and the family, measured as the percentage of single parent families, appeared to increase both the property and violent crime rate. When interactions were computed and estimated, the conditional effects were salient in one of the three interactions (economy-education) for the property crime rate, and in two of the three interactions (economy-education, economy-polity) for the violent crime rate. The theme underlying the significant interactions concerned the non-economic institution of education, an institution which has not been assessed in any of the empirical tests of IAT. Education lessened the impact of the economy on property and violent crime, while the polity-economy interaction reduced the impact of violent crime. These particular findings may point to the fact that some of the institutions may be more important in explaining certain types of crime. This was particularly evident for the polity – economy interaction which significantly reduced violent crime rates, but failed to reduce property crime rates. This result is similar to the one reported by Messner and Rosenfeld (1997b) who found that a decommodification index based on levels and patterns of welfare expenditures reduced homicide rates.

While we have no direct measure of education, the operationalization as the percentage of college enrollments appears to be having some sort of socializing influence. It may very well be that the institution of college is transmitting a respect for formal learning and the pursuit of knowledge in such a way that such values are transmitted to others in the population. In turn, higher college enrollments could create a larger educated work force (National Research Council, 1993: 32). Without formal measures, however, this assertion is purely speculative and only survey-based research with individuals in college will bring evidence to bear on this front. In a similar vein, the polity seems to be able to curtail the effect of the poverty level on the violent crime rate by providing some of the means of survival to its members. Interestingly, when the percentage of the population receiving public aid was at its lowest, the effect of the poverty level on the violent crime rate was 10.94; however, when public aid recipients was at its highest level, the conditional effect of the poverty level on violent crime was -35.94. Clearly, then, there are some steps that both the education and the polity can take to curb the criminogenic influence of economic dominance.

Nevertheless, when different variable operationalizations were constructed for both the polity and education noneconomic institutions, these results did not hold up. That is, at both the additive and interactive levels, our alternative specifications did not significantly influence either property or violent crime rates. These null findings point to a broader issue within IAT, and perhaps within criminological theory in general. Deciding on how to indirectly measure variables must be undertaken with extreme caution and respect for alternative specifications. As we have shown, the conclusions one draws from an indirect empirical test is extremely sensitive to the operationalizations of key variables. Had we not examined different measurements for education and polity, we would have been left with one set of conclusions that did not hold up with varying measurement strategies. Clearly, the most important direction for future work on IAT is in the theoretical and measurement realm, an issue which we return to shortly.

We should point out a few limitations with our data. First, our data were not collected by government officials to specifically test IAT and as such, the empirical test reported on in this paper is a conservative one given our measurement and operationalization of IAT constructs. Second, our data do not contain measures for the important notions of culture and anomie, both central concepts in IAT, and we were forced to assume that culture was invariant. In response to this, some observers may suggest that our inclusion of both economic and noneconomic institutions operate simply as control variables once culture has been added to the model. Measuring culture and anomie, of course, is not solely problematic of IAT as it has been mentioned as a problem in testing classic strain and anomie theories of crime. The measurement strategy for such concepts is, perhaps, the most difficult problem facing researchers who are interested in testing IAT (e.g., Chamlin & Cochran, 1996; Rosenfeld & Messner, 1997). Finally, our data do not contain specific information on race and gender. Given Messner and Rosenfeld's (1997a) discussions on this issue, future research should make every effort to obtain such information for comparison purposes.

Even though our assessment does not connote a comprehensive test of IAT, we have been able to examine some propositions emanating from the theory and such preliminary assessments are important when testing new theoretical advances (Chamlin & Cochran, 1995: 414). Therefore, we believe that these limitations do not render a fatal flaw in our attempt to examine IAT, and we would offer that the results from this analysis are supportive of future research regarding IAT, one centering on the construction of a data set which attempts to measure the key concepts and institutions put forth in IAT, as well as other noneconomic institutions such as religion which are not fully developed in the theory. We acknowledge that this is not an easy endeavor, but the collection of original data is the only way by which more formal tests of the theory can be undertaken. With this in mind, we see a number of promising avenues for future research.

First, both race and gender could play a significant role in IAT. In terms of race, research suggests that blacks and whites share an overwhelming support for the American Dream as a prescription for their own American lives (Hochschild, 1995:55). She (1995:56-57) reports that poor blacks are as likely to endorse the American Dream as more well-off blacks. Given that poverty rates for blacks are much higher than they are for whites (Donzinger, 1996:26), and that births to unmarried black women are higher than births to unmarried white women by a factor of over 2 to 1 (Blumstein, 1993:15), it may be the case that black males are disproportionately over-represented in crime rates as a result of these factors. To us, it appears that IAT may be an excellent predictor for such differences and we encourage this future application.

IAT may also be able to explain the over-representation of males in crime rates relative to females. For example, Messner and Rosenfeld (1997a:79) argue that women are more engaged than males in the family institution in that they perform the bulk of family tasks. As a result, this greater engagement in family life should lead to different cultural orientations – women are more likely to balance economic values with other values. The logical extension of this position would suggest that women and men hold different interpretations of the *American Dream* (Messner & Rosenfeld, 1997:80). In fact, some support exists for this claim. In a study of high school seniors, Beutel and Marini (1995) report that male students were more likely to be materialistic and competitive while female students were more likely to express compassion and indicate a willingness to forego personal rewards to help others in need. The impact of noneconomic and economic factors on crime across gender could be easily assessed through a series of multiple group models and we encourage its application in future research. On a related point, by arguing that family ties are tenuous for young black males, Messner and Rosenfeld (1997a) suggest that the intersection of race and gender may be worthy of future research, and we see no reason to disagree.

With regard to community structure, it is plausible that certain neighborhoods such as those that are poor or have low social control/cohesion have higher crime rates and as a result, could be disproportionately influenced by economic and noneconomic institutions (Wilson, 1996). For example, poor neighborhoods that are characterized by low social cohesion could have higher rates of unemployment and divorce than more affluent and informally controlled neighborhoods leading to a breakdown in many types of informal control (e.g., Taylor, 1997). In addition, given the low income of residents in such neighborhoods, they may be more likely to be in need of social welfare assistance. Similar to gender, multiple group models could easily assess this issue. Another possible avenue of research concerns the impact of IAT variables on different types of crime such as white collar crime. The scope conditions with which IAT can explain different types of crime would stengthen the generality of the theory.

Finally, we encourage the exploration of the utility of IAT to explain rates of crime cross-nationally. For example, countries such as Ireland, China, and Russia would make for interesting case studies for a variety of reasons. Ireland, for example, has a very low homicide rate (McCullagh, 1996; Wilbanks, 1996). While some would attribute this to the presence of strong religious ties (a noneconomic institution), other factors, such as the minimal presence of guns could be affecting the homicide rate. China and Russia have recently made segway into a market economy and it would be interesting to see how crime rates respond to such large economical changes. Early indications from China seem to suggest that factory owners are having trouble deciding whether or not to lay off factory workers, or retain workers but lose profits (Langfitt, 1997). IAT may serve to be a useful description of the dynamic changes ongoing in such places

REFERENCES

Agnew, R. (1992). Foundation for a general strain theory of crime and delinquency. *Criminology* 30: 47-87.

Beutel, A.M. & Mooney Marini, M. (1995). Gender and values. *American Sociological Review* 60:436-448.

Bernard, T.J. (1987). Testing structural strain theories. *Journal of Research in Crime and Delinquency* 24:262-280.

Blau, J.R. & Blau, P.M. (1982). The cost of inequality: Metropolitan structure and violent crime. *American Sociological Review* 47:114-129.

Blumstein, A. (1993). Making rationality relevant: The American Society of Criminology 1992 Presidential Address. *Criminology* 31:1-16.

Bonger, W.A. (1916). *Criminality and economic conditions.* Boston, MA: Little Brown.

Breusch, T.S. & Pagan, A.R. (1979). A simple test for heteroskedasticity and random coefficient variation. *Econometrica* 47:1287-1294.

Chamlin, M.B. & Cochran, J.K. (1995). Assessing Messner and Rosenfeld's institutional anomie theory: A partial test. *Criminology* 33:411-429.

Chamlin, M.B. & Cochran, J.K. (1996). Reply to Jensen. *Criminology* 34: 129-131.

Chamlin, M.B. & Cochran, J.K. (1997). Social altruism and crime. *Criminology* 35:203-228.

Cohen, L.R. & Felson, M. (1979). Social change and crime rate trends: A routine activity approach. *American Sociological Review* 44:588-608.

Derber, C. (1992). *Money, murder, and the American Dream: Wilding from Main Street to Wall Street.* Boston, MA: Faber and Faber.

Donzinger, S.R. (1996). *The real war on crime: The report of the National Criminal Justice Commission.* New York, NY: Harper Collins.

Esping-Andersen, G. (1990). *The three worlds of welfare capitalism.* Princeton, NJ: Princeton University Press.

Fiala, R. & LaFree, G. (1988). Cross-national determinants of child homicide. *American Sociological Review* 53:432- 445.

Flanagan, T.J. & Maguire, K. (1992). *Sourcebook of criminal justice statistics 1991.* Washington, D.C.: U.S. Department of Justice.

Gartner, R. (1990). The victims of homicide: A temporal and cross-national comparison. *American Sociological Review* 55:92-106.

Gottfredson, M.R. & Hirschi, T. (1990). *A general theory of crime.* Stanford, CA: Stanford University Press.

Glueck, S. & Glueck, E. (1950). *Unraveling juvenile delinquency.* New York, NY: The Commonwealth Fund.

Greene, W.H. (1995). *LIMDEP Version 7.0.* User's manual. Bellport, NY: Econometric Software.

Hirschi, T. (1995). The family. In: Wilson, J.Q. & Petersilia, J., eds. *Crime.* San Francisco, CA: ICS Press.

Hirschman, A.O. (1992). *Rival views of market society and other recent essays.* Cambridge, MA: Harvard University Press.

Hochschild, J.L. (1995). *Facing up to the American Dream: Race, class and the soul of the nation.* Princeton, NJ: Princeton University Press.

Jaccard, J., Turrisi, R. & Wan, C.K. (1990). *Interaction effects in multiple regression.* Newbury Park, CA: Sage.

Jensen, G.F. (1996). Comment on Chamlin and Cochran. *Criminology* 34: 129-131.

Langfitt, F. (1997). China eases into market economy. *The Baltimore Sun*, September 19: 2A.

Lynch, J. (1995). Crime in international perspective. In: Wilson, J.Q. & Petersilia, J., eds. *Crime*. San Francisco, CA: ICS Press.

McCullagh, C. (1996). *Crime in Ireland*. Cork, Ireland: Cork University Press.

Menard, S. (1995). A developmental test of Mertonian anomie theory. *Journal of Research in Crime and Delinquency* 32: 136-174.

Merton, R.K. (1968). *Social theory and social structure*. New York, NY: Free Press.

Merton, R.K. (1997). On the evolving synthesis of differential association and anomie theory: A perspective from the sociology of science. *Criminology* 35: 517-525.

Messner, S.F. (1982). Poverty, inequality, and the urban homicide rate: Some unexpected findings. *Criminology* 20:103-114.

Messner, S.F. & Rosenfeld, R. (1994). *Crime and the American Dream*. Belmont, CA: Wadsworth.

Messner, S.F. & Rosenfeld, R. (1997a). *Crime and the American Dream*. Second Edition. Belmont, CA: Wadsworth.

Messner, S.F. & Rosenfeld, R. (1997b). Political restraint of the market and levels of criminal homicide: A cross-national application of institutional anomie theory. *Social Forces* 75:1393-1416.

National Research Council (1993). *Losing generations: Adolescents in high-risk settings*. Washington, D.C.: National Academy Press.

Neter, J. Wasserman, W. & Kutner, M.K. (1989). *Applied linear regression models*. Second Edition. Burr Ridge, IL: Irwin.

Rosenfeld, R. & Messner, S.F. (1995). Crime and the American Dream: An institutional analysis. In: Adler, F. & Laufer, W.S., eds. *Advances in criminological theory*. Volume 6. New Brunswick, NJ: Transaction.

Rosenfeld, R. & Messner, S.F. (1997). Markets, morality, and an institutional-anomie theory of crime. In: Passas, N. & Agnew, R., eds. *The future of anomie theory*. Boston, MA: Northeastern University Press.

Sampson, R. & Laub, J. (1993). *Crime in the making*. Cambridge, MA: Harvard University Press.

Sampson, R. & Lauritsen, J.L. (1994). Violent victimization and offending: Individual-, situational-, and community-level risk factors. In: Reiss, A. & Roth, J., eds. *Understanding and preventing violence: Volume 3 Social Influences*. Washington, D.C.: National Academy Press.

Shaw, C.R. & McKay, H.D. (1969). *Juvenile delinquency and urban areas*. Chicago, IL: University of Chicago Press.

Sims, B. (1997). Crime, punishment, and the American Dream: Toward a Marxist integration. *Journal of Research in Crime and Delinquency* 34:5-24.

Taylor, R.B. (1997). Social order and disorder of street blocks and neighborhoods: Ecology, microecology, and the systemic model of social disorganization. *Journal of Research in Crime and Delinquency* 34: 113-155.

United States Bureau of Census (1990). *Census of the Population*. Washington, D.C.: Bureau of Census.

United States Bureau of Census (1992). *Statistical abstracts of the United States*. Washington, D.C.: Bureau of Census.

United States Bureau of Census (1993). *Statistical abstracts of the United States*. Washington, D.C.: Bureau of Census.

United States Bureau of Census (1996). *Statistical abstracts of the United States*. Washington, D.C.: Bureau of Census.

United States Department of Housing and Urban Development (1996). *Moving up to the American Dream: From public housing to private homeownership*. Washington, D.C.: Department of Housing and Urban Development.

United States National Center for Education Statistics (1996). *Statistical abstracts of the United States*. Washington, D.C.: National Center for Education Statistics.

Wilbanks, W. (1996). Homicide in Ireland. *International Journal of Comparative and Applied Criminal Justice* 20:59-75

Wilson, W.J. (1996). *When work disappears: The world of the new urban poor*. New York, NY: Knopf.

Received October 1997

Alex Piquero
Temple University
Department of Criminal Justice
Gladfelter Hall (5th floor)
Philadelphia, PA. 19122
USA

Nicole Leeper Piquero
University of Maryland
Department of Criminology
2220 LeFrak Hall
College Park, MD. 20742
USA

[12]

SOCIAL INSTITUTIONS AND VIOLENCE: A SUB-NATIONAL TEST OF INSTITUTIONAL ANOMIE THEORY*

MICHAEL O. MAUME
University of North Carolina at Wilmington

MATTHEW R. LEE
Mississippi State University

Messner and Rosenfeld's institutional anomie theory is grounded in the assumption that relatively higher crime rates in the United States are due to (1) the overwhelming influence of economic motives and institutions in society, and (2) the subjugation of all other social institutions to cultural economic interests (e.g., the American Dream). Our analysis is designed to extend the limited body of empirical research on this theory in several ways. First, we seek to test the utility of institutional anomie theory for predicting crime rates across aggregate units within *the United States (counties). Second, we draw out the theory's emphasis on* instrumental *crime and suggest that measures of noneconomic social, political, familial, religious, and educational institutions will be particularly relevant for explaining instrumental as opposed to expressive violence. Third, in contrast to prior research, we develop conceptual reasons to expect that these factors will primarily* mediate *(as opposed to moderate) the relationship between economically motivating pressures and instrumental violence. Our negative binomial regression analyses of data from the Supplementary Homicide Reports and various censuses indicate that the measures of noneconomic institutions perform well in explaining both instrumental and expressive homicides, but that these measures mediate the impact of economic pressures (as measured by the Gini coefficient of family income inequality) to commit instrumental violence most strongly. Further, we find only very limited support for the more popular moderation hypothesis.*

KEYWORDS: Anomie, institutional anomie theory, social institutions, violence, instrumental homicide

* A previous draft of this paper was presented at the 2001 meeting of the American Society of Criminology in Atlanta, GA. We appreciate helpful comments from Richard Rosenfeld, Scott Phillips, T. David Evans, Kent Kerley, and the journal's reviewers on previous drafts of this manuscript. Direct correspondence to Michael O. Maume, Dept. of Sociology & Criminal Justice, University of North Carolina at Wilmington, Wilmington, NC 28403-5978, maume@uncw.edu.

A compelling issue facing American criminologists in the waning years of the twentieth century and the onset of the next has been the decline in crime rates. From 1993 to 1999, the homicide rate in the United States dropped 40%. Despite a number of arguments put forth to explain this decline (see Blumstein and Rosenfeld, 1998; Blumstein and Wallman, 2000; LaFree, 1999) the fact is that the United States remains "exceptional" in its level of lethal violence, compared with other nations. In *Crime and the American Dream*, Messner and Rosenfeld (2001) propose a version of anomie theory to explain why Americans are so much more plagued by serious crime than other nations. Their "institutional" anomie theory builds on Merton's (1938) landmark theory by detailing the role of culture and social structure in a more complete manner than Merton's original formulation. Recent tests of this theory have not only found support for its components, but also have demonstrated its utility for explaining variations in crime across U.S. states (Chamlin and Cochran, 1995; Piquero and Piquero, 1998).

We seek in this paper to extend the limited but growing body of research on institutional anomie theory in a number of ways. First, we argue that prior tests of the theory have underestimated its potential for explaining macrolevel variation in crime rates by restricting their focus to states and nations. As we detail below, smaller aggregate units such as counties also exhibit their own institutional characteristics, and the presence of noneconomic institutions within these smaller units may provide protective effects against crime. Second, we extend the work of prior research by focusing on the links between institutional anomie and violence using homicides disaggregated according to apparent motivation of the offender (i.e., instrumental or expressive). As we explicate below, IAT is strongly geared toward explaining crimes that are instrumental in nature. Third, we expand the range of measures of noneconomic institutions considered in previous research. Finally, in contrast to the more popular hypothesis stating that noneconomic institutions moderate the effects of economic pressures on instrumental crime, we present conceptual reasons for expecting that noneconomic institutions will primarily mediate the effects of the economy on instrumental violence.

INSTITUTIONAL ANOMIE THEORY

Institutional anomie theory is rooted in Robert Merton's anomie theory (Merton, 1938). Basic anomie theory argues against the idea that the causes of crime are found in individual pathologies. Rather, Merton argued that the source of crime is to be found in the ways that society is organized. Merton focused on two aspects of society: (1) cultural goals and values expressed in American society and passed on from generation to generation (e.g., the "American Dream) and (2) social structure. Merton argued that the system of stratification in the United States is a source of both social and income inequality. Further, the realities of inequality, and the failure of many to meet the expectations set forth by culturally approved goals of success such as the American Dream, produce the condition of *anomie* in society. Merton characterized anomie as endemic—part of a society's very structure. As an outcome of this disjunction between culturally approved success goals and the inequality in structural means to achieve those goals, anomie, Merton (1938) argued, was likely to have a disproportionate impact on people at the bottom of the social hierarchy (e.g., the poor). Although noting that the modal adaptation to anomie is conformity to normative goals and means, Merton argued that several "deviant" adaptations to anomie were likely to result in criminal behavior. For example, *innovation* involves the acceptance of the American Dream, but the pursuit of "illegitimate" means, when faced with blocked legitimate opportunities (e.g., work, college), to achieve this goal (Merton, 1938).

Steven Messner and Richard Rosenfeld introduced their own variant of Merton's anomie theory—institutional anomie theory (IAT)—in the first edition of their book, *Crime and the American Dream* (1994). IAT is not simply an extension of Merton's anomie theory (e.g., Dubin, 1959), but a critique as well. Although they accept Merton's argument that motivations for crime stem from unequal access to legitimate means for success, they argue that the overarching problem is the American Dream itself. The nature of the American Dream—fetishism of money, success by any means necessary—is a prime example of culture setting up a structure where "at all social levels, America is organized for crime" (Messner and Rosenfeld, 2001:5). Messner and Rosenfeld argue that the drive to succeed entails criminogenic consequences for the lower and upper classes alike. Thus, providing more equitable access to legitimate opportunities in the economic domain will not only fail to reduce crime, but may in fact *increase* crime rates by increasing emphasis on the cultural goal of economic success (Chamlin and Cochran, 1997).

Their version of anomie theory turns to other aspects of society—namely, noneconomic familial, educational, and political institutions—to produce a more complete explanation of serious crime. Whereas in other capitalist societies the desire for financial profit is offset by strong adherence to institutions such as church and family, Messner and Rosenfeld (2001:68) argue that noneconomic institutions in the United States are subjugated by the economy in what they refer to as the "institutional balance of power." This subjugation occurs through (1) the "devaluation of noneconomic institutional functions and roles"—for example, education is frequently achieved in the interest of pursuing a career, rather than the goal of learning for learning's sake; (2) "accommodation to economic requirements by other institutions"—such as the timing of pregnancy and childbearing to coincide with career moves or interests; and (3) "penetration of economic norms into other institutional domains"—such as the tendency to view college students as "customers" in the "business" of higher education (see Messner and Rosenfeld, 2001:70–76 for a more extensive discussion). Overall, the "*exaggerated* emphasis on monetary success" in American society denigrates alternative standards by which success in life may be judged (Messner and Rosenfeld, 2001:69). These propositions are summarized in Figure 1, which is a graphic representation of the theory adapted from Messner and Rosenfeld (2001).

Figure 1. Institutional Anomie Theory (Adapted from Messner and Rosenfeld, 2001)

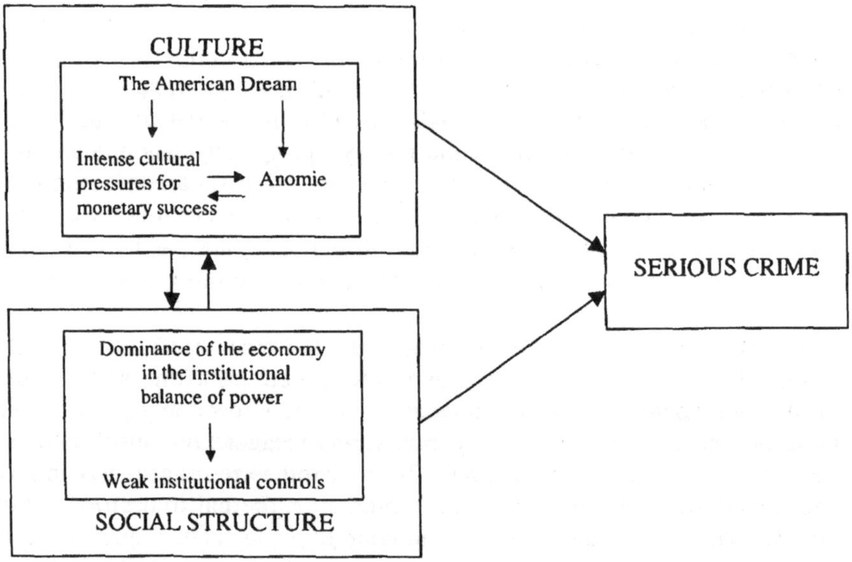

As shown in the model in Figure 1, serious crime is an outcome of the dual influence of culture and social structure in general, and, more specifically, mechanisms going on in each of these spheres. On the cultural side, the emphasis on the American Dream leads to both intense cultural pressures for monetary success and an increase in anomie. The dominance of the economy in the social structure, as noted above, weakens the regulatory efficacy of noneconomic institutions (e.g., the family, education, and the polity). Serious crime is a result of this weakening, in terms of both the loss of "normative control associated with culture" and "the more external type of social control associated with social structure [i.e., active participation in social institutions]" (Messner and Rosenfeld, 2001:78). Therefore, one avenue for the remediation of serious crime is a strengthening of noneconomic institutions to achieve a more equitable balance with the economy. Messner and Rosenfeld (2001:101) argue that "this institutional vitalization would, in turn, temper the anomic qualities and the intense pressures for monetary success associated with the American Dream."

REVIEW OF STUDIES TESTING IAT

Despite its potential utility as a tool for explaining and reducing crime, there have been only a few attempts to assess the empirical validity of IAT. Messner and Rosenfeld, (2001) provide little guidance on how the theory should be tested. Moreover, one could argue that beyond providing evidence "consistent" with their theory (Messner and Rosenfeld, 1997, described below), the authors have not attempted a comprehensive empirical assessment of their theory. Also, as Chamlin and Cochran (1995) note, the cultural dimensions of the theory—particularly anomie and the corresponding cultural pressures for monetary success—are impossible to measure given the available structural data on macrosocial units. Therefore, tests of the theory, including the present one, are partial tests with the potential of providing, at most, a preponderance of evidence in favor of IAT.

Chamlin and Cochran (1995) conducted the first direct test of IAT. Using data from 50 U.S. states, they tested the effects of the major structural components of IAT (indicators of the economy and other noneconomic institutions—family, polity, and religion) on "instrumental" (i.e., property) crime rates in 1980. They hypothesized that the economy and noneconomic institutions would interact, such that indicators of the family, religion, and the polity would condition the relationship between poverty and crime across states. Their findings support this general hypothesis, even after alternative specifications using different combinations of the theoretical indicators are employed. Chamlin and Cochran (1995) conclude by encouraging researchers to use available data to test IAT.

In Messner and Rosenfeld's (1997) own paper applying the theory, the authors link their work on IAT with research by Esping-Andersen (1990) on market societies to argue that the "decommodification of labor" in societies, or the freedom of individuals to make life choices without the constraints of the market, is inversely related to homicide. Specifically, decommodification, operationalized in terms of the degree to which nations prioritize entitlement (welfare, social security) expenditures, is framed as a mechanism that buffers the effects of the economy and thus, in IAT terms, balances more equitably the economy with noneconomic social institutions. Using data from 45 countries, Messner and Rosenfeld (1997:1407–1408) find that their arguments are supported by the data, and they conclude that their research "lends credibility to [IAT] and helps to empirically distinguish this perspective from more conventional stratification-based accounts of variation across societies in the level of homicide." We find Messner and Rosenfeld's arguments concerning decommodification to be a compelling and important avenue for direct tests of the theory. Given its attention to both economic and political concerns, the authors argue that the concept is an indicator of the *balance* between these two institutions.

Two more recent studies that test IAT theory are based on state-level and nation-level data. Piquero and Piquero (1998) follow Chamlin and Cochran's approach closely, but with 1990 data, to test IAT across states within the United States. The major differences in the two papers are Piquero and Piquero's (1998) use of several indicators of education, the omission of religious measures, and the decision to model both violent and property crimes. Although Piquero and Piquero's modeling approach follows Chamlin and Cochran's (1995), their findings with regard to property crime are somewhat divergent. They find only the multiplicative terms involving indicators of education and the economy to be significant predictors of property crime rates. However, some of these differences may be due to the differences in the research designs already noted, as well as the fact that Chamlin and Cochran included robbery in the calculation of their property crime rates. Piquero and Piquero include robbery in their violent crime rates, whose models detect interaction effects between the economy and the polity, as well as between the economy and education.

Savolainen's (2000) research uses two cross-national data sets to apply IAT to the thesis that welfare expenditures will condition the association between income inequality and homicide rates. Savolainen (2000:1037) finds that, in fact, the relationship between income inequality and homicide is much stronger when welfare support is low: "Because of their generous welfare programs, the nations that appear to be immune to the detrimental effects of economic inequality have a very small or nonexistent underclass population."

Besides these direct tests of IAT, there have been a few studies that have indirectly found support for the theory. The first, a study by Hannan and DeFronzo (1998), proposes that county-level welfare support (measured using both welfare payments and the proportion of residents receiving welfare) will condition the impact of economic deprivation on crime. Based on data from 406 U.S. counties, the authors find that this is the case, and they conclude that their findings support IAT's "argument that welfare frees people from total reliance on market forces, thus limiting anomie and enhancing the social control functions of non-economic institutions" (Hannon and DeFronzo, 1998:389). Second, Chamlin and Cochran (1997) used IAT to help frame their hypotheses on the relationship between social altruism and crime. They define social altruism as "the conviction that societies can teach their members to value and perform behaviors that promote the welfare of others" (p. 208). They argue further that altruism is likely to vary within the United States across local political units (e.g., cities). Using data on 279 cities, they find that the level of altruism across localities (measured using aggregate contributions to charity) is negatively correlated with both property and violent crime rates. Interestingly, though, the authors find (on the basis of indirect effects analysis) that altruism does not mediate the effects of any of the several included structural predictors on either property or violent crime (see also Chamlin and Cochran, 2001).

The direct tests of IAT by Chamlin and Cochran (1995) and Piquero and Piquero (1998) are the most comprehensive so far in seeking to measure the balance of power between economic and noneconomic social institutions. Before describing our own strategy in measuring this institutional balance, we assess the utility of IAT for explaining the variation in one type of serious crime—homicide—across macrosocial units within the United States.

INSTITUTIONAL ANOMIE AND ECONOMIC CRIMES

The question of whether IAT is a general theory, suited to explain a wide variety of crime, is addressed early on in Messner and Rosenfeld's discussion. They state that one boundary condition of their theory is that it is intended to explain "serious" crimes, or "violations of criminal law involving significant bodily injury, the threat of bodily injury, or, in the case of nonviolent offenses, significant economic harm to victims, both individual and collective" (Messner and Rosenfeld, 2001:42). Thus, less serious crimes (e.g., misdemeanors) fall outside the scope of the theory. Chamlin and Cochran's (1995) test of IAT used property crime rates (including robbery, burglary, larceny, and auto theft) as the dependent variable. This decision seems to be a direct result of their interpretation of the theory (p. 413):

> Messner and Rosenfeld (1994) are quite clear about the types of

behavior that their perspective is designed to predict and explain. Specifically, institutional anomie theory pertains to rates of "criminal behavior with an instrumental character, behavior that offers monetary rewards" within the United States (pp. 68, 85). Thus, both common-law and white-collar offenses, as long as they are profit motivated, fall within the scope of Messner and Rosenfeld's theoretical approach.

Chamlin and Cochran (1995) operationalize "profit motivated" offenses as property offenses. But this approach overlooks the fact that many violent crimes have economic motives. In fact, Messner and Rosenfeld devote a great deal of space in their book to one of the most serious crimes in any society—murder. They indicate that they have murder and other "serious" crimes in mind when taking account of the utility of their theory, but they frame their explanation for lethal violence as the outcome of illegitimate opportunity structures in which violence is often instrumental. For example, Anderson's (1999) research documenting the "code of the street" makes a clear connection between illegal drug markets and violence. He finds that, "for the most desperate people . . . the underground economy of drugs and crime often emerges to pick up the slack. To be sure, the active participants in this economy are at serious risk of violence, death, and incarceration" (p. 108). In the next section, we attempt to make the distinction in types of homicide clearer.

INSTRUMENTAL AND EXPRESSIVE HOMICIDES

Any discussion of economic motives and violent crime must distinguish between what are known as instrumental and expressive forms of violence. First applied to the study of homicides by Block and Zimring in 1973, this dichotomy classifies the circumstances and motives of homicides into two types. *Instrumental* homicides entail lethal violence in pursuit of some material gain. Hence, the "violence" is only instrumental to some material goal. The typical homicide in this category would be a murder committed in the course of another felony (e.g., robbery). *Expressive* homicides are committed in the context of an argument, a lover's quarrel, or a fit of rage. Examples of expressive homicides include arguments over money, crimes of passion, revenge killings, and child murders (Block and Block, 1991). In all cases, the violence involved in expressive murders is considered by the murderer as the primary end, in and of itself, to be achieved (Block et al., 2000).

This dichotomy has been subject to scrutiny and criticism since its application to homicides (see, e.g., Cooney and Phillips, 2002). One might argue, for example, that these circumstances are just a proxy for, or overlap quite a great deal with, the victim-offender relationship categorization of homicides (i.e., intimate, acquaintance and stranger homicides). Although it is true that instrumental homicides are more likely to involve offenders and victims who do not know each other, and expressive homicides are more likely to involve acquaintances and intimates, the association between circumstances and relationship is not perfect. In fact, Decker (1996) and Varano and Cancino (2001) have found, based on data from St. Louis and Chicago, that "deviant homicides"—both expressive murders involving strangers and instrumental murders involving acquaintances and intimates—made up as many as 40% to 50% of all homicides. Varano and Cancino (2001), looking at Chicago homicides from 1975 to 1995, found that minority males and gang-related homicides were overrepresented among deviant homicides. Therefore, it is incorrect to argue that victim-offender relationship is a proxy for circumstances, for in fact the two attributes are capturing different dynamics in homicide (cf. Marleau and Hamilton, 1999).

A more substantial critique of the instrumental/expressive distinction is offered by Daly and Wilson (1988), Polk (1994), and Felson and Messner (1996), who argue in their own ways that a large share of offenders have some sort of instrumental goal in mind when engaging in any form of lethal or nonlethal violence. Nevertheless, in one way or another, these authors' own work has shown either that the circumstances of lethal violence differ significantly from nonlethal violence or that typologies of lethal violence are at least useful departure points, with finer grained classifications as the eventual destination. Therefore, we agree with Block and Block (1991) that the instrumental/expressive dichotomy is a useful classification, and we argue that it is applicable to macrolevel homicide research.

RESEARCH STRATEGY

We are in agreement with the studies reviewed above that IAT is a viable and testable theory of serious crime. One goal of this paper is to test the applicability of IAT for explaining homicide by type. In doing so, we expect that IAT will be better suited to (or have more explanatory power for) predicting instrumental than expressive homicides. In addition, our test of IAT departs from previous tests in two significant ways: (1) We hypothesize that the relationships among the structural components of the theory encompass two possible causal mechanisms: moderation and mediation; (2) we propose that IAT is a valid theory for explaining variations in crime across "local" macrosocial units (or subnational units), such as counties. We describe our specific reasoning for these two departures below. Overall, we tie both of these modifications into what we believe are the two strongest contributions of Messner and Rosenfeld's theory: (1) the recognition of the institutional structure of society and its relation to culture and (2) the study and theorizing about crime across macrosocial units of analysis.

CAUSAL MECHANISMS

Our approach to operationalizing this test of IAT departs from previous tests in that we hypothesize two possibilities by which social institutions may have an impact on rates of lethal violence. Based on our reading of Messner and Rosenfeld (2001), we suggest that the key structural variables described by the theory may be linked by one of two causal mechanisms: moderation or mediation. Baron and Kenny (1986:1174) define moderation to be the case where one (or more) variable(s) "affects the direction and/or strength of the relation between an independent or predictor variable and a dependent or criterion variable." Likewise, "a given variable may be said to function as a mediator to the extent that it accounts for the relation between the predictor and the criterion" (Baron and Kenny, 1986:1176). The reasoning behind these two mechanisms and corresponding hypotheses are presented below. As Savolainen (2000) points out, the model of IAT (adapted in Figure 1, above) is not really concrete enough to determine the nature of the structural model intended by Messner and Rosenfeld (2001). Nevertheless, our close reading of their work leads us to support two possible hypotheses derived from the structural components of IAT.[1]

MODERATION

The first possible scenario with respect to IAT is that of *moderation*, whereby the impact of noneconomic institutions on homicide is thought to be dependent on the dominance of the economy in a given aggregate unit. This is the approach to testing IAT taken in the studies by Chamlin and Cochran (1995), Piquero and Piquero (1998), and Savolainen (2000) described above. Noneconomic institutions are viewed as moderating influences on the relationship between the economic sector and crime (i.e., operationalized with multiplicative terms based on economic and noneconomic measures). For example, Chamlin and Cochran (1995:415) "expect an improvement in economic conditions to result in a reduction of instrumental crime only when there is a simultaneous strengthening of

1. This two-pronged strategy is not without precedent in the criminology literature. For example, Kaufman and Widom (1999) take a similar approach in attempting to determine the relationship between childhood victimization and running away and delinquency in adolescence. Their results find more support for moderation than mediation. Like them, we found the logic established by Baron and Kenny (1986) to be useful in preparing this section of our paper.

noneconomic institutions." Put another way, strong noneconomic institutions would be expected to diminish the anomic influence of the economy on serious crime. This moderator approach, Savolainen (2000:1025–1026) argues, is implied to a great extent by Messner and Rosenfeld's descriptions of the institutional balance of power as "the interplay of the economy and other social institutions" (1997:1408) and of the "functions of institutions" as "overlapping and interdependent" (2001:66). This leads to our first hypothesis.

Hypothesis 1: The strength of noneconomic institutions will *moderate* the influence of the economy on homicide.

Mediation

We believe that the theory suggests another possible causal link: an elaboration process where noneconomic institutions are expected to mediate the relationship between the economy and homicide. As we pointed out above, the authors of the theory are not very clear on how the major components of their theory should fit together empirically.[2] In fact, Messner and Rosenfeld's (1997) own work testing IAT employs an elaborated modeling approach to test the mediating effects of decommodification on cross-national homicide, which suggests that strategies for modeling the theory are still open to debate. Why might noneconomic institutions have a mediating, rather than a moderating, effect? Unlike moderation, which suggests that the simultaneous interplay of social institutions is a key determinant of serious crime, mediation suggests a causal chain with an initial path linking the economy (represented by a variable treated as fully exogenous) to noneconomic institutions, and a second path associating noneconomic institutions with crime. Further, full mediation would only exist if, when controlling for noneconomic institutions, the relationship between the economy and homicide becomes insignificant. Although this last condition is often an unrealistic expectation in nonexperimental research, we argue that partial mediation is a reasonable possibility and that the causal chain interpretation of IAT is plausible.

Looking at the first path, from the economy to noneconomic institutions, the basic hypothesis is that the dominance (strength) of the economy will have a direct impact on the functioning of noneconomic institutions.

2. This confusion is not limited to the theory's authors. Despite their analysis of moderating effects based on hypotheses derived from IAT, Chamlin and Cochran (1995:414) interpret Messner and Rosenfeld's analytical model of IAT as follows: "Social structure (the dominance of the economic structure) weakens institutional controls. Culture and social structure are hypothesized to influence each other. Lastly, anomie and weak institutional controls *mediate* the effects of culture and social structure on rates of instrumental crime, respectively" [emphasis added].

The moderation thesis highlights the "interplay" among social institutions that has implications for rates of serious crime (see Savolainen, 2000); however, Messner and Rosenfeld (2001:70) argue that the economy has an "unusual dominance" among social institutions in the United States, and that this dominance "diminishes the capacity of other institutions, such as the family, education, and the political system, to curb criminogenic cultural pressures and to impose controls over the behavior of members of society" (p. ix). This subjugation occurs primarily through the (1) "devaluation," (2) "accommodation," and (3) "penetration" described by Messner and Rosenfeld and in our above review of IAT. Besides their own arguments, Sims' (1997) attempt to integrate IAT with Marxist theory sheds further light on the dominance of the economy in the United States and other capitalist societies. Derived from Marx's theory of history, her argument is that economic dominance is to be expected; specifically, Marx proposed a metaphor for societies in which social structures can be thought of as buildings, which are composed of base structures and superstructures. Sims (1997:9) interprets this metaphor as such: "Like a building with different levels rising up and out of its base foundation, societies are formed with the economic mode of production providing the base foundation for its social institutions [i.e., political, judicial, philosophical, religious, artistic, family, community, education, and economic]." A Marxian interpretation of modern social institutions would therefore highlight the impact of the economy on the nature of noneconomic institutions. In relation to IAT, we infer from this that the characteristics of the economy in a social system not only shape the character of social institutions, but also that the economy will continue to have a direct impact on how other institutions function and are able to effectively control criminal behavior.

This leads us to the second major link of the causal chain: the direct effect of noneconomic institutions on serious crime. Messner and Rosenfeld (2001), following from the points made above, argue that the dominance of the economy will have unwanted consequences for noneconomic institution, specifically, the ability of noneconomic institutions to carry out their dual roles of (1) socialization and (2) social control, both of which will be hampered by the anomic influences of the economy. The weakening of these two functions will have direct consequences for rates of serious crime. This part of their theoretical discussion has clear ties with the social disorganization tradition in criminological theory, particularly in their argument that, "at the institutional level, the dominance of the economy in the institutional balance of power fosters weak social control" (Messner and Rosenfeld, 2001:77; see also Sims, 1997:12). As such, a mediation argument is not only in the spirit of IAT but of social disorganization theory as well, given the latter theory's view of economic deprivation as a disorganizing influence on collective social ties in both neighborhoods (Sampson and Groves, 1989) and larger units of analysis (Shihadeh and Steffensmeier, 1994), as well as the vitality of "local institutions" (Peterson et al., 2000).[3] Elsewhere in their book, Messner and Rosenfeld (2001:82) seem to solidify support for this second path in a partial summary of their theory: "Based on the logic of our explanation of crime, weakened institutional support and control are, *in turn*, associated with high levels of criminal involvement" [emphasis added].

Finally, noneconomic institutions may turn out to be at least partial mediators of the direct effects of the economy on serious crime. In their description of the decommodification of labor, Messner and Rosenfeld (1997:1394) quote Esping-Anderson's (1990) view of the concept as a mechanism that "promote[s] reliance on, *or insulation from*, pure market forces [emphasis added]." Chamlin and Cochran (1997:208), in their paper on altruism and crime, use IAT as one theoretical leg on which to set their argument that "the more communities can enmesh their citizens in mutual ties of trust, empathy, and obligation, the more they can *insulate* their citizens from macro-social precipitators of crime [emphasis added]." Therefore, it seems reasonable to conclude that noneconomic institutions may serve as a buffer, or insulator, against unchecked economic influence on serious crime. This leads to our mediation hypothesis:

> *Hypothesis 2*: The strength of noneconomic institutions will *mediate* the influence of the economy on homicide.

This hypothesis can be further specified as a set of directional statements, as follows:

> *Hypothesis 2a*: An increase in the dominance of the economy will lead to a decrease in the strength of noneconomic institutions, such that there will be a negative relationship between indicators of the economy and noneconomic institutions.

> *Hypothesis 2b*: A weakening of noneconomic institutions will make homicide more likely, such that there will be a negative association between noneconomic indicators and measures of homicide.

A key point made by Messner and Rosenfeld (2001:79) is that "institutions vary with respect to the extent to which they impose restraints on

3. Adding more confusion to discussion and application of these two causal mechanisms in the criminological literature, Peterson et al. (2000:55) state that their evaluation of economic deprivation, local institutions, and neighborhood crime examined "whether different types of local institutions *mediate* the relationship between economic deprivation and overall as well as different types of violent crime" [emphasis added]. They also use the term, mediate, at several other points in their paper (pp. 32–35); however, their multivariate analyses employ interaction terms composed of economic deprivation and measures of local institutions, which actually test moderating and not mediating effects.

individuals, and the nature of this variation reflects the larger culture." Thus, it appears that a causal link to criminal *behavior* would require individual-level measures of constructs akin to social bonding theory (e.g., attachment, commitment); however, hypothesized (as it should be) at a purely macrosocial level, IAT makes a direct link between the strength of economic and noneconomic institutions and rates of serious crime among human collectives. In addition, we contend that the two theoretical possibilities described are not necessarily competing hypotheses. It is entirely possible that both the moderation and mediation hypotheses, or only one (or none), hold in the analyses to follow.

COUNTIES AS UNITS OF ANALYSIS

As noted above, prior tests of IAT have been conducted at the nation and state levels of analysis. Yet we believe that the explanatory power and analytical flexibility of the theory have been underestimated. Therefore, we also propose that IAT is a valid theory for explaining variations in crime across "local" macrosocial units (or subnational units), such as counties.

Counties as Social Systems

Longstanding traditions in sociology assert either directly or indirectly that local macrosocial units exhibit their own institutional arrangements, and that the balance between economic and noneconomic institutions varies considerably across subnational units within the United States. In one of the earliest sociological studies of life in the United States, Tocqueville (1969) observed that local communities, such as townships and counties, had a significant degree of autonomy to offer early American citizens. This observation strongly influenced later sociological views on the nature and character of community. According to Bernard (1962:41), the local community, such as a county or city, may be viewed as a social system:

> consisting of a set of subsystems—including local government, an economy, and educational system, a recreational system, and so on . . . . The local community itself, in turn, is part of a larger system—economic, political, religious, or other. For communities are not self-sufficient, autonomous entities, independent and unrelated to other communities. They are integral parts of a larger national community—which, in turn, is itself part of an international community . . . . The existence of systems operating in structured communities results in order. Even among animals this order can be called a social order. But only among human beings can we speak of this social order as

> also *normative*. It is at this point that human communities part company with all others. For social order in human communities is institutionalized. Both structures and systems operate within an institutional framework.

Of course, the notion of an institutional framework is essential to Messner and Rosenfeld's IAT, and current theorizing in other areas of social science is also in agreement with Bernard's (1962) proposition that local communities have their own institutional structures. For example, Tolbert et al. (1998:406) tie together work by Putnam (1993) and Etzioni (1996) in asserting that these structures "create various levels of civic engagement across locales and differences in local levels of socioeconomic well-being" (see also Lyson and Tolbert, 1996). In other words, local communities in the United States are characterized to a relevant extent by diversity in their institutional structures, with some places, for example, enjoying a good deal more prosperity than others (Nielsen and Alderson, 1997). This current strain of theorizing further argues that "the burden of sheltering workers, providing opportunities, and maintaining welfare [has shifted] from the nation-state to the local community" (Tolbert et al., 1998:402). We argue, therefore, that criminologists be urged to entertain the possibility that IAT is applicable to local communities, at least within the United States.

Applying IAT at the County Level of Analysis

Based in part on the previous discussion, we propose that the structural components of IAT are applicable and testable at the county level of analysis. To extend support for this argument, we offer some additional points to consider. First, it must be stressed that Messner and Rosenfeld (2001) are never completely clear on the appropriate level of analysis for testing their theory. For example, they (2001:26) state at one point in their book that "the primary *analytical* focus of this book . . . is on variation in rates of crime at the level of nation-states" [emphasis added]. Yet they also suggest at a few points in their book that the boundary conditions of IAT are extendable to levels of analysis within the United States. For example, in differentiating their approach from individual-level explanations of criminal behavior, Messner and Rosenfeld (2001:37) point out that the purpose of their theory is "to explain *macrolevel* differences (that is, differences across groups or populations) in rates of the most serious types of crime." Although the focus is primarily on national-level rates, at a later point in their book, Messner and Rosenfeld (2001:80) apply their theoretical arguments to within-U.S. differences in serious crime rates by gender and race categories:

> It is also important. . .to ask whether the theoretical framework we

> have proposed for explaining the distinctive position of the United States when considered in international perspective can also account for the social distribution of crime within the nation. We believe that the logic of our argument is compatible with observed differences in crime rates across social categories in American society.

We argue that their logic is also compatible with differences in homicide rates across American space. A reasonable criticism of this approach is that it may violate the "spirit," if not the "letter," of IAT (Savolainen, 2000:1037). We acknowledge this criticism, but we argue that no persuasive arguments have been presented thus far that would deter the application of this theory to subnational levels. Both Chamlin and Cochran (1995) and Piquero and Piquero (1998) have opened the door to such a strategy. Chamlin and Cochran (1995:417), in justifying their use of states as units of analysis, argue that IAT "focuses on social dynamics that are likely to operate across various levels of official aggregation." This line of reasoning corresponds quite well with the general conclusion made by Land et al. (1990) that many of the structural covariates of homicide will exhibit similar effects across various units of aggregation.

Second, we believe that the specific components of IAT upon which existing research has relied thus far may be found and measured at the "local" level of analysis. We have already argued that local communities have their own institutional structures, but we assert as well that the relationships between economic and noneconomic institutions specified by IAT should hold across local communities as well. Messner and Rosenfeld (1997) argue that industrialized nation-states are market societies, wherein a certain degree of commodification shapes social life within those societies. Logan and Molotch (1987:2) extend a similar argument in their work on the political economy of "place," stating that the "extreme commodification of place touches the lives of all and influences virtually every cultural, economic, and political institution that operates on the urban scene." Hearkening back to Tocqueville's observations, Logan and Molotch (1987:147) argue that "compared to most other industrial societies, the United States organizes land use in a unique manner, both in the extent of authority given to private developers and in the extreme independence of local government agencies." Thus, we are likely to see variation in the institutional balance of power, as well as homicides, across local communities—particularly in the United States.[4]

Third, counties offer several methodological advantages over other units

4. There is certainly precedent outside the IAT literature for applying theories originally formulated at the nation-state level to subnational units. For example, Dunaway (1996) applies world-systems theory to the problem of explaining the development

of analysis. Counties are more numerous than states, and thus they present more potential for achieving statistical power and less chance of encountering various estimation problems such as multicollinearity and outlying or influential cases. Also, restricting our sample to metropolitan counties (see below) allows us to draw reasonable comparisons with prior macrolevel research employing metropolitan counties (e.g., DeFronzo and Hannon, 1998), and it circumvents estimation problems encountered when a great number of rural counties with zero homicides are included in the sample. Finally, employing counties as the unit of analysis affords us the opportunity to derive some potentially useful new measures of noneconomic institutions (detailed below) from existing data sources.

DATA AND MEASURES

To carry out our research strategy, we employ cross-sectional data for U.S. counties and county equivalents with populations of 100,000 or greater circa 1990. Our analytical focus is on the effects of the prevalence of and commitment to both economic and noneconomic institutions on serious violent crime, homicide in particular. We derive our measure of total homicides from the Supplementary Homicide Reports offender file (Fox, 2000). More specifically, we extracted the number of homicides for 1990, 1991, and 1992. In addition, we acknowledge that very few homicides are committed by people under the age of 10 or over the age of 64 years. We therefore analyze age-specific homicide rates for those homicides committed by people between the ages of 10 and 64. As we detail below, homicide is a rare event, and so we follow recent work by Osgood (2000) and Osgood and Chambers (2000) for constructing our homicide rates.

In addition to using a total homicide rate, we also attempt to extend prior research by focusing on homicides that are instrumental in nature. As Messner and Rosenfeld (2001) indicate, the cultural pressures to commit crime may stem from the dominance of the economy over noneconomic institutions. Our reading of the theory therefore is that IAT is generally geared toward explaining instrumental homicides. We thus use the Supplementary Homicide Reports to construct an instrumental homicide rate, and, for comparative purposes, an expressive homicide rate extracting data for the same years as the total homicide rate. Adhering to prior research that focuses on classifying homicides by circumstance (Miethe and Drass, 1999; Williams and Flewelling, 1988), we identify as

of southern Appalachian counties in the United States. In addition, a number of studies have applied Durkheim's nation-level theory of suicide to explain intranational variation in suicide rates in the United States (Bankston et al., 1983; Breault, 1986; Cutchin and Churchill, 1999; Kowalski et al., 1987).

instrumental in nature all felony-murders and suspected felonies (e.g., robbery-murders), as well as gangland and youth gang killings. Additionally, homicides that had the following circumstance codes are identified as *expressive*: lovers' triangles; killed by babysitter; brawl under alcohol; brawl under drugs; argument over money; other arguments. In homicide events involving multiple offenders, the SHR classifies circumstance based on the "first" offender. The instrumental and expressive homicide rates are constructed in a manner analogous to that for the total homicide rate.

It is important to acknowledge that there are limitations to the Supplementary Homicide Reports. Most notable of these are that not all agencies participate in the reporting program, and that for some homicides, the circumstance codes are unknown. The countervailing factors in support of using these data, however, are numerous. First, most law enforcement agencies in the United States do in fact participate in this reporting program. Second, the proportional frequency with which homicides are reported to the police is much higher than for any other crime. Hence, the degree of measurement error is lower than that found in data for other measures of criminal activity (such as robbery or aggravated assault). Third, the clearance rate for homicide is also much higher than for any other crime, providing a more complete portrait of offenders than can typically be gleaned from alternative data sources. Fourth, we are aware of no alternative sources of homicide data providing counts for a large sample of major metropolitan areas in the United States that allows the partitioning of homicides into subcategories (in our case, instrumental and expressive). And so although the data do present a conservative estimation of the prevalence of homicide, they represent the best source of information available for the present purposes.

INDEPENDENT VARIABLES

Our measure of the influence and structure of the *economy* in a local area is based on previous work on IAT (particularly Messner and Rosenfeld, 1997), and it is measured as the Gini coefficient of family income inequality. We base our choice of inequality as an operationalization of the strength and dominance of the economy in the emphasis of both IAT and Mertonian anomie theory on stratification and its key role in generating anomic conditions.[5] This measure is derived from the 1990 Census of

5. Both Chamlin and Cochran (1995) and Piquero and Piquero (1998) used alternative indicators of the economy, including income inequality (Gini) and a measure of absolute poverty. Although all of the analyses in this paper use the Gini coefficient as the single indicator for the economy, we conducted additional analyses (not shown here) that substituted poverty (measured as the proportion of individuals in the county living below the poverty level). With a few minor exceptions, our results were identical to the ones presented below.

Population and Housing Summary Tape File 3C.

As noted above, we use the Gini coefficient of income inequality as our indicator of the influence and structure of economic conditions on crime rates. There is some debate among criminologists regarding what the Gini coefficient actually captures (see, e.g., Bailey, 1984). Does it measure the dominance of the economy? Does it measure the imbalance among institutions? Does it really measure the degree to which the market economy is unfettered and hence dominant in the institutional balance of power? These competing interpretations reflect the tension among Mertonian anomie theory and IAT pointed out by Bernburg (2002). According to this analyst, the assertion that inequality, as a measure of social stratification in a collectivity, is a source of pressure to commit crime is firmly grounded in Mertonian theory, whereas the view that inequality reflects the degree of dominance the economy has in the institutional balance of power is an additional perspective contributed by IAT.[6] Because we use inequality as a measure of the strength and dominance of the economy, and tie this to the idea that the strength of noneconomic institutional structures may hinder this effect, our conceptual framework is more tightly associated with IAT than with Mertonian anomie theory.

Drawing on prior research and theoretical statements of IAT, we derive several measures tapping the presence of noneconomic institutions and commitment to these institutions across counties. To measure participation in the *political* sphere, we employ a measure of average voter turnout for the 1988 and 1992 presidential elections. This measure is consistent with prior research, and it is expected that greater levels of voter turnout will be associated with lower rates of instrumental homicide.

Lack of commitment to the *family* as a noneconomic institution is measured as the rate of divorce among people 15 years and older. Prior research uses similar measures such as the proportion of families that are female headed, but our initial analyses indicate that this measure is highly collinear with some other measures in the model. Measures of divorce are widely used in macrolevel research on crime (see Blau and Blau, 1982; Rosenfeld et al., 2001), and it is expected that homicide rates will be higher where family disintegration is more prevalent.

Other measures designed to tap into cross-community variation in support for noneconomic institutions are the average *educational* expenditures per person of school age for 1987 and 1992 in the county, and the rate of adherence to civically engaged *religious* denominations. Educational expenditure data are derived from the USA Counties data archive and the population data are drawn from STF 3C of the 1990 U.S. Census of Population and Housing. The religion measure is based on work by

6. We would also like to thank the reviewers for pointing out this distinction.

Tolbert et al. (1998), and it is derived from the 1990 Census of Churches. Civically engaged religious denominations are those whose members evidence high levels of involvement in civic and voluntary associations such as labor unions, professional associations, fraternal organizations, service clubs, hobby or garden clubs, or sports clubs or teams. The construction of this measure is described in the appendix of Tolbert et al.'s (1998) article, which lists the following denominations as those with extraordinary civic engagement: African Methodist Episcopal Zion, American Baptist, Church of Christ, Congregational Christian, Disciples of Christ, Episcopal, Jewish, Latter-Day Saints, Lutheran, Methodist, Presbyterian, and Unitarian.

In addition to these measures, some recent research has suggested that the level of social welfare generosity varies inversely with crime rates across macrosocial units. This is evident in the work of Messner and Rosenfeld (1997) as well as of Hannon and DeFronzo (1998). We therefore construct a measure of welfare generosity based in part on the work of Hannon and DeFronzo (1998). Specifically, their study employs an index of welfare generosity and prevalence employing two measures derived from Special Summary Tape File 17 (Poverty Areas in the United States) of the U.S. Census. The items in their index are a measure of the average monthly welfare payments per poor person adjusted for cost of living (as the average proportion of local incomes devoted to rent), and the proportion of poor families receiving welfare. They then standardize these measures and average them into an index. Although we were able to closely replicate their measures, our analysis of these data revealed two concerns. Specifically, the measures have algebraically opposite correlations with our dependent variables of interest, and the measure of welfare generosity exhibited a strong "V" shaped relationship with our homicide rates that is not well captured with a standard quadratic specification.[7] The level of welfare payments has a strong inverse relationship with all of our homicide rates, until it reaches its third quartile, at which point the relationship changes direction and becomes a strong positive relationship with the homicide rates. To address this issue, we created indicator variables for each quartile of the welfare generosity distribution and examined

7. With our data, the means and standard deviations for adjusted monthly welfare payments (Mean = $255.31. S.D. = $59.54) and proportion of poor families receiving aid (Mean = .34, S.D. = .10) nearly mirror those of Hannon and DeFronzo ($260.51, $67.06 and 33%, 11%, respectively), who have a slightly different sample. Although our two measures are positively associated with one another (r = .435**), in our data, they share different relationships with the dependent variables. For example, the correlations between the welfare generosity measure and logged total, instrumental, and expressive homicide rates are r = –.147**, –.094*, and –.148**, whereas the corresponding correlations for the measure of the proportion of poor families receiving aid are r = .236**, .265**, and .222**, respectively.

a series of models to probe for collapsibility in the distribution. These models reveal that the effects of the first through third quartiles of the welfare generosity measure are well summarized with a single indicator variable. Our final measure of welfare expenditures is then a dummy variable coded 1 for the counties in the first three quartiles of the welfare payment distribution, capturing low to moderate levels of monthly welfare payments per poor person, and 0 for counties with high levels of welfare payments. We expect this measure to exhibit a negative association with homicide, meaning that counties that provide less in welfare benefits will have lower homicide rates. Taken together, these measures are designed to tap into the strength of five main noneconomic socializing institutional structures in the United States: the polity, religion, the family, education, and the social welfare system.

The main effects of our theoretical variables on homicide rates may be biased if we fail to control for the influence of other known covariates of the homicide rate. Therefore, we include in the multivariate models that follow measures of population structure (the average of standardized scores of the logged population size and density), the proportion of the county population in the crime-prone age groups (proportion age 15–29), the proportion of the county population that is black, and an indicator variable for counties in the southern region. The final sample size is 454 counties with populations of 100,000 or more residents.

Table 1 presents the descriptive portion of our analysis, providing in the first two columns the means and standard deviations for each of the variables implemented in the multivariate models below. The average homicide rate is 7.6 per 100,000 people, with a standard deviation slightly exceeding this, suggesting a great deal of variation across urban counties. When the total homicide rate is partitioned out into instrumental and expressive homicide rates, it is apparent that expressive homicides are the more frequent of the two (mean = 4.75). The measures of the presence of and commitment to various noneconomic institutions indicate that an average of 54% of the eligible population turned out to vote for the 1988 and 1992 presidential elections in these counties, almost a quarter of the county population on average belongs to what we have defined as civically engaged denominations, the average county level expenditure per school age person is $4,516.89, the average monthly cost of living adjusted welfare payment per poor person is $255.13 (and because we employ the indicator variable detailed above in the multivariate models, 75% of the counties have low to moderate levels of welfare payments), and around 8% of those 15 years of age and older are divorced.

The main indicator of the motivating pressure of the economic sphere of social life, the Gini coefficient of family income inequality, has a mean of .40. Finally, the control variables indicate that on average our sample of counties is about 11% black, nearly a quarter of the population is in the 15 to 29 year old age range, and 35% of the counties are in the South.

Table 1. Descriptive Statistics and Selected Correlations

	Mean	St. Deviation	r*
Dependent Variables			
Homicide Rate	7.55	8.64	
Instrumental Homicide Rate	2.80	3.88	
Expressive Homicide Rate	4.75	5.31	
Theoretical Variables			
Voter Turnout	0.54	0.09	–.291**
Civically Engaged Adherents	0.24	0.11	–.037
Educational Expenditures	4,516.89	1,071.08	–.214**
Divorce Rate	0.08	0.02	.275**
Welfare Expenditures	255.31	59.54	–.356**
Gini Coefficient	0.40	0.03	
Control Variables			
Age 15-29	0.24	0.04	
Percent Black	0.11	0.12	
Population Structure	1.55	.58	
South	0.35		

* Zero-order correlations between Gini coefficient and theoretical variables.
** $p < .01$.

ANALYTIC STRATEGY AND RESULTS

Given that homicide is a rare event, and homicide disaggregated by our instrumental and expressive classification scheme generates even lower rates, our estimation strategy needs to take into account the non-normal distribution of the outcomes of interest. Current practice in the macrolevel criminological literature is to employ a Poisson-based estimation strategy (see Lee and Ousey, 2001; Osgood, 2000; Osgood and Chambers, 2000). Poisson estimators are well suited for rare event data because even in the face of skewed distributions, they still provide more efficient estimates than ordinary least-squares regression. The straightforward Poisson estimator entails the restrictive assumption that the mean and variance of the dependent variables are equal. In our case, the variances exceed the means for all three of our homicide measures. When this is the case, the data are overdispersed, and the negative binomial variant of the Poisson estimator, which allows the introduction of an error term into the model, is more appropriate. Additionally, although negative binomial regression is more frequently used to model counts of rare events, it can also be adapted to model the *rate* of rare events by including a measure tapping the natural logarithm of the population at risk as an offset variable. In our case, the offset variable is the natural logarithm of the population age 10 to 64 years old. In the models below, we therefore employ a negative binomial estimation strategy to predict the rates of total, instrumental, and expressive homicide in our sample of urban counties.

A typical problem that arises in research using aggregate data is multicollinearity, or the presence of high correlations among independent variables. Multicollinearity can generate misleading estimates and inappropriate inferences. To address this problem, we reestimated all of the models reported below with an ordinary least-squares estimator to secure variance inflation factors (VIFs). Allison (1999) suggests that VIFs in excess of 2.5 should be taken as indicative of a potential multicollinearity problem. All VIFs for the reported models are below 2.05, clearly indicating that multicollinearity is not problematic with these data.

The logic of our conceptual model suggests two potentially competing processes. The first process is that of mediation, where we expect our theoretical measures (voter turnout, civically engaged religious adherents, educational expenditures, the divorce rate, and welfare expenditures) to at least partially mediate or reduce the effect of the Gini coefficient of income inequality on the homicide measures. The second process is one of moderation, where we expect that the effect of the Gini coefficient on the homicide measures will vary systematically according to the level of each of the theoretical variables.

According to Baron and Kenny (1986), to effectively demonstrate a mediation effect, the Gini coefficient must first have the expected correlation with the mediation variables. Hence, in the third column in Table 1, we present the correlations between each theoretical variable and the Gini coefficient. As expected, these correlations indicate that as the level of income inequality increases, voter turnout, educational, and welfare expenditures decrease, and the divorce rate increases. Only the measure of civically engaged religious adherents does not exhibit a statistically significant negative correlation with the Gini coefficient. These correlations lend initial support to our theoretical model, because they indicate that high levels of income inequality depress political participation, reduce educational expenditures, reduce the level of social welfare benefits distributed, and elevate the level of family disruption.

Further following the logic of mediation, we implement a strategy of sequential or elaboration models. In this tactic, we first regress the various dependent variables on the Gini coefficient and the control variables. We then elaborate these models by including the cluster of measures of noneconomic institutions. To provide support for the mediation hypotheses, these models need to demonstrate that the effect of the Gini coefficient of income inequality on homicide rates is weakened with the inclusion of our measures of noneconomic institutions. We also caution readers that full mediation (reducing the effect of the Gini coefficient on homicide rates to zero) is not necessary to demonstrate a mediation effect. Under this scenario, the effect of the Gini coefficient is fully indirect, being transmitted through the noneconomic institution measures. However, a partial mediation effect, where there is a substantively observable reduction in the Gini coefficient between reduced and full models, is also possible. In this case, the effect of the Gini coefficient on homicide rates is not completely indirect, but partially indirect (through the noneconomic institution measures) and partially direct. In short, a partial mediation effect will also be consistent with the logic of our theoretical model.

To our knowledge, there is no method available for testing the significance of the change in an independent variable's effects between models when the nonlinear nature of the negative binomial distribution is taken into account. We therefore focus on the degree of substantive reduction observed in the Gini coefficient by calculating the percentage change from the reduced model to the full model. Booth and Osgood (1993) employ a similar strategy. Given this strategy and our conceptual focus on instrumental violence, we expect the reduction in the effect of the Gini coefficient to be most pronounced for instrumental homicide rates.

Table 2 presents the results of the first series of models predicting the total homicide rate. The first row for each variable is the negative binomial coefficient, and the second row is the standard error of the coefficient. Model 1 reveals that three of the five variables have statistically significant effects on the total homicide rate, and each is in the expected algebraic direction. These coefficients are readily interpretable as standardized effects, which is desirable because the standard deviations for the measures vary dramatically across counties. For example, to determine the percentage change in the total homicide rate for a one standard deviation change in the Gini coefficient, the following formula is applied:

$$((e^{bk*Sk})-1)*100$$

where b is the coefficient associated with the *k*th variable and S is the standard deviation of the variable of interest. In this case, the coefficient is multiplied by the standard deviation of the variable (11.793*.03); this value (.353) is then exponentiated (1.4244), subtracted by 1, and multiplied by 100. Thus, for model 1, a one standard deviation change in the Gini coefficient is associated with a 42.44% increase in the total homicide rate. Likewise, a one standard deviation increase in the percentage of the population that is black is associated with a 55.7% increase in the total homicide rate. Homicide rates are also higher where the population size is larger and where the population is more densely settled. The proportionate reduction in the log likelihood from the intercept-only specification to the full model is 7%, according to the pseudo R^2 statistic.

The second model in this table is designed to examine two issues. First, do the measures of noneconomic institutions have statistically significant associations with the homicide rate, and second, does controlling for the presence of these institutions mediate the effect of economic inequality on homicide? With respect to the first question, these data indicate that four of the five indicators of noneconomic institutions have the expected statistically significant effect on the homicide rate. For example, a single standard deviation increase in the rate of voter turnout (9%) is associated with an 18% decline in the homicide rate. The corresponding figures for civically engaged religious denominations and the divorce rate are –8.83% and +38.72%, respectively. In addition, the coefficient for the welfare expenditures measure (–.356) indicates that homicide rates are on average roughly one-third lower in urban counties where welfare payments are disbursed at low to moderate levels than where welfare payments are disbursed at high levels. Consistent with our expectations then, these data indicate that total homicide rates are lower where voter turnout is high, where a larger proportion of the population is associated with civically engaged religious denominations, and where welfare payments are disbursed at low to moderate levels. In contrast, and as expected, homicide rates on average are higher where divorce is more prevalent. The only noneconomic institution variable that does not perform as expected is our measure of educational expenditures per pupil. The pseudo R^2 statistic for this model is 9%, which represents a 2% raw increase in the variance explained, but a 28% proportional increase in the variance explained.

The second notable feature of Model 2 in Table 2, and the first test of our mediation hypotheses, is the reduction in the effect of the Gini coefficient from Model 1 to Model 2. The effect of Gini is reduced 34.38% with the addition of the noneconomic institution measures. The coefficient indicates that a one standard deviation increase in the Gini coefficient when controlling for the influence of the noneconomic institution measures is associated with a 26.13% increase in the total homicide rates (as opposed to a 42.44% change in the previous model). The 34% reduction is substantively large, and our interpretation is that the noneconomic institution measures partially, but not completely, mediate the effect of the Gini coefficient on the total homicide rate. In other words, economic pressures appear to both directly and indirectly (through the deterioration of the socially organizing and socially controlling functions of the noneconomic institutional structures) elevate violent crime in urban areas of the United States.[8]

Table 2. Negative Binomial Regression Models Predicting Total Homicide Rate in 454 Urban Counties

	Model 1	Model 2	Model 3	Model 4	Model 5	Model 6	Model 7
Gini Coefficient	11.793**	7.738**	8.239**	7.275**	7.859**	7.830**	15.308**
	(1.308)	(1.271)	(1.329)	(1.306)	(1.287)	(1.392)	(2.965)
Age 15–29	.271	–.135	–.211	–.006	–.114	–.124	–.116
	(1.271)	(1.146)	(1.152)	(1.137)	(1.145)	(1.148)	(1.135)
Percent Black	3.691**	3.920**	3.828**	4.061**	3.917**	3.910**	4.049**
	(.471)	(.430)	(.432)	(.440)	(.430)	(.434)	(.423)
Population Structure	.212**	.147*	.152*	.131	.150*	.147*	.137*
	(.071)	(.068)	(.068)	(.069)	(.068)	(.068)	(.068)
South	.046	.105	.120	.088	.117	.104	.132
	(.096)	(.098)	(.099)	(.099)	(.100)	(.099)	(.098)
Voter Turnout		–2.222**	–2.259**	–2.147**	–2.164**	–2.233**	–1.886**
		(.509)	(.510)	(.511)	(.516)	(.513)	(.515)
Civically Engaged Adherents		–.841*	–.867**	–.895**	–.850**	–.839*	–.943**
		(.334)	(.333)	(.337)	(.335)	(.334)	(.331)
Educational Expenditures		–.000	–.000	–.000	–.000	–.000	–.000
		(.000)	(.000)	(.000)	(.000)	(.000)	(.000)
Divorce Rate		16.366**	15.578**	16.760**	16.117**	16.292**	16.264**
		(2.341)	(2.415)	(2.350)	(2.372)	(2.383)	(2.303)
Welfare Expenditures		–.356**	–.366**	–.367**	–.355**	–.357**	3.127*
		(.093)	(.093)	(.093)	(.093)	(.094)	(1.234)
Voter Turnout* Gini			15.557				
			(12.487)				
Civically Engaged Adherents* Gini				–17.028			
				(10.687)			
Educational Expend-itures* Gini					.000		
					(.001)		
Divorce Rate* Gini						11.516	
						(70.977)	
Welfare Expenditures* Gini							–8.969**
							(3.178)
Pseudo R^2	.07	.09	.09	.09	.09	.09	.09
% Reduction in Gini Coefficient		**34.38%**					

+ $p < .10$; * $p < .05$; ** $p < .01$.

The second main hypothesis we investigate is that noneconomic institutions will moderate the effects of the economy on crime rates. We follow what has become standard practice in prior research on IAT and specify interaction models to test this hypothesis. To avoid problems with multicollinearity, we simply compute the product terms using deviations from

8. All of the elaboration models reported here were reexamined with an OLS regression estimator predicting the logged rate of each outcome. These auxiliary models confirm that the large reductions observed in the negative binomial context were also observed in the OLS context. Additionally, standard tests for the significance of change in regression coefficients across nested OLS models reveal that the reductions in the effect of the Gini coefficient are statistically significant for total, instrumental, and expressive homicide rates. See Clogg et al. (1995:1273–1276) for computation of significance tests.

the mean for each variable (with the exception of the dummy variable for welfare expenditures). Models 3 through 7 in Table 2 display the results of these specifications. Interestingly, the only variable to interact with the Gini coefficient is our measure of welfare expenditures. The negative coefficient suggests that the effect of economic pressures on total homicide rates is significantly weaker in counties with low to moderate levels of welfare disbursements (that is, in the part of the distribution where welfare payment levels are directly linearly associated with declining homicide rates). And so although the other measures of noneconomic institutions (voter turnout, civically engaged religious adherents, and divorce rates) appear to only mediate the relationship between the economy and crime rates, the level of welfare payments as a means of insulating the population from economic pressures both mediates and moderates the effect of the economy on crime.

Although we consider these results supportive of our expectations, our reading of IAT suggests that the beneficial effects of noneconomic institutions in terms of mediating the link between economic inequality and homicide rates may be observed most directly for instrumental homicides. Although the results in Table 2 using the total homicide rate appear supportive, this rate masks the substantial differences in the motivations for homicide clearly illustrated in Table 1 when comparing the mean rates of instrumental and expressive homicide. To address this issue that has been neglected by prior research, we reestimate the models presented in Table 2—substituting the instrumental homicide rate for the total homicide rate—and present the results of these models in Table 3.

Similar to the previous table, the results for Model 1 in Table 3 indicate that economic inequality, the proportion of the population that is black, and the population structure are all significantly and positively related to the instrumental homicide rate. It is also notable that the model fit, as reflected in the pseudo R^2 statistic, is comparable (8%). Turning to our key test of the mediation hypotheses, Model 2 in Table 3 reveals a pattern consistent with that observed for the total homicide rate in Table 2. The data indicate that voter turnout, the presence of civically engaged religious adherents, and welfare payment levels are all associated with lower instrumental homicide rates, whereas high divorce rates are associated with higher instrumental homicide rates. The point estimates indicate that a one standard deviation increase in voter turnout and civically engaged adherents is associated with reductions in the instrumental homicide rate of 14% (voter turnout) and 10% (civically engaged adherents), whereas instrumental homicide rates are approximately one-third lower in counties where welfare payments are at low to moderate levels. Similarly, a one standard deviation increase in the divorce rate is associated with a 43.4% increase in the homicide rate. The inclusion of these variables also results

Table 3. Negative Binomial Regression Models Predicting Instrumental Homicide Rate in 454 Urban Counties

	Model 1	Model 2	Model 3	Model 4	Model 5	Model 6	Model 7
Gini Coefficient	9.303**	5.284**	5.616**	4.755**	5.455**	5.026**	11.646**
	(1.544)	(1.526)	(1.570)	(1.558)	(1.551)	(1.648)	(3.459)
Age 15–29	–.858	–.574	–.587	–.407	–.552	–.589	–.533
	(1.398)	(1.342)	(1.344)	(1.336	(1.344)	(1.342)	(1.338)
Percent Black	4.378**	4.750**	4.682**	4.921**	4.750**	4.776**	4.870**
	(.527)	(.491)	(4.934)	(.505)	(.493)	(.496)	(.488)
Population Structure	.419**	.300**	.304**	.279**	.304**	.302**	.285**
	(.081)	(.078)	(.079)	(.080)	(.079)	(.079)	(.079)
South	–.135	–.017	–.002	–.035	.003	–.013	.010
	(.108)	(.113)	(.114)	(.113)	(.115)	(.113)	(.113)
Voter Turnout		–1.680**	–1.700**	–1.616**	–1.602**	–1.650**	–1.388*
		(.584)	(.585)	(.586)	(.589)	(.588)	(.594)
Civically Engaged Adherents		–.949*	–.964*	–1.028*	–.971*	–.960*	–1.055*
		(.409)	(.408)	(.410)	(.409)	(.410)	(.408)
Educational Expenditures		.000	.000	.000	.000	.000	.000
		(.000)	(.000)	.000	(.000)	(.000)	(.000)
Divorce Rate		18.034**	17.477**	18.406**	17.730**	18.294**	18.090**
		(2.700)	(2.764)	(2.702)	(2.717)	(2.755)	(2.673)
Welfare Expenditures		–.371**	–.381**	–.387**	–.372**	–.366**	2.606
		(.108)	(.109)	(.109)	(.108)	(.109)	(1.454)
Voter Turnout* Gini			12.994				
			(14.861)				
Civically Engaged Adherents* Gini				–21.085			
				(12.646)			
Educational Expenditures* Gini					.001		
					(.001)		
Divorce Rate* Gini						–35.312	
						(85.087)	
Welfare Expenditures* Gini							–7.658*
							(3.738)
Pseudo R^2	.08	.10	.10	.10	.10	.10	.10
% Reduction in Gini Coefficient		**43.2%**					

+ $p < .10$; * $p < .05$; ** $p < .01$.

in a 3% raw change in the pseudo R^2 statistic, which is a 42.85% proportional change in the variance explained.

The feature of this table standing in starkest contrast to the prior table is that the inclusion of the noneconomic institution measures reduces the effect of the Gini coefficient on instrumental homicide rates by 43.2%. This is substantially larger than the reduction in the coefficient for total homicide rates, and it provides what we consider to be strong support for a partial mediating effect of noneconomic institutions on instrumental homicide rates.

Following the logic of our prior models, it is again evident in Models 3 through 7 that the only variable that moderates the effect of the Gini coefficient on instrumental homicide rates is welfare expenditures. And like the effect for total homicide rates, the negative interaction term indicates

Table 4. Negative Binomial Regression Models Predicting Expressive Homicide Rate in 454 Urban Counties

	Model 1	Model 2	Model 3	Model 4	Model 5	Model 6	Model 7
Gini Coefficient	13.031**	9.002**	9.797**	8.628**	9.072**	9.369**	17.566**
	(1.562)	(1.556)	(1.650)	(1.605)	(1.577)	(1.688)	(3.693)
Age 15-29	1.007	.076	−.072	.172	.085	.130	.073
	(1.562)	(1.425)	(1.437)	(1.419)	(1.425)	(1.428)	(1.412)
Percent Black	3.360**	3.530**	3.397**	3.633**	3.526**	3.487**	3.670**
	(.564)	(.528)	(.529)	(.540)	(.528)	(.532)	(.519)
Population Structure	.120	.086	.092	.073	.087	.084	.080
	(.084)	(.083)	(.083)	(.084)	(.084)	(.083)	(.084)
South	.131	.147	.165	.135	.153	.142	.176
	(.117)	(.123)	(.123)	(.123)	(.125)	(.123)	(.122)
Voter Turnout		−2.543**	−2.610**	−2.478**	−2.510**	−2.586**	−2.190**
		(.628)	(.630)	(.632)	(.638)	(.632)	(.634)
Civically Engaged Adherents		−.769+	−.814*	−.798+	−.774+	−.767+	−.873*
		(.408)	(.406)	(.411)	(.409)	(.408)	(.405)
Educational Expenditures		−.000	−.000	−.000	−.000	−.000	−.000
		(.000)	(.000)	(.000)	(.000)	(.000)	(.000)
Divorce Rate		15.559**	14.401**	15.896**	15.399**	15.240**	15.449**
		(2.870)	(2.972)	(2.891)	(2.927)	(2.918)	(2.827)
Welfare Expenditures		−.343**	−.355**	−.351**	−.342**	−.351**	3.589*
		(.114)	(.114)	(.114)	(.114)	(.115)	(1.537)
Voter Turnout* Gini			22.121				
			(15.669)				
Civically Engaged Adherents* Gini				−13.051			
				(13.339)			
Educational Expenditures* Gini					.000		
					(.001)		
Divorce Rate* Gini						47.324	
						(86.031)	
Welfare Expenditures* Gini							−10.117*
							(1.590)
Pseudo R^2	.05	.07	.07	.07	.07	.07	.07
% Reduction in Gini Coefficient		**30.92%**					

+ $p < .10$; * $p < .05$; ** $p < .01$.

that the effect of income inequality on instrumental homicide rates is significantly weaker where welfare payments have their strongest depressing effect.

We round out our analysis in Table 4, which presents the results of analogous models predicting the rate of expressive homicide. Similar to the two prior tables, Model 1 indicates that the rate of expressive homicide is higher where economic inequality and the size of the black population are greater. Model 2 elaborates this model with the inclusion of the various measures of noneconomic institutions. Although four of the five variables entered into the elaborated equation are statistically significant and in the expected direction, the reduction in the coefficient for the Gini index is much more modest than that observed for the previous two tables (30.92%). This implies that our indicators of noneconomic institutions have a larger role in mediating the effect of the economy on instrumental homicide rates than on expressive or total homicide rates. In addition, the interaction models reveal that the role of welfare payments in moderating the effect of income inequality on expressive homicide rates is similar to that observed for the other outcomes examined.

DISCUSSION AND CONCLUSIONS

Our analysis was designed to extend prior research on IAT in several ways. First, we built on prior research by employing a lower level of analysis than prior studies—counties. Our rationale for this was both practical and conceptual. We argued that the strategy of prior research employing states as the unit of explanation fails to capture meaningful heterogeneity within states. More importantly, however, we argued that it is reasonable to conceptualize counties as social systems with their own unique institutional dynamics. Our claim that IAT is flexible enough to be applied to subnational units is consonant with a broader trend in macrocriminological research. For example, Land et al. (1990) argue that good theories will exhibit explanatory power across multiple levels of explanation, and Shihadeh and Steffensmeier (1994) make the argument that cities can be conceptualized as both "units of stratification and social control." In addition, we focused exclusively on urban counties because the large bulk of all homicide occurs in urban locales, and because most previous macrolevel research focuses on urban areas.

Second, prior research on the explanatory power of IAT for violence focuses either on total violent crime rates or an aggregate measure of homicide. However, as homicide researchers are increasingly becoming aware, the failure to disaggregate or partition homicide rates into meaningful subcategories can mask potentially important variations in the effects of predictor variables. Further, IAT appears to have particular salience for instrumental homicide rates because of its implicit economically based motivation. Hence, we disaggregated our measure of total homicide into instrumental and expressive homicides.

Third, we slightly extend the range of predictor variables tapping the prevalence of and commitment to noneconomic institutions. In particular, we derived measures of the number of educational expenditures per school age person and the rate of adherence to civically engaged religious denominations. Finally, our reading of the theory suggests that the effects of economic inequality on homicide will be attenuated in the presence of noneconomic institutions (the mediation effect), which is different from the more popular expectation of prior research positing that the effects of economic inequality (or poverty) on crime varies according to the level of noneconomic institutions (the moderation effect).

Overall, our analysis provides rather consistent support for our expectations. To summarize, our negative binomial regression models indicate that the economy as operationalized by the Gini coefficient of family income inequality is a strong predictor of variation in rates of urban total, instrumental, and expressive homicide. Moreover, the majority of our measures of noneconomic institutions performed well in explaining variation in all three rates of homicide, the exception being the measure of educational expenditures. But perhaps most interesting are the final two findings from these analyses. As expected, our data indicate that the presence of noneconomic institutions has a particularly pronounced mediating effect on the link between income inequality and instrumental homicide, accounting for almost half of the direct association. However, we find only very limited support for the moderation hypothesis. Indeed, only the level of welfare expenditures serves to constrain the effect of income inequality on homicide rates. In light of these series of findings, we conclude that noneconomic institutions appear to play an important role in buffering the effects of economic motivation on instrumental violence.

Although our results largely support IAT, the analyses do potentially suffer from some limitations. Our focus on the most serious form of violence, homicide, coupled with our desires to classify homicides according to the apparent motive of the offender and to analyze data for a large sample of urban areas, left us with no choice but the Supplementary Homicide Reports in terms of data sources. The limitations of the SHR described above are well known.

We believe that researchers should continue to refine tests of IAT to build on the few tests that have already been published and were described above. In particular, we hope that IAT will be seen as a viable theory for macro level research carried out at the subnational level. As noted by Piquero and Piquero (1998), the constructs operationalized in tests of IAT thus far do not differ significantly from those of other theories at the macrolevel, particularly economic deprivation theories. One issue that remains is the appropriate modeling strategy: Does IAT require the modeling of interaction terms measuring its structural, or institutional, components? We believe that this is still an open question, but argue, with the support of prior research, that one modeling strategy does not necessarily obviate the use of another (e.g., elaboration modeling) to provide support for IAT. A second issue is the appropriate subnational unit of analysis. Some may argue that cities, SMSAs, or states are more appropriate levels of analysis for testing IAT at a subnational level. In particular, the rationale we put forth in this paper could easily be modified to argue for the treatment of central cities as social systems.

In addition, we argued that the application of IAT to serious "instrumental" crime does not restrict the scope of the theory to property crimes.

We encourage additional research seeking to refine measurement of the dependent variable in most criminological research—namely, crime—and offer one type of distinction in lethal violence (instrumental vs. expressive homicides) as a step in this direction. We agree with others who have pointed out the need for disaggregating crime rates, but argue that there are additional avenues for linking mainstream theories to types of homicide beyond race and sex disaggregation. Combining methods of disaggregation would be the most likely choice for determining the suitability for particular theories. One recent example of this is a paper by Martinez (2000), which explains the differing impacts of immigration on Latino homicide victimization by type (stranger vs. acquaintance) using deprivation and social disorganization perspectives.

In conclusion, we argue that IAT is in fact a viable theory for explaining homicide rates across macrosocial units within the United States, and may in fact be well suited for integration with other macrolevel theories, such as systemic social disorganization theory (Bursik and Grasmick, 1993; Rose and Clear, 1998). Such integration might not only lead to a more comprehensive structural explanation of crime, but also may help crystallize policy implications at the macrolevel as well. Similar to IAT, disorganization theory posits that a weakening of institutional controls (e.g., family, school) is a major contributor to higher crime rates. Like many potentially effective crime prevention remedies, the rebalancing of economic and noneconomic institutions to offset the criminogenic consequences of the American Dream may in fact have to take root at the local level before we are able to characterize American exceptionalism in serious crime as a thing of the past.

REFERENCES

Allison, Paul
1999 Multiple Regression: A Primer. Thousand Oaks, Calif.: Pine Forge Press.

Anderson, Elijah
1999 Code of the Street: Decency, Violence, and the Moral Life of the Inner City. New York: W.W. Norton.

Bailey, William C.
1984 Poverty, inequality, and city homicide rates. Criminology 22:531–550.

Bankston, William B., H. David Allen, and Daniel S. Cunningham
1983 Religion and suicide: A research note on sociology's 'one law.' Social Forces 62:521–528.

Baron, Reuben M. and David A. Kenny
1986 The moderator-mediator variable distinction in social psychological research: Conceptual, strategic, and statistical considerations. Journal of Personality and Social Psychology 51:1173–1182.

Bernard, Jessie
1962 American Community Behavior. Revised ed. New York: Holt, Rinehart, and Winston.

Bernburg, Jón Gunnar
2002 Anomie, social change and crime: A theoretical examination of institutional-anomie theory. British Journal of Criminology 42:729–742.

Blau, Judith R. and Peter M. Blau
1982 The cost of inequality: Metropolitan structure and violent crime. American Sociological Review 47:114–129.

Block, Carolyn Rebecca and Richard L. Block
1991 Beginning with Wolfgang: An agenda for homicide research. Journal of Crime and Justice 14:31–70.

Block, Carolyn Rebecca, Christine Ovcharchyn Devitt, Edmund R. Donoghue, Roy J Dames, and Richard L. Block
2000 Are there types of intimate partner homicide? Presentation at the Homicide Research Working Group Annual Symposium. Chicago, Ill., June 24–27.

Block, Richard E. and Franklin E. Zimring
1973 Homicides in Chicago, 1965-1970. Journal of Research in Crime and Delinquency 10:1–7.

Blumstein, Alfred and Richard Rosenfeld
1998 Explaining recent trends in U.S. homicide rates. Journal of Criminal Law & Criminology 88:1175–1216.

Blumstein, Alfred and Joel Wallman (eds.)
2000 The Crime Drop in America. New York: Cambridge University Press.

Booth, Alan and D. Wayne Osgood
1993 The influence of testosterone on deviance in adulthood: Assessing and explaining the relationship. Criminology 31:93–117.

Breault, K. D.
1986 Suicide in America: A test of Durkheim's theory of religious and family integration, 1933-1980. American Journal of Sociology 92:628–656.

Bursik, Robert and Harold G. Grasmick
1993 Neighborhoods and Crime: The Dimensions of Effective Community Control. New York: Lexington Books.

Chamlin, Mitchell B. and John K. Cochran
1995 Assessing Messner and Rosenfeld's institutional anomie theory: A partial test. Criminology 33:411–429.
1997 Social altruism and crime. Criminology 35:203–228.
2001 Social altruism and crime revisited: A note on measurement. Journal of Crime and Justice 24:59–72.

Clogg, Clifford C., Eva Petkova, and Adamantios Haritou
1995 Statistical methods for comparing regression coefficients between models. American Journal of Sociology 100:1261–1293.

Cooney, Mark and Scott Phillips
2002 Typologizing violence: A Blackian perspective. International Journal of Sociology and Social Policy 22:75–108.

Cutchin, Malcolm P., and Robert R. Churchill
1999 Scale, context, and causes of suicide in the United States. Social Science Quarterly 80:97–114.

Daly, Martin and Margo Wilson
1988 Homicide. New York: Aldine de Gruyter.

Decker, Scott H.
1996 Deviant homicide: A new look at the role of motives and victim-offender relationships. Journal of Research in Crime and Delinquency 33:427–449.

DeFronzo, James and Lance Hannon
1998 Welfare assistance levels and homicide rates. Homicide Studies 2:31–45.

Dubin, Robert
1959 Deviant behavior and social structure: Continuities in social theory. American Sociological Review 24:147–164.

Dunaway, Wilma
1996 The First American Frontier: Transition to Capitalism in Southern Appalachia, 1700-1860. Chapel Hill: University of North Carolina Press.

Esping-Andersen, Gosta
1990 The Three Worlds of Welfare Capitalism. Princeton, N.J.: Princeton University Press.

Etzioni, Amitai
1996 The New Golden Rule: Community and Morality in a Democratic Society. New York: Basic Books.

Felson, Richard B. and Steven F. Messner
1996 To kill or not to kill? Lethal outcomes in injurious attacks. Criminology 34:519–545.

Fox, James Alan
2000 Uniform Crime Reports [United States]: Supplementary Homicide Reports, 1976–1998 [Computer file]. ICPSR version. Boston, Mass.: Northeastern University, College of Criminal Justice [producer], Ann Arbor, Mich.: Inter-university Consortium for Political and Social Research [distributor].

Hannon, Lance and James DeFronzo
1998 The truly disadvantaged, public assistance, and crime. Social Problems 45:383–392.

Kaufman, Jeanne G. and Cathy Spatz Widom
1999 Childhood victimization, running away, and delinquency. Journal of Research in Crime and Delinquency 36:347–370.

Kowalski, Gregory S., Charles E. Faupel, and Paul D. Starr
1987 Urbanism and suicide: A study of American counties. Social Forces 66:85–101.

LaFree, Gary
1999 Declining violent crime rates in the 1990s: Predicting crime booms and busts. Annual Review of Sociology 25:145–168.

Land, Kenneth C., Patricia L. McCall, and Lawrence E. Cohen
1990 Structural covariates of homicide rates: Are there any invariances across time and social space? American Journal of Sociology 95:922–963.

Lee, Matthew R. and Graham C. Ousey
2001 Size matters: Examining the link between small manufacturing, socioeconomic deprivation, and crime rates in nonmetropolitan communities. Sociological Quarterly 42:581–602.

Logan, John R. and Harvey L. Molotch
1987 Urban Fortunes: The Political Economy of Place. Berkeley: University of California Press.

Lyson, Thomas and Charles Tolbert
1996 Small manufacturing and nonmetropolitan well being. Environment and Planning A 28:1779–1794.

Marleau, Jude and Alayne Hamilton
1999 Demanding to be heard: Women's use of violence. Humanity and Society 23:339–358.

Martinez, Ramiro, Jr.
2000 Immigration and urban violence: The link between immigrant Latinos and types of homicide. Social Science Quarterly 81:363–374.

Merton, Robert
1938 Social structure and anomie. American Sociological Review 3:672–682.

Messner, Steven F. and Richard Rosenfeld
1994 Crime and the American Dream. Belmont, Calif.: Wadsworth.
1997 Political restraint of the market and levels of criminal homicide: A cross-national application of institutional-anomie theory. Social Forces 75:1393–1416.
2001 Crime and the American Dream. 3d ed. Belmont, Calif.: Wadsworth.

Miethe, Terance D. and Kriss A. Drass
1999 Exploring the social context of instrumental and expressive homicides: An application of qualitative comparative analysis. Journal of Quantitative Criminology 15:1–21.

Nielsen, Francois and Arthur S. Alderson
1997 The Kuznets curve and the great U-turn: Income inequality in U.S. counties, 1970 to 1990. American Sociological Review 62:12–33.

Osgood, D. Wayne
2000 Poisson-based regression analysis of aggregate crime rates. Journal of Quantitative Criminology 16:21–43.

Osgood, D. Wayne and Jeff M. Chambers
2000 Social disorganization outside the Metropolis: An analysis of rural youth violence. Criminology 38:81–115.

Peterson, Ruth D., Lauren J. Krivo, and Mark A. Harris
2000 Disadvantage and neighborhood violent crime: Do local institutions matter? Journal of Research in Crime and Delinquency 37:31–63.

Piquero, Alex and Nicole Leeper Piquero
1998 On testing institutional anomie theory with varying specifications. Studies on Crime and Crime Prevention 7:61–84.

Polk, Kenneth
1994 Why Men Kill: Scenarios of Masculine Violence. New York: Cambridge University Press.

Putnam, Robert D.
1993 Making Democracy Work: Civic Traditions in Modern Italy. Princeton, N.J.: Princeton University Press.

Rose, Dina and Todd Clear
1998 Incarceration, social capital, and crime: Implications for social disorganization theory. Criminology 36:441–479.

Rosenfeld, Richard, Steven R. Messner, and Eric P. Baumer
2001 Social capital and homicide. Social Forces 80:283–309.

Sampson, Robert J. and W. Byron Groves
1989 Community structure and crime: Testing social-disorganization theory. American Journal of Sociology : 774-802.

Savolainen, Jukka
2000 Inequality, welfare state, and homicide: Further support for the institutional anomie theory. Criminology 38:1021–1042.

Shihadeh, Edward S. and Darrell J. Steffensmeier
1994 Economic inequality, family disruption, and urban black violence: Cities as units of stratification and social control. Social Forces 73:729–751.

Sims, Barbara
1997 Crime, punishment, and the American dream: Toward a Marxist integration. Journal of Research in Crime and Delinquency 3:5–24.

Tocqueville, Alexis de
1969 Democracy in America. G. Lawrence, (Transl.) J. P. Mayer (ed.). New York: Harper and Row.

Tolbert, Charles M., Thomas A. Lyson, and Michael D. Irwin
1998 Local capitalism, civic engagement, and socioeconomic well-being. Social Forces 77:401–427.

Varano, Sean Patrick and Jeffrey Michael Cancino
2001 An empirical analysis of deviant homicides in Chicago. Homicide Studies 5:5–29.

Williams, Kirk R. and Robert L. Flewelling
1988 The social production of criminal homicide: A comparative study of disaggregated rates in American cities. American Sociological Review 53:421–431.

Michael O. Maume is an Assistant Professor at the University of North Carolina at Wilmington. His areas of research interest are macrosocial correlates of lethal violence, communities and crime, and life course criminology. He has recently been the co-author of articles published in *Rural Sociology*, *Homicide Studies*, and *Violence Against Women*.

Matthew R. Lee is an Associate Professor of Sociology and a Research Fellow with the Social Science Research Center at Mississippi State University. His areas of interest are macro-criminology and violence. Recent research appears in *Justice Quarterly*, *The Sociological Quarterly*, *Criminology*, *Rural Sociology*, and various other journals.

[13]

Decommodification and Homicide Rates in the 20th-Century United States

CANDICE BATTON
University of Nebraska–Omaha
GARY JENSEN
Vanderbilt University

This study uses time-series regression techniques to examine the impact of decommodification on homicide rates in the United States from the institutional anomie perspective. Although recent studies have examined the impact of decommodification on cross-national variations in homicide rates, little attention has been paid to historical trends in this relationship. Our findings support institutional anomie theory when decommodification is conceptualized as a historically variant and contextual variable. No support was found for more intricate specifications measuring annual variation in the level of decommodification, and no support was found for alternative modes of periodization. Finally, the results also point to a temporal shift in the correlates of homicide rates between the two distinct historical periods, and the results have methodological implications for conducting time-series analyses.

The conservative political climate of American society for the past several decades has been characterized by the belief that government welfare programs have failed to lessen the social problems they were constructed to solve. Such programs have been referred to disparagingly as "social engineering," and those committed to the use of government as a tool for solving social problems have been stigmatized as liberals. Yet, although the political shift away from welfare state policies benefiting the disadvantaged has been

AUTHORS' NOTE: We would like to thank the anonymous reviewers for their helpful comments on earlier drafts of this article. An earlier version of this article was presented at the annual meeting of the Homicide Research Working Group in Chicago, Illinois, June 2000. Direct all correspondence to Candice Batton, Department of Criminal Justice, University of Nebraska, 540 N. 16th Street, 1100 NRC, Lincoln, NE 68588-0630.

gaining momentum, it is far from clear that the programs lumped together under this rubric actually failed.

One of the most recent assessments of societal variations in homicide reported an inverse relationship between measures of the magnitude of social programs designed to insulate citizens from market forces and homicide rates. Messner and Rosenfeld (1997b) proposed that national policies of decommodification (i.e., government policies designed to free people from the harsher exigencies of a market economy) have had a dampening effect on violence rates. Controlling for other correlates, the more a nation invests in decommodification, the lower its homicide rate. Such findings run counter to the notion that government social engineering has either failed or magnified social problems.

Messner and Rosenfeld's (1997b) research suggests that variation in government policies affect homicide rates among societies, but relatively little is known about the effects of variation over time within societies. The present study takes steps in that direction by assessing the impact of decommodifying social policies on U.S. homicide rates during the 20th century. If Messner and Rosenfeld's theory applies to variation over time, changes in social welfare policies should lower homicide rates or weaken links between fluctuations in market forces and homicide.

The Concept of Decommodification

The concept of decommodification is based on the assumption that the economy affects the structure and organization of all other social institutions (e.g., polity, family, education) and social relations in society. The degree to which economic fluctuations affect other institutions and relations is related to the level of control the state exercises over the economy and the extent to which it attempts to mediate the effects of economic fluctuations. In a capitalist society, market events and fluctuations are likely to have a greater impact during periods when state regulation and control over the economy are minimal than at times when the state takes a more active role in ameliorating the effects of economic swings.

Economic fluctuations also affect the lives of individuals as they rely on their participation in the market for sustenance and support. In a free market society characterized by a laissez-faire attitude and the absence of social welfare policies, changes in the economy or an individual's labor force participation are likely to have a direct and immediate impact on the individual's activities within other institutional realms. For example, both acquiring and losing a job are related to a person's ability to support himself or herself and to provide for a family. Job status and income also affect educational and leisure opportunities. Thus, a free market economy exerts a constraining influence on individuals in terms of the structure and organization of their lives.

Decommodification refers to the totality of measures intended to have a stabilizing effect on market societies, such as the adoption and implementation of social welfare policies and programs. These policies are intended to balance power between the economy and the polity, thus ameliorating the harsher consequences of market activity and economic fluctuations on the lives of individuals. As Esping-Andersen (1990) noted, decommodification "refers to the degree to which individuals, or families, can uphold a socially acceptable standard of living independently of market participation" (p. 37). Messner and Rosenfeld (1997b) expanded this conception, stating that "decommodified social policies permit actions and choices by citizens—to get married, have children, seek higher education, engage in political activity—that are, in principle, unconstrained by market considerations" (p. 1394). Decommodification involves more than funding social welfare programs; it also has a quality dimension regarding social rights and ease of access to entitlements (Esping-Andersen, 1990, p. 47).

Decommodification and the Theory of Institutional Anomie

Messner and Rosenfeld (1997b) proposed that the concept of decommodification can be integrated with their theory of institutional anomie, which focuses on the interplay between culture, social structure, and crime. According to this theory, crime rates are likely to be higher when cultural goals emphasize financial success and material wealth but simultaneously de-emphasize conduct norms prescribing appropriate institutionalized means for achieving those goals (Merton, 1968; Messner & Rosenfeld, 1997b, p. 1396). Such anomic pressures are nourished and sustained by a particular institutional arrangement in which other social institutions become subservient to the economy. More specific, economic dominance leads to (a) the devaluation of noneconomic institutional functions and roles, (b) the prioritizing of economic obligations and expectations during times of role conflict, and (c) the penetration of economic norms into other institutional domains (e.g., reliance on extrinsic rewards in school, idea that government should be run more like a business). Economic dominance promotes high crime rates because (a) it contributes to a rising sense of anomie as other institutions become less capable of fulfilling their responsibilities to establish and maintain respect for social norms and (b) it weakens the control exerted by noneconomic roles as they become decreasingly attractive in comparison to economic roles. The theoretical implication is that decommodification will have a dampening effect on a society's crime and violence rates as it (a) reduces the dominance of the economic system and helps restore a sense of institutional balance and (b) works to de-emphasize concerns regarding financial loss and job trouble because social welfare policies ease the urgency and devastation linked with financial hardship.

Although Messner and Rosenfeld (1997b) were among the first to focus specifically on the criminogenic effects of decommodification,[1] Carlson and Michalowski (1997) noted that several criminological theories (i.e., Marxian, conflict, opportunity, strain, social disorganization, routine activities) share in the idea that "economic distress generated by rises in unemployment will increase crimes against both persons and property" (p. 210). As Carlson and Michalowski noted, property crime analyses tend to be based on rational choice models of behavior given distressing economic conditions. In contrast, violent crime analyses tend to see violence and aggression as nonrational and expressive responses to rising levels of anger and frustration generated by worsening economic conditions that affect the opportunity structure.[2] Although some violent acts may stem from economic distress, the primary means by which economic downturns affect violence rates is through their impact on general social conditions and the manner in which people engage in their routine activities (i.e., where, how, how often, and with whom). During economic downturns, general societal conditions are more facilitating of violence and aggression than are conditions in an improving economy.

Messner and Rosenfeld's (1997b) findings are consistent with institutional anomie theory, but support for decommodification effects is weak. First, the bivariate homicide-decommodification relationship is significant for advanced capitalist nations only when the United States is included in the sample. When the United States is excluded, the relationship becomes nonsignificant. Second, in the multivariate analysis, models were tested on three different samples, one of which excludes Syria, an outlier for homicide rates. When Syria is excluded, the model fit improves slightly, but the magnitude of the decommodification effect on homicide rates diminishes. If excluding one outlier (Syria) weakens decommodification effects on homicide rates, the exclusion of another (i.e., the United States) could diminish the effects even more, perhaps to the point of nonsignificance. When the impact of the United States on the bivariate analyses is considered in conjunction with the notion that its extreme decommodification and homicide rate scores may be unduly influencing the results of the multivariate analyses, the importance of further research on decommodification and homicide is even more apparent.[3]

Messner and Rosenfeld (1997b, p. 1401) noted that a society's level of decommodification is not likely to vary much in the short run. However, evidence of changes in the level of decommodification should be more apparent for longer spans of time. From the institutional anomie perspective, homicide rates should be affected as decommodification shifts the institutional balance of power in society away from the economy and limits the impact of economic fluctuations on the lives of individuals. For example, with decommodification, economic deprivation and market fluctuations are less likely to result in rash acts of aggression. Furthermore, because decommodification contributes to the restoration of value and respect for noneconomic roles, it should indirectly function to increase the web of social control mechanisms regulating aggression.

Decommodification in the United States

It is difficult to identify a specific date heralding the start of decommodification in the United States as the tradition of helping those in need reaches back to colonial times (Social Security Administration, 1997, p. 1). However, the need for social welfare became increasingly apparent in the early 1900s as urbanization and industrialization resulted in greater numbers of people living away from their families. Also, vaccines and advances in public health and sanitation contributed to rapid population growth and a growth in aged persons. For the most part, increasing demands for assistance were addressed on an "as needed" basis at the state and local levels (although some funds were available through federal grants and loans) and consisted of targeted measures, such as mothers' pensions, old age assistance, and aid for the blind.

Although a few provisions had been made in the way of veterans' benefits and a civil service retirement system for federal employees, it was not until the early 1930s, following the stock market crash and the onset of the Great Depression, that the federal government became integrally involved in the development and administration of social welfare programs (Social Security Administration, 1997, p. 2). Beginning in 1933, the federal government initiated several antidepression measures including the Emergency Banking Relief Act, the Economy Act, the Civilian Conservation Corps, the Federal Emergency Relief Administration, and the Agricultural Adjustment Administration (Urdang, 1996). Although many of these measures were intended to deal with the immediate economic crisis, a commitment to more general social welfare policies and programs by the federal government came in 1935 with the passage of the Social Security Act (Social Security Administration, 1997).

Social security is rooted in the concept of social insurance, which refers to eligibility for benefits as a matter of right rather than solely because of need (Social Security Administration, 1997). In its pure form, all persons should be eligible for benefits as a right extending from citizenship or labor force participation. In the United States, social security was implemented with the intent of providing two specific types of social insurance coverage: dependency due to old age and unemployment. This focus is not surprising because the Great Depression had destroyed the life savings of many elderly and had greatly diminished employment opportunities (Social Security Administration, 1997). Benefit payments for old-age, survivors', and disability insurance (OASDI) were slated to begin in 1942, but a 1939 amendment allowed a start date of 1940. Although eligibility for OASDI benefits was originally determined by former social security contributions and labor force participation, benefits were extended to the dependents of deceased and retired workers in 1939, representing a shift in focus from the individual worker to protection of the family. In the 1950s, coverage was expanded to disabled workers and their dependents and to more occupations. By the mid-1960s, OASDI boasted nearly universal coverage, and its format remains largely unchanged (Social Security Administration, 2000).

Unemployment insurance and workers' compensation are also major aspects of social insurance. Although the first program was in Wisconsin in 1932, national unemployment insurance provisions were made in 1935 with the Social Security Act, with programs in place by 1937 (Social Security Administration, 1997). Unemployment insurance is intended to provide partial income replacement to workers who are involuntarily unemployed. Thus, the right to benefits stems from labor force participation. Similarly, workers' compensation provides benefits to persons unable to work due to injuries on the job. Although the first workers' compensation law was passed in 1908 providing for federal civilian employees working in hazardous conditions, it was 1949 before all states had provisions for injured workers (Social Security Administration, 1997).

Social insurance is only one component of social welfare programming. A second major category consists of veterans' benefits, which date back to 1789 following the Revolutionary War. By the late 1800s, benefits included provisions for medical and hospital care and pensions for disabled veterans and the dependents of deceased service men. Benefits were extended following World War I (WWI) to include disability compensation, life insurance, and vocational rehabilitation (Department of Veterans' Affairs, 2000). They were again expanded in 1944 following World War II (WWII) to include extensive educational and home loan benefits.

A third aspect of social welfare programming is public aid, which refers to money distributed on the basis of need. Perhaps, the most well-known are the Food Stamp Program, initiated in 1961 and made permanent in 1964, and the Supplemental Security Income Program, which was initiated in 1974 with the goal of assisting needy persons who are aged, blind, or disabled. Another large component of public aid is geared toward needy children and families, such as the Temporary Assistance for Needy Families Program, which replaced Aid to Families and Dependent Children in 1997.

A fourth aspect of social welfare programming consists of health and medical services. Although discussions over national health care have gone on since the early 1900s, it was not until 1965 that the first government health insurance programs were established under Medicare and Medicaid. Medicare is aimed primarily at disabled workers, the aged, and their dependents and includes provisions for a variety of medical and health services (e.g., hospital services, nursing facility care, home health services, hospice care, physician services). Medicaid provides similar benefits but is geared toward assisting low-income persons and families and also includes prenatal and child health care.

Housing aid is another form of social welfare, which primarily consists of money for public-housing projects and subsidized rent. The first low-rent public-housing programs in the United States were initiated in 1933 as part of the public works programs set in motion during the Great Depression. Subsequent housing acts in 1949 and 1954 provided for the massive urban renewal programs of the 1950s.

In addition to the aforementioned programs, social welfare programming also includes money for education and a number of other miscellaneous programs. Education benefits are the only social welfare benefits that are largely indirect and afforded on the basis of citizenship as opposed to need or labor force participation. Benefits are indirect in that education expenditures are largely for new school construction, although a small portion are for adult vocational educational services. Beyond the major types of programs already mentioned, social welfare also includes funding for a variety of other programs, such as school lunch programs, energy usage programs, aid for Native Americans, and money for child placement and adoption services among other things.

Expectations

Institutional anomie theory suggests that decommodification should have a dampening effect on violence rates as social welfare policies and programs function to buffer society and individuals from the harshest effects of economic downturns. In consideration of this, a negative decommodification-homicide relationship is expected. Although the passage of the 1935 Social Security

Act largely hailed the beginning of decommodification in the United States, it is likely that the impact of decommodifying policies and programs was not felt until the post-WWII period because of delays in their implementation in conjunction with the effects of WWII. In the following, we consider the issues involved in measuring temporal variation in the level of decommodification and examine its impact on homicide rates over time.

DATA AND METHOD

Data

This study analyzes U.S. data for 1900 to 1997. The start and end dates have both historical and methodological rationales. Until recently, national homicide data were only available back to 1933. However, by using econometric-forecasting techniques, Eckberg (1995) estimated homicide rates for 1900 to 1932. Thus, the use of 1900 as the starting point is at least partially due to the availability of new data, an analysis of which allows an assessment of early 20th-century violence rates and a comparison with later periods. Examining the entire 20th century also facilitates an assessment of whether the factors that affect U.S. lethal violence rates are historically constant or temporally variant across different time periods.

Although new data afford new opportunities for analysis, it is important to note that there are limitations associated with analyzing national-level data. Perhaps, most important is that national data obscure differences that may exist at local, state, and regional levels. Time-series analyses of differentially aggregated data would undoubtedly provide a more in-depth understanding of temporal and spatial variations in homicide rates. For example, city- or county-level data might facilitate a more in-depth discussion of the decommodification-homicide relationship by allowing for comparisons between rural and urban areas, which often experience shifts in market forces differently because of employment in different segments of the labor force. Unfortunately, often such data do not exist from the past because of less systematic record-keeping systems, changes in coding procedures, and natural processes that have destroyed data. Although such limitations should be acknowledged, we still feel that valuable insights can be gained by analyzing national-level data. Furthermore, an analysis of national-level U.S. data will facilitate comparisons with Messner and Rosenfeld (1997b), who also focused on nations.

Measures

Dependent Variable

One of the most widely discussed methodological issues in historical studies of violence levels is the availability, validity, and reliability of data. In comparison to assault, rape, and robbery, homicide is advantageous as an indicator of historical violence levels because it is less subject to definitional ambiguity, it is more likely to be reported to authorities, and it indexes other forms of violence (Gurr, 1981; Hansmann & Quigley, 1982; Riedel, 1990). The primary sources of U.S. data are the Vital Statistics (http://www.cdc.gov/nchs/nvss.htm), compiled by the National Center for Health Statistics (NCHS) from coroner and medical examiner reports, and the Uniform Crime Reports (http://www.fbi.gov/ucr/ucr.htm), compiled by the Federal Bureau of Investigation from police reports.

Although neither source is flawless,[4] we use NCHS data.[5] First, comparisons suggest that they are more accurate than Uniform Crime Reports data, especially before 1949, as they are less dependent on estimation procedures (Cantor & Cohen, 1980; Zahn & McCall, 1999). Second, Eckberg (1995) recently used Vital Statistics data to estimate U.S. homicide rates for 1900 to 1932, which had not been previously available. In calculating estimates, Eckberg (p. 4) accounted for the composition of the early death registration area, which largely excluded southern and western states where homicide rates were highest. He also adjusted for differences in the proportions of urban and rural areas in the registration area and nonregistration area states. Although these data should be used cautiously,[6] it likely provides a more accurate portrayal of early 1900s homicide than other sources. In sum, homicide rate data came from Eckberg for 1900 to 1932 and from NCHS annual mortality tables for 1933 to 1997.[7]

Independent Variables

Decommodification. Messner and Rosenfeld (1997b) used a decommodification index based on summed z scores for (a) social welfare expenditure levels as a percentage of gross domestic product (GDP), (b) average annual per capita expenditures on social welfare, and (c) percentage of social welfare expenditures allocated to employment injuries. These items were selected based on results from a principal components factor analysis of the items in Esping-Andersen's (1990) decommodification index. In an attempt to replicate and extend Messner and Rosenfeld's findings, Savolainen (2000) also used this measure. To facilitate comparisons, we created a time-series decommodification index consisting of the same factors spanning from 1929 to 1995. To control for inflation and changes in the value of the dollar over time, per capita expenditures were divided by the 1982 to 1984 Consumer Price Index and multiplied by 100 to convert all of the data into constant 1982 to 1984 dollars. Consumer Price Index data were taken from the Bureau of Labor Statistics Web site (http://www.stats.bls.gov/cpi/home.htm).

Control Variables

Alcohol consumption. Although this study focuses on decommodification effects, several control variables are included because of previous research findings; the first of which is alcohol consumption, which R.N. Parker (1995) and Jensen (2000) have found to affect violence. Although data are available for most of the 1900s, prohibition era consumption rates are generally not available, and estimates may be suspect (Jensen, 2000; Wood, 1926). Therefore, we join others in using cirrhosis death rates per 100,000 as a proxy for alcohol consumption (Cook & Tauchen, 1982; Goode, 1994; Jensen, 2000; Levine & Reinarman, 1991; Miron & Zwiebel, 1991). The data are from *Historical Statistics of the United States* (*HSUS*) (U.S. Bureau of the Census, 1975) for 1900 to 1970, *Vital Statistics* (National Center for Health Statistics, 1982) and issues of the *Statistical Abstract of the United States* (*SAUS*) (published by the U.S. Bureau of the Census) for 1971 to 1994, and NCHS Web site tables (http://www.cdc.gov/nchs/datawh/statab/unpubd/mortabs) for 1995 to 1997.

Prohibitionist legislation. Prohibitionist legislation refers to measures that restrict or ban alcoholic beverage sales to entire populations or specific groups, such as total bans in specific geographical areas, restrictions on public-drinking facilities (e.g., bars, saloons), and minimum-age purchase and possession laws. Both Batton (1999) and Jensen (2000) have found a relationship between prohibitionist legislation and homicide rates in historical studies. The effects are controlled for with a count variable reflecting the number of states with prohibitionist legislation in effect in any given year constructed with data from Cashman (1981).

Mob murders. During Prohibition, the United States witnessed an increase in murders associated with the illegal liquor trade because of the rise of organized crime and mob conflict over territories and distribution (Batton, 1999; Gurr, 1989; Jensen, 2000). The effects of organized crime and mob activity on homicide rates are controlled for with a dummy variable reflecting years in which mob-perpetrated murders involving the illegal liquor trade were high.

Immigration. Historical studies have found that the homicide rate increases during periods of heavy immigration (Lane, 1999). To control for this, the percentage of the U.S. resident population composed of newly admitted immigrants was included in the analyses. Data on immigration are from *HSUS* (1900-1970) and *SAUS* (1971-present).

Unemployment rates. Market events and fluctuations are argued to exert a constraining influence on individuals by affecting labor force participation opportunities. At an aggregate level, these effects should be reflected in changing unemployment rates (i.e., percentage of civilian labor force unemployed) over time. Thus, unemployment rates are included as an indicator of the impact that shifting market forces have on individuals and the conditions in which they live. As noted earlier, numerous other studies have also examined unemployment effects on crime. In a review of 63 studies, Chiricos (1987) found evidence of a significant unemployment-crime relationship in a large portion of studies, with most reporting a positive relationship. Unemployment data were taken from *HSUS*, *SAUS*, and the Bureau of Labor Statistics Web site (http://www.bls.gov/blshome.htm). Prior to the Great Depression, unemployment fluctuated between 2% and 12% but reached nearly 25% in the 1930s. From the early 1940s into the 1980s, it increased, peaking around 10%. Since then, unemployment has declined to 4% to 5%.

Divorce rates. Several studies have found a relationship between rates of homicide and divorce including Gartner (1990), Kposowa and Breault (1993), and Messner and Golden (1992). Divorce rates are the number of divorces per 1,000 persons in the population and are included to control for the effects of levels of social integration (or disintegration) on violence rates. Data were taken from the U.S. Bureau of the Census (1931) for 1900 to 1929, *Vital Statistics* for 1930 to 1982, and *SAUS* for 1983 to 1997.

Armed forces. In a study of Prohibition and violence rates, Jensen (2000) found a negative effect on homicide for percentage in the armed forces. Furthermore, the military has historically provided young adults, especially males who are the primary actors in homicides, with a means of supporting themselves. Thus, percentage of the population on active military duty is included as a control. The data were extracted from *HSUS* (1900-1970) and *SAUS* (1971-1997).

Postwar period. Both Gurr (1989) and Zahn and McCall (1999) have found homicide rates tend to surge briefly following the United States's involvement in war. To control for this, a dummy is included for periods following the United States's involvement in a foreign war (i.e., WWI, WWII, Korean War, Vietnam, and the Persian Gulf).

Age structure of the population. Although research on the impact of the age structure on homicide has produced mixed results, a number of studies have found a relationship, including Blau and Golden (1986), Gurr (1989), and Land, McCall, and Cohen (1990). We control for changes in the age structure by including percentage of the population composed of 15 to 24 year olds and percentage of the population 65 or older. Data were taken from *HSUS* (1900-1959) and the Centers for Disease Control Web site (http://www.cdc.gov/nchs/data) (1960-1997).

Analytical Approach

Detrending is often seen as a simple solution for the problems posed to time-series analyses by autocorrelation and non-stationarity. However, detrending can be problematic because it changes the nature of the data, which has implications for hypothesis testing. At a conceptual level, researchers often start with a theory about historical trends but then use differenced data to test hypotheses. This is problematic because the researcher is no longer examining historical trends; the data now represent annual fluctuations (Jensen, 1997, p. 47). When differenced data are used to test theories about long-term historical change, it is not surprising that the original theory is often disconfirmed. Often overlooked is that the theory has been disconfirmed by procedures that remove or adjust most of the history of the phenomenon to be explained (Jensen, 1997).

We test for stationarity and the presence of unit roots using Augmented Dickey-Fuller tests. The results indicate several of the series contain unit roots in levels[8] and are difference stationary processes. In consideration of problems posed by nonstationarity, we difference our data. However, we also attempt to model the effects of trends and eliminate autocorrelated error terms through the inclusion of theoretically and historically relevant variables. By inspecting the residuals plot and thinking more deeply about history and theory, potential missing variables can often be discerned because the spans of time in which the dependent variable is consistently underestimated or overestimated become apparent (Jensen, 2000). In sum, we perform analyses on both level and differenced measures.

The relationship between decommodification and homicide rates is examined using ordinary least squares time-series regression techniques with E-views (2001) software. Several tests for autocorrelation are used. To test for first-order processes in basic models, we use the Durbin-Watson statistic. For models with a lagged endogenous term and to test for higher order processes, we use Durbin's h,[9] the Breusch-Godfrey LM test (with up to three lags), and the Box-Ljung Q statistics associated with the autocorrelation and partial autocorrelation functions in the correlograms.

TABLE 1
Least Squares Models Predicting 1929 to 1995 Homicide Rates With an Index of Annual Changes in Decommodification Based on Both Level (Y_t) and Differenced (Y_{t-1}) Measures

	Y_t	Y_{t-1}
Intercept	1.390	–.009
Decommodification index	.147	.094
Lagged endogenous term	.811***	.477***
AR(1)	.584**	—
Adjusted R^2	.961	.194
Durbin-Watson *d*	1.925	1.919
Durbin's *h*	—[a]	.872
Breusch-Godfrey LM test (three lags)		
F values	.146	.030
Obs*R^2	.486	.099
N	66	66

NOTE: AR = autoregressive.
a. Durbin's *h* not calculated; see Note 10.
** Significant at $\alpha = .01$. *** Significant at $\alpha = .001$.

FINDINGS

Impact of Decommodification

Institutional anomie theory suggests decommodification should result in lower homicide rates because it (a) buffers the impact of market events and fluctuations and (b) shifts the institutional balance of power, which diminishes anomic pressures and strengthens social control mechanisms. In Table 1 we examine the relationship between homicide rates and the decommodification index used by both Messner and Rosenfeld (1997b) and Savolainen (2000). In both the level and differenced measure models, autocorrelation could only be accounted for by including a lagged endogenous term.[10] An autoregressive term had to be included in the levels model as well. The Durbin's *h* and Breusch-Godfrey LM tests found no evidence of autocorrelation. The results indicate a positive but nonsignificant relationship between decommodification and homicide rates from 1929 to 1995 regardless of whether levels (b = .147, α = .193) or first differences (b = .094, α = .652) are analyzed. Although these findings appear to contradict the notion that decommodification has a dampening effect on homicide rates, an index of fluctuations in annual expenditures on social welfare programming may not be the best means of conceptualizing temporal changes in levels of decommodification.

Aminzade (1992) and Griffin (1992) noted that it is important to properly conceptualize time when conducting historical research. In further explicating this idea, Isaac and Leicht (1997, p. 31) distinguished between temporally extensive and intensive analytic regimes. With the former, time units are used only to chronologically order observations and manipulate sample elements. This approach has been criticized for being ahistorical because models spanning long time periods are presented as causally invariant as well as theoretically and historically undifferentiated. In contrast, temporally intensive regimes treat time as central and as requiring theoretical justification. Isaac and Leicht identified two temporally intensive analytic regimes, but of particular interest here is the conceptualization of time as historical context. From this perspective, time is important in that different historical periods are presumed distinct in terms of their social structure and organization, which affect causal pathways. Historically differentiated periods are presumed to exhibit continuity within periods but discontinuity between periods.

Time as historical context pertains to decommodification as it is a macro-level process that changes the structure and organization of society as it results in a shift in the institutional balance of power as the state increasingly buffers changes in the economic realm. Because of its broad-sweeping, pervasive impact, we conceptualize decommodification as a contextual variable that not only affects homicide rates but also the manner in which other factors affect homicide rates. The implication is that different historical periods should be differentiated.

Central to the analysis is identifying the temporal transition points and determining the nature of causality within the different periods (Isaac & Leicht, 1997). Although the passage of decommodifying legislation began in the mid-1930s, most programs were not implemented until the late 1930s and early 1940s, at which time the United States was becoming involved in WWII. Theoretically and historically, WWII is better conceptualized as the end of the earlier era because the 1930s were marked by escalating conflict in Europe and increasing awareness of potential

U.S. involvement in the war. In addition, WWII has been credited with ending the severe economic depression of the 1930s. To test the notion that the end of WWII marked the transition, Chow breakpoint tests were performed controlling for immigration, divorce, cirrhosis deaths, and size of the youthful population. A lagged endogenous term was included to account for autocorrelation. To fully cover the period of interest, breakpoints from 1930 to 1950 were tested. The test statistics were significant ($\alpha = .05$) for every year from 1930 to 1950 for the levels model and for 1930 to 1946 for the differences model. Although the results do not point to a specific transition year, they do strongly support the notion that structural change occurred.

Next, we analyzed recursive regression models for the early period by starting in 1900 and adjusting the end date 1 year at a time from 1930 to 1950. The models were composed of variables found to be associated with homicide rates in previous research with consideration given to their historical relevance. Nonsignificant variables were eliminated from the models in an attempt to identify the best fitting model. Models were then compared in terms of model fit, coefficients, and autocorrelation in an attempt to empirically identify the best end date. This process was completed for both the early and late periods (with the start date being adjusted 1 year at a time from 1930 to 1950) and with both level and differenced measures. Although the results vary slightly, the best models for both periods (regardless of measure type) pointed to a transition at or toward the end of WWII. For the early period, the best fit was for end dates of 1945 and 1946 in levels and 1943 to 1945 in differences. For the late period, the best fit was for start dates of 1943 to 1951 in levels and 1944 to 1946 in differences.[11] Based on these findings, we differentiate between two historical periods: 1900 to 1945 and 1946 to 1997. This model is consistent with Brenner's (1976) research, which indicated a stronger relationship between economic trends and violence in the United States, Canada, England, Wales, and Scotland following WWII than before the war.[12]

Time as historical context implies continuity within but discontinuity between temporal periods, meaning the factors associated with homicide rates in one historical period are likely distinct from those in other periods (Isaac & Leicht, 1997). The association between a particular variable and homicide rates may be comparable in both periods, exist in only one period, or change directions across periods. In consideration of this, the historical relevance of variables found to be related to homicide rates in previous research was considered in constructing models. For example, Prohibition and mob violence involving bootlegging was expected to affect early 20th-century homicide rates but not late period rates. Conversely, divorce rates (as an indicator of social integration) were expected to have a stronger effect following WWII as divorce became a more common form of marital dissolution. In the early 1900s, divorces were rare, and marital dissolution often stemmed from abandonment or the death of a spouse from either natural or accidental causes. For each period, the best fitting model was developed, and nonsignificant variables were removed.

The results presented in Table 2 indicate a high degree of within period consensus for the differenced and level measure models. For the early period, a significant relationship was found in both models for unemployment, cirrhosis deaths, and an age structure variable. Similarly, the late period models both included cirrhosis deaths, immigration, and a lagged endogenous term. The greatest within period difference was found for the early period in that several factors were found to be associated with homicide rates in levels (i.e., immigration, prohibitionist legislation, mob murder activity, postwar period, percentage in military) but not in first differences. This may be a statistical artifact stemming more from the poorer quality of early 1900s data than real differences in the results yielded by level and differenced measures.

Of particular interest to this study are the between period differences as they allow an assessment of the impact of decommodification on homicide rates. Market events and fluctuations exert a constraining influence on individuals by effecting opportunities for labor force participation. At an aggregate level, the effects of shifting market forces should be reflected in trends in unemployment rates over time. In consideration of this, a positive unemployment-homicide relationship should exist in the early 1900s due to the absence of social welfare policies that would buffer the negative effects of economic downturns. However, the unemployment-homicide relationship should disappear following the implementation of decommodifying policies and programs as the harsher effects of economic fluctuations on society

TABLE 2
Least Squares Models Predicting 20th-Century Rates of Homicide in the United States Based on Both Level (Y_t) and Differenced (Y_{t-1}) Measures

	1900-1945		*1946-1997*	
	Y_t	Y_{t-1}	Y_t	Y_{t-1}
Intercept	23.891***	00.354*	–01.571***	00.009
Unemployment rates	.117***	.075**	–.091**	—
Cirrhosis death rates	.619***	.508**	.207***	.199*
Immigration rates	117.132***	—	310.614***	215.403**
Divorce rates	—	—	.497***	.626**
Prohibitionist legislation	.070***	—	—	—
Mob murders (dummy)	1.129***	—	—	—
Postwar period (dummy)	–.792*	—	—	—
Percentage of population in the armed forces	–18.748**	—	—	—
Percentage of population age 15 to 24	–134.722***	—	—	—
Percentage of population age 65 or older	—	–473.532**	—	—
Lagged endogenous term	—	–.402**	.616***	.390**
MA(3)	—	—	–.559***	—
Adjusted R^2	.896	.337	.983	.460
Durbin-Watson *d*	2.386	1.792	1.943	2.157
Durbin's *h*	—	.813	.241	.966
Breusch-Godfrey LM test (3 lags)				
F values	0.637	0.099	0.657	1.902
Obs*R^2	2.448	0.361	2.290	5.969
N	46	44	52	52

* Significant at $\alpha = .05$. ** Significant at $\alpha = .01$. *** Significant at $\alpha = .001$.

and individuals are absorbed and diminished by social welfare programs.

The results in Table 2 are consistent with these expectations in that rates of unemployment and homicide are positively related in the early period for both the level ($b = .117$, $\alpha = .001$) and differenced ($b = .075$, $\alpha = .01$) models. In both cases, the model fit is good with adjusted R^2 values of .896 and .337 in Columns 1 and 2, respectively.[13] For the levels model, the Durbin-Watson statistic is 2.386, which falls in the inconclusive region ($d_U = 2.22$, $d_L = 2.71$) and prevents rejection of the null hypothesis of no autocorrelation. However, the Q statistics and the Breusch-Godfrey LM test indicate no autocorrelation ($\alpha = .05$). For the differenced model, the Q statistics, Durbin's *h*, and the Breusch-Godfrey LM test all indicate no autocorrelation.[14] In contrast to the early period, the unemployment-homicide relationship in the late period becomes negative for the levels model ($b = -.091$, $\alpha = .05$) and disappears entirely for the differences model ($b = .009$, $\alpha = .86$). In both models, a lagged endogenous term was included to account for autocorrelation as well as a moving average (MA)(3) term[15] for the levels model. Also, adjusted R^2 values of .983 (levels) and .460 (differences) indicate good model fits.[16]

Although the absence of an unemployment effect for the 1945 to 1997 differences model supports institutional anomie theory, the negative effect in the levels models was unexpected. Insight can be gained by considering the nullifying effects of social welfare on unemployment in conjunction with the characteristics of homicide victims and offenders. Because decommodification is argued to affect homicide by ameliorating the harsh consequences of market fluctuations, its benefits should be greatest for adults who make up the bulk of the labor force and homicide victims and offenders. However, in recent decades, more young people have become involved in violent crimes (except for a slight late-1990s decline) (Regoli & Hewitt, 2000; Siegel & Senna, 2000; Zahn & McCall, 1999). Juveniles are less likely than adults to directly experience the impact of market events because most reside at home due to their minor status, are financially supported by parents, and do not participate extensively in the labor market. Thus, increasing juvenile violence may function to obscure, or mask, the effects of unemployment on homicide.

Recursive regression coefficients support this idea in that increases in juvenile violence rates occurred at approximately the same time the unemployment-homicide relationship became negative and significant.[17] Although the increase in juvenile violent offending began in 1983 to 1985, the surge was greatest from 1987 to 1994 when juvenile arrests for violent crime increased 79% but the juvenile population only increased 7% (Snyder, 1998; Snyder & Sickmund, 1999). The increase was even greater for juvenile murder arrests, which doubled between 1987 and 1993 (Snyder & Sickmund, 1999). Since 1994, juvenile violence has receded despite continued growth in the juvenile population (Snyder, 1998, Snyder & Sickmund, 1999). Although available data are insufficient for definitively assessing the youth violence effect on the unemployment-homicide relationship, entering juvenile murder rates into the equation for 1975 to 1995 eliminates the negative unemployment-homicide relationship.[18]

Rising levels of juvenile violence is not the only factor that may be contributing to a negative unemployment-homicide relationship in the mid-1980s. First, it was at this time homicides increasingly involved drug-related and unknown circumstances (Zahn & McCall, 1999).[19] Also, relatively low-unemployment levels in the 1980s tended to obscure high-nonemployment levels as greater numbers of working age males dropped out of the labor force entirely (Carlson & Michalowski, 1997; Currie, 1997).[20] Finally, post-WWII changes in the gender composition of the labor force may affect the unemployment-homicide relationship. To the extent that both primarily involve males, a diminishing relationship would be expected as more females joined the labor force and, as a result, comprised a greater portion of both the employed and unemployed.[21]

Alternative Model of Periodization

An alternative model of periodization was recently proposed by Carlson and Michalowski (1997) based on phases of capitalist development (i.e., exploration, consolidation, and decay) that are argued to differentially affect the nature of social institutions and social relations in society. In their study of unemployment and crime, Carlson and Michalowski identified four contextually distinct temporal periods corresponding to these phases between 1933 and 1992 during which there was variation in the strength and direction of the unemployment-crime relationship. To identify the most accurate model of historical contextual effects, we examined the homicide-unemployment relationship during each of the four periods.

Bivariate analyses largely replicate their findings in that the unemployment-homicide relationship was positive and weak ($b = .167$, $\alpha = .000$) during exploration (1933-1947), nonsignificant ($b = -.115$, $\alpha = .211$) during consolidation (1948-1966), positive and weak-moderate ($b = .329$, $\alpha = .020$) during decay (1967-1979), and nonsignificant ($b = -.034$, $\alpha = .854$) but in the expected direction during recent exploration (1980-1992). However, as Jensen (2000) found in his study of Prohibition, alcohol, and murder, conclusions based on bivariate analyses may be erroneous because they fail to take into account the potential effects of counterveiling causal influences. Therefore, it is important to include other potentially relevant variables in regression modeling because they may affect the impact of other variables. In fact, in a later unemployment-imprisonment study, Michalowski and Carlson (1999) also included controls for other factors that might affect imprisonment even though the effect of unemployment during the aforementioned periods was of particular interest. When we included controls for immigration, divorce, and cirrhosis deaths,[22] the unemployment-homicide relationship remained positive and significant during early exploration ($b = .338$, $\alpha = .001$) but became nonsignificant for the latter three periods: $b = .057$ ($\alpha = .118$) for 1948 to 1966, $b = -.107$ ($\alpha = .457$) for 1967 to 1979, and $b = -.045$ ($\alpha = .788$) for 1980 to 1992. The absence of significant unemployment effects in the latter three periods indicates continuity during this span of time rather than discontinuity.

In addition to examining the direction and significance of the unemployment coefficient, we also performed Chow breakpoint tests, which test for structural change in a model by comparing the sum of squared residuals obtained from fitting a single equation for the sample period (e.g., 1900-1997) with those from separate equations (e.g., 1900-1945, 1946-1997). In both Carlson and Michalowski (1997) and the present study, Chow tests support the model of periodization proposed. However, we urge caution in interpreting these results based on our finding that almost every potential breakpoint was significant.[23] The limitations of Chow breakpoint tests are not well documented, but the test requires advance knowledge of the breakpoint (Calkin, 1999; Hansen, 2001). It is possible that the test requires a more precise breakpoint than is possible to identify in a discussion of long-term changes in the structure and organization of society. Although social scientists attempt to identify precise times at which change occurs, in reality, societal change is something that tends to be more gradual. Another limitation is that the Chow test assumes the error terms are normally distributed, homoskedastic, and the same for all models (Greene, 1993; Gujarati, 1988). Interestingly, if the parameters are expected to differ across models, the error term variance is not likely to be the same for each equation, which is problematic for the results. Furthermore, the Chow test does not shed light on whether model differences stem from changes in the intercepts, coefficients, or the error term variance.

Our findings concerning periodization have two important implications. First, the results indicate that at least in violence studies, the post-WWII period is better conceptualized as a single historical era than as three developmentally distinct eras. Second, the significant positive effect of unemployment for 1933 to 1947 is consistent with results from our early 20th-century model. Although we agree a turning point was reached in the mid-1940s, marking the transition to a new era, we argue that the turning point initiating this period occurred prior to 1933. Although 1933 ended Prohibition, the economic structure was largely unchanged with the United States in the midst of the Great Depression at this time. Although some social welfare programs were enacted in the early to mid-1930s, many were not implemented until later. In the earlier 1900s, before the onset of the depression, the economy was growing but largely stable as industrial modes of production increasingly dominated the urban landscape and agriculturally based work diminished. In consideration of this continuity, we suggest a turning point denoting the start of this era that is closer to the turn of the 20th century.[24] This is further supported by the finding that the effect of unemployment is positive in the early 1900s whether time is defined as a single period (1900-1945, 1900-1947) or as two periods (1900-1932, 1933-1947).

CONCLUSIONS

This study has attempted to assess claims made by institutional anomie theorists that decommodification has a dampening effect on lethal violence due to its stabilizing influences on the larger social structure of society, which result in a shift in the institutional balance of power and a reduction in economic dominance. Although Messner and Rosenfeld (1997b) and, more recently, Savolainen (2000) found support for this perspective in their cross-national analyses, our goal was to evaluate the relevance of the theory for explaining variation over time. Toward that end, we assessed the impact of decommodification on violence in the United States by studying the relationship between homicide and both unemployment and social welfare program expenditures during the 20th century. Our findings indicate that the conceptualization and modeling of temporal variation in decommodification is important in understanding its impact on lethal violence rates over time.

There are different ways of conceptualizing time in studies of historical change. Due to its pervasive impact on the larger social structure and organization of society, decommodification was conceptualized as a contextual and historically variant factor; the effects of which were captured by differentiating between historical periods, or analytic regimes, and then allowing causal structures to vary across them. This approach is consistent with Isaac and Leicht (1997) who noted, "Historically differentiated periods . . . [may be] grounded in particular institutional configurations" (p. 31). We also found empirical support in that the homicide models were characterized by continuity within periods, as indicated by good model fits, and discontinuity between periods, suggesting the presence of a turning point. Of particular interest was the shift in the unemployment-homicide relationship between the two temporal regimes, distinguished by their level of decommodification.

Attempts to test an alternative mode of periodization, specified by Carlson and Michalowski (1997) in a recent study of the unemployment-crime relationship, lend further empirical support to our model of two contextually distinct historical periods. Our failure to find significant differences in the unemployment-homicide relationship during the latter three Fordist periods (i.e., 1948-1966, 1967-1979, 1980-1992) suggests continuity during this time rather than discontinuity marked by historical contingencies. Furthermore, our analyses suggest the first Fordist period (1933-1947) would be better conceptualized as beginning in the early 20th century based on the positive unemployment-homicide relationship from 1900 to 1945.

Although our findings support institutional anomic theory when decommodification is conceptualized as a contextual factor that affects the social structure and organization of society, more intricate analyses of temporal variation in decommodification and homicide rates were less supportive. More specific, in analyses of the decommodification index used by Messner and Rosenfeld (1997b) and Savolainen (2000), no relationship was detected between changing levels of decommodification and homicide rates, regardless of whether level or differenced measures were analyzed. Also, although not reported here, alternative measures of annual variation in decommodification were examined to determine if particular types of social welfare programming affected homicide rates more or less than others.[25] When the effects of each program (i.e., social insurance, veterans' benefits, health and medical care, public aid, housing assistance, unemployment and workers' compensation, OASDI) were examined separately, few significant relationships were identified, and there was no consistent pattern to the results.

In Messner and Rosenfeld's (1997b) cross-national study, the decommodification-homicide relationship was heavily dependent on the inclusion of the United States. When this is considered in conjunction with the failure of the present study to find strong decommodification effects in more intricate time-series analyses of homicide, it suggests limitations for either institutional anomie theory or measures of decommodification. Although more precise measures may be able to detect societal level differences at one point in time, they may be inappropriate for measuring temporal changes in decommodification levels within a society, which are likely to be more subtle and less apparent in both intricate analyses and shorter spans of time. Instead, studies of temporal change in decommodification will have to view it as a large-scale social process, influencing the very structure and organization of society.[26] A second possibility is that institutional anomie theory may not be particularly applicable to violence. Although it has been applied to homicide, Messner and Rosenfeld (1997a, 1997b) originally postulated it as a theory of crime. Some researchers argue that crime and violence are distinct phenomena requiring unique explanations (Zimring & Hawkins, 1997). However, it should be noted that Savolainen (2000) recently found support for an institutional anomie approach to studying homicide.

Although we have focused on changes in the unemployment-homicide relationship across periods as evidence of the impact of decommodification, there were other homicide correlates as well. In the early 1900s, homicide rates were associated with immigration, unemployment, prohibitionist legislation, alcohol consumption (i.e., cirrhosis death rates), mob violence, postwar periods, population age structure, and percentage in the armed forces.

Following WWII and the implementation of decommodifying social policies, several factors drop from the model including postwar periods, population age structure, armed forces participation, mob violence, and prohibitionist legislation. Although immigration and cirrhosis deaths continue as correlates, the effect of unemployment shifts, and divorce rates enter the model.

The temporal shift in homicide correlates coincides with developments in criminological theory. Pre-WWII theories (Merton, 1938; Sutherland, 1939) tended to focus on economic factors and social class in the explanation of crime and delinquency. By the late 1950s (Nye, 1958) and 1960s (Burgess & Akers, 1966; Hirschi, 1969), theory and research were shifting to the family and family breakdown. By the mid-1970s, social control and social-learning theories were gaining popularity, both stressing family relationships and discounting economic and class variables. More recently, Agnew's (1992) reformulated strain theory focuses on anger from family conflict rather than structurally induced economic change.

We focus on homicide because it is central to Messner and Rosenfeld's (1997b) study and because it is one of the few violence measures for which fairly valid and reliable data are available from the early 20th century. However, it is important to keep in mind that national-level data likely obscure some important facets of the impact of decommodification on violence rates that might be detected if city-, county-, or state-level data (for example) were available. To the extent that these data are available, investigating these issues is an important avenue for future research.

A second potential direction for future research involves the integrated homicide-suicide theory recently revitalized by Unnithan, Huff-Corzine, Corzine, and Whitt (1994), which suggests homicide and suicide rates are related through two sets of causal mechanisms. Although forces of production affect the total number of homicides and suicides in a society, forces of direction affect the expression of lethal violence, or the risk of homicide relative to suicide. One avenue for future research would be to investigate trends in the homicide-suicide relationship and the impact (if any) of decommodifying social policies and programs on suicide rates as well as homicide rates.

NOTES

1. Messner and Rosenfeld (1997b) use the term *decommodification*, but others have also considered the impact of post-WWII economic trends and institutional changes on crime rates, such as Cappell and Sykes (1991); LaFree, Drass, and O'Day (1992); and LaFree (1998).

2. For more information on violence-economic distress research, see Carlson and Michalowski (1997), Chiricos (1987), Messner and Rosenfeld (1999), and K.F. Parker, McCall, and Land (1999).

3. We focus on the impact of decommodification on homicide rates to (a) assess the applicability of institutional anomie theory to violence and (b) facilitate comparisons with Messner and Rosenfeld (1997b) who also examined homicide rates in a cross-national test of this theory. However, the emphasis on shifting market forces and the impact of economic distress on social conditions could readily be applied to property crime rates, and assessing the applicability of institutional anomie theory to historical trends in both property and violent crimes would be a fruitful avenue of investigation.

4. In general, early 1900s data are problematic in that (a) they did not become fully national until 1933 and there are often inconsistencies (b) over time from coding procedure changes and (c) across jurisdictions from differences in the training, funding, and practices of the local offices from which the data originate. For a more complete review of homicide data quality issues, see Cantor and Cohen (1980), Rand (1993), Riedel (1999), and Zahn and McCall (1999).

5. Vital Statistics homicides are slightly higher than Uniform Crime Reports figures because the National Center for Health Statistics (NCHS) uses a medical (as opposed to legal) definition of homicide, which includes justifiable homicides (i.e., peace officer or private citizen killing a person committing a felony). Justifiable homicides cannot be distinguished from criminal homicides prior to 1949. However, they account for a very small proportion of homicides, and rates plotted from both sources are highly correlated (i.e., Pearson's $r = .98$ for 1936-1975) (Cantor & Cohen, 1980, p. 133).

6. Eckberg (1995) identified three potential problems with estimating national homicide rates from death registration area data. First, the models for the earliest years may have large error terms and lack precision due to the small number of states on which they are based. However, even the weakest models have substantial predictive power because the death registration area data are not independent of national data. Second, forecast estimates closer to the period on which the equation is based are more accurate because they rely on fewer interim estimates. Although caution should be used, Eckberg argued that early estimates are more accurate than the unadjusted data. Third, undercounting is a problem because homicides and suicides were often counted as accidental deaths if local authorities had insufficient information.

7. NCHS data for each year between 1933 and 1992 were extracted from annual Vital Statistics of the United States reports corresponding to each year, which are compiled by the NCHS (formerly known as the National Office of Vital Statistics) and published by the Public Health Service in Washington, D.C. Data for 1993 to 1997 were extracted from the data warehouse section of the NCHS Web site (http://www.cdc.gov/nchs/datawh).

8. Note that one problem with unit root tests is a bias against rejecting the null hypothesis of nonstationarity and the presence of a unit root (Davidson & MacKinnon, 1993; Kwiatkowski, Phillips, Schmidt, & Shin, 1992).

9. When the number of observations multiplied by the standard error of the lagged term squared exceeds one, Durbin's *h* is not a valid test for serial correlation. This was only a problem for the Y_t model (1.25) in Table 1. (See Ostrom, 1990, for more information.)

10. Attempts to account for autocorrelation with substantive variables were unsuccessful, likely, because structural change occurred during 1929 and 1995 making it difficult (if not impossible) to identify variables with constant effect for the entire period.

11. The adjusted R^2 values for the early period were .896 for both 1945 and 1946 (levels) and .341 (1943), .340 (1944), and .337 (1945) (differences). For the late period, the values ranged from .978 to .980 (1943-1951) (levels) and were .478 (1944), .478 (1945), and .459 (1946) (differences).

12. A 1960 breakpoint was also tested because of improvements in data quality. The Chow results were significant, but fits for pre- and post-1960 models were not as strong as those for the 1946 breakpoint. As is later discussed, we urge caution with the Chow test results.

13. It is not uncommon for models based on levels to have high R^2 values; they should be interpreted cautiously. See Davidson and MacKinnon (1993) and Hibbs (1974).

14. To determine if the early homicide rate model was affected by combining data from Eckberg (1995) and NCHS, which could have distinct error structures, a dummy was included in the model (0 = 1933-1945, 1 = 1900-1932). The results indicate no evidence of imputation effects for Eckberg's estimates in that the dummy was nonsignificant and the model fit and autocorrelation tests remained largely unchanged in both levels and differences.

15. Ostrom (1990) argued that higher order moving average (MA) processes are quite rare. However, in models without the MA(3) term, Durbin's h ($h = 1.904$), the Breusch-Godfrey LM test ($F = 3.357$, Obs*$R^2 = 9.868$), and the Q statistics found autocorrelation at the 3-year lag at $\alpha = .05$ but not at $\alpha = .01$. Based on these findings, we include an MA(3) term but note that the coefficients and model fit ($R^2 = .979$) are unchanged when it is excluded from the model.

16. We also examine business failure rates, expecting the relationship with homicide rates to be similar to unemployment as both are indicators of market force trends. The results are similar in that the effect of business failure rates in the early period was positive ($b = .018$, $\alpha = .01$) for the levels model, and although the coefficient was positive for the differences model ($b = .007$, $\alpha = .118$), it was nonsignificant. In the late period, business failure rates (like unemployment rates) exhibited a negative relationship in the levels model ($b = -.004$, $\alpha = .05$) and a negative, but nonsignificant, relationship in the differences model ($b = -.005$, $\alpha = .293$). In sum, alternative market force indicators yield similar results.

17. The E-views (2001) recursive coefficients make it possible to observe changes in the relationship between two variables over time controlling for the effects of other regressors. For 1946 to 1997, the recursive coefficients indicate no unemployment-homicide relationship until the early to mid-1980s, at which time the relationship became negative and statistically significant.

18. Although positive, the juvenile murder rate coefficient is not significant. In addition to unemployment, cirrhosis rates also become nonsignificant. Importantly, these findings should be viewed with caution as they are based on an abbreviated sample (1975-1995) that lacks theoretically and historically meaningful temporal bounds due to data availability.

19. To test this notion, drug-related arrest rates were entered into the equation. In levels, total ($b = -.002$, $\alpha = .067$), juvenile ($b = -.002$, $\alpha = .190$), and adult ($b = -.002$, $\alpha = .127$) arrest rates nullified the impact of unemployment, but contrary to expectations, their impact was negative (and almost significant for total rates). The same results were found with differenced measures.

20. To test this notion, we included percentage of population not in the labor force for all persons and young males (16 and older, 20 and older, respectively). In both levels and differences, the effect was nonsignificant.

21. To test this idea, we included male and female unemployment rates in the model. Both male ($b = .077$, $\alpha = .05$) and female ($b = -.094$, $\alpha = .05$) unemployment rates had negative effects on homicide in levels indicating no support. The model fits were largely unchanged.

22. The same controls were used for all four periods (a) because of the overlap between our second period and Carlson and Michalowski's (1997) last three periods and (b) as a means of including some controls in the first period without adding all of the factors we had identified as relevant for the early period, which would severely damage the statistical integrity of the model.

23. The Chow test results supported the models of structural change proposed by both Carlson and Michalowski (1997) (1933-1947, 1948-1966, 1967-1979, 1980-1992) and the present study (1900-1945, 1946-1997). To enhance our understanding of the breakpoints, we replicated their results using 1933 to 1992 data and tested the significance of the breakpoints between each period as well as breakpoints for 5 years in either direction. For example, breakpoints from 1943 to 1953 were tested for the period 1933 to 1966. The results were far from clear in that all the breakpoints were at least partially significant ($\alpha = .05$ for either the *F* or *LR* statistic). The results were the same for 1948 to 1979 in testing for 1962 to 1972 breakpoints; all were significant. For 1966 to 1992, breakpoints at 1975 to 1981 were nonsignificant but were significant for 1983 to 1985. These results are based on levels, but similar results were obtained with differenced measures. As noted earlier, several of the breakpoints tested to differentiate between the two periods we proposed were also significant. In consideration of these findings, we urge caution in interpreting the Chow results of both studies.

24. We use 1900 as a starting point, but a few years before or after 1900 may be more appropriate. However, the absence of reliable data makes it virtually impossible to study national trends prior to 1900.

25. It could be hypothesized that programs (e.g., unemployment, workers' compensation, veterans' benefits) benefiting high-homicide risk groups (i.e., young males) might dampen violence rates more than those (i.e., old-age, survivors', and disability insurance; Medicare) primarily benefiting low-risk groups (i.e., elderly, children, disabled). Conversely, more general programs providing health and medical care and housing assistance, for example, may be hypothesized to have a greater impact on violence because they benefit a larger segment of society. Programs that elevate the standard of living of those most in need benefit the individual as well as the larger society by alleviating pressure on persons who would typically provide care for needy children and aged parents, for example. Furthermore, they diminish the financial and social hardships that society would incur if these groups were to slide farther into poverty (e.g., homelessness, malnutrition and starvation, death and disease). To assess these ideas, the effects of two variables (i.e., expenditures as percentage of gross domestic product, per capita expenditures) were examined in separate equations (1945-1995) for each program type. As noted, few significant relationships were identified, and there was no consistent pattern to the results.

26. Other decommodification measures were also examined including regressing social welfare expenditures on gross domestic product and then using the residuals as an indicator of relatively low (or high) expenditures given the state of the economy. The residuals slightly improved the model fit but were nonsignificant. In a similar vein, social welfare expenditures were regressed on unemployment to identify times of relatively low expenditures given unemployment rates. The residual measures suppressed the unemployment effect but were nonsignificant and only slightly improved the model fit.

REFERENCES

Agnew, R. (1992). Foundations for a general strain theory of crime and delinquency. *Criminology, 30*, 47-87.

Aminzade, R. (1992). Historical sociology and time. *Sociological Methods and Research, 20*, 456-480.

Batton, C. (1999). *The stream analogy: An historical study of lethal violence rates from the perspective of the integrated homicide-suicide model*. Unpublished doctoral dissertation, Vanderbilt University.

Blau, P., & Golden, R. (1986). Metropolitan structure and criminal violence. *Sociological Quarterly, 27*, 15-26.

Brenner, H. (1976). *Effects of the economy on criminal behaviour and the administration of criminal justice in the United States, Canada, England and Wales and Scotland*. Rome: United Nations Social Defense Research Institute.

Burgess, R., & Akers, R. (1966). A differential association-reinforcement theory of criminal behavior. *Social Problems, 14*, 128-147.

Calkin, D. (1999). *Historic resource production from USDA Forest Service northern and intermountain regional lands* (PNW-RN-540). Retrieved September 7, 2001, from the U.S. Department of Agriculture, Forest Service Web site: www.fs.fed.us/pnw/pubs/rn_540.pdf

Cantor, D., & Cohen, L. (1980). Comparing measures of homicide trends: Methodological and substantive differences in the Vital Statistics and Uniform Crime Report time series (1933-1975). *Social Science Research, 9*, 121-145.

Cappell, C., & Sykes, G. (1991). Prison commitments, crime, and unemployment: A theoretical and empirical specification for the United States, 1933-1985. *Journal of Quantitative Criminology, 7*, 155-199.

Carlson, S., & Michalowski, R. (1997). Crime, unemployment, and social structures or accumulation: An inquiry into historical contingency. *Justice Quarterly, 14*, 209-239.

Cashman, S. (1981). *Prohibition: The lie of the land*. New York: Free Press.

Chiricos, T. G. (1987). Rates of crime and unemployment: An analysis of aggregate research evidence. *Social Problems, 34*, 187-212.

Cook, P., & Tauchen, G. (1982). The effects of liquor taxes on heavy drinking. *Bell Journal of Economics, 13*, 379-390.

Currie, E. (1997). Market, crime, and community: Toward a mid-range theory of post industrial violence. *Theoretical Criminology, 1*, 147-172.

Davidson, R., & MacKinnon, J. (1993). *Estimation and inference in econometrics*. New York: Oxford University Press.

Department of Veterans' Affairs. (2000). *A history of supporting veterans*. Retrieved June 6, 2000, from www.va.gov/About_VA/history/vafhis.htm

E-views (Version 4.0) [Computer software]. (2001). Irvine, CA: Quantitative Micro Software.

Eckberg, D. (1995). Estimates of early twentieth-century U.S. homicide rates: An econometric forecasting approach. *Demography, 32*, 1-16.

Esping-Andersen, G. (1990).*The three worlds of welfare capitalism*. Princeton, NJ: Princeton University Press.

Gartner, R. (1990). The victims of homicide: A temporal and cross-national comparison. *American Sociological Review, 55*, 92-106.

Goode, E. (1994). *Deviant behavior* (4th ed.). Englewood Cliffs, NJ: Prentice Hall.

Greene, W. (1993). *Econometric analysis* (2nd ed.). New York: Macmillan.

Griffin, L. (1992). Temporality, events, and explanation in historical sociology. *Sociological Methods and Research, 20*, 403-427.

Gujarati, D. (1988). *Basic econometrics* (2nd ed.). New York: McGraw-Hill.

Gurr, T. R. (1981). Historical trends in violent crime: A critical review of the evidence. In M. Tonry & N. Morris (Eds.), *Crime and justice: An annual review of research, Vol. 3* (pp. 295-353). Chicago: University of Chicago Press.

Gurr, T. R. (1989). Historical trends in violent crime: Europe and the United States. In T. R. Gurr (Ed.), *Violence in America: The history of crime* (pp. 21-54). Newbury Park, CA: Sage.

Hansen, B. (2001). The new econometrics of structural change: Dating breaks in U.S. labor productivity. *Journal of Economic Perspectives*. Retrieved September 7, 2001, from www.ssc.wisc.edu/~bhansen/papers/breaks.pdf

Hansmann, H., & Quigley, J. (1982). Population heterogeneity and the sociogenesis of homicide. *Social Forces, 61*, 206-224.

Hibbs, D. (1974). Problems of statistical estimation and causal inference in time-series regression models. In American Sociological Association (Ed.), *Sociological methodology* (pp. 252-308). San Francisco: Jossey-Bass.

Hirschi, T. (1969). *Causes of delinquency*. Berkeley: University of California Press.

Isaac, L., & Leicht, K. (1997). Regimes of power and the power of analytic regimes: Explaining U.S. military procurement Keynesianism as historical process. *Historical Methods, 30*, 28-45.

Jensen, G. (1997). Time and social history: Problems of atemporality in historical analyses with illustrations from research on early modern witch hunts. *Historical Methods, 30*, 46-57.

Jensen, G. (2000). Prohibition, alcohol, and murder: Untangling countervailing mechanisms. *Homicide Studies, 4*, 18-36.

Kposowa, A., & Breault, K. (1993). Reassessing the structural covariates of U.S. homicide rates. *Sociological Focus, 26*, 27-46.

Kwiatkowski, D., Phillips, P., Schmidt, P., & Shin, Y. (1992). Testing the null hypothesis of stationarity against the alternative of a unit root: How sure are we that economic time series have a unit root? *Journal of Econometrics, 54*, 159-178.

LaFree, G. (1998). *Losing legitimacy: Street crime and the decline of social institutions in America*. Boulder, CO: Westview.

LaFree, G., Drass, K., & O'Day, P. (1992). Race and crime in postwar America: Determinants of African-American and White rates, 1957-1988. *Criminology, 30*, 157-188.

Land, K., McCall, P., & Cohen, L. (1990). Structural covariates of homicide rates: Are there any invariates across time and social space? *American Journal of Sociology, 95*, 922-963.

Lane, R. (1999). *Violent death in the city: Suicide, accident, and murder in nineteenth century Philadelphia*. Cambridge, MA: Harvard University Press.

Levine, H. G., & Reinarman, C. (1991). From Prohibition to regulation: Lessons from alcohol policy for drug policy. *Milbank Quarterly, 69*, 461-494.

Merton, R. (1938). Social structure and anomie. *American Sociological Review, 3*, 672-682.

Merton, R. (1968). *Social theory and social structure*. New York: Free Press.

Messner, S., & Golden, R. (1992). Racial inequality and racially disaggregated homicide rates: An assessment of alternative theoretical explanations. *Criminology, 30*, 421-445.

Messner, S., & Rosenfeld, R. (1997a). *Crime and the American dream*. Belmont, CA: Wadsworth.

Messner, S., & Rosenfeld, R. (1997b). Political restraint of the market and levels of criminal homicide: A cross-national application of institutional anomie theory. *Social Forces, 75*, 1393-1416.

Messner, S., & Rosenfeld, R. (1999). Social structure and homicide: Theory and research. In M. D. Smith & M. A. Zahn (Eds.), *Homicide: A sourcebook of social research* (pp. 27-41). Thousand Oaks, CA: Sage.

Michalowski, R., & Carlson, S. (1999). Unemployment, imprisonment, and social structures of accumulation: Historical contingency in the Rusche-Kircheimer hypothesis. *Criminology, 37*, 217-249.

Miron, J., & Zwiebel, J. (1991). Alcohol consumption during Prohibition. *Economics and Drugs, 81*, 242-247.

Nye, I. (1958). *Family relationships and delinquent behavior.* New York: John Wiley.

Ostrom, C. (1990). *Time series analysis: Regression techniques.* Newbury Park, CA: Sage.

Parker, K. F., McCall, P. L., & Land, K. C. (1999). Determining social structural predictors of homicide: Units of analysis and related methodological concerns. In M. D. Smith & M. A. Zahn (Eds.), *Homicide: A sourcebook of social research* (pp. 107-124). Thousand Oaks, CA: Sage.

Parker, R. N. (1995). *Alcohol and homicide: A deadly combination of two American traditions.* Albany: State University of New York Press.

Rand, M. R. (1993). The study of homicide caseflow: Creating a comprehensive homicide data set. In C. R. Block & R. L. Block (Eds.), *Questions and answers in lethal and non-lethal violence: Proceedings of the Homicide Research Working Group* (pp. 103-118). Washington, DC: Government Printing Office.

Regoli, R., & Hewitt, J. (2000). *Delinquency in society.* Boston: McGraw-Hill.

Riedel, M. (1990). Nationwide homicide data sets: An evaluation of the Uniform Crime Reports and National Center for Health Statistics data. In D. L. MacKenzie, P. J. Baunach, & R. R. Roberg (Eds.), *Measuring crime: Large-scale, long-range efforts* (pp. 175-208). Albany: State University of New York Press.

Riedel, M. (1999). Sources of homicide data: A review and comparison. In M. D. Smith & M. A. Zahn (Eds.), *Homicide: A sourcebook of social research* (pp. 75-95). Thousand Oaks, CA: Sage.

Savolainen, J. (2000). Inequality, welfare state, and homicide: Further support for the institutional anomie theory. *Criminology, 38*, 1021-1042.

Siegel, L., & Senna, J. (2000). *Juvenile delinquency: Theory, practice, and law* (7th ed.). Belmont, CA: Wadsworth.

Snyder, H. (1998). *Juvenile arrests 1997* (NCJ173938). Washington, DC: Office of Juvenile Justice and Delinquency Prevention.

Snyder, H., & Sickmund, M. (1999). *Juvenile offenders and victims: 1999 national report* (NCJ178257). Washington, DC: Office of Juvenile Justice and Delinquency Prevention.

Social Security Administration. (1997). *Social Security programs in the United States.* Washington, DC: Government Printing Office.

Social Security Administration. (2000). *What is the history of the Social Security system in the United States?* Retrieved June 4, 2000, from www.ssa.gov/policy/pubs/BGP/bgphistory.html

Sutherland, E. (1939). *Principles of criminology.* Philadelphia: J.B. Lippincott.

U.S. Bureau of the Census. (1931). *Marriage and divorce 1929: Statistics of marriages, divorces, and annulments of marriage.* Washington, DC: Government Printing Office.

U.S. Bureau of the Census. (1975). *Historical statistics of the United States, colonial times to 1970, bicentennial edition.* Washington, DC: Government Printing Office.

Unnithan, P., Huff-Corzine, L., Corzine, J., & Whitt, H. (1994). *The currents of lethal violence: An integrated model of suicide and homicide.* Albany: State University of New York Press.

Urdang, L. (1996). *The timetables of American history.* New York: Simon & Schuster.

Wood, C. (1926). *A criticism of national Prohibition.* Washington, DC: Association Against the Prohibition Amendment Incorporated.

Zahn, M. A., & McCall, P. L. (1999). Trends and patterns of homicide in the 20th-century United States. In M. D. Smith & M. A. Zahn (Eds.), *Homicide: A sourcebook of social research* (pp. 9-23). Thousand Oaks, CA: Sage.

Zimring, F., & Hawkins, G. (1997). *Crime is not the problem: Lethal violence in America.* New York: Oxford University Press.

Candice Batton *is an assistant professor in the Department of Criminal Justice at the University of Nebraska–Omaha. Her research interests are in the area of lethal violence, both homicide and suicide. Of particular interest are historical trends in lethal violence rates. Her work on lethal violence has appeared in* Homicide Studies, Criminology, *and* Deviant Behavior.

Gary Jensen *is a professor of sociology at Vanderbilt University. He specializes in empirical tests of theories of deviance and control and is currently studying variations in (a) early modern witch hunts, (b) international homicide rates, and (c) the social ecology of gangs.*

[14]

SOCIAL ALTRUISM AND CRIME*

MITCHELL B. CHAMLIN
University of Cincinnati

JOHN K. COCHRAN
University of South Florida

Drawing on the theoretical statements of Braithwaite (1989), Cullen (1994), Messner and Rosenfeld (1994), this research examines the influence of social altruism on the level of crime for a sample of U.S. cities. The multivariate analyses clearly indicate that the ratio of contributions to the United Way to aggregate city income, a behavioral approximation of the cultural value of altruism, is inversely related to property and violent crime rates. The implications of these findings for the reduction of crime are discussed.

Most macro-social theories of crime can be thought of as embracing either one of two basic conceptual insights to explain and predict variations in rates of crime. The first, which we refer to as the motivational insight, recognizes that various structural and cultural conditions can set into motion causal processes that motivate members of particular groups or strata to disproportionately engage in criminal behavior. Specifically, the failure of conventional society to provide sufficient legitimate avenues to secure culturally defined success goals (Cloward, 1959; Merton, 1938), the frustration produced by ascribed inequalities (Blau, 1994; Blau and Blau, 1982), adherence to a subcultural value system that condones the use of force to settle interpersonal disputes (Curtis, 1975; Gastil, 1971; Hackney, 1969), as well as the dehumanizing effects of capitalism (Bonger, 1916), have all been variously identified as generating macro-social motivations for crime.

The second conceptual insight, which we refer to as the opportunity insight, recognizes that the social and physical structures of ecological units can affect crime rates by influencing the attractiveness of potential targets to motivated offenders. For example, the social control variant of opportunity theory focuses on the interrelationships among community characteristics, informal social control, and target attractiveness. Ostensibly, structural conditions that impede communication and the formation of

* We would like to thank Frank Cullen, John Wooldredge, Paul Mazerolle, Kenneth Land, and the anonymous reviewers for their input and Linda Naiditch, Director of Market Information and Analysis for the United Way of America, for her assistance.

affective interpersonal relationships within communities inhibit the creation and maintenance of local institutions that could strengthen the level of informal social control, thereby increasing rates of crime and delinquency (Bursik and Grasmick, 1993; Kornhauser, 1978; Sampson and Wilson, 1995; Shaw and McKay, 1969).

Alternatively, environmental opportunity theories focus on the interrelationships among the social and physical ecology of communities, the day-to-day activities of individuals, and the distribution of crime. Accordingly, the concern is not so much with how the social structure affects local institutions, but rather how specific features of a community's infrastructure, as well as the structure of social relations, affects the convergence in time and space of potential offenders and targets of crime (Brantingham and Brantingham, 1991; Cohen and Felson, 1979; Felson, 1994; Newman, 1971).

Currently, one can begin to discern the emergence of a third insight that has the potential to extend the understanding of the relationship between social conditions and crime beyond that provided by traditional macro-social motivational and opportunity theories of crime—the social altruism insight. *Social altruism*, as we define it, refers to the willingness of communities to commit scarce resources to the aid and comfort of their members, distinct from the beneficence of the state (see Piliavin and Charng, 1990; Simmons, 1991).

Empirically, we hypothesize that social altruism varies inversely with crime. To be sure, this is not a novel idea (Angell, 1942, 1947). Indeed, as we discuss below, we believe that the concept of social altruism is a synthetic term that can be used to organize, and subject to empirical evaluation, a common theme that is integral to the recent theoretical contributions of Braithwaite (1989), Cullen (1994), and Messner and Rosenfeld (1994).

SOCIAL ALTRUISM AS AN ORGANIZING CONSTRUCT

In *Crime, Shame, and Reintegration*, Braithwaite (1989) advances the idea that variations in crime rates are inextricably tied to the manner in which communities respond to law violations. At one end of the continuum, communities that engage in punishment strategies that tend to isolate, dehumanize, and otherwise stigmatize offenders also tend to exacerbate the crime problem. Ostensibly, societal reactions of this sort (disintegrative shaming) minimize the deterrent effects of punishment by inadvertently destroying mutual bonds of respect and caring that promote repentance and a return to conformity. As a result, disintegrative shaming tends to solidify the criminal self-concept, increase the attractiveness of criminal subcultures, and thereby, increase the rate of illegal behavior (Braithwaite, 1989:54–55, 1993).

At the other end of the punishment continuum, communities that engage in reintegrative shaming—formal and informal sanctioning, followed by overt efforts to reaccept transgressors into conventional society—are expected to experience relatively low rates of crime. When punishment admonishes the offense rather than the offender, much like that which occurs within the family setting, feelings of guilt, embarrassment, and a desire to reform are likely to ensue. Hence, the more a community punishes in a manner that reinforces, rather than destroys, interdependencies among individuals, the more it will enjoy lower rates of crime (Braithwaite, 1989:56–68).

Our primary interest in Braithwaite's approach, however, is not with the relationship between the styles of social control and crime rates, but rather with the social conditions that produce differential patterns of social control. According to Braithwaite (1989), the likelihood that a community's social control practices will tend to resemble one form of shaming instead of another is determined in no small part by the cultural context in which it operates. Specifically, social systems that foster values that teach their members that they have social and moral obligations to others above and beyond those produced by self-motivated relationships of social exchange (communitarian societies), are most likely to exercise reintegrative shaming. Within such communities reintegrative shaming is likely to occur because those enforcing social norms, as well as the offender, maintain a stake in the latter's continued participation in the community (Braithwaite, 1989, 1993; Makkai and Braithwaite, 1994).

In contrast, social systems that promulgate values that encourage the pursuit of particularistic interests (individualistic societies) are most likely to rely on disintegrative shaming to control crime. According to Braithwaite (1989:86–87), individualistic societies tend to disrupt the informal networks that facilitate the use of reintegrative shaming techniques. Consequently, they must rely on the coercive power of the state to sanction offenders in ways that, more often than not, stigmatize and isolate them from conventional society.

Thus, the theory of reintegrative shaming clearly implicates the cultural climate of the community (the communitarianism-individualism continuum) in the production of crime rates. From the perspective of crime reduction, two causal linkages seem readily apparent. First, insofar as communitarian social systems are better able to shame offenders into renouncing their antisocial behaviors, recidivism and, consequently, the overall rate of crime, should decline. Second, insofar as communitarian social systems instill a sense of moral and social obligation to others, they are likely to discourage initial acts of criminality before they occur, thereby reducing the overall rate of crime (Braithwaite, 1989, especially pp. 61–65).

Messner and Rosenfeld (1994) also offer theoretical insights into the development of a social altruism perspective of crime. Like Braithwaite, they propose that culturally prescribed values that stress individualism, particularly those associated with the procurement of material rewards, play a pivotal role in the production of crime across macro-social units. However, in contrast to Braithwaite, their concern is not with the causal linkages between culture and styles of social control (i.e., shaming) and crime, but rather with understanding how cultural values accentuate structurally induced anomic pressures to engage in crime.

In brief, Messner and Rosenfeld's institutional anomie theory embraces, as a point of departure, Merton's (1938, 1957) basic observations concerning the criminogenic influence of conventional society. According to Merton, American culture places a preeminent emphasis on monetary rewards (i.e., the "American Dream"). Although socially approved methods for acquiring property are also instilled in the populace, a preoccupation with the "ends" often relegates the norms associated with the "means" to a position of lesser importance. Thus, in the context of blocked opportunities, the contradictions between the values concerning means and ends produce a state of anomie, which in turn, frees some segments of society to engage in criminal activities to procure monetary goals.

The above notwithstanding, Messner and Rosenfeld question Merton's decision to restrict his analysis of the relationship between social structure and anomie to only one facet of this dimension of the social system, the legitimate opportunity structure. Following Durkheim (1897:254–256), they argue that an expansion of economic opportunities, rather than mitigating the level of anomie in society, may actually intensify culturally induced pressures to use extralegal means to acquire monetary rewards. Insofar as economic vitality reinforces the societal preoccupation with the goal of material success, it is likely to heighten the level of anomie within a collectivity (Messner and Rosenfeld, 1994:62, 99–101). Hence, Messner and Rosenfeld (1994:108) conclude that the elimination of structural impediments to legitimate opportunities cannot, in and of itself, do much to reduce crime rates.

Rather than focusing simply on the inability of the economy to provide universal access to material rewards, Messner and Rosenfeld's theoretical schema explores the criminogenic effects of the triumph of values that define success in terms of the accumulation of assets over the values that define success in terms of more altruistic endeavors. Drawing heavily on Marxist theory, they argue that the cultural penchant for pecuniary gain is so all-encompassing that the major social institutions (i.e., the polity, the church, the schools, and the family) lose their ability to regulate passions and behaviors. Instead of promulgating and cultivating other social goals, these institutions primarily support the quest for material success. For example, rather than promoting a greater concern for the commonweal, "the very purpose of government tends to be conceptualized in terms of its capacity to facilitate the individual pursuit of economic prosperity" (Messner and Rosenfeld, 1994:79). Thus, to the extent that social institutions are subservient to the economic structure, they fail to provide alternative definitions of self-worth and achievement that could serve as countervailing forces against the anomic pressures of the American Dream.

From this perspective, significant crime reduction can only be accomplished through the revitalization of noneconomic institutions and the consequent reaffirmation of cultural values that inculcate the belief that there is more to a successful life than the insatiable quest for more goods and services (Messner and Rosenfeld, 1994:102–111; see also Veblen, 1889). Put in the context of this discussion, this means that communities that can more effectively instill values that result in their members finding satisfaction in more altruistic pursuits (e.g., parenting, serving the community) are likely to be less anomic and thereby suffer lower rates of crime (p. 110).

A third theoretical statement that complements Braithwaite's discussion of communitarianism, as well as Messner and Rosenfeld's notions concerning the social validation of noneconomic roles, is Cullen's social support paradigm. In his presidential address to the Academy of Criminal Justice Sciences, Cullen (1994) argues that social support is an implicit, but often neglected, causal factor that can account for variations in social control, individual involvement in crime, and crime rates. It is the latter outcome that concerns us here.

Within the macro-social context, Cullen characterizes social support in terms of the ability of communities to provide social networks that provide both instrumental and expressive resources to cope with the exigencies of daily life (1994:531–537). So construed, social support is hypothesized as serving as a bulwark against numerous structural sources of crime. Consider, for example, the well–established statistical relationship between family disruption and crime rates. Most research, rooted in the social disorganization tradition, interprets this association in terms of the impact of family structure on a community's capacity to provide informal social control. Ostensibly, family disruption, as well as other structural antecedents of social disorganization, decrease the supervision of youth and property, as well as participation in local associations, thereby producing high rates of crime (Messner and Sampson, 1991; Sampson 1986, 1987). However, the finding that family disruption promotes higher rates of crime is equally compatible with a social support interpretation. As Cullen (1994:535) aptly notes, "high rates of family disruption may operationalize not only adults' ability to exert surveillance over youths but also the availability to youths of both adult support networks and the opportunity to develop intimate relations." Alternatively, communities that can provide effective social support, either through the family or other institutions, encourage conformity. Thus, Cullen concludes that the more social support there is in a community, the lower the rate of crime (p. 534).

SYNTHESIS

The core insight that is subsumed within each of the approaches discussed above is the conviction that societies that can teach their members to value and perform behaviors that promote the welfare of others—that is, social altruism—will experience lower rates of crime. Thus, whether they are variously described as communitarian (Braithwaite, 1989), culturally regenerated (Messner and Rosenfeld, 1994), or socially supportive (Cullen, 1994), the more communities can enmesh their citizens in mutual ties of trust, empathy, and obligation, the more they can insulate their citizens from macro-social precipitators of crime. To be sure, there is some disagreement across the three theoretical statements about the intervening mechanisms that link social altruism to crime rates. Nonetheless, each of these causal processes—methods of shaming (Braithwaite, 1989), anomie (Messner and Rosenfeld, 1994), and social support (Cullen, 1994)—share the common notion that societies that most effectively balance the pursuit of individualistic agendas with a concern for the needs of others will be most successful in establishing and teaching social values that inhibit their members from engaging in criminal activities.

Currently, we are aware of no empirical studies that have directly examined the relationship between social altruism, as codified here, and rates of behavior, including crime. However, there is indirect evidence, from the philanthropic literature, as well as from ecological analyses of crime, that could be viewed as amenable to our social altruism thesis.

There is a substantial body of theory and research, rooted in a variety of social science disciplines, concerning social altruism (Piliavin and Charng, 1990; Simmons, 1991). Unfortunately, most of this literature focuses on the biological (Allison, 1992), social-psychological (Radley and Kennedy, 1995), and economic (Feldstein and Taylor, 1976) determinants, rather than the consequences, of charitable activities. However, a growing body of research indicates that the performance of beneficent behaviors promotes their repetition and, more important, the acceptance of pro-altruistic values (Callero et al., 1987; Piliavin and Charng, 1990; Simmons, 1991). For example, Piliavin and Charng (1990) report, based on a review of several recent studies, that blood donors are more likely to give money to charities, do volunteer work, and participate in charitable fund-raising activities than are nondonors. Moreover, Callero et al. (1987) report that prior blood donation indirectly promotes future donations through the development of altruistic attitudes. Thus, it appears that good work spawns additional good work, as well as a concern for the welfare of others. Of course, whether the development of altruistic values affects the performance of other types of behavior remains an empirical question. Nonetheless, these findings are compatible with the hypothesis that social altruism, insofar as it nurtures values that are antithetical to the victimization of others, can reduce the rate of crime.

Various macro-social examinations of crime lend further credence to our ideas concerning the social altruism-crime relationship. For example, a number of studies report that structural conditions that could conceivably obstruct the formation of altruistic values (e.g., geographic mobility, family disruption, and cultural heterogeneity) tend to be associated with high rates of crime (Bursik and Webb, 1982; Crutchfield et al., 1982; Sampson and Groves, 1989). It should be noted that these findings are also consistent with other causal processes, such as a reduction in informal social control, and therefore must be regarded as suggestive.

Clearly, one must locate and analyze more proximate indicators of social altruism before commenting further on its relationship to crime. This study seeks to address this deficiency by assessing the impact of a measure of social altruism, controlling for the effects of variables derived from motivational and opportunity theories, on variations in crime rates for a sample of U.S. cities.

PROCEDURES

The initial sample for this investigation consists of 354 (86%) of the 410 U.S. cities that reported collecting at least $1 million in contributions to their United Way campaigns. This choice reflects two concerns. First, larger social aggregations, such as states, are probably too heterogeneous to allow for an assessment of macro-social theory (Bailey, 1984). Second, as a practical matter, our measure of social altruism is only available for these cities. Missing values (primarily for the crime measures) reduces the final sample size to 273 for the personal, and 279 for the property, crime rate equations.

SOCIAL ALTRUISM

As noted above, we conceptualize social altruism as the willingness of communities to commit, distinct from the beneficence of the state, scarce resources to aid and comfort their members. We exclude governmental activities, such as transfer payments, from our definition because state-sponsored assistance programs might not reflect the humanitarianism of localities. Rather, they tend to be determined by a multiplicity of interests and decisions that are made at federal, state, and local levels (Chamlin, 1992; Isaac and Kelly, 1981; Piven and Cloward, 1971; Schram and Turbett, 1983).

To capture a spirit of local voluntarism, we operationalize social altruism in terms of contributions to a local charitable institution. The presumption here is that the more members of a community donate their limited financial resources to help others, especially those within the same community, the greater the level of social altruism. Among the numerous philanthropic organizations in the United States, we believe that United Way most closely approximates our concept of social altruism. Not only does it derive most of its funds from locally organized solicitations, but it also stresses the values of personal responsibility and communitarianism (Brilliant, 1990; Green, 1987).

Indeed, the use of monetary contributions to local charities to measure social altruism is not without precedent. For example, Angell (1942, 1947), in an attempt to identify the structural determinants of social integration among U.S. cities, included pledges to local Community Chests, a precursor of the United Way, as the primary structural indicator of the willingness of citizens to make economic sacrifices for the welfare of others. Thus, similar to Angell, we operationalize social altruism in terms of the quantity of financial contributions to the yearly United Way campaigns.

Specifically, social altruism is measured as the ratio of the two-year average of money collected during the 1992–1993 and 1993–1994 United Way campaigns to the aggregate income (1990). We use a two-year average to minimize the effects of idiosyncratic yearly fluctuations in contributions. We deflate this figure by aggregate city income to take into account local differences in the capacity to donate money.

The national office of the United Way of America requests that the local organizations report their contribution figures in the following, standardized form: (gross campaign receipts plus transfers and designations from other United Ways) minus transfers and designations to other United Ways. Unfortunately, our source for the contribution data, *The Chronicle of Philanthropy*, provides no information about the compliance rate of cities from which they collected information. To assess the reliability of the data reported in *The Chronicle of Philanthropy*, we requested and received comparable data from the national office of the United Way of America for cities that reported standardized campaign receipts ($N = 328$). The zero-order correlations between the contribution data for the United Way of America subsample of cities and the full sample, for both time periods, exceed +.98. Hence, we are confident that the vast majority of local organizations reported standardized contributions figures to *The Chronicle of Philanthropy*. Since the use of the financial data from the

United Way of America would generate sample attrition above and beyond that produced by the missing data for the crime variables, we decided to continue to use the 354-city sample.

DEPENDENT VARIABLES

In light of the dearth of theory and prior research concerning the social altruism-crime relationship, we decided to explore the possibility that the effects of social altruism might vary across offense categories. Hence, the following analyses model the effects of social altruism and other structural predictors on property and violent crime rates (1994). Following convention, the property crime rate is measured as the total number of burglaries, larcenies, and motor vehicle thefts per 100,000 population, and the violent crime rate is measured as the total number of homicides, robberies, aggravated assaults, and forcible rapes per 100,000 population.

CONTROL VARIABLES

Following previous research (e.g., Blau and Blau, 1982; Jackson, 1984; Jacobs, 1982; Sampson, 1986, 1987; Sampson and Groves, 1989), we include seven control variables in the model specifications to account for causal processes identified by motivational, opportunity, and compositional theories. We also include three additional control variables that are likely to affect the level of social altruism and crime rates across municipalities.

A number of motivational theories contend that economic deprivation has a substantial impact on the level of crime across macro-social units. For example, traditional Marxist theory (Bonger, 1916) and anomie theory (Cloward, 1959; Merton, 1938) suggest that blocked opportunities produce frustration and thereby motivate the disadvantaged to engage in crime to satisfy their material needs.

Given the ongoing debate concerning the relative importance of absolute and relative deprivation as predictors of crime (see Bailey, 1984; Messner, 1982; Williams, 1984), our models include measures of both dimensions of economic deprivation. Absolute deprivation is measured as the percentage of families below the poverty level (1990). Relative economic deprivation is measured by the Gini index of economic concentration (1989).

Alternatively, opportunity theories of crime focus on the relationships among the physical and social structures of ecological units, informal social control, and crime. For instance, urbanism theory, including the social disorganization approach, suggests that structural conditions that impede communication and the formation of affective interpersonal relationships foster higher rates of crime. Neighborhoods, as well as larger social areas, that have large, heterogenous populations and that possess few economic resources have difficulties creating and maintaining social institutions that discourage criminal victimizations (Bursik and Grasmick, 1993; Crutchfield et al., 1982; Fischer, 1975; Kornhauser, 1978; Mayhew and Levinger, 1976; Shaw and McKay, 1969; Tittle, 1989; Wirth, 1938).

To take into account the predictions of urbanism theory, the model specifications include two measures of population heterogeneity, as well as a measure of population size. The first indicator of population heterogeneity, racial heterogeneity, is measured as the percentage of the population that is black (1990). The second, ethnic heterogeneity, is measured as the percentage of the population that is foreign born. The third urbanism variable, population size, is measured as the total number of inhabitants in each city (1990).

Another variant of opportunity theory, the routine activity approach, suggests that household structure affects levels of capable guardianship and target suitability. Specifically, single-person households are hypothesized to simultaneously decrease guardianship, but increase target attractiveness, thereby increasing rates of crime, especially those involving theft (Cohen and Felson, 1979; Sampson, 1987; Sampson and Wooldredge, 1987). Household structure is measured as the percentage of single-person households (1990).

Various indicators of the age structure of the population are often included as control variables because of the individual-level finding that young adults tend to be disproportionately involved in crime as both victims and offenders (e.g., Jackson, 1984; Jacobs, 1982; Land et al., 1990). The presumption here is that what is true for individuals is also true for social aggregates. While this may not be so (Alker, 1969), we include the percentage of the population aged 18 to 24 (1990) to control for the possibility of an age-related compositional effect.

Lastly, the model specifications also include measures of residential mobility, family disruption, and regional location.[1] Each of these variables has been found to significantly affect crime rates (Blau and Blau, 1982; Crutchfield et al., 1982; Messner, 1982; Sampson and Groves, 1989). To the extent that these variables are also related to social altruism, their exclusion from the analyses could lead to model misspecification error. Clearly, there is reason to suspect that this might be the case. For example, Braithwaite (1989:94–99) contends that residential mobility, along with other dimensions of urbanism, reduces communitarianism. Family disruption, insofar as it reduces participation in local institutions (Sampson

1. The cities included in the sample are distributed across the four census regions as follows: 22% are located in the Northeast, 28% are located in the Midwest, 38% are located in the South, and 12% are located in the West.

and Groves, 1989), is likely to have a similar effect on communitarianism. Historically, the South has evidenced a strong propensity to provide considerably less public and private resources to mitigate various social problems. Racial discrimination, as well as a more pervasive disregard for the poor, appears to motivate the actions of Southerners (Chamlin, 1992; Schiller, 1973). Consequently, it is likely that each of these factors could affect the level of social altruism.

Residential mobility is measured as the percentage of persons five years of age and older living in different locations in 1990 and 1985. Family disruption is measured as the percentage of persons 15 and older who are divorced. The southern location is measured as a dummy variable, where 1 = South and 0 = non-South.

SOURCES

Information concerning the official count of property and personal crimes was obtained from the Uniform Crime Reports (Federal Bureau of Investigation, 1995). The dollar value of contributions to the United Way was ascertained from *The Chronicle of Philanthropy* (1994). With the exception of residential mobility and the percentage of divorcees, data for each of the control variables, as well as the income distributions used to calculate the Gini index, were obtained from *The County and City Data Book* (Bureau of the Census, 1994). Residential mobility was calculated from data ascertained from Table 172 of *The Census of Population: Social and Economic Characteristics* (Bureau of the Census, 1993). The percentage of divorcees was calculated from data gathered from Table 64 of *The Census of Population: General Population Characteristics* (Bureau of the Census, 1992).

RESULTS

ANALYTIC STRATEGY AND MODEL ADEQUACY

The analysis proceeds as follows. First, because theory (Braithwaite, 1989; Cullen, 1994) and research (Crutchfield et al., 1982; Sampson and Groves, 1989) suggest that there is a causal relationship between the social structure and social altruism, we regress the latter on the entire set of structural predictors. Second, because we suspect that the effects of a number of social characteristics on crime, particularly urbanism, residential mobility, and cultural heterogeneity, are mediated by social altruism, we regress property and violent crime rates on the full set of predictors.

Table 1 presents the final models of the effects of the structural predictors on United Way contributions, and Table 2 presents the effects of the structural predictors and social altruism on property and violent crime rates. Inspection of the descriptive statistics, as well as the residual analyses, reveal no problems with the ordinary least squares (OLS) solutions for the United Way contributions or property crime rates. As is reported in Tables 1 and 2, the Breusch–Pagan test indicates that the disturbance terms generated by these equations are homoscedastic.

The model for violent crimes, however, is another matter. The initial, linear specification produces heteroscedastic errors ($X^2 = 44.56, p < .05$). Further investigation indicated that the violation of the normality assumption for the violent crime rate is responsible for this problem. To induce normality, we transformed the violent crime rates by their natural logarithms. Thus, the final model for violent offenses, which is reported in column 2 of Table 2, is in semilog form.

We also explored the extent to which multicollinearity, especially among the measures of the racial and economic composition of cities, affects the parameter estimates. First, we examined the correlation matrix for evidence of multicollinearity (see Appendix 1). Only two correlations exceed .60; the correlations between the percentage of families below the poverty level and the percentage of blacks (.64) and the Gini index (.61), respectively, were the strongest. Fortunately, reestimating each of the equations, removing each of the predictors, one at a time, from each of the models, produces minute fluctuations in the standard errors and no noticeable changes in the findings. Second, we examined the variance inflation factor (VIF) scores. None of the VIF scores, for any of the models, exceeds four. Since a VIF value in excess of 10 is generally considered evidence of multicollinearity (Neter et al., 1990), we conclude that the VIF scores indicate that collinearity is not a problem. Third, in recognition of the various criticisms of VIF scores (see Maddala, 1992), we also examined the collinearity diagnostics developed by Belsley et al., (1980). Experiments reveal that a condition index threshold of approximately 30 suggests the existence of potentially harmful collinearity and a variance-decomposition proportion of 0.5 or greater should be used to identify dependencies among the predictor variables. Based on these decision rules, we find no evidence of multicollinearity among the predictors included in each of the three final models.

UNITED WAY CONTRIBUTIONS

To reiterate, Braithwaite (1989) and Cullen (1994) suggest that a number of structural factors, particularly those associated with urbanization, inhibit the development of social altruism. Table 1, which presents the results of the OLS regression analysis of United Way contributions, allows us to evaluate this contention.

Table 1. OLS Regression Estimates for the Effects of the Structural Predictors on United Way Contributions

	United Way Contributions
Percent Black	.05[a]*
	.32[b]
	4.38[c]
Percent Aged 18–24	.01
	.01
	.14
Poverty	.12*
	.27
	3.44
Gini Index	−13.44*
	−.22
	−2.72
Percent Foreign Born	.05*
	.14
	2.58
Single-Person Households	.22*
	.40
	6.87
Population Size[d]	−.00*
	−.22
Percent Divorced	−.06
	−.05
	−.84
Residential Mobility	−.01
	.04
	−.51
South	−1.02*
	−.21
	−3.19
Constant	1.77
Adjusted R^2	.36
Breusch-Pagan Test	.47[e]
N	302

[a] Metric coefficient.
[b] Standardized coefficient.
[c] *T* value.
[d] For ease of presentation, the unstandardized coefficients for population size are expressed in units per 1000.
[e] Fail to reject the null hypothesis that the disturbance terms are homoscedastic at $p < .05$.
* $p < .05$.

Table 2. OLS Regression Estimates for Property and Violent Crime Rates

	Property Crime	Violent Crime (log)
United Way Contributions	−132.03[a]*	−.03*
	−.12[b]	−.10
	−2.00[c]	−1.97
Percent Black	61.93*	.03*
	.40	.53
	5.46	8.32
Percent Aged 18–24	−36.92	−.17
	−.08	−.12
	−.95	−1.67
Poverty	2.01	.03*
	.01	.23
	.05	3.33
Gini Index	13616.11*	.33
	.21	.02
	2.51	.22
Percent Foreign Born	82.00*	.03*
	.22	.23
	4.02	4.85
Single-Person Households	31.12	.02*
	.05	.11
	.82	2.06
Population Size[d]	−.01*	.00
	−.13	.03
	−2.34	.58
Percent Divorced	389.84*	.07*
	.32	.18
	5.01	3.34
Residential Mobility	48.68*	.01
	.15	.10
	2.11	1.64
South	348.69	.05
	.07	.03
	0.98	.51
Constant	−6724.06*	3.99*
Adjusted R^2	.40	.57
Breusch-Pagan Test	17.55[e]	8.54[e]
N	279	273

[a] Metric coefficient.
[b] Standardized coefficient.
[c] *T* value.
[d] For ease of presentation, the unstandardized coefficients for population size are expressed in units per 1000.
[e] Fail to reject the null hypothesis that the disturbance terms are homoscedastic at $p < .05$.
* $p < .05$.

In general, the findings are consistent with the proposition that the disruptive effects of urbanization reduce the level of social altruism across U.S. cities. Specifically, five of the seven significant parameter estimates are in the expected direction. Both measures of cultural heterogeneity, the percentage of blacks ($\beta = .32, p < .05$) and the percentage of foreign born ($\beta = .14, p < .05$) are positively related to United Way contributions. As predicted, population size ($\beta = -.22, p < .05$), a somewhat crude measure of urbanization, negatively affects United Way contributions. The measure of economic equality ($\beta = -.22, p < .05$), which Cullen (1994:534) argues retards the development of social support within communities (what we deem social altruism), negatively affects United Way contributions. Lastly, the dummy variable for southern location ($\beta = -.21, p < .05$), which we have suggested reflects a regional propensity to refrain from providing financial assistance to others, is negatively related to the dependent measure.

The only significant partial coefficients that can be interpreted as being contrary to our initial predictions are those for the percentage of single-person households ($\beta = .40, p < .05$) and poverty ($\beta = .27, p < .05$). Insofar as poverty and single-person households inhibit the formation of strong ties to the community (Sampson and Groves, 1989), one would have anticipated finding that poverty impedes, rather than promotes, contributions to charitable institutions. It may be, however, that the positive relationship between each of these two structural predictors and United Way contributions may capture the influence of social need. That is to say, that poverty and household structure, net of other factors, might reflect the objective demand for assistance from the larger community. Hence, as poverty and the percentage of single-person households increase, so too might the willingness of the community to contribute to the less fortunate. Regardless, the overall pattern of findings is clear. As hypothesized, structural conditions that would be expected to obstruct the establishment of communitarianism appear to diminish the performance of altruistic behavior.

PROPERTY AND VIOLENT CRIME RATES

As noted above, Table 2 presents the findings from the OLS regression analyses of property and violent crime rates. The first column reports the effects of the structural predictors and United Way contributions on property crime rates, and the second reports the effects on violent crime rates.

Two patterns of interest emerge from the analyses. First and foremost, United Way contributions, net of other factors, negatively affect property ($\beta = -.12, p < .05$) and violent ($\beta = -.10, p < .05$) crime rates. While the magnitude of the standardized coefficients is relatively small compared to the other predictors, the coefficients are quite stable. That is to say, altering the model specifications does not reduce the parameter estimates for the effects of United Way contributions to statistical insignificance.

Second, the results for the control variables tend to support the predictions derived from motivational and opportunity theories and are comparable to those reported in prior research (e.g., Bailey, 1984; Jacobs, 1982; Land et al., 1990; Messner and Golden, 1992). However, the negative relationship between population size and property crime is somewhat anomalous and is not readily interpretable.

Consistent with various motivational theories, the indicators of relative and absolute deprivation significantly affect the dependent measures. However, it appears that the relationship between economic conditions and crime varies across dimensions of deprivation, as well as categories of crime. Specifically, the Gini index is positively related to property crimes, but it has no effect on violent crimes. In contrast, poverty is directly related to the violent crime rate, but it has no appreciable impact on property offenses.

As predicted by the opportunity theories of crime, measures of racial and ethnic heterogeneity and the percentage divorced positively affect each of the crime rates, while the percentage of single-person households and residential mobility positively affect the property crime rate.

Contrary to expectations, population size is negatively related to property crime rates. Further examination of the final models revealed no problems with outliers, any failures to account for nonlinearities, nor other evidence of model specification error. Hence, we conclude that this finding is not a mere artifact of the data analyses.

While the negative partial effect for population size is somewhat disconcerting, it is not without precedent in the research literature (Bailey, 1984; Jackson, 1984; Messner and Sampson, 1992). Moreover, given that population size is included in the models as a statistical control and therefore is only peripherally related to the theoretical impetus of this study, we decline offering any post-hoc speculations about the processes producing this result.

Lastly, to determine the extent to which social altruism mediates the effects of the structural predictors on crime, we performed two path analyses. For clarity of presentation, Tables 3 and 4 report the total, indirect (via United Way contributions), and direct effects of the structural predictors on property and violent crime rates, respectively.

As is clear from inspection of Table 3, the measure of social altruism does not mediate the effects of any of the structural variables on the property crime rates. The indirect effects are invariably small and none of

Table 3. Direct and Indirect Effects of the Predetermined Variables on Property Crime Rates

Predetermined Variable	Total Effect	Indirect Effect via United Way Contributions	Direct Effect
United Way Contributions	–.12	—	–.12*
		—	–2.00[a]
Percent Black	.37	–.04	.40*
		–1.82	5.46
Percent Aged 18–24	–.09	–.01	–.08
		–.14	–.95
Poverty	–.03	–.03	.00
		–1.73	.05
Gini Index	.24	.03	.21*
		1.61	2.51
Percent Foreign Born	.21	–.02	.22*
		–1.59	4.02
Single-Person Households	.00	–.05	.05
		1.92	.82
Population Size	–.10	.03	–.13*
		1.88	–2.34
Percent Divorced	.38	.06	.32*
		.77	5.01
Residential Mobility	.15	.00	.15*
		.46	2.11
South	.09	.03	.07
		1.69	.98

[a] *T* value.
* $p < .05$.

them is statistically significant (see Allison, 1995, for the computational formulas for determining the statistical significance of indirect effects).

Although most of the indirect effects of the structural predictors on the rate of violent crime tend to be modest, as seen in Table 4, one is statistically significant. Consistent with Braithwaite's (1989) discussion of the disintegrative influence of urbanism, population size indirectly increases the violent crime rate by inhibiting social altruism ($\rho = .022$, $p < .05$). However, this result must be viewed with some skepticism. Given that we estimated 20 indirect effects, we cannot rule out the very real possibility that finding one significant intervening relationship merely reflects chance variation.

In sum, while this study fails to sustain the contention that social altruism mediates the influence of structural conditions on crime, it does support the core theoretical hypothesis concerning the relationship between social altruism and crime. The multivariate analyses clearly indicate that,

Table 4. Direct and Indirect Effects of the Predetermined Variables on Violent Crime Rates

Predetermined Variable	Total Effect	Indirect Effect via United Way Contributions	Direct Effect
United Way Contributions	−.10	—	−.10*
		—	−1.97[a]
Percent Black	.50	−.03	.53*
		−.23	8.32
Percent Aged 18–24	−.12	−.00	−.12
		−1.43	−1.67
Poverty	−.20	−.03	.23*
		−1.66	3.33
Gini Index	.04	.02	.02
		1.62	.22
Percent Foreign Born	−.12	−.01	.23*
		−1.84	4.85
Single-Person Households	.07	−.04	.11*
		−1.90	2.06
Population Size	.05	.02*	.03
		3.50	.58
Percent Divorced	.19	.01	.18*
		.75	3.34
Residential Mobility	.14	.04	.10
		.57	1.64
South	.05	.02	.03
		1.70	.51

[a] *T* value.
* $p < .05$.

net of other factors, United Way contributions negatively affect both property and violent crime rates. The implications of these findings for crime reduction strategies, as well as future research, are discussed below.

DISCUSSION

Drawing on the theoretical statements of Braithwaite (1989), Cullen (1994), and Messner and Rosenfeld (1994), this research examines the influence of social altruism on the level of crime for a sample of U.S. cities. The multivariate analyses clearly indicate that the ratio of United Way contributions to aggregate city income, a behavioral approximation of the cultural value of altruism, is inversely related to both property and violent crime rates. Assuming, for the sake of argument, that these findings are not simply an artifact of the research design, they strongly suggest that communities that effectively teach their members to respect and engage in behaviors that promote the welfare of others enjoy relatively lower rates of crime.

To be sure, it is one thing to discern a statistical relationship between a measure of social altruism and crime and quite another to translate this finding into meaningful social policy. Part of the reason that opportunity theories are, in our view, gaining ascendancy over motivational theories of crime is because they engender attractive and relatively innocuous crime prevention strategies. For example, environmental criminologists have long argued that construction designs that minimize dead space and maximize public surveillance can substantially reduce the incidence of crime (Brantingham and Brantingham, 1991; Felson, 1994).

In contrast, the policy implications of motivational theories invariably call for a substantial reformation of the social structure. Even if such a metamorphosis is possible, it may not accomplish as much as motivational theorists anticipate. As Durkheim (1897) and, more recently, Messner and Rosenfeld (1992:99–101) note, increasing the degree of social, racial, and economic equality may redistribute social rewards among different members of society, but it would not diminish the aggregate level of criminal motivation within a collectivity.

Unfortunately, the incentive that makes the elimination of social and economic inequality exceedingly problematic—the desire to maximize one's own self-interest—has also been identified as inhibiting social altruism (Allison, 1992; Andreoni, 1989). From a rational choice perspective, altruistic behavior, insofar as it entails a net economic loss, is likely to be rejected as counterproductive.

The above notwithstanding, it may be possible to manipulate the rewards associated with charitable giving in a way that encourages the development of altruistic values and, consequently, the reduction of crime. Two observations gleaned from the philanthropic literature guide our thinking.

First, a growing body of research indicates that increasing the tax deductibility of charitable contributions fosters individual donations to philanthropic organizations at a rate that, in some models, more than compensates for the loss to the federal treasury (Feldstein and Taylor, 1976; Reece, 1979; Reece and Zieschang, 1985; Taussig, 1967). Hence, it may be possible to exploit, in a cost-efficient manner, the profit-maximizing tendencies of individuals to encourage altruistic behavior. Second, as discussed above, it appears that altruistic behavior, regardless of its initial impetus, tends to lead to further altruistic behavior as well as the acceptance of pro-altruistic values (Callero et al., 1987; Piliavin and Charng, 1990; Simmons, 1991).

Taken together, these patterns suggest that it may be possible to build altruistic values by first stimulating beneficent behavior by appealing to an individual's enlightened self-interest (e.g., modifying the tax code). Once people engage in philanthropic behavior, regardless of their original reasons for doing so, they are likely to continue to repeat those behaviors and develop altruistic values.

This is not to say, of course, that all individuals engage in altruistic pursuits only when it is in their economic interests to do so. Clearly, such is not the case (Allison, 1992; Piliavin and Charng, 1990). Thus, it may be prudent to complement economic incentives with appeals to more noble sentiments, such as the National Football League's commercials for the United Way (Andreoni, 1989). What we are suggesting, however, is that it is possible to instill and nurture altruistic norms and values, regardless of the countervailing pressures that seem to be endemic to Western societies (Braithwaite, 1989:86–97).

In sum, the implications of this study are straightforward. Clearly, the findings presented in this study should be replicated with other samples and, most important, with alternative indicators of social altruism. If, however, subsequent investigations tend to confirm our initial findings concerning the relationship between social altruism and crime, society should consider initiating social policies, such as the ones identified above, that motivate individuals to perform beneficent acts.

REFERENCES

Alker, Hayward R., Jr.

1969 A typology of ecological fallacies. In Mattei Dogan and Stein Rokkan (eds.), Quantitative Ecological Analysis in the Social Sciences. Cambridge, Mass.: MIT Press.

Allison, Paul D.

1992 The cultural evolution of beneficent norms. Social Forces 71:279–301.

1995 Exact variance of indirect effects in recursive linear models. In Peter V. Marsden (ed.), Sociological Methodology. Washington, D.C.: American Sociological Association.

Andreoni, James

1989 Giving with impure altruism: Applications to charity and Ricardian equivalence. Journal of Political Economy 97:1447–1458.

Angell, Robert C.

1942 The social integration of selected American cities. American Journal of Sociology 67:575–592.

1947 The social integration of American cities of more than 100,000 population. American Sociological Review 12:335–342.

Bailey, William C.

1984 Poverty, inequality, and city homicide rates: Some not so unexpected findings. Criminology 22:531–550.

Belsley, David A., Edwin Kuh, and Roy E. Welsch
1980 Regression Diagnostics. New York: John A. Wiley & Sons.

Blau, Peter M.
1994 Structural Contexts of Opportunities. Chicago: University of Chicago Press.

Blau, Judith R. and Peter M. Blau
1982 The cost of inequality: Metropolitan structure and violent crime. American Sociological Review 83:114–129.

Bonger, Willem
1916 Criminality and Economic Conditions. Boston: Little, Brown.

Braithwaite, John
1989 Crime, Shame, and Reintegration. Cambridge, England: Cambridge University Press.
1993 Shame and modernity. The British Journal of Criminology 33:1–18.

Brantingham, Paul J. and Patricia L. Brantingham (eds.)
1991 Environmental Criminology. Prospect Heights, Ill.: Waveland Press.

Brilliant, Eleanor L.
1990 The United Way. New York: Columbia University Press.

Bureau of the Census
1992 Census of Population: General Population Characteristics. Washington, D.C.: U.S. Government Printing Office.
1993 Census of Population: Social and Economic Characteristics. Washington, D.C.: U.S. Government Printing Office.
1994 County and City Data Book. Washington, D.C.: U.S. Government Printing Office.

Bursik, Robert J., Jr., and Harold G. Grasmick
1993 Neighborhoods and Crime. New York: Lexington Books.

Bursik, Robert J., Jr., and Jim Webb
1982 Community changes and patterns of delinquency. American Journal of Sociology 88:244–42.

Callero, Peter L., Judith H. Howard, and Jane A. Piliavin
1987 Helping behavior as role behavior: Disclosing social structure and history in the analysis of prosocial action. Social Psychology Quarterly 50:247–256.

Chamlin, Mitchell B.
1992 Intergroup threat and social control: Welfare expansion among states during the 1960s and 1970s. In Allen E. Liska (ed.), Social Threat and Social Control. Albany: State University of New York Press.

Cloward, Richard A.
1959 Illegitimate means, anomie, and deviant behavior. American Sociological Review 24:164–176.

Cohen, Lawrence E. and Marcus Felson
1979 Social change and crime rate trends: A routine activity approach. American Sociological Review 44:588-608.

Crutchfield, Robert D., Michael R. Geerkin, and Walter R. Gove
1982 Crime rate and social integration: The impact of metropolitan mobility. Criminology 20:467–478.

Cullen, Francis T.
1994 Social support as organizing concept for criminology: Presidential address to the Academy of Criminal Justice Sciences. Justice Quarterly 11:527–559.

Curtis, Lynn A.
1975 Violence, Race, and Culture. Lexington, Mass.: D.C. Heath.

Durkheim, Emile
1897 Suicide. 1951. New York: Free Press.

Federal Bureau of Investigation
1995 Crime in the United States. Uniform Crime Reports. Washington, D.C.: U.S. Government Printing Office.

Feldstein, Martin and Amy Taylor
1976 The income tax and charitable contributions. Econometrica 44:1201–1221.

Felson, Marcus
1994 Crime and Everyday Life. Thousand Oaks, Calif.: Pine Forge Press.

Fischer, Claude S.
1975 Toward a subcultural theory of urbanism. American Journal of Sociology 80:1319–1341.

Gastil, Raymond D.
1971 Homicide and a regional culture of violence. American Sociological Review 36:412–427.

Green, Calvin E.
1987 United Way at 100. New York: The Newcomen Society of the United States.

Hackney, Sheldon
1969 Southern violence. American Historical Review 74:906–925.

Isaac, Larry and William Kelly
1981 Racial insurgency, the state, and welfare expansion: Local and national evidence from postwar United States. American Journal of Sociology 86:1348–1386.

Jackson, Pamela I.
1984 Opportunity and crime: A function of city size. Sociology and Social Research 68:173–193.

Jacobs, David
1982 Inequality and economic crime. Sociology and Social Research 66:12–28.

Kornhauser, Ruth R.
1978 Social Sources of Delinquency. Chicago: University of Chicago Press.

Land, Kenneth C., Patricia L. McCall, and Lawrence E. Cohen
1990 Structural covariates of homicide rates: Are there any invariances across time and space? American Journal of Sociology 95:922–963.

Maddala, G. S.
1992 Introduction to Econometrics. New York: Macmillan.

Makkai, Toni and John Braithwaite
1994 Reintegrative shaming and compliance with regulatory standards. Criminology 32:361–385.

Mayhew, Bruce H. and Roger L. Levinger
1976 Size and density of interaction among human aggregates. American Journal of Sociology 82:86–110.

Merton, Robert K.
1938 Social structure and anomie. American Sociological Review 3:672–682.
1957 Social Theory and Social Structure. 1968. New York: Free Press.

Messner, Steven F.
1982 Poverty, inequality, and the urban homicide rate: Some unexpected findings. Criminology 20:103–114.

Messner, Steven F. and Reid Golden
1992 Racial inequality and racially disaggregated homicide rates: An assessment of alternative theoretical explanations. Criminology 30:421–445.

Messner, Steven F. and Richard Rosenfeld
1994 Crime and the American Dream. Belmont, Calif.: Wadsworth.

Messner, Steven F. and Robert J. Sampson
1991 The sex ratio, family disruption, and rates of violent crime: The paradox of demographic structure. Social Forces 69:693–713.

Neter, John, William Wasserman, and Michael R. Kutner
1990 Applied Linear Statistical Models. Homeland, Ill.: Irwin.

Newman, Oscar
1971 Defensible Space. New York: Macmillan.

Piliavin, Jane A. and Hong-Wen Charng
1990 Altruism: A review of recent theory and research. Annual Review of Sociology 16:27–65.

Piven, Frances Fox and Richard A. Cloward
1979 Regulating the Poor. New York: Vintage.

Radley, Alan and Marie Kennedy
1995 Charitable giving by individuals: A study of attitudes and practice. Human Relations 6:685–709.

Reece, William S.
1979 Charitable contributions: New evidence on household behavior. The American Economic Review 69:142–151.

Reece, William S. and Kimberly D. Zieschang
1985 Consistent estimation of the impact of tax deductibility on the level of charitable contributions. Econometrica 53:271-293.

Sampson, Robert J.
1986 Crime in cities: The effects of formal and informal social control. In Albert J. Reiss, Jr., and Michael Tonry (eds.), Crime and Justice. Chicago: University of Chicago Press.
1987 Urban black violence: The effect of male joblessness and family disruption. American Journal of Sociology 93:348–382.

Sampson, Robert J. and W. Byron Groves
1989 Community structure and crime: Testing social-disorganization theory. American Journal of Sociology 94:774–802.

Sampson, Robert J. and William Julius Wilson
1995 Toward a theory of race, crime, and urban inequality. In John Hagan and Ruth D. Peterson (eds.), Crime and Inequality. Stanford, Calif.: University of Stanford Press.

Sampson, Robert J. and John D. Wooldredge
1987 Linking the micro- and macro-level dimensions of lifestyle-routine activity and opportunity models of predatory victimization. Journal of Quantitative Criminology 3:371–393.

Schiller, Bradley R.
1973 The Economics of Poverty and Discrimination. Englewood Cliffs, N.J.: Prentice-Hall.

Schram, Stanford F. and J. Patrick Turbett
1983 Civil disorder and welfare expansion: A two-step process. American Sociological Review 48:408–414.

Shaw, Clifford R. and Henry D. McKay
1969 Juvenile Delinquency and Urban Areas. Chicago: University of Chicago Press.

Simmons, Roberta A.
1991 Presidential address on altruism and sociology. The Sociological Quarterly 32:1–22.

Taussig, Michael K.
1967 Economic aspects of the personal income tax treatment of charitable contributions. National Tax Journal 20:1–19.

The Chronicle of Philanthropy
1994 Donations reported by 354 United Ways for 1993–94. The Chronicle of Philanthropy 6:26–27.

Tittle, Charles R.
1989 Influences on urbanism: A test of predictions from three prespectives. Social Problems 36:270–288.

Veblin, Thorstein
1889 The Theory of the Leisure Class. 1934. New York: Macmillan.

Williams, Kirk R.
1984 Economic sources of homicide: Reestimating the effects of poverty and inequality. American Sociological Review 49:283–289.

Wirth, Louis
1938 Urbanism as a way of life. American Journal of Sociology 40:1–24.

Mitchell B. Chamlin is Associate Professor of Criminal Justice at the University of Cincinnati. His current research focuses on the elaboration of macro-level theories of crime and crime control.

John K. Cochran is Associate Professor of Criminology at the University of South Florida. His research interests are in the social control functions of religion, and the examination of issues in macrosocial deterrence and rational choice theories. He has recently published in *Journal of Research in Crime and Delinquency* and *Justice Quarterly*.

Appendix 1. Zero-Order Correlations by Crime Type

	1	2	3	4	5	6	7	8	9	10	11	12
1	—	.11	–.16	.02	–.26	.43	.52	.22	.64	–.13	.33	.65
2	.13	—	.36	–.06	–.09	–.06	.11	.08	.08	–.07	–.07	.19
3	–.15	.37	—	–.15	.11	–.19	–.03	–.11	–.01	–.01	.02	.12
4	.02	–.07	–.16	—	–.01	.01	–.04	.26	.05	–.42	.07	.24
5	–.27	–.10	.10	–.01	—	.02	.04	.02	–.28	.60	–.14	–.14
6	.42	–.06	–.20	.01	.03	—	.48	–.05	.18	–.08	–.19	.29
7	.52	.11	–.03	–.04	.04	.48	—	.34	.60	.26	.11	.44
8	.22	.09	–.11	.27	.02	–.05	.34	—	.11	.13	.40	.23
9	.64	.09	–.01	.05	–.27	.18	.61	.11	—	–.03	.33	.55
10	–.13	–.07	–.01	–.41	.60	–.07	.26	.13	–.02	—	–.01	–.20
11	.32	–.07	.02	.07	–.14	–.18	.11	.40	.33	–.01	—	–.19
12	.44	.01	.05	.33	.06	.33	.41	.21	.33	–.11	–.06	—

NOTES: The upper triangle reports the zero-order correlations between the structural predictors, United Way contributions, and the natural log of the violent crime rate (N = 273). The lower triangle reports those for the structural predictors, United Way contributions, and the property crime rate (N = 279).

1 = percent black, 2 = population size, 3 = percent foreign born, 4 = percent divorced, 5 = residential mobility, 6 = South, 7 = Gini index, 8 = single-person households, 9 = poverty, 10 = percent aged 18–24, 11 = United Way contributions, and 12 = crime rate.

All correlations greater than ± .12 are statistically significant at $p < .05$.

Part IV
Crime and Institutional Dynamics at the Local Level

[15]

LOCAL POLITICS AND VIOLENT CRIME IN U.S. CITIES*

THOMAS D. STUCKY
Indiana Purdue University - Fort Wayne

Recent research has begun to examine the effects of politics on crime. However, few studies have considered how local political variation is likely to affect crime. Using insights from urban politics research, this paper develops and tests hypotheses regarding direct and conditional effects of local politics on violent crime in 958 cities in 1991. Results from negative binomial regression analyses show that violent crime rates vary by local political structures and the race of the mayor. In addition, the effects of structural factors such as poverty, unemployment, and female-headed households on violent crime depend on local form of government and the number of unreformed local governmental structures. Implications for systemic social disorganization and institutional anomie theories are discussed.

KEYWORDS: Local politics, violent crime, social disorganization, institutional anomie

For most of the twentieth century, criminological studies paid little attention to politics. For instance, Bursik (1988) notes that classic social disorganization theory focuses nearly exclusively on *internal* community dynamics. Shaw and McKay (1972) assumed that the ecological factors affecting community development and social mobility patterns were natural processes (Bursik and Grasmick, 1993). Therefore, the context surrounding a community, such as the political environment, had little to do with community organization. Bursik (1988, 1989) argues that this is a significant shortcoming, because local governmental decisions can greatly affect community development patterns and ultimately crime. Similarly, Bursik and Grasmick (1993:53–55) suggest that governmental decisions regarding zoning and land use are likely to have important consequences

* This research was supported by a National Science Foundation dissertation improvement award (#SES-0002291), and the Center for Criminology and Socio-legal Studies at the University of Iowa. Crime and police expenditure data were obtained through the Inter-University Consortium for Political and Social Research (study # 9028). Neither the consortium nor the original collectors of the data bear any responsibility for the analysis or interpretations presented here. I am very grateful to Karen Heimer, Kevin Leicht, Celesta Albonetti, Robert Baller, Peverill Squire, the editor of *Criminology*, and anonymous reviewers for helpful comments on earlier drafts of this paper.

for residential stability and property values. Likewise, classic anomie theory focuses little attention on politics. However, a recent reformulation of anomie theory—institutional anomie theory—suggests that the impact of the economy on crime depends on the relative strengths of economic and noneconomic institutions such as the polity (Messner and Rosenfeld, 1997a, 1997b). Cross-national (Savolainen, 2000) and state-level research (Chamlin and Cochran, 1995) testing institutional anomie theory suggests that politics can have direct and conditional effects on crime. In addition, other recent research suggests that aspects of local politics such as the race of the mayor can have direct effects on interracial homicide (Jacobs and Wood, 1999), police killings of minorities (Jacobs and O'Brien, 1998), and violence against police (Jacobs and Carmichael, 2002).

Because recent criminological research has begun to suggest that politics and crime are related, I argue that a fuller consideration of the implications of variation in local politics is in order. To date, few criminological studies have considered the patterned ways that local political variation could affect crime or included direct measures of local politics. A voluminous body of urban politics research (summarized below) suggests that variation in local politics can have consequences for a number of social and political outcomes such as city council representation, voter turnout, and the responsiveness of city government to local concerns, which I argue are likely to affect crime rates. In the next section, I briefly discuss some of the ways politics has been discussed in recent systemic social disorganization and institutional anomie research, highlighting the need for more direct examination of how local political dynamics affect crime directly and conditionally. In addition, I discuss a few recent city-level studies that have included direct measures of local politics. Next, I discuss the impact of city politics on political and social outcomes. Then, I use insights from this research to generate some testable hypotheses on the relationship between local politics and crime.

POLITICS IN PREVIOUS CRIMINOLOGICAL RESEARCH

As noted above, classic social disorganization theory did not consider the relationship between the neighborhood and the larger community context. Recent research in systemic social disorganization theory has begun to address this lacuna. In particular, recent social disorganization research has focused on the role of public control in crime (Bursik and Grasmick, 1993; McNulty and Holloway, 2000; Velez, 2001). Public control refers to the ability of neighborhoods to secure external resources through ties with the local government and police (Bursik and Grasmick, 1993:17–18). Thus, systemic social disorganization theory predicts that neighborhood crime rates will depend, in part, on the ability of neighborhoods to extract resources from the city government. Consistent with this, Peterson et al. (2000) find that certain types of local institutions promote or inhibit violent crime rates in Columbus, Ohio neighborhoods. Not surprisingly, they find that bars have a criminogenic effect. However, they find that local recreation centers have a strong inhibiting effect on violent crime, but only in extremely disadvantaged areas. Peterson et al. (2000) argue that certain local institutions mediate the link between disadvantage and violent crime. Libraries and recreation centers provide greater opportunity for interaction among community residents and structure their time—thereby enhancing social control and reducing violent crime. Bars, on the other hand, are expected to increase the opportunity for crime and victimization. To the extent that communities can increase their local institutional base and fight the encroachment of disorganizing institutions such as bars, public control will be enhanced and violent crime will be reduced. Similarly, McNulty and Holloway (2000) find that the proximity to local public housing projects explains much of the race-violent crime relationship in 1990 census block groups in Atlanta. They argue that public housing projects anchor disadvantage and foster crime-prone areas within the city. Bursik (1989) finds that the placement of public housing projects in Chicago in the 1970s occurred in the least stable neighborhoods, which he argues were least able to organize politically to block construction. Thus, public housing is related to crime, and the placement of public housing depends on local political decisions. Finally, Velez (2001)—in a 60-neighborhood study across three cities—finds that public control reduces the risk of personal victimization, and this effect is strongest in very disadvantaged neighborhoods. Even small increases in public control lead to reductions in personal victimization risk in very disadvantaged areas, which traditionally have little public control. Because researchers have only recently begun to address mechanisms of public control, research has not yet systematically addressed the possibility that variation in local politics could affect public control. However, if public control is about the relationship between neighborhoods and the city government, then examining the *internal* determinants of neighborhood organization only addresses half the relationship. The *external* political environment is also likely to affect the ability of neighborhoods to develop the ties with local government necessary to increase public control and reduce crime. Thus, it makes sense to consider the structures and processes that are likely to affect city political responses to community attempts to secure resources.

Similarly, institutional anomie has begun to address the relationship of politics and crime. Institutional anomie theory suggests that the high crime rate in the United States is due to the overwhelming strength of economic institutions over noneconomic institutions such as the schools, churches, and the polity (Messner and Rosenfeld, 1997a). In a cross-national study of homicide rates, Messner and Rosenfeld (1997b) find a relationship between political restraint of the market and homicide. Homicide rates were lower in countries where the government protected citizens from the "vicissitudes of the market" through welfare programs. Similarly, Savolainen (2000) finds that the effect of inequality on homicide depends on the strength of the welfare state across countries. Specifically, the impact of inequality on homicide decreased as the strength of a country's welfare state increased. Chamlin and Cochran (1995), in a state-level test of institutional anomie, found that the effect of poverty on property crime decreased as voter turnout increased. Thus, these studies suggest that crime depends on the relative strengths of political and economic institutions. These studies point to the critical role of governmental structure in determining crime at the national level. However, to date, institutional anomie research has not considered variation in local politics. If variation in local politics affects the ways that governments protect citizens from market forces, then one must consider local as well as national politics. The urban politics research discussed below suggests that patterned variation in local politics across cities can have political and social consequences that I argue affect crime and the relationship between deprivation and crime.

In short, both institutional anomie and systemic social disorganization theory suggest the importance of examining the relationship between politics and crime but have not adequately considered how variation in *local* politics could affect crime. To date, only a few studies have examined how variation in local politics affects crime. This is perhaps because of the unit of analysis in previous research examining politics. Although national-level (Messner and Rosenfeld, 1997b; Savolainen, 2000), state-level (Chamlin and Cochran, 1995), and neighborhood-level (McNulty and Holloway, 2000; Velez, 2001) analyses yield important insights, they are not well suited for capturing the effects of variation in city-level politics.

Recently, a few studies of crime have included direct measures of variation in local politics. For example, Shihadeh and Flynn (1996) suggest that the political strength of groups within the city will have important consequences for crime. In a study of segregation and black crime rates in 150 large cities in 1990, they suggest that, "[b]lack isolation from whites may also lead to political . . . disenfranchisement of black neighborhoods (p. 1332). Black social isolation may inhibit the ability of communities to procure services from the city government. This isolation inhibits the ability of the community to organize against crime. The authors suggest that one resource communities can have within the city is representation on city councils. Thus, cities with greater black political empowerment should have lower crime because they are able to garner important resources to limit the effects of isolation and thereby reduce crime. Similarly, Rosenfeld et al. (2001), in a study of social capital and homicide, include the proportion of the voting age population that voted as a measure of civic engagement. They argue that, "high levels of civic engagement should strengthen social organization, and promote informal social control, thereby yielding lower levels of crime and violence" (Rosenfeld et al., 2001:286). Thus, areas with high civic engagement should be better able to secure external resources such as policing necessary to control crime. They note that social disorganization, strain, and anomie theories suggest the relevance of social capital for reducing crime. One component of social capital—civic engagement—is related to politics. However, these authors do not account for the possibility that aspects of the structure of political systems could affect levels of civic engagement. Evidence from political science research suggests that it can. For instance, research suggests that nonpartisan voting systems depress voter turnout (Alford and Lee, 1968; Karnig and Walter, 1977, 1983). Jacobs et al. have also included direct measures of local political variation in three recent studies of city-level violence. Jacobs and O'Brien (1998) find that police killings of citizens are lower in cities with African-American mayors. Jacobs and Carmichael (2002) find that citizen killings of police and nonlethal assaults against police are less likely in cities with African-American mayors. Finally, Jacobs and Wood (1999) find that interracial homicides are affected by the presence of an African-American mayor. They find that whites kill blacks more often in cities with African-American mayors, whereas blacks kill whites less often in cities with African-American mayors. Thus, aspects of local politics clearly have implications for crime.

The consideration of certain aspects of politics in recent research on systemic social disorganization and institutional anomie theories and other recent city-level research discussed above represent important first steps in understanding the relationship of politics and crime. However, more work can be done to explain how local politics affects crime. I argue the best way to do that is to consider research on the causes and consequences of variation in local politics. In the next section, I briefly review urban politics research on the consequences of progressive era reforms.

CITY POLITICAL STRUCTURES, REPRESENTATION, AND PUBLIC POLICY

One dominant theme in studies of urban politics has been the impact of progressive era reforms on local politics.[1] During the nineteenth century,

1. For overviews of the history of progressive era reforms, see Banfield and Wilson, 1963; Fox, 1977; Griffith, 1974; Hofstadter, 1955.

local government was dominated by patronage politics, where city officials traded favors for votes (see Banfield and Wilson, 1963). In the early twentieth century, reformers sought to limit the influence of machine politics by introducing changes in local government (Bridges and Kronick, 1999; Knoke, 1982). This discussion is limited to the three most common reforms. The first was to change *form of government* from an elected mayor to an appointed city manager.[2] The second reform was to change *electoral systems* from district-based city council elections to at-large elections where council members were elected to represent the city as a whole. Finally, reformers sought to reduce machine politics by making elections formally *nonpartisan*. Table 1 provides operational definitions of the local political structures discussed. Because the term "reform" has strong normative connotations, it is important to bear in mind that no normative preference is suggested in the use of the term in this context. It is retained here only because it is the standard term used in political science literature on the topic. To reduce the normative baggage associated with calling cities with mayor-council forms of government, partisan electoral procedures and geographically based city council elections "unreformed", I will refer to these as *traditional* local governmental structures below.

Although the overt goal of reform was to produce governments concerned with the good of the entire city, a strong underlying theme was the desire of middle-class businessmen to limit the political influence of working class, poor, and immigrant groups (Bridges and Kronick, 1999; Hofstadter, 1955). In the South, reformism became virtually synonymous with exclusion of blacks from the political process. Indeed, the link between electoral systems and black city council representation was so strong that court cases challenged the constitutionality of at-large election procedures (see Bullock and MacManus, 1993). In the next section, I discuss research that has examined the effects of variation in the three major elements of reformism—form of government, partisanship of elections, and city council electoral procedures—on political and social outcomes.

LOCAL POLITICAL STRUCTURES AND REPRESENTATION

Urban politics research has extensively examined the effect of various electoral systems on black city council representation. Early research suggested that at-large elections produced lower black representation than district elections (see Welch, 1990 for an overview). In district systems, black candidates need only appeal to a small group of voters, who are more likely to be of similar race due to patterns of residential segregation.

2. Council-manager cities have mayors, but they are usually selected from among city council members rather than being directly elected and do not drive policy as they do in mayor-council cities.

Table 1. Local Political Structures

CITY FORM OF GOVERNMENT	
Mayor/Council	Head of government is elected
Council/City Manager	Head of government is appointed professional administrator
Commission	Group of elected officials collectively govern
ELECTORAL SYSTEM	
District	Council members elected based on geographical area within city
At-large	All council members elected by whole city
Mixed	Some council members elected at large and others by district
PARTISANSHIP	
Partisan	Local or national political party appears on the ballot in general election
Nonpartisan	Local or national political party does not appear on the ballot in general election

Some evidence suggests that the effect of at-large elections on black city council representation has declined in recent years, particularly outside the South (Bullock and MacManus, 1993; Sass and Mehay, 1995; Welch, 1990). However, Sass and Pittman (2000) found that the trend toward increasing black representation through the early 1990s stagnated later in the 1990s.

Extant research also suggests that partisanship of elections can affect the race and socioeconomic status of city council members (Bledsoe and Welch, 1985; Welch and Bledsoe, 1986, 1988). Partisan systems moderately favor the representation of poor and minority groups on city councils (Welch and Bledsoe, 1988) because political parties provide an important organizational resource that the poor and minorities can use to mobilize voters. In addition, because voters do not have party cues to follow in voting, name recognition becomes much more important in nonpartisan elections. Therefore, nonpartisan elections favor candidates with greater resources to advertise. Finally, nonpartisan local elections depress voter turnout (Alford and Lee, 1968; Karnig and Walter, 1977, 1983). All of these factors moderately favor the election of white, middle-, and upper-class city council members in nonpartisan elections.

Although research suggests that local political structures can affect who is elected to political office, it is reasonable to ask whether this has any policy implications. Many argue that there are good reasons to be skeptical about the potential influence of minority representation on local policy outcomes because of the need for coalition-building and the economic constraints that many cities face (e.g., Karnig and Welch, 1980:150–152; Santoro, 1995:795). Despite these constraints, some research suggests that increased black representation in city government could affect the kinds of policies implemented (e.g., Browning et al., 1984; Campbell and Feagin, 1975; Cole, 1976; Karnig and Welch, 1980). In particular, a large research literature has examined the relationship between local black representation and black municipal employment. Although not unequivocal, evidence suggests that increases in black city council and mayoral representation increase black municipal employment (Dye and Renick, 1981; Eisinger, 1982), particularly black police employment (Kerr and Mladenka, 1994; Salzstein, 1989).

LOCAL POLITICAL STRUCTURE AND POLICY OUTCOMES

Another line of research has examined whether structures of local government have any direct effect on local public spending (e.g., Liebert, 1974; Lineberry and Fowler, 1967; Lyons, 1978; Morgan and Pelissero, 1980; Morgan and Watson, 1995). For instance, Lineberry and Fowler (1967) found that city taxation and expenditure levels were more responsive to socioeconomic and racial cleavages in traditional cities, which they argue was because of the necessity of satisfying the local electorate to maintain office. Similarly, Lyons (1978) argues that minority and poor-driven calls for increases in city services are more likely to be heeded in mayor-council cities, whereas middle- and upper-class tax-paying homeowners will likely drive expenditures down in council-manager or commission cities. However, in a widely cited study, Morgan and Pelissero (1980) found no differences in overall spending between reformed and traditional cities.

More recent studies have suggested that local political structures can affect municipal spending patterns, but the relationship is conditional. For instance, Wong (1988) argues that local *redistributive* spending is the type most likely to be affected by organized interest groups within the city and reformed local governments reduce the ability of organized groups to affect the political process. Thus, reformed governments might not affect city expenditures for road construction but could reduce the responsiveness of the government to pressure for increases in public welfare spending. Similarly, Sharp (1991) finds that the link between local economic distress and economic development policy depends on the level of responsiveness of the city government, which in turn, depends (in part) on whether the government is reformed. Finally, Langbein et al. (1996) argue that the effect of city council election procedures on spending will depend on whether the proposed expenditure benefits the whole city or only certain areas. They argue that cities with geographic city-council representation automatically represent the preferences of geographically concentrated groups better than at-large cities. Therefore, district cities will be more likely to favor spending where the benefit is geographically concentrated, whereas at-large cities will favor spending on programs benefiting the whole city.

Finally, a few studies have examined the effect of reformism on the policy preferences of local officials. For example, Hansen (1975) found that the level of agreement between local officials and voters on local issue priorities depended on the competitiveness of local elections and citizen political participation, which in turn depended partly on partisanship of elections. Similarly, Shumaker and Getter (1983) found that city elites are most likely to respond favorably to advantaged groups in the city. However, party competition and a strong democratic party—which are less likely to be found in reformed cities—reduced the responsiveness bias favoring advantaged groups.

In sum, evidence suggests that the three major components of progressive era reform—form of government, partisanship, and city council electoral rules—can have political and social implications. Urban politics research suggests that traditional local governmental structures somewhat enhance the election of the poor and blacks to city councils, which, in turn, can affect public policies. In addition, these structures of local government can directly affect spending patterns, economic development policies, the distribution of services within a city, and the responsiveness of local governments to the poor and minorities. Although criminological research has only recently begun to address the impact of various local political structures on crime, prior research has suggested a number of ways that local politics may have consequences for crime. In the next section, I develop some testable hypotheses on the relationship between local politics and crime.

LOCAL POLITICS AND CRIME

FORM OF GOVERNMENT

City *form of government* is one source of local institutional political variation that has been posited to have direct criminal justice implications. Wilson and Boland (1978) find that police in council-manager cities are more aggressive than in mayor-council cities, as indicated by the number of traffic citations written. They argue that the police departments in commission and city manager cities are more insulated from politics than in cities with elected mayors. Because elected mayors must satisfy the local electorate to maintain office, citizens are likely to have more leverage in trying to impact the policies of the police than in cities with managers appointed by the city council or commission governments that have no individual head of government to hold accountable. Thus, to the extent that city governmental form inhibits responsiveness of the police to citizen pressure, one would expect less positive relationships with the police. Jacobs and Wood (1999) and Jacobs and Carmichael (2002) suggest that interracial violence is higher in cities where black political efficacy is lower. If form of government affects the responsiveness of the police to minority groups, then one would expect decreased feelings of political efficacy and increased crime in city manager and commission cities.

In addition, because mayors must be re-elected, they must be concerned with the potential swing vote that organized groups represent. City managers and commissioners are likely to feel less pressure to respond to "squeaky wheels" within parts of the city, because they are concerned with the city as a whole. Consistent with this, Lyons (1978) argues that minority and poor-driven calls for increases in city services are more likely to be heeded in mayor-council cities. Therefore, on average, one would expect that mayors would be more attentive to pressure from citizen groups to provide the services that poor and minority areas need, which Velez (2001) suggests leads to increased public control and lower crime. As a consequence, *ceteris paribus*, crime rates should be lower in mayor/council cities. Therefore, my first hypothesis is as follows: *Cities with mayor/council structures will have lower crime rates than those with council/manager or commission governments.*

CITY COUNCIL ELECTORAL SYSTEMS

Another source of local political variation likely to affect the ties between citizens and local officials is the structure of the local electoral system. As noted above, the weight of the evidence suggests that *physical* representation of poor and minority groups is greatest in cities with geographically-oriented electoral systems (Sass and Pittman, 2000; Welch, 1990; Welch and Bledsoe, 1988; Zax, 1990). Although the link between increased physical representation of minorities on city councils and minority *policy* representation is not unambiguous, there is clear evidence that district council members consider their own district their highest priority, whereas at-large council members see the whole city as their constituency (Welch and Bledsoe, 1988). No research that I am aware of compares crime across different city council electoral schemes. However, Rose and Clear (1998) suggest that the political organization of a community may be a critical factor in community organization against crime and that local political participation is more likely to the extent that community residents believe that participation will produce results. Bledsoe (1986) finds that district-based elections were associated with higher political efficacy for blacks. In other words, blacks are more likely to feel they have a say in local government in cities with district-based elections than at-large elections. Recall that Jacobs and Wood (1999) suggest that black political efficacy reduces violence against whites. Therefore, to the extent that district systems enhance the responsiveness of city council members to district-based concerns and increase the political efficacy of minority groups, one would expect crime to be lower in district than at large cities.

Another reason for this may be the way that city resources are allocated. If, as Wong (1988) suggests, organized interest groups affect redistributive spending within the city, then city political structures that maximize local interest group organization should produce the most redistributive spending. Because district cities represent the preferences of geographically concentrated groups better than at-large cities (Langbein et al., 1996), one might expect more redistributive spending in district cities than at-large cities, *ceteris paribus*. Recent research suggests that redistributive spending is directly related to crime. For instance, DeFronzo (1997) found that AFDC payments per recipient were directly negatively related with homicide. Thus, my second hypothesis is as follows: *Cities with district-based electoral systems will have lower crime rates than cities with at-large elections elections.*

PARTISANSHIP OF ELECTIONS

As discussed above, extant research suggests that partisan systems favor somewhat greater physical representation of poor and minority city council candidates (Welch and Bledsoe, 1988) and increase voter turnout (Alford and Lee, 1968; Karnig and Walter, 1977, 1983). Research also suggests that partisanship enhances the responsiveness of local officials to citizen concerns (Hansen, 1975; Shumaker and Getter, 1983). Thus, one would expect that partisan elections should enhance the ability of citizen groups to cement ties to local public officials and secure public resources, which previous research suggests will be tied to reductions in crime (e.g. Velez, 2001). If partisan elections enhance the ties of the local community with elected officials and increase the ability of communities to obtain the resources needed for public control, one would expect partisan cities to have lower crime rates, *ceteris paribus*. Thus, my third hypothesis is as follows: *Cities with partisan elections will have lower crime rates.*

Throughout the preceding discussion of the effects of local governmental structure, I argued that certain political structures enhance the responsiveness of the local government. It stands to reason that if these traditional local institutional structures can enhance governmental responsiveness individually and reduce crime, they could also have a cumulative effect. It seems plausible that crime will be reduced as the number of these unreformed or traditional city governmental structures increases.

Thus, my fourth hypothesis is as follows: *As the number of traditional local political structures increases, crime rates will decrease.*[3]

INTERACTION OF LOCAL POLITICS, SOCIAL STRUCTURE, AND CRIME

Extant research suggests considerable empirical support for the relationship between social structural factors such as poverty and family disruption and crime (e.g., Land et al., 1990; Miethe et al., 1991; Parker and McCall, 1999; Sampson, 1985, 1987). There are a number of plausible explanations for this link. For instance, systemic social disorganization theory suggests that social structural factors such as poverty and family disruption lead to a breakdown in community social control, which leads to crime (Bursik, 1988, 2000; Bursik and Grasmick, 1993). However, Rose and Clear (1998) argue that not all poor communities are disorganized. They suggest that the political organization of a community may be a critical factor in community organization against crime. They point to the existence of well-developed internal *political institutions* as key factors affecting the ability of the community to address problems that arise. This suggests that political organization could provide a buffer against the criminogenic effects of structural factors such as poverty and family disruption.

The urban politics research discussed above suggests that there may be structural reasons why some poor and minority communities may be more able to affect the political process than others. For instance, Lyons (1978) argues that mayor-council governments are more responsive to organized poor and minority group pressure because of the swing vote these groups represent. This variation in responsiveness to poor and minority groups is likely to have important consequences for the structural factors previously associated with social disorganization and institutional anomie, such as poverty and family disruption. Thus, in mayor-council governments, citizen pressure on local officials may produce needed resources in the community to reduce the effects of poverty or limit family disruption. Recall that Velez (2001) found that increases in public control reduce victimization most in the most disadvantaged communities. If Lyons (1978) is correct, poor communities in mayor-council cities will be better able to secure needed resources for public control and reduce crime. Therefore, local form of government is likely to affect the relationship between deprivation

3. It is important to keep in mind that these unreformed governmental structures are posited to lead to responsiveness rather than being direct indicators of governmental responsiveness.

and crime rates. Thus, my fifth hypothesis is as follows: *The effect of deprivation on crime rates will be lower in cities with mayor/council forms of government.*

Institutional anomie theory suggests that the crime-producing effects of economic conditions depend on the strength of noneconomic institutions. Research at both the national and state levels has found that the effect of the economy on crime depends on political factors. Recall that Savolainen (2000) finds that the effect of inequality on homicide depends on the strength of the welfare state. Similarly, at the state level, Chamlin and Cochran (1995) found that the effect of poverty on crime depended on voter turnout. Thus, previous institutional anomie research at the national and state level suggests that the effect of the economy on crime is conditioned by politics. However, research to date has not examined the interaction of social structure, *local politics*, and crime.

As noted above, research suggests that cities with partisan elections, elected mayors, and district-based city councils will be more responsive to the needs of poor and minority groups (e.g., Hansen, 1975; Shumaker and Getter, 1983). It also seems plausible that the increased responsiveness in these traditional political structures could affect the relationship between structural deprivation and crime. For instance, recall Wong's (1988) assertion that redistributive spending will be more likely in district cities and DeFronzo's (1997) finding that welfare payments per capita were directly related to homicide. If district cities are more generous with welfare payments, then one can expect them to have lower violent crime than at-large cities. Likewise, previous research suggests that voter turnout is higher in partisan cities. Because previous research has shown a relationship among voter turnout, poverty, and crime at the state level, it seems worthwhile to examine whether the same relationship inheres at the local level. As noted above, institutional anomie research suggests a national-level link interaction among the economy, politics and crime. The research discussed here suggests that this may translate to the city level as well. Thus, my sixth hypothesis is as follows: *As the number of traditional local political structures increases, the effect of deprivation on crime will decrease.*

RACE OF LOCAL OFFICIALS

To this point, the discussion has focused on characteristics of local political *structure*. The urban politics research, discussed above, also examined the effect of *actors* within the system. As noted above, although some research questions their potential influence (see Karnig and Welch, 1980:150-152; Santoro, 1995:795), some evidence suggests that minority local officials can affect local policies (e.g., Browning et al., 1984; Campbell and Feagin, 1975; Karnig and Welch, 1980). For instance, Browning et al. (1984) found that black city council representation was associated with the creation of civilian police review boards, and other research suggests that black representation increases black police employment (Dye and Renick, 1981; Kerr and Mladenka, 1994; Salzstein, 1989). A few previous studies have suggested direct connections between minority representation and crime.

For instance, Shihadeh and Flynn (1996) suggest that the political strength of groups within the city will have important consequences for crime. They argue that black social isolation may also lead to political exclusion of black neighborhoods. In particular, they examine the level of black representation on city councils. To quantify black political empowerment within cities, Shihadeh and Flynn (1996) measure of black city council representation equity, which is the proportion of city council members that are black, divided by the proportion of city's voting age population that is black. Values less than one indicate that the black community is politically underrepresented, and values equal to or greater than one suggest that the black community is politically empowered. Thus, cities with greater black political empowerment should have lower crime because they are able to garner important resources to limit the effects of isolation and thereby reduce crime. Although Shihadeh and Flynn (1996) did not find consistent effects of black political empowerment on black violence, it is worth considering whether other measures of local minority political strength matter for crime. It seems plausible that *absolute* black political empowerment could be more important than relative equity of council representation. For example, according to their equity measure, a city with a 5% black population would be over-represented on a city council if 1 council member out of 10 was black. However, an absolute measure would predict the power of that single black council member to affect policy to be small. Therefore, it is worthwhile to examine different measures of black political empowerment on city council to determine if there are differences in crime rates. Thus, my seventh hypothesis is as follows: *Crime rates will be lower in cities with higher black city council representation.*

Studies have also suggested that the race of the mayor can have direct criminal justice consequences. For instance, Salzstein (1989) finds that cities with black mayors have higher black police employment and are more likely to institute civilian review boards for police. One would expect that increased minority involvement in the police force and the institution of civilian review boards would enhance the quality of the relationship between the minority community and the police. Research by Jacobs et al. suggests that the race of the mayor has direct implications for crime. They find that minority killings by police (Jacobs and O'Brien, 1998) and both lethal and nonlethal violence against police (Jacobs and Carmichael, 2002) are less likely in cities with African-American mayors. Jacobs and Carmichael (2002) suggest that the link between the race of the mayor and crime may be due to the perception of injustice by minorities. They suggest that some crimes result from feelings of injustice, and this sense of injustice leads to lashing out against the perceived majority—the most visible agents of which are the police. The presence of a black mayor reduces these feelings of injustice and increases feelings of political efficacy (Bobo and Gilliam, 1990). Therefore, it is reasonable to expect that the presence of a black mayor may reduce black feelings of injustice and lead to more positive relationships between the minority community and the police, ultimately reducing crime. Thus, my eighth hypothesis is as follows: *Crime rates will be lower in cities with black mayors.*

SUMMARY

In sum, recent city-level studies have suggested that politics may play a role in crime. Urban politics research suggests that local politics can affect minority political representation, responsiveness of the city government to organized groups within the city, and policy outcomes. I argue that this variation in governmental responsiveness will affect crime rates. The research discussed above suggests that the structures and processes of local government can affect policies of the police and crime. In the next section, I discuss the data and methods used to test the hypotheses discussed above.

DATA AND METHODS

To assess the hypotheses discussed above, I selected the 1071 cities with 25,000 or more residents in 1990 listed in the *County and City Databook, 1994* (U.S. Department of Commerce, 2000). Missing data reduced the sample size by about 11% to 958. However, other than having a slightly larger mean population (104,000 vs. 88,000), the missing cases do not appear to affect the demographic characteristics of the sample. The dependent variable is measured in 1991, and predictor variables are measured in 1990 (unless otherwise noted) so that the temporal ordering of measured variables would correspond to the implied causal ordering of arguments. The details of variable construction are discussed below.

MEASURES

The current study measures crime using the crimes known to the police from the Uniform Crime Reports (UCR) (U.S. Department of Justice, 2000) because it is the only crime measure available for a sufficient number of cities to provide variation in local political structures and is considered a reasonably accurate reflection of serious crime (Gove et al., 1985;

LaFree, 1998). Following other recent studies (McNulty and Holloway, 2000; Peterson et al., 2000; Velez, 2001), I examine violent crime in 1991, which includes murder, rape, robbery, and aggravated assault.

All city institutional political variables were obtained from the 1991 Form of Government (FOG) survey conducted by the International County/City Management Association (Urban Data Service, 1992) (see Appendix A for questionnaire items).[4] For the analyses reported below, I created a categorical variable indicating city form of government called *mayor-council*, coded 1 for cities with mayor/council governments and 0 for council-manager and commission cities.[5] City council electoral procedures were captured in the at-large variable. *At-large* is coded 1 if all city council members are nominated and elected to serve the whole city, and 0 otherwise. Thus, the excluded reference category includes cities where at least some members of the council are elected to represent geographic areas within the city. *Partisan* is coded 1 if the political party affiliation of candidates appears on the ballot in local general elections, and 0 otherwise. Finally, to capture the cumulative effects of these local political structures, I create a variable, *traditional government structure index*, where 1 is added to the index for each unreformed local political structure (mayor-council, district or mixed, and partisan). Therefore, this variable ranges from 0 to 3. Unfortunately, information on local political structures was missing for a number of cities in the sample. To reduce the number of missing cases and the possibility that reporting errors on the FOG survey impact the analyses, the 1981, 1986, and 1996 FOG surveys (Urban Data Service, 1982, 1987, 1997) were examined. Where there was consistency in a political structure before and after 1991, that value was substituted for the missing 1991 value. Where any ambiguity remained, calls were placed to each mayor or city clerk's office to verify the political structures in 1991, whether missing or seemingly the result of reporting error on the FOG survey. In addition, the race of city officials was available in the FOG survey for 722 cities in the sample. Therefore, I created a categorical variable called *black mayor*, coded 1 if the city's mayor was African-American in 1991, and 0 otherwise. I also created a measure of black city council representation. *Black city council proportion* is the number of black city council members divided by the total number of city council members.

Previous research has also identified a number of social structural factors that are related to crime such as poverty and family disruption (Land

4. This raises potential causal order issues. However, it is unlikely that the current crime rate will be an important factor in cities changing their form of government.

5. Only 11 cities in the sample had commission governments. It is also possible to have town meeting and representational town meeting forms of government, but no cities in the sample had either form.

et al., 1990). However, in preliminary OLS analyses using separate variables, variance inflation factors (VIF) exceeded 10, indicating severe multicollinearity (Neter et al., 1996). Therefore, following previous research (e.g., Land et al., 1990; Parker and McCall, 1999), I create an index, which I call *deprivation*. Principal components analyses produced a factor with the following indicators: percent poor in 1989, percent unemployed in 1991, percent of owner-occupied homes in 1990, and percent of female-headed households in 1990. Factor loadings for all variables were quite high: .72 to .91. I generated factor scores for each city based on the four variables listed above. Following social disorganization theory, the percentage of the city's population that was foreign born in 1990 is included separately as a measure of ethnic heterogeneity. In addition, the percentage of the city's population that is black and the percentage that is Hispanic are also included as separate independent variables (both natural logged to reduce skewness).[6] Including the deprivation index in analogous OLS regression equations substantially reduced maximum VIFs (less than 4.0 in all reported results), suggesting that multicollinearity did not affect reported results.

Population density and percent population change have also been linked to crime in prior research (see Land et al., 1990). Therefore, *percent population change* (from 1980 to 1992) and *population density* (rate of 1992 population per square mile) are included in reported analyses. Also, prior research on the distribution of crime across the life course suggests that crime commission rises through the teen years and then declines throughout adulthood (see Gottfredson and Hirschi, 1990 for a review). Failure to control for the size of the *youthful population* could mean that differences in crime across cities could be due to variation in the size of the most crime-prone population. Therefore, the natural log of the percentage of population age 18 to 24 in 1990 is included. Another variable included in many previous city-level analyses of crime is regional location (e.g., Parker and McCall, 1999; Shihadeh and Flynn, 1996). *South* is a categorical variable coded 1 for cities in southern states (AL, AR, FL, GA, KY, LA, MD, MS, NC, SC, VA, and TX) and 0 otherwise. Few previous city-level studies of crime have included any measure of local finances. However, one major tool city governments have to deal with local problems is through expenditures. It seems plausible that cities that spend more on their citizens will have lower crime rates. Recall, DeFronzo (1997) found that AFDC payments per recipient were significantly negatively related to homicide in 141 cities. Unfortunately, welfare expenditures were not available for a sufficient number of cities in the sample. Therefore, the

6. Alternative models that included percent black in the deprivation index produced similar results.

impact of overall *city expenditures* per resident will be assessed. This variable is measured as city expenditures (in dollars) per resident in the 1990–1991 fiscal year.[7] Because reported crime could be a function of policing levels (see Levitt, 1998), I also include a measure of *police spending*, which is the city expenditures for policing per resident (in hundreds of dollars) in the 1990–1991 fiscal year. Finally, to address potential unobserved heterogeneity, the natural log of violent crimes in 1990 is included in all reported models.[8] This provides a stringent test for explanatory variables in the model because prior violent crime explains a large proportion of the variance in the dependent variable (Morenoff et al., 2001). See Appendix B for means and standard deviations and Appendix C for bivariate correlations of variables used in the analyses.

STATISTICAL MODELS

Preliminary analyses showed that the dependent variable is highly skewed. This is probably due to the large range in the size of cities included in the sample. The smallest cities in the sample had only 25,000 residents, whereas the largest cities had more than 1 million residents. Although previous research has often dealt with this issue through log transformation of the dependent variable, Osgood (2000) shows the superiority of Poisson-based models for aggregate crime rate data. Transforming Poisson regression of counts into the rate data of interest in the current study is accomplished by including the natural log of the population in 1991 in the linear model and fixing the coefficient to 1, following standard practice in discussions of Poisson-based analyses (see Gardner et al., 1995; Osgood, 2000; Osgood and Chambers, 2000). The Poisson model also assumes that the linear model adequately explains the variation in violent crime across cities. In essence, the Poisson model assumes that there is no residual dispersion left to explain, once the explanatory variables are included in the model. The negative binomial models reported in Table 2 avoid this unrealistic assumption by including an estimated dispersion parameter to account for residual variance.[9]

7. This again raises the issue of causal order. However, because city budgets take time to develop, current city expenditures are more likely to influence crime rates than the reverse.

8. For an example, see Table 5 of Sampson and Raudenbush (1999).

9. The advantage of including this parameter in the model is that when there is no overdispersion in the model, the parameter estimate is 0 and the negative binomial model reduces to the Poisson model.

RESULTS

Table 2 presents the results of four negative binomial regression equations predicting the rate of violent index crimes per 100,000 residents in 1991. Equation (1) includes several variables suggested by prior research to be related to crime. To assess overall model fit, one can use a likelihood ratio test, which is computed as twice the difference between the log-likelihoods of the models being compared. This value is then compared with the χ^2 distribution, with degrees of freedom equal to the difference in the number of parameters between the two models being compared (Osgood and Chambers, 2000). In this case, equation (1) is being compared with a model with only a dispersion parameter and an intercept. The χ^2 value = 1491.4, which is highly significant ($p < .0001$), suggesting that the model fits the data very well.

Turning to the effects of individual variables, as expected, violent crime in the previous year is strongly positively associated with violent crime in the current year in all equations in Table 2 ($p < .0001$). Also (as shown in the deprivation index), structural factors such as female-headed households, poverty, and unemployment are highly significantly positively associated with crime rates ($p < .0001$). In the negative binomial model, the beta coefficient refers to the proportional change in the dependent variable when the independent variable changes by one unit (Cameron and Trivedi, 1998). Therefore, one would expect violent crime to be 26% higher for each unit increase in the deprivation index—which is approximately a standard deviation because this is an index. Both the natural log of the percent of the population that is black and the natural log of the percent of the population that is Hispanic are highly significantly related to the natural log of violent crime rates in 1991 ($p < .0001$), net of the other factors in the model. Thus, violent crime increases as the percentage of African-Americans and Hispanics in the population increases. However, percent foreign born, percent population change, and population density are not significantly related to violent crime rates in 1991, net of prior violent crime and the other factors in the model. Percent of the population age 18–24 is strongly *negatively* related to violent crime in all reported results, net of the other factors in the model. It is possible that the individual link between age and crime does not translate to higher levels of aggregation. In other words, it could be that younger cities have aggregate crime-reducing effects that run counter to the individual relationship between age and crime. Cities located in southern states have significantly higher violent crime rates than cities in nonsouthern states, even controlling for the other factors in equation (1) ($p < .05$). Contrary to expectations, police spending is actually significantly *positively* related to crime ($p < .0001$). This could be because the variables are measured contemporaneously, but it is unlikely that current violent crime rates affect current police spending because local budgets take time to develop. As predicted, overall city expenditures are significantly negatively related to violent crime rates ($p < .0001$) across all models reported in Table 2. Thus, controlling for the other factors in the model, cities with higher expenditures per resident have lower violent crime rates. It appears that, when it comes to violent crime, cities get what they pay for.

Equation (2) adds the local political structural variables discussed above. Contrary to hypothesis 1, mayor-council cities do not have significantly lower violent crime rates than council-manager and commission cities ($p = .1534$), controlling for the other factors in the model (although the coefficient is in the expected direction). Consistent with hypothesis 2, city council electoral procedures appear to be significantly related to crime. Cities with purely at-large council elections have significantly higher violent crime rates ($p < .01$) than cities where some or all of the council members are elected to represent geographic districts within the city. Thus, net of prior crime and the other factors in the model, one would expect violent crime to be 8.3% ($e^{.080}$) higher in purely at-large cities than those with some form of geographically based city council representation. Contrary to hypothesis 3, partisan cities did not have significantly lower violent crime rates than nonpartisan cities, controlling for the other factors in the model, although the variable did approach significance ($p = .105$) and was in the predicted direction.

Consistent with hypothesis 5, the effect of social factors such as poverty, unemployment, and family disruption on violent crime depends on the local form of government. The significant negative value ($p < .01$) for the interaction term between the deprivation index and mayor-council means that the structural factors included in the index have less of an impact on violent crime in mayor-council cities, controlling for prior violent crime and the other factors in the model. To illustrate this, consider the differences in predicted violent crime rates by form of government. Because the mayor-council variable has a value of 0 in council-manager and commission cities, the interaction term drops out of the prediction equation for those cities. Thus, the effect of structural deprivation on violent crime rates in council-manager and commission cities is the main effect for the deprivation index. In mayor-council cities, the addition of the coefficient for the interaction term (–.096) reduces the effect of structural indicators of deprivation on violent crime rates by 31% (.096/.309) over council-manager and commission cities, controlling for the other factors in the model. It is also interesting to note that the effect of the southern region variable drops to nonsignificance once the political structural variables are

Table 2. Negative Binomial Regression of City Violent Crime on Social Structure, Local Political Structures, and Race of Elected Officials

VARIABLE	Eq. (1)	Eq. (2)	Eq. (3)	Eq. (4)
Constant	–8.0043****	–8.0641****	–7.9689****	–8.0880****
	(0.1096)	(0.1115)	(0.1100)	(0.1240)
Violent Crime Rate 1990	0.3558****	0.3596****	0.3572****	0.3698****
	(0.0148)	(0.0149)	(0.0146)	(0.0172)
Deprivation Index	0.2630****	0.3094****	0.3099****	0.3249****
	(0.0214)	(0.0243)	(0.0263)	(0.0299)
Percent Black (Ln)	0.1003****	0.1139****	0.1132****	0.1085****
	(0.0129)	(0.0132)	(0.0130)	(0.0161)
Percent Hispanic (Ln)	0.0645****	0.0573****	0.0570****	0.0679****
	(0.0144)	(0.0143)	(0.0143)	(0.0166)
Percent Foreign Born	–0.0012	–0.0036	–0.0033	–0.0044
	(0.0023)	(0.0023)	(0.0023)	(0.0027)
Percent Population Change	–0.0001	–0.0003	–0.0003	–0.0000
	(0.0003)	(0.0003)	(0.0003)	(0.0003)
Percent Age 18-24 (Ln)	–0.2522****	–0.2756****	–0.2718****	–0.2523****
	(0.0422)	(0.0421)	(0.0420)	(0.0468)
Population Density	–0.0011	–0.0008	–0.0008	–0.0004
	(0.0006)	(0.0006)	(0.0006)	(0.0008)
South	0.0851*	0.0573	0.0556	0.0683
	(0.0363)	(0.0365)	(0.0364)	(0.0422)
Police Spending	0.1427****	0.1260****	0.1269****	0.1724****
	(0.0328)	(0.0320)	(0.0323)	(0.0363)
City Expenditures	–0.1180****	–0.1048***	–0.1003***	–0.1001**
	(0.0281)	(0.0279)	(0.0280)	(0.0339)
Local Political Structures				
Mayor/Council		–0.0453		
		(0.0317)		
Partisan		–0.0606		
		(0.0374)		
At-Large		0.0801**		
		(0.0304)		
Deprivation*Mayor/Council		–0.0957**		
		(0.0296)		
Traditional Govt. Structures Index			–0.0628****	–0.0575**
			(0.0154)	(0.0179)
Deprivation*Traditional Govt. Structures Index			–0.0343*	–0.0609***
			(0.0138)	(0.0177)
Black Elected Officials				
Black Council Proportion				–0.1010
				(0.1777)
Black Mayor				–0.1871*
				(0.0864)
N	958	958	958	722
Log-Likelihood	10661091.4	10661105.5	10661103.2	5165258.9
Likelihood Ratio χ^{2a}	1491.4****	28.2***	23.6***	4.63^{+}

NOTE: Standard errors in parentheses.
$^{+}$ $p < .10$; * $p < .05$; ** $p < .01$; *** $p < .001$; **** $p < .0001$ (2-tailed tests).
a χ^2 in equation 1 refers to LR comparison with intercept only model, χ^2 in equations (2) and (3) refer to LR comparison with equation 1, χ^2 in equation (4) refers to LR comparison with equation (3) model with N of 722.

included in the model.[10] Thus, some of the regional differences in crime between southern and nonsouthern states found in previous studies could have been due to the failure to control for variation in local politics.

Equation (3) substitutes the traditional government structure index to capture the cumulative effects of mayor-council forms of government, partisan elections, and district- based city council representation. The traditional government structures index is significantly negatively related to violent crime ($p < .0001$), controlling for prior violent crime and the other factors in the model. Thus, consistent with hypothesis 4, as the number of traditional local political structures increases, violent crime decreases. Equation (4) also includes the interaction between traditional government structures index and the deprivation index. Consistent with hypothesis 6, the coefficient for this interaction term is negative and significant ($p < .05$). Substantively, this means that the effect of poverty, unemployment, marital disruption, and homeownership on violent crime weakens as the number of representation enhancing local political structures increases.

RACE OF LOCAL PUBLIC OFFICIALS AND CITY VIOLENT CRIME RATES

In addition to the effect of local political structures on physical representation of blacks, the research discussed above suggests that the race of local officials may also affect local policies and crime. Consistent with Jacobs' recent research (Jacobs and Carmichael, 2002; Jacobs and Wood, 1999; Jacobs and O'Brien, 1998) and Shihadeh and Flynn (1996), I hypothesized that black local officials would enhance the ties of poor, minority residents to the local government, which, in turn, should reduce violent crime. Equation (4) includes the black city council proportion variable and the categorical variable for whether the mayor is black, following hypotheses 7 and 8.[11] As noted above, race of mayor and city council member information was only available for 722 cities in the sample. However, the results from equation (4) are substantively similar to equation (3), suggesting that the model is not sensitive to the sample. Contrary to hypothesis 7, the proportion of the city council that is black is not significantly related to crime. Equation (4) also includes a dichotomous measure of the race of the mayor, coded 1 if the city's mayor was black, and 0 otherwise.

10. I also tested to see if region interacted with the political effects discussed here. No significant interactions between local politics and region were found.

11. Previous research in urban politics limited samples to cities with 5% or 10% black populations, assuming that blacks must make up a sufficient proportion of the electorate to obtain the threshold of support necessary for election (e.g., Karnig, 1979; Karnig and Welch, 1982; Welch, 1990). This appears to be unduly restrictive because 26 cities with less than 5% black populations and 61 cities with less than 10% black populations in the current sample had black city council members.

Consistent with hypothesis 8, having a black mayor is significantly related to violent crime. Thus, net of prior violent crime, local political structures, and the other factors in the model, one would expect violent crime to be 20.6% ($e^{.187}$) lower in cities with an African-American mayor.[12]

CONCLUSION

In sum, the current study considered the effect of variation in local political arrangements on violent crime rates across cities. This study found that local politics had direct and conditional effects on violent crime. Specifically, the study found that violent crime rates were lower in cities where at least some city council members are elected to serve geographic districts. Thus, there appears to be something about district-based city council representation that reduces violent crime. The urban politics research discussed above suggests that this may be because district-based political representation enhances the responsiveness of local governments, which may, in turn, lead to policies that reduce violent crime. Likewise, violent crime went down as the number of unreformed or what I termed traditional local political structures increased. This offers more evidence for the notion that certain local political arrangements enhance or inhibit the accessibility of local officials in ways that affect crime. In addition, the effects of structural indicators of deprivation, such as poverty and family disruption, on violent crime were lower in cities with mayor-council forms of government and as the number of traditional local governmental structures increased. Thus, there appears to be something about certain local governmental structures that weakens the relationship between deprivation and crime. The study also found that, controlling for prior violent crime, local political structures and the other factors in the model, cities with African-American mayors had lower violent crime rates. This is consistent with previous research showing that the race of the mayor can affect crime (e.g., Jacobs and Carmichael, 2002; Jacobs and Wood, 1999).

These results have implications for systemic social disorganization and institutional anomie theories. Systemic social disorganization theory suggests that political organization may be a source of community social control that helps reduce crime. Likewise, institutional anomie theory suggests that the effect of the economy on crime depends on the strength of political institutions. However, neither perspective has considered the

12. An alternative model substituting Shihadeh and Flynn's (1996) black city council population ratio produced similar results. In addition, although the correlation between percent black and the black city council proportion is high (.83), alternative models that reduced the potential for multicollinearity by including percent black in the deprivation index yielded similar results. Finally, models that included black mayor, black city council proportion, or ratio variables separately produced substantively similar results.

possibility that there may be *patterned* variation in local politics that could affect crime. The urban politics research discussed above and the results of the current study suggest that both institutional anomie and systemic social disorganization perspectives could profit from examination of how the direct and conditional effects of local politics on violent crime.

Recent research from the institutional anomie perspective has begun to consider the direct and conditional effects of politics on crime. For example, Savolainen (2000) found that cross-national variation in homicide rates depended in part on the strength of the welfare state. Likewise, Chamlin and Cochran (1995) found that the relationship between economic conditions and crime depended on the strength of noneconomic institutions. The current study showed that *local* political variation affects violent crime and the relationship between economic conditions and crime. Therefore, future research on institutional anomie needs to further specify the dimensions of noneconomic institutions and how these affect crime directly and the relationship between economic institutions and crime. In particular, this study also suggests that future institutional anomie research should focus on *local* variation in the strength of economic and noneconomic institutions.

This study also has implications for research from the systemic social disorganization perspective. As noted above, recent research in the systemic social disorganization tradition has focused on public control, which refers to the ability of neighborhoods to secure external resources through ties with the local government and police (Bursik and Grasmick, 1993). Thus, systemic social disorganization theory predicts that neighborhood crime rates will depend, in part, on the ability of neighborhoods to extract resources from the city government. However, extant studies focus nearly exclusively on the internal aspects of public control. The results of the current study suggest that future research on public control needs to focus on the external aspects of this relationship and examine the role local governmental structure plays in constraining or enabling local community organization and the responsiveness to community demands for services.

Similarly, some have recently begun to argue that politics has an impact on *parochial* levels of control as well. Recent work by Sampson and Morenoff and their colleagues (Morenoff et al., 2001; Sampson and Raudenbush, 1999; Sampson et al., 1997) suggests that collective efficacy is one important source of local community control that mediates the effect of social structural disadvantage on crime. Similarly, Rosenfeld et al. (2001) include voter turnout as one indicator of civic engagement in their measure of social capital. However, no criminological studies have addressed the possibility that local political variation could *systematically* affect parochial control. The urban politics literature suggests some good reasons to believe that local politics is likely to have patterned effects on parochial control as well. For instance, as noted above, nonpartisan elections depress voter turnout—one of Rosenfeld et al.'s, (2001) measures of civic engagement. Likewise, Bledsoe (1986) found that district elections were associated with higher political efficacy for blacks. In other words, blacks are more likely to feel they have a say in local government in cities with district-based elections than at-large elections. Thus, how local politics affects parochial control should be addressed in the future as well.

This study also has wider implications for criminology. It suggests the value of considering how local politics structures the relationships among citizens, the local government, and the police. For instance, given recent attention to community policing (e.g., Skogan and Hartnett, 1997), it seems reasonable to wonder whether local political structures affect the likelihood of implementation and success of community policing programs. Research suggests that the adoption of community policing programs often occurs as the result of community pressure (Zhao, 1996). If reformed local governments make elites less tuned to the priorities of the citizens, reformed governments could be less likely to implement community policing or develop and maintain the relationships with poor communities to make it successful. Finally, segregation is an important issue in both studies of race and crime (Peterson and Krivo, 1993; Shihadeh and Flynn, 1996) and black city council representation (Vedlitz and Johnson, 1982). Future studies will examine the joint impacts of race, residential segregation, and local politics on violent crime.

It is important to recognize the limitations of the current study. First, the urban politics studies discussed here do not predict dramatic differences across cities based on variation in local political structures. However, Velez (2001) argues that in high-crime areas, even small increases in external resources can reduce victimization rates. Thus, even if the differences between reformed and traditional governments are not dramatic, they may be enough to have an impact on violent crime. Second, the current study employed relatively crude measures of politics due to limited data availability. Future studies will need to find measures that are better able to directly measure the responsiveness of local governments and the effect of this responsiveness on crime. For instance, data on variation in the policy outputs of various local governments such as community block grants or welfare spending would provide a better picture as to the mechanisms through which local politics affects crime. In addition, future studies will need to examine how party politics affects the outcomes discussed here. For instance, given the Republican focus on law and order in recent years (e.g., Jacobs and Helms, 1996), it is reasonable to wonder whether the party of local officials affects crime.

In sum, criminological studies have recently begun to consider the impact of local political structural variation on violent crime. Historians of urban politics have suggested that one of the goals of reform was to reduce the political clout of the poor and minorities. The empirical studies discussed above suggest that there are some lingering differences in the way local governments respond to citizen pressure based on differences in local governmental structure. The results of the current study suggest that this affects city-level variation in violent crime. The importance of local political structures for violent crime in the current study also suggests the value of expanding on traditional explanations of crime by applying insights from research outside mainstream criminology.

REFERENCES

Alford, Robert and Eugene Lee
1968 Voting turnout in American cities. American Political Science Review 62:796–813.

Banfield, Edward and James Q. Wilson
1963 City Politics. New York: Vintage Books.

Bledsoe, Timothy
1986 A research note on the impact of district/at-large elections on black political efficacy. Urban Affairs Quarterly 22:166–174.

Bledsoe, Timothy and Susan Welch
1985 The effect of political structures on the socioeconomic characteristics of urban city council members. American Politics Quarterly 13:467–483.

Bobo, Lawrence and Franklin D. Gilliam
1990 Race, sociopolitical participation, and black empowerment. American Political Science Review 84:377–393.

Bridges, Amy and Richard Kronick
1999 Writing the rules to win the game: The middle-class regimes of municipal reformers. Urban Affairs Review 34:691–706.

Browning, Rufus, Dale Rogers Marshall, and David H. Tabb
1984 Protest is not Enough: The Struggle of Blacks and Hispanics for Equality in Urban Politics. Berkeley: University of California Press.

Bullock, Charles S. III and Susan A. MacManus
1993 Testing assumptions of the totality-of-the-circumstances test: An analysis of the impact of structures on black descriptive representation. American Politics Quarterly 21:290–306.

Bursik, Robert. J.
1988 Social disorganization and theories of crime and delinquency: Problems and prospects. Criminology 26:519–551.
1989 Political decision-making and ecological models of delinquency: Conflict and consensus. In Steven F. Messner, Marvin D. Krohn, and Allen E. Liska (eds.), Theoretical Integration in the Study of Deviance and Crime. Albany: State University of New York Press.
2000 The Systemic Theory of Neighborhood Crime Rates. In Sally S. Simpson (ed.), Of Crime and Criminality. Thousand Oaks, Calif.: Pine Forge Press.

Bursik Jr., Robert J. and Harold G. Grasmick
1993 Neighborhoods and Crime: The Dimensions of Effective Community Control. New York: Lexington Books.

Cameron, A. Colin and Pravin K. Trivedi
1998 Regression Analysis of Count Data. Cambridge University Press.

Campbell, David and Joe R. Feagin
1975 Black politics in the South: A descriptive analysis. The Journal of Politics 37:129–162.

Chamlin, Mitchell B. and John K. Cochran
1995 Assessing Messner and Rosenfeld's institutional anomie theory: A partial test. Criminology 33:411–429.

Cole, Leonard
1976 Blacks in Power. Princeton, N.J.: Princeton University Press.

DeFronzo, James
1997 Welfare and homicide. Journal of Research in Crime and Delinquency 34:395–406.

Dye, Thomas R. and James Renick
1981 Political power and city jobs: Determinants of minority employment. Social Science Quarterly 62:475–486.

Eisinger, Peter K.
1982 Black employment in municipal jobs. American Political Science Review 76:380–392.

Fox, Kenneth
1977 Better City Government: Innovation in American Urban Politics 1850–1927. Philadelphia: Temple University Press.

Gardner, William, Edward P. Mulvey, and Esther C. Shaw
1995 Regression analyses of counts and rates: Poisson, overdispersed Poisson, and negative binomial models. Psychological Bulletin 118:392–404.

Gottfredson, Michael R. and Travis Hirschi
1990 A General Theory of Crime. Stanford, Calif.: Stanford University Press.

Gove, Walter R., Michael Hughes, and Michael R. Geerken
1985 Are uniform crime reports a valid indicator of the index crimes? An affirmative answer with minor qualifications. Criminology 23:451–510.

Griffith, Ernest S.
1974 The Progressive Years and their Aftermath, 1900–1920. New York: Praeger.

Hansen, Susan Blackall
1975 Participation, political structure and concurrence. The American Political Science Review 69:1181–1199.

Hofstadter, Richard
1955 The Age of Reform. New York: Random House.

Jacobs, David and Jason T. Carmichael
2002 Subordination and violence against state control agents: Testing political explanations for lethal assaults against the police. Social Forces 80:1223–1251.

Jacobs, David and Ronald E. Helms
1996 Toward a political model of incarceration: A time-series examination of multiple explanations of prison admission rates. American Journal of Sociology 102:323–357.

Jacobs, David and Robert M. O'Brien
1998 The determinants of deadly force: A structural analysis of police violence. American Journal of Sociology 103:837–862.

Jacobs, David and Katherine Wood
1999 Interracial conflict and interracial homicide: Do political and economic rivalries explain white killings of blacks or black killings of whites? American Journal of Sociology 105:157–190.

Karnig, Albert K.
1979 Black resources and city council representation. Journal of Politics 41:134–149.

Karnig, Albert K. and Oliver Walter
1977 Municipal elections: Registration, incumbent success and voter participation. In Municipal Yearbook, 1977 Washington, D.C: International City Management Association.
1983 Decline in municipal voter turnout. American Politics Quarterly 11:491–506.

Karnig, Albert K. and Susan Welch
1980 Black Representation and Urban Policy. Chicago, Ill.: University of Chicago Press.
1982 Electoral structure and black representation on city councils. Social Science Quarterly 63:99–114.

Kerr, Brinck and Kenneth R. Mladenka
1994 Does politics matter? A time-series analysis of minority employment patterns. American Journal of Political Science 38:918–943.

Knoke, David
1982 The spread of municipal reform: Temporal, spatial, and social dynamics. American Journal of Sociology 87:1314–1339.

LaFree, Gary D.
1998 Losing Legitimacy: Street Crime and the Decline of Social Institutions in America. Boulder, Colo.: Westview Press.

Land, Kenneth C., Patricia L. McCall, and Lawrence E. Cohen.
1990 Structural covariates of homicide rates: Are there any invariances across time and social space? American Journal of Sociology 95:922–963.

Langbein, Laura I., Philip Crewson, and Charles Neil Brasher
1996 Rethinking ward and at-large elections in cities: Total spending, the number of locations of selected city services and policy types. Public Choice 88:275–293.

Levitt, Steven D.
1998 The relationship between crime reporting and police: Implications for the use of uniform crime reports. Journal of Quantitative Criminology 14:61–81.

Liebert, Roland J.
1974 Municipal functions, structure, and expenditures: A reanalysis of recent research. Social Science Quarterly 54:765–783.

Lineberry, Robert L. and Edmund P. Fowler
1967 Reformism and public policies in American cities. The American Political Science Review 61:701–716.

Lyons, William
1978 Reform and response in American cities: Structure and policy reconsidered. Social Science Quarterly 59:118–132.

McNulty, Thomas L. and Steven R. Holloway
2000 Race, crime and public housing in Atlanta: Testing a conditional effect hypothesis. Social Forces 79:707–729.

Messner, Steven F. and Richard Rosenfeld
1997a Crime and the American Dream, 2d ed. Belmont, Calif.: Wadsworth.
1997b Political restraint of the market and levels of criminal homicide: A cross-national application of institutional-anomie theory. Social Forces 75:1393–1416.

Miethe, Terance D., Michael Hughes, and David McDowall
1991 Social change and crime rates: An evaluation of alternative theoretical approaches. Social Forces 70:165–185.

Morenoff, Jeffrey D., Robert J. Sampson, and Steven W. Raudenbush
2001 Neighborhood inequality, collective efficacy, and the spatial dynamics of urban violence. Criminology 39:517–559.

Morgan, David R. and John P. Pelissero
1980 Urban policy: Does changing structure matter? The American Political Science Review 74:999–1006.

Morgan, David R. and Sheilah S. Watson
1995 The effects of mayoral power on urban fiscal policy. Policy Studies Journal 23:231–243.

Neter, John, Michael H. Kutner, Chistopher J. Nachtsheim, and William Wasserman.
1996 Applied Linear Statisical Models, 4th ed. Boston, Mass.: McGraw-Hill.

Osgood, D. Wayne
2000 Poisson-based regression analysis of aggregate crime rates. Journal of Quantitative Criminology 16:21–43.

Osgood, D. Wayne and Jeff M. Chambers
2000 Social disorganization outside the metropolis: An analysis of rural youth violence. Criminology 38:81–115.

Parker, Karen F. and Patricia L. McCall
1999 Structural conditions and racial homicide patterns: A look at the multiple disadvantages in urban areas. Criminology 37:447–477.

Peterson, Ruth D. and Lauren J. Krivo
1993 Racial segregation and homicide. Social Forces 71:1001–1026.

Peterson, Ruth D., Lauren Krivo, and Mark A. Harris
2000 Disadvantage and neighborhood violent crime: Do local institutions matter? Journal of Research in Crime and Delinquency 37:31–63.

Rose, Dina R. and Todd R. Clear
1998 Incarceration, social capital, and crime: Implications for social disorganization theory. Criminology 36:441–479.

Rosenfeld, Richard, Steven F. Messner, and Eric Baumer
2001 Social Capital and Homicide. Social Forces 80:283–309.

Salzstein, Grace Hall
1989 Black mayors and police policies. Journal of Politics 51:525–544.

Sampson, Robert J.
1985 Race and criminal violence: A demographically disaggregated analysis of urban homicide. Crime and Delinquency 31:47–82.
1987 Urban black violence: The effect of male joblessness and family disruption. American Journal of Sociology 93:348–382.

Sampson, Robert J. and Stephen W. Raudenbush
1999 Systemic social observation of public spaces: A new look at disorder in urban neighborhoods. American Journal of Sociology 105:603–651.

Sampson, Robert J., Stephen Raudenbush, and Felton Earls
1997 Neighborhoods and violent crime: A multilevel study of collective efficacy. Science 277:918–924.

Santoro, Wayne A.
1995 Black politics and employment policies: The determinants of local government affirmative action. Social Science Quarterly 76:795–806.

Sass, Tim R. and Stephen L. Mehay
1995 The Voting Rights Act, district elections, and the success of black candidates in municipal elections. The Journal of Law and Economics 38:367–392.

Sass, Tim R. and Bobby J. Pittmann, Jr.
2000 The changing impact of electoral structure on black representation in the South, 1970–1996. Public Choice 104:369–388.

Savolainen, Jukka
2000 Inequality, welfare state, and homicide: Further support for the institutional anomie theory. Criminology 38:1021–1043.

Sharp, Elaine B.
1991 Institutional manifestations of accessibility and urban economic development policy. The Western Political Quarterly 44:129–147.

Shaw, Clifford R. and Henry D. Mckay
1972 Juvenile Delinquency and Urban Areas. Revised ed. Chicago, Ill.: University of Chicago Press.

Shihadeh, Edward S. and Nicole Flynn
1996 Segregation and crime: The effects of social isolation on the rates of black urban violence. Social Forces 74:325–352.

Shumaker, Paul and Russell W. Getter
1983 Structural sources of unequal responsiveness to group demands in American cities. The Western Political Quarterly 36:7–29.

Skogan, Wesley G. and Susan M. Hartnett
1997 Community Policing, Chicago Style. New York: Oxford University Press.

Urban Data Service
1982 Municipal Form of Government—1981. Survey Conducted by the International City Management Association, Washington, D.C.
1987 Municipal Form of Government—1986. Survey Conducted by the International City Management Association, Washington, D.C.
1992 Municipal Form of Government—1991. Survey Conducted by the International City Management Association, Washington, D.C.
1997 Municipal Form of Government—1996. Survey Conducted by the International City Management Association, Washington, D.C.

U.S. Department of Commerce. Bureau of the Census
2000 County and City Data Book [United States], 1994 (Computer file). Washington, D.C: U.S. Department of Commerce, Bureau of the Census. University of Virginia website. Available: http://fisher.lib.virginia.edu/ccdb/city94.html 1994, (Accessed, August 2000).

U.S. Department of Justice, Federal Bureau of Investigation
2000 Uniform Crime Reporting Program Data: 1975-1997 [Offenses Known and Clearances by Arrest, various years] (Computer file). Compiled by the U.S. Department of Justice, Federal Bureau of Investigation. ICPSR ed. Ann Arbor, MI: Inter-university Consortium for Political and Social Research (producer and distributor), 2000.

Vedlitz, Arnold and Charles A. Johnson
1982 Community racial segregation, electoral structure and minority representation. Social Science Quarterly 63:729–736.

Velez, Maria B.
2001 The role of public social control in urban neighborhoods: A multi-level analysis of victimization risk. Criminology 39:837–863.

Welch, Susan
1990 The impact of at-large elections on the representation of blacks and hispanics. Journal of Politics 52:1050–1075.

Welch, Susan and Timothy Bledsoe
1986 The partisan consequences of nonpartisan elections and the changing nature of urban politics. American Journal of Political Science 30:128–139.
1988 Urban Reform and Its Consequences. Chicago, Ill.: University of Chicago Press.

Wilson, James Q. and Barbara Boland
1978 The effect of the police on crime. Law and Society Review 12:367–390.

Wong, Kenneth K.
1988 Economic constraint and political choice in urban policymaking. American Journal of Political Science 32:1–18.

Zax, Jeffrey S.
1990 Election methods and black and hispanic city council membership. Social Science Quarterly 71:339–355.

Zhao, Jihong
1996 Why Police Organizations Change: A Study of Community Oriented Policing. Washington, D.C.: Police Executive Research Forum.

1132 STUCKY

Thomas D. Stucky is an Assistant Professor of Public and Environmental Affairs at Indiana-Purdue University at Fort Wayne. His research interests are at the intersection of politics and crime and criminal justice, specifically the relationship between politics and crime/policing, and state-level trends in imprisonment and correctional spending. Please address all correspondence to Thomas D. Stucky, Public and Environmental Affairs, Indiana-Purdue University, 2101 E. Coliseum Blvd., Fort Wayne, IN 46805, stuckyt@ipfw.edu.

Appendix A. Summary of ICMA Fog Survey Questions Used to Construct Local Institutional Political Variables

MAYOR/ COUNCIL

Question 1: Indicate your current form of government as defined by your charter, ordinance, or state law.

1. Mayor/Council
2. Council/Manager
3. Commission
4. Town Meeting
5. Representative Town Meeting

DISTRICT

Question 29: Indicate the number of council members selected by each of the following methods?

1. Nominated and elected at large
2. Nominated by ward or district and elected at large
3. Nominated by ward or district and elected by ward or district
4. Other
   a. Total council members listed in 1 – 4.

PARTISAN

Question 21: Does the political party affiliation of candidates for board or council appear on the ballot in a local general election?

1. No
2. Yes

Appendix B. Univariate Statistics for Variables Reported in Table 2

	N	Mean	S. D.	Min.	Max.
Violent Crime 91	958	796.11	691.84	2.33	4301.0
Violent Crime 90	958	762.51	684.75	21.96	4353.0
Population	958	104183	304946	25001	7322564
Population Density	958	3784.0	3202.0	11.0	44043.0
Percent 18-24	958	12.39	6.64	5.10	65.6
Police Exp/Resident	958	11.68	5.29	3.28	75.16
City Exp/Capita	958	874.55	565.08	161.00	7154.00
Percent Black	958	11.99	15.31	0.08	89.95
Percent Hispanic	958	10.42	15.15	0.20	93.9
Deprivation Index	958	0.007	0.972	–2.11	3.617
Pct. Owner Occupied Homes	958	57.79	12.54	21.63	91.54
Percent Poor	958	12.72	7.38	1.11	43.20
Percent Unemployed	958	6.46	2.66	1.90	19.70
Pct. Female Headed Households	958	18.16	6.92	5.61	51.72
Pct. Population Change	958	23.38	47.13	–23.20	587.70
Pct. Foreign Born	958	9.26	9.78	0.20	70.40
Black City Council Prop.	722	0.081	0.13	0	.75

Appendix C. Bivariate Correlation Matrix*

	1	2	3	4	5	6	7	8	9	10	11	12	13	14	15	16	17	18	19
1. Violent Crime 91	1.00																		
2. Violent Crime 90	.94*	1.00																	
3. Population	.26*	.25*	1.00																
4. Population Density	.21*	.23*	.24*	1.00															
5. % 18-24	-.02	-.02	-.01	.02	1.00														
6. Police Expenditures	.39*	.41	.19*	.27*	-.10	1.00													
7. Expend/Capita	.24*	.25*	.27*	.15*	-.01	.49*	1.00												
8. Percent Black	.66*	.67*	.15*	.08*	.04	.23*	.22*	1.00											
9. Percent Hispanic	.22*	.22*	.09*	.41*	-.02	.13*	-.06*	-.11*	1.00										
10. Depriv. Index	.66*	.65*	.17*	.25*	.32*	.17*	.23*	.63*	.25*	1.00									
11. % Own-Occ. Homes	-.4*	-.39*	-.16*	-.38*	-.51*	-.25*	-.31*	-.31*	-.23*	-.73*	1.00								
12. Percent Poor	.54*	.53*	.12*	.06	.42*	.03	.08*	.52*	.24*	.91*	-.57*	1.00							
13. Percent Unemployed	.56*	.56*	.12*	.19*	.1*	.05	.10*	.5*	.33*	.87*	-.42*	.79*	1.00						
14. Pct Female Head House.	.72*	.71*	.18*	.25*	.11*	.27*	.33*	.8*	.07*	.9*	-.57*	.74*	.72*	1.00					
15. % Pop. Chg	-.15*	-.13*	-.05	.17*	-.09*	-.11*	-.12*	-.20*	.12*	-.28*	.17*	-.23*	-.20*	-.33*	1.00				
16. % Foreign Born	.14*	.17*	.12*	.62*	-.02*	.34*	.04	-.13*	.74*	.07*	-.25*	-.02	.09*	-.03	.04	1.00			
17. Traditional Govt. Index	.13*	.11*	.14*	-.01	.06	-.07*	.15*	.30*	-.27*	.25*	-.12*	.19*	.19*	.34*	-.3*	-.29*	1.00		
18. Black City Council Prop.	.57*	.59*	.17*	.07	.07	.17*	.20*	.83*	-.08*	.54*	-.28*	.45*	.43*	.66*	-.25*	-.11*	.26*	1.00	
19. Black Mayor	.39*	.4*	.26*	.17*	.05	.2*	.17*	.40*	.05	.32*	-.17*	.21*	.28*	.39*	-.05	.03	.04	.46*	1.00

* $p < .05$ (two-tailed test), N= 958 for all variables except Black City Council Proportion and Black Mayor (N=722).

[16]

DISADVANTAGE AND NEIGHBORHOOD VIOLENT CRIME: DO LOCAL INSTITUTIONS MATTER?

RUTH D. PETERSON
LAUREN J. KRIVO
MARK A. HARRIS

This article explores whether local institutions matter for controlling neighborhood violence. Disadvantaged neighborhoods have difficulty attracting and maintaining conventional institutions that help control crime. At the same time, institutional settings that are conducive to violence are more prevalent. This article assesses whether certain local institutions provide a mechanism linking economic deprivation and residential instability to criminal violence. Rates of total and individual violent crimes are examined for census tracts in Columbus, Ohio for 1990. The findings show that communities may reduce violent crime somewhat by developing a larger base of certain types of local institutions (e.g., recreation centers) and preventing the encroachment of others (i.e., bars). Still, such institutional mechanisms do not explain why economic deprivation and residential instability are strongly linked to violent crime. This suggests that efforts to substantially reduce violence in local communities must counter the macro-structural forces that increase economic deprivation and lead to inner-city decline.

Scholars have long sought to understand the sources and consequences of living in poor and deteriorated inner-city neighborhoods (Jargowsky 1997; Lynn and McGeary 1990; Massey and Denton 1993; Wilson 1987, 1996). One of the most feared outcomes of local disadvantage is heightened violent crime, and many studies have found a strong association between these two conditions (Almgren et al. 1998; Crutchfield, Glusker, and Bridges 1999; Curry and Spergel 1988; Krivo and Peterson 1996; McNulty 1999; Messner and Tardiff 1986; Patterson 1991; Sampson, Raudenbush, and Earls 1997;

This article was presented at the annual meeting of the American Society of Criminology, San Diego, November 1997. We would like to thank Robert L. Kaufman for consultation and Richard J. Lundman for comments on an earlier version of this article. This research was partially funded by the Committee on Urban Affairs and the Urban Assistance Program, The Ohio State University. The Columbus Police Department's Community Education Unit generously provided data on crime in city census tracts. We are especially grateful to Ted A. Oshodi, the Department's Crime Prevention Program Coordinator.

Warner and Pierce 1993). Recently, scholars have become interested in exploring this relationship in more detail because the number of impoverished neighborhoods in the United States has increased sharply since 1970 (Abramson, Tobin, and VanderGoot 1995; Jargowsky 1994, 1997; Jargowsky and Bane 1990, 1991; Kasarda 1993). At the same time, the prevalence of poverty has risen in many already poor inner-city areas. This growing concentration of poverty and disadvantage has heightened concern among scholars, policymakers, and community leaders for understanding better the criminal consequences of high levels of local disadvantage, particularly for explaining why such a relationship exists.

Set in the context of social disorganization theory, most efforts to elucidate the link between disadvantage and neighborhood crime have focused on the role of informal control as the mediating factor. High rates of deprivation are said to reduce informal control mechanisms, which, in turn, lead to increased crime including violence. Some have attempted to explore empirically these linkages by examining local associational ties, an indirect measure of informal social control (Bellair 1997; Greenberg, Rohe, and Williams 1982; Macoby, Johnson, and Church 1958; Sampson and Groves 1989; Simcha-Fagan and Schwartz 1986; Warner and Rountree 1997). These researchers demonstrate that local social ties often predict crime and violence but do not necessarily *explain* the relationship between poverty and criminal behavior. In addition, Sampson et al. (1997) attempt to measure more directly informal social control among neighbors. They find that collective efficacy (a measure that combines informal social control and social cohesion) accounts for a large portion of the effect of concentrated disadvantage on perceived and actual violent crime victimization in Chicago neighborhoods.

Although these studies have provided important insights regarding neighborhood violence, they do not address a central concern of the literature on urban decline that Wilson (1987, 1996) and others (Kornhauser 1978) view as key to explaining high levels of social dislocation in the inner city. Specifically, contemporary social disorganization perspectives point to the local institutional base as also mediating between social conditions and violent crime. Disadvantaged neighborhoods have difficulty attracting and maintaining the types of local institutions that impede violent behavior by providing community stability, social control, and alternative activities to occupy the time of residents. Yet, researchers have seldom examined empirically whether institutions provide these intervening links to violent crime rates. In light of this gap in our understanding of the disadvantage-crime relationship, one objective of this article is to assess whether select local institutions provide important mechanisms linking disadvantage to high criminal violence.

Public housing projects are one part of the institutional fabric of some poor neighborhoods. Yet, it is unclear whether an observed relationship between public housing and crime is due to the fact that the traditional structural sources of social disorganization (poverty and turnover) are present in public housing because low income is a requirement for residency, or because other features of public housing make it a "breeding ground for crime and violence." Massey and Kanaiaupuni (1993) have demonstrated that the presence of public housing in a neighborhood has a strong effect in concentrating poverty within that community (see also Carter, Schill, and Wachter 1998; Holloway et al. 1998). In this way, public housing may contribute to social disorganization and in turn violence, simply because of its association with higher economic deprivation. If this were the case, we would not expect a unique effect of this factor on crime when social disorganization variables are taken into account. Another objective of this article is to examine the merits of this claim. The following section outlines in detail the conceptual arguments for our consideration of institutional and housing factors.

CONCEPTUAL ARGUMENTS

The general theoretical rationale for exploring the institutional context of neighborhood violence stems from social disorganization theory (Kornhauser 1978; Shaw and McKay 1969) and Wilson's (1987, 1996) work on concentrated poverty, social isolation, and urban social dislocation. Social disorganization broadly defined "refers to the inability of a community structure to realize the common values of its residents and maintain effective social controls" (Sampson and Groves 1989:777). Ultimately, social disorganization has its foundation in broad social conditions, in particular, economic deprivation, population heterogeneity, and residential turnover. The local institutional base is presumed to mediate between these conditions and crime (Kornhauser 1978). Disadvantaged communities lack many of the economic and social resources for developing and maintaining stable organizations. Employers that provide jobs and retail services are unlikely to find it profitable to locate in poorer neighborhoods. Indeed, many inner-city areas have been devastated by economic disinvestment of a range of businesses (Squires 1994; Wilson 1996). Residents of disadvantaged areas also lack the power to demand that local government and private agencies develop institutions to meet community needs and to fight the development of establishments, such as bars, that foster deviant behavior. As a result, basic institutions like stores, banks, libraries, and recreational facilities that provide stable regular access to jobs and routine retail and social services may be far less prevalent in disadvantaged communities, whereas problematic enterprises such as taverns may proliferate (Covington 1999; Zahn 1998). The lack of institutional capacity, in turn, impedes the ability of communities to exercise social control and to provide necessary routes to valued goals. The result is heightened crime, violence, and delinquency.

Wilson (1987, 1996) also emphasizes the important consequences of weak institutional structures in disadvantaged communities. As he argues, the extreme concentration of disadvantage in some neighborhoods creates a distinctly different social-structural milieu characterized by a high degree of social isolation—"lack of contact or of sustained interaction with individuals and institutions that represent mainstream society" (Wilson 1987:60). In fact, more impoverished areas have a particularly difficult time sustaining the basic community institutions that socialize residents to maintain regular daily schedules of work and school, and that provide social control of residents' behavior. In this way, Wilson views the weakening of local institutions as a "key mediating [link] between economic displacement and the crystallization of patterned deviant behavior" (Sullivan 1993:11; see also Short 1997). Thus, the basic logic of Wilson's argument is quite similar to social disorganization theory; extreme economic deprivation impedes the ability of communities to sustain basic institutional structures that connect individuals to valued roles within society and inhibit crime and violence.

To specify the link to crime more fully, communities that lack strong and viable institutions have fewer conventional role models as well as fewer formal and informal mechanisms for controlling crime. When local organizations that link individuals to each other and to broader political and economic institutions are less prevalent, commitments to mainstream values are less likely to be encouraged, socialization to conformity is undermined, and the resulting *indirect* social control is weakened (Hagedorn 1991; Wacquant 1993). Furthermore, many local institutions provide organized activities that structure individuals' time and allow them to have direct oversight of each other. When conventional institutions are few in number, this avenue of reduction and control of crime and violence is weakened. Community members also have fewer mechanisms for becoming connected and identified with each other when they lack formal settings in which to congregate and spend time. As such, families, neighbors, and other primary groups have fewer contexts in which to form networks that foster *direct* control by intervening in crimes and supervising youth activities (e.g., hanging out and truancy) that may evolve into violent encounters.

A number of local institutions should be primary in mediating between disadvantage and crime. Recreation centers and libraries provide places and activities where people can gather, thereby structuring time and observing each other in public. To the degree that these institutions offer organized activities, they place local residents in settings that promote and facilitate the sharing of common values and goals. As this occurs, community networks are more likely to form and fulfill control functions.

Some local economic institutions such as banks and retail stores may help to stabilize communities and reduce violent crime by providing gathering places and community oversight. In addition, they may provide jobs for residents who, in turn, serve as conventional role models by following regularized work schedules. The presence of employment and retail establishments could help to connect local areas with larger political and economic institutions such as business associations and government agencies, including social service organizations and the police. In this way, they may enhance the ability of neighborhoods to gain services and protection that help reduce crime. The existence of economic institutions may also make the community appear viable to outsiders and residents feel like the neighborhood is a good place to live. Thus, there are visible signs that the community is "in control."

In contrast to institutions that provide stability and control, some institutions actually may encourage criminal and violent behavior. Bars provide such a setting. Like street corners, bars are places where idle individuals may spend significant amounts of time and where nonconventional role modeling and defensive posturing may become prevalent. In bars, individuals are not only involved in a situation of company that may be conducive to criminal activity but they also may be intoxicated and as such exhibit impaired judgement and "weaken[ed] internal social control" (Roncek and Maier 1991:726). Parker and Rebhun (1995) have elaborated a selective disinhibition perspective on alcohol consumption and homicide. They note that "the disinhibiting effect of alcohol is to undermine the operation of active constraint" in situations where there is potential violence (p. 35). In macro-level tests of this perspective, they find that alcohol availability has an important influence on homicide and that it intensifies the effect of other predictors including poverty (Parker 1995; Parker and Rebhun 1995). Impaired judgment and disinhibition could produce violence within bars themselves. However, such states could also affect the level of violence within the local community as people leave drinking establishments, return to their residences, and potentially act violently on the streets and in their homes. Beyond the effects of alcohol consumption, the proliferation of bars and taverns may be an indication that the community is unable to limit their presence via zoning, local options, or other legal mechanisms; the presence of bars may be an indirect indicator of social disorganization. If bars have the presumed positive effect on crime, the relationship may not be linear. An additional bar in an area with few or no bars may increase crime more than an additional tavern in a community that is already replete with such drinking establishments.

Despite the theoretical bases for expecting that local institutions mediate the relationship between economic deprivation and criminal violence, little research examines this issue directly. A few analyses present accounts of inner-city communities pointing to the lack of strong positive institutions.

These studies suggest that such an institutional dearth is linked to numerous local problems including heightened crime. Hagedorn (1991) describes a single zip code (20 by 20 square blocks) in Milwaukee that is rife with drug, violence, and gang problems as being totally devoid of basic institutions.

> This area has no large chain grocery stores. There are no banks or check-cashing stores in the entire zip code area. Bars and drug houses are in plentiful supply and the area has the highest number of Milwaukee drug arrests. Still, in 1989, this zip code area did not have a single alcohol/drug treatment facility. Even community agencies are located overwhelmingly on the periphery of 53206, circling the neighborhoods they serve, but not a part of them. (P. 534)

Similarly, Messner and Rosenfeld (1997) note a police officer's description of institutional barrenness in Englewood, an especially crime-ridden and destitute neighborhood in Chicago:

> Do you see any hardware stores? Do you see any grocery stores? Do you see any restaurants? Any bowling alleys? There is nothing here. . . . Everything we take for granted—a laundromat, a cleaners, anything. It's not here. . . . What do these kids have to do? Nothing. (P. 34)

This quote mirrors descriptions presented by Wilson (1996) of a number of impoverished Chicago neighborhoods. Despite the poignancy of these accounts, studies have not examined the contribution of such a dearth of institutions, independent of economic deprivation, to violent crime within these types of communities.

The only other analyses exploring local institutions and crime examine the role of bars (Roncek and Bell 1981; Roncek and Maier 1991; Roncek and Pravatiner 1989; Zahn 1998). For Cleveland, Roncek and his colleagues found that blocks with higher numbers of taverns have higher rates of all types of index offenses (Roncek and Bell 1981; Roncek and Maier 1991). More important, the effect of bars consistently was stronger than that for other community characteristics. In San Diego, they found the same pattern of more crime on blocks with bars, although the effect is somewhat weaker (Roncek and Pravatiner 1989). Zahn (1998) also noted a strong association between bars and homicide in Phoenix, Philadelphia, and St. Louis. Beyond these studies, scholars have not explored the empirical linkages between the presence of various types of institutions and neighborhood crime.

As noted above, public housing is an important component of the social fabric of some neighborhoods that may be linked to local crime. Some discussions of public housing for cities like Chicago, St. Louis, and Newark might lead one to expect a strong independent effect of public housing on crime because of its poor construction, management, maintenance, and layout (Popkin et al. 1995; Rainwater 1970; Sampson 1990; Skogan and Annan 1993; Vergara 1997). These conditions provide a visible sign of neighborhood decline and may signal to "troublemakers" that the buildings are out of anyone's control (Kelling and Coles 1996; Skogan 1990; Wilson and Kelling 1982). Yet, this description does not hold for much of public housing (e.g., Holzman 1996). Projects vary in size and physical quality. Many developments are smaller, and a considerable number of units are structurally sound and relatively well maintained. Indeed, such housing may be as sturdy or sturdier than private market dwellings in the same or similar areas of the city.[1] If so, the presence of public housing would not have the independent influence on crime suggested by descriptions of a handful of large, troubled projects in a few cities. Rather, any association with heightened criminal violence would occur through public housing's strong connection with other factors such as the social disorganization variables of economic deprivation and residential instability (Sampson 1990).

Several studies have demonstrated that public housing explicitly concentrates poverty and related disadvantages (Carter et al. 1998; Holloway et al. 1998; Massey and Kanaiaupuni 1993; Sampson 1990). By design, public housing is inhabited by persons in poverty, especially the poorest segments of the impoverished, thereby necessarily increasing the poverty rate within neighborhoods where such housing is located. In addition, public housing commonly was built in already poor neighborhoods because of substantial mobilization against locating the poor in middle-class areas (Bickford and Massey 1991). As such, communities in which there are public housing projects frequently have high poverty rates. Residential turnover also tends to be high in neighborhoods where housing projects are located (Bursik 1989; Sampson 1990). Under conditions of high poverty and population turnover, residents of communities with housing projects are less able to form networks of formal and informal social control, and hence have more difficulty controlling crime.

Little systematic research has explored the effect of public housing on crime, and most available studies are quite dated. A few investigations have examined crime *within* projects (Newman 1972; Rainwater 1970). However, public housing also may influence crime levels in the overall neighborhood in which the housing is located and in adjacent areas. Only Farley's (1982) study of St. Louis; Bursik's (1989) study of Chicago; and Roncek, Bell, and Francik's (1981) study of Cleveland have analyzed this possibility. The results of these studies are mixed. Farley (1982) found that neither violent nor property crime rates are significantly higher in areas with public housing projects (of varying types) within, or adjacent to them, compared to the city as a whole. In contrast, Bursik (1989) showed that public housing is associated with higher rates of juvenile delinquency in communities, although its effect is indirect through increased population turnover in the neighborhood. Finally, Roncek et al. (1981) showed that blocks in Cleveland with a housing project adjacent to them have a statistically higher incidence of violent but not property crime. Further research is needed to reconcile these differing findings and more fully illuminate the role of public housing in neighborhood crime.

DATA AND METHOD

Sample and Data

The analyses here examine the influence of economic deprivation, local institutions, and public housing on violent index crime rates for census tracts in Columbus, Ohio, for 1990. There are a total of 215 census tracts in Columbus, although many are split across municipal boundaries and thus are only partially within the city limits. Our analysis includes the 177 tracts (or portions of tracts) with at least 700 persons within the city.[2] This minimum size allows us to construct reliable crime rates and measures of other tract characteristics. Census tracts do not necessarily correspond to neighborhoods in a socially meaningful sense. However, they are the best local areas for which the required data are available, and they have been used in a number of prior analyses of urban crime (Crutchfield 1989; Crutchfield et al. 1999; Kohfeld and Sprague 1988, 1990; Krivo and Peterson 1996; McClain 1989). It could be argued that smaller areas such as block groups or blocks would be a preferable unit of analysis for examining the influence of some institutions. For example, bars and public housing might have greater effects on violent acts that take place within these settings or in the immediately surrounding area. However, data limitations and substantive interest preclude considering smaller units. Tracts are the smallest unit for which Columbus crime data are available. Furthermore, our substantive arguments about the role of institutions in mediating the effect of structural characteristics on crime pertain to broader community areas. Finally, for any institution that might have a stronger effect in smaller locales, the choice of tracts simply provides a more conservative test of its influence.

Data for the sociodemographic independent variables are from the 1990 U.S. Censuses of Population and Housing Summary Tape File 3A (U.S. Bureau of the Census 1991). The Columbus Police Department (1994) provided counts for reported index violent crimes for tracts within the city. These violent crime data are the same as those reported in the Federal Bureau of Investigation's (FBI) Uniform Crime Reports (UCR) except that they are broken down by census tract. We use data from published volumes and other publicly available local sources to ascertain the presence of important social institutions within tracts. Lists by address of major retail chain grocery stores and banks were obtained from the 1990 telephone directory. A list of local public libraries by address was obtained from the Directory of Ohio Libraries (State Library of Ohio 1990). Lists of other institutions by address were acquired from the following sources: (1) city recreation centers from the Columbus Department of Parks and Recreation; (2) bars and other establishments with liquor licenses from the State of Ohio Department of Liquor Control, with supplemental information gained in a variety of ways (see below); and (3) public housing projects from the Columbus Metropolitan Housing Authority. The addresses of these institutions were geocoded to their census tract locations by Geographic Data Technology, Inc. (GDT).[3] The operationalizations of dependent and independent variables are presented in Table 1.

Crime Rates

Rates for the FBI's violent index crimes (homicide, forcible rape, robbery, aggravated assault) provide the dependent variables. We calculate the overall rate of serious violent crime and separate rates for homicide, rape, robbery, and aggravated assault. Following common practice, three-year (1989 through 1991) average crimes per 1,000 population (per 1,000 females for rape) are calculated to minimize the impact of annual fluctuations and increase the likelihood of having sufficient incidents to construct reliable rates for small areas (Messner and Golden 1992; Sampson 1985, 1987).[4]

Neighborhood Institutions and Public Housing

We include measures of four types of neighborhood institutions: recreation centers, libraries, retail/employment, and bars. The first three are types of stabilizing institutions that have the potential to link individuals to larger sociopolitical entities and to structure time and activities in ways that facilitate interaction, observation, and socialization. Retail/employment institutions also provide local economic opportunities. By contrast and as noted above, bars likely have a crime-producing influence. These four types of establishments do not include all institutions of possible importance. However, they have the elements that are considered to foster (or hinder) formal and informal social control and enable the community to realize common goals.

Operationally, the institution variables represent total counts of each institutional type (libraries, recreation centers, retail/employment, and bars) located within the census tract or within an adjacent tract.[5] As indicated above, libraries and recreation centers are those identified in official sources for the city of Columbus. Retail/employment institutions are chain grocery

TABLE 1: Operationalizations of Dependent and Independent Variables

Variable	*Operationalization*
Violent crime rate	Three-year (1989-91) average of index violent crimes (homicide, rape, robbery, aggravated assault) per 1,000 population
Homicide rate	Three-year (1989-91) average of homicides (murders and nonnegligent manslaughter) per 1,000 population
Rape rate	Three-year (1989-91) average of forcible rapes per 1,000 females
Robbery rate	Three-year (1989-91) average of robberies per 1,000 population
Assault rate	Three-year (1989-91) average of aggravated assaults per 1,000 population
Tract age	1990 minus initial year tracted (range 0-60)
Percentage young males	Percentage of the total tract population that is male and 15 to 24 years of age
Percentage Black	Percentage of the total tract population that is Black
Public housing	1 = Public housing project in the tract or in an adjacent tract 0 = No public housing project
Economic deprivation	Index composed of the average *z*-scores of the following four indicators: Percentage of tract population below the poverty line Percentage of tract families that are female headed Percentage of tract civilian noninstitutionalized persons 16 years and older who are either unemployed or not in the labor force Percentage of tract civilian noninstitutionalized persons 16 and older who are employed in professional or managerial occupations
Residential instability	Index composed of the average *z*-scores of the following three indicators: Percentage of tract-occupied housing units that are renter occupied Percentage of tract population five years or older that moved between 1985 and 1990 Percentage of tract housing units that are vacant
Recreation centers	Number of recreation centers in the tract or in an adjacent tract
Libraries	Number of libraries in the tract or in an adjacent tract
Retail/employment institutions	Number of chain grocery stores and banks in the tract or in an adjacent tract
Bars	Number of bars in the tract or in an adjacent tract (square root)

stores and banks. Bars are establishments with liquor licenses where drinking is the primary activity. We employed a two-stage process to identify bars.

Retail establishments holding a State of Ohio liquor license for drinking on the premises such as a restaurant, private club, or night club were first identified. Next, each establishment was considered to be a bar when (1) the name given in the Department of Liquor Control documents included club, lounge, bar, or tavern; (2) it was listed as a club, lounge, bar, or tavern in the Columbus Yellow Pages; (3) knowledgeable sources agreed that the establishment was a bar; or (4) it was confirmed as such via telephone survey. This operationalization excludes establishments that have liquor licenses for consumption on the premises but where drinking is not the primary activity, for example, restaurants, bowling alleys, and the like.[6] Finally, we create a dummy variable for public housing that distinguishes tracts without any public housing projects from those with at least one project in the tract or in an adjacent tract.[7]

None of the measures noted above provides a truly complete definition of the hypothesized social control mechanisms. Ideally, it would be helpful to have a more comprehensive set of retail establishments (i.e., local as well as chain businesses and a wider range of types of establishments). It would also be useful to know not only the prevalence of each institutional type but also levels of participation (including employment within the local retail establishments) and the nature of available programs provided by local organizations (e.g., after-school child care, youth groups, sports leagues, neighborhood associations). Unfortunately, it would be very difficult and costly to collect data that measure these aspects of the various institutions. Consequently, we use counts as indirect proxies for these more specific characteristics of organizations that should help to control crime. Given the limitations of the indicators, our results must be interpreted cautiously. Still, any significant effects are likely conservative estimates of the influence of institutions that would be much stronger if the quality of the measures were better.

Other Independent Variables

To capture aspects of the structural sources of social disorganization, we include measures of economic deprivation and residential instability. We use an index of economic deprivation because of substantial intercorrelations among a number of census tract indicators of this construct and following the recommendations and practices of recent analysts (Bursik and Grasmick 1993; Land, McCall, and Cohen 1990; Messner and Golden 1992; Morenoff and Sampson 1997). This index is operationalized as the average of the standardized (z) scores for the following four variables: (1) percentage of the population in poverty, (2) percentage of families headed by females, (3) percentage of civilian noninstitutionalized persons age 16 and older who are either unemployed or not in the labor force, and (4) percentage of civilian noninstitutionalized persons age 16 and older who are employed in professional or managerial occupations (reverse coded).[8] Exploratory factor analysis confirmed that the individual indicators reflect the same underlying construct.

Following conceptual arguments of Wilson (1987, 1996) and recent empirical evidence that disadvantage has a particularly strong effect on *violent* crime when it is extremely high (Krivo and Peterson 1996), we carefully explored whether the relationship between economic deprivation and violence is nonlinear and found this to be the case. In particular, the effect of economic deprivation on criminal violence is moderate, positive, and linear until disadvantage reaches extreme levels; after this point, the slope escalates dramatically. To specify properly this form of nonlinearity, our models allow for different slopes *within* these two portions of the deprivation distribution. Specifically, we include two variables to capture the separate slopes: (1) the economic deprivation slope—deprivation index value for tracts with economic deprivation up to 1 standard deviation above the mean (.86) and 0 otherwise, and (2) the extreme economic deprivation slope—deprivation index value for tracts with economic deprivation greater than 1 standard deviation above the mean (>.86) and 0 otherwise. This specifies the economic deprivation effect as a spline function.[9]

In addition to economic deprivation, we include a measure of residential instability. This is a composite index composed of the average *z*-scores of the following three variables: residential mobility (percentage of residents five years of age and older living in a different dwelling five years ago), rental occupancy (percentage of occupied housing units that are renter-occupied), and the vacancy rate (percentage of all housing units that are vacant). Exploratory factor analysis confirmed that the individual indicators reflect the same underlying construct (see also Bursik and Grasmick 1993; Morenoff and Sampson 1997).

The analysis also includes three control variables: the percentage of the tract population that is male and in the crime-prone ages (15-24), the percentage of the tract population that is Black, and tract age. Note that percentage Black captures the tract-level association of minority concentration with criminal violence, rather than being a measure of ethnic heterogeneity. The age of the tract is measured as 1990 minus the census decade in which the current area was first officially tracted within the city of Columbus. This city was initially divided into tracts in 1930 and has expanded considerably since that time. Thus, tract age varies from 0 for areas incorporated into the city only in 1990 to 60 for tracts within the city continuously since 1930. The control for tract age is necessary because there may be unmeasured characteristics of older areas (e.g., economic decline, poor housing) that are associated with both institutions and increased violent crime. Due to historical growth patterns, older tracts may have more libraries, recreation centers, and other institutions. Consequently, without a control for tract age, we could find a positive effect of institutions on violent crime that reflects the unmeasured characteristics rather than, as we argue, the social control influence of institutions.

Statistical Analyses

Our basic model specifies that violent crime is a function of economic deprivation, residential instability, public housing, neighborhood institutions, and control variables. We use ordinary least squares (OLS) regression to estimate models of overall and different types of violent index crimes. To capture the potential nonlinear effect of bars in which an additional tavern leads to a larger increase in violence when there are few bars than when bars are already numerous, we take the square root of this independent variable.[10] Multicollinearity often is problematic in analyses of aggregate units. As noted above, this is the main reason for using indices of economic deprivation and residential instability. Careful examination of condition indices and variance-decomposition proportions revealed no problems from multicollinearity in the parameter estimates presented below (Belsley, Kuh, and Welsch 1980).

RESULTS

Descriptive and Bivariate Results

Table 2 presents the zero-order correlation matrix of all of the variables along with their means and standard deviations. The means show that for Columbus in 1990 the overall violent crime rate was 11.8 per 1,000. The bulk of these violent crimes was robberies and assaults (means of 6.1 and 4.4, respectively). With regard to the institutional variables of interest, more than one-third (37 percent) of tracts has at least one public housing project in or adjacent to it. Columbus census tracts have an average of just less than one recreation center and .54 libraries in or nearby. However, these numbers mask the fact that about 37 percent ($n = 65$) of tracts have no recreation center and 54 percent ($n = 96$) have no library. At the same time, about a quarter of areas have more than two recreation centers, but very few places have more than a single library nearby. There is an average of eight retail/ employment establishments per tract, with eight tracts having no such institutions. Finally, there is an average of nine bars per tract, with only one-fifth of areas having three or fewer drinking establishments in or nearby (only 3 percent have none, $n = 5$).

TABLE 2: Correlations, Means, and Standard Deviations of Dependent and Independent Variables: Census Tracts in Columbus, 1990

	Violence Rate	*Homicide Rate*	*Rape Rate*	*Robbery Rate*	*Assault Rate*	*Tract Age*	*Percent Young Males*	*Percent Black*	*Public Housing*	*Economic Deprivation*	*Extreme Deprivation*	*Residential Instability*	*Recreation Centers*	*Libraries*	*Retail*	*Bars (square root)*
Violent crime rate	1.000															
Homicide rate	.757	1.000														
Rape rate	.902	.642	1.000													
Robbery rate	.937	.640	.789	1.000												
Aggravated assault rate	.936	.767	.876	.757	1.000											
Tract age	.535	.386	.436	.534	.477	1.000										
Percent young males	.085	–.076	.150	.141	.015	.110	1.000									
Percent Black	.602	.620	.578	.421	.704	.205	–.080	1.000								
Public housing	.423	.283	.380	.370	.428	.199	–.039	.282	1.000							
Economic deprivation slope[a]	.423	.331	.422	.354	.435	.442	.252	.451	.360	1.000						

Extreme economic deprivation slope[a]	.779	.681	.701	.611	.856	.397	−.043	.575	.388	.189	1.000					
Residential instability	.427	.184	.447	.465	.326	.152	.471	.089	.073	.019	.303	1.000				
Recreation centers	.463	.390	.410	.367	.509	.470	−.055	.392	.338	.398	.459	.015	1.000			
Libraries	.377	.339	.350	.333	.371	.358	−.089	.206	.220	.300	.359	.021	.513	1.000		
Libraries	.377	.339	.350	.333	.371	.358	−.089	.206	.220	.300	.359	.021	.513	1.000		
Retail/ employment institutions	−.009	−.129	−.012	.103	−.121	.068	−.028	−.300	.003	−.311	.004	.164	.009	.122	1.000	
Bars (square root)	.563	.355	.531	.566	.490	.538	.285	.164	.341	.326	.445	.368	.576	.475	.336	1.000
Mean	11.807	.242	1.940	6.116	4.443	39.887	8.470	25.27	.367	−.242	.242	.000	.972	.537	8.232	2.765[b]
SD	11.760	.292	2.017	6.043	5.278	18.122	6.271	29.57	.483	.550	.566	.850	.968	.649	6.795	1.210

a. The means and standard deviations for items that make up the economic deprivation index are 18.22 (16.69) for percentage below poverty, 25.49 (16.11) for percentage female-headed families, 35.38 (13.60) for percentage total jobless, and 17.23 (11.01) for percentage professionals.
b. The mean of the absolute number of bars is 9.1, with a standard deviation of 7.7.

The zero-order correlations show that, as expected, economic deprivation, residential instability, and public housing all have positive associations with each type of violent crime. This is also true for tract age and percentage Black. Young age structure has a positive but weak relationship with all types of violent crime except homicide; its association with murder is weak and negative ($r = -.08$). Contrary to theoretical expectations, recreation centers and libraries have positive rather than negative associations with crime, perhaps due to their relationship with tract age. Retail/employment institutions generally have the anticipated negative associations with all types of violence, whereas areas with more bars have higher levels of violent crime. Note that the presence of public housing has a moderate association with economic deprivation but only a minimal correlation with residential instability.

Multivariate Results: Overall Violent Crime

Table 3 presents the results of OLS models examining the effects of public housing, economic deprivation, residential instability, and neighborhood institutions on overall rates of violent crime. We first examine a model that explores the additive effects of the explanatory variables. This model allows us to assess whether the effect of public housing on violent crime remains after accounting for its association with other census tract conditions, whether institutions have independent effects on violence, and whether any such effects account for the strong influence of deprivation.

This model demonstrates that, as measured here, public housing does not have an independent influence on violent crime. When controlling for other factors, the presence of public housing is not significant. Furthermore, its net effect is weak ($\beta = .06$) and substantially smaller than its standardized bivariate association with violent crime ($r = .42$, see Table 2). In results not reported in the table, we determined that this reduction is heavily due to the association of public housing with economic deprivation rather than to its relationship with residential instability. When the disadvantage variables are excluded from the model presented in Table 3, public housing has a large significant effect on violence. In contrast, its influence is the same as that reported in Model 1 when only residential instability is excluded.

Regarding the social disorganization variables, residential instability is significantly associated with heightened rates of violent crime. Economic deprivation also has a positive effect; however, the nature of this relationship is more complex. Recall that economic deprivation has a nonlinear effect estimated as a spline function, with different slopes for extreme and nonextreme portions of the deprivation distribution. The two coefficients show that economic deprivation leads to much more substantial increases in violence in tracts where disadvantage is extremely high ($b = 8.7$) than in other

TABLE 3: Regression of Violent Crime Rates on Social Disorganization, Public Housing, Institution, and Control Variables: Census Tracts in Columbus, 1990

	Model 1		*Model 2*	
	b (SE)	β	b (SE)	β
Tract age	.110**	.170	.111**	.170
	(.031)		(.031)	
Young males	–.170	–.090	–.155	–.083
	(.090)		(.088)	
Percent Black	.086**	.216	.091**	.229
	(.021)		(.021)	
Public housing	1.526	.063	1.257	.052
	(1.046)		(1.019)	
Economic-deprivation slope	2.893**	.212[a]	2.404*	.176[a]
	(1.195)		(1.174)	
Extreme-economic-deprivation slope	8.739**	.639[a]	8.211**	.601[a]
	(1.178)		(3.129)	
Residential instability	3.196**	.231	3.229**	.234
	(.645)		(.627)	
Recreation centers	–1.034	–.085	–.012	–.001
	(.644)		(.705)	
Libraries	.338	.019	.100	.005
	(.823)		(.808)	
Retail/employment institutions	–.025	–.014	–.034	–.020
	(.079)		(.078)	
Bars (square root)	1.650**	.170	1.290*	.133
	(.609)		(.613)	
Recreation Centers * Extreme Economic Deprivation			–2.795**	–.331
			(.811)	
Bars (square root) * Extreme Economic Deprivation			1.497*	.312
			(.796)	
Constant	1.164		1.092	
Adjusted R^2	.772		.785	
(N = 177)				

a. The betas for the economic-deprivation slope variables were calculated by using the standard deviation of the *continuous* economic-deprivation index (s = .860).
*$p < .05$. **$p < .01$.

areas (b = 2.9). Thus, the same amount of change in economic deprivation leads to three times the increase in violent crime in the most disadvantaged areas. Note that the social disorganization variables are among the strongest predictors of violence (see the βs). Only racial composition has as strong an effect as these factors. Furthermore, extreme economic deprivation has by far the strongest influence (β = .64) and a very sizable absolute effect. Once economic disadvantage reaches extreme levels, one additional unit of the index leads to a dramatic increase of 8.7 violent crimes per 1,000 residents (nearly three-quarters the mean rate). Clearly, these effects for deprivation and instability are significant and strong even though they are net of institutional prevalence.

Examining the parameters for the individual institution variables shows a mixed pattern. Recreation centers, libraries, and retail/employment institutions do not have significant effects on levels of criminal violence. Although the effects of recreation centers and retail establishments are in the expected negative direction, apparently these institutions do not have the overall stabilizing influence implied in prior literature. By contrast, a greater prevalence of bars in Columbus tracts is related to higher levels of violent crime. This result is consistent with arguments that bars are contexts that generate nonconventional activities both within the taverns and in the areas surrounding them; drinking is more prevalent, and inhibitions and social control are presumably undermined. Thus, we find that the one institution that is considered to heighten crime has the anticipated effect. Also, its influence is moderate, tied with tract age for the fifth strongest of the 11 variables.

To further explore the ways in which institutions affect crime, we conducted additional analyses to assess whether institutions interact with economic deprivation. The findings reveal that bars and recreation centers both interact with extreme deprivation. The results including these two significant interactions are reported as Model 2. These show that recreation centers have virtually no effect on violent crime when deprivation is very low to moderate (for the main effect, $b = -.01$). However, these institutions have a sizable negative influence in areas of extreme disadvantage. For example, when extreme disadvantage is at its lowest level (.86), the effect of recreation centers is large (i.e., $b = -.01 + [-2.80 * .86] = -2.42$). And, as extreme deprivation becomes more severe, the crime-reducing influence of recreation centers on violence steadily increases. The interaction with bars demonstrates that the number of drinking establishments has a positive influence on violent crime at all levels of disadvantage, but this effect is significantly and increasingly greater in extremely disadvantaged than other areas.

To illustrate more clearly the patterns of these interactions, we calculated predicted rates of violent crime for tracts with low (–.86), average (0), and extreme (.86) economic deprivation and varying numbers of both bars (2, 6, and 20) and recreation centers (0, 1, and 2). In computing the predicted rates, we hold tract age, percentage young males, percentage Black, public housing, residential instability, libraries, and retail/employment institutions constant at their mean tract levels. The results are shown in Table 4. Looking first at areas with no recreation centers (panel A), tracts with low levels of deprivation and very few bars (2) have violent crime rates of 6.5 per 1,000, well below the Columbus mean of 11.8. When the number of bars changes to a

TABLE 4: Predicted Violent Crime Rates by Level of Economic Deprivation, Number of Bars, and Number of Recreation Centers

	Number of Bars		
	Few (2)	*Moderate (6)*	*Numerous (20)*
Panel A: zero recreation centers			
Economic deprivation			
Low	6.5	7.8	10.4
Average	8.6	9.9	12.5
Extreme	17.4	20.1	25.3
Panel B: one recreation center			
Economic deprivation			
Low	6.5	7.8	10.5
Average	8.6	9.9	12.5
Extreme	15.1	17.7	22.9
Panel C: two recreation centers			
Economic deprivation			
Low	6.5	7.9	10.5
Average	8.6	9.9	12.5
Extreme	12.7	15.3	20.5

moderate level (6), the violent crime rate increases by only 1.3 per 1,000 (to 7.8). And when the number of bars is quite extensive (20), the crime rate is only another 2.6 per 1,000 higher.[11] Note that all tracts with low levels of deprivation experience levels of violent crime below the mean, with bars playing only a small role in intensifying local violence. Areas of average economic deprivation have higher violent crime rates. However, bars play the same modest role in increasing criminal violence in such census tracts (predicted rates are 8.6, 9.9, and 12.5 for areas with few, moderate, and numerous numbers of bars, respectively).

The picture is quite different in areas with extreme economic deprivation and no recreation centers. Here, violent crime is consistently above average regardless of the number of bars. However, in extremely disadvantaged tracts, increases in the number of bars lead to notably greater increments in violent crime than is the case in other tracts. The violent crime rate increases by 2.7 (from 17.4 to 20.1) when going from few to a moderate number of bars and by another 5.2 (to 25.3) when bars become numerous. In brief, bars appear to be a breeding ground for violent crime in areas that also confront the many problems associated with substantial levels of economic deprivation.

Panels B and C, where there are one or two recreation centers, also show the strong effects of both deprivation and bars on violence. However, comparing the three panels indicates the additional importance of the interaction between recreation centers and extreme deprivation. When deprivation is low or average, recreation centers do not alter the violent crime rate. To illustrate, the rate of violence is 6.5 in low-deprivation areas without a recreation center in or nearby, and the same is true of low-deprivation tracts with one or two such facilities. In contrast, the presence of recreation centers in extremely disadvantaged areas serves to reduce violent crime. For example, extremely disadvantaged tracts with few bars and *no* recreation centers have a violent crime rate of 17.4 per 1,000 compared with that of 15.1 per 1,000 when there is *one* recreation facility and 12.7 when there are *two* such centers. Thus, the addition of a recreation center to an extreme-deprivation tract leads to a *decrease* in violent crime of 2.3 per 1,000 population (about one-fifth of the average rate). This is true no matter how many bars are present. As a result, the effect of extreme deprivation is weaker in areas with one or more recreation centers in or nearby than is the case when none is present. Therefore, recreation centers do appear to help counter the violence-producing effects of extreme deprivation so that when they are present, overall levels of violence do not reach the peak rates observed in extreme-deprivation areas that lack these institutions.

Individual Violent Crimes

To examine whether the patterns found for general levels of violence apply across different types of violent crime, we performed the same OLS regression analyses separately for rates of homicide, rape, robbery, and aggravated assault. The results from the interaction models are presented in Table 5. Overall, the findings for the individual crimes show similarities in the effects of a number of key variables with those reported for total rates. Net of other factors, the *presence* of public housing has a negligible and nonsignificant effect on all four crimes. Except for homicide, this is due to public housing's strong association with economic deprivation (results not reported). Also consistent with earlier findings, libraries and retail/employment institutions generally do not influence the levels of different types of violent crime. The one exception is that the number of retail establishments has a significant negative effect on assault, although this association is relatively weak ($\beta = -.07$).

The remaining important patterns found in these models are more complex. As with overall violence, economic deprivation, recreation centers, and bars all influence the various types of violent crime, and these effects are conditional. However, the specific patterns of these interactions vary across the four individual crimes. For homicide, neither of the two interactions is significant. With regard to rape and robbery, recreation centers have a notable

TABLE 5: Regressions of Rates of Homicide, Rape, Robbery, and Aggravated Assault on Social Disorganization, Public Housing, Institutions, and Control Variables: Census Tracts in Columbus, Ohio 1990

	Homicide		*Rape*		*Robbery*		*Aggravated Assault*	
	b (SE)	β	b (SE)	β	b (SE)	β	b (SE)	β
Tract age	.002	.096	.006	.056	.085**	.255	.021*	.074
	(.001)		(.006)		(.021)		(.011)	
Young males	–.006	–.131	–.007	–.021	–.072	–.074	–.064*	–.076
	(.003)		(.018)		(.061)		(.032)	
Percentage Black	.003**	.284	.018**	.269	.036**	.177	.042**	.237
	(.001)		(.004)		(.015)		(.008)	
Public housing	–.019	–.031	.077	.019	.989	.079	.263	.024
	(.036)		(.206)		(.709)		(.373)	
Economic-deprivation slope	.041	.122[a]	.505*	.215[a]	.846	.121[a]	1.214**	.200[a]
	(.042)		(.237)		(.817)		(.430)	
Extreme-economic-deprivation slope	.329**	.970[a]	.904	.386[a]	.813	.116[a]	6.371**	1.039[a]
	(.112)		(.632)		(2.178)		(1.146)	
Residential instability	.014	.040	.608**	.256	2.105**	.296	.790**	.127
	(.022)		(.127)		(.436)		(.230)	
Recreation centers	–.040	–.133	.097	.047	–.297	–.048	.317	.058
	(.025)		(.142)		(.491)		(.258)	
Libraries	.030	.067	.070	.023	.185	.020	–.160	–.020
	(.029)		(.163)		(.563)		(.296)	
Retail/employment institutions	–.003	–.071	–.003	–.010	.025	.028	–.053*	–.068
	(.003)		(.016)		(.054)		(.029)	

(continued)

TABLE 5: Continued

	Homicide		*Rape*		*Robbery*		*Aggravated Assault*	
	b (SE)	β	b (SE)	β	b (SE)	β	b (SE)	β
Bars (square root)	.042*	.174	.190	.114	.739*	.148	.419*	.096
	(.022)		(.124)		(.426)		(.224)	
Recreation Centers * Extreme Economic Deprivation	.039	.184	–.774**	–.534	–1.512**	–.348	–.964**	–.254
	(.029)		(.164)		(.565)		(.297)	
Bars (square root) * Extreme Economic Deprivation	–.047	–.397	.471**	.572	1.156*	.469	.217	.099
	(.028)		(.161)		(.554)		(.291)	
Constant	.057		.443		–.388		1.034	
Adjusted R^2	.555		.703		.606		.857	
(N = 177)								

a. The betas for the economic-deprivation slopes were calculated by using the standard deviation of the *continuous* deprivation index (s = .860).
$^*p < .05$. $^{**}p < .01$.

and increasingly negative effect in extremely deprived tracts but no effect in less disadvantaged areas. Bars also have a more sizable and growing positive influence in more than less deprived areas. For aggravated assault, only recreation centers interact with extreme deprivation such that these facilities reduce violence in extremely disadvantaged but not other areas. These patterns can be seen more clearly in Figure 1, which shows the predicted rates of the four individual violent crimes by level of disadvantage, number of bars, and number of recreation centers. As above, all other variables are held constant at their mean tract levels.

The results for homicide differ most from those for total and the other three types of violent crime. Extreme deprivation significantly increases killings, and bars neither add to nor intensify this effect. An influence of bars is apparent only among areas of low deprivation. Although recreation centers seem to reduce homicide slightly in these areas, this influence is not significant (see Table 5). Rape and robbery show different patterns that are more like each other and the overall violence results. In particular, whether deprivation is low or extreme, areas with many bars have higher rape and robbery rates than census tracts with few bars (see the height of the shaded bars compared with the white ones). However, in areas of extreme deprivation, the impact of bars on rape and robbery is particularly large. Rape and robbery rates are at least one and a half times higher in areas of extreme deprivation with numerous bars than in their counterparts with few bars. The impact of bars is much more muted in low-deprivation tracts. As with total violence, recreation centers reduce robbery and rape in extremely disadvantaged areas, thereby diminishing the violence-producing influence of economic deprivation.

The final graph in Figure 1 shows a pattern for assault that is slightly different from the previous two crimes. Bars have a modest significant effect on increasing assaults that is similar in low and extremely deprived tracts. Furthermore, recreation centers decrease assaults somewhat within the most deprived areas, leading to a slightly reduced but still very large influence of economic deprivation on this type of violence.

CONCLUSIONS

Recent literature has highlighted the importance of the institutional base within neighborhoods for explaining why economic deprivation is linked to high rates of crime. Both social disorganization theory and Wilson's underclass perspective point to the potential centrality of community institutions in connecting individuals to valued roles within society and reinforcing the ability of residents to exercise social control. In this view, it is hypothesized

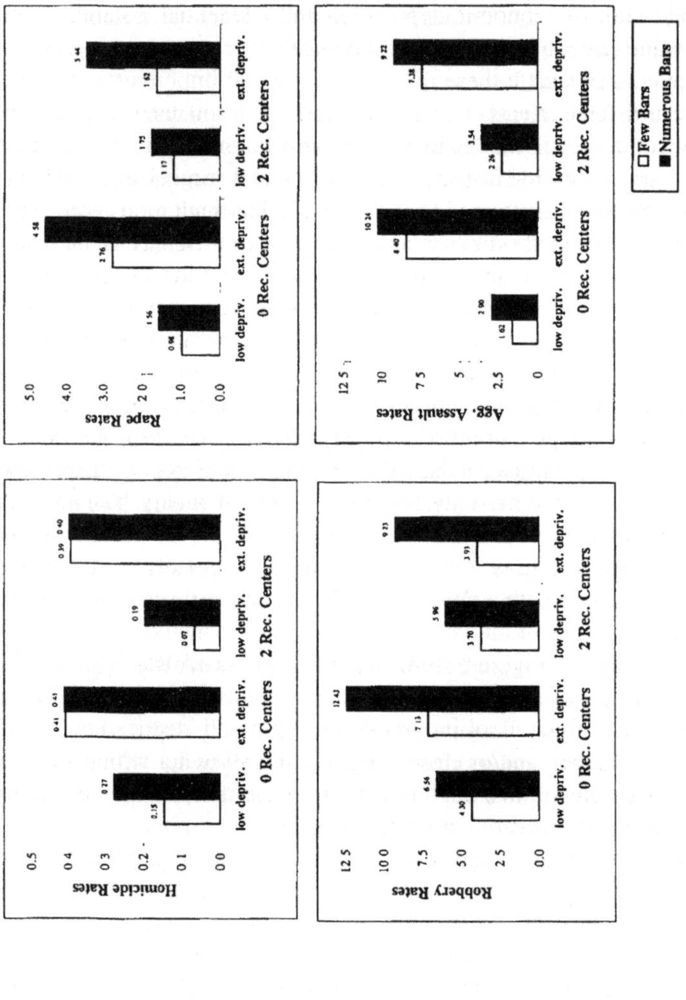

Figure 1: Predicted Rates of Homicide, Rape, Robbery, and Aggravated Assault by Level of Deprivation, Number of Bars, and Number of Recreation Centers: Census Tracts in Columbus, 1990

that economically disadvantaged neighborhoods lack the institutional capacity to foster realization of common values and control crime. We evaluated this argument by examining whether different types of local institutions mediate the relationship between economic deprivation and overall as well as different types of violent crime. We also sought to clarify how the presence of public housing is related to criminal violence. Is public housing simply another indicator of economic deprivation and residential instability, or is there a unique effect of this factor on violence?

Our findings elucidate these questions in several important ways. First, they indicate that the effects of economic deprivation and residential instability on violent crime are independent of the institutional structures explored here. In models including institutions, these social disorganization variables remain strong and significant. This is because the institutions themselves only have limited effects on violence, at least as measured here. In particular, the presence of retail/establishments and libraries is not associated with general or specific rates of violence. One interpretation of this finding is that such institutions truly are unrelated to criminal violence because they lack sufficient breadth and power of social influence to either add to the crime reducing characteristics of advantaged areas or combat the crime-generating conditions of disadvantaged areas. Thus, institutions may provide positive resources for communities but these do not, in turn, sufficiently alter the conditions (e.g., residential mobility, housing and school quality, business location) that Wilson and others view as key to crime and other social dislocations.

Alternatively, we may not have identified significant relationships because our measures are simply too crude to capture the crime-controlling aspects of the local institutional base. We were able to include only counts of libraries and major chain establishments. Although difficult to obtain, indicators that tap the prevalence of a wider range of public services and businesses (e.g., youth and after-school programs, locally based businesses) and that measure participation and/or employment would allow for stronger tests of the theoretical contentions. Such tests might yield more support for claims that institutions do stabilize communities and curtail crime.

In contrast to libraries and retail establishments, we find that a greater prevalence of recreation centers does reduce violent crime somewhat at least in the most economically disadvantaged areas.[12] In these contexts, areas with more recreation centers have lower rates of rape, robbery, and aggravated assault. This is not obvious to most observers of urban neighborhoods because violence remains startlingly high in light of the stronger effect of disadvantage. However, our findings strongly suggest that rates of violence would be even higher in some of the most economically deprived areas if these tracts had fewer recreation centers. These findings are evident even though recreation centers are also measured as a simple count of facilities.

Perhaps this result emerged because the very presence of recreation centers is a better indicator than the other institutional measures of the availability of programming that serves social control functions. Still, the number of recreational facilities is not a direct indicator of such programming. Therefore, the fact that even modest effects are identified here may indicate that the potential of local institutional mechanisms to reduce crime is even greater than demonstrated in this investigation. If so, policies that bolster the availability of institutions that provide meaningful recreational and other social activities within disadvantaged areas may serve communities well in their fight against crime.

Still, such public service institutions work against substantial obstacles in light of the generally important effect of bars in increasing violence. With the exception of homicide in extremely disadvantaged areas, tracts with more bars have higher levels of every type of violent crime irrespective of their level of economic deprivation. These effects are often sizable in magnitude. However, with our data, it is impossible to determine whether the bars' effect is due to disinhibition, defensive posturing and social interaction in situated company, or the fact that numerous bars are signs of disorder and weak community control. All are possibilities that require attention in future research.

The difficulty in determining why bars are important is further complicated by the fact that the prevalence of bars does not have a uniform effect. Bars have stronger effects on violence in extremely deprived areas but only for robbery and rape. No prior theory or research helps to make sense of this pattern. Why would selective disinhibition encourage only more robbery or rape? Parker and his colleagues argue for the possibility of stronger effects of alcohol consumption for crimes with a weaker normative base (Parker 1995; Parker and Auerhahn 1999; Parker and Rebhun 1995). However, it seems likely that the normative structures opposing robbery and rape are quite strong and stronger even than those for assaults where bars do not have as great an effect in areas of extreme disadvantage. But even if incorrect, it is unclear why the differential effects for bars occur only in areas of extreme disadvantage. Clearly analysts need to explore the varying nature of individual types of violent crimes in disadvantaged communities with and without many bars to determine how the situation of violent transactions and other aspects of the local context differentially affect the various crime types. Such research should also explore the reasons for the more pronounced levels of assault (and homicide) in extremely deprived tracts with no or few bars because this, too, could provide part of the explanation for the observed patterns. In areas of extreme deprivation, assaults and homicide are already so high that bars do not contribute as large an addition to these types of violence. Future researchers should explore whether defensive posturing, role modeling, or institutional weaknesses not explored in this article help explain the particularly important effects of deprivation on homicide and assault.

Public housing is another part of the institutional fabric of communities that we argued would contribute to violent crime. As noted, prior research was ambiguous as to whether this effect is due totally to the obvious association of public housing with economic deprivation and residential instability. Our results using a measure that captures the presence of public housing in or adjacent to a tract suggest that the relationship between public housing and violent crime is indirect. Public housing does not significantly influence violent crime when aspects of social disorganization, particularly economic deprivation, are controlled. Thus, public housing policies that have led to the development of projects that concentrate deprivation may have inadvertently contributed to the crime problem of neighborhoods. That is, our results imply that current policies seeking to decentralize publicly supported housing may reduce neighborhood crime rates. We caution, however, that to date, there is no clear evidence about how such policies would affect local crime or other social problems. Ludwig, Duncan, and Hirschfield (1999) demonstrate that moving seriously deprived families to low-poverty neighborhoods reduces teen involvement in violent crime but increases property offending. Galster and Zobel's (1998) review of studies of dispersed low-income housing programs (Gautreaux-type Section 8 housing dispersal, Scattered-Site Public Housing, and Moving to Opportunity demonstrations) indicates that the evidence regarding their consequences is highly inconclusive. Studies have shown that individual movers benefit in numerous ways from dispersal to low-poverty neighborhoods, including in terms of reduced crime and fear of crime in their own residential communities (see also Rosenbaum and Popkin 1991; Rosenbaum, Kulieke, and Rubinowitz 1988). However, whether overall levels of crime in a city or metropolitan area are reduced through such shifts of residents is unknown because this depends on the nature of the relationship between poverty and crime.

In sum, we began with the question of whether local institutions matter for controlling neighborhood violence. The findings provide some support for such institutional effects. One of the "stabilizing" institutions that we consider (recreation centers) has a crime-reducing impact in extremely disadvantaged areas. Thus, local communities may help to reduce their crime problems by developing a larger internal institutional base, but we caution that additional research is needed to specify more fully what types of institutions, and programs within them, will have the most payoff. Gains in reducing violence would also be forthcoming from preventing the encroachment of large numbers of drinking establishments or other settings where individuals spend significant amounts of idle time and engage in behaviors that may impair judgment. The current direction of policies to dismantle and restructure public housing developments also may decrease violent crime in communities through its impact in deconcentrating poverty. Most important, though, and consistent with much previous research, the key determinants of neighborhood crime appear to be economic deprivation and residential instability. Therefore, in the final analysis, efforts to reduce crime must counter the macro-structural forces that increase economic deprivation and lead to inner-city decline.

NOTES

1. Knowledgeable experts indicate that this is the case for public housing in the city that is the site of this research, Columbus, Ohio (Hartman 1999; Holloway 1999).

2. Most of the excluded units are split tracts that are almost entirely in a suburb and extend only very slightly over the city line. Hence, the size of the city population in these tracts is quite small. Other excluded tracts, including the downtown area, simply have small residential populations. Three additional tracts are excluded because their populations reside predominantly in institutions or group quarters (e.g., prisons, college dormitories).

3. Geographic Data Technology, Inc. (GTD) is a private company that performs geocoding of address data to Census and Federal Information Processing Standards (FIPS) codes. To perform the geocoding, this organization uses its own private software, Software Designer's Kit, in conjunction with 1990 TIGER files updated for post-1990 street changes and corrected for errors such as incorrect street spellings. We chose this corporation because it has a much higher address-matching rate and greater accuracy in coding than alternatives available to us (ARC/INFO and original 1990 TIGER files).

4. The Federal Bureau of Investigation (FBI) defines forcible rape as carnal knowledge of a female. Therefore, the denominator for our rape measure consists of females rather than the total population. However, the total violent crime rate includes rapes of females in the numerator along with the other violent crimes but still uses the total population as the denominator. We explored an alternate operationalization of the total violent crime rate in which we summed the rape rate per 1,000 females with the other three individual violent crimes per 1,000 total population. Both operationalizations of this dependent variable yielded the same pattern of results. Along different lines, the use of the resident population of the tract as the denominator does not take into account the possibility that residents are not the only individuals at risk of victimization within any tract. Nonresidents may be victimized while in the area (Boggs 1965). Hence, the victimization rates analyzed here are not truly risk rates; technically, they are rates of prevalence rather than rates of incidence.

5. A tract is considered as adjacent when it borders (fully or partially) a given other tract. Thus, each tract may have multiple adjacent tracts. We identified which tracts are adjacent by carefully examining a map of all census tracts in the city of Columbus and determining which tracts share borders.

6. This two-stage procedure was necessary because a careful examination of the types of liquor licenses obtained by particular establishments determined that these did not distinguish the businesses by their primary activity. Thus, well-known restaurants might have bar or tavern liquor licenses and vice versa.

7. Our measure of public housing includes only structures managed by the Columbus Metropolitan Housing Authority and does not include alternative types of subsidized housing such

as Section 8 apartments. Of note, in constructing the public housing variable, we considered alternative and more refined categories, for example, 0, 1-3, and 4+ projects. Using the alternative categorization provided similar conclusions to those that are presented below. Therefore, we report findings for the more parsimonious operationalization. Two other alternatives were also considered—the number and percentage of public housing units in the tract. However, because the overwhelming majority of areas does not have public housing, these variables have very high proportions of zero values. In light of these distributions, the use of the dichotomous dummy variable captures what appears to be the substantively important distinction, the presence or absence of public housing.

8. The professionals/managers' variable indicates greater economic deprivation when they are less (rather than more) prevalent. Therefore, the standardized score for this variable was reverse coded before incorporating it into the index of economic deprivation.

9. This specification follows that suggested by Goodman (1979) for exploring alternative forms of the relationship between education and earnings. This also follows Krivo and Peterson's (1996) analysis of extreme neighborhood disadvantage and urban crime. Note that the economic deprivation slope measures are not simply a trichotomous dummy variable operationalization; rather, they take on their continuous values (not simply 1) *within* the respective extreme and nonextreme portions of the disadvantage distribution. In brief, these variables specify a functional form in which the slope of economic deprivation is allowed to differ between tracts with extreme levels of deprivation and tracts with lower levels of disadvantage.

10. We use the square root rather than a logarithmic transformation because there are areas with no bars, and one cannot take the log of zero.

11. Recall that the number of bars is operationalized as a square root and hence its effect on violent crime decreases as the number of bars increases. This is why the predicted crime rate increases by only twice the amount when going from moderate to numerous bars (i.e., the increase of 2.6) as when going from few to moderate bars (i.e., the increase of 1.3), even though the number of bars themselves increases by more than three times the amount in the former (14 bars) than the latter (4 bars) case.

12. Throughout this analysis, we have assumed that violence is produced by the social variables that we consider. Yet, our independent and dependent variables are measured contemporaneously. Thus, it is possible that crime could affect neighborhoods in such a way as to reduce the number or presence of stabilizing institutions (i.e., public authorities or business executives may decide not to locate institutions in heavily crime-ridden areas, or existing businesses may relocate and public services may be closed down as crime and violence become a problem in an area). Although this could be the case, careful examination of the location of recreation centers in Columbus shows that a large number of such facilities are, in fact, still currently located in tracts in the older more central areas of the city, which also have the highest levels of violent crime. (This can be seen in the positive bivariate correlations of recreation centers with crime.) Thus, it seems unlikely that the reverse causal order described above holds for the institutional variable found to be significant here.

REFERENCES

Abramson, Alan J., Mitchell S. Tobin, and Matthew R. VanderGoot. 1995. "The Changing Geography of Metropolitan Opportunity: The Segregation of the Poor in U.S. Metropolitan Areas, 1970-1990." *Housing Policy Debate* 6:45-72.

Almgren, Gunnar, Avery Guest, George Immerwahr, and Michael Spittel. 1998. "Joblessness, Family Disruption, and Violent Death in Chicago, 1970-90." *Social Forces* 76:1465-93.

Bellair, Paul E. 1997. "Social Interaction and Community Crime: Explaining the Importance of Neighbor Networks." *Criminology* 35:677-703.

Belsley, David A., Edwin Kuh, and Roy E. Welsch. 1980. *Regression Diagnostics: Identifying Influential Data and Sources of Collinearity.* New York: John Wiley.

Bickford, Adam and Douglas S. Massey. 1991. "Segregation in the Second Ghetto: Racial and Ethnic Segregation in American Public Housing, 1977." *Social Forces* 69:1011-36.

Boggs, Sarah L. 1965. "Urban Crime Patterns." *American Sociological Review* 30:899-908.

Bursik, Robert J., Jr. 1989. "Political Decision-Making and Ecological Models of Delinquency: Consensus and Conflict." Pp. 105-17 in *Theoretical Integration in the Study of Deviance and Crime: Problems and Prospects*, edited by S. Messner, M. Krohn, and A. Liska. Albany: State University of New York Press.

Bursik, Robert J. and Harold G. Grasmick. 1993. "Economic Deprivation and Neighborhood Crime Rates." *Law and Society Review* 27:263-83.

Carter, William H., Michael H. Schill, and Susan M. Wachter. 1998. "Polarisation, Public Housing and Racial Minorities in US Cities." *Urban Studies* 35:1889-1911.

Columbus Police Department. 1994. *UCR Offense Reports: Selected Offenses by Census Tract, 1989-1992.* Columbus, OH: Columbus Police Department.

Covington, Jeanette. 1999. "African American Communities and Violent Crime: The Construction of Race Differences." *Sociological Focus* 32:7-24.

Crutchfield, Robert D. 1989. "Labor Stratification and Violent Crime." *Social Forces* 68: 489-512.

Crutchfield, Robert D., Ann Glusker, and George S. Bridges. 1999. "A Tale of Three Cities: Labor Markets and Homicide." *Sociological Focus* 32:65-83.

Curry, G. David and Irving A. Spergel. 1988. "Gang Homicide, Delinquency, and Community." *Criminology* 26:381-405.

Farley, John E. 1982. "Has Public Housing Gotten a Bum Rap? The Incidence of Crime in St. Louis Public Housing Developments." *Environment & Behavior* 14:443-77.

Galster, George and Ann Zobel. 1998. "Will Dispersed Housing Programmes Reduce Social Problems in the US?" *Housing Studies* 13:605-22.

Goodman, Jerry D. 1979. "The Economic Returns of Education: An Assessment of Alternative Models." *Social Science Quarterly* 60:269-83.

Greenberg, Stefanie W., William M. Rohe, and Jay R. Williams. 1982. *Safe and Secure Neighborhoods: Physical Characteristics and Informal Territorial Control in High and Low Crime Neighborhoods.* Washington, DC: U.S. Department of Justice, National Institute of Justice.

Hagedorn, John M. 1991. "Gangs, Neighborhoods, and Public Policy." *Social Problems* 38:529-42.

Hartman, Patricia. 1999. Personal Communication (July) with Vice President for Property Services, Ohio Capital Corporation for Housing, Columbus, OH.

Holloway, Steven R. 1999. Personal Communication (July). Department of Geography, University of Georgia, Athens.

Holloway, Steven R., Deborah Bryan, Robert Chabot, Donna M. Rogers, and James Rulli. 1998. "Exploring the Effect of Public Housing on the Concentration of Poverty in Columbus, Ohio." *Urban Affairs Review* 33:767-89.

Holzman, Harold R. 1996. "Criminological Research on Public Housing: Toward a Better Understanding of People, Places, and Spaces." *Crime & Delinquency* 42:361-78.

Jargowsky, Paul A. 1994. "Ghetto Poverty among Blacks in the 1980s." *Journal of Policy Management* 13:288-310.

———. 1997. *Poverty and Place: Ghettos, Barrios, and the American City.* New York: Russell Sage.

Jargowsky, Paul A. and Mary Jo Bane. 1990. "Ghetto Poverty: Basic Questions." Pp. 16-67 in *Inner-City Poverty in the United States*, edited by Laurence E. Lynn, Jr. and Michael G. H. McGeary. Washington, DC: National Academy Press.

———. 1991. "Ghetto Poverty in the United States, 1970-1980." Pp. 235-73 in *The Urban Underclass*, edited by Christopher Jencks and Paul E. Peterson. Washington, DC: The Brookings Institution.

Kasarda, John D. 1993. "Inner-City Concentrated Poverty and Neighborhood Distress: 1970 to 1990." *Housing Policy Debate* 4:253-302.

Kelling, George L. and Catherine M. Coles. 1996. *Fixing Broken Windows: Restoring Order and Reducing Crime in Our Communities*. New York: Martin Kessler Books.

Kohfeld, Carol W. and John Sprague. 1988. "Urban Unemployment Drives Urban Crime." *Urban Affairs Quarterly* 24:215-41.

———. 1990. "Demography, Police Behavior, and Deterrence." *Criminology* 28:111-36.

Kornhauser, Ruth Rosner. 1978. *Social Sources of Delinquency: An Appraisal of Analytic Models*. Chicago: University of Chicago Press.

Krivo, Lauren J. and Ruth D. Peterson. 1996. "Extremely Disadvantaged Neighborhoods and Urban Crime." *Social Forces* 75:619-50.

Land, Kenneth C., Patricia L. McCall, and Lawrence E. Cohen. 1990. "Structural Covariates of Homicide Rates: Are There Any Invariances across Time and Social Space?" *American Journal of Sociology* 95:922-63.

Ludwig, Jens, Greg J. Duncan, and Paul Hirschfield. 1999. "Urban Poverty and Juvenile Crime: Evidence from a Randomized Housing-Mobility Experiment." Working Paper, Georgetown University and Northwestern University/University of Chicago Joint Center for Poverty Research.

Lynn, Lawrence E., Jr. and Michael G. H. McGeary, eds. 1990. *Inner-City Poverty in the United States*. Washington, DC: National Academy Press.

Macoby, Eleanor E., Joseph P. Johnson, and Russell M. Church. 1958. "Community Integration and the Social Control of Juvenile Delinquency." *Journal of Social Issues* 14:38-51.

Massey, Douglas S. and Nancy A. Denton. 1993. *American Apartheid: Segregation and the Making of the Underclass*. Cambridge, MA: Harvard University Press.

Massey, Douglas S. and Shawn M. Kanaiaupuni. 1993. "Public Housing and the Concentration of Poverty." *Social Science Quarterly* 74:109-22.

McClain, Paula D. 1989. "Urban Black Neighborhood Environment and Homicide: A Research Note on a Decade of Change in Four Cities, 1970-1980." *Urban Affairs Quarterly* 24: 584-96.

McNulty, Thomas L. 1999. "The Residential Process and the Ecological Concentration of Race, Poverty, and Violent Crime in New York City." *Sociological Focus* 32:25-42.

Messner, Steven F. and Reid M. Golden. 1992. "Racial Inequality and Racially Disaggregated Homicide Rates: An Assessment of Alternative Theoretical Explanations." *Criminology* 30:421-47.

Messner, Steven F. and Richard Rosenfeld. 1997. *Crime and the American Dream*. 2d ed. Belmont, CA: Wadsworth.

Messner, Steven F. and Kenneth Tardiff. 1986. "Economic Inequality and Levels of Homicide: An Analysis of Urban Neighborhoods." *Criminology* 24:297-317.

Morenoff, Jeffrey D. and Robert J. Sampson. 1997. "Violent Crime and the Spatial Dynamics of Neighborhood Transition: Chicago, 1970-1990." *Social Forces* 76:31-64.

Newman, Oscar. 1972. *Defensible Space: Crime Prevention through Urban Design*. New York: Collier-Macmillan.

Parker, Robert Nash. 1995. "Bringing 'Booze' Back In: The Relationship between Alcohol and Homicide." *Journal of Research in Crime and Delinquency* 32:3-38.

Parker, Robert Nash and Kathleen Auerhahn. 1999. "Drugs, Alcohol, and Homicide: Issues in Theory and Research." Pp. 176-191 in *Homicide: A Sourcebook of Social Research*, edited by M. Dwayne Smith and Margaret A. Zahn. Thousand Oaks, CA: Sage.

Parker, Robert Nash with Linda Anne Rebhun. 1995. *Alcohol and Homicide: A Deadly Combination of Two American Traditions*. Albany: State University of New York Press.

Patterson, E. Britt. 1991. "Poverty, Income Inequality, and Community Crime Rates." *Criminology* 29:755-76.

Popkin, Susan J., Lynn M. Olson, Arthur J. Lurigio, Victoria E. Gwiasda, and Ruth G. Carter. 1995. "Sweeping Out Drugs and Crime: Residents' Views of the Chicago Housing Authority's Public Housing Drug Elimination Program." *Crime and Delinquency* 41:73-99.

Rainwater, Lee. 1970. *Behind Ghetto Walls: Black Family Life in a Federal Slum*. Chicago: Aldine.

Roncek, Dennis W. and Ralph Bell. 1981. "Bars, Blocks, and Crime." *Journal of Environmental Systems* 11:35-47.

Roncek, Dennis W., Ralph Bell, and Jeffrey M. A. Francik. 1981. "Housing Projects and Crime: Testing a Proximity Thesis." *Social Problems* 29:151-66.

Roncek, Dennis W. and Pamela A. Maier. 1991. "Bars, Blocks, and Crimes Revisited: Linking the Theory of Routine Activities to the Empiricism of 'Hot Spots.'" *Criminology* 29:725-53.

Roncek, Dennis W. and Mitchell A. Pravatiner. 1989. "Additional Evidence That Taverns Enhance Nearby Crime." *Sociology and Social Research* 73:185-88.

Rosenbaum, James E., Marilynn J. Kulieke, and Leonard S. Rubinowitz. 1988. "White Suburban Schools' Responses to Low-Income Black Children: Sources of Successes and Problems." *The Urban Review* 20:1-41.

Rosenbaum, James E. and Susan J. Popkin. 1991. "Employment and Earnings of Low-Income Blacks Who Move to Middle-Class Suburbs." Pp. 342-56 in *The Urban Underclass*, edited by Christopher Jencks and Paul E. Peterson. Washington, DC: The Brookings Institution.

Sampson, Robert J. 1985. "Race and Criminal Violence: A Demographically Disaggregated Analysis of Urban Homicide." *Crime and Delinquency* 31:47-82.

———. 1987. "Urban Black Violence: The Effect of Male Joblessness and Family Disruption." *American Journal of Sociology* 93:348-82.

———. 1990. "The Impact of Housing Policies on Community Social Disorganization and Crime." *Bulletin of the New York Academy of Medicine* 66:526-33.

Sampson, Robert J. and W. Byron Groves. 1989. "Community Structure and Crime: Testing Social-Disorganization Theory." *American Journal of Sociology* 94:774-802.

Sampson, Robert J., Stephen W. Raudenbush, and Felton Earls. 1997. "Neighborhoods and Violent Crime: A Multilevel Study of Collective Efficacy." *Science* 277:918-24.

Shaw, Clifford and Henry McKay. 1969. *Juvenile Delinquency and Urban Areas*. Rev. ed. Chicago: University of Chicago Press.

Short, James F., Jr. 1997. *Poverty, Ethnicity, and Violent Crime*. Boulder, CO: Westview.

Simcha-Fagan, Ora and Joseph E. Schwartz. 1986. "Neighborhood and Delinquency: An Assessment of Contextual Effects." *Criminology* 24:667-703.

Skogan, Wesley G. 1990. *Disorder and Decline: Crime and the Spiral of Decay in American Neighborhoods*. Berkeley: University of California Press.

Skogan, Wesley G. and Sampson Annan. 1993. "Drug Enforcement in Public Housing." Pp. 162-174 in *Drugs and the Community: Involving Community Residents in Combating the Sale of Illegal Drugs*, edited by R. C. Davis, A. J. Lurigio, and D. P. Rosenbaum. Springfield, IL: Charles C Thomas.

Squires, Gregory D. 1994. *Capital and Communities in Black and White: The Intersections of Race, Class, and Uneven Development*. Albany: State University of New York Press.

State Library of Ohio. 1990. *Directory of Ohio Libraries*. Columbus, OH: State Library.

Sullivan, Mercer L. 1993. "Puerto Ricans in Sunset Park, Brooklyn: Poverty amidst Ethnic and Economic Diversity." Pp. 1-25 in *In the Barrios: Latinos and the Underclass Debate*, edited by Joan Moore and Raquel Pinderhughes. New York: Russell Sage.

U.S. Bureau of the Census. 1991. *Census of Population and Housing, 1990: Summary Tape File 3A*. Washington, DC: U.S. Bureau of the Census.

Vergara, Camilo Jose. 1997. *The New American Ghetto*. New Brunswick, NJ: Rutgers University Press.

Wacquant, Lois J. D. 1993. "Urban Outcasts: Stigma and Division in the Black American Ghetto and the French Urban Periphery." *International Journal of Urban and Regional Research* 17:366-83.

Warner, Barbara D. and Glenn L. Pierce. 1993. "Reexamining Social Disorganization Theory Using Calls to the Police as a Measure of Crime." *Criminology* 31:493-517.

Warner, Barbara D. and Pamela Wilcox Rountree. 1997. "Local Social Ties in a Community and Crime Model: Questioning the Systemic Nature of Informal Social Control." *Social Problems* 44:520-36.

Wilson, James Q. and George L. Kelling. 1982. "Broken Windows: The Police and Neighborhood Safety." *The Atlantic Monthly* March:29-38.

Wilson, William Julius. 1987. *The Truly Disadvantaged: The Inner City, the Underclass, and Public Policy*. Chicago: University of Chicago Press.

———. 1996. *When Work Disappears: The World of the New Urban Poor*. New York: Knopf.

Zahn, Margaret. 1998. "Homicide and Public Policy." Ninth Annual Walter C. Reckless Memorial Lecture, Columbus, OH: Criminal Justice Research Center, Ohio State University.

[17]

THE ROLE OF PUBLIC SOCIAL CONTROL IN URBAN NEIGHBORHOODS: A MULTI-LEVEL ANALYSIS OF VICTIMIZATION RISK*

MARÍA B. VÉLEZ
The Ohio State University

This study introduces public social control into multilevel victimization research by investigating its impact on household and personal victimization risk for residents across 60 urban neighborhoods. Public social control refers to the ability of neighborhoods to secure external resources necessary for the reduction of crime and victimization. I find that living in neighborhoods with high levels of public social control reduces an individual's likelihood of victimization, especially in disadvantaged neighborhoods. Given the important role that residents of disadvantaged neighborhoods can play in securing public social control, this contingent finding suggests that disadvantaged neighborhoods can be politically viable contexts.

Community policing and mobilization case studies emphasize that residents of disadvantaged neighborhoods can address problems of disorder and crime, fear of crime, and poor city services by securing ties to public officials and the police (Dawley, 1992; Henig, 1982; Kelling and Coles, 1996; Medoff and Sklar, 1994; Podolfskey and DuBow, 1981; Rabrenovic, 1996; Rooney, 1995; Skogan and Hartnett, 1997). Residents in a disadvantaged Chicago neighborhood (Englewood), for example, worked with local police and others to reduce robberies occurring around currency exchanges by placing an Automatic Transfer Machine inside the neighborhood police station (Skogan and Hartnett, 1997:183). Similarly, Dawley

---

* An earlier version of this paper was presented at the 1999 American Society of Criminology meetings in Toronto, Ontario. I am very grateful to Wayne Santoro, Ruth D. Peterson, Paul E. Bellair, Lauren J. Krivo, Christopher Browning, Robert L. Kaufman, Townsand Price-Spratlen, Mark Harris, and the Editor and anonymous reviewers of *Criminology* for helpful comments on earlier drafts of this paper. Support for this research was provided by a grant from the National Consortium on Violence Research (NCOVR); NCOVR is supported under Grant SBR9513040 from the National Science Foundation. This analysis uses data from the Police Services Study that were made available by the Inter-University Consortium for Political and Social Science Research. The data from the Police Services Study, Phase II, 1977: Rochester, St. Louis, and St. Petersburg, were originally collected by Elinor Ostrom, Roger B. Parks, and Gordon Whittaker of Indiana University. Neither the collectors of the original data nor the consortium bear any responsibility for the analysis or interpretations presented here.

(1992) documented how a local organization secured funding from the City of Chicago and other sources to create recreational activities for youth in another crime-ridden Chicago community (Lawndale). These recreational services helped transform the neighborhood into a safer place for residents. Both accounts illustrate public social control—what Bursik and Grasmick (1993:17–18) conceptualized as the ability of neighborhoods to solicit and secure external resources by establishing ties to local governmental officials and the police department.

This study introduces public social control into multilevel victimization research by investigating its impact on household and personal victimization risk for residents across 60 neighborhoods in three metropolitan areas. Multilevel victimization models examine simultaneously the impact of contextual and individual-level factors on the likelihood of victimization risk (Kennedy and Forde, 1990; Miethe and McDowall, 1993; Miethe and Meier, 1994; Rountree et al., 1994; Sampson and Wooldredge, 1987; Smith and Jarjoura, 1989). Incorporating public social control into multilevel models of victimization provides a unique contribution because most studies conceptualize contextual factors only in terms of economic, demographic, and familial conditions. By assessing the impact of public social control, this study comments on the extent to which victimization is shaped, at least partially, by the broader political dynamics of a city. As such, this study is consistent with theoretical efforts that emphasize how political decision making by elites has influenced neighborhood dynamics, like public housing placement (Bursik, 1989; Logan and Molotch, 1987; McNulty and Holloway, 2000), social and physical disorder (Skogan, 1990), and residential race segregation (Massey and Denton, 1993).

In assessing the role of public social control, I pay particular attention to whether its benefits in reducing victimization risk are greater in disadvantaged neighborhoods than in neighborhoods with more affluence. One may anticipate such an outcome given differences in levels of public social control found in disadvantaged versus affluent neighborhoods. Disadvantaged neighborhoods typically have relatively low levels of public social control (Anderson, 1999; Skogan and Hartnett, 1997). Given these "floor" levels, any increase in neighborhood ties to public officials and external resources would represent a meaningful enrichment that, in turn, should translate into a significant reduction of victimization risk. Affluent neighborhoods, in contrast, already enjoy high or "ceiling" levels of public social control. Incremental improvements in public social control are unlikely to diminish an already low risk of victimization. If public social control does indeed offer an effective solution to criminal victimization in disadvantaged neighborhoods, it would suggest that neighborhoods that face the greatest structural barriers can be politically viable given the key role that residents play in securing public social control or in facilitating community policing strategies (e.g., Goldstein, 1990; Henig, 1982; Piquero et al., 1998).

THE ROLE OF COMMUNITY SOCIAL CONTROL IN THE VICTIMIZATION PROCESS

Community social control refers to the ability of a community to regulate itself by regulating the behavior of residents and visitors (Bursik and Grasmick, 1993). Social disorganization theory proposes that community social control mediates the effect of neighborhood disadvantage on crime (Bursik, 1988; Shaw and McKay, 1942). Empirically, this means that the effect of neighborhood conditions such as poverty on crime and victimization should disappear or substantially diminish when community social control is taken into account (Bellair, 1997, 2000; Sampson and Groves, 1989; Sampson et al., 1997; Warner and Rountree, 1997).

In examining this hypothesis, researchers have focused primarily on local social ties—relationships *among* residents—as important sources of community social control. Specifically, studies have emphasized the respective impact of neighboring and informal social control on crime (Bursik and Grasmick, 1993). Neighboring refers to the extent of social interaction among neighbors such as chatting or getting together. Research demonstrates that higher levels of neighboring are associated with lower crime rates (Bellair, 1997, 2000; Sampson and Groves, 1989; Warner and Rountree, 1997). Informal social control refers to the ability of local neighborhoods to supervise the behavior of residents (Bursik and Grasmick, 1993; Hunter, 1985). Informal social control may take on a variety of forms, including neighbors watching out for each other and calling the police at the first sign of trouble (Bursik and Grasmick, 1993; Elliott et al., 1996; Greenberg et al., 1982; Sampson and Groves, 1989; Sampson et al., 1997, 1999). Sampson et al. (1997), for instance, found that social cohesion accompanied by the willingness to intervene on behalf of the neighborhood's interest led to important reductions in crime and victimization in Chicago neighborhoods.

The focus on ties established among neighborhood residents, however, means that few social disorganization studies have investigated how ties to public officials and the police—another dimension of community social control—influence crime and victimization (Bursik and Grasmick, 1993). A notable exception is Bursik (1989), who examined whether the placement of new housing projects, a reflection of city-level decision making, was related to crime across Chicago neighborhoods. Bursik (1989:117) found that city officials placed new housing projects in residentially unstable neighborhoods, which were "presumably unable to organize and negotiate an effective defense against their construction." In turn, the placement of housing projects in residentially unstable neighborhoods led to substantial increases in neighborhood delinquency rates through further increases in instability. Bursik's findings suggest that political decision making is consequential for neighborhood levels of crime and victimization. An important implication of his study is that residents must establish ties to city elites in order to influence political decisions that affect their neighborhoods, including their levels of crime.

Two bodies of literature note the importance of public social control. First, research on community policing documents how such programs allow the police to cultivate relationships with residents of mostly poor urban neighborhoods (Goldstein, 1990; Kelling and Coles, 1996; Piquero et al., 1998; Skogan, 1990; Skogan and Hartnett, 1997; Skolnick and Bayley, 1986). The success of police efforts at reducing crime, however, often hinges upon community involvement in the city-sponsored program. Kelling and Coles (1996), for instance, documented how the mayor and police chief of Baltimore set up a task force of city agencies and community associations to meet regularly with community residents in a disadvantaged neighborhood (Boyd Booth). With city support, residents in turn were able to board up abandoned buildings, remove neighborhood trash, and fence off walkways to impede drug-dealing efforts. These actions helped reduce violent crime by 56% in three years (Kelling and Coles, 1996). Building relationships with the police offers residents more than just reductions in crime. Skogan (1990), for example, found that community policing efforts in Newark led to residents' increased satisfaction with their neighborhoods and the police as well as a decrease in residents' fear of crime.

Second, research on neighborhood mobilization examines strategies that residents can use to establish ties to city officials and thus shape political decision making (Dawley, 1992; Henig, 1982; Medoff and Sklar, 1994; Rabrenovic, 1996; Rooney, 1995). Because residents from disadvantaged neighborhoods do not typically start off with strong ties to city governments and the police (Henig, 1982), these studies show that residents must first mobilize to gain the attention of city officials. The importance of communities being well organized suggests that local social ties (relationships among neighbors) play an important role in the formation of public social control. Once residents have garnered the city's attention, they often are able to secure city-allocated resources. For example, frustrated by the city's ineffective efforts to address crime in a disadvantaged neighborhood in Schenectady, New York (Hamilton Hill), a group of women formed Clean Sweep United to bring attention to neighborhood crime (Rabrenovic, 1996). Among other tactics, group members organized a lunch on the mayor's stoop to highlight the fact they could not do the same safely in their neighborhood. Such actions compelled the mayor and the district attorney to abandon the use of plea bargaining and implement stricter sentencing for drug-related cases. Similarly, residents of a disadvantaged Boston community (Roxbury) pressured the city to remove abandoned cars that had long plagued their neighborhood. A local resident posed as a volunteer for the mayor's reelection campaign to obtain pro-mayor bumper stickers that were then later placed on the abandoned cars; an embarrassed city hall removed the cars the next day (Medoff and Sklar, 1994). Taken together, both the community policing and neighborhood mobilization literatures demonstrate that public social control can alter meaningfully the living conditions of disadvantaged neighborhoods.

THE CONTINGENT NATURE OF PUBLIC SOCIAL CONTROL

It is likely that the importance of establishing ties between neighborhood residents and local public officials is greatest in disadvantaged communities. Two related factors support this perspective. First, the infusion of outside resources such as increased police protection should lead to greater reductions in victimization in neighborhoods that lack the internal resources necessary to effectively regulate the behavior of residents and visitors. Unlike more privileged areas, disadvantaged neighborhoods often lack internal resources like informal social control given the magnitude of the structural problems they face (Anderson, 1990, 1999; Henig, 1982; Krivo and Peterson, 1996; Sampson et al., 1999; Wilson, 1987, 1996). For instance, residents from disadvantaged neighborhoods cannot address problems like abandoned and dilapidated buildings or widespread joblessness without the assistance and resources from city officials. Thus, when ties are established between neighborhoods and local government officials and the police, the resources that accompany this relationship should be most rewarding for reducing victimization in disadvantaged neighborhoods.

Given the serious nature and number of problems facing disadvantaged neighborhoods, a second reason for expecting an enhanced effect of public social control lies in the amount of public social control found in disadvantaged versus affluent neighborhoods. As noted earlier, disadvantaged neighborhoods typically have low levels of public social control (Anderson, 1999; Skogan and Hartnett, 1997). Not only do many disadvantaged neighborhoods lack city-allocated resources (Massey and Denton, 1993), but many inner city residents of poor neighborhoods also feel alienated from the police and local judicial system (Anderson, 1999). Given such "floor" levels of public social control, it seems reasonable to expect that even a small increase in public social control would represent a significant improvement and likely lead to a significant reduction of victimization risk. In contrast, because more affluent neighborhoods already have high or "ceiling" levels of public social control, it seems unlikely that incremental improvements would translate into large reductions to an already low risk of victimization.

The work by Skogan and Hartnett (1997) exemplifies this "enhanced effects" view of public social control in disadvantaged neighborhoods. The authors assessed the effectiveness of community policing in five Chicago neighborhoods. They found that Morgan Park, an affluent neighborhood with alliances to local political entities, reported the fewest program impacts. Skogan and Hartnett (1997) speculated that the lack of significant improvement from community policing initiatives was due to the fact that Morgan Park simply started off with fewer crime-related problems and already enjoyed a favorable relationship with local public officials. In contrast, community policing efforts had dramatic impacts in Englewood and Austin, two highly disadvantaged neighborhoods. Skogan and Hartnett (1997) concluded that the importance of community policing in these two neighborhoods was due to the fact that these communities began with more serious problems and weaker relationships to city agencies. These findings suggest that an enhanced effect of public social control is likely in disadvantaged neighborhoods because they have the most to gain from securing ties and resources from public officials and police.

INCORPORATING PUBLIC SOCIAL CONTROL INTO MUILTILEVEL VICTIMIZATION MODELS

I assess the impact of public social control along with local social ties within a multilevel victimization model. Multilevel victimization models draw on two theoretical perspectives. First, researchers use routine activities theory to explore the *microlevel* factors associated with an individual's probability of victimization. Routine activities theory highlights the role of situational factors and posits that an individual's probability of criminal victimization increases with the convergence of exposure to motivated offenders, target suitability, and the absence of capable guardians (Cohen and Cantor, 1980; Cohen et al., 1981; Miethe and Meier, 1994; Miethe et al., 1987). Individuals who leave their homes unoccupied, for example, report more household burglaries than do individuals who stay at home and essentially serve as guardians of their home (Cohen and Cantor, 1980).

Second, multilevel victimization studies use social disorganization theory to understand the impact of *neighborhood* conditions on victimization. Social disorganization models focus on how neighborhoods with high levels of poverty, residential mobility, racial/ethnic heterogeneity, and family disruption yield heightened levels of crime and victimization (Bursik, 1988; Shaw and McKay, 1942). Sampson and Groves (1989), for example, found that neighborhoods with poor socioeconomic conditions had higher burglary victimization rates than did more affluent neighborhoods. Multilevel victimization studies also draw on recent reformulations of social disorganization theory that incorporate the view that many inner-city neighborhoods are socially isolated (Anderson, 1990, 1999; Skogan, 1990; Wilson, 1987, 1996). This perspective attributes the unusually high crime rates in extremely disadvantaged neighborhoods to acute levels of social isolation (Wacquant and Wilson, 1989; Wilson, 1987, 1996). Consistent with this view, Krivo and Peterson (1996) found that extremely disadvantaged neighborhoods in Columbus, Ohio, had violent crime rates 12 and 16 times greater than did neighborhoods with moderate and low levels of disadvantage, respectively.

Drawing from these micro level and neighborhood-level explanations of victimization risk and crime rates, researchers now view victimization risk as a result of both the social forces in an individual's neighborhood and an individual's routine activities (Kennedy and Forde, 1990; Miethe and McDowall, 1993; Miethe and Meier, 1994; Rountree et al., 1994; Sampson and Wooldredge, 1987; Smith and Jarjoura, 1989). Sampson and Wooldredge (1987), for example, found that residents who lived in communities with high levels of family disruption and who spent nights outside the home were more likely to experience predatory victimization. Similarly, Miethe and Meier (1994) found that individuals who resided in poor neighborhoods and who engaged in dangerous activities like going to bars at night faced heightened risks of violent and property victimization.

In sum, I extend previous multilevel victimization studies by integrating public social control into models of victimization risk. Specifically, I examine the impact of public social control on victimization risk while taking into account neighborhood disadvantage, local social ties, and an individual's routine activities. Because case studies about neighborhood mobilization and community policing indicate that public social control has brought about numerous neighborhood improvements in several disadvantaged neighborhoods, I also test whether the impact of public social control on victimization is enhanced by neighborhood disadvantage.

DATA AND METHODS

I use data from the Police Services Survey, conducted in 1977, to examine an individual's likelihood of criminal victimization.[1] This data set

1. Although the data used here are more than 20 years old, they nonetheless are applicable to the circumstances researchers find in today's neighborhoods. Our current understanding of disadvantaged neighborhoods largely comes from Wilson (1987, 1996), whose arguments about the concentration of disadvantage rely on the dramatic social and economic transformations that took shape during the 1970s. For example,

is well suited for understanding the role of public social control because it was part of a larger evaluation of police services provided to neighborhoods. The survey contains information from 12,015 households located in 60 residential neighborhoods across three Standard Metropolitan Statistical Areas (SMSAs): Rochester, New York; Tampa-St. Petersburg, Florida; and St. Louis, Missouri.[2] Because the survey was designed to evaluate police services to these households, police beats serve as the geographical marker for each neighborhood. The average population of the police beat is 9,500, and the average land area is about two square miles, making these beats reasonable approximations of neighborhoods (Bellair, 1997; Smith, 1982; Smith and Jarjoura, 1989). For each neighborhood, a random sample of household telephone numbers was obtained; the target was approximately 200 interviews per neighborhood. The completion rate varied slightly by neighborhood, but in all cases, it exceeded 80% (Smith, 1982:82). From each household sampled, one adult member was interviewed and acted as a spokesperson for the household. It is important to acknowledge that this sample is limited because it only includes information from three SMSAs. Because these areas were chosen to reflect the distribution of police departments from small- to medium-sized SMSAs in the United States, these data can be considered reasonably representative of similarly sized SMSAs (see Smith, 1982).[3]

In order to construct measures of neighborhood conditions and community social control, I aggregated responses to survey questions within each of the 60 neighborhoods by using the geographical identifier for each household. The within-area sample for the Police Services Study is very large; the average number of respondents in a given neighborhood is 202 (ranging from 106 to 259 respondents). Thus, theoretically relevant variables at the community level can be constructed reliably.

---

the number of Chicago communities with concentrated poverty increased from 16 in 1970 to 26 in 1980; this includes an increase of eight new extremely poor neighborhoods during this 10-year period. Given that the 1970s were the site for much of these structural dislocations, it seems reasonable to expect that the processes uncovered by this 1977 survey can speak to, and are consistent with, the processes of today's neighborhoods.

2. In the Police Services Study, the SMSAs of Rochester, New York; Tampa-St. Petersburg, Florida; and St. Louis, Missouri were selected based on cost constraints and logistic considerations from a larger sample of 34 large metropolitan areas (Smith, 1982). Based on the racial and economic composition of neighborhoods across these three SMSAs, 60 neighborhoods were chosen, corresponding closely to cluster sampling (Smith, 1982). Once the neighborhoods were selected, a random sample of households was chosen and surveyed.

3. Nonetheless, future research should examine public social control across a larger number of SMSAs that better represent SMSA sizes and geographic regions of the contemporary United States.

VARIABLES AND MEASURES

DEPENDENT VARIABLES

Victimization. Respondents were asked if their homes had ever been burglarized and if someone in the household had been assaulted or mugged in the past 12 months. Using this information, I computed a dichotomous variable for *household victimization* by coding respondents whose home had been burglarized as 1, 0 otherwise. Similarly, I constructed a dichotomous measure of *personal victimization* by distinguishing respondents who reported an assault or mugging (1) from those who had not (0). Because this analysis is concerned with how neighborhood context affects the probability of victimization, I included only assaults and muggings that respondents reported to have taken place in their homes, on their blocks, or in their neighborhoods (see Miethe and McDowall, 1993; Miethe and Meier, 1994; Rountree et al., 1994; Smith, 1982).

INDEPENDENT VARIABLES

Community Social Control. Drawing on the work of Bursik and Grasmick (1993), I conceptualized *public social control* as community ties to the local government and the police, two institutions that control resources beneficial to neighborhood life. I measured public social control with respondents' answers to the following four questions: (1) "The local government is concerned about your neighborhood" (1 = strongly agree or agree; 0 = otherwise); (2) "A person can get satisfaction out of talking to the public officials in your community" (1 = strongly agree or agree; 0 = otherwise); (3) "Do you think that your police department tries to provide the kind of services that people in your neighborhood want?" (1 = yes; 0 = no); and (4) "How would you rate the overall quality of police services in your neighborhood?" (1 = outstanding, good or adequate; 0 = inadequate, poor or nonexistent). For each neighborhood, responses to each question were summed to create a percentage of residents satisfied with local governmental officials and the police; these percentages were standardized (converted to z-scores) and summed. Reliability analysis indicates that these four measures form a robust unidimensional construct (Cronbach's alpha = .94). High scores on this measure indicate that residents' perceived a favorable relationship with local public officials and the police. Although this measure is limited because it is based on perceptions about respondents' ties to local governmental officials, it seems reasonable to expect that this perception is based on first-hand experiences with how such political entities have responded to community issues in the past.[4]

4. An avenue for future research is to examine actual interactions between

I measured *local social ties* with an index based on the percentage of residents in each neighborhood who got together with their neighbors at least once a year (see Bellair, 1997) and the percentage of residents in each neighborhood who asked neighbors to watch their homes while they were away for a few days. These two measures were then standardized and summed (Cronbach's alpha = .84). High scores on the index of *local social ties* represent communities that have high levels of neighboring coupled with an abundance of neighbors watching out for each other.

Neighborhood Conditions. I examined three neighborhood conditions prominent in social disorganization studies. I constructed an index of neighborhood *disadvantage* that standardized and summed the percentage of households with incomes below $5,000 per year (the lowest income category available to respondents); the percentage of residents without a bachelor's degree; and the percentage of households that comprise single parents with children under the age of 18 (Cronbach's alpha = .74). To capture a neighborhood's level of racial/ethnic *heterogeneity*, I subtracted from one the sum of the squared proportion of residents in each of the following racial or ethnic groups: whites, African Americans, and other minorities (see Bellair, 1997; Sampson and Groves, 1989; Warner and Pierce, 1993; Warner and Rountree, 1997). High scores on this measure indicate neighborhoods that are racially and ethnically heterogeneous, and low scores indicate neighborhoods that are more racially and ethnically homogeneous.[5] A neighborhood's level of *residential stability* is the mean number of years that respondents have resided in their neighborhoods (see Bellair, 1997).

Routine Activities. I measured an individual's routine activities in three ways. To capture a respondent's *exposure to offenders*, I controlled for respondents' perceptions about the level of crime in their neighborhood. Specifically, I distinguished between residents who reported an increase in neighborhood crime within the past year (1) from respondents who reported that neighborhood crime had stayed the same or decreased (0). Target attractiveness is indicated by respondents' yearly *family income*, a seven-category variable that ranges from an income below $5,000 (1) to an income that is more than $30,000 (7) (see Kennedy and Forde, 1990; Miethe and McDowall, 1993; Miethe and Meier, 1990; Rountree et al., 1994). I measured capable guardianship by distinguishing between respondents who *live alone* (1) from those who live with other adults (0)

residents and the local government and police as well as the distribution of resources across neighborhoods.

5. The formula for calculating racial/ethnic heterogeneity is $1-\Sigma p_1^2$, where p_1 is the proportion of the total population of the police beat in a given racial/ethnic group.

(see Miethe and McDowall, 1993; Miethe and Meier, 1994; Rountree et al., 1994).

Controls. I controlled for three respondent attributes that are associated with criminal victimization: race/ethnicity, sex, and age. I constructed two dummy variables for race/ethnicity: *African-American* and *other minority*.[6] White respondents comprised the reference category. *Female* respondents were coded as 1, and males as 0. *Age* was measured in years. To account for any differences across the three SMSAs, I included two dummy variables for the SMSAs of *Rochester* and *St. Louis*. Following Bellair (1997), these cities are compared with the Tampa-St. Petersburg SMSA, the reference category. The Appendix presents the bivariate correlations.

ANALYTIC STRATEGY

A typical concern with multilevel data is the correlation of cases within each neighborhood leading to biased standard errors. To account for the clustering of cases within each unit, I estimated random-effects logistic regression models. This procedure ensures that the coefficients and standard errors are unbiased, making reliable hypothesis testing possible. For each regression equation, I report metric and semi-standardized coefficients. The semi-standardized coefficient ($SS^{\mathcal{L}}$) indicates the amount of change in the log odds of the likelihood of victimization associated with a one-standard-deviation change in the independent variable (Kaufman, 1996).[7] I explored the potential for multicollinearity by examining the Variance Inflation Factor (VIF) scores, condition indices, and variance decomposition proportions (Belsley et al., 1980). In all models, the VIF scores were lower than 5 and the condition indices were lower than 20, indicating that multicollinearity does not adversely affect the parameter estimates in the analysis.

Given that I am particularly interested in the role of public social control in highly and extremely disadvantaged communities, it is important to consider how many such neighborhoods actually enjoy high levels of public social control. Figure 1 separates neighborhoods into low, high, or extreme levels of disadvantage and shows the percentage of neighborhoods within each category that has high levels of public social control. (High levels of public social control refer to neighborhoods that scored

6. Respondents that identified themselves as Latino (N = 92), Native American (*N* = 47), or other (*N* = 42) were collapsed into one category because their numbers were too small for reliable analysis of the independent groups.

7. The semi-standardized coefficient is computed as $SS_j^{\mathcal{L}} = b_j * S_j$, where S_j is the standard deviation of X_j.

Figure 1 Percentage of Neighborhoods with High Levels of Public Social Control

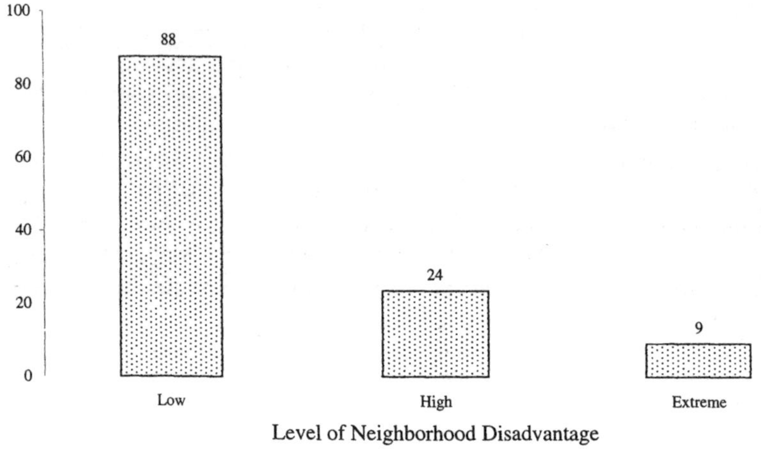

above the mean on the public social control index.) As one would expect, neighborhoods with low levels of disadvantage are most likely to have high levels of public social control. Of the 32 neighborhoods with low disadvantage, 28 have high levels of public social control (88%). Although high levels of public social control tend to be concentrated in areas with affluence, nonetheless 4 of the 17 highly disadvantaged neighborhoods also report high levels of public social control (24%). As Figure 1 indicates, extremely disadvantaged neighborhoods are the least likely to enjoy the benefits of high public social control in that only 1 of 11 neighborhoods enjoys high levels of public social control. Yet that 9% of extremely disadvantaged neighborhoods have high levels of public social control suggests that ties to local public officials and the police *can* be established even in places that are faced with the greatest structural disadvantage. The presence of high levels of public social control in disadvantaged neighborhoods indicates that there is sufficient variation across these contexts to make the testing of the interaction between public social control and neighborhood disadvantage substantively meaningful.

I present four equations for each dependent variable. Model 1 (a and b) examines the effects of neighborhood conditions on household or personal victimization, net of an individual's routine activities and controls. Model 2 (a and b) introduces local social ties into the equations. Model 3 (a and b) adds public social control, and Model 4 (a and b) tests for an interaction between public social control and neighborhood disadvantage.[8] To create

8. I also tested for an interaction between neighborhood disadvantage and local social ties, but it was not significant (results not shown).

Table 1. Means and Standard Deviations of Independent and Dependent Variables

	Whole Sample (N = 60)		Low Disadvantage (N = 32)		High Disadvantage (N = 17)		Extreme Disadvantage (N = 11)	
	Mean	S.D.	Mean	S.D.	Mean	S.D.	Mean	S.D.
Panel A: Neighborhood-Level Data								
Neighborhood Conditions								
Disadvantage	.00	2.45	–1.91	1.16	1.22	.80	3.68	1.03
Poverty (%)	18.06	12.63	8.53	4.77	23.91	6.68	36.77	8.10
Family Disruption (%)	5.46	3.01	4.06	1.88	5.75	3.26	9.07	2.14
College Educated (%)	35.81	17.07	47.55	12.96	24.64	10.45	18.88	7.41
Heterogeneity	.20	.18	.13	.14	.27	.20	.31	.17
Residential Stability	12.28	3.73	11.22	3.03	13.37	4.49	13.72	3.41
Local Social Ties								
Local Social Ties	.00	1.85	1.21	1.27	–1.12	1.47	–1.81	1.14
Neighboring (%)	59.56	8.78	64.21	7.06	54.37	8.34	54.19	6.46
Neighbors Watch Out (%)	72.59	8.48	78.42	5.12	68.16	6.00	62.50	5.55
Public Social Control								
Public Social Control	.00	3.68	2.41	2.58	–2.08	2.52	–3.78	2.72
Satisfied Talking with Public Officials (%)	49.30	10.30	56.04	8.52	43.53	6.10	38.60	3.64
Satisfied with Police Services (%)	62.76	11.70	69.14	10.46	58.05	6.33	51.46	9.81
Confidence in Local Government (%)	68.90	10.56	74.64	8.26	63.79	8.63	61.65	10.02
Police Responsive to Community (%)	83.21	8.06	88.56	3.71	78.83	6.47	74.41	7.99
	Whole Sample (N = 9829)		**Low Disadvantage (N = 5299)**		**High Disadvantage (N = 2603)**		**Extreme Disadvantage (N = 1927)**	
	Mean	S.D.	Mean	S.D.	Mean	S.D.	Mean	S.D.
Panel B: Individual-Level Data								
Victimization								
Household	.07	.26	.05	.23	.07	.26	.12	.32
Personal	.03	.16	.01	.12	.03	.18	.06	.23
Assault	.02	.13	.01	.10	.02	.14	.03	.18
Robbed	.01	.11	.00	.05	.01	.13	.03	.16
Routine Activities								
Exposure to Offenders (=1)	.22	.41	.18	.39	.27	.44	.24	.43
Family Income	3.03	1.67	3.65	1.69	2.53	1.38	1.99	1.18
Live Alone (=1)	.22	.41	.16	.37	.27	.44	.31	.46
Controls								
African American (=1)	.27	.45	.09	.29	.32	.46	.72	.45
Other Minority (=1)	.02	.12	.01	.11	.02	.13	.02	.13
White (=1)	.71	.45	.90	.30	.67	.47	.26	.44
Female (=1)	.58	.49	.56	.50	.58	.49	.63	.48
Age (years)	47.67	17.87	46.89	16.98	47.63	18.71	49.86	18.90
Rochester, NY	.18	.38	.16	.37	.23	.42	.15	.35
St. Louis, MO	.43	.50	.39	.49	.45	.50	.52	.50
Tampa-St. Petersburg, FL.	.39	.49	.44	.50	.32	.47	.33	.47

NOTE: Low disadvantaged neighborhoods are below the mean on the index of disadvantage. High disadvantaged neighborhoods are between the mean and one standard deviation above the mean on the index of disadvantage. Extreme disadvantaged neighborhoods are one standard deviation above the mean on the index of disadvantage.

this interaction term, I first mean-centered the component variables and then created a product term (Aiken and West, 1991). In all four models, public social control and neighborhood disadvantage are mean-centered.

FINDINGS

Table 1 provides the means and standard deviations for the dependent and independent variables. The first and second columns present descriptive statistics pertaining to all neighborhoods (Panel A) and all individuals in the sample (Panel B). To show how key measures vary across neighborhoods with divergent levels of disadvantage, I split the sample according to whether respondents lived in neighborhoods with low, high, or extreme disadvantage. Following Krivo and Peterson (1996), neighborhoods that scored below the mean on the index of disadvantage were considered to have low disadvantage; neighborhoods that scored between the mean and one standard deviation above the mean on the index of disadvantage were considered to have high disadvantage; and neighborhoods that scored one standard deviation or more above the mean on the index of disadvantage were considered to have extreme disadvantage.

As revealed earlier in Figure 1, Panel A of Table 1 details important disparities in public social control across the 60 neighborhoods. For example, 56% of residents in communities with low levels of disadvantage are satisfied talking with public officials, but only 44% and 39% of residents in highly or extremely disadvantaged neighborhoods, respectively, are satisfied with public officials. Similarly, almost 70% of residents from neighborhoods with low levels of disadvantage report satisfaction with police services, whereas police satisfaction is reported by only 58% and 51% of residents in highly disadvantaged and extremely disadvantaged neighborhoods, respectively. In addition, Table 1 shows that highly and extremely disadvantaged neighborhoods embody a variety of characteristics conducive to victimization risk. Compared with low levels of neighborhood disadvantage, for instance, disadvantaged neighborhoods have higher levels of heterogeneity (Panel A) and people living alone (Panel B) as well as lower levels of local social ties (Panel B). Given the prevalence of these and other factors, it is not surprising that Panel B shows that individuals living in neighborhoods with low levels of disadvantage report anywhere from about one and one-half to six times fewer household and personal victimizations than do residents from highly or extremely disadvantaged neighborhoods.[9]

9. With *residential stability* as the exception, all means for noncontrol variables in neighborhoods with low levels of disadvantage are statistically different from means in highly or extremely disadvantaged neighborhoods ($p < .05$, two-tailed).

Table 2 presents the results of logistic equations predicting an individual's likelihood of household or personal victimization. Although not central to this study, I first turn to the role of routine activities in an individual's risk of victimization. Model 1a shows a heightened risk of household victimization for individuals who have exposure to offenders, high family incomes, and who live alone. The pattern is largely similar for personal victimization, given that Model 1b demonstrates that exposure to offenders and family income are important predictors of personal victimization. Noteworthy, the effects of these routine activities on both household and personal victimization persist as local social ties and public social control are entered into the models. That an individual's routine activities play an important role in victimization risk, net of neighborhood conditions and community social control, lends support to the view purported by multilevel victimization studies that victimization risk is a byproduct of both the social forces in individuals' neighborhoods and their routine activities.

Turning to the role of neighborhood conditions, Model 1 (a and b) shows that neighborhood disadvantage enhances an individual's likelihood of household and personal victimization. This finding is consistent with multilevel victimization research that has found that individuals residing in disadvantaged neighborhoods have higher risks of victimization than do individuals living in less disadvantaged neighborhoods (Kennedy and Forde, 1990; Miethe and McDowall, 1993; Miethe and Meier, 1994; Rountree et al., 1994; Sampson and Wooldredge, 1987; Smith and Jarjoura, 1989). As we would expect, this effect of neighborhood disadvantage is mediated by local social ties for household victimization (Model 2a) and by public social control for personal victimization (Model 3b). Results also indicate that heterogenous neighborhoods are contexts that increase individuals' likelihood of household victimization, even after adjusting for local social ties and public social control.

Individuals living in neighborhoods with high levels of local social ties are less likely to report household or personal victimization (Model 2 [a and b]). Consistent with social disorganization research, these findings indicate that an effective strategy to reduce victimization is to foster the social interaction of residents so that they watch out for each other (e.g., Sampson et al., 1997; Warner and Rountree, 1997). Note, however, that the effect of local social ties is much stronger for personal than for household victimization. In fact, the semi-standardized coefficient for personal victimization is almost two times larger than is the semi-standardized coefficient for household victimization. A likely explanation for this disparity is that personal but not household crimes typically occur in visible public spaces. As such, personal crimes may be more subject than household

Table 2. Random-Effects Logistic Regression of Household or Personal Victimization on Neighborhood Conditions, Community Social Control, Routine Activities, and Controls (N = 9,829)

	Household Victimization Models				Personal Victimization Models			
	1a	2a	3a	4a	1b	2b	3b	4b
	b SSℒ	b SSℒ	b SSℒ	b SSℒ	b SSℒ	b SSℒ	b SSℒ	b SSℒ
Neighborhood Conditions								
Disadvantage	.092**	.050	.014	–.013	.184***	.108*	.027	–.016
	.224	.120	.035	–.032	.447	.263	.065	–.039
	(.032)	(.041)	(.047)	(.046)	(.044)	(.053)	(.052)	(.057)
Heterogeneity	1.108**	.887*	1.096**	1.424	.079	–.378	.246	.439
	.197	.160	.195	.253	.014	–.067	.044	.078
	(.374)	(.388)	(.408)	(.414)	(.490)	(.497)	(.463)	(.476)
Residential Stability	.003	.004	.005	.004	–.003	–.005	.013	.012
	.011	.010	.018	.016	–.012	–.019	.050	.045
	(.017)	(.017)	(.017)	(.017)	(.023)	(.022)	(.019)	(.020)
Community Social Control								
Local Social Ties	. . .	–.103⁺	–.066	–.072	. . .	–.190**	–.081	–.114⁺
		–.190	–.122	–.134		–.352	–.150	–.211
		(.063)	(.067)	(.065)		(.083)	(.073)	(.075)
Public Social Control	. . .	. . .	–.039⁺	–.039⁺	. . .	. . .	–.106***	–.098**
			–.143	–.142			–.389	–.360
			(.027)	(.026)			(.033)	(.033)

Table 2. Continued

	Household Victimization Models				Personal Victimization Models			
	1a	2a	3a	4a	1b	2b	3b	4b
	b $SS^{\mathcal{L}}$	b $SS^{\mathcal{L}}$	b $SS^{\mathcal{L}}$	b $SS^{\mathcal{L}}$	b $SS^{\mathcal{L}}$	b $SS^{\mathcal{L}}$	b $SS^{\mathcal{L}}$	b $SS^{\mathcal{L}}$
Public Social Control*								
Disadvantage	. . .	. . .	. . .	–.017**	. . .	. . .	. . .	–.017*
				–.163				–.154
				(.007)				(.009)
Routine Activities								
Exposure to Offenders (=1)	.950***	.946***	.939***	.946***	.793***	.785***	.762***	.772***
	.389	.390	.385	.388	.325	.322	.312	.316
	(.084)	(.084)	(.084)	(.084)	(.131)	(.131)	(.130)	(.131)
Family Income	.077**	.079**	.082**	.077**	–.205***	–.198***	–.185***	.193***
	.128	.130	.137	.129	–.343	–.331	–.308	.323
	(.030)	(.030)	(.030)	(.030)	(.054)	(.054)	(.054)	(.054)
Live Alone (=1)	.251*	.250**	.257**	.255**	–.312	–.312	–.290	–.289
	.104	.010	.106	.105	–.129	–.129	.120	–.120
	(.103)	(.103)	(.103)	(.103)	(.169)	(.168)	(.168)	(.168)
Controls								
African American (=1)	.037	.033	.016	–.024	–.108	–.104	–.186	–.239
	.017	.010	.007	–.010	–.048	–.046	–.084	–.107
	(.114)	(.114)	(.114)	(.114)	(.172)	(.169)	(.163)	(.166)
Other Minority (=1)	–.814^{+}	–.823*	–.820*	–.844	–.176	–.190	–.205	–.223
	–.100	–.100	–.101	–.104	–.022	–.023	–.025	–.027
	(.467)	(.467)	(.467)	(.467)	(.530)	(.530)	(.526)	(.528)
Female (=1)	.112^{+}	.114^{+}	.117^{+}	.113	–.120	–.116	–.105	–.110
	.055	.060	.058	.056	–.059	–.057	–.052	–.055
	(.085)	(.085)	(.085)	(.084)	(.132)	(.132)	(.130)	(.130)

Table 2. Continued

	Household Victimization Models				Personal Victimization Models			
	1a	2a	3a	4a	1b	2b	3b	4b
	b SS 𝓛	b SS 𝓛	b SS 𝓛	b SS 𝓛	b SS 𝓛	b SS 𝓛	b SS 𝓛	b SS 𝓛
Age (years)	–.023***	–.023***	–.023***	–.023	–.032***	–.032***	–.032***	–.032***
	.409	–.410	–.410	–.416	–.572	–.573	–.567	–.576
	(.003)	(.003)	(.003)	(.003)	(.004)	(.004)	(.004)	(.004)
Rochester, NY	–.058	–.170	–.173	–.298	.456*	.214	.228	.092
	–.022	–.070	–.066	–.114	.166	.082	.088	.035
	(.174)	(.184)	(.181)	(.182)	(.243)	(.247)	(.211)	(.227)
St. Louis, MO	.161	.049	.013	–.180	.473	.036	.157	–.050
	.080	.020	.006	–.089	.219	.018	.078	–.025
	(.135)	(.184)	(.187)	(.195)	(.197)	(.252)	(.224)	(.251)
Constant	–2.534	–2.373	–2.553	–2.584	–2.090	–1.791	–.262	–2.174
X^2	277.69***	282.90***	286.66***	298.04***	169.43***	186.94***	224.75***	234.28***
Log Likelihood	–2344.81	–2343.54	–2342.53	–2339.71	–1096.83	–1124.83	–1121.08	–1119.41
df	12	13	14	15	12	13	14	15

NOTE: Standard error in parentheses. $^{+}$ $p < .10$; * $p < .05$; ** $p < .01$; *** $p < .001$ (one-tailed).

crimes to the guardianship provided by neighbors (Miethe and McDowall, 1993; Miethe et al., 1987; Rountree et al., 1994).

The effect of local social ties on victimization is altered when public social control is included into the equations (Models 3 and 4 [a and b]). As Model 3a shows, the effect of local social ties is mediated completely by public social control for household victimization. The pattern is somewhat different for personal victimization. In Model 3b, the effect of local social ties disappears with the introduction of public social control but regains marginal significance when the interaction of public social control and neighborhood disadvantage is included in Model 4b. That public social control largely mediates the effect of local social ties lends support to the idea that establishing ties to public officials and the police is most likely in neighborhoods where residents already have established social connections with each other.

Central to this study, Model 3 (a and b) shows that public social control plays an important role in diminishing victimization risk. This finding suggests that neighborhoods with strong ties to public officials and the police are able to secure city resources that effectively diminish victimization risk. This view is consistent with Bursik and Grasmick's (1993:38) argument that a key way to affect the "nature of neighborhood life" is for neighborhoods to negotiate with local governmental officials and the police. More generally, the importance of public social control demonstrates that an individual's probability of victimization risk is shaped to a great extent by the broader political dynamics of the city. But as was the case for local social ties, the effect of public social control is much stronger for personal than for household victimization. For example, the semi-standardized coefficient for personal victimization is more than two times larger than its counterpart for household victimization. Given that personal crimes occur typically in public spaces, they seem more vulnerable than do household crimes to the actions of residents and public agents of social control.

Model 4 (a and b) further explicates the nature of the effect of public social control on victimization risk by including the interaction between public social control and neighborhood disadvantage. For both household and personal victimization, public social control yields greater benefits for the reduction of victimization as neighborhood disadvantage increases.[10]

10. Given that public social control and neighborhood disadvantage overlap to such an extent ($r = -.77$), it is important to explore whether the significant interaction between public social control and neighborhood disadvantage is simply due to a nonlinear effect of public social control on victimization risk. I tested for this nonlinearity by constructing a squared term for public social control; creating a product term between public social control-squared and neighborhood disadvantage; and including these terms in the regression models one at a time as well as with the base terms of

Figures 2 and 3 provide a visual depiction of this interaction. The lines marked by squares represent the predicted effect of public social control on household (Figure 2) and personal (Figure 3) victimization in neighborhoods with extreme disadvantage, holding all other variables constant at their means. The lines marked by triangles show this same relationship for neighborhoods with high disadvantage. Both lines depict strong negative slopes, which means that increases in public social control are associated with large reductions in victimization risk for residents of highly and extremely disadvantaged neighborhoods. In neighborhoods with low levels of disadvantage, the lines marked by diamonds in Figures 2 and 3 show that increases in public social control are less effective in reducing household and personal victimization (below their already low levels).[11]

This enhanced effect of public social control indicates that public social control is particularly important in disadvantaged neighborhoods—places where it is needed most. This suggests that a key component of neighborhood "success" hinges on the ability of residents to work with more powerful outside institutions that are equipped to allocate much needed resources to disadvantaged neighborhoods. This observation is consistent with numerous case studies that have highlighted the importance of public social control for disadvantaged neighborhoods in Chicago as well as in cities like Baltimore, Newark, and Boston (Dawley, 1992; Kelling and Coles, 1996; Medoff and Sklar, 1994; Podolefsky and DuBow, 1981; Skogan, 1990; Skogan and Hartnett, 1997).

CONCLUSION

Recent multilevel victimization studies have demonstrated that disadvantaged neighborhood conditions increase dramatically an individual's probability of victimization (Kennedy and Forde, 1990; Miethe and McDowall, 1993; Miethe and Meier, 1994; Rountree et al., 1994; Sampson and Wooldredge, 1987; Smith and Jarjoura, 1989). Community policing

public social control and neighborhood disadvantage. Neither the public social control squared-term nor the product term between public social control-squared and neighborhood disadvantage was significant, providing no evidence for a curvilinear relationship.

11. Statistical tests of the public social control slopes for extreme and high levels of neighborhood disadvantage indicate that the effects are significantly different from zero ($b = -.06$, $t = 2.18$ and $b = -.08$, $t = -.2.57$ for household victimization; $b = -.12$, $t = -4.33$ and $b = -.14$, $t = -4.46$ for personal victimization). By contrast, the line marked by diamonds in Figure 2 shows that public social control has a slight negative effect on household victimization in neighborhoods with low levels of disadvantage, but it is not statistically different from zero ($b = -.02$, $t = -.67$). The line marked by diamonds in Figure 3 depicts a negative (although weaker) effect on personal victimization in neighborhoods with low levels of disadvantage; it is statistically different from zero ($b = -.08$, $t = -.2.83$).

Figure 2 The Effect of Public Social Control on Household Victimization

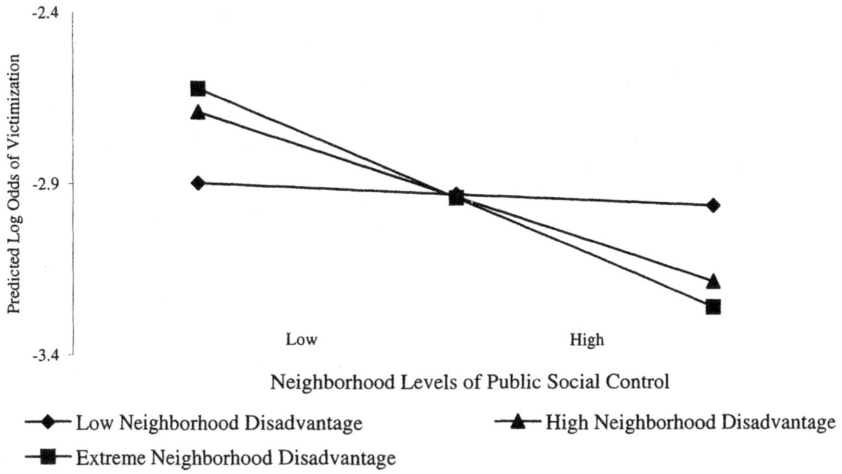

Figure 3 The Effect of Public Social Control on Personal Victimization

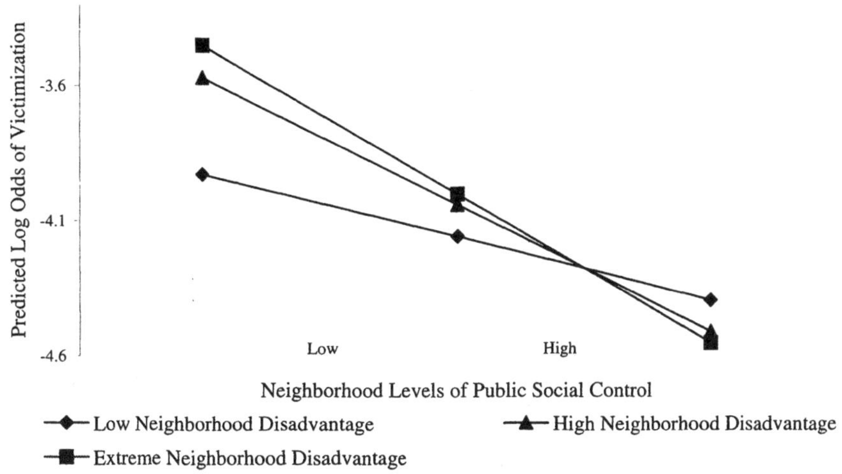

and mobilization case studies suggest that a way to counteract this heightened level of victimization is through public social control (Dawley, 1992; Henig, 1982; Kelling and Coles, 1996; Medoff and Sklar, 1994; Podolfskey and DuBow, 1981; Rabrenovic, 1996; Rooney, 1995; Skogan and Hartnett, 1997). Public social control refers to the ability of neighborhoods to solicit and secure external resources by establishing ties between neighborhoods and local governmental officials and police departments (Bursik, 1989; Bursik and Grasmick, 1993; Hunter, 1985). In turn, the resources that accompany these ties should bring about reductions in crime and victimization. Using a multilevel model, this study assessed the impact of public social control on household and personal victimization risk for residents across 60 neighborhoods in three SMSAs. Net of a variety of neighborhood and individual-level characteristics, I find that public social control reduces household and personal victimization risk. In fact, public social control yields greater benefits in neighborhoods with prevalent structural disadvantage than in neighborhoods with more affluence. This enhanced effect suggests that the establishment of neighborhood ties to local public officials results in the infusion of resources, such as increased educational services for youth, needed to counteract the heightened levels of victimization found in disadvantaged neighborhoods.

Not only does this finding point to public social control as an avenue for community betterment, it also has implications for our understanding of the political viability of disadvantaged neighborhoods. In contrast to the view that residents from high poverty areas are necessarily alienated from political institutions and have apathetic attitudes toward the political process, the enhanced effect of public social control suggests that disadvantaged neighborhoods can be politically viable contexts (see Berry et al., 1991). This observation is supported most clearly by the important role that residents of disadvantaged neighborhoods play in establishing public social control. The literature on neighborhood mobilization stresses the influence that residents of disadvantaged neighborhoods can bring to bear on local politicians when they are organized and use pressure tactics (Dawley, 1992; Henig, 1982; Medoff and Sklar, 1994; Rabrenovic, 1996; Rooney, 1995). Such actions, in turn, often have compelled authorities to allocate resources to disadvantaged neighborhoods.

Similarly, although the literature on community policing shows that police departments may initiate ties to residents, such work also emphasizes the crucial role that residents play in making community policing programs successful (Kelling and Coles, 1996; Podolfskey and DuBow, 1981; Skogan and Hartnett, 1997). Indeed, a major goal of community policing is to foster neighborhood self-help and community mechanisms of informal social control that set in motion the process for neighborhoods to take ownership of their communities (Goldstein, 1990; Skogan, 1998).

Thus, even if residents do not initiate public social control, its *potency* appears anchored with the unified actions of residents in disadvantaged neighborhoods. As such, my findings suggest an "empowered" view of residents living in disadvantaged neighborhoods given their ability to take active roles in curtailing levels of victimization and crime.

Our understanding of public social control would be furthered by investigating the conditions under which ties are secured and resources are allocated. For example, future research should explore how such neighborhood characteristics as racial/ethnic composition and levels of political mobilization affect the likelihood that residents acquire public social control. For instance, Skogan and Hartnett (1997) found that community policing efforts in a predominantly African-American neighborhood were more successful than in a Latino neighborhood. This suggests that predominantly Latino neighborhoods face unique structural and cultural constraints that make difficult the fostering of ties with the police. Uncovering the mechanisms that lead to public social control is important given its implication for our understanding of the conditions under which disadvantaged neighborhoods can be politically viable contexts. How public social control is secured is important given that it effectively buffers residents of disadvantaged neighborhoods from much of the structural forces that lead to their heightened levels of victimization risk.

REFERENCES

Aiken, Leona S. and Stephen G. West
1991 Multiple Regression: Testing and Interpreting Interactions. Newbury Park, Calif.: Sage.

Anderson, Elijah
1990 Streetwise: Race, Class, and Change in an Urban Community. Chicago: University of Chicago Press.
1999 Code of the Street: Decency, Violence, and the Moral life of the Inner City. New York: W.W. Norton.

Bellair, Paul E.
1997 Social interaction and community crime: Examining the importance of neighbor networks. Criminology 35:677–701.
2000 Informal surveillance and street crime: A complex relationship. Criminology 38:137–169.

Belsley, David A., Edwin Kuh, and Roy E. Welsch
1980 Regression Diagnostics: Identifying Influential Data and Sources of Collinearity. New York: John Wiley & Sons.

Berry, Jeffrey, Kent E. Portney, and Ken Thomson
1991 The political behavior of poor people. In Christopher Jencks and Paul E. Peterson (eds.), The Urban Underclass. Washington, D.C.: Brookings Institution.

Bursik, Robert J., Jr.
1988 Social disorganization and theories of crime and delinquency: Problems and Prospects. Criminology 26:519–551.
1989 Political decision-making and ecological models of delinquency: Conflict and consensus. In Steven F. Messner, Marvin D. Krohn, and Allen E. Liska (eds.), Theoretical Integration in the Study of Deviance and Crime. Albany: State University of New York Press.

Bursik, Robert J., Jr. and Harold G. Grasmick
1993 Neighborhoods and Crime. New York: Lexington Books.

Cohen, Lawrence E. and David Cantor
1980 The Determinants of larceny: An empirical and theoretical study. Journal of Research in Crime and Delinquency 17:140–159.

Cohen, Lawrence E., James R. Kluegel, and Kenneth C. Land
1981 Social inequality and predatory criminal victimization: An exposition and test of a formal theory. American Sociological Review 46:505–524.

Dawley, David
1992 A Nation of Lords: The Autobiography of the Vice Lords. Prospect Heights, Ill.: Waveland Press.

Elliott, Delbert S., William Julius Wilson, David Huizinga, Robert J. Sampson, Amanda Elliot, and Bruce Ranking
1996 The effects of neighborhood disadvantage on adolescent development. Journal of Research in Crime and Delinquency 33:389–426.

Goldstein, Herman
1990 Problem-Oriented Policing. Philadelphia: Temple University Press.

Greenberg, Stephanie W., William M. Rohe, and Jay R. Williams
1982 Safe and Secure Neighborhoods: Physical Characteristics and Informal Territorial Control in High and Low Crime Neighborhoods. Washington, D.C.: National Institute of Justice.

Henig, Jeffrey
1982 Neighborhood Mobilization: Redevelopment and Response. New Brunswick, N.J.: Rutgers University Press.

Hunter, Albert J.
1985 Private, parochial and public school orders: The problem of crime and incivility in urban communities. In Gerald D. Suttles and Mayer N. Zald (eds.), The Challenge of Social Control: Citizenship and Institution Building in Modern Society. Norwood, N.J.: Ablex Publishing.

Kaufman, Robert L.
1996 Comparing effects in dichotomous logistic regression. Social Science Quarterly 77:90–109.

Kelling, George L. and Catherine M. Coles
1996 Fixing Broken Windows: Reducing Order and Reducing Crime in Our Communities. New York: Touchstone.

Kennedy, Leslie W. and David R. Forde
1990 Routine activities and crime: An analysis of victimization in Canada. Criminology 28:137–151.

Krivo, Lauren J. and Ruth D. Peterson
1996 Extremely disadvantaged neighborhoods and urban crime. Social Forces 75:619–650.

Logan, John R. and Harvey L. Molotch
1987 Urban Fortunes: The Political Economy of Place. Berkeley, Calif.: University of California Press.

Massey, Douglas and Nancy Denton
1993 American Apartheid: Segregation and the Making of the Underclass. Cambridge, Mass.: Harvard University Press.

McNulty, Thomas L. and Steven R. Holloway
2000 Race, crime, and public housing in Atlanta: Testing a conditional effect hypothesis. Social Forces 79:707–729.

Medoff, Peter and Holly Sklar
1994 Streets of Hope: The Fall and Rise of an Urban Neighborhood. Boston, Mass.: South End Press.

Miethe, Terance D. and David McDowall
1993 Contextual effects in models of criminal victimization. Social Forces 71:741–759.

Miethe, Terance D. and Robert F. Meier
1990 Opportunity, choice, and criminal victimization: A test of a theoretical model. Journal of Research in Crime and Delinquency 27:243–266.
1994 Crime and Its Social Context: Toward an Integrated Theory of Offenders, Victims, and Situations. Albany: State University of New York Press.

Miethe, Terance D., Mark C. Stafford, and J. Scott Long
1987 Social differentiation in criminal victimization: A test of routine activities/lifestyle theories. American Sociological Review 52:184–194.

Piquero, Alex, Jack Greene, James Fyfe, Robert J. Kane, and Patricia Collins
1998 Implementing community policing in public housing developments in Philadelphia: Some early results. In Geoffrey P. Alpert and Alex Piquero (eds.), Community Policing: Contemporary Readings. Prospect Heights, Ill.: Waveland Press.

Podolefsky, Aaron and Frederic DuBow
1981 Strategies for Community Crime Prevention: Collective Responses to Crime in Urban America. Reactions to Crime Project, Center for Urban Affairs, Northwestern University. Springfield, Ill.: C.C. Thomas.

Rabrenovic, Gordana
1996 Community Builders: A Tale of Neighborhood Mobilization in Two Cities. Philadelphia: Temple University Press.

Rooney, Jim
1995 Organizing the South Bronx. Albany: State University of New York Press.

Rountree, Pamela Wilcox, Kenneth Land, and Terance D. Miethe
1994 Macro-micro integration in the study of victimization: A hierarchical logistic model analysis across Seattle neighborhoods. Criminology 32:387–414.

Sampson, Robert J. and W. Byron Groves
1989 Community structure and crime: Testing social disorganization theory. American Journal of Sociology 94:774–802.

Sampson, Robert J. and John D. Wooldredge
1987 Linking the micro- and macro-level dimensions of lifestyle-routine activity and opportunity models of predatory victimization. Journal of Quantitative Criminology 3:371–393.

Sampson, Robert J., Jeffrey D. Morenoff, and Felton Earls
1999 Beyond social capital: Spatial dynamics of collective efficacy for children. American Sociological Review 64:633–660.

Sampson, Robert J., Stephen W. Raudenbush, and Felton Earls
1997 Neighborhoods and violent crime: A multilevel study of collective efficacy. Science 277:918–924.

Shaw, Clifford R. and Henry D. McKay
1942 Juvenile Delinquency and Urban Areas. Chicago, Ill.: The University of Chicago Press.

Skogan, Wesley G.
1990 Disorder and Decline: Crime and the Spiral of Decay in American Neighborhoods. Berkeley, Calif.: University of California Press.
1998 Community policing in Chicago. In Geoffrey P. Alpert and Alex Piquero (eds.), Community Policing: Contemporary Readings. Prospect Heights, Ill.: Waveland Press.

Skogan, Wesley G. and Susan M. Hartnett
1997 Community Policing, Chicago Style. New York: Oxford University Press.

Skolnick, Jerome and David H. Bayley
1986 The New Blue Line: Police Innovation in Six American Cities. New York: Free Press.

Smith, Douglas A.
1982 Invoking the Law: Determinants of Police Arrest Decisions. Unpublished Dissertation. Bloomington, Ind.: Indiana University.

Smith, Douglas A. and G. Roger Jarjoura
1989 Household characteristics, neighborhood composition and victimization risk. Social Forces 68:621–640.

Wacquant, Loic and William Julius Wilson
1989 The cost of racial and class exclusion in the inner city. Annals of the American Academy of Political and Social Science 501:8–25.

Warner, Barbara D. and Glenn L. Pierce
1993 Reexamining social disorganization theory: Using calls to the police as a measure of crime. Criminology 31:493–517.

Warner, Barbara D. and Pamela Wilcox Rountree
1997 Local social ties in a community and crime model: Questioning the systemic nature of informal social control. Social Problems 44:520–536.

Wilson, William Julius
1987 The Truly Disadvantaged: The Inner City, the Underclass, and Public Policy. Chicago, Ill.: The University of Chicago Press.
1996 When Work Disappears: The World of the New Urban Poor. New York: Random House.

María B. Vélez is a Doctoral Student in sociology at The Ohio State University. Her current research examines the determinants and consequences of public social control in Chicago neighborhoods. Her general research interests include the interrelationships among crime, disadvantage, and race/ethnicity; linking neighborhood crime and victimization to city political processes; and multilevel models of crime and victimization. Direct Correspondence to María Vélez, Department of Sociology, 300 Bricker Hall, 190 North Oval Mill, The Ohio State University, Columbus, OH 43210 (e-mail: velez.17@osu.edu).

Appendix. Bivariate Correlation Matrix

	1	2	3	4	5	6	7	8	9	10	11	12	13	14	15	16
1. Household Victimization	1.00															
2. Personal Victimization	.07*	1.00														
3. Disadvantage	.08*	.09*	1.00													
4. Heterogeneity	.09*	.05*	.50*	1.00												
5. Residential Stability	.00	.03*	.30*	.01	1.00											
6. Public Social Control	–.08*	–.11*	–.77*	–.29*	–.06*	1.00										
7. Local Social Ties	–.10*	–.10*	–.70*	–.56*	–.30*	.58*	1.00									
8. Exposure to Offenders	.13*	.08*	.07*	.05*	.04*	–.10*	–.10*	1.00								
9. Family Income	.01	–.05*	–.48*	–.21*	–.16*	.39*	.32*	.00	1.00							
10. Live Alone	.01	–.01	.18*	.09*	.04*	–.12*	–.13*	–.01	–.33*	1.00						
11. African American	.07*	.07*	.56*	.44*	.10*	–.48*	–.52*	.00	–.23*	.05*	1.00					
12. Other Minority	–.02*	–.00	.03*	.05*	.01	–.01	.00	–.01	–.01	–.02*	–.08*	1.00				
13. Female	.01	–.01	.05*	.01	.02*	–.04*	.01	.04*	–.19*	.15*	.03*	–.01	1.00			
14. Age	–.10*	–.08*	.06*	–.04*	.14*	–.02*	–.03*	.03*	–.32*	.22*	–.10*	–.03*	.05*	1.00		
15. Rochester, NY	–.01	.01	–.03*	–.09*	.22*	–.04*	.04*	.10*	–.04*	.01	–.11*	.03*	.03*	–.01	1.00	
16. St. Louis, MO	.04*	.04*	.09*	.22*	.15*	.02*	–.53*	.02*	–.01	.01	.24*	–.06*	–.09*	–.03*	–.41*	1.00

NOTE: * $p < .05$ (two-tailed).

[18]

INDUSTRIAL SHIFT, POLARIZED LABOR MARKETS AND URBAN VIOLENCE: MODELING THE DYNAMICS BETWEEN THE ECONOMIC TRANSFORMATION AND DISAGGREGATED HOMICIDE*

KAREN F. PARKER
Department of Criminology, Law and Society
University of Florida

KEYWORDS: labor markets, inequality, race, urban violence, concentrated disadvantage

Industrial restructuring marks the removal of a manufacturing and production-based economy in urban areas, which had served as a catalyst in concentrating disadvantage and polarizing labor markets since the 1970s. Although scholars have established a relationship between concentrated disadvantage—poverty, joblessness, racial residential segregation—and urban violence in cross-sectional studies, this literature has yet to estimate whether economic restructuring contributed to the change in urban homicide over time. Modeling this relationship requires an analytical strategy that incorporates specific indicators of (race and gender) polarized labor markets, separate from indicators of urban disadvantage, on disaggregated homicides while taking into account the growing dependency of urban cities on formal social control (via police presence and rise in incarceration). In this

This project was supported by Grant 2001-IJ-CX-0008 awarded by the National Institute of Justice, U.S. Department of Justice. Conclusions drawn from research findings and points of view expressed in this document are those of the author's and do not necessarily reflect positions of the U.S. Department of Justice. I would like to thank Patricia McCall, John MacDonald, Aaron Griffin and Alex Piquero for their suggestions on earlier versions of the paper; Mari DeWees for her assistance with data collection; and Ray Paternoster and the anonymous reviewers for their kind and helpful comments. Direct correspondence to: Karen F. Parker, Department of Criminology, Law and Society, University of Florida, Gainesville, Florida 32611-5950, email: kparker@crim.ufl.edu.

study I provide a theoretical rationale for linking industrial restructuring to urban homicide. Using a multivariate strategy to capture the shift in labor market forces and disaggregated homicides from 1980 to 1990, I also estimate the impact of this relationship. The results provide evidence of the industrial shift and documents both the decline in manufacturing jobs for black males and black females and a growth in the service sector opportunities for white males only. I also find that industrial restructuring had a unique impact on disaggregated homicide beyond what has previously been established in cross-sectional studies.

Industrial restructuring was the catalyst for the concentration of disadvantage and violence found in urban areas since the 1970s. This claim, emphasized by Wilson (1987) and Massey et al. (1993, 1994), marks the polarization of labor markets and increased joblessness of recent decades. Most indicative of the industrial shift was a gradual decline in manufacturing jobs which meant fewer employment options for many minority groups and led to a more gender-segregated labor market structure (see Glass et al., 1988; Kasarda, 1983; Smith and Tienda, 1987; Wilson and Wu, 1993). The primary goal behind this research is to examine whether industrial restructuring contributed to the change in urban violence over time.

Examining the relationship requires a dynamic analysis over time. This is currently missing from the literature. In this study I pursue two objectives. First, I estimate the impact of the economic transformation on disaggregated homicides using a multivariate change model that captures the shift in labor force sectors and disaggregated homicides from 1980 to 1990. Second, I attempt to establish the importance of incorporating race- and gender-specific characteristics in labor market indicators, independent of concentrated disadvantage, in the study of urban violence. I then estimate the impact of labor market polarization and industrial restructuring on the change in homicide offending for specific groups: white males, white females, black males and black females. Meeting these two aims allows me to determine whether these groups were affected differently by the economic transformation, as is argued in much of the urban economy literature.

REVIEW OF LITERATURE: RACE, GENDER AND INDUSTRIAL RESTRUCTURING

In The Truly Disadvantaged (1987) Wilson writes that blacks were defenseless against the changes in the urban economy. His later work (1991) summarizes his concerns:

> The *shift* [emphasis added] from goods-producing to service-producing industries, the increasing polarization of the labor market into low-wage and high-wage sectors, innovations in technology, the relocation of manufacturing industries out of central cities, and periodic recessions have forced up the rate of black joblessness (unemployment and nonparticipation in the labor market). (Wilson, 1991:640)

Scholars have demonstrated that poverty levels in urban neighborhoods differ significantly by race. Evidence of strong patterns of residential segregation have also emerged (Massey and Denton, 1988, 1993; Wilson, 1987), independent of economic status (Massey et al. 1987). For many blacks, labor market marginalization and joblessness only heightened the disadvantages they already faced (see Kasarda, 1989, 1992; Ricketts and Sawhill, 1988; Wilson, 1996). For example, Wilson (1987) claims that black male joblessness is the single greatest factor influencing the decline in marriageability. High rates of mortality, incarceration and military service among young black men also increased that imbalance (South, 1992; Wilson, 1996). Joblessness has thus been linked in criminological literature to family disruption and urban crime rates (see Almgren et al., 1998; Krivo et al., 1998; Sampson, 1987). It is significant that much of this research focuses on the disadvantages associated with black male joblessness.

Minority females have also faced labor market dislocation and consequences associated with industrial restructuring. That is, evidence suggests that the shift from manufacturing to service sectors in many urban areas was felt differently along gender lines (see Glass et al., 1988; Haynie and Gordon, 1999; Smith and Tienda, 1987; Wilson and Wu, 1993). Hsueh and Tienda (1996), for example, find strong evidence of labor force instability among women compared to men, and minorities compared to nonminorities (see also Tienda and Lii, 1987). Moreover, the levels of economic disadvantage that black and white women face differ significantly (see examples in Tienda et al., 1987). Smith and Tienda (1987) find that Hispanic and black women faced greater declines in jobs than their Asian and white counterparts. According to Kletzer (1991), black women were more likely than white to work in the manufacturing sector and other low-skilled service industries that saw significant losses in employment. Because of high levels of economic marginalization and labor force fluctuations among women (Browne, 1997; Ihlanfledt and Sjoquist, 1989), as well as the greater dependency of black women on low-level service industries, it is important to incorporate race- and gender-specific labor market characteristics when estimating the impact of changes in the urban economy on homicide.

This gap in the literature was the impetus for this study. First, we do not know how the shift in the industrial sector (that is, manufacturing and service industries), which both polarized the labor market along race and gender lines and heightened urban disadvantage, affects homicide disaggregated by race and gender. Scholars have long argued for distinct race and gender patterns in criminological behavior (see Hawkins, 1987; Hill and Crawford, 1990; Simpson, 1991; Simpson and Elis, 1995). This paper responds by incorporating both race- and gender-specific indicators.

Second, the unique impact of industrial restructuring on urban violence remains unknown because previous studies tended to be cross sectional, thus overlooking the importance of Wilson's assertions about a shift in the urban economy. Shihadeh and Ousey's (1998) examination of the links between industrial restructuring and urban violence from 1970 to 1990 is the only exception. Although their work establishes a demonstrable relationship between the urban economy and race-specific homicide, it lacked in measures of industrial sectors (for example, manufacturing and service), which is central to capturing industrial restructuring. This research moves beyond previous studies in important ways. First, because much of the existing research is cross sectional, I use a modeling strategy that estimates the impact of change in industrial and other factors on change in disaggregate homicides while accounting for the discrete, highly skewed nature of disaggreagated homicide data. I also incorporate detailed race- and gender-specific measures of manufacturing and service sector employment, which allows me to document any changes in the urban economy involving these groups and the polarization in labor markets. Finally, studies have also generally failed to control for important aspects of formal social control in urban areas (Mosher, 2001). These conditions, such as the rise in incarceration and greater dependency on police, have also changed significantly over time. I have tried to incorporate these considerations.

INDUSTRIAL RESTRUCTURING AND DISAGGREGATED HOMICIDE: THEORETICAL LINKS

Industrial restructuring can theoretically be linked to urban homicide in several specific ways (see also Shihadeh and Ousey 1998 for theoretical arguments). First, consistent with the Chicago school tradition and claims made in the social disorganization literature, structural disadvantage can block the development of formal and informal ties necessary to social control. Researchers find that structural conditions, such as family instability and poverty, contribute to urban violence (Crutchfield and Pitchford, 1997; Krivo and Peterson, 1996; Parker and McCall, 1997, Parker and McCall, 1999; Sampson, 1987). Recent literature documents that the economic transformation in urban areas both disadvantaged minority women (Browne, 1997; Hsueh and Tienda, 1996; McCall, 2000) and produced a racially segregated residential environment (Anderson,

1990; Massey and Eggers, 1990; Massey, Gross and Shiuya, 1994; Wilson, 1996). Taken together, these conditions can impede the development of organizations, both social and business, and the ability to maintain effective social controls (Bursik and Grasmick, 1993) that influence violent crime (Crutchfield, 1989). Because industrial sectors represent important economic and organizational structures in urban areas, any restructuring of the urban economy is likely to influence homicide among specific groups differently.

A second theoretical linkage captures the long-held belief found in sociological writings—including Marxist, conflict and strain theories—concerning the impact of poverty on crime. These theories rely on the notion that deprivation, either relative or absolute, heightens feelings of anger and frustration that result in aggression. According to Blau and Blau (1982), when an economically polarized environment is coupled with ascribed (racial) inequality, the potential for violence becomes more pronounced. Given that blacks faced the greatest loss of jobs from the removal of manufacturing jobs over time, deprivation (that is, joblessness and poverty) could exacerbate frustration and contribute to the change in disaggregated homicide among blacks from 1980 to 1990.

A third possibility takes into account the greater use and dependency on formal social control. In line with Bursik and Grasmick (1993), Rose and Clear (1998) provide evidence that community dependency on formal mechanisms of social control, via incarceration and police presence, can further weaken organizational and family structures, which results in more rather than less crime. Furthermore, researchers have demonstrated a disproportionate concentration of police in black urban areas (see Jackson and Carroll, 1981; Liska et al., 1981) and the rise in incarceration over time (Bureau of Justice Statistics, 1996), particularly among black males (Lynch and Sabol, 1997). Thus, it appears that at the same time industrial restructuring was most pronounced in urban areas, these areas were also growing more dependent on state social control. This is an important consideration because, for example, a rise in black male incarceration can reduce the pool of potential spouses (Anderson, 1999; Wilson, 1987; Wilson, 1996) and change the economic and population composition of urban areas. In this way, changes in state social control can affect race-and gender-specific homicides differently over time.

HYPOTHESES

Overall, I argue that labor market polarization and industrial restructuring may be more relevant to explaining the shift or change in race- and gender-specific homicides over time than previously demonstrated. A key assertion in this research is that labor market opportunities differ significantly for race- and gender-specific groups, which contributes to disparate levels in disaggregated homicide. I expect to find considerable change in labor market and industrial structures over the 1980 to 1990 period, with much of this change affecting the patterns of homicide among black men and women relative to white. Specifically, I offer two hypotheses based on the urban economy literature.

> H1: A decline in employment of black males in manufacturing will contribute to a change (rise) in homicide involving black males because they depend on this sector more than other groups.
>
> H2: Growth in the service industry, particularly providing employment options for black females, will be inversely related to the change in homicide involving black females.

The shift in economic sectors will not only cause labor markets to become increasingly polarized and segmented along race and gender lines, but also be related to the geographic concentrations of disadvantage in urban areas. While urban disadvantage and social disorganization approaches offer specific predictions concerning the relationship between structural conditions and violence, common to each is the emphasis on place over personal characteristics. As Sampson and Wilson (1995) originally argued, I propose that the relationships between structural conditions and urban violence are the result of racial differences in the ecological context of urban areas (see also Krivo and Peterson, 2000). To take the geographic concentration of urban disadvantage and how levels of disadvantage can be more extreme in black areas into account, I hypothesize that:

> H3: Growing levels of urban disadvantage—the spatial concentration of poverty, income inequality, racial residential segregation, and dependency on public assistance payments—will have a positive impact on the change (rise) in black male and black female homicides over time.

Acknowledging the racial invariancy of the social disorganization perspective, I hypothesize separately that:

> H4: As urban areas become increasingly racially concentrated and socially disorganized (that is, inequality, divorce, residential instability and sex ratios), these structural conditions will have a positive impact on the change in homicides for all groups.

Finally, the rise in incarceration and police presence in urban areas during the 1980s and 1990s are significant to this study. These two factors represent a greater dependency on formal social control mechanisms, predominantly in black concentrated areas, which can positively (rather than negatively) affect violence.

> H5: An increase in incarceration and police presence over time in the sample of urban cities will have a positive impact on the change (rise) in black homicides as compared to white homicides, regardless of gender.

Before outlining the data and methodological strategy, I provide some rationale for estimating the dynamic relationship between industrial restructuring and urban homicide from 1980 to 1990. First, Wilson's work documents the shift in industrial and economic sectors since the 1970s, but I am influenced by his 1991 claim that the shift in some industrial sectors and urban conditions—that is, family and organizational structures—may be complicated and subtle. Because some changes in the urban economy are likely to be gradual, the outcomes and consequences of these conditions (for example, homicide) may be as well, highlighting the importance of estimating periods that extend beyond the 1970s (Wilson, 1991). Moreover, much of Wilson's work incorporates 1980 census data (see, for example, Wacquant and Wilson, 1989; Wilson, 1991). Second, Kasarda's work (1983, 1992) argues that the shift in labor markets—the transformation of urban cities from places of production, manufacturing and distribution to an administrative, information-based, highly skilled service economy—were irreversible. That is, the change in economic sectors is likely to continue, if not increase, throughout the 1980s and 1990s. Thus, examining the 1980 to 1990 period should capture the dynamic impact of the industrial shift on urban homicide.

DATA AND METHODS

DATA SOURCES

The unit of analysis is U.S. cities with a population of 100,000 or more in 1980. This sampling generated 168 cities that were matched in the 1990 data to allow for a within-city comparison over time. There are three major sources of data. For the dependent variables, the source of data is the Supplementary Homicide Report (SHR) of the Federal Bureau of Investigation's Uniform Crime Report (UCR) program (Fox, 1996).[1] This

1. Because this study employs the SHR as one of its primary data sources, all of the limitations associated with its use apply. Specifically, researchers have noted incomplete and inconsistent reporting of SHR data (Pampel and Williams, 2000; Maltz, 1999; Reidel, 1989). Also, variability in the priority agencies give to reporting SHR information as well as variability in coding procedures across police departments impact the validity of SHR data (Maltz, 1999; Maxfield, 1989).

is considered to be the richest database for homicide research (Pampel and Williams, 2000). The UCR is also the source of information on the number of police officers in each city circa 1980 and 1990. The second major data source is the 1980 and 1990 Census of Population: Social and Economic Characteristics (U.S. Bureau of the Census, 1983, 1994). These data sources are essential because they provide comparable indictors during the periods of interest. Third, the Bureau of Justice Statistics' Census of State Adult Correctional Facilities (1979) and the Census of State and Federal Adult Correctional Facilities (1990) are the primary sources of information for the race-specific incarceration measures.

DEPENDENT VARIABLES

This study limits the dependent measures to single offender/single victim murders and nonnegligent manslaughters to avoid issues of ambiguity and measurement error associated with classifying multiple victims and offenders, particularly in analysis involving different racial classifications (Flewelling and Williams, 1999; Messner and Golden, 1992; Williams and Flewelling, 1987, 1988).[2] To minimize the impact of random year-to-year fluctuations in homicide incidents, and because of the level of race and gender specificity offered in this study, the four measures are averages based on 5 years of data surrounding decennial periods in 1980 (1977–1981) and 1990 (1987–1991).[3] I acknowledge the problem of missing data on offenders' race in the SHR data and that homicides are few to rare in the case of white females, which raises

---

Alternative data sources such as vital statistics have been examined in comparison to the SHR (UCR), with studies reporting general agreement between the data sources at the national level (Reidel, 1999; Wiersema et al., 2000).

2. Consistent with much of the past homicide research based on SHR data, this study limits its attention only to single offender-single victim murders and nonnegligent manslaughters. While the author acknowledges the importance of examining homicide cases involving multiple offenders and/or victims, literature suggests that homicides involving multiple offenders and/or victims typically differ significantly from one-on-one events (see Block, 1985; Cheatwood, 1993; Cheatwood and Block, 1990; Clark, 1995). Also Flewelling and Williams (1999) note that issues and inconsistencies can arise for scholars when examining multiple offender and/or victim incidents in disaggregated homicide studies in terms of how best to count these incidents. Finally, my examination of SHR data reveals that cases involving multiple offenders comprise a relatively small portion of homicide events, which leads me to believe the exclusion of these cases does not introduce a bias into the analysis. In light of these issues, I choose to exclude multiple offender and/or victim cases from the analysis.
3. In 1990, Florida did not report data to the uniform crime reporting program for one or more of the 5 years of interest to this study, which reduces the sample of cities in the analyses (see Krivo and Peterson, 2000 for more information).

several methodological concerns in multivariate modeling. I deal with these issues in two ways.

First, when offender race was not known, an imputation algorithm developed by Williams and Flewelling (1987) was used to "extrapolate the characteristics of the known cases to those with missing information" (p. 426).[4] Second, the dependent variables are used as counts rather than rates so that the appropriate statistical techniques can be used in estimating rare aggregate level events and/or dealing with overdispersion (that is, mean/variance inequality) in the data (see Osgood, 2000). The dependent variables are thus computed as the average homicide counts for a given race- and gender-specific group in 1980 and 1990.

INDEPENDENT VARIABLES

I generate race- and gender-specific measures of industrial restructuring and labor market stratification. First, I calculate manufacturing employment by dividing the number of race- and gender-specific persons in manufacturing by the total number of those aged 16 and older. (Occupations within manufacturing include precision, production, craft and repair workers; operators; fabricators and laborers.) Service industry employment is calculated in the same way.

To estimate the geographic concentration of urban disadvantage for racial groups, I incorporate measures consistent with previous cross-sectional studies on disaggregated homicide (Krivo and Peterson, 1996; Messner and Golden, 1992; Parker and McCall, 1999).[5] That is, race-specific measures of poverty (the percentage of the population that lives

---

4. I thank the Center for the Study and Prevention of Violence at the University of Colorado and Kirk Williams for helping me with these data. In terms of method for dealing with missing information via the adjusted procedure offered by Williams and Flewelling (1987), I am aware of alternative methods (Messner et al., 2002; Pampel and Williams, 2000). My read of this literature, however, leads me to conclude that the procedure used in this study is just as good as the others. In fact, there is no evidence supporting one method over the others; rather studies report more similarities across techniques than differences.
5. Unlike the labor market indicators, there is no evidence that indicators of urban disadvantage vary by gender in addition to race. Because Wilson and other urban economy researchers reviewed here clearly document both race and gender dimensions in labor market opportunity structures (such as black male joblessness, black female service industry involvement, etc.), I incorporate both race- and gender-specific labor market indicators. On the other hand, much of the urban disadvantage literature focuses on the spatial concentration of disadvantage in predominantly black areas (see Krivo and Peterson, 2000; Massey et al., 1987; Massey and Eggers, 1990, Massey et al., 1994; Wilson, 1987) and thus this literature requires the use of race-specific (rather than race- and gender-specific) measures in the analysis.

below the poverty level) and income inequality (via Gini Index of Income Concentration), racial residential segregation (the index of dissimilarity), and the percentage of race-specific female-headed households receiving public assistance payments have been included in this study.

A measure of black concentration is included to take into account the change in the minority group population and racial composition of cities over time. Black concentration is calculated as the percentage of the black population. I include a measure of the percentage of the population with Hispanic origins as a control measure.

The measures of social disorganization in cities are economic inequality, divorced males, residential stability and sex ratio. The measure of divorced males is a race- and gender-specific indicator of the number of divorced males in the race-specific male population aged 15 years or older. Residential stability is tallied as time in the same residence for the previous 5 years. The sex ratio is calculated as the number of race-specific males per 100 females (see Messner and Sampson, 1991). To estimate existing inequalities between race- and gender-specific groups, I use two ratio measures. All groups are aged 16 or older. First is the ratio of employed (black/white) males to employed (black/white) females. Second is the ratio of (black/white) professional or managerial males to (black/white) professional or managerial females.

Finally, I offer two measures of formal social control efforts in urban areas. They include police presence and a race-specific measure of the incarcerated population. The police presence measure is computed as a rate based on the average number of police officers in each city in 1980 (1979–1981) and 1990 (1989–1991) per 100,000 population.[6] The race-specific incarceration measure is based on state-level census data counts of correctional facilities' incarcerated populations. Specifically, this measure is a proportion computed by taking the number of black (white) persons from each facility within a given state, then dividing that number by the total incarcerated (in custody) population in 1980 and 1990.

Preliminary analyses reveal that the explanatory variables associated with urban disadvantage were highly correlated (see Land et al., 1990 for details), which led me to use confirmatory factor analysis and combine these measures into a composite index called the urban disadvantage/segregation index. Specifically, this index includes two race-specific measures of economic deprivation (that is, poverty and income inequality) racial residential segregation and the race-specific measure of public assistance. The two ratio measures of race- and gender-specific

6. Mean substitution was used for some police officer data in 1990 in situations where data were missing for 1 out of the 3 years. Mean substitution was not used in cases where data for 2 out of the 3 years were missing. Rather these cases were treated as missing data. No mean substitution was used in the police officer data circa 1980.

inequality were also combined based on factor loadings that well exceeded a .500 score.[7] Descriptive information for each of the detailed measures and indices are found in the Appendix.

INDUSTRIAL RESTRUCTURING: THE EVIDENCE

Table 1 presents the extent of change in disaggregated homicide, labor market sectors, and other urban conditions from 1980 to 1990. In order to show the percentage of change in the indicators over time, I compute change scores by subtracting a given indicator in 1980 from 1990, divide that value by 1980 and then multiply by 100. I also report a t-test statistic to establish whether a given predictor in 1980 differs significantly from that predictor in 1990. I highlight some of the key findings here.

First, on average for the sample of cities, homicide offending increased over time for three of four groups: white males, black males, and black females. Of these groups, homicide events involving black males increased the most from 1980 to 1990 (37.3 percent), followed by black females (15.4 percent) and white males (2.1 percent). The offending of white females decreased slightly over time, a change that was statistically significant.

Poverty levels and income inequality increased for both blacks and whites over time and I find a significant decrease in urban levels of racial residential segregation. In fact, the residential segregation between blacks and whites decreased considerably (-27.3 percent), which others have also found (see Farley and Frey, 1994). On the other hand, the percentage of black female-headed families on public assistance decreased significantly from 1980 to 1990 (-2 percent) as the percentage of white families increased (31.9 percent). When these measures are combined into the composite indices, the differences in public assistance and racial segregation translate into significant racial differences in the urban disadvantage/segregation composite measure scores. That is, the indices reveal that the concentration of urban disadvantage decreased for blacks (-16.85 percent) but increased for whites (113.4 percent).

Significant changes in industrial sectors are found across the four groups, which supports Wilson's claim of industrial restructuring. In terms of manufacturing employment, the results reveal that black females faced the greatest job loss over time (-25.6 percent), followed by white females

7. After the above indices were computed, I re-examined the bivariate correlations for evidence of collinearity and partialling among the regressors (see Land et al., 1990), as well as performed collinearity diagnostics in a series of cross-sectional regression analyses to obtain variance inflation factors (VIFs). Neither the VIFs nor correlations revealed problems in the multivariate analysis. In fact, none of the VIF associated with the parameter estimates exceed a value of 4 (values ranged from 1.062 to 3.703 across the models).

(-23.1 percent), white males (-13.9 percent) and then black males (-5.8 percent), though black males made up the largest segment of this industry's employed population during both the 1980s and 1990s (see Appendix). Although the actual change in manufacturing employment for black males was smaller than the other groups, the overall high levels of joblessness for this group could account for low levels of change over time.

Table 1. Indicators in Homicide Models, 1980–1990

	Change Scores		T Scores	
	White	Black	White	Black
Homicide count[a]				
Males	2.1	37.3	-.796	3.04*
Females	-1.0	15.4	2.98*	2.87*
Urban disad./Segregation index	113.14	-16.85	-28.23*	19.43*
Income Inequality	18.0	9.9	-49.6*	-17.3*
Poverty	7.1	8.4	-3.68*	-3.04*
Racial resid. segregation	-27.3	-27.3	22.1*	22.1*
Public assistance payments	31.9	-2.0	-4.27*	5.24*
Manufacturing employment[a]				
Males	-13.9	-5.8	11.43*	50.27*
Females	-23.2	-25.6	4.10*	11.47*
Service industry[a]				
Males	5.0	-4.8	-2.44*	-.37
Females	-2.8	-5.5	1.67	4.97*
Black concentration	25.0	25.0	-9.62*	-9.62*
Inequality index[a]	-18.7	124.9	4.98*	-2.05*
Divorced males[a]	45.2	107.3	-6.22*	-4.45*
Ratio of males to females[a]	1.7	.4	-6.77*	-.56
Residential stability	95.9	95.9	7.28*	7.28*
Police Presence	4.7	4.7	-3.99*	-3.99*
Incarcerated population	-11.5	3.4	12.81*	-4.71*
Percent Hispanic	33.6	33.6	-10.04*	-10.04*

[a] indicates that measure is race- and gender-specific
* $p < .05$

When accounting for gender, previous literature states that women were more likely to be employed in low-skilled service/retail occupations (see, for example, Tienda et al., 1987). My research yields the same findings (see Appendix), the change scores reveal a decline in service sector employment among white females (-2.8 percent), black females (-5.5 percent) and black males (-4.8 percent). White males, on the other hand, have become more numerous in the service industry over time (5.0 percent). White males, then, are benefiting from the industrial shift—one that marks a growth in administrative, highly skilled information-oriented service positions in urban cities (Kasarda, 1992). In addition, the decline in service jobs among black and white women would seem to reflect the reduction in low-skilled service and retail occupations that some researchers suggest (see Goldin, 1990; McCall, 2000). Overall, this table indicates evidence of industrial restructuring and an increasingly polarized labor market in urban cities over time. I now turn to the multivariate models that estimate the dynamic impact of the industrial shift on urban homicide.

DYNAMIC MULTIVARIATE MODELS OF CHANGE

I provide multivariate models to capture the impact of the economic transformation on disaggregated homicide from 1980 to 1990. Initial statistical diagnostics revealed that the more standard ordinary least squares (OLS) modeling technique or change score model should not be used because of the distributional nature of the disaggregated homicide data and because I utilize homicide counts instead of rates. The approach I choose is a Poisson-based regression procedure, preferred over OLS regression when the assumptions for this technique are not met (see Osgood, 2000). In terms of the race- and gender-specific dependent variables, the highly skewed and rare white female homicide counts call for a Poisson modeling procedure. This technique, however, is not suitable when the homicide data are overdispersed, as they are for the remaining three dependent variables (black male, black female and white male homicide counts). A solution is the negative binomial form of the Poisson procedure (see Osgood, 2000).

While there is no consensus regarding the best way to model change in the social science literature (Firebaugh and Beck, 1994; Kessler and Greenberg, 1981; Hausman, Hall and Griliches, 1984), I estimated a pooled cross-sectional time series equation in this study (via STATA, Version 7). The fixed-effects (fe) specification of the negative binomial and Poisson modeling procedure was employed to meet the research aims and based on statistical evidence. First, STATA documentation indicates that the "xtnbreg, fe" procedure can be used to estimate the time-series information in the data; thus answering questions concerning the effect of x when x changes within unit (STATA, 2003), which is central to this research effort.[8] Second, the appropriateness of fixed-effects (fe) over

8. The specific procedure used in STATA was "xtnbreg, fe" (and "xtpois, fe" in the case of the white female homicide counts). According to STATA documentation, there are two kinds of information in cross-sectional time-series data (STATA, 2003; http://www.stata.com/support/faqs/). The first type of cross-sectional information reflects the change between units and the "xtnbreg, be" procedure can be used to answer questions about the effect of x when x changes between units. This procedure, therefore, estimates the cross-sectional information in the data. The other type is time-series or within-unit information. To estimate the time-series information in the data, the "xtnbreg, fe" procedure can be used to answer

random-effects (re) estimator can be established using Hausman's specification test (Hausman, Hall and Griliches, 1984; Maddala, 1983). The results of this test statistic are reported in Table 2. Overall, a fixed-effects modeling design enables me to assess the influence of time varying covariates on the change in race and gender-specific homicides within a city (Hausman et al., 1984). A control variable for time was added to the models to fix the effects across the decennial points (referred to as "period effect for 1990"). In addition, the log of the city's race- and gender-specific population was included as an exposure variable and its coefficient was constrained to equal 1 (STATA, 2003). This method converts the counts of homicide into the equivalent of a rate for each city (Maddala, 1983; Osgood, 2000).

Table 2 presents the results of the change analysis. Models 1 and 2 display the parameter estimates of change in black male and black female homicides, and Models 3 and 4 present the impact of the coefficients on the change in white male and white female homicide equations.

Support is found for the differential influence of the industrial shift on the change in disaggregated homicide but not in the hypothesized direction. First, change in industrial markets (via the decline in black male manufacturing employment) contributes significantly to the change in black male homicide. At the same time, no significant impact was found on the homicide offending of the other race- and gender-specific groups, which supports the first hypothesis. However, the change in manufacturing jobs for black males significantly decreases the change in black male homicide over time—not the expected direction. Second, the shift toward a service-based economy significantly influences the change in homicide involvements of black females only. Specifically I find that the change in service industry has a positive impact on the change in black female homicides over time, which is not in the predicted direction (see hypothesis 2). One explanation for this finding is that while the economic transformation was characterized by growth in the service industry, much of the growth was in administrative, information-based technologies (see Kasarda, 1992), which did not increase job opportunities or economic status of minority women. In fact, these data revealed a growth in service

---

questions concerning the effect of x when x changes within unit. Because I am interested in estimating the impact of change in a covariate (x) on the change in the dependent variable within a given city, the fixed-effect (fe) procedure was used in this study. Moreover, the Hausman specification test provided statistical evidence of the appropriateness of the fixed-effect (fe) over random-effects (re) procedure. Generally researchers prefer to use the random-effects model because it allows for the estimation of variables that are constant within unit. However, this modeling procedure requires that the ui terms be treated as random variables and that they follow the normal distribution. This assumption is not likely to be valid in most cases and it was not found to be true with these data.

sector employment for white males but a significant decline among black females during this time period (see Table 1), which supports this interpretation. That is, the actual shift (growth) in the service sector neither increased the employability of black females nor advanced their economic status, which translates into more (instead of less) homicide offending over time.

Table 2. Conditional regression coefficients (and z-scores) for homicides, 1980 and 1990

	Black		White	
	Male Model 1	Female Model 2	Male Model 3	Female Model 4[b]
Manufacturing Employment[a]	-.013* (-1.81)	.008 (.39)	.004 (.67)	-.042 (-1.02)
Service Industry[a]	.014 (.83)	.022* (1.47)	.008 (.22)	.031 (.64)
Urban Disadvantage-Segregation Index	-.019** (-2.92)	-.025** (-2.75)	-.000 (-.01)	.019 (.85)
Inequality Index[a]	-.019 (-.84)	-.005 (-.11)	.175 (1.07)	.048 (.16)
Black Concentration	-.035** (-2.56)	-.036* (-2.27)	-.003 (-.23)	.071* (1.75)
Divorced Males[a]	-.001 (-.40)	-.004 (-1.07)	.009* (1.76)	.008 (.76)
Ratio of Males to Females[a]	.009 (.59)	.018 (.76)	-.002 (-.11)	-.014 (-.35)
Residential Stability	-.005 (-1.00)	-.011 (-1.17)	-.009** (-2.78)	-.009 (-1.33)
Police Presence	-.005** (-2.99)	-.006** (-3.15)	-.003** (-2.36)	-.004 (-.97)
Incarcerated Population	-.109 (-.08)	2.82* (1.66)	-1.66* (-1.82)	-2.38 (-1.25)
Percent Hispanic (log)	-.126 (-.96)	-.489** (-2.73)	.005 (.03)	-.120 (-.26)
Period Effect for 1990	-1.06** (-2.73)	-1.47** (-2.64)	-.537* (-1.60)	-.537 (-.87)
Constant	-3.79	-4.54	-6.79	–
Log-Likelihood	-423.74**	-239.86**	-352.31**	-121.12**
Hausman Test	26.99**	31.80**	68.47**	24.00*
N	240	228	256	252

* $p < .05$ ** $p < .01$

[a] denotes that measure is race- and gender-specific; all other measures are race-specific with the exception of control measures; South not included in fixed-effects models because the measure is not time varying

[b] Poisson Model (otherwise Negative Binomial)

Homicides among whites, male and female, were not influenced by the change in labor market forces in urban areas from 1980 to 1990, which is consistent with the previous literature and supports my theoretical predictions. In addition, the findings that industrial restructuring has a significant impact on black females, like black males, support previous literature (see, for example, Browne, 1997; Ihlanfledt and Sjoquist, 1989), as well as my theoretical arguments of the importance of estimating both race- and gender-specific changes in labor market structures.

Interestingly, I find that the change in urban disadvantage/segregation significantly contributes to the change in black male and black female homicide counts over time. It is important to recall that black urban disadvantage/segregation decreased from 1980 to 1990, with much of the decline in concentrated disadvantage among blacks being due to the simultaneous decrease in racial residential segregation (see also Farley and Frey, 1994). As a result, the change (decrease) in concentrated black disadvantage had a significant inverse effect on black male and black female homicide counts over time. Thus, when black disadvantages decline, so does black homicide offending. On the other hand, white urban disadvantage does not significantly impact the change in white gender-specific homicide offending. These findings provide evidence that the spatial concentration of disadvantage in urban areas is a significant predictor of the change in black gender-specific homicides as compared to white gender-specific homicide offending (hypothesis 3). These findings also support my research claim that labor market polarization and industrial restructuring have a unique impact on the shift or change in disaggregated homicide over time, independent of urban disadvantage indicators.

In Table 2, I find also that the changing nature of racial composition in the urban population impacts the change in disaggregated homicide over time, while race- and gender- specific based forms of inequality (via inequality index) do not. For example, the change (increase) in black concentration levels of urban areas has a statistically significant effect on the change in black male, black female and white female homicides from 1980 to 1990. More specifically, I find that black concentration has a negative impact of the change in black gender-specific homicides but a positive influence on white female homicides. On the other hand, while the ethnic (Hispanic) composition of urban areas has increased significantly from 1980 to 1990 (34 percent), this shift in population composition influences the change in black female homicide offending only.

Among the social disorganization indicators, I find that the change in divorced males and stability among urban residents significantly affect the change in white male homicides only. More specifically, the increase in white divorced males had a positive impact on the change (increase) in white male homicides, while the increase in the residential stability of the urban population had a negative impact on the change in white male homicides. While I hypothesized that social disorganization indicators would similarly impact the homicide counts for each race-and gender-specific groups (see hypothesis 4), whereby the impact of these indicators would be more consistent across the disaggregated models, the findings are largely consistent with findings in previous studies.

I estimate the impact of change in formal social control on homicide because greater dependency on formal social control could result in negative outcomes (such as an increase in violence) over time. The hypothesis is partially supported in this research (hypothesis 5). I find the shift (increase) in the presence of police from 1980 to 1990 has a significant, inverse impact on the change (increase) in homicide events for three of four race-and gender-specific groups. That is, the change in police presence over time had a negative impact on the change in homicide offending among black males, black females and white males. On the other hand, I find that the shift in the race-specific incarcerated population differentially influences the change in homicide offending across the racial groups. For example, white incarceration is inversely related to the change in white female homicides while the increase in black incarceration is positively related to the change (decrease) in black male homicides. As hypothesized, these findings suggest that there is a potential for negative outcomes as a result from the greater dependency on incarceration in urban cities (see Rose and Clear, 1998); this relationship, however, holds true only among blacks as compared to whites.

CONCLUSION

The dynamic multivariate models show that the industrial shift contributed to the change in urban homicide over time. That is, this research finds that race- and gender-specific groups felt the consequences of economic transformation differently, which contributes to the disparate levels in disaggregated homicide offending over time. More specifically, the shift in labor market sectors and the increasing polarization of labor market opportunities are influential measures when estimating the change in disaggregated homicide solely among black males and black females. This research highlights the importance of modeling change, incorporating distinct measures of the polarization of labor markets and implementing a statistical modeling strategy that can account for the uniquenesses found in disaggregated homicide data.

I provide evidence that the economic transformation of urban areas had an unprecedented impact on disadvantaged blacks in urban areas. For example, the change in urban disadvantage/segregation yield similar affects on the change in black gender-specific homicides, while the industrial shift, which marked the removal of manufacturing jobs from urban communities, was felt differently along race and gender lines. That is, a change in manufacturing employment had a significant impact on the change in black male homicides, while the shift toward a high skilled, administrative service economy positively influenced the homicide counts of black females over time. By coupling gender dynamics with race when investigating labor market opportunities, I find that black males were not alone when experiencing job loss or declining employment opportunities within industrial sectors. Black females also experienced significant disadvantages over time, which translated into an increase in homicide offending for this specific group.

My attempt to capture the impact of industrial restructuring on disaggregated homicides from 1980 to 1990 also reveals the industrial shift and change in levels of concentrated disadvantage has a more pronounced impact on blacks than whites. That is, the trend toward an increasingly stratified labor market and the industrial shift did not contribute to the change in white male or white female homicides in significant ways. Rather, this research reveals that white males benefited from the move toward a service economy over time and highlights the importance of modeling industrial restructuring separately from concentrated disadvantage in the study of urban violence. It also documents a significant relationship between formal social control and disaggregated homicide over time. I therefore argue that it is not only important to control for the influences of formal social control in studies of urban homicide but also that future research should explore possible interrelationships between formal social control, informal social control and urban violence.

This study is not without its limitations. While these limitations are largely related to the measures and data utilized in this study, other weaknesses surface such as a lack of policy-relevant indicators. For example, because this study focuses on multiple U.S. cities in order to provide a more systematic study of the relationship between industrial restructuring and urban homicide, I was not able to include important policy efforts in the local area. It is clear that criminal justice policies and procedures (via police presence and deployment) have considerable influence on the incidents of violence within different neighborhoods and areas of a given city. In addition, local areas are engaging in policy-driven actions to build the economic base of their areas (Wilson, 1996) and these efforts are likely to echo into other areas, such as drug and crime rates. An estimation of how policy efforts by criminal justice officials and local groups contribute to the changing (declining) nature of crime and violence within a given area is beyond this current study.

In addition, while this research provides empirical evidence that economic restructuring contributed to the increase in urban homicide from 1980 to 1990 differentially across race and gender-specific groups, recent studies document that homicides are declining in urban areas (see Blumstein and Wallman, 2000). It is not clear what role the industrial shift and changing economic climate of urban areas plays in the reduction of urban violence since the mid 1990s. Efforts to further model this dynamic process by including 2000 census data has only become more crucial as a result of the research findings presented here.

REFERENCES

Almgren, Gunnar, Avery Guest, George Inmerwahr and Michael Spittel
1998 Joblessness, family disruption, and violent death in Chicago, 1970–1990. Social Forces. 76:1465–1493.

Anderson, Elijah
1990 Streetwise: Race, Class and Change in an Urban Community. Chicago: University of Chicago Press.

Blau, J., and P. M. Blau
1982 The cost of inequality: Metropolitan structure and violent crime. American Sociological Review 47:114–29.

Block, C.R.
1985 Lethal Violence in Chicago over Seventeen Years. Chicago: Illinois Criminal Justice Information Authority.

Blumstein, Alfred and Joel Wallman
2000 The Crime Drop in America. Cambridge University Press.

Browne, Irene
1997 Explaining the black-white gap in labor force participation among women heading households. American Sociological Review 62:236–252.

Bureau of Justice Statistics
1996 Correctional Population in the United States, 1994. Executive Summary. Washington, DC.

Bursik, Robert J. Jr. and Harold Grasmick
1993 Neighborhoods and Crime: The Dimensions of Effective Community Control. New York: Lexington Books.

Cheatwood, Derral
1993 Notes on the theoretical, empirical and policy significance of multiple offender homicides. In A.V. Wilson (ed), Homicide: The Victim/Offender Connection. Cincinnati, OH: Anderson Publishing.

Cheatwood, D. and K. Block
1990 Youth and homicide: An investigation of the age factor in criminal homicide. Justice Quarterly, 7:265–92.

Clark, Richard
1995 Lone versus multiple offending in homicide: Differences in situational context. Journal of Criminal Justice, 23:451–460.

Crutchfield, Robert D.
1989 Labor stratification and violent crime. Social Forces 68:489–512.

Crutchfield, Robert D. and Susan Pitchford
1997 Work and crime: The effects of labor stratification. Social Forces 76:93–118.

Farley, Reynolds and W.H. Frey
1994 Changes in the segregation of whites from blacks during the 1980s: Small steps toward a more integrated society. American Sociological Review 59:23–45.

Firebaugh, Glenn, and Frank D. Beck
1994 Does economic growth benefit the masses? American Sociological Review 59(5):631–653.

Flewelling, Robert L. and Kirk R. Williams
1999 Categorizing homicide: The use of disaggregated data in homicide research. In M. Dwayne Smith and Margaret A. Zahn (eds), Homicide: A Sourcebook of Social Research. Thousand Oaks, CA: Sage Publications.

Fox, James Alan
1996 Uniform Crime Reports [United States]: Supplementary Homicide Reports, 1976–1994.[Computer file]. ICPSR 6754.

Glass, Jennifer, Marta Tienda and Shelley A. Smith
1988 The impact of changing employment opportunity on gender and ethnic earnings inequality. Social Science Research 17:252–276.

Goldin, Claudia
1990 Understanding the Gender Gap. New York: Oxford University Press.

Hausman, Jerry, Bronwyn H. Hall and Zvi Griliches
1984 Econometric models for count data with an application to the patents-R & D relationship. Econometrica 52(4):909–938.

Hawkins, Darnell
1987 Beyond anomalies: Rethinking the conflict perspective on race and criminal punishment. Social Forces 65(3):719–745.

Haynie, D. and B. Gordon
1999 A gendered context of opportunity: Determinants of poverty across urban and rural labor markets. The Sociological Quarterly 40 (2):177–189.

Hill, Gary D. and Elizabeth M. Crawford
1990 Women, race and crime. Criminology 28 (4): 601–626.

Hsueh, Sheri and Marta Tienda
1996 Gender, ethnicity and labor force instability. Social Science Research 25:73–94.

Ihlanfledt, Keith and David Sjoquist
1989 The impact of job decentralization on the economic welfare of central city blacks. Journal of Urban Economics 32:70–91.

Jackson, Pamela and Leo Carroll
1981 Race and the war on crime. American Sociological Review 46:290–305.

Kasarda, John D.
1983 Entry-level jobs, mobility, and urban minority unemployment. Urban Affairs Quarterly 19:21–40.
1989 Urban industrial transition and the underclass. The Annals of the American Academy of Political and Social Sciences. 501:26–47.
1992 The severely distressed in economically transforming cities. In Adele V. Harrell and George E. Peterson (eds.), Drugs, Crime, and Social Isolation: Barriers to Urban Opportunity. Washington, DC: The Urban Institute.

Kessler, Ronald C., and David F. Greenberg
1981 Linear Panel Analysis: Models of Quantitative Change. New York: Academic Press.

Kletzer, Lori G.
1991 Job displacement, 1979–1986: How blacks fared relative to whites. Monthly Labor Review, July:17–25.

Krivo, Lauren and Ruth D. Peterson
1996 Extremely disadvantaged neighborhoods and urban crime. Social Forces 75:619–648.
2000 The structural context of homicide: Accounting for racial differences in process. American Sociological Review 65(4):547–559.

Krivo, Lauren J., Ruth D. Peterson, Helen Rizzo, and John R. Reynolds
1998 Race, segregation and the concentration of disadvantage: 1980–1990. Social Problems 45(1):61–79.

Land, Kenneth C., Patricia L. McCall, and Larry E. Cohen
1990 Structural covariates of homicide rates: Are there any invariances across time and social space? American Journal of Sociology 95:922–963.

Liska, Allen, Joseph Lawrence and Michael Benson
1981 Perspectives on social order: the capacity of social control. American Journal of Sociology 87:413–426.

Liska, Allen, John Logan and Paul Bellair
1998 Race and violent crime in the suburbs. American Sociological Review 63:27–38.

Lynch, James and William Sabol
1997 Did Getting Tougher on Crime Pay? Crime Policy Report. Washington, DC: The Urban Institute State Policy Center.

McCall, Leslie
2000 Gender, the labor market and the educational wage gap. American Sociological Review 65(2):234–255.

Maddala, G. S.
1983 Limited-dependent and qualitative variables in econometrics. New York: Cambridge University Press.

Massey, Douglas and Nancy Denton
1993 American Apartheid: Segregation and the Making of the Underclass. Cambridge, Mass,: Harvard University Press.
1988 The dimensions of residential segregation. Social Forces 67:281–315.

Massey, Douglas and M.L. Eggers
1990 The ecology of inequality: Minorities and the concentration of poverty, 1970–1980. American Journal of Sociology 95:(5) 1153–1188.

Massey, Douglas, Gretchen A. Condran and Nancy A. Denton
1987 The effect of residential segregation on black social and economic well-being. Social Forces 66:29–56.

Massey, Douglas, Andrew B. Gross and Kumiko Shibuya
1994 Migration, segregation and the concentration of poverty. American Sociological Review 59:425–445.

Maltz, Michael D.
1999 Bridging gaps in police crime data: A discussion paper from the BJS Fellows Program. Report No. NCJ–1176365, Bureau of Justice Statistics. Washington, DC: Office of Justice Programs, U.S. Department of Justice.

Maxfield, Michael G.
1989 Circumstances in supplementary homicide reports: Variety and validity. Criminology 27: 671–696.

Messner, Steven F., Glenn Deane and Mark Beaulieu
2002 A log-multiplicative association model for allocating homicides with unknown victim-offender relationships. Criminology 40(2):457–479.

Messner, Steven F. and Reid M. Golden
1992 Racial inequality and racially disaggregated homicide rates: An assessment of alternative theoretical explanations. Criminology 30(3):421–447

Messner, Steven F, and Robert J. Sampson
1991 The sex ratio, family disruption and rates of violent crime: The paradox of demographic structure. Social Forces 69(3):693–713.

Mosher, Clayton
2001 Predicting drug arrest rates: Conflict and social disorganization. Crime & Delinquency 47:84–104.

Osgood, Dwayne W.
2000 Poisson-based regression analysis of aggregated crime rates. Journal of Quantitative Criminology, 16:21–44.

Pampel, Fred C. and Kirk R. Williams
2000 Intimacy and homicide: Compensating for missing data in the SHR. Criminology 38:661–680.

Parker, Karen F. and Patricia L. McCall
1997 Adding another piece to the inequality-homicide puzzle: The impact of structural inequality on racially disaggregated homicide rates. Homicide Studies 1:35–60.
1999 Structural conditions and racial homicide patterns: A look at the multiple disadvantages in urban areas. Criminology 37(3):447–473.

Reidel, Marc
1989 National homicide datasets: An evaluation of UCR and NCHS data. In D.L. MacKenzie, P.J. Baunach, and R.R. Roberg (eds),

Measuring Crime: Large Scale, Long-Range Efforts. Albany, NY: SUNY Press.

Ricketts, Erol L., and Isabel V. Sawhill
1988 Defining and measuring the underclass. Journal of Policy Analysis and Management 7: 316–325.

Rose, Dina and Todd Clear
1998 Incarceration, social capital and crime: Implications for social disorganization theory. Criminology 36:441–479.

Sampson, Robert J.
1987 Urban back violence: The effect of male joblessness and family disruption. American Journal of Sociology 93(2):348–382.

Sampson, R.J., and W.J. Wilson
1995 Race, crime, and urban inequality. In Crime and Inequality, edited by John Hagan and Ruth D. Peterson (pp. 37–54). Stanford, CA: Stanford University Press.

Shihadeh, Edward and Graham Ousey
1998 Industrial restructuring and violence: The link between entry-level jobs, economic deprivation and black and white homicide. Social Forces 77:185- 206.

Simpson, Sally S.
1991 Caste, class and violent crime: Explaining differences in female offending. Criminology 29(1):115–136.

Simpson, Sally and Lori Elis
1994 Is gender subordinate to class? An empirical assessment of colvin and pauly's structural marxist theory of delinquency. Journal of Criminal Law and Criminology 85 (2):453–480.

Smith, Shelley A., and Marta Tienda
1987 The doubly disadvantaged: Women of the U.S. labor force. In Working Women, 2nd ed., edited by Ann Stromberg and Shirley Harkess. Palo Alto, CA: Mayfield Publishers.

South, Scott J.
1992 For love or money? Sociodemographic determinants of the expected benefits from marriage. In The Changing American Family, edited by Scott J. South and Stewart Tolnay (pp. 171–194). Boulder, CO: Westview Press

STATA
2003 Cross-Sectional Time-Series Reference Manual. STATA Press.

Tienda, Marta and D.T. Lii
1987 Minority concentration and earnings inequality: Blacks, Hispanics and Asians compared. American Journal of Sociology 93:141–165.

Tienda, Marta, Shelley Smith, and Vilma Ortiz
1987 Industrial restructuring, gender segregation, and sex differences in earnings. American Sociological Review 52:195–210.

U.S. Bureau of the Census
1983 Census Of Population And Housing, 1980 [United States]: Summary Tape File 1a [Computer file]. Washington, DC: U.S. Dept. of Commerce, Bureau of the Census, 1982. ICPSR 7941.

U.S. Bureau of the Census
1994 Census of Population and Housing, 1990 [United States]: Summary Tape File 1a [Computer file]. Washington, DC: U.S. Dept. of Commerce, Bureau of the Census, 1991. ICPSR 9575.

U.S. Dept. of Justice, Bureau of Justice Statistics
1979 Census of State Adult Correctional Facilities, 1979 [Computer file]. Conducted by U.S. Dept. of Commerce, Bureau of the Census. 2nd ICPSR ed. Ann Arbor, MI: Inter–university Consortium for Political and Social Research, 1997. ICPSR 7852

U.S. Dept. of Justice, Bureau of Justice Statistics.
1990 Census of State And Federal Adult Correctional Facilities, 1990 [Computer file]. Conducted by U.S. Dept. of Commerce, Bureau of the Census. 2nd ICPSR ed. Ann Arbor, MI: Inter–university Consortium for Political and Social Research, 2001. ICPSR 9908.

Wacquant, L., and W. Wilson
1989 The cost of racial and class exclusion in the inner city. Annals of the American Academy of Political and Social Science 501:8–25.

Wiersema, Brian, Colin Loftin, and David McDowall
2000 A comparison of supplementary homicide reports and national vital statistics system homicide estimates for U.S. counties. Homicide Studies, 4:317–340.

Williams, Kirk and Robert L. Flewelling
1987 Family, acquaintance, and stranger homicide: Alternative procedures for rate calculations. Criminology 25:543–560.
1988 The social production of homicide: A comparative study of disaggregated rates in American cities. American Sociological Review 53:421–431.

Wilson, W.J.

1987 The Truly Disadvantaged: The Inner City, the Underclass and Public Policy. Chicago: University of Chicago Press.

1991 Another look at the truly disadvantaged. Political Science Quarterly 106 (4):639–656.

1996 When Work Disappears: The World of the New Urban Poor. New York: Alfred A. Knopf.

Wilson, F., and L. Wu

1993 A Comparative Analysis of the Labor Force Activities of Ethnic Populations, Proceedings of the Annual Research Conference of the U.S. Bureau of the Census. Washington, DC: U.S. Government Printing Office.

Karen F. Parker is associate professor of sociology in the Department of Criminology, Law and Society at the University of Florida. Her current research interests include exploring structural disadvantage effects on urban violence, examining the contextual and spatial dynamics of racial profiling in Miami communities, and incorporating dimensions of race and gender labor market segregation into the study of urban homicide.

Appendix. Means, Overall and Within Sample Standard Deviations for Indicators Included in the Race- and Gender-Disaggregated Homicide Models

	White Males			White Females			Black Males			Black Females		
	Overall Mean	Overall St. Dev.	Within St. Dev.	Overall Mean	Overall St. Dev.	Within St. Dev.	Overall Mean	Overall St. Dev.	Within St. Dev	Overall Mean	Overall St. Dev.	Within St. Dev.
Homicide Count[a]	23.9	67.9	7.7	1.99	3.9	.83	40.5	107.8	14.2	5.9	12.9	2.2
U. Disad/Segr Index	18.7	7.2	4.8	18.7	7.2	4.8	64.7	31.9	28.3	64.7	31.9	28.3
Manufacturing Employment[a]	35.9	10.5	4.1	9.6	9.1	5.6	44.7	11.7	6.6	14.4	7.12	3.4
Service Industry[a]	9.9	2.9	1.0	15.0	6.9	4.5	18.4	14.0	8.9	26.6	8.8	3.8
Black Concentration	19.8	17.2	1.5	19.8	17.2	1.5	19.8	17.2	1.5	19.8	17.2	1.5
Inequality Index[a]	.84	.89	.87	.84	.89	.87	1.9	2.4	1.7	1.9	2.4	1.7
Divorced Males[a]	8.6	4.7	3.2	8.6	4.7	3.2	11.7	13.4	9.8	11.7	13.4	9.8
Ratio of Males to Females[a]	93.3	5.7	1.5	93.3	5.7	1.5	93.8	15.5	3.6	93.8	15.5	3.6
Residential Stability	51.9	20.2	14.3	51.9	20.2	14.3	51.9	20.2	14.3	51.9	20.2	14.3
Police Presence	211.1	84.9	15.6	211.1	84.9	15.6	211.1	84.9	15.6	211.1	84.9	15.6
Incarcerated Population	.460	.15	.04	.460	.15	.04	.433	.15	.02	.433	.15	.02
Percent Hispanic	1.6	1.3	.19	1.6	1.3	.19	1.6	1.3	.19	1.6	1.3	.19

[a] denotes that measure is race- and gender-specific

Part V
Implications for Punishment

[19]

The Political Economy of Imprisonment in Affluent Western Democracies, 1960–1990

John R. Sutton
University of California

Research showing an association between business cycles and imprisonment is suspect on both theoretical and empirical grounds. Most research on this topic uses an impoverished notion of business cycles and pays no attention to differences in the institutional contexts of economic policymaking. This article reexamines this issue using data from 15 affluent capitalist democracies observed over 30 years, from 1960 to 1990. Pooled regression techniques are used to test hypotheses regarding the effects of business cycles, political power, and the structure of labor market institutions. Results from simple models show the expected associations between business cycles and imprisonment rates, but these associations disappear in models that include measures of politics and institutional structure. This suggests that the business cycle–imprisonment relationship is not causal but is instead an artifact of antecedent differences between neoliberal and corporatist societies.

Over the last three decades, the busiest line of empirical research on imprisonment has treated incarceration rates as a function of macroeconomic trends. This research builds on a Marxian theoretical foundation laid in the 1930s by Rusche and Kirchheimer (Rusche 1978; Rusche and Kirchheimer 1968), who argued that the function of prisons in capitalist societies is to manage surplus labor. Since the 1970s, dozens of studies have tested the derivative hypothesis that the imprisonment rate moves inversely with the business cycle, rising during recession and declining during economic expansion. Most results confirm the expected association (Chiricos and DeLone 1992), and many scholars believe the "Rusche–Kirchheimer hypothesis" (henceforward RK) is amply supported. Others are skeptical, arguing that tests of RK are based on narrow samples or misspecified statistical models (e.g., D'Alessio and Stolzenberg 1995; Parker and Horowitz 1986; Sutton 2000). If an empirical association exists between recession and imprisonment rates, it is by no means clear how it should be interpreted. Scholars in the RK tradition have suggested that recession may be linked to imprisonment rates as a result of increased crime (unemployed people steal), by the legitimating function of the state (unemployed people make revolutions), or by the agency of official decision makers (judges give harsher sentences to unemployed people). So far we have no way to sort out these alternative interpretations, since "the research has left many if not most of the key theoretical issues unexamined" (Chiricos and DeLone 1992: 432).

I find three chronic weaknesses in the RK literature that call not just for skepticism, but for

---

Direct all correspondence to John R. Sutton, University of California Santa Barbara, Department of Sociology, Santa Barbara CA 93106 (sutton@soc.ucsb.edu). This research was supported by grants #SES-9122424 and SBR-9510936 from the U.S. National Science Foundation. Conclusions drawn from the analysis reflect the viewpoint of the author, and not NSF. Earlier versions of this paper were presented to the Sociology Department at Princeton University in November, 2000; at the meetings of the American Sociological Association in August, 2001; to the Sociology Department at the University of California, Davis, in October, 2001; and to the Sociology Department at the University of Illinois-Chicago in January 2003. The author is grateful to *ASR* editors and reviewers, Bill Bielby, Ryken Grattet, Heather Haveman, John Meyer, and members of the Inequality, Institutions, and Networks seminar at UCSB for their advice and comments on earlier drafts.

a fundamental rethinking of the prison-economy relationship. One weakness is a persistent lack of attention to the state and the dynamics of social policy making. Holding crime constant, rates of incarceration are most powerfully and proximally influenced by policies that determine the kinds of behaviors that are criminalized and the administrative capacity of criminal justice agencies. These are institutional phenomena: what Wilkins (Wilkins 1991; Wilkins and Pease 1987) calls the "social demand for punishment" cannot be explained away in terms of class interest or elite conspiracy. There is now good evidence from outside the RK tradition of discursive, ideological, and political factors that influence penal policy independently of economic trends, including the development of social welfare schemes (Garland 1985), the production of criminological knowledge and the routes by which it is incorporated into penal policy (Savelsberg 1994), the organization of the life course (Sutton 2000), institutionalized patterns of inequality (Wilkins 1991; Wilkins and Pease 1987), and partisan political alignments (Jacobs and Helms 1996; Sutton 1987; von Hofer 2003). This work is not theoretically integrated, and—perhaps in reaction to the stifling influence of RK—it tends not to address economic effects on incarceration. But the findings from this research point toward a provocative generalization: Demand for punishment seems to be highest in societies that have a strong commitment to individualistic means of social achievement and a correspondingly weak capacity for collective responses to inequality.

A second weakness is that the RK research is based on an impoverished notion of the economy. This is partly a problem of model specification: following Rusche and Kirchheimer's emphasis on labor surplus, most studies rely on a single predictor of imprisonment rates, usually unemployment (Chiricos and DeLone 1992: Appendix A). This is naïve because business cycles are multidimensional phenomena, comprising several empirical trends that are often independent of each other and that have different implications for class-based social divisions. This is not a difficult problem to remedy in empirical terms, since additional indicators of business cycles are readily available. But it points to a deeper theoretical problem: RK research implicitly assumes that all capitalist economies are the same and that business cycles are wholly exogenous to other kinds of social processes. This ignores a large and growing body of research in sociology, political science, and macroeconomics that focuses on differences in the institutional foundations of Western capitalist economies and the consequences of these differences for economic performance. This research shows that the variation in the strength and organization of national labor movements, the balance of power among class-based political parties, and the relative centralization of labor markets are consequential for a wide range of macroeconomic outcomes, including employment and growth (e.g., Esping-Andersen 1990; 1999; Garrett 1998; Western 1997). The empirical RK research has overlooked these institutional differences; indeed the research overwhelmingly has focused on societies of the United States and Britain (Chiricos and DeLone 1992: Appendix A), which are exemplars of market liberalism (Esping-Andersen 1990). Little attention has been paid to the European corporatist democracies, where labor market trends are less volatile, welfare state protections are stronger, and incarceration rates are lower.

A third weakness is that, just as the RK research ignores differences across capitalist economies, it ignores institutional adaptations. Rusche and Kirchheimer themselves treated the emergent welfare states of the early 20th century as no different than the poor law regimes that accompanied early industrial capitalism. The majority of the recent RK research ignores the move to Keynesian economic management that began in the 1950s; more importantly, the economic restructuring of the last 30 years has received scant attention. The global oil shocks of 1973 and 1979–80 and the recessions that followed challenged the assumptions of Keynesianism and encouraged a wide-ranging set of adaptations among the advanced capitalist countries. Scholarly opinion is divided about how deep and transformative these adaptations have been, and their debates have implications for our understanding of the economy-imprisonment relationship. According to the "globalization thesis" (Garrett 1998, ch. 1), increasing capital mobility and incorporation into world markets have pushed the European social democracies toward American-style market liberalism (Kitschelt 1994; Piven 1991), while other scholars argue that differences between liberal and social democratic regimes have persisted in spite of new economic pressures (Esping-Andersen 1999; Garrett 1998). There is a parallel debate in the punishment literature. Wacquant (1999; 2001) has argued that, as European states adjust to more turbulent labor markets, they also imitate the United States by adopting more punitive means of managing inequality. Research by Western and his colleagues (Western and Beckett 1998; Western and Beckett 1999; Western and Guetzkow 2002; Western and Pettit 2000) suggests on the contrary that mass imprisonment is embedded in the U.S. labor market in ways that are not easily exportable. The systematic comparative work required to sort out these arguments has not yet been performed.

The implications of this critique can be summarized briefly: (1) The existing RK research suffers from empirical misspecification and theoretical narrowness; (2) since punishment practices and labor market trends both are shaped by antecedent institutional factors, the observed association between them may well be spurious; and (3) an adequate account of the relationship between the economy and the prison must incorporate both differences among capitalist democracies and adaptations occurring over time. I address each of these issues and develop an alternative model of the relationship of imprisonment to the economy in the next section. This model operates on two levels. On the first level, it offers a more nuanced representation of the behavior of business cycles than has been employed in the RK research, which in turn will permit more exacting analyses of their relationship to imprisonment. On the second level, the model identifies salient institutional differences between liberal and corporatist policy regimes—especially political power and the organization of labor markets—that are likely to influence both incarceration and employment trends. My argument in brief is that incarceration and employment are interdependent because both are embedded in wider institutional frameworks that shape social policy in modern Western societies. More specifically, I argue that incarceration rates are higher in countries where capacities for regulating the macroeconomy and containing inequality are weak. I test this model on data from 15 capitalist democracies observed over 30 years, from 1960 to 1990. This assures that the analysis captures both relatively stable differences among social policy regimes and adaptations to watershed economic challenges.

RETHINKING THE ECONOMY–IMPRISONMENT RELATIONSHIP

Respecifying Business Cycles

For our purposes, it is convenient, and reasonably faithful to the macroeconomics literature, to think of business cycles as having three empirically distinct dimensions: growth, employment, and inflation. In the textbook scenario, these dimensions are related in the following way: economic growth produces wealth, stimulating demand for goods, services, and labor; eventually wages and/or consumption may rise faster than the economy's productive capacity, leading to inflation; inflation creates a disincentive for productive investment, leading to slower growth, and, eventually, higher rates of unemployment. Real economies do not move in such a lockstep fashion; the potential independence of these trends provides much of the grist for macroeconomic research and suggests great care in generating hypotheses about imprisonment, particularly in a cross-national context. Most of the empirical macroeconomics research focuses on the dynamic properties of single economies; indeed, the United States often serves as exemplar. In my discussion, I will describe the standard expectations about business cycle behavior, but I will also emphasize the growing literature that offers comparative analyses across several economies.

EMPLOYMENT. I begin with the issue of employment because it is central to the RK hypothesis. The most commonly used indicator is the unemployment rate, but a well-known limitation of official unemployment rates is that they count only people who are active in the labor force—usually people who are either working or out of work but collecting unemployment benefits. Unemployment rates do not include people who have never participated in the labor force or who have dropped out because of a perceived lack of opportunities. In the adult population, most labor-force nonparticipants are women. However, the labor-force nonparticipant group also includes a high concentration of young, poorly educated, low-skilled, and socially marginal men—precisely the group that would be most at risk of imprisonment. Indeed, such high-risk candidates are probably more highly concentrated among discouraged workers than among the officially unemployed. Labor-force participation rates provide a useful (inverse) measure of the relative size of the population that is excluded from work. Elmeskov and Pichelmann (1993) analyzed the empirical relationship between labor-force participation and official unemployment rates, and they find a loose negative relationship among OECD (Organisation for Economic Cooperation and Development) countries over the long run: high unemployment tends to coincide with low participation in the labor force (OECD 1991). Still, their data show a few exceptions (notably Sweden), and the patterns of association between the time series vary dramatically across countries. Thus, the two measures seem to capture different dimensions of labor-market slack. Since rising rates of labor-force participation signify expanding economic opportunities, we should expect a negative association with prison growth. I will focus on *male* labor-force participation rates to capture the population most at risk of crime and imprisonment.[1]

GROWTH. Total economic output, typically measured by per capita gross domestic product (GDP), is the most general and frequently used indicator of macroeconomic performance, and GDP growth is the most common indicator of business cycle movement. Economic growth is a major determinant of unemployment rates; an association described by "Okun's law," one of the best-known predictions in macroeconomics.[2] However, as a great deal of empirical work has shown, Okun's law is not a law, but a variable. Comparative analysis by Moosa (1997) shows systematic differences across countries and over time: cycles of GDP and unemployment growth are more tightly related in the United States, Canada, and the United Kingdom than in Japan and continental Europe, where corporatist protections help buffer labor markets. And some evidence shows that linkages are becoming tighter overall (Okun's coefficient is rising) as worker protections have eroded in many countries. GDP growth is likely to show direct negative effects on prison growth. But we also should attend to possible indirect effects mediated by unemployment. If the orthodox interpretation of the RK hypothesis is correct—that is, labor surplus per se is responsible for variation in imprisonment rates—then labor market effects should persist even when productivity growth is included in the equation. Otherwise, the productivity effect is likely to overwhelm any observed effects of labor markets.

INFLATION. Inflation—a general increase in prices—typically is a byproduct of rapid growth, particularly when the economy is producing near its upper limit of output. Growth fuels consumer optimism, hence demand; but if productivity cannot keep pace, prices for a finite stock of goods and services are bid upwards, reducing real incomes. Generally, since inflation makes people poorer, we might expect a positive association between inflation and imprisonment. Indeed, the logic of Okun's popular "misery index" (the sum of inflation and unemployment rates) suggests that the two trends should have convergent impacts. Lessan (1991) found such a pattern in a time-series analysis of U.S. imprisonment data.

However, macroeconomic theory predicts that inflation and unemployment are inversely related. The anticipated trade-off between inflation and unemployment is formalized in the "Phillips curve," a cornerstone of macroeconomic theory and monetary policy since the 1950s (Dornbusch, Startz, and Fischer 1998, ch. 16). The logic of the Phillips curve implies that the two trends are unlikely to have convergent effects on incarceration rates. Indeed, without straying far from the spirit of the RK hypothesis, it is reasonable to predict that inflation has a *negative* impact on incarceration. This is

[1] Data on unemployment rates by gender are not available for the earlier years covered by this study. This is probably a minor problem, since male and female unemployment rates tend to move together. Trends in labor-force participation vary sharply: across the countries analyzed here, male participation rates have fallen and female participation rates have risen.

[2] Specifically, Okun's law predicts that when real GDP growth is over the annual trend of 2.25 percent, unemployment will decline by .5 percent for every 1 percent of additional GDP growth (Okun 1962).

because inflation reduces inequality by redistributing wealth and income from creditors to debtors (Dimelis and Livada 1999; Dornbusch, Startz, and Fischer 1998:518–21; Johnson and Shipp 1999). The hardest hit creditors tend to be large institutions, such as banks, insurance companies, and investment firms, as well as wealthy individuals who derive substantial income from equity stocks. Many businesses are net debtors, but so are most families, particularly those at the lower end of the income distribution. Indexing protects the real incomes of most workers and pensioners from erosion, and, if unemployment is low, even non-indexed wages are likely to rise. Wages aside, inflation tends to raise effective incomes because it makes long-term borrowing—for furniture, cars, homes, and educational expenses—more attractive. Conversely, *dis*inflation has profound adverse consequences, mainly for lower-income persons. A relevant example of this is the tight money policies adopted by the United States and other rich countries in an attempt to end the inflationary binge of the 1970s—a strategy that, in the early 1980s, led to a deep recession and the highest unemployment rates in the postwar period.

I also attend to two kinds of effects that expand the basic business cycle model and provide a theoretical bridge to the institutional effects that are my main interest. First, looming behind the RK hypothesis—indeed all arguments deriving from Marx—is the idea that incarceration is related to economic inequality. The implicit logic of the RK argument is that recession raises imprisonment rates by widening class divisions and aggravating social tensions; unemployment is one mechanism of immiseration, but is not the thing itself. Wilkins (1991; Wilkins and Pease 1987) frames the association between imprisonment and inequality in different terms: he argues that incarceration is a form of stratification, a "negative reward" that is allocated through the same social processes that allocate positive rewards like income, education, and health care. Thus the "public demand for punishment" is likely to be higher in societies that tolerate high levels of inequality. Both the RK and Wilkins hypotheses predict a positive association between inequality and imprisonment rates.

Second, it is also important to factor in the effects of social protection schemes designed to buffer individuals from the impact of recessions. Macroeconomic theory suggests that social benefits, such as unemployment compensation, influence rates of unemployment by raising the "reservation wage" (the wage that offers an adequate incentive for an unemployed worker to accept a job). Also, more generous benefits may embolden employed workers to press for higher wages even in the face of rising unemployment. Whatever the mechanism, substantial research has shown that the more generous the benefit and the longer it persists, the higher the rate of unemployment (Scarpetta 1996:51–2). This suggests a positive association between benefits and imprisonment, mediated by unemployment. However, Cantor and Land (1985) show that we could expect a direct negative effect because unemployment benefits reduce incentives for crime (hence the risk of imprisonment) among insured workers. This suggests that, at least in the short term, higher spending on unemployment benefits should counteract the tendency of rising unemployment to push crime and imprisonment rates up The expected association in this scenario is negative.

Rethinking Labor Markets

This section develops two arguments I posed in the introduction. The first is that business cycles are not exogenous. Rates of employment, growth, and inflation are affected by institutional differences between neoliberal and corporatist economies; this means that, at the very least, tests of the effects of business cycles on imprisonment are misspecified unless they control for these antecedent differences. The second and more ambitious argument is that the association between imprisonment and business cycles is spurious, that in fact, institutional differences directly affect both. Recall Wilkins's (1991) suggestion that imprisonment rates and inequality covary. I have already introduced this idea as a testable hypothesis, but viewed in the larger context of Wilkins's work, it is a tautology, since he conceptualizes imprisonment as a *form* of inequality. The question then becomes, What determines the level of tolerance for inequality—including punishment rates—across societies and over time? To pose the question in this way implies that neoliberalism and corporatism are not just alternative techniques of macroeconomic management, but alternative policy regimes that are organized around fundamentally different institutional logics (Friedland and Alford 1991). Neoliberalism defers to the logic of the market: inequality, unemployment, and crime are treated as the natural results of competitive individualism, the state's prescribed role is reactive, and social policies are invidious, even overtly punitive. Corporatist societies are organized around the logic of cooperation, so the state plays a more active role in managing inequality and social policies are aimed at socializing economic risks and rewards. This notion of alternative policy regimes is not new, in fact it is fundamental to the political economy and welfare state literatures (e.g., Esping-Andersen 1990; 1999; Garrett 1998; Hicks 1988; Hicks and Kenworthy 1998; Huber, Ragin, and Stephens 1993; Kenworthy 2002). What is new here is the attempt to bring the issue of imprisonment under the same theoretical umbrella.

I intend to specify the dimensions of market logic, its alternatives, and its likely consequences for imprisonment. To these ends I draw on an extended debate among economists, political scientists, and sociologists about how labor markets and economic performance are related to inequality. The debate focuses on labor market rigidity, which refers primarily to the existence and extent of institutional constraints on open bidding for jobs, wages, and working conditions between firms and individual workers, but also includes redistributive programs that can affect the supply and cost of labor. Labor market rigidity is not a purely technical matter but is rather deeply political: the purpose of regulatory and redistributive policies is to mitigate the impacts of labor market failure on workers and their families, thus their major advocates are labor unions and leftist political parties. Neoclassical economists argue that constraints of this sort are likely to erode economic performance because they raise wages above market-clearing rates and increase the costs of hiring and firing employees. From this point of view, the welfare-state protections and neocorporatist labor regimes that took shape in varying degrees in the 1950s and 1960s were sustainable only because Western economies were relatively closed to outside influences; the 1973–1974 oil shock was a signal that the global market would ultimately have its way, and the dramatic rebound of the U.S. economy after the 1980–1981 recession was evidence for many that the worst-tasting medicine produces the best results. On the other side of the debate, a stream of literature running from Calmfors and Driffil (1988; Calmfors 1993) and Esping-Andersen (1990; 1999) to Garrett (1998) has attacked the idea that U.S.-style market liberalism is the only road to economic health. Their work suggests that highly centralized social-democratic regimes can achieve high levels of growth, keep inflation in check, *and* reduce inequality by encouraging wage restraint across the entire economy.

Both sides of this debate help to specify the causal scenarios to be tested in this analysis. The neoclassical argument suggests how labor market structure might effect imprisonment indirectly: If economic performance is inversely related to incarceration rates (the RK hypothesis is true), *and* labor market regulation erodes economic performance, then the net effect of regulation is positive. Thus, highly regulated corporatist economies are likely to experience higher imprisonment rates in the long run. This scenario is logically consistent, but prima facie implausible, since the United States and the United Kingdom, the two developed countries with the weakest regulatory regimes, also have the highest average rates of incarceration. The revisionist interpretation suggests an entirely different causal scenario: Regulation may reduce the amplitude of business cycles, thus indirectly holding down incarceration rates—again, if RK is true. More importantly, if corporatist regulatory strategies are symptomatic of a deeper institutional logic that informs a broad range of social policies, then we will probably see direct negative effects on incarceration rates.

The following hypotheses capture the tension in this debate. I focus on two sources of labor market rigidity that figure prominently in the literature—the political power of labor movements and social democratic parties, and the capacity of corporatist institutions to coordinate labor markets.

UNION STRENGTH. Stronger union organization enhances the collective power of workers to influence wage-setting and other policies that are friendly to workers and their families. The general expectation among mainstream economists is that unrestrained wage demands by powerful unions will erode economic performance. This effect, they argue, accounts in part for high unemployment rates in Europe since the 1970s; conversely, recovery in the 1980s and 1990s is partly attributable to union decline (e.g., Layard, Nickell, and Jackman 1991; Nickell 1997; Scarpetta 1996). Extending this logic, union strength should be positively associated with prison growth and should attenuate any observed impact of business cycles. There is, however, an alternative account. Research by Hicks (1988) and Alvarez, Garrett, and Lange (Alvarez, Garret, and Lange 1991; Garrett 1998; Garrett and Lange 1986; Lange and Garrett 1985; Lange and Garrett 1986) concludes that union strength contributes to economic growth *and* improvements in income equality when it is complemented by labor party control of government. Boreham, Hall, and Leet (1996) find that, among OECD countries, stronger union sectors are associated with higher levels of redistributive social spending, independent of political party effects. There is no research on the effects of unionization on imprisonment, nor have I found evidence that labor unions have been directly influential on criminal justice issues. But it is clear from the existing research that labor unions are more than wage-bargaining agents, they are also collective political actors that are inimically opposed to the logic of the market. Strong unions imply greater working-class influence in domestic politics, which is likely to encourage cooperative and redistributive social policies and discourage policies that are unfriendly to their constituents—and it is difficult to think of a less worker-friendly policy than imprisonment. On these grounds, I anticipate a negative association between union strength and imprisonment rates.

PARTISAN POLITICS. There is a substantial and hotly debated literature on partisan influences on macroeconomic policy. As Alvarez et al. (1991:531–40) elegantly summarize, one side argues that the mix of unemployment and inflation is influenced by which party is in power, because left parties are more averse to unemployment and right parties are more averse to inflation; the other side argues that both the left and right parties are inclined to court the "median voter," so partisan effects cancel out and market forces prevail. The mere existence of this debate is sufficient reason to incorporate partisan effects in the analysis, if only as a control. In the literatures on political economy and social policy, the role of left (social democratic and labor) parties has drawn the most attention. Comparative research shows that left parties encourage more redistributive social policies (Hicks and Misra 1993; Hicks and Swank 1992; Korpi 1989), tighter regulation of labor markets (Garrett 1998; Hicks 1988), and a preference for inflation over unemployment (Hibbs 1997). Thus, there is good reason to suspect that these parties exert an antecedent influence on factors that are likely to affect imprisonment rates. There is also evidence that, at least among the Anglo-American democracies, dominance by right parties encourages prison growth directly (Jacobs and Helms 1996; Sutton 1987; 2000). This implies a direct negative effect of left parties, but their specific impact has not been tested because the United States lacks a true party of the left. Data from a wider range of countries will permit such a test; I anticipate a negative association between left party rule and prison expansion.

CORPORATIST LABOR MARKET INSTITUTIONS. Capitalist countries vary widely in their structural capacity to coordinate labor market transactions. Neoliberal democracies like the United States and the United Kingdom rely primarily on market mechanisms to set wages, the terms of employment, and eligibility for social benefits, and interest groups play no formal role in economic policymaking. In corporatist regimes, wage rates, work rules, and policies concerning employment security and social protection are set by negotiations among "peak associations" representing workers (through their unions and union federations), employers (through industry associations or federations spanning the entire private economy), and the state. Thus, corporatism is a set of structural arrangements through which workers, employers, and the state are jointly engaged in forging economic policies that are applied in a coordinated way across the entire economy (Hicks and Kenworthy 1998).

There are grounds to expect both indirect and direct effects of corporatist institutions on incarceration trends. A hypothesis of indirect effects arises from the standard macroeconomic view that coordination impedes economic performance. In this view, centralized wage setting—a signal feature of corporatist economies—reduces employers' flexibility in responding to changing market conditions and to the varying circumstances of workers in different occupations and industries. As a result, growth suffers and unemployment rises. One particularly interesting and influential version of this argument is the "insider-outsider theory." Lindbeck and Snower (1989) have argued that employed, unionized workers (insiders) have a power advantage over unemployed workers and workers in the informal sector (outsiders): The cost of replacing protected workers is high, so insiders have an incentive to push for wage increases even in the face of a recession. This is likely to raise unemployment rates and hinder economic recovery. If we append this argument (corporatism leads to deeper and longer recessions) to the RK hypothesis (recessions push incarceration rates up), we should expect a net positive effect of corporatism on incarceration, mediated by business cycles. This hypothesis is *prima facie* dubious, because it does not explain Canada, the United States, and the United Kingdom—countries that rank at or near the bottom of any measure of corporatism, and at or near the top in prison growth—but multivariate tests could possibly reveal an underlying effect of this sort.

Since the 1980s, a rising chorus of scholars has criticized the neoclassical view, offering considerable evidence that centralized wage-setting and union consultation can yield efficient economic performance.[3] The core of the revisionist argument is that salutary compromises are more likely when economic risk is nationalized. Under such conditions, union confederations are willing to accept modest (noninflationary) wage increases in return for favorable employment policies and a strong social safety net, and employers are inclined to accept labor market regulation in return for predictable levels of inflation and protection from labor unrest. This suggests a net negative effect of corporatism on incarceration that may operate indirectly, through enhanced economic performance (again, if the RK hypothesis is true), or directly, as part of a tendency toward more equalitarian social policy.

This effect may not be linear. In a pair of frequently cited articles, Calmfors and Driffil (1988; 1993) put forward a more subtle argument that both market-based and corporatist labor arrangements can perform efficiently; pathologies are most likely to arise at intermediate (industry) levels of labor market coordination, where unions are powerful enough to distort market forces and competition among unions and industries discourages wage restraint. Comparative research by Scarpetta (1996) shows just such a "hump-shaped" effect of coordination on several indicators of unemployment; by simple extension, this suggests a similar, but indirect, U-shaped effect of corporatism on incarceration. But this hypothesis also leaves Canada, the United States, and the United Kingdom dangling conspicuously. An opposite and more intuitively sensible hypothesis is suggested by Lindbeck and Snower's "insider-outsider" imagery, particularly as employed by Esping-Andersen (1999; 2000a; 2000b). Even in relatively inclusive corporatist countries, risks are not shared equally across the whole society, but only among those with a collective voice. Corporatist institutions can aggravate the insider-outsider problem in broad political and social terms, because workers in core occupations and industries may use their bargaining advantage to monopolize the benefits of regulated labor markets, leaving outsider workers to experience high rates of unemployment, limited social protection, and generally weak attachments to supportive institutions. Esping-Andersen's (2000b) empirical analyses show that, although labor market regulation does not cause mass unemployment, it does affect the *shape* of unemployment, with particularly harsh impacts on the young and unskilled. As long as the economy is growing, expansion of the core can create new opportunities for outsiders and reduce competition between the two sectors; but recession is likely to lead to shrinkage in core opportunities, deepened segmentation, and rising inequality. Women workers are likely to be positioned as outsiders, but so are younger workers, ethnic minorities, immigrants, and guestworkers—groups that also experience a higher than average risk of incarceration. This leads to another curvilinear hypothesis, this time with a U-shaped functional form. Imprisonment rates

[3] Kenworthy and Hicks (Hicks and Kenworthy 1998; Kenworthy 2002) summarize these studies and provide extensive citations.

are likely to be highest in the market liberal societies, where competitive individualism sets the tone for social policy, and in highly corporatist countries, where group competition between insiders and outsiders is institutionalized. I expect imprisonment rates to be lower in the middle, where neither model predominates.

DATA AND METHODS

The data for this study comprise time series for 15 countries observed from 1960 to 1990. The sample includes five Anglo-American liberal democracies (Australia, Canada, New Zealand, the United Kingdom, and the United States), four Scandinavian social democracies (Denmark, Finland, Norway, and Sweden), and six European corporatist democracies (Austria, Belgium, France, Germany [F.R.G.], and the Netherlands). The sample was stratified in this way to maximize variation on key economic and labor-market variables while still maintaining a focus on the most developed economic systems. Panels are unbalanced in minor ways due to missing data. German imprisonment data begin in 1961, and New Zealand unionization data only run from 1961 to 1986. These imbalances are irrelevant for the estimation procedures used here.

The dependent variable is imprisonment rates, measured as a ratio of the number of inmates per 100,000 population. For the purposes of this analysis, I use aggregate imprisonment rates, combining sentenced and remand inmates, and inmates in local jails as well as those in penitentiaries. Although this measure is used commonly in scholarly and policy literatures, it is problematic because it collapses several analytically distinct processes operating at different points in the criminal justice process. As Pease's "stocks" and "flows" imagery suggests (Andre and Pease 1994; Pease 1992; Pease 1994), the prison population at any given time is a function of admission rates and the effective length of incarceration, which in turn are affected by the incidence of crime as well as official decisions regarding arrest, pretrial detention, charging, conviction, sentencing, and release, all of which may operate independently. A thorough accounting of imprisonment trends requires the pairing of an appropriate numerator (prison populations or admissions, for example) with a proximal denominator (the incidence of crime, convictions, or sentences). Thus Pease (1994:125) contends that a measure of the prison population as a ratio to the national population "is useless for all practical and intellectual purposes" (see also Pease 1992; Young 1986; Young and Brown 1993).

There are several grounds, both practical and theoretical, for defending the measure used here. Prison admission rates, arguably a better measure and clearly more sensitive than inmate population rates, are wholly unavailable for five of the countries in the sample and only spottily available for three more. Counts of arrests and convictions are similarly unavailable. Separate counts of remand populations are not available at all for Canada, and are only partial for two other countries. Even if the data could be gathered, the distinction between sentenced and remand populations would be meaningless, and probably fatally biased, because of differences in national legal conventions. Unlike Common Law systems, continental European countries count convicted prisoners as being on remand until all of their appeals are exhausted, making cross-national distinctions between sentenced and remand populations impossible (Pease 1994:127). Finally, the most skeptical scholars (but also Lynch 1987; Pease 1992; 1994), are motivated by a concern for "punitiveness"—a protean concept whose meaning varies, depending on the theoretical and ideological agenda of the user (Pease 1994:118). Because of severe data limitations, analyses in this vein must use cross-sectional data from small samples of countries, so even the most insightful results remain quite tentative. My goals are different, and in some ways simpler. I am explicitly interested in the dynamics of incarceration, and the need to assemble substantial time series from different countries justifies some sacrifice of depth for breadth. If aggregation at this level obscures important subprocesses, the cost will be a weakening of estimated effects, raising the risk of Type I errors—an acceptably conservative risk. Moreover, I am not concerned with abstract "punitiveness," but with the concrete reality of incarceration. Wilkins, (1991:13), whose "market model" of imprisonment informs my own approach, uncomplicates the issue nicely: "The incarceration rate represents the proportion of individuals who have lost their liberty by reason of the deployment of the criminal law. The incarceration rate is an excellent proxy for many other measures of societies' responses to acts defined as crimes; moreover it is generally available, simple, and highly variable" (see also Wilkins and Pease 1987:20).

Imprisonment data were drawn from several different sources. For most countries, statistical yearbooks provided baseline figures that were, in some cases, supplemented or replaced by other sources. Government statistical agencies in Canada, Germany, and the Netherlands provided data directly, and Australian yearbook data were supplemented with data published by the Australian Institute of Criminology (Mukherjee et al. 1989) and in Biles (1982). The definitive source for Scandinavian criminal justice systems is von Hofer (1997); Austrian data are from Hanak and Pilgram (1991); and Belgian data are from Snacken (1991). For European countries from 1970 on, data have been cross-checked with figures published by the Council of Europe (1990). Figure 1 presents running boxplots of imprisonment rates among the countries studied here. Panel 1a includes data from all 15 countries in the sample; it is dominated by U.S. observations, which appear as a high and upwardly accelerating series of outliers. The remaining panels focus on subsamples of countries, clustered in terms of Esping-Andersen's (1990) regime typology; the United States is excluded so that graphs can be redrawn on a common and more revealing scale. The graphs suggest modest differences across groups: Even without the United States, average imprisonment rates are higher in the Anglo-American countries (panel 1b). Apparent differences in trends between Scandinavian and central European countries (panels 1c and 1d) arise from two countries: Finnish incarceration rates are exceptionally high through the 1960s (von Hofer 2003), and Dutch rates are consistently low.

Descriptive statistics and correlations for all variables, and detailed definitions of independent variables and sources of data, are listed

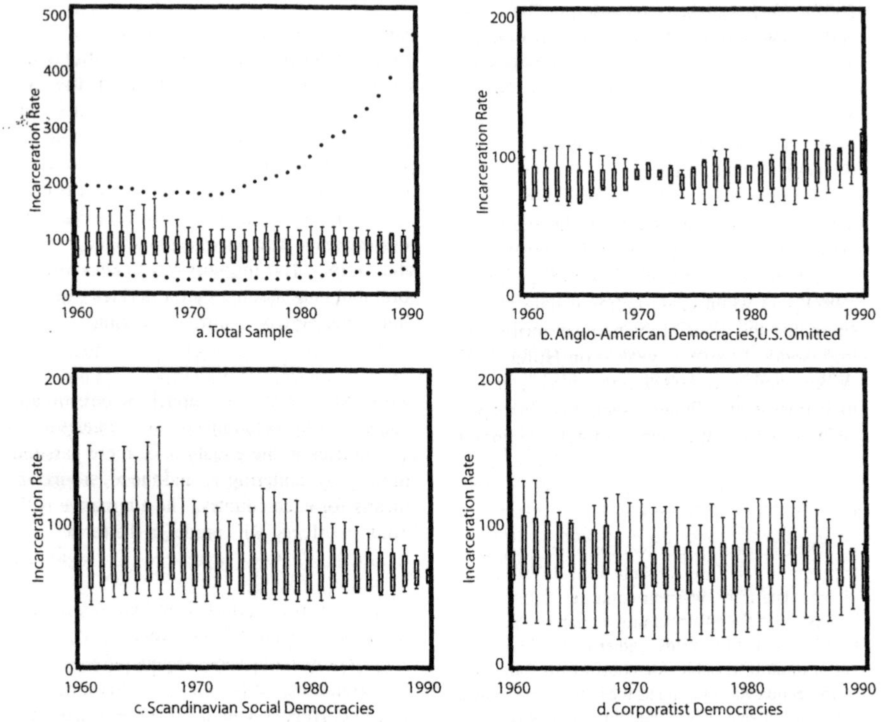

Figure 1. Box Plots of Imprisonment Rates in 15 Affluent Capitalist Democracies

in appendix tables. Business cycles are represented by four standard indicators: *unemployment rates* are calculated as the number of officially unemployed workers as a percentage of the active labor force, *male labor-force participation* is the percentage of males age 15–64 who are in the labor force, *economic growth* is measured in terms of real per capita gross domestic product (in 1985 U.S. dollars), and *inflation* is calculated from within-country GDP deflators. To supplement these standard indicators, I use a quintile-based Gini index of *income inequality* compiled from various sources by Nielsen and Alderson (1995),[4] and the influence of *social benefits* is represented by spending on unemployment compensation as a percentage of GDP. Three variables represent institutional effects. *Union strength* is measured as union density, the number of union members as a percentage of the active labor force (Golden, Lange, and Wallerstein 1997). *Left dominance* is indicated by a measure of the proportion of total cabinet seats held by left (labor and social democratic) parties (Swank 2002). *Corporatism* is represented by Hicks and Kenworthy's (2002) wage-coordination measure, a synthetic index that captures the comprehensiveness of business and union federations, centralization of the wage-bargaining process, and cooperation among unions, employers, and the state.

It is important, finally, to control for the incidence of crime. Recession might encourage crime, although the research literature is ambiguous on this matter (Box 1987; Chiricos 1987); and while cross-national data tend to show that the association between crime and imprisonment is very weak (von Hofer 2003; Wilkins and Pease 1987), it is probably unwise to dismiss it out of hand. I seek, insofar as possible, to derive estimates of effects on imprisonment that are independent of criminogenic effects, so to this end I use homicide rates (the number of homicides per 100,000 population) as a control. This is far from an ideal indicator, since the relationship of homicide rates to other kinds of crime rates is problematic, and tends to vary across countries (Zimring and Hawkins 1997). Unfortunately there are no preferable alternatives, since comparable data on other types of crimes are not available for all of the countries and years in the sample. The two virtues of homicide rates are, first, that fairly accurate data are available from modern societies over long stretches of time (Monkkonen 1989), and, second, because homicides are so conspicuous, they are likely to have an exaggerated influence on public perceptions of crime and on crime-control policies (Zimring and Hawkins 1997).

Pooled time-series models raise special difficulties because the observations are related to each other in both space and time. The basic model can be expressed as follows:

$$y_{it} = \alpha + \beta x_{it} + \varepsilon_{it}, \quad (1)$$

which differs from the standard regression model in terms of the subscripts, with i denoting cross-sectional units (countries, in this case) and t denoting time (in this case years). The problem here is that the observations are not independent; most conspicuously for cross-national studies in which $N < T$, there is likely to be unobserved heterogeneity due to stable but unmeasured differences across the countries in the sample. The simplest way to deal with this problem is to assume that α is fixed over time but varies across countries, yielding

$$y_{it} = \alpha_i + \beta x_{it} + \varepsilon_{it}. \quad (2)$$

This fixed effects (FE) model can be estimated using OLS by including dummy variables for N-1 countries in the equation, or more parsimoniously by centering y_{it} and the x_{it} around the means for each country. The alternative is the random effects (RE) model in the form

$$y_{it} = \alpha + \beta x_{it} + \nu_i + \varepsilon_{it}, \quad (3)$$

in which ν_i is a random disturbance that is stable through time within country i. The RE model is preferable if one seeks to generalize to a larger population, but the implicit assumption that ν_i is uncorrelated with the other regressors may be untenable (Greene 1997:632–33). A

[4] The Gini data include two "technical" variables that control for biases arising from differences in income data from different countries (Nielsen and Alderson 1995: 684): a dummy variable for income data based on households (rather than individuals), and a dummy variable for coefficients calculated from decile data. I included these technical indicators in all models where the Gini index is used as a regressor, but omit their coefficients from the tables.

Hausman test using the present data (in the full model in Table 1 below) showed significant and systematic differences between the FE and RE estimates, indicating that FE is preferable. The models presented below also correct for heteroskedasticity (a likely problem due to size differences among the countries and wide divergences in imprisonment trends) and first-order autocorrelation. These corrections make very little qualitative difference in the final results.[5]

Indicators of incarceration rates, unemployment rates, male labor-force participation rates, unemployment benefits, union density, and homicide rates are in levels, logged to limit undue influence from outliers. The Gini, left cabinet dominance, and corporatism variables are also measured in levels form (not logged). Left cabinet dominance is smoothed using running averages from t–2 to t–1. This follows common practice in the comparative social welfare literature (Hicks and Swank 1992); substantively, this transformation recognizes that "policy lags" (Dornbusch, Startz, and Fischer 1998) are likely to delay the full impact of shifts in left-party power. The GDP and inflation variables are expressed in proportional change terms as $\ln(X_t/X_{t-1})$. The GDP measure is differenced to provide a measure of growth, a more appropriate indicator of business cycles; inflation is implicitly a measure of change in the value of money.

The full estimation model, with signs on the coefficients that indicate hypothesized effects, is the following:

[5] Models are estimated using Stata's xtgls procedure; data are mean-centered within panels. Tables showing unreported results are available from the author.

Table 1. FE/GLS Estimates of Effects of Selected Variables on Imprisonment Rates

	Heteroskedastic				Heteroskedastic AR(1)
Error Structure	1	2	3	4	5
Unemployment Rates	.0428*	.0640***	.0557**	.0224	.00960
	(.0171)	(.0178)	(.0180)	(.0186)	(.0198)
Male Labor Force Participation	.554**	–.0718	.0937	.114	–.201
	(.195)	(.178)	(.168)	(.162)	(.204)
GDP Growth		–.335	–.383*	–.294	–.150
		(.197)	(.187)	(.178)	(.105)
Inflation		–1.09***	–.548**	–.699***	–.357*
		(.185)	(.167)	(.162)	(.142)
Income Inequality		.595**	.517**	.162	.0726
		(.202)	(.173)	(.181)	(.200)
Unemployment Benefits		–.0604*	.0132	.0240	.00183
		(.0283)	(.0285)	(.0292)	(.0309)
Union Density			–.472***	–.457***	–.504***
			(.0361)	(.0363)	(.0588)
Left Party Cabinet Dominance			–.0347**	–.0274*	–.0246
			(.0130)	(.0133)	(.0153)
Neocorporatism				–.800***	–.710***
				(.144)	(.177)
Neocorporatism^2				.433***	.402**
				(.111)	(.117)
Homicide Rates	.0700	.127**	.214***	.174***	.0975**
	(.0398)	(.0403)	(.0363)	(.0357)	(.0308)
Intercept	1.71	4.38***	5.34***	5.66***	7.29***
	(.900)	(.798)	(.752)	(.731)	(.953)
Wald χ^2	11.83**	187.81***	359.06***	410.02***	137.28***

Note: Standard errors appear in parentheses. AR = autoregressive; FE = fixed effects; GDP = gross domestic product; GLS = generalized least squares.
$*p < .05$; $**p < .01$; $***p < .001$ (two-tailed tests)

$$\ln(IMP) = \beta_0 + \beta_1 \times \ln(UNEMP_{t-1}) - \beta_2 \ln(MLFP_{t-1}) - \beta_3 \times \ln(GDP_t/GDP_{t-1}) - \beta_4 \times \ln(DEFL_t/DEFL_{t-1}) + \beta_5 \times GINI - \beta_6 \times \ln(UNBEN_{t-1}) - \beta_7 \times \ln(DENSITY_{t-1}) - \beta_8 \times (NEOCORP_{t-1}) + \beta_9 \times (NEOCORP_{t-1})^2 - \beta_{10} \times ma(LEFT_{t-2,\,t-1}) + \beta_{11} \times \ln(HOM_{t-1}),$$

where IMP = imprisonment rate, UNEMP = unemployment rate, MLFP = male labor force participation rate, GDP = real gross domestic product per capita, DEFL = country-specific GDP deflator, GINI = Gini inequality scores, UNBEN = unemployment benefits as a percentage of GDP, DENSITY = union density, NEOCORP = the Hicks-Kenworthy neocorporatism measure, LEFT = left-party share of cabinet seats, HOM = homicide rates, and *ma* is the moving average operator.

RESULTS

Table 1 shows results from the regression analysis. My modeling strategy is to begin with simple specifications that emphasize aggregated individual-level factors, then to incorporate structural factors that are expected to have antecedent effects. The first model represents the conventional version of the Rusche-Kirchheimer (RK) argument. It contains only labor supply variables—unemployment and labor-force participation—along with a control for homicide rates. Model 2 offers a more comprehensive version of RK by incorporating GDP growth and inflation as additional measures of business cycles, along with indicators of income inequality and spending on unemployment benefits. Model 3 takes into account the political strength of labor unions and left parties, and model 4 includes the polynomial measure of corporatist labor market structures. Models 1 through 4 are robust GLS estimates from mean-centered data; model 5 adds a correction for autocorrelation.

Model 1 conforms in part to the expectations of the RK hypothesis, and in part not. On the one hand, high unemployment is significantly associated with high rates of imprisonment. The association is rather weak: On average a one percent difference in unemployment rates corresponds to only a .04 percent difference in incarceration rates. On the other hand, male labor-force participation shows an unexpectedly positive and quite strong effect, indicating that imprisonment rates are higher when a greater proportion of men are active in the labor market (or, the equivalent, when fewer have dropped out). These perplexing findings may partly be artifacts of the high inverse correlation between unemployment and male participation rates ($r = -.83$),[6] but also, as subsequent results show, of an underspecified model.

Model 2 paints a more coherent picture. Here the unemployment effect appears a bit stronger and the labor-force participation effect drops away entirely. GDP growth shows no effect, but the coefficients for inflation rates, income inequality, and unemployment benefits are all significant and in the hypothesized directions. The inflation effect appears powerful: When the buying power of local currency drops by one percent (inflation rises), the imprisonment rate is on average about one percent lower. Higher income inequality is associated with higher imprisonment rates, and more generous spending on unemployment insurance appears to push imprisonment rates down (to about the same degree as unemployment *rates* push imprisonment upward). Results so far suggest that, at the very least, the RK hypothesis needs to be elaborated to incorporate not only labor supply, but also aggregate inequality and downward-redistributive social policies.

The third model reveals some powerful influences of political power. The coefficients for union density and left-party dominance are both negative and significant, indicating that strong unions and strong social democratic parties contribute independently to lower rates of incarceration. Just as important, inclusion of union and left party effects suggests that earlier results were partly spurious. The estimated effects of unemployment and income inequality are both cut by about 13 percent, but remain significant. The inflation effect drops by half, and that for

[6] When the participation variable is dropped from model 1, the unemployment effect goes nonsignificant; when unemployment is dropped, the participation effect is cut by half but remains significant. Dropping one or the other makes no difference in more complex models.

unemployment benefits disappears. The reasonable interpretation of these shifts is that unions and left parties affect trends in employment and redistribution as well as trends in imprisonment. For reasons that are not clear, but are probably unimportant, the negative coefficient for GDP growth becomes just significant in model 3. The curvilinear effect of neocorporatism is added to the equation in model 4. As expected, the coefficient for the linear term is negative and that for the squared term is positive; both are significant, suggesting a U-shaped association. This addition significantly improves the overall fit of the model, even though it weakens the estimated effects of most downstream variables. Effects of unemployment rates, GDP growth, and income inequality all shrink below significance. Coefficients for union density and left party strength grow smaller—the former slightly, the latter by almost 25 percent—but remain significant. The inflation coefficient grows rather markedly, but model 5 suggests this might be artifactual. Model 5 includes the same set of variables, but adds a correction for autocorrelation. Here the inflation coefficient is cut by half and the left party effect drops a bit, becoming insignificant; effects of union density and neocorporatism remain strong and significant.

Most of these findings can be summarized briefly. In harmony with prior studies, they show associations between imprisonment rates and labor surplus, as well as with inflation and more general patterns of inequality. But they show also that these associations are mostly byproducts of higher-order effects arising from the distribution of political power and the institutional structure of labor markets. Union density—and, in some models, left party power—show direct negative effects on imprisonment rates and also attenuate the influence of business cycles, inequality, and social benefits. This suggests that strong unions and social democratic parties exert political influence in support of a range of ameliorative social policies, including less punitive responses to crime. Of the two forms of political power studied here, union influence appears to be more consequential and robust; but the left party effect should not be dismissed as an artifact of autocorrelation. In a separate model that truncates the observation period in 1985, the left party effect rebounds strongly while other results are qualitatively unchanged. This supports observations in the qualitative literature that left parties in many countries moved toward a law-and-order stance during the 1980s (Downes and Morgan 1997; Tham 1995; 2001; Träskman 1995; Victor 1995; von Hofer 2003).

Accounting for neocorporatist arrangements further weakens downstream effects, including those of political power. The direct effects of neocorporatism are less readily interpretable. The observed curvilinear association might indicate, as I hypothesized, that imprisonment rates are highest (net of other effects) in countries that are either very low or very high in terms of labor market centralization, but this can only be determined by examining the functional form of the association. Figure 2 uses the coefficients in

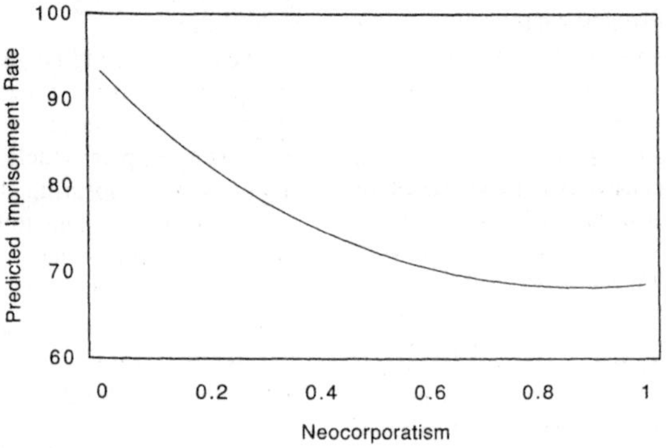

Figure 2. Predicted Imprisonment Rates by Level of Neocorporatism

model 5 to plot predicted rates of imprisonment across different levels of neocorporatism, with all other regressors set at their means.

It is apparent that the association is not U-shaped, but negative with a declining slope. The lowest predicted imprisonment rate—about 68 per 100,000—corresponds to a neocorporatism score of .90, or about the 80th percentile. The strongest association appears in the lower half of the distribution, where neocorporatism scores range from .005 to .61; differences in the upper half of the distribution are negligible. This can be put in more concrete terms by thinking about the range of neocorporatism scores among different countries in the sample. Those consistently scoring below the median range from the United States (mean score = .079) to France (mean score = .425), with other Anglo-American democracies and Italy falling between these extremes. Observations for the Scandinavian social democracies, Austria, and Germany are always in the upper half of the distribution, and those for the Netherlands (mean score = .66) and Belgium (mean score = .73) fall around the median. This pattern of covariation is thus mainly linear, but it also seems to reflect categorical differences that make countries with highly centralized labor markets uniformly resistant to high levels of imprisonment. The choice between linear and categorical interpretations is interesting, but in this case moot. The appropriate conclusion is simply that, net of other measured effects, imprisonment rates are highest in market societies and lowest in societies with strong systems of labor market regulation.[7]

DISCUSSION

This article has challenged the prevailing orthodoxy on the relationship between the prison and the economy in two ways. The first was to respecify and test the RK hypothesis using more nuanced indicators of economic performance and a broader sample of countries than previous studies have employed. The second was to place the business cycle-imprisonment relationship in a larger context by analyzing the impact of political power and labor market institutions. I proposed a model that treated the association between labor surplus and imprisonment not as causal, but as an artifact of wider structural differences in policy regimes among the advanced Western democracies. This model was informed by debates among economists, sociologists, and political scientists about the impact and viability of market liberal and neocorporatist forms of labor market organization. Concatenation of neoclassical economics with the RK model (odd bedfellows, perhaps, but logically consistent) leads to the prediction that powerful unions, strong left parties, and highly regulated labor markets will indirectly drive imprisonment rates up, as a byproduct of weakened economic performance. The alternative model predicted that these same factors will discourage high imprisonment rates directly, as part of a broader orientation to inclusive and equalitarian forms of social policy. This argument differs from those of RK and neoclassical economics by taking both prisons and labor markets seriously as institutions, not just economic instrumentalities. This means that employment, no less than criminality, is a moral status; and that in the rationalized orders of modern societies, the articulation of labor markets and prisons with welfare regimes and macroeconomic policies influences the distribution of both economic opportunity and moral reputability.

The most striking pattern in these results is the apparently strong impact of unemployment, inflation, income inequality, and unemployment benefits in simpler models, followed by declining or even disappearing effects in models that include measures of institutional structure. The effect of unemployment benefits disappears when union and left party strength are controlled, probably because both of these collective actors try to push compensation rates up. The effects of unemployment and inequality are fully accounted for by the combined influence of political power and labor market structure. This pattern provides strong evidence that

[7] The fact that the United States is an outlier in terms of both incarceration rates and labor market regulation raises the question of whether the strong estimated effect at the low end of the neocorporatism scale results from differences between the United States and other countries rather than across the entire distribution. As a test, I estimated model 5 on data that omitted the U.S. observations. Coefficients for the neocorporatism variables declined about 25 percent in absolute value but remained significant, and there were no qualitative differences in the rest of the model. The effect is robust.

previous tests of the RK hypothesis are at best incomplete, and at worst wholly misspecified; in particular, the effect of labor surplus seems wholly spurious. The most persistent business-cycle effect is the decelerative influence of inflation. One could interpret this as an instrumental effect whereby downward redistribution of wealth reduces incentives for crime, hence the need for punishment; but this interpretation is undercut if one accepts homicide rates as an effective control for crime in these models. Given the larger pattern of results, the more likely interpretation is that inflation is to a large degree a political outcome that reflects the preferences of unions and left parties for redistribution over inequality.

All of the hypotheses regarding institutional variables were supported under one or another model specification. The finding that incarceration rates are inversely related to the scope of union organization, and often to the power of left parties, offers strong evidence that criminal justice is responsive to working class influence over social policy. Corporatist labor market arrangements further encourage collaborative, cross-class solutions to a wide range of social policy issues, including, apparently, less punitive responses to crime. Thus, while imprisonment rates are not responsive to fluctuations in labor *supply*, they are very sensitive to variation in labor market *structure*. A labor market in this sense is not just a site for economic transactions, but a set of institutionalized power relationships that establish a framework for negotiations between workers and employers, define the broad outlines of the stratification system, and set normative expectations about government's role in managing the economy. As Western and Beckett have argued (1999), the prison is not a response to the labor market, but one of its constituent elements; my results show that in modern western democracies, imprisonment trends are related both to the distribution of political power and to the kinds of structures that are used to govern the distribution of employment, social protection, and social status.

This analysis is not the last word on the business cycle-imprisonment relationship. As Spitzer (1975) pointed out, the association of labor surplus to incarceration rates is probably stronger, and perhaps directly causal, for certain high-risk subpopulations—especially poorly educated young men who are also ethnic minorities or immigrants. This line of inquiry requires finer-grained data than those used here. Even at lower levels of aggregation, however, the effect of labor surplus is probably not exogenous. Analyses by Sampson and Laub (1993) and Western and Pettit (2000) point to a reciprocal relationship: Among individuals, joblessness increases the risk of crime and incarceration; but involvement with the criminal justice system also increases subsequent joblessness.

These findings suggest the need for a broader theoretical canvas on which to paint the sociology of crime and punishment. For reasons that have been well analyzed by Savelsberg (1994), criminological research has for some time been parochialized and cut off from broader currents in sociological thought, particularly in the United States. As Durkheim recognized (1933), research on punishment taps into fundamental social processes of solidarity and exclusion, stratification, and power. Further and more systematic attention to the ways punishment is embedded in social policy regimes will not only contribute to more sophisticated theories of criminality, but will also enrich analyses of the economy and the state. Crime and punishment are too important to be left to the criminologists.

John R. Sutton *is Professor of Sociology at the University of California-Santa Barbara. His research has focused on organizational responses to changing legal environments, the history of social control institutions in the United States, and most recently on the relationship of imprisonment to life-course institutions and opportunity structures in modern Western societies.*

APPENDIX

Table A. Variable Descriptions and Sources

Variable	Description	Source
Imprisonment rates	Inmates per 100,000 population (natural log, at *t*)	Various (see text)
Unemployment rates	Unemployed persons as percent of total working population (natural log, at *t–1*)	Golden (1997); NZ data from ILO (1955–1990)
Male labor force participation rates	Males in the labor force as percent of males age 15–64 (natural log, at *t–1*)	OECD (1991)
GDP	Real GDP per capita (proportional change from *t–1* to t)	Summers and Heston (1995)
Inflation	Proportional change (from *t–1* to *t*) in GDP deflator	Summers and Heston (1995)
Income inequality	Quintile-based Gini index	Nielsen and Alderson (1995)
Unemployment benefits	Expenditures on unemployment compensation as a percentage of GDP (natural log, at *t–1*)	International Labour Office (1961–92)
Union density	Union members as percent of total labor force (natural log, at *t–1*)	Golden (1997); NZ data from Western (1997)
Left party dominance	Proportion of total cabinet seats held by left parties (average from *t–1* to *t*)	Swank (2002)
Neocorporatism	Hicks-Kenworthy wage coordination measure (at *t–1*)	Hicks and Kenworthy (2002)
Homicide rates	Number of homicides per 100,000 population (natural log, at *t–1*)	World Health Organization (1951–64; 1962–88)

Table B. Correlations and Descriptive Statistics for Variables Used in the Analysis

	1	2	3	4	5	6
1. Incarceration rate	1.000	—	—	—	—	—
2. Unemployment rate	0.105	1.000	—	—	—	—
3. Male labor force participation	–0.039	–0.834	1.000	—	—	—
4. GDP growth	0.007	–0.108	0.247	1.000	—	—
5. Inflation	–0.245	0.112	–0.303	–0.316	1.000	—
6. Quintile-based Gini	0.166	–0.476	0.528	0.187	–0.193	1.000
7. Unemployment benefits	0.037	0.856	–0.756	–0.148	0.083	–0.465
8. Union density	–0.574	0.118	–0.129	–0.125	0.275	–0.227
9. Left cabinet dominance	–0.035	0.086	–0.133	–0.122	0.179	–0.037
10. Neocorporatism	–0.360	–0.662	0.549	0.142	–0.025	0.151
11. Neocorporatism^2	–0.221	–0.554	0.481	0.119	0.048	0.253
12. Homicide rate	0.115	0.508	–0.572	–0.259	0.305	–0.268
Mean	4.308	1.492	4.467	0.026	0.049	.343
SD	0.152	0.507	0.047	0.023	0.027	.0354

	7	8	9	10	11	12
7. Unemployment benefits	1.000	—	—	—	—	—
8. Union density	0.160	1.000	—	—	—	—
9. Left cabinet dominance	0.129	–0.052	1.000	—	—	—
10. Neocorporatism	–0.602	0.180	0.076	1.000	—	—
11. Neocorporatism^2	–0.603	0.127	0.139	0.832	1.000	—
12. Homicide rate	0.514	0.224	0.081	–0.463	–0.362	1.000
Mean	0.433	3.801	0.336	0.559	0.426	0.891
SD	0.279	0.159	0.306	0.061	0.066	0.147

Note: All figures are based on panel-centered data.

REFERENCES

Alvarez, R. Michael, Geoffrey Garrett, and Peter Lange. 1991. "Government Partisanship, Labor Organization and Macroeconomic Performance." *American Political Science Review* 85:539–56.

Andre, Glenn and Ken Pease. 1994. "Using Routine Statistics in Estimating Prison Population for Policy Assessment." *Canadian Journal of Criminology* 36:137–47.

Biles, David. 1982. "Crime and Imprisonment: An Australian Time Series Analysis." *Australian and New Zealand Journal of Criminology* 15:133–53.

Boreham, Paul, Richard Hall, and Martin Leet. 1996. "Labour Movements and Welfare States: A Reconsideration of How Trade Unions Influence Social Change." *Australian and New Zealand Journal of Sociology* 32:1–20.

Box, Steven. 1987. *Recession, Crime and Punishment*. Totowa, NJ: Barnes & Noble.

Calmfors, Lars. 1993. "Centralization of Wage Bargaining and Macroeconomic Performance." *OECD Economic Studies* 21:161–91.

Calmfors, Lars and John Driffill. 1988. "Bargaining Structure, Corporatism, and Macroeconomic Performance." *Economic Policy* 6:13–61.

Cantor, David and Kenneth C. Land. 1985. "Unemployment and Crime-Rates in the Post-World War II United States: A Theoretical and Empirical Analysis." *American Sociological Review* 50:317–32.

Chiricos, Theodore G. 1987. "Rates of Crime and Unemployment: An Analysis of Aggregate Research Evidence." *Social Problems* 34:187–212.

Chiricos, Theodore G. and Miriam A. DeLone. 1992. "Surplus Labor and Punishment: A Review and Assessment of Theory and Evidence." *Social Problems* 39:421–46.

Council of Europe. 1990. *Prison Information Bulletin No. 15*. Strasbourg: Council of Europe.

D'Alessio, Stewart J. and Lisa Stolzenberg. 1995. "Unemployment and the Incarceration of Pretrial Defendants." *American Sociological Review* 60:350–9.

Dimelis, Sophia and Alexandra Livada. 1999. "Inequality and Business Cycles in the U.S. and European Union Countries." *International Advances in Economic Research* 5:321–38.

Dornbusch, Rudiger, Richard Startz, and Stanley Fischer. 1998. *Macroeconomics*. Boston, MA: McGraw-Hill/Irwin.

Downes, David and Rod Morgan. 1997. "Dumping the 'Hostages to Fortune'? The Politics of Law and Order in Post-War Britain." Pp. 87–134 in *The Oxford Handbook of Criminology*, edited by Mike Maguire, Rod Morgan, and Robert Reiner. Oxford: Clarendon Press.

Durkheim, Emile. 1933. *Division of Labor in Society*. New York: Free Press.

Elmeskov, Jorgen and Karl Pichelmann. 1993. "Interpreting Unemployment: The Role of Labour-Force Participation." *OECD Economic Studies* 21:139–60.

Esping-Andersen, Gosta. 1990. *The Three Worlds of Welfare Capitalism*. Princeton, NJ: Princeton University Press

Esping-Andersen, Gøsta. 1999. *Social Foundations of Postindustrial Economies*. Oxford ; New York: Oxford University Press.

———. 2000a. "Regulation and Context: Reconsidering the Correlates of Unemployment." Pp. 99–112 in *Why Deregulate Labour Markets?*, edited by Gosta Esping-Andersen and Marini Regini. Oxford ; New York: Oxford University Press.

———. 2000b. "Who Is Harmed by Labour Market Regulations?: Quantitative Evidence." Pp. 66–98 in *Why Deregulate Labour Markets?*, edited by Gosta Esping-Andersen and Marini Regini. Oxford ; New York: Oxford University Press.

Friedland, Roger and Robert R. Alford. 1991. "Bringing Society Back In: Symbols, Practices, and Institutional Contradictions." Pp. 232–266 in *The New Institutionalism in Organizational Analysis*, edited by Walter W. Powell and Paul J. DiMaggio. Chicago, IL: University of Chicago Press.

Garland, David. 1985. *Punishment and Welfare: A History of Penal Strategies*. Brookfield, VT: Gower.

Garrett, Geoffrey. 1998. *Partisan Politics in the Global Economy*. New York: Cambridge University Press.

Garrett, Geoffrey and Peter Lange. 1986. "Performance in a Hostile World: Economic Growth in Capitalist Democracies, 1974–1982." *World Politics* 38:517–45.

Golden, Miriam, Peter Lange, and Michael Wallerstein. 1997. *Union Centralization among Advanced Industrial Societies: An Empirical Study* [MRDF] (http://www.shelley.polisci.ucla.edu/data).

Greene, William H. 1997. *Econometric Analysis*. Upper Saddle River, NJ: Prentice Hall.

Hanak, Gerhard and Arno Pilgram. 1991. *Der Andere Sicherheitsbericht: Ergänzungen Zum Bericht Der Bundesregierung*. Vienna, Austria: Verlag für Gesellschaftskritik.

Hibbs, Douglas A. 1997. "Political Parties and Macroeconomic Policy." *American Political Science Review* 71:1467–87.

Hicks, Alex. 1988. "Social Democratic Corporatism and Economic Growth." *Journal of Politics* 50:677–704.

Hicks, Alexander and Lane Kenworthy. 1998. "Cooperation and Political Economic Performance in Affluent Democratic Capitalism." *American Journal of Sociology* 103:1631–1672.

———. 2002. *Hicks-Kenworthy Economic*

Cooperation Variables [MRDF] (http://www.emory.edu/SOC/lkenworthy).

Hicks, Alexander M. and Joya Misra. 1993. "Political Resources and the Growth of Welfare in Affluent Capitalist Democracies, 1960–1982." *American Journal of Sociology* 99:668–710.

Hicks, Alexander M. and Duane H. Swank. 1992. "Politics, Institutions, and Welfare Spending in Industrialized Democracies, 1960–82." *American Political Science Review* 86:649–74.

Huber, Evelyne, Charles Ragin, and John D. Stephens. 1993. "Social Democracy, Christian Democracy, and the Welfare State." *American Journal of Sociology* 99:711–49.

International Labour Office. 1955–1990. *Year Book of Labour Statistics*. Geneva: ILO.

———. 1961–92. *The Cost of Social Security*. Geneva: ILO.

Jacobs, David and Ronald E. Helms. 1996. "Toward a Political Model of Incarceration: A Time-Series Examination of Multiple Explanations for Prison Admission Rates." *American Journal of Sociology* 102:323–57.

Johnson, David S. and Stephanie Shipp. 1999. "Inequality and the Business Cycle: A Consumptionist Viewpoint." *Empirical Economics* 24:173–80.

Kenworthy, Lane. 2002. "Corporatism and Unemployment in the 1980s and 1990s." *American Sociological Review* 67:367–88.

Kitschelt, Herbert. 1994. *The Transformation of European Social Democracy*. New York: Cambridge University Press.

Korpi, Walter. 1989. "Power, Politics, and State Autonomy in the Development of Social Citizenship." *American Sociological Review* 54:309–28.

Lange, Peter and Geoffrey Garrett. 1985. "The Politics of Growth." *Journal of Politics* 47:792–827.

———. 1986. "The Politics of Growth Reconsidered." *Journal of Politics* 48:257–74.

Layard, Richard, Stephen Nickell, and Robert Jackman. 1991. *Unemployment: Macroeconomic Performance and the Labour Market*. Oxford: Oxford University Press.

Lessan, Gloria T. 1991. "Macro-Economic Determinants of Penal Policy: Estimating the Unemployment and Inflation Influences on Imprisonment Rate Changes in the United States, 1948–1985." *Crime, Law and Social Change* 16:177–98.

Lindbeck, Assar and Dennis Snower. 1989. *The Insider-Outsider Theory of Employment and Unemployment*. Cambridge, MA: MIT Press.

Lynch, James P. 1987. "Imprisonment in Four Countries." Bureau of Justice Statistics, Washington DC.

Monkkonen, Eric H. 1989. "Diverging Homicide Rates: England and the United States, 1850–1857." Pp. 80–101 in *Violence in America, Vol. I: The History of Crime*, edited by Ted Robert Gurr. Newbury Park, CA: Sage Publications.

Moosa, Imad A. 1997. "A Cross-Country Comparison of Okun's Coefficient." *Journal of Comparative Economics* 24:335–56.

Mukherjee, Satyanshu, Anita Scandia, Dianne Dagger, and Wendy Matthews. 1989. *Source Book of Australian Criminal and Social Statistics, 1804–1988*. Canberra, Australia: Australian Institute of Criminology.

Nickell, Stephen. 1997. "Unemployment and Labor Market Rigidities: Europe Versus North America." *Journal of Economic Perspectives* 11:55–74.

Nielsen, François and Arthur S. Alderson. 1995. "Income Inequality, Development, and Dualism: Results from an Unbalanced Cross-National Panel." *American Sociological Review* 60:674–701.

OECD. 1991. *Historical Statistics 1960–1989*. Paris: OECD.

Okun, Arthur M. 1962. "Potential Gnp: Its Measurement and Significance." *Proceedings, Business and Economic Statistics Section of the American Statistical Association*:89–104.

Parker, Robert Nash and Allan V. Horowitz. 1986. "Unemployment, Crime, and Imprisonment: A Panel Approach." *Criminology* 24:751–73.

Pease, Ken. 1992. "Punitiveness and Prison Populations: An International Comparison." *Justice of the Peace* N.V.:405–8.

———. 1994. "Cross-National Imprisonment Rates: Limitations of Method and Possible Conclusions." *British Journal of Criminology* 34:116–30.

Piven, Frances Fox. 1991. *Labor Parties in Postindustrial Societies*. New York: Oxford University Press.

Rusche, Georg. 1978. "Labor Market and Penal Sanction: Thoughts on the Sociology of Criminal Justice." *Crime and Social Justice* 4:2–8.

Rusche, Georg and Otto Kirchheimer. 1968. *Punishment and Social Structure*. New York: Russell and Russell.

Sampson, Robert J. and John H. Laub. 1993. *Crime in the Making: Pathways and Turning Points through Life*. Cambridge, MA: Harvard University Press.

Savelsberg, Joachim. 1994. "Knowledge, Domination, and Criminal Punishment." *American Journal of Sociology* 99:911–43.

Scarpetta, S. 1996. "Assessing the Role of Labor Market Policies and Institutional Settings on Unemployment." *OECD Economic Studies* 26:43–98.

Snacken, Sonja. 1991. "Belgium." Pp. 29–71 in *Imprisonment Today and Tomorrow: International Perspectives on Prisoners' Rights and Prison Conditions*, edited by Dirk van Zyl Smit and

Frieder Dünkel. Boston, MA: Kluwer Law and Taxation Publishers.

Spitzer, Steven. 1975. "Toward a Marxian Theory of Deviance." *Social Problems* 22:638–51.

Summers, Robert and Alan Heston. 1995. *Penn World Tables 5.6* [MRDF] (http://www.nber.org/pub/pwt56).

Sutton, John R. 1987. "Doing Time: Dynamics of Imprisonment in the Reformist State." *American Sociological Review* 52:612–30.

———. 2000. "Imprisonment and Social Classification in Five Common-Law Democracies, 1955–1985." *American Journal of Sociology* 106:350–86.

Swank, Duane. 2002. *Political Strength of Political Parties by Ideological Group in Capitalist Democracies* [MRDF] (http://www.marquette.edu/polisci/Swank.htm).

Tham, Henrik. 1995. "From Treatment to Just Deserts in a Changing Welfare State." Pp. 89–122 in *Beware of Punishment: On the Utility and Futility of Criminal Law*, edited by Annika Snare. Oslo, Norway: Scandinavian Research Council for Criminology.

———. 2001. "Law and Order as a Leftist Project?: The Case of Sweden." *Punishment & Society* 3:409–26.

Träskman, Per Ole. 1995. "The Dragon's Egg–Drugs-Related Crime Control." Pp. 147–72 in *Beware of Punishment: On the Utility and Futility of Criminal Law*, edited by Annika Snare. Oslo, Norway: Scandinavian Research Council for Criminology.

Victor, Dag. 1995. "Politics and the Penal System: A Drama in Progress." Pp. 68–88 in *Beware of Punishment: On the Utility and Futility of Criminal Law*, edited by Annika Snare. Oslo, Norway: Scandinavian Research Council for Criminology.

von Hofer, Hanns. 1997. *Nordic Criminal Statistics: 1950–1995*. Stockholm, Sweden: Department of Criminology, Stockholm University.

———. 2003. "Prison Populations as Political Constructs: The Case of Finland, Holland and Sweden." *Journal of Scandinavian Studies in Criminology and Crime Prevention* 4:21–38.

Wacquant, Loic. 1999. "'Suitable Enemies': Foreigners and Immigrants in the Prisons of Europe." *Punishment & Society* 1:215–22.

———. 2001. "Deadly Symbiosis: When Ghetto and Prison Meet and Mesh." *Punishment & Society* 3:95–134.

Western, Bruce. 1997. *Between Class and Market: Postwar Unionization in the Capitalist Democracies*. Princeton, NJ: Princeton University Press.

Western, Bruce and Katherine Beckett. 1998. "The Free Market Myth: Penal Justice as an Institution of the US Labour Market." *Berliner Journal Fur Soziologie* 8:159+.

———. 1999. "How Unregulated Is the U.S. Labor Market? The Penal System as a Labor Market Institution." *American Journal of Sociology* 104:1030–60.

Western, Bruce and Josh Guetzkow. 2002. "Punitive Policy and Neoliberalism in the U.S. Labor Market." Presented at the annual meeting of the American Sociological Association, August, Chicago, IL.

Western, Bruce and Becky Pettit. 2000. "Incarceration and Racial Inequality in Men's Employment." *Industrial and Labor Relations Review* 54:3–16.

Wilkins, Leslie T. 1991. *Punishment, Crime and Market Forces*. Aldershot, England: Dartmouth Publishing Company.

Wilkins, Leslie T. and Ken Pease. 1987. "Public Demand for Punishment." *International Journal of Sociology and Social Policy* 7:16–29.

World Health Organization. 1951–64. *Statistiques Epidemiologiques Et Demographiques Annuelles*. Geneva, Switzerland: WHO.

———. 1962–88. *World Health Statistics Annual*. Geneva, Switzerland: WHO.

Young, W. 1986. "Influences Upon the Use of Imprisonment: A Review of the Literature." *The Howard Journal* 25:125–36.

Young, Warren and Mark Brown. 1993. "Cross-National Comparisons of Imprisonment." Pp. 1–50 in *Crime and Justice: A Review of Research*, vol. 17, edited by Michael Tonry. Chicago, IL: University of Chicago Press.

Zimring, Franklin and Gordon Hawkins. 1997. *Crime Is Not the Problem: Lethal Violence in America*. New York: Oxford University Press.

[20]

INCARCERATION, SOCIAL CAPITAL, AND CRIME: IMPLICATIONS FOR SOCIAL DISORGANIZATION THEORY*

DINA R. ROSE
TODD R. CLEAR
Florida State University

This study is a theoretical exploration of the impact of public social control on the functioning of local social controls. Set within the framework of social disorganization and systemic theory, the study argues that an overreliance on incarceration as a formal control may hinder the ability of some communities to foster other forms of control because they weaken family and community structures. At the ecological level, the side effects of policies intended to fight crime by controlling individual behavior may exacerbate the problems they are intended to address. Thus, these communities may experience more, not less, social disorganization.

It is commonly accepted that in the absence of effective controls, crime and disorder flourish. Controls can operate at the individual, family, neighborhood, and state levels; and the safest neighborhoods are thought to be those in which controls work at each of these levels. This study is a theoretical exploration of the impact of state social control on the functioning of family and neighborhood social controls. We argue that state social controls, which typically are directed at individual behavior, have important secondary effects on family and neighborhood structures. These, in turn, impede the neighborhood's capacity for social control. Thus, at the ecological level, the side effects of policies intended to fight crime by controlling individual criminals may exacerbate problems that lead to crime in the first place.

We recognize that to some readers our argument is entirely plausible, perhaps even obvious. "After all," they might say, "everyone knows that current socioeconomic policy produces structural damages to the poor, creating a permanent underclass." Yet other readers will find our argument curious or even counterintuitive. How can it be bad for neighborhood life to remove people who are committing crimes in those very neighborhoods? We discuss a topic on which today's informed observers

* Special thanks to Robert J. Bursik, Jr., Theodore Chiricos, Gary Kleck, and two anonymous reviewers for their comments on earlier drafts of this article. Thanks also to Karen Lepik for editorial and research assistance. An earlier version of this article was presented at the 1996 Annual Meeting of the American Sociological Association.

hold opposing views and on which there is little direct empirical evidence. We argue that a substantial body of indirect evidence exists on the expected social impacts of high incarceration rates, and that this evidence is well established within ecological frameworks of neighborhood life. To develop this theoretical line of reasoning, we move from the individualist paradigm that dominates contemporary thought about crime and crime policy, as exemplified by "criminal careers" and "criminal incapacitation" (see Blumstein et al., 1986; and Zimring and Hawkins, 1995) to a more inclusive ecological model of crime, crime control, and neighborhood life.

Ecological theories of crime seek to explain spatial variations in urban crime rates by exploring differences in the capacity for control across areas. Social disorganization theory, for example, attributes crime and disorder to impaired local controls at the neighborhood level. As a result, some communities are unable to self-regulate. In their study of neighborhood-level control, social disorganization theorists have largely ignored the impact of public, or state control, on processes of neighborhood organization and subsequent opportunities for crime. This is because formal public controls are thought of as responses to crime. Yet, there is clearly a relationship between the use of local and public controls. When local controls are impaired, communities must rely more heavily upon the controls of the state. Partly this is because there is more crime in these areas so the communities need the added strength of formal law enforcement in their response to crime. However, it may be that increased state efforts shift control resources from local to public, thus making state efforts more necessary. For instance, in high-crime neighborhoods, a concentration of police efforts removes large numbers of residents from the neighborhood. It is assumed that measures taken by the state, such as arresting and imprisoning offenders, will make communities safer by removing dangerous residents and by enabling those remaining to shore up their local controls. This may not always be the case. Rather, these practices may undermine the kinds of networks that form the basis of local control. Inherent in our analysis is the view that offenders have complex relationships to the networks in which they are embedded. They may contribute both positively and negatively toward family and neighborhood life. Their removal in large numbers alters those networks both positively and negatively. In highly organized communities, where levels of crime are low, action by the criminal justice system may enhance neighborhood networks overall by fostering ties between residents who now feel safer. In highly disorganized areas, however, action by the criminal justice system may damage neighborhood structure by disrupting network ties of offenders and nonoffenders and fostering alienation among residents and between the neighborhood and the state. In the latter case, the impact on local social control of the removal of residents is similar in nature (though different in kind) to Wilson's (1987) observation that communities experience a loss of control due to the out-migration of middle-class families. In this study we explore the hypothesis that an overreliance on formal controls may hinder the ability of some communities to foster other forms of control. As a result, these communities may experience more, not less, social disorganization.

SOCIAL DISORGANIZATION THEORY, SOCIAL CONTROL AND CRIME

In the search to explain spatial variation in crime rates, social disorganization theorists have explored the structural characteristics associated with crime. Shaw and McKay's (1942) social disorganization theory, and more recently work done by Bursik (1986, 1988), Sampson (1985, 1986a, 1986b, 1986c, 1987), and others, focuses on group adaptations to social processes such as urbanization and shifting patterns of economic growth, rather than concentrating on individual criminality. The essence of this theory is that some communities are unable to effectively self-regulate due to the damaging effects of certain environmental characteristics. This condition leads to a disrupted neighborhood organizational structure, which subsequently attenuates residents' ties to each other and to the community. As a result, some residents no longer submit to normative social controls.

Disorganized communities are unable to realize the common values of their residents and are unable to solve commonly experienced problems (Kornhauser, 1978) because they cannot establish or maintain consensus concerning values, norms, roles, or hierarchical arrangements among their members (Kornhauser, 1978; Shaw and McKay, 1942). As a control theory, social disorganization theory assumes that one common goal residents in all neighborhoods share is the desire to live in an area that is safe to inhabit (Bursik and Grasmick, 1993:15). We assume all residents desire this since even offenders do not wish to be victimized.

Researchers working within this theoretical domain have focused their efforts on identifying which ecological conditions are most associated with crime. Attention has commonly been centered on such variables as poverty, residential mobility, ethnic heterogeneity, population, and structural density. The state of disorganization remains latent, only to be inferred by the existence of these destabilizing factors.

Recently, attempts have been made to explore the "black box" of disorganization. Sampson (1987) and Sampson and Groves (1989) have investigated the mediating effects of guardianship, community attachment, and informal social control. They have shown that integration and social ties are important mediators between social conditions and crime. For instance, Sampson (1988) finds that integration is indicated by individuals' local friendships, their attachment to the community and their participation in local activities. Integration fosters participation, which fosters deeper integration. Whereas these scholars focus their efforts on identifying *dimensions* of control, Bursik and Grasmick (1993) have identified different *levels* of control. They merge systemic and social disorganization theories to examine the mediating role of private, parochial, and public controls. Bursik and Grasmick's extension of disorganization theory shows how ecological factors influence different levels of control. Social control, they argue, represents an effort by neighborhood residents to regulate the behavior of both locals and outsiders to achieve the goal of a safe living environment. Figure 1 shows their "Basic Systemic Model of Crime." This is a model of the structure of social resources that produce crime. It is composed of three panels of theoretical effects. The first panel is derived from the work of Shaw and McKay (1942) and contains the traditional social disorganization constructs: socioeconomic composition, residential stability, and racial/ethnic heterogeneity. The second panel comprises external resources and primary and secondary relational networks. It is an amalgam of the human/social capital construct derived from Wilson's work (1987, 1996). This panel represents the interplay between local familial and voluntary groups and forces external to the neighborhood that may affect neighborhood life. The final panel, drawn

Figure 1. Bursik and Grasmick's Basic Systemic Model of Crime

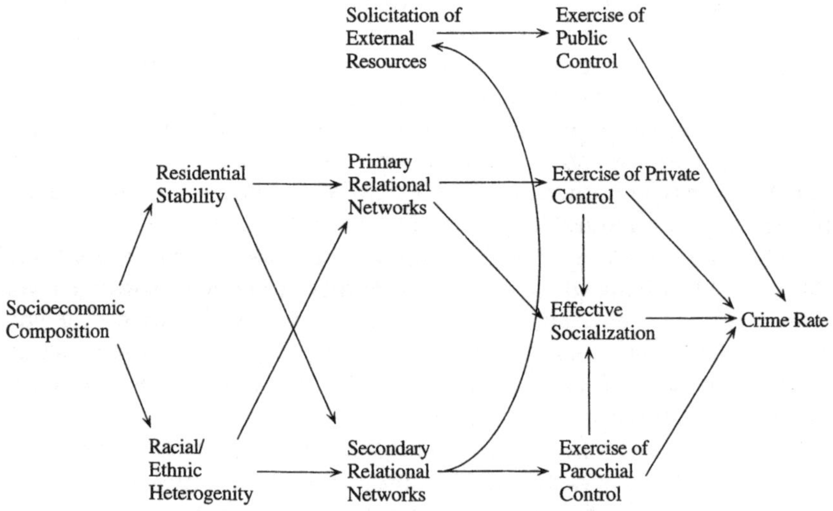

From Bursik and Grasmick (1993).

from Hunter's work (1985), is a classification of the levels of social control by which communities carry out self-regulation.

Private control occurs among intimates and primary groups, such as family members or very close friends. Control stems from the allocation or threatened withdrawal of sentiment, social support, and mutual esteem. Parochial controls are the kinds of supervision and surveillance of places that occur naturally within communities, as people interact in normal day-to-day routines (see Felson, 1996). They encompass the broader, local, interpersonal networks, including the relationship among local institutions, such as stores, schools, and churches. For instance, Sampson et al. (1997) identified several examples of informal community control tactics, such as willingness to intervene to prevent truancy or street-corner loitering by teenagers or confrontation of individuals who are damaging public property or disturbing the neighborhood. Control is located in the effectiveness of these groups and in the capacity of neighbors to supervise each other. Public controls involve the networks developed between the neighborhood and outside agencies, including those operated by the criminal justice and other governmental systems. Control is a function of the ability of the neighborhood to secure public goods and services from sources outside the neighborhood (Bursik and Grasmick, 1993:16–17).

These efforts by Sampson (1987), Sampson and Groves (1989), and Bursik and Grasmick (1993) highlight the significance of networks in neighborhood control. Sampson and Sampson and Groves primarily focus their efforts on components of the primary and parochial levels. They recognize that the extent to which individual residents are integrated and tied to the neighborhood influences its capacity to self-regulate. Conversely, when residents' ties are attenuated, when they feel anonymous and isolated, local control is difficult to achieve. Social control becomes compromised because there is a lack of community interaction and shared obligation. As a result, the community is weakened and can no longer intervene on behalf of the neighborhood (Sampson, 1987). Bursik and Grasmick add to this the idea that public control plays a role in neighborhood regulation to the extent that relations between the community and the state determine the type and quality of services and resources provided. We would add that networks between these actors influence the community's receptivity to coercive controls and determine whether the two engage in a largely cooperative or adversarial relationship.

While it is tempting to think about these as three distinct levels of control, they are implicitly linked because they are interdependent. For instance, parochial controls are far more effective when they exist within environments with strong private controls. As a form of control, the Parent-Teachers' Association's (PTA) functioning in the neighborhood will have more impact on a child's behavior when parents of various children know and interact with each other, because information shared at the parochial level reinforces interactions at the private level. However, when parents do not attend PTA meetings, this organization ceases to serve as a mechanism for parochial control.

By contrast, public controls can operate in the neighborhood without regard for private and parochial controls, although often not as well. For instance, the police can do their jobs regardless of the state of the local PTA. Further, police can make the streets safe so residents can attend the local PTA meeting. They cannot, however, make residents want to attend that meeting. Only well-functioning private controls can manage that.

Black (1976) was one of the first to suggest a relationship between formal and informal controls as part of his larger theory about the quantity and style of law. His work recognizes the distinction between governmental and nongovernmental control and proposes the importance of both for effective regulation. He argued, as we do, that as informal social controls deteriorate, formal controls increase. We note that empirical results have provided only mixed support for Black's hypothesis. Leesan and Sheley (1992) recently attributed this to the fact that most studies (Braithwaite and Biles, 1980; Gottfredson and Hindelang, 1979; Kruttschnitt, 1980–81; Massey and Myers, 1989; Myers, 1980; Smith, 1987) have been conducted at the microsociological level. Their macrosociological level study, however, fared little better.

The lack of support found for the link between informal and formal controls might be attributed to the way in which control is conceptualized. Black considered informal control to be primarily familial and intimate. Lessan and Sheley (1992) use homicide and suicide rates as an indicator of the loss of community nongovernmental control over its members because they assumed these acts occur in the context of familial and intimate violence. This operationalization only vaguely connects to the broader ideas of informal social control, and it omits the role of parochial controls, which we view as essential. The interplay among all three types of control is important for effective community self-regulation, and a simple, recursively linear model is insufficient to test these relationships.

An overreliance on public controls may diminish the capacity of private and parochial controls as communities learn to rely on outsiders. While it is assumed that neighbors who call the police to control excessive noise have summoned public controls to shore up private and parochial controls, they actually may have replaced parochial with public control. Perhaps more significantly, policies and practices of public control agencies can directly attack the functioning of lower levels of control by disrupting the networks of association and the resources on which private and parochial controls rely. For instance, in 1996, President Clinton announced that the federal government would be funding community-based policing, through neighborhood crime watches and foot patrols, as part of community revitalization efforts. Although these programs are community based, they are often thinly veiled, "top-down" policy models in which the formal social control agencies assign duties and sanctions for the neighborhood group to impose on its members. When the focus of community policing derives from the biases of the formal control agency, tensions among residents of the neighborhood escalate, as does the hostility between the community and the police (Goetz, 1996). This is particularly true in disorganized communities, where the relationships among the levels of control are fragile.

THE NONRECURSIVE MODEL

In its current form, the Bursik and Grasmick model is recursive, suggesting the traditional form of the crime control relationship: Communities that experience less social disorganization experience less crime. Our argument is that the public controls (the third panel) feed back upon most of the elements of the Basic Systemic Model. Thus, we argue for a reciprocal model in which public control influences the exogenous variables in the model. Figure 2 is a revision of Bursik and Grasmick's Basic Systemic Model illustrating our idea. It incorporates a feedback loop into a theory of the impact of crime control on neighborhood structures and its subsequent impact on self-regulation. It also subsumes primary and secondary relational networks and the solicitation of external resources under the heading "human and social capital." We return to this point below.

Our model specifies a reciprocal relationship between public social control and human and social capital and between public social control and the endogenous variables socioeconomic status, residential stability, and racial/ethnic heterogeneity through levels of incarceration. Bursik and Grasmick make the argument that residential mobility and racial/ethnic heterogeneity affect the relational networks that are the basis of control because both conditions make it difficult for residents to establish and maintain ties within the neighborhood. Further, both decrease the ability and willingness of individuals to intervene in criminal events on behalf of their neighbors due to individual anonymity and alienation and, possibly, due to hostility or mistrust between different groups. In addition, mobility and heterogeneity potentially impair the socialization of youths, who are presumably exposed to multiple standards and forms of behavior rather than to one, unified code (Bursik and Grasmick, 1993:35–36).

Traditionally, Shaw and McKay (1942) believed that the key factor influencing residential mobility and ethnic heterogeneity was the socioeconomic composition of the neighborhood. Shaw and McKay believed poor neighborhoods were multiethnic and transient because they were the first stopping ground of new immigrants, who tended to move on when they

Figure 2. A Nonrecursive Model of Crime Control, Social Disorder, and Crime

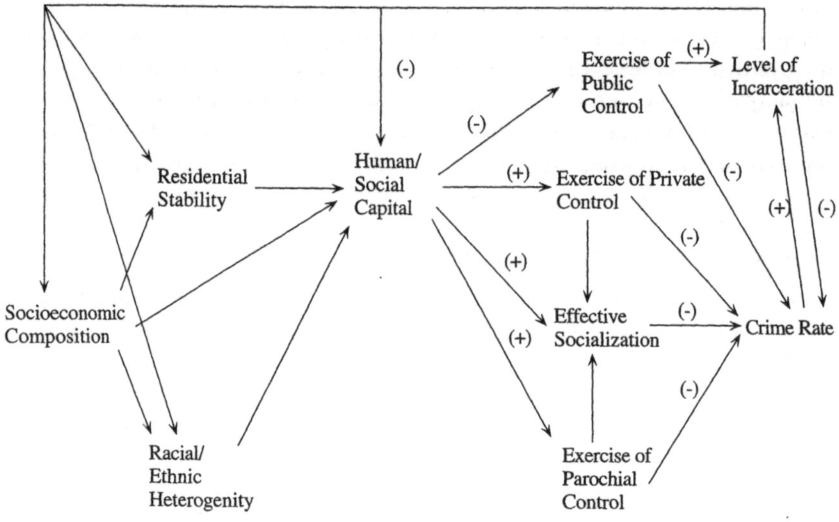

Adapted from Bursik and Grasmick (1993).

were financially able. Today, although contemporary researchers tend to model all three variables as equally exogenous, they continue to subscribe to the idea that disorganized communities are ethnically heterogeneous and residentially mobile because they are poor. Current work on the urban underclass, poverty, and residential segregation questions the chances of upward mobility for certain segments of the population (Anderson, 1990; Massey, 1990; Wilson, 1987). Thus, economic opportunities may not be driving residential mobility trends in some of today's poorer neighborhoods. Rather, other forces may be at work, forces producing entrenched deficits in social capital.

Our modification of Bursik and Grasmick's Basic Systemic Model is aligned with recent attempts by researchers to move beyond simple recursive models of crime to incorporate the nonrecursive or systemic features of the phenomenon. For the most part, work on nonrecursive models has dealt with the causes and effects of crime. For instance, Cook (1986:6–19) describes a "feedback loop" in which individuals limit their exposure to potential victimization as a result of their assessment of the likelihood of their being victimized, and in so doing, reduce the number of criminal opportunities. This takes the form of a market in which the volume of crime is partly determined by an interaction between potential victims who adapt their self-protection efforts based upon the probability of victimization and potential criminals who adapt their rate of offending based upon the overall quality of criminal opportunities. Skogan (1986, 1990) argues that levels of crime increase fear, which results in psychological and physical withdrawal from the neighborhood. This in turn weakens informal control, damages the organizational life and mobilization capacity of the neighborhood, and deteriorates business conditions. Wilson (1996) has argued that these forces also lead to the economic abandonment of inner cities, which produces further deterioration. These changes result in more crime and lead to a change in the composition of the population.

Within the social disorganization tradition, researchers have begun to examine the reciprocal relationship between community structure and crime rates with the understanding that social disorganization produces crime, which then produces more disorganization. Sampson et al. (1997) found that in very disadvantaged neighborhoods, decreases in collective efficacy (informal social controls and social cohesion within a neighborhood) result in a significant decrease in residential stability, which in turn increases the poverty of those neighborhoods. The so-called "broken windows" thesis (Wilson and Kelling, 1982), for example, is that the visible existence of minor criminal events conditions beliefs about more basic public safety and softens potential offenders' self-controls against criminal conduct. Likewise, Rose's (1995) analysis of crime and neighborhood organization in Chicago identified a reciprocal model in which neighborhood organizations affect opportunities for crime, the existence of which influences the need for renewed organizational efforts, which in turn alters subsequent opportunities for crime. Gottfredson and Taylor (1988) have shown that neighborhood characteristics affect individual arrest probabilities of prison releasees, even after their personal characteristics are controlled. The import of this line of inquiry is that crime trends are not independently linear, but must be understood contextually within local communities, especially with regard to other forms of self-regulation (see Bursik and Grasmick, 1993). In this vein, a recent paper by Taylor (1997) shows how the parochial controls described by Bursik and Grasmick are mediated by street-block characteristics.

Bursik and Grasmick (1993:57–59) note that their systemic model may be incomplete because of a failure to incorporate the degree to which crime and delinquency affect a neighborhood's capacity for social control. We add that it may be incomplete because of its failure to incorporate the feedback effect of the key systemic feature of public social controls.

The nonrecursive nature of the relationship between crime and community suggests that a simple recursive model of removing offenders to improve neighborhood life fails to consider the feedback effect of public social control on the system of communities and crime. To the degree the feedback effects weaken community structure, there would then be unintended consequences of crime control strategies that damage neighborhood self-regulation.

We argue that one of those forces is incarceration, for it affects the three disorganizing factors originally identified by Shaw and McKay (1942). First, incarceration alters the socioeconomic composition of the neighborhood by influencing vital local resources, such as labor and marriage markets. (We consider these and other impacts of incarceration in more detail below.) Second, in many areas penal practices are a key factor influencing mobility in and out of the neighborhood. Every entrant into prison is someone exiting a neighborhood; every release from prison returns someone to a neighborhood. Finally, incarceration influences heterogeneity. Shaw and McKay, and others since them, have examined the impact of racial and ethnic heterogeneity on social organization because of the assumption that different ethnic groups represent different norms and values. Today, in many poor communities, there is racial homogeneity (these areas often are primarily black) but a heterogeneity of norms and values still exists (see Anderson, 1990, for a review of this argument). Not only do incarceration trends open opportunities for entrance of newcomers (with potentially different norms and values) into the neighborhood, but they increase opportunities for individuals to be socialized into prison subcultures. One might think that the removal of offenders would increase the cultural homogeneity of the neighborhoods they leave behind. However, well over 90% of prison admissions are eventually released after an average prison stay of about two years (Clear and Cole, 1997). Upon their return to the community, the stronger deviant orientation of prison releasees increases local cultural heterogeneity, thereby increasing disorganization.

THE RECIPROCAL EFFECTS OF INCARCERATION

Since 1973, the incarceration rate has grown from about 90 per 100,000 to over 400 per 100,000; prisoners have increased from 350,000 to more than 1.5 million. Though the accumulation of additional prisoners has been gradual, the net impact of this profound shift in the collective experience of incarceration is important to understand. Growth in imprisonment has disproportionately affected the poor and people of color. When controlling for age and social class, it has been estimated that a minimum of 10% of *underclass* African-American males aged 26 to 30 were incarcerated in 1986 (Lynch and Sabol, 1992)—a number that has certainly grown with the prison population's growth (about double) since that time. In 1992 alone, 1 in 27 African-American males aged 16 to 34, living in metropolitan areas and contiguous counties, was admitted to prison

(Lynch and Sabol, 1997). In 1994, approximately 9% of *all* African-Americans were under some form of correctional supervision (incarcerated or on probation or parole) (Bureau of Justice Statistics, 1996). Approximately 7% of all African-American males aged 20 to 50 are currently in prison (Bureau of Justice Statistics, 1995). Overall, the lifetime probability of an African-American male going to state or federal prison is 29% (Bonczar and Beck, 1997). The residential segregation of African-Americans in urban communities means that some of their neighborhoods have suffered war-level casualties in parenting-age males during the increase in imprisonment since 1973, when far fewer African-American males were incarcerated.

Our view builds on Wilson (1987), who argues that the out-migration of the middle class has resulted in neighborhoods without sufficient economic and social foundations for effective social control. These communities, he argues, are characterized by "joblessness, lawlessness, low-achieving schools" and increasing social isolation from mainstream society (Wilson 1987:58). Further, it is the impact of joblessness on social isolation that is crucial to understanding the underclass. Without a financially stable middle class (and no way to create a new one), these communities have neither the residents who socialize their youngsters to conventional norms and values, nor the ability to sustain local institutions.

The goal of Wilson's analysis was to account for the growth of severe poverty, and he begins by examining the events that disrupt a fully functioning community. Our analysis begins where he left off; it examines events that disrupt low-functioning neighborhoods. Communities hardest hit by incarceration are already depleted and each resource is vital. Compared to healthy neighborhoods, ones with sufficient supplies of human and social capital, disorganized areas most likely suffer exponentially with each additional network disruption. We expect, then, the same type of effect on communities from the out-migration of residents (even those who offend) as did Wilson, but with greater magnitude because of the fragile nature of the neighborhood.

A great deal depends, of course, on whether the active offender is viewed as a neighborhood asset or a liability. It is logical to assume that the loss of criminal males benefits communities simply because they are residents who are committing crimes. Their removal, then, could be seen as a positive act by the state: Criminals are gone, communities are safer and informal controls are now free to blossom. But if offenders are not *solely* a drain—if they are resources to some members of the community and if they occupy roles within networks that form the basis for informal social control—their removal is not solely a positive act, but also imposes losses on those networks and their capacity for strengthened community life.

Research shows offenders represent both assets and liabilities to their communities. A good example is provided by the conflicting perspectives that emerge from street ethnographies of criminal behavior. Some studies paint a dim picture, such as Fleisher's (1995) description of the lives of a sample of serious offenders who passed through Lompoc Prison, California, while he was an administrator there. He describes men who are disconnected from legitimate society and whose personal relationships are characterized by cycles of violence, complete amorality of conduct, and irremedial bouts of alcoholism and drug addiction. His conclusion is that only a policy of lengthy imprisonment makes sense for these men. Yet, this pessimistic view must be contrasted to studies of inner-city youth gangs that document the violent criminal lifestyle of gang members even while they show the connections of these young men to children, families, and others in their neighborhoods. In one study, a majority of active gang members were fathers, and a minority were employed in legitimate jobs though most worked sporadically (Decker and Van Winkle, 1996). Though the gang isolates the young man from pro-social elements of community life, those connections are still seen as valuable by gang members and their families alike, partly due to the mutually supportive relations gang members have with others in their community (e.g., see Venkatesh, 1997).

Portraits drawn by the ethnographers cannot be simply summarized. Clearly, some offenders offer little or nothing of value to their neighborhoods and much that is damaging to them. However, there are just as clearly offenders who occupy positions in socialization and social control networks of their own, and whose removal to prison disrupts those networks. In addition, as the growth in imprisonment in recent years is increasingly a result of the incarceration of drug offenders rather than violent offenders (Irwin and Austin, 1996), the removal of potential assets may be increasing. That is, these men may be offenders who leave their communities for prison and take with them the support they have been providing to networks that sustain private and parochial controls in those neighborhoods.

Fishman's (1990) study of the partners of incarcerated men is a portrait of the complexities of offenders' contributions to their families and associates. Many of the women in her study exhibit a strong commitment to their male partners and put enormous effort into maintaining intimate ties across prison walls. Some women's lives seem to improve with the man's removal, others clearly deteriorate. While the women display admirable fortitude when confronted with the loss of their partners, for almost all of them this represents a challenge to their resources and a profound interruption in their lives. Nor is the removal of criminal parents uniformly positive for their children. Lowenstein's (1986) research on the children of incarcerated men finds evidence of significant psychological stress and acting out among some children following their fathers' incarceration, while others exhibited fewer symptoms of stress. MaCoun and Reuter's (1991) study of street-level drug dealers finds that these offenders had both legitimate and illegitimate sources of income in order to meet daily living expenses. Sullivan's (1989) ethnography of young offenders finds the same complex pattern of economic involvement in crime and legitimate enterprise, and it shows that these young men contribute to the financial welfare of families and others in their neighborhoods. Maher's (1991) ethnography of crack-using mothers shows that even within this group of impaired crack addicts there are many who make a great effort to provide parenting to their children.

These studies confirm that some active offenders whose crimes make them eligible for incarceration are financial assets to their families and their communities. They contribute directly to the welfare of their families and other intimates in the same way noncriminal males do, although perhaps they provide fewer total dollars. This contribution helps explain why a study conducted a generation ago (Clear et al., 1971) found that over half of a sample comprised of one month's admissions to the Indiana Department of Corrections reported that their families went onto public assistance immediately following their imprisonment. Other street ethnographies show how young male offenders often live within tight associational networks of families and children, and they act as resources to those networks (e.g., McCall, 1994; Shakur, 1993). Recent research on gangs (Jankowski, 1991; Venkatesh, 1997) shows gang members in multidimension roles—some detrimental and some beneficial to the neighborhood.

Our point is not that offenders be romanticized as "good citizens," but rather that they not be demonized. A view of them as "merely bad" is a one-sided stereotype that not only ignores the assets they represent to the networks within which they live, but also fails to account for the benefits they contribute to their environments. It also fails to recognize the damage done to other relational networks when they are incarcerated, networks often consisting of nonoffending family members, relatives, and friends. One reason disorganized communities are disorganized is because they do not have the strong bonds and dense social relationships that are important to social control (Kornhauser, 1978:45). This makes the fragile linkages in those areas even more important. To say that offenders contribute to their communities is not to say they are ideal relatives and neighbors. It does recognize, however, their contribution exists, and in disorganized areas with low levels of control partly due to weak ties, the contribution of offenders may not be that much less than their nonoffending neighbors.

Socially organized areas have sufficient assets and resources to overcome the loss of an offender's asset in order to remove the offender's liability from the neighborhood. In socially disorganized areas, however, assets are already sufficiently depleted that the neighborhood feels the loss of the asset just as it rejoices in the loss of the liability. Further, bouts of incarceration tend to produce individuals more hostile to legal legitimacy, less willing to work, and less able to get a job—conditions that increase that individual's role as a liability and diminish him as an asset. Add to this mix potentially hostile and antagonistic relations with the police and the state and incarceration trends may serve to exacerbate a neighborhood's social isolation. The question is, To what degree is this true? To respond to this question, we first consider the role of social and human capital in building informal social control.

SOCIAL AND HUMAN CAPITAL: THE IMPORTANCE OF PLACE

Social disorganization theory is implicitly based upon the notions of social and human capital, even if the terms have not been explicitly adopted. *Social capital* refers to the social skills and resources needed to effect positive change in neighborhood life. It is the aspect of structured groups that increases the capacity for action oriented toward the achievement of group goals (Hagan, 1994). Goals are accomplished by transforming resources gathered in one forum, for one purpose, into resources for another forum and for another purpose (Coleman, 1988). The essence of social disorganization theory is that disruptions of both formal and informal processes of social control impede a neighborhood's ability to self-regulate (Bursik, 1988). Social capital is the essence of social control for it is the very force collectives draw upon to enforce order. It is what enables groups to enforce norms and, as a result, to increase their level of informal control. Disorganized communities, then, suffer from crime and other negative conditions partly because they have insufficient supplies of social capital.

In Bursik and Grasmick's Basic Systemic Model, the solicitation of external resources and both primary and secondary relational networks (the three factors directly influencing the three levels of control) are elements of social capital. We discuss them in terms of this broader category in order to emphasize the idea that socially organized communities need integrated networks at many different levels for effective self-regulation. In socially organized areas resources accumulated at one level can become resources for control at another level. This does not occur so readily in socially disorganized areas.

Social capital works by facilitating certain actions and constraining others. It stems from a sense of trust and obligation created through interaction among community members and serves to reinforce a set of prescriptive norms. Thus, social capital effectively unites individuals within a neighborhood, thereby initiating and enhancing a sense of collectivity (Coleman, 1988). High levels of social capital augment the ability and efficacy of the community to sanction transgressors. In communities with large supplies of social capital, for example, adolescents are encouraged to complete their education, discouraged from stealing cars, and sanctioned appropriately in informal and intimate relationships. Sampson and Laub (1993) recently concluded that social investment (or social capital) in institutional relationships dictates the salience of informal social control at the individual level. More important, they found that trajectories of crime and deviance can be modified by these bonds. It follows that communities rich in social capital also will experience relatively low levels of disorganization and low levels of crime. It has been shown, for instance, that immigrant groups rich in human and social capital are more able to promote self-employment than their more capital-poor counterparts (Sanders and Nee, 1996). This, then, insulates the neighborhood from the link between unemployment and crime.

Social capital relies upon (and in turn promotes) human capital. *Human capital* refers to the human skill and resources individuals need to function effectively, such as reading, writing, and reasoning ability. It is the capital individuals acquire through education and training for productive purposes (Hagan, 1994). In a sense, social capital contextualizes human capital (and vice versa) because neighborhoods rich in social capital exert more control over individual residents, thus helping to produce more highly educated, employable, and productive members of the community. Neighborhoods deficient in social capital are areas conducive to crime because they are characterized by many individuals who are undereducated, unemployed, and more likely to be criminal. Thus, communities rich in social capital also are communities rich in human capital. Conversely, those without one, tend also to be without the other. Recent research provides evidence to support these relationships. For instance, disrupted network ties (the basis for social capital), which limit access to noncash resources, have been shown to be a primary determinant of whether women are working or are on welfare (Edin and Lein, 1997). Farkas et al. (1997) recently found that differences in cognitive skills (human capital) explain a large part of the pay differences between ethnic groups. They conclude that these differences arise largely from social sources such as school, family, and neighborhood experiences, all of which are key components of social capital.

What this amounts to is that where people live greatly affects their lives. By providing an environment either rich or deficient in resources, place of residence affects tangibly the quality of day-to-day life (Sullivan, 1989). Place of residence also influences the range of opportunities people find available because area affects the quality and extent of their personal networks. Environments rich in human capital promote the development of social capital (and vice versa), and these are the areas in which residents, both individually and collectively, are able to solve problems.

Neighborhoods are the focal point for satisfying daily needs through informal support networks. For instance, place of residence is an important source of informal networks of people who provide important products and services (such as child care) and alter life chances with job referrals and political connections (or, of course, criminal contacts). While this informal marketplace sometimes operates through monetary exchange, more often it operates through barter, where reciprocity is the currency of exchange (Logan and Molotch, 1987). This system is especially important for the poor, who rely more upon each other for these types of resources because they tend to be less spatially liberated than the well-to-do (Wellman, 1979). As a result, poor people draw upon this network more frequently than people in affluent areas, and poor people are particularly damaged when their interpersonal networks are disrupted. This type of endogeneous exchange further becomes irrelevant if it does not carry with it the external connection to economic and political structures that foster community (Logan and Molotch, 1987). In the aggregate, the impact of social disruptions on the neighborhood can be devastating.

Not much is known about the networks so fundamental to social capital and social control. On the individual level, research has explored the impact of network disruption on the quality of life. For instance, Kessler and McLeod (1984) and Conger et al. (1993) show that women suffer psychological distress from "network" events, life events that do not occur to them but to members of their networks, and that men are more distressed by work and financial events. Within criminology, not much work has focused on the nature of networks and their impact on residents and communities, other than to assume enhanced networks lead to increases in social control. Variables measuring integration and social ties have been included in social disorganization analyses (Sampson and Groves, 1989) with an eye to determining their importance in preventing crime. In this study, we ask the opposite question: How much disruption can networks sustain before they fail to function?

Events that disrupt the relational networks and systems so fundamental to the development and maintenance of social capital reduce the neighborhood's ability to self-regulate. Within social disorganization, studies including integration and network ties have used continuous variables because social disorganization is thought to be linear. Most research on networks also assumes that networks affect individuals in a linear fashion.

This work analyzes changes resulting from incremental additions to the network. With one exception, the question of thresholds has not been addressed. Berkman and Syme (1979) show that an individual with only one person in the network has roughly the same mortality rate as someone with 20. Thus, there is a threshold effect between zero and one. We extrapolate from this that other networks probably operate similarly and that at the community level a minimum number of healthy networks is needed for the neighborhood to function effectively. When a sufficient number of individual networks is disrupted, the community is disrupted too. We do not speculate on what that number is, though it can be answered empirically. There may even be a tipping point; that is, a small number of offenders may be removed with little ill effect because remaining networks are minimally affected. But after some point of removing males, the remaining networks have taken sufficient hits that their capacity to function in ordinary social controls is severely dampened. Indeed, this threshold may be lower in the most disorganized communities, where networks may be thin to begin with and thus more vulnerable to disruption. In other words, social capital contextualizes the impact of network disruption through incarceration. Not only do disorganized communities have more networks disrupted through incarceration, the impact may be stronger in these neighborhoods because they have a lower threshold due to depleted supplies of social capital.

LEGITIMATE SYSTEMS OF NEIGHBORHOOD ORDER

The potential for unintended consequences of imprisonment is made plain by a "systems" model in which criminals are seen as embedded in various interpersonal, family, economic, and political systems. While there are many networks and systems at work in the community, our point is best illustrated by exploring three important legitimate systems of neighborhood order: family, economic, and political. Familial systems are the most important source of private social controls. Economic and political systems set the context within which parochial social controls flourish or wane. We investigate these systems as direct ways in which incarceration affects a neighborhood's capacity for informal social control. In addition, we also propose ways in which incarceration influences illegitimate systems within the community.

We have listed ways in which the unintended consequences of incarceration might be expected to affect these systems within the neighborhood infrastructure. While one or another of these factors by itself may seem trivial in its relationship to crime, their combined effects may potentially be devastating. The purpose of this review is not to build a fully developed theory of such relationships. Rather, it is to begin building this theory by showing how disrupting a large number of networked systems through incarcerating consequential portions of a neighborhood's population can promote, rather than reduce, crime.

Familial Systems

Communities that contribute higher rates of members to incarceration experience higher rates of family disruption, single-parent families, and births to young, single adults (Lynch and Sabol, 1992). The close association between these factors and the removal of high rates of young males from these underclass, racial-minority communities suggests a plausible hypothesis that one is, in part, a product of another (or at least that they are mutually reinforcing phenomena). What are the implications of this pattern?

It is well established that children suffer when parents are removed from the home. What is less clear is the nature and extent of disruption that follows an incarceration. Studies of this problem have tended to focus on mothers (Gabel, 1992), but there have also been a few attempts to document the impacts of imprisonment of fathers (Brodsky, 1975; Carlson and Cervera, 1992; Fishman, 1990; King, 1993; Lowenstein, 1986). The studies show that the negative psychological and circumstantial impact on children from the removal of a parent for incarceration is similar in form though not in degree to that produced by removal due to divorce or death. Further, Hagan (1996) shows that theories of strain, socialization, and stigmatization each confirm the potential for negative developmental outcomes when a father is imprisoned.

It might be argued that removal of a criminally active father improves the environment of the remaining sons. This is not clear from the data. One study (Smith and Clear, 1997) of a male, jail intake sample finds preliminary evidence for the existence of substantial positive parenting prior to incarceration. After the male's imprisonment, the responses of the jailed inmate's family to his incarceration include address changes because the remaining family moved into more cramped quarters and new school districts; family disruption, including the arrival of new male roles into the family replacing the inmate; reduced time for maternal parenting due to taking secondary employment; and so on. Thus, we need not demonstrate the positive parenting skills of active offenders. Rather, all of these factors are potentially disruptive forces for the family, and each tends to disturb family cohesiveness, which studies show would predict serious delinquency (Sampson, 1987).

Children's internalization of social norms may also be disrupted by high levels of incarceration. Changes in parental working conditions and family circumstances are known to affect children's social adjustment and norm transmission across generations (Parcel and Menaghan, 1993). Adult crime is also connected both to childhood experience and to changes in adult social bonds (Laub and Sampson, 1993). School success is linked to family structure, which has an effect independent of social class and parenting style in impoverished families (Vacha and McLaughlin, 1992). Teachman et al.'s (1997) longitudinal survey found an interaction between social capital, as measured by family structures and parental interaction with their children and their children's schools, and the drop-out rate of high school students. From this, we can deduce that if a parent is incarcerated, and the stability of the family is thus jeopardized, the remaining parent has less time for interaction with the children or the school, increasing the chances of dropout.

At a most basic level, the absence of males restricts the number of adults available to supervise young people in the neighborhood. While it is commonly assumed that criminally active adults are less capable or willing guardians, there is no evidence to support this. In fact, Venkatesh (1997) reports that although many problems within the housing project he studied were gang related, gang members involved in criminal activity tended to be accepted because they contributed to the well-being of the community in a variety of ways. For instance, they acted as escorts or protectors, renovated basketball courts, and discouraged truancy. These factors eroded perceptions of them as social deviants partly because their roles as sons and brothers helped residents to view them as "only temporarily" bad and partly because the gang helped the community in tangible ways.

The presence of large numbers of unsupervised youth is predictive of serious crime at the neighborhood level (Sampson and Groves, 1989). A recent study (Carlson and Cervera, 1991) shows women had to rely on family and friends to fill the role of their incarcerated husbands in terms of money, companionship, and babysitting. Clearly, some offenders are wholly negative influences on their children. Street ethnographies have shown, however, that active offenders are not always damaging parents. One might plausibly conclude that the parenting skills of many who live in disorganized communities, among them offenders, are problematic. However, one would be unwise to assume, and it would contradict current wisdom on child development, that the absence of such a parent improves the child's situation. Unfortunately, research on the parenting skills of offenders, either pre- or post-incarceration, does not exist to our knowledge.

The incarceration of large numbers of parent-age males also restricts the number of male partners available within the neighborhood. This means that mothers find more competition for partners and parents for their children. In the context of more competitive parental situations, mothers may feel reluctant to end relationships that are unsuitable for children partly because prospects for a suitable replacement are perceived as poor. Males under these odds may also feel less incentive to remain in committed parenting partnerships.

It is known that abusive relationships with parents contribute to later delinquency. Early childhood abuse results in earlier criminal activity, increased risk of an arrest during adolescence (by more than 50%), and adults with twice as many arrests as control groups (Widom, 1994). Even in the case of offenders who are abusers, the question is whether their removal ends the child's experience of abuse. If males eliminated from the home are replaced with others who continue to abuse, the trade is a net negative. Where the remaining family unit is forced to choose from a thinning stock of males, the options may not be attractive. For those women who end abusive relationships and live alone, the neighborhood implications may also be problematic: A substantial body of research finds that violent crime is higher in localities with high rates of single-parent households (Pope, 1979; Roncek, 1981; Sampson, 1985), and one study shows that rates of out-of-wedlock births predict levels of incarceration across time in the United States (Jacobs and Helms, 1996). While it is undetermined whether single-parent households are producing the violent offenders or merely serve as easier targets for violent offenders (Roncek, 1981), either scenario resulting from fewer males is detrimental to the neighborhood.

This chain of negative effects on the family—the socialization unit of private social control—contributes to the gradual reduction of social capital within a community. None of these changes by itself "causes" delinquency, but such disruptions are associated with earlier and more active delinquent careers. Their effects would be expected to be additive and in more extreme levels of removal of males, interactive.

Economic Systems

Fagan's (1997) exhaustive review of legal and illegal work illustrates that it is simplistic to view offenders as solely illegally employed. Research shows that many, if not most, criminals also have legal employment so that their removal from the neighborhood removes a worker from the local economy. Fagan recognizes the argument that removing a single offender who held a legal job frees that position for another (potentially nonoffending) resident. However, in local areas where a high proportion of residents engage in both legal and illegal work, Fagan notes that removing many individuals may devastate the local economy. Even if sending an offender to prison does free the legitimate job for someone else, at best this simply shifts the economic benefit of the job from one community household to another, with no net benefit to the neighborhood as a whole. In large numbers, however, it ravages supplies of local human capital and leaves a gap in employable residents. The result is that numerous household units suffer specific losses and the community suffers a net loss. Even families that reap the individual benefit of newly available employment suffer the indirect costs of depleted neighborhood economic strength.

Family members earning money contribute to the welfare of their families, and this remains true even when some of those earnings are from criminal activity (such as drug sales). Edin and Lein (1997) show that in an effort to sustain their families, mothers rely upon regular, substantial financial help from people in their personal networks because neither welfare nor low-paying jobs provide sufficient income to cover expenses. In this study, 69 to 91% of the respondents reported they had received money from members in their networks, 40 to 55% had received cash from their families, 24 to 32% received cash from their boyfriends, and 27 to 41% received cash from their child's father. Incarceration removes from the neighborhood many of the men who provide some type of support to these women.

Prior to incarceration, most prisoners are an economic resource to their neighborhoods and immediate families. Sullivan's work (1989) suggests that in impoverished neighborhoods, a work-age male generates economic activity that translates into purchases at the local deli, child support, and so forth. This economic value is generated in a variety of endeavors, including off-the-books work, intermittent illicit drug trade, theft, welfare, and part-time employment. Once arrested and incarcerated, this economic value is transformed and transferred. It is transformed into penal capital—the demand for salaried correctional employees to provide security. It is also transferred to the locality of the prison, where the penal system's employees reside and live. Thus, in the case of New York, a resident of Bedford-Stuyvesant, arrested and convicted, is transformed from, say, a $12,000 resource in his community to a $30,000 resource in an upstate village. This type of transfer of wealth applies to as many as 70% of New York State's 69,000 inmates (Clines, 1992).

What happens to a neighborhood that experiences a steady growth in these transfers of its wealth? Economic hardship is one of the strongest geographic predictors of crime rates. The socially imbedded nature of crime and unemployment suggests that those communities suffering deprivation experience greater criminal involvement among residents (Hagan, 1993). Therefore, it is reasonable to assume that a neighborhood experiencing economic loss as a result of incarceration will experience an increase in crime (Wilson, 1987). In fact, studies have documented the impact of a community's economic well-being on its level of criminality. Covington and Taylor (1991) show that violent crime is associated with a community's relative deprivation, and Block (1979) found a link between a community's crime rate and its ratio of wealthy to impoverished residents. These studies confirm that social processes damaging a neighborhood's economic viability may also tend to raise its level of crime. In addition, the level of community-wide labor force participation may be even more important than an individual's employment in shaping individual criminality (Crutchfield and Pitchford, 1997).

Imprisonment not only has an economic effect on the community that was home to the prisoner, it also affects the prisoner's level of human capital directly. Grogger (1995) demonstrated that merely being arrested has a short-term, negative impact on earnings, while Freeman (1992) has shown that suffering a conviction and imprisonment has a permanent impact on earning potential. Individuals suffering from insufficient supplies of human capital are destined to have low-level jobs, which not only do not pay well, but offer no vision for the future. Individuals whose jobs hold no future have less of a stake in conformity and are more likely to engage in criminal activity (Crutchfield, 1997). Experience with the criminal justice system, then, contributes to the very inequality in economic means that promotes street crime in the first place (Braithwaite, 1979). Thus, the criminal justice system leaves economic scars on its clients long after its formal involvement in their lives has ended.

In addition, to the extent incarceration primarily removes young men from the neighborhood, it also increases the likelihood of single-parent families being headed by women. Recent research (Browne, 1997) shows that long-term exposure to welfare, lack of work experience, and having never been married characterize disarticulation from mainstream society for women, a condition contributing to earning differences between black and white women. Thus, large-scale incarceration of men may influence the earning power of the women they leave behind.

The macroeconomics of crime policy also damage inner-city communities by shifting government funding priorities away from those communities toward penal institutions. The harsh budgetary politics of the 1990s has corresponded to equally harsh punitive politics in which correctional expenditures have grown by billions of dollars annually while money to support schools, supplement tuition, provide summer jobs for teens, and so forth all received cuts. The latter provide meager supports for communities already hard hit by crime and justice, and they become even more meager still. Whatever role these social programs play in propping up informal networks of social control is eliminated with the depletion of their funding.

In addition, these policies may even motivate the communities hardest hit by budget cuts to accept or encourage criminal behavior in order to sustain what little sense of community remains. A recent study of an urban housing project found that members of a community council that was set up, ironically, to discuss gang-related problems within the project would "borrow" money from local gang leaders to sponsor community-oriented activities (Venkatesh, 1997).

Political Systems

Communities vary in the means they use to deal with problems. While it is generally perceived that poor communities do not organize, some clearly do (Henig, 1982). Researchers have found collective activity, covering a broad range of activities and approaches, in all types of neighborhoods (Podolefsky and DuBow, 1980). Variation in collective action can be attributed to several factors. For instance, the extent to which communities rely upon authority structures or formal social control varies according to differences in the racial and class composition of the community (Bennett, 1995). The degree to which residents perceive that they receive inadequate police services is also related to their propensity to organize locally (Henig, 1982). The political capacity of the community may be a critical factor, too, particularly for communities that have fewer internal resources and need to increase their external resources (Bennett, 1995). In other words, communities vary in their desire and their capacity to organize. The extent to which a neighborhood has developed a network of political and social institutions prior to the occurrence of a specific threat helps to determine whether the community will be able to mobilize collective action against the threat (Henig, 1982).

Bursik and Grasmick's (1993:52) systemic model of social control shows that it is the interrelationship between community institutions and between community organizations and outside agencies that draws upon and produces social capital. Areas with well-developed networks are able to acquire externally based goods and services that enhance their ability to fight crime locally. Communities without such programs may not have extensive connections to the wider community or may not know how to obtain external funding and other necessary resources (Bursik and Grasmick, 1993:15). In addition, most successful programs build upon existing networks, and disrupting these networks may damage already fragile programs.

For the disruption of networks through incarceration to affect the functioning of neighborhood programs and efforts at social control, we need not make the argument that offenders are active participants in local political efforts. Rather, we need only make the argument that their removal disrupts the networks of other individuals who otherwise might participate.

Males who are removed from the community are related to many of those left behind. They are brothers, fathers, uncles. Podolefsky and

DuBow (1980) find that residents who define the crime problem as stemming from inside the neighborhood advocate different control tactics than do residents who see crime as coming from outside. To the extent residents define the problem as stemming from inside the neighborhood, they are inclined to develop a social-problems approach to crime reduction; to the extent they define the problem as coming from outside the neighborhood, they are likely to define a victimization approach. A social-problems approach focuses on improving social conditions thought to be the root of crime, such as youth problems, job opportunities, and neighborhood environmental improvement. A victimization approach focuses on protective and surveillance behavior and on efforts to increase sanctions for offenders. Policymakers who may not understand that residents make this distinction often implement victimization-approach strategies when the community would prefer a social-problems approach.

One factor determining participation in local political structures is belief in their efficacy. In disorganized communities there is reason to suspect residents do not believe that the state's justice agencies work on their behalf. Most minority children can tell stories of racism in the criminal justice system, and the validation of these tales is apparent to the eye. One-in-three African-American males in his twenties is under some form of formal justice system control; in many cities, half of this group are subjects of the system (Mauer, 1995). Many are casualties of the war on drugs. Instituted at the national level, this war was fought at the local level. In a comprehensive review of drug policy, Goetz (1996) points out that policy is often driven by the conscious political strategy of politicians rather than by levels of crime. Further, the spatial impact of this war has been a concentrated increase in criminal justice activity in lower income, inner-city neighborhoods. Just as Lessan and Sheley (1992) found that military wars are associated with increases in arrests due to increased local surveillance and decreased tolerance of deviance, the drug war may also have spilled over into increased arrests for nondrug offenses, as police scour the streets for evidence of drug crimes. Each of these drug offenders eventually returns to the community further criminalized by prison experiences. Moreover, the alienation of otherwise law-abiding residents who no longer feel part of a society that is so hostile to the drug economy (one dimension of Wilson's social isolation) leaves them less likely to participate in local political organizations or to submit to the authority of more formal ones.

The overwhelming presence of American criminal justice in these communities goes a long way to defining the meaning of the state for this segment of society. The state is most likely to be encountered as a coercive agent of control rather than a "fair" agent of justice, and when this is true people are less likely to conform their behavior to the requirements of the law (Tyler, 1990).

Communities with high rates of incarceration may spawn beliefs about the state that are contentious. In Philadelphia, a small cadre of police (perhaps as few as 10) was found to have been planting evidence and falsifying testimony to achieve convictions in African-American neighborhoods (New York Times, 1996). Already nearly 200 convictions have been overturned and dozens of wrongfully incarcerated offenders have been released from prison, including a grandmother whose conviction was obtained through planted drugs as a way to teach her drug-dealing grandson "a lesson." In the past few years, this crew has been responsible for nearly 2,000 convictions that authorities are reviewing for illegality. One can imagine the impressions of the criminal justice system formed by the victims of the perhaps 1,000 false imprisonments, and the impressions of their children, siblings, spouses, and in-laws. The effect of malfeasance of the law within these communities is geometric. This is one of the reasons why it would surprise few to learn that many inner-city young people define the power of the state as a nemesis to be avoided rather than an ally to be cultivated. In the community, disillusionment with the political structure probably erodes residents' feeling of empowerment and reduces their willingness to participate in local politics. As a result, the call for citizen involvement may fall on deaf ears.

There is another level at which this negative political impact may operate: It may reduce deterrence. Finckenauer's (1982) study of Rahway prison's "Scared Straight" program found that those exposed to the harsh, accusatory taunting by the lifers actually had more delinquency than a comparison group not exposed to the program. Finckenauer concluded from this that the Scared Straight program failed as a deterrent. But we may ask whether the results are not even more disquieting. Most who study prison life believe there are significant brutalizing effects to imprisonment that impair prisoners' inclinations to conform to the law. Strongly suggestive evidence (Cochran et al., 1994) exists, for example, that the use of the death penalty has brutalizing effects on the general public. Is it not more reasonable to expect that the broader exposure of specific publics to the realities of prison life also brutalizes them in a similar way?

Stated in another way, part of the deterrent power of the prison may be strengthened by the mystery that surrounds it. Once experienced, prison, no matter how harsh, is transformed from an awful mystery to a real-life ordeal that has been suffered and survived. High recidivism rates are consistent with the idea that prison experiences fail to deter. Fear of prison (especially among the middle class who have not experienced it) may be most potent when it is an unacquainted fear.

In minority communities, prison is a part of life. A black 10-year-old is likely to have at least one (and likely more) ex-cons among his fathers, uncles, brothers, and neighbors. The lesson is that prison is not awesome, but is survivable. Widespread use of prison is tantamount to a widespread reassurance that prison is "normal." Thus, the politics of imprisonment may be a combination of increasing resentment and decreasing marginal gain. Turning dominant cultural symbols upside down, there is even the claim that inner-city residents accrue street status from surviving prison (Shakur, 1993).

ILLEGITIMATE SYSTEMS

To this point we have discussed only the legitimate components of neighborhood structure that promote self-regulation. But high levels of incarceration also affect illegitimate local activity in unintended ways—to mangle Tip O'Neill's famous observation about politics, we might say that "all street crime is local." By saying this, we mean that with the exception of some rare instances of violent crime, all criminality is contextual, embedded in interpersonal and group relations. These relations may be seen as illegitimate systems that operate at the neighborhood level, also subject to the effects of incarceration.

Crime is often a group phenomenon (see Reiss, 1988). Young males commit much of their street-level acquisitional crime in groups—muggings, burglaries, robberies, and so forth. Nearly all drug crime, from sales to consumption, is a group activity. In fact, Warr (1996) has shown recently that delinquents belong to multiple groups, but only for a brief period. Each group, then, is constantly undergoing a process of reconfiguration and renewal with new members. Further, he finds that it is the configuration of the group that determines which member will instigate the offense rather than a stable set of "hardened" delinquents continually motivating others into crime. This raises the question of what happens when the criminal justice system removes one member of a criminal group. The hope is that the disruption will be sufficient to end the activities of the group and/or that the general deterrent effect will be sufficient to dissuade others from participating. It may often be, however, that the group continues its criminal activity as before. The group may even recruit a replacement member in order to carry out criminal functions at continuing levels. For every group that replaces removed members, little or no crime prevention is achieved by the incarceration of the initial member.

This is almost certainly the case with drug-related crime. Offenders serving sentences for drug crimes have skyrocketed from less than 10% of a much smaller prison stock in 1980 to about one-third of the population in 1996 (Bureau of Justice Statistics, 1997). Drug demand fluctuates for a variety of reasons, but it is largely unaffected by who is around to sell the drugs, as long as someone is willing to do the job—when the economic reasons for selling drugs persist, the criminal actions of the group go on largely uninterrupted (Caulkins et al., 1997). This may be worse than a mere wash, however. Implicit within the replacement idea is "recruitment", that is, a young male otherwise at the margin of criminal groups becomes more intimately associated with them. In the case of drug crime, for example, a young male who otherwise might have been in school or in search of legal work is instead recruited into the drug trade. This male, who might have left young adulthood without close association with crime groups, instead becomes initiated into criminal enterprise—with lifelong implications. The results of criminal replacement may sometimes include augmentation of a criminal career.

DISCUSSION

The thesis of this study has been that an overreliance on formal controls may increase disorganization by impeding other forms of control. High incarceration rates may contribute to rates of criminal violence by the way they contribute to such social problems as inequality, family life deterioration, economic and political alienation, and social disorganization. Concentrated within certain communities, high levels of incarceration undermine social, political, and economic systems already weakened by the low levels of human and social capital produced under conditions such as high rates of poverty, unemployment, and crime. Further impairing these damaged systems means that communities with scarce supplies of human and social capital are unable to produce the resource they so greatly need. The result is a reduction in social cohesion and a lessening of those communities' capacity for self-regulation.

The counterproductive capacity of excessive incarceration helps explain the conundrum of contemporary penal policy: Incarcerating ever more offenders has not produced a consistent decrease in crime rates. Since 1973, the number of offenders incarcerated in prisons and jails has increased every year, from about 350,000 to over 1.5 million. But crime has fluctuated during that time period. Today's decreases were preceded by years of increases, and those increases were themselves preceded by a period of first increase and then decrease. By contrast, incarceration has done nothing but increase at an essentially stable rate. This suggests that crime control is not directly related to incarceration, because the social control capacity of the growth in imprisonment has been blunted by other social forces. We have argued that the impact of concentrated incarceration rates on social disorganization is one of those forces.

This extension of social disorganization theory has important theoretical and policy-related implications. Theoretically, it means that simple recursive studies of disorganization may be inadequate. The growing body of evidence suggests that communities are embedded in a system that reflects and continually reproduces levels of disorganization. It also means that one must look to additional sources of disorganization. Clearly, empirical research should be conducted to test the central tenets of this study.

Our hypotheses could be tested directly by investigating the linkages between the effects of a concentration of high incarceration rates and the net impact on family and social life, analyzed at the neighborhood level. For instance, if communities suffering from the removal of a large number of adult males through incarceration could be shown to suffer subsequently from higher rates of single-parent families, more out-of-wedlock births, an increase in residential mobility for the remaining family members, and higher crime, that would begin to provide empirical evidence supporting our theoretical case that a reliance on incarceration is one of the social conditions leading to crime. This is a conclusion other researchers (see Lynch and Sabol, 1992, for example) have already begun to draw. To develop fully an empirical test of a nonrecursive process requires data organized by neighborhoods, and such data are not yet currently available. (For an explication of the lack of such data and a description of the problems in collecting them, see Bursik and Grasmick, 1993.) A further testing of our argument awaits the availability of suitable data.

If our hypothesis has some value, it raises enormous implications for social policy on crime. For one thing, it confirms the common aphorism about prison construction, that society cannot build its way out of the crime problem. It also explains why this is so: The more society builds prisons, the more it cultivates the crime problem for which building is proposed as a solution. A crime control strategy that looks only to coerce compliance from members of communities and that ignores the ways in which it can strengthen the neighborhood's internal mechanism of social control is worse than neutral. It is self-defeating.

There is reason to think this pattern applies primarily (perhaps even exclusively) to the most resource-poor communities. These areas suffer from the most crime partly because they lack enough social and human capital in the first place. As a result, they suffer the most from incarceration and its unintended consequences. Stronger communities produce fewer offenders because they suffer from fewer of the environmental conditions conducive to crime. Also, because stronger communities have larger supplies of human and social capital, they have stronger foundational structures and, as a result, suffer from less crime. Incarceration is a crime control strategy that works for these communities because there are fewer offenders. Of these, few are removed (most stay within local formal control systems such as probation) and the disruption caused by their absence is minimal.

By contrast, high-crime neighborhoods are also high-incarceration neighborhoods. In these places, children are more likely to experience family disruption, lack of parental supervision, property devoid of effective guardians, and all other manner of deteriorated informal social controls that otherwise deflect the young from criminal behavior. This is the point Etzioni (1996) recently made when he argued that an overreliance on external control agencies actually weakens the capacity of communities to exert their own self-management. The prison can never be a substitute for absent adults, family members, and neighbors in making places safe.

We emphasize that our position does not suggest a wholesale rejection of incarceration; we do not believe in instituting policies that leave communities at risk. Imprisonment of people who threaten the personal safety of residents may well decrease the demand for self-regulation and thereby increase its relative effectiveness. But many (if not most) offenders occupy an actual or potential relationship to private and parochial control systems. They are, for example, parents, employees, neighbors, and so forth. Removing these residents eliminates their actual and potential role in neighborhood self-regulation. The result is that formal and public social control policies based upon the extensive use of incarceration contain, at the neighborhood level, the seeds of their own demise.

Our position is that society must consider the relationships among various forms of control so that it can employ practices that maximize the effectiveness of each level of control. This is not as radical an idea as it may appear. Neighborhood-based approaches are nothing new to justice agencies. The most obvious examples are community-based policing strategies that establish partnerships with neighborhood groups and residents (Robinson, 1996). These strategies define crime-related problems very broadly and seek to work with neighborhood members at every step in confronting crime. The result is not that neighborhood members "turn over" their crime problem to an external formal control agency, but rather that their actions are incorporated into a broader anticrime effort. Under community policing approaches, law enforcement comes to be defined as a local activity, and law enforcers align themselves with resident groups and individuals. Equally important, the police come to define their own successes not in terms of mere arrests, but in terms of the quality of life of the residents they serve.

We make a distinction between the top-down community policing strategies we criticized earlier and the bottom-up approaches to which we refer here. The "get tough" community policing approach involving street sweeps and the widespread use of arrests may undercut private and parochial social control processes. By contrast, the kind of policing philosophy of Charleston Police Chief Reuben Greenberg (Butterfield, 1996) illustrates what we mean by providing supports for these neighborhood systems of self-regulation. Children found after curfew or in truancy are not arrested but returned to their parents or the school. Law enforcement officials are available to monitor (and presumably advise) parental disciplinary actions with their children. Controversial as these programs are, they also link public social control efforts to the existing private capacities for self-regulation. Further, they are being shown to work. Boston Police Commissioner Paul Evans recently attributed his city's decline in violence to the combined strength of neighborhood involvement and aggressive policing. This collaborative effort between the police and local groups, leaders and residents, works, he says, because, "arresting people without involving the community in the overall effort is counterproductive" (Herbert, 1997).

Approaches such as these that have the capacity for enriching human and social capital and that build foundational systems offer promise of strengthening neighborhood capacities to confront crime, and criminal justice agencies have begun moving in this direction. For instance, the Coordinating Council on Juvenile Justice and Delinquency Prevention (1996:10) report on violence prevention lists as one of its main goals the strengthening and mobilizing of communities, which "means enabling residents to recognize and solve their own problems and creating opportunities for everyone to take responsibility for finding solutions." The American Probation and Parole Association (1996) lists 15 exemplary programs in which probation and parole agencies work in tandem with neighborhood groups to deal with local crime problems. When prosecutors move their offices into the local neighborhood and focus on quality-of-life problems in those areas, they find themselves asked to deal with a range of problems far broader than serious, felony crime (Boland, 1996). In Vermont (Perry and Gorczyk, 1997), the Department of Corrections requires all offenders to engage in some form of community reparative labor, such as repairing substandard housing or providing services to the elderly or incapacitated. Braithwaite's (1989) theory of "reintegrative shaming" has kindled "family conferencing" approaches with juvenile delinquents, in which a group of local citizens preside over a process involving young offenders and their victims aimed at offenders' learning the consequences of their misdeeds and re-committing to abstain from the behavior in the future (Van Ness and Strong, 1997). Some have described the appearance of these and myriad other new, local justice programs as heralding the arrival of a new ideal of "community justice" (Clear and Karp, 1998).

Noncriminal justice approaches may also be used to strengthen community self-regulation around crime. New York City's Beacon Community Center Program is a school-based, multipurpose, violence prevention strategy that addresses "a wide range of critical needs of at-risk youth" in school settings. It focuses on preventing violence, drug abuse, and other social problems by identifying individual, family, school, peer group, and community risk factors for crime and seeking to enhance protective mechanisms to avoid them (McGillis, 1996). The Vera Institute (Shapiro, 1997) operates an experimental family drug crisis center that has as one of its specific aims the amelioration of problems encountered by families of addicts who become involved in the criminal justice system. This is a direct attempt to reduce and control the social damage caused by coercive criminal justice responses to crime.

These various strategies are different from each other in a number of important respects, of course, but for our purposes they all share critical common components. They retain offenders in their communities, treat offenders as potential resources to strengthen communities, use local resources to transform offenders into social capital, and thereby strengthen the capacity for self-regulation within these localities. Until this type of community justice strategy becomes the norm, communities hard hit by crime will continue to be hard hit by crime control responses. And, if our theory is correct, the system will ever grow from its own seeds.

REFERENCES

American Probation and Parole Association
1996 Restoring hope through community partnerships: The real deal in crime control. Perspectives 20(2):40–42.

Anderson, Elijah
1990 Streetwise: Race, Class and Change in an Urban Community. Chicago: University of Chicago Press.

Bennett, Susan F.
1995 Community organizations and crime. The Annals of the American Academy of Political and Social Science 539:72–84.

Berkman, Lisa and Leonard Syme
1979 Social networks, host resistance, and mortality: A nine-year follow-up study of Alameda County residents. American Journal of Epidemiology 109:684–694.

Black, Donald
1976 The Behavior of Law. Orlando, Fla.: Academic Press.

Block, Richard
1979 Community, environment and violent crime. Criminology 17:46–57.

Blumstein, Alfred, Jacqueline Cohen, Jeffrey A. Roth, and Christy A. Visher
1986 Criminal Careers and "Career Criminals." Washington, D.C.: National Academy Press.

Boland, Barbara
1996 What is community prosecution? NIJ Journal 231:35–40.

Bonczar, Thomas P. and Allen J. Beck
1997 Lifetime Likelihood of Going to State or Federal Prison. Washington, D.C.: Bureau of Justice Statistics.

Braithwaite, John

1979 Inequality, Crime and Public Policy. London: Routledge & Kegan Paul.

1989 Crime, Shame and Reintegration. New York: Cambridge University Press.

Braithwaite, John and David Biles

1980 Empirical verification and Black's The Behavior of Law. American Sociological Review 45:334–338.

Brodsky, Stanley

1975 Families and Friends of Men in Prison. Lexington, Mass.: Lexington Books.

Browne, Irene

1997 The black-white gap in labor force participation among women. American Sociological Review 62:236–252.

Bureau of Justice Statistics

1995 Prisoners in 1994. Washington, D.C.: Bureau of Justice Statistics.

1996 Correctional Populations in the U.S., 1994. Executive Summary. Washington, D.C.: Bureau of Justice Statistics.

1997 Prisoners in 1996. Washington, D.C.: Bureau of Justice Statistics.

Bursik, Robert J., Jr.

1986 Ecological stability and the dynamics of delinquency. In Albert J. Reiss, Jr., and Michael Tonry (eds.), Communities and Crime. Chicago: University of Chicago Press.

1988 Social disorganization and theories of crime and delinquency: Problems and prospects. Criminology 26:519–551.

Bursik, Robert J., Jr., and Harold G. Grasmick

1993 Neighborhoods and Crime: The Dimensions of Effective Community Control. New York: Lexington Books.

Butterfield, Fox

1996 An ivy leaguer becomes a southern law policeman. New York Times, January 18:18.

Carlson, Bonnie and Neil Cervera

1992 Inmates and Their Wives. Westport, Conn.: Greenwood Press.

Caulkins, Jonathon P., C. Peter Rydell, William L. Schwabe, and James Chiesa

1997 Mandatory Minimum Drug Sentences: Throwing Away the Key or the Taxpayer's Money? Santa Monica, Calif.: RAND.

Clear, Todd R. and George F. Cole

1997 American Corrections. 4th ed. Belmont, Calif.: Wadsworth.

Clear, Todd R. and David Karp

1998 The community justice ideal. Final report to the National Institute of Justice from the Institute for Communitarian Policy Studies (draft), Florida State University, Tallahassee.

Clear, Val B., Todd R. Clear, and V. Scott Clear

1971 Eight million dollars: The hidden costs of incarceration. Anderson College (mimeo), Indiana.

Clines, Francis X.

1992 Ex-inmates urge return to areas of crime to help. New York Times, December 23:1ff.

Cochran, John K., Mitchell B. Chamlin, and Mark Seth
1994 Deterrence or brutalization? An impact assessment of Oklahoma's return to capital punishment. Criminology 32(1):107–134.

Coleman, James
1988 Social capital and the creation of human capital. American Journal of Sociology 94 Supplement:S95-S120.

Conger, Rand D., Frederick O. Lorenz, Glen H. Elder, Jr., Ronald L. Simons, and Xiaojia Ge
1993 Husband and wife differences in response to undesirable life events. Journal of Health and Social Behavior 34:71–88.

Cook, Philip J.
1986 The demand and supply of criminal opportunities. In Michael Tonry and Norval Morris (eds.), Crime and Justice: An Annual Review of Research. Vol. 7. Chicago: University of Chicago Press.

Coordinating Council on Juvenile Justice and Delinquency Prevention
1996 Combating Violence and Delinquency: The National Juvenile Justice Action Plan. Summary Report on the Prevention of Violence. Washington, D.C.: U.S. Department of Justice, Office of Justice Programs.

Covington, Jeannette and Ralph B. Taylor
1991 Fear of crime and urban residential neighborhood: Implications of between- and within-neighborhood sources of current models. Sociological Quarterly 32:231–249.

Crutchfield, Robert D. and Susan R. Pitchford
1997 Work and crime: The effects of labor stratification. Social Forces 76:93–118.

Decker, Scott H. and Barrik Van Winkle
1996 Life in the Gang: Family, Friends and Violence. New York: Cambridge University Press.

Edin, Kathryn and Laura Lein
1997 Work, welfare, and single mothers' economic survival strategies. American Sociological Review 62(2):253–266.

Etzioni, Amatai
1996 The responsive community: A communitarian perspective. American Sociological Review 61:1–11.

Fagan, Jeffrey
1997 Legal and illegal work: Crime, work and unemployment. In Burton Weisbrod and James Worthy (eds.), Dealing with Urban Crises. Evanston, Ill.: Northwestern University Press.

Farkas, George, Paula England, Keven Vicknair, and Barbara Stanek Kilbourne
1997 Cognitive skill, skill demands of jobs, and earnings among young European American, African American, and Mexican American workers. Social Forces 75:913–940.

Felson, Marcus
1996 Those who discourage crime. In John E. Eck and David Weisburd (eds.), Crime and Place: Crime Prevention Studies. Vol. 4. Albany, N.Y.: Harrow and Heston.

Fishman, Laura
1990 Women at the Wall. Albany, N.Y.: SUNY Press.

Finckenauer, James O.
1982 Scared Straight: The Panacea Phenomenon. Englewood Cliffs, N.J.: Prentice-Hall.

Fleisher, Mark S.
1995 Beggars and Thieves: Lives of Urban Street Criminals. Madison: University of Wisconsin Press.

Freeman, Richard B.
1992 Crime and unemployment of disadvantaged youth. In Adele Harrell and George Peterson (eds.), Drugs, Crime and Social Isolation: Barriers to Urban Opportunity. Washington, D.C.: Urban Institute.

Gabel, Stewart
1992 Children of incarcerated and criminal parents: Adjustment, behavior and prognosis. Bulletin of American Academic Psychiatry Law 20:33–45.

Goetz, Edward G.
1996 The U.S. war on drugs as urban policy. International Journal of Urban and Regional Research 20:539–550.

Gottfredson, Stephen D. and Michael Hindelang
1979 A study of the behavior of law. American Sociological Review 44:3–18.

Gottfredson, Stephen D. and Ralph B. Taylor
1988 Community contexts and criminal offenders. In Tim Hope and Margaret Shaw (eds.), Communities and Crime Reduction. London: Her Majesty's Stationery Office.

Grogger, Jeffrey
1995 The effect of arrests on the employment and earnings of young men. Quarterly Journal of Economics 110(1):51–71.

Hagan, John
1993 The social embeddedness of crime and unemployment. Criminology 31:465–492.
1994 Crime and Disrepute. Thousand Oaks, Calif.: Pine Forge Press.
1996 The next generation: Children of prisoners. In Vera Institute, The Unintended Consequences of Incarceration. New York: Vera Institute of Justice.

Henig, Jeffrey R.
1982 Neighborhood Mobilization: Redevelopment and Response. New Brunswick, N.J.: Rutgers University Press.

Herbert, Bob
1997 The keys to cutting crime. The New York Times, October 2:A15.

Hunter, Albert J.
1985 Private, parochial and public social orders: The problem of crime and incivility in urban communities. In Gerald D. Suttles and Mayer N. Zald (eds.), The Challenge of Social Control: Citizenship and Institution Building in Modern Society. Norwood, N.J.: Aldex Publishing.

Irwin, John and James Austin
1996 It's About Time: America's Prison Population Crisis. Belmont, Calif.: Wadsworth.

Jacobs, David and Ronald E. Helms
1996 Toward a political model of incarceration: A time series examination of multiple explanations for prison admission rates. American Journal of Sociology 102:323–357.

Jankowski, Martin Sanchez
1991 Islands in the Street: Gangs and American Urban Society. Berkeley: University of California Press.

Kessler, Ronald and Jane D. McLeod
1984 Sex differences in vulnerability to undesirable life events. American Sociological Review 49:620–631.

King, Anthony E. O.
1993 The impact of incarceration on African American families: Implications for practice. Journal of Contemporary Human Service 73:145–153.

Kornhauser, Ruth Rosner
1978 Social Sources of Delinquency: An Appraisal of Analytic Models. Chicago: University of Chicago Press.

Kruttschnitt, Candace
1980–81 Social Status and Sentences of Female Offenders. Law & Society Review 2:247–265.

Laub, John H. and Robert J. Sampson
1993 Turning points in the life course: Why change matters to the study of crime. Criminology 31:301–325.

Lessan, Gloria T. and Joseph F. Sheley
1992 Does law behave? A macrolevel test of Black's propositions on change in law. Social Forces 70:655–678.

Logan, John R. and Harvey L. Molotch
1987 Urban Fortunes: The Political Economy of Place. Berkely: University of California Press.

Lowenstein, Ariela
1986 Temporary single parenthood—The case of prisoner's families. Family Relations 35:79–85.

Lynch, James P. and William J. Sabol
1992 Macro-social changes and their implications for prison reform: The underclass and the composition of prison populations. Paper presented at the American Society of Criminology, New Orleans, November 5.
1997 Did Getting Tougher on Crime Pay? Crime Policy Report. Washington, D.C.: The Urban Institute State Policy Center.

MaCoun, Robert and Peter Reuter
1991 Are the wages of sin $30 an hour? Economic aspects of street-level drug dealing. Crime and Delinquency 38:477–491.

Maher, Lisa
1991 Punishment and welfare: Crack cocaine and the regulation of mothering. In Clarice Feinman (ed.), The Criminalization of a Woman's Body. New York: Haworth.

Massey, Douglas S.
1990 American apartheid: Segregation and the making of the underclass. American Journal of Sociology 96:329–357.

Massey, James L. and Martha A. Myers
1989 Patterns of repressive social control in post-reconstruction Georgia, 1882–1935. Social Forces 68:458–488.

Mauer, Mark
1995 African American Males and the Criminal Justice System, 1995. Washington, D.C.: The Sentencing Project.

McCall, Nathan
1994 Makes Me Wanna Holler: A Young Black Man in America. New York: Random House.

McGillis, Daniel
1996 Beacons of Hope: New York City's School-Based Beacon Community Centers. NIJ Focus. Washington, D.C.: National Institute of Justice.

Myers, Martha A.
1980 Predicting the Behavior of Law: A Test of Two Models. Law & Society Review 4:835–857.

New York Times
1996 Philadelphia feels effects of inquiry, March 24:A-35 (national edition).

Parcel, Toby L. and Elizabeth G. Menaghan
1993 Family social capital and children's behavior problems. Social Psychology Quarterly 56:120–135.

Perry, John G. and John F. Gorczyk
1997 Restructuring corrections: Using market research in Vermont. Corrections Management Quarterly 1:3:26–35.

Podolefsky, Aaron and Frederik DuBow
1980 Strategies for Community Crime Prevention: Collective Responses to Crime in Urban America. Reactions to Crime Project, Center for Urban Affairs. Evanston, Ill.: Northwestern University.

Pope, Carl E.
1979 Victimization rates and neighborhood characteristics: Some preliminary findings. In William H. Parsonage (ed.), Perspectives in Victimology. Beverly Hills, Calif.: Sage.

Reiss, Albert J., Jr.
1988 Co-offending and criminal careers. In Michael Tonry and Norval Morris (eds.), Crime and Justice: An Annual Review of Research. Vol 10. Chicago: University of Chicago Press.

Robinson, Laurie
1996 Linking community-based initiatives and community justice: The Office of Justice Programs. NIJ Journal. 231:4–7.

Roncek, Dennis
1981 Dangerous places: Crime and residential environment. Social Forces 60:74–96.

Rose, Dina R.
1995 Fighting back against crime and disorder: An examination of neighborhood-based organizations and social disorganization theory. Unpublished dissertation, Department of Sociology, Duke University, Durham, N.C.

Sampson, Robert J.
1985 Neighborhoods and crime: The structural determinants of personal victimization. Journal of Research in Crime and Delinquency 22:7–40.
1986a Crime in cities: The effects of formal and informal social control. In Albert J. Reiss, Jr., and Michael Tonry (eds.), Communities and Crime. Chicago: University of Chicago Press.
1986b The effects of urbanization and neighborhood characteristics on criminal victimization. In Robert M. Figlio, Simon Hakim, and George F. Rengert (eds.), Metropolitan Crime Patterns. Monsey, N.Y.: Criminal Justice Press.
1986c Neighborhood family structure and risk of personal victimization. In James Byrne and Robert J. Sampson (eds.), The Social Ecology of Crime. New York: Springer-Verlag.
1987 Communities and crime. In Michael R. Gottfredson and Travis Hirschi (eds.), Positive Criminology. Beverly Hills, Calif.: Sage.
1988 Local friendship ties and community attachment in mass society: A multilevel systemic model. American Sociological Review 53:766–779.

Sampson, Robert J. and W. Byron Groves
1989 Community structure and crime: Testing social disorganization theory. American Journal of Sociology 94:744–802.

Sampson, Robert J. and John H. Laub
1993 Crime in the Making: Pathways and Turning Points Through Life. Cambridge, Mass.: Harvard University Press.

Sampson, Robert J., Stephen W. Raudenbush, and Felton Earls
1997 Neighborhoods and violent crime: A multilevel study of collective efficacy. Science 277:918–924.

Sanders, Jimy M. and Victor Nee
1996 Social capital, human capital and immigrant self-employment. American Sociological Review 62:231–249.

Shakur, Sanyika
1993 Monster: The Autobiography of an L.A. Crip. New York: Atlantic Monthly Press.

Shapiro, Carol
1997 La Bodega. New York: Vera Institute of Justice.

Shaw, Clifford R. and Henry D. McKay
1942 Juvenile Delinquency and Urban Areas. Chicago: University of Chicago Press.

Skogan, Wesley
1986 Fear of crime and neighborhood change. In Albert J. Reiss, Jr., and Michael Tonry (eds.), Communities and Crime. Chicago: University of Chicago Press.
1990 Disorder and Decline: Crime and the Spiral of Decay in American Neighborhoods. New York: The Free Press.

Smith, Douglas A.
1987 Police response to interpersonal violence: Defining the parameters of legal control. Social Forces 65:76–82.

Smith, Margaret and Todd R. Clear
1997 Fathers in prison: Interim report. Draft report to the Edna McConnel Clark Foundation by the Rutgers University School of Criminal Justice, Newark, N.J.

Sullivan, Mercer L.
1989 Getting Paid: Youth, Crime and Work in the Inner City. Ithaca, New York: Cornell University Press.

Taylor, Ralph B.
1997 Social order and disorder of street blocks and neighborhoods: Ecology, microecology and the systemic model of social disorganization. Journal of Research in Crime and Delinquency 34(1):113–155.

Teachman, Jay D., Kathleen Paasch, and Karen Carver
1997 Social capital and the generation of human capital. Social Forces 75:1343–1359.

Tyler, Tom
1990 Why People Obey the Law. New Haven, Conn.: Yale University Press.

Vacha, Edward F. and T. F. McLaughlin
1992 The social structural, family, school and personal characteristics of at-risk students: Policy recommendations for school personnel. Journal of Education 174(3):9–25.

Van Ness, Daniel and Karen Strong
1997 Restorative Justice. Cincinnati, Ohio: Anderson.

Venkatesh, Sudhir Alladi
1997 The social organization of street gang activity in an urban ghetto. American Journal of Sociology 103:82–111.

Warr, Mark
1996 Organization and instigation in delinquent groups. Criminology 34:11–37.

Wellman, Barry
1979 The community question: The intimate networks of East Yorkers. American Journal of Sociology 84:1201–1231.

Widom, Kathy Spatz
1994 Childhood victimization and risk for adolescent problem behaviors. In Robert D. Ketterlinus and Michael E. Lamb (eds.), Adolescent Problem Behaviors: Issues and Research. New York: Earlbaum.

Wilson, James Q. and George Kelling
1982 Broken windows. Atlantic Monthly, March:29–38.

Wilson, William Julius
1987 The Truly Disadvantaged. Chicago: University of Chicago.
1996 When Work Disappears: The World of the New Urban Poor. New York: Knopf.

Zimring, Franklin and Gordon Hawkins
1995 Incapacitation: Penal Confinement and the Restraint of Crime. New York: Oxford University Press.

Dina R. Rose is an Assistant Professor in the School of Criminology and Criminal Justice at Florida State University. Her Ph.D. in sociology is from Duke University. She has published work on community disorganization, social control, and juvenile delinquency. Her current research interests include community control, social policy, and homelessness.

Todd R. Clear is Professor and Associate Dean, School of Criminology and Criminal Justice, Florida State University. His Ph.D. in criminal justice is from The University at Albany. Among his publications are *Harm in American Penology* and *Controlling the Offender in the Community*. His current research interests include incarceration policy, alternatives to imprisonment, and community justice.

Name Index